WHAT COMES NATURALLY

WHAT COMES NATURALLY

Miscegenation Law
and the Making of Race in America

Peggy Pascoe

OXFORD
UNIVERSITY PRESS

OXFORD
UNIVERSITY PRESS

Oxford University Press, Inc., publishes works that further
Oxford University's objective of excellence
in research, scholarship, and education.

Oxford   New York
Auckland   Cape Town   Dar es Salaam   Hong Kong   Karachi
Kuala Lumpur   Madrid   Melbourne   Mexico City   Nairobi
New Delhi   Shanghai   Taipei   Toronto

With offices in
Argentina   Austria   Brazil   Chile   Czech Republic   France   Greece
Guatemala   Hungary   Italy   Japan   Poland   Portugal   Singapore
South Korea   Switzerland   Thailand   Turkey   Ukraine   Vietnam

Copyright © 2009 by Peggy Pascoe

Published by Oxford University Press, Inc.
198 Madison Avenue, New York, NY 10016

www.oup.com

First issued as an Oxford University Press paperback, 2010

Oxford is a registered trademark of Oxford University Press

Library of Congress Cataloging-in-Publication Data
Pascoe, Peggy.
What comes naturally : miscegenation law and
the making of race in America / Peggy Pascoe.
p. cm.
Includes bibliographical references and index.
ISBN 978-0-19-977235-3 (pbk.)
1. Racially mixed people—Legal status, laws, etc.—United States—History.
2. Miscegenation—United States—History.
3. Interracial marriage—United States—History. I. Title.
KF4755.P37 2008
346.7301'6—dc22
2008018035

Printed in the United States of America
on acid-free paper

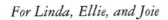

For Linda, Ellie, and Joie

Contents

MAPS

WHAT COMES NATURALLY

INTRODUCTION

THIS BOOK EXAMINES two of the most insidious ideas in American history. The first is the belief that interracial marriage is unnatural. The second is the belief in white supremacy. When these two ideas converged, with the invention of the term "miscegenation" in the 1860s, the stage was set for the rise of a social, political, and legal system of white supremacy that reigned through the 1960s and, many would say, beyond.

Marriage may not be the first thing that comes to mind when considering America's entrenched history of racism—slavery, the denial of voting rights, and the segregation of railroads and schools have all attracted more attention. I want to suggest, however, that this very inattention to interracial marriage is an indication of how thoroughly and effectively the concept of "miscegenation" was woven into the fabric of American law and society. Between the 1860s and the 1960s, Americans saw their opposition to interracial marriage as a product of nature rather than a product of politics. The more natural opposition to interracial marriage seemed, the easier it was for it to serve as the bottom line of white supremacy and the most commonsense justification for all other forms of race discrimination.

The term "miscegenation" first appeared during the presidential election of 1864, in a pamphlet written by two New York politicos who wanted to replace the older term for interracial sex and marriage, "amalgamation," which they considered inadequate because it had been borrowed from something else (the mixture of metals). Insisting that it was important to have an independent term, one that referred to the "mixture of two or more races" and nothing else, they combined *miscere* (mix) and *genus* (race) to form the new, more scientific-sounding "miscegenation."[1]

The term "miscegenation" caught on quickly, providing the rhetorical means of channeling the belief that interracial marriage was unnatural into the foundation of post–Civil War white supremacy. This is how a Virginia court put it in 1878, when it voided the marriage of a Black man and a White woman: "The purity of public morals, the moral and physical development of both races, and the highest advancement of our cherished southern civilization, under which two distinct races are to work out and accomplish the destiny to which the Almighty has assigned them on this continent—all require that they should be kept distinct and separate, and that connections and alliances so unnatural that God and nature seem to forbid them, should be prohibited by positive law, and be subject to no evasion."[2] For nearly a century afterward, the notion that "miscegenation" was "unnatural" stood as the taken-for-granted basis of American laws and policy, the legal embodiment of the nearly unanimous White opposition to intermarriage.

Marriage proved to be such a fruitful ground for the growth of white supremacy because it reached well beyond the realm of romance. As a social institution, marriage links individual desire to social respectability and financial responsibility; it also links citizens and their dependents to the state. Because it stretches seamlessly from romance to respectability to responsibility, marriage has extraordinary power to naturalize some social relationships, and to stigmatize others as unnatural. When societies decide who can and who can't legally marry, they determine who is and isn't really part of the family. These inclusions and exclusions take place at such an intimate level that they shape what seems natural and, in turn, what is stigmatized as unnatural.

The claim that interracial marriage was unnatural drew much of its power from cultural assumptions about the nature of race, so much so that miscegenation law provides a premier locus for studying the history of race in America. In the North and South, states usually banned marriages between Whites and Blacks, but in the American West, to which the laws were extended in the late nineteenth century, legislatures prohibited (depending on the state) marriages between Whites and American Indians, native Hawaiians, Chinese, Japanese, Filipinos, Koreans, and Hindus. These laws provide a virtual road map to American legal conceptions of race; they spotlight the multiracial framework of white supremacy that emerged after the Civil War and stood at the center of American law into the 1960s.

Still, this is not a story about race alone. The claim of unnaturality held the extraordinary power that it did because when it came to interracial marriage, claims about the nature of race were interwoven with claims about the nature of gender and sexuality. From the moment that the term "miscegenation" was invented, Americans were haunted by the flip side of the claim that interracial marriage was unnatural: the possibility that interracial marriage might be perfectly natural, every bit as natural, some couldn't resist saying, as the attraction between men and women. The two men who coined the term "miscegenation" laid out the Black/White version of this possibility in the form of a parody of the ideas of famous anti-slavery activists. "The sympathy Mr. Greeley, Mr. Phillips, and Mr. Tilton feel for the negro," they explained, "is the love which the blonde bears for the black; it is a love of race, a sympathy stronger to them than the love they bear to woman. It is founded upon natural law. We love our opposites. It is in the nature of things that we should do so, and where nature has free course, men like those we have indicated, whether anti-slavery or pro-slavery, conservative or radical, democrat or republican, will marry and be given in marriage to the most perfect specimens of the colored race."[3]

From the 1860s through the 1960s, the American legal system elevated the notion that interracial marriage was unnatural to commonsense status and made it the law of the land. During this period miscegenation law channeled property, propriety, personal choice, and legitimate procreation into one very particular kind of monogamous marital pair: couples that were made up of one White man and one White woman, whose sameness of race was required by law and whose difference in sex was taken entirely for granted. The more Whites believed that interracial marriage was unnatural, the more they assumed that the marriage of one White man to one White woman was the only kind of marriage worthy of the name—and the more they saw their own marriages as the fortunate result of individual romantic preference rather than the obligatory outcome of a legal system steeped in gendered assumptions about race and heterosexuality.

What Comes Naturally tells the history of race, gender, and sexuality as they intertwined in the rise and fall of miscegenation law. In chapter 1, I trace the historical links between marriage, property, and citizenship, the line between illicit sex and marriage, and the passage of early laws against interracial marriage, showing how the collapse of slavery and the invention of the term "miscegenation" made interracial marriage a hotly contested issue during the Civil War and Reconstruction.

In chapters 2 through 4, I show how the claim that interracial marriage was unnatural ended this debate by allowing miscegenation laws to become so taken for granted that they seemed to be the obvious, inarguable foundation for post–Civil War white supremacy. Appellate court judges trumpeted the claim that interracial marriage was unnatural and immoral, while state legislatures passed laws that brought Whites, Blacks, Indians, and Asian Americans all within the reach of miscegenation law, and courts enforced the laws by placing individuals in each of these categories. By stigmatizing interracial relationships as illicit sex rather than marriage, judges separated interracial intimacy from the notions of contract, choice, and civil rights otherwise associated with marriage and citizenship. As a result, interracial couples were deprived of the protection of the Fourteenth Amendment to the U.S. Constitution, which guarantees "equal protection of the laws," and miscegenation laws appeared to be the embodiment of constitutional equality.

In chapter 5, I show how the claim that interracial marriage was unnatural was then turned into bureaucratic procedures that made interracial marriage statistically invisible. By linking bans on interracial marriage to the issuance of marriage licenses, state officials charged with local health and welfare turned local marriage license clerks into the gatekeepers of white supremacy. Building on the racial terminology in the text of miscegenation laws, and on the work of race scientists, county clerks designed procedures that made race classifications appear to be simple common sense rather than scientific nonsense.

In chapters 6 through 8, I examine the half-century-long campaign to overturn miscegenation laws and uproot the claim that interracial marriage was unnatural. The first steps were taken between 1913 and 1927 by the NAACP, which invented a way to oppose miscegenation laws without also endorsing interracial marriage. By combining an innovative attack on the "nature" of race (in the form of black inferiority) with much more traditional claims about the "nature" of gender (in the form of the protection of women), NAACP leaders set the terms for much of the debate that followed, even during the 1940s and 1950s when the NAACP tried to avoid the issue altogether. Between 1930 and 1960, the campaign against the laws moved forward by fits and starts, showing the tension between civil rights organizations, including the Los Angeles Catholic Interracial Council (LACIC), the Japanese American Citizens League (JACL), the ACLU, and the NAACP, over when to challenge the laws, which races to foreground, whether interracial marriage was a "natural" or a "civil" right, and whether to hold fast to the politics of respectability or take direct aim at the sexualization of miscegenation law. It was not until all these questions had been resolved—and until the NAACP wholeheartedly reentered the fray in the 1964 case of *McLaughlin v. Florida*—that the stage was finally set for the critics to succeed. In 1967, the U.S. Supreme Court declared miscegenation laws unconstitutional in the case of *Loving v. Virginia.*

In chapter 9, I trace the post-*Loving* dismantling of miscegenation law and show how White opposition to interracial marriage finally waned. By a remarkable process of forgetting the many miseries miscegenation law had engendered, Americans came to celebrate the *Loving* decision not only as a triumphant victory over white supremacy but also as a harbinger of color-blindness. In the years since, a variety of political actors have tried to harness the symbolic power of *Loving* to one cause or another—putting a multiracial category in the census, legalizing same sex marriage, or ending affirmative action—while the justices of the U.S. Supreme Court continue to debate the meaning of *Loving* for race and constitutional equality. In the conclusion, I tell the story of the last two miscegenation provisions to be removed from state constitutions (in South Carolina and Alabama, in 1998 and 2000), offer some thoughts on the many legacies of miscegenation law, and suggest that colorblindness should be considered a racial ideology of its own rather than the obvious solution to the problem of white supremacy.

Studies of miscegenation law started appearing even before the *Loving* decision and have been appearing ever since, with an explosion of work during the past decade. Scholars have developed two quite different approaches to the subject. The first is rooted in the politics of civil rights and the tenets of liberal individualism. Echoing the arguments used by lawyers who fought against miscegenation law in the 1950s and 1960s, these scholars describe the laws as examples of the establishment of racial "caste" and treat them as a subset of the history of segregation, with strong emphasis—and sometimes exclusive focus—on Blacks and Whites in the American South. As they tell it, the history of miscegenation law is a tragic denial of the rights of personal choice, a sad story of the folly of placing explicit racial categories in the law. The campaign to overturn miscegenation laws becomes part and parcel of the history of civil rights for African Americans, rendered in narratives that flow from one court battle to another, reaching a climax with *Loving v. Virginia*. In these studies, *Loving* marks the moment when the last of the segregation-era race categories were removed from the law; it stands for the triumph of romantic individualism over the forces of prejudice. The extent of interracial intimacy serves as a prime, even uniquely revealing, indicator of social progress, the springboard for discussions about the rise of colorblind racelessness and the possibilities of multiracialism.[4]

A second, newer approach has grown up piece by piece, alongside this civil rights story line, among scholars steeped in critical race and critical cultural studies. Its goal is to reveal the power of the law in shaping identities and producing "race," or, sometimes, to reveal the cultural obsession with interracial sex and marriage that lay just beneath the seeming taboos and silences.[5] Centering the links between racial formations and sex, gender, and family formations, these scholars explore the processes of racialization, sexualization, and naturalization, examining all the groups mentioned in miscegenation laws; they have even begun to explore the significance of the groups that were *not* mentioned in the laws.[6] Rather than limiting their focus to racial "caste" and de jure segregation, they examine the broader phenomenon of white supremacy, show how the passage of miscegenation laws became a routine aspect of American state-making, and raise questions about the promotion of colorblindness.[7]

What Comes Naturally reflects this latter approach; it is my attempt to marshal the extensive legal and archival record into a narrative that is as powerful and compelling as—if also broader and ultimately more persuasive than—the Black and White civil rights story line. As I will show, the history of miscegenation law stretches from the passions of White male slaveholders and fur traders to the halls of state legislatures; from sensational newspaper scandals about White women and Japanese American men to the actions of local district attorneys; from the machinations of White relatives eager to take property away from Black or Indian women to the process of race-making in criminal, civil, and probate courts; from the eager hopes of Filipino immigrant laborers and the confusion of marriage license clerks to the intricate design of the modern American administrative state.

To bring the national scale and multiracial breadth of miscegenation law clearly into focus, I have opened each chapter in this book with a discussion of a particular incident that occurred in a location—Texas, Indiana, Oregon, Arizona, California, New York, and Florida—that has so far received much less attention from scholars than Alabama and Virginia, the two southern states that take pride of place in most studies. The history of miscegenation law reaches well beyond the categories of Black and White, as even the invention of the term "miscegenation" shows. The politicos who invented "miscegenation" put forth two roughly parallel words. "Miscegenation," which denoted mixtures of "two or more races," was an immediate hit, but "melaleukation," which denoted mixtures between "the white and black races," never caught on.[8]

Miscegenation law reached well beyond the South. When the term "miscegenation" was invented, laws prohibiting interracial marriage were in effect not only there but also in Maine and Rhode Island; in Michigan, Illinois, and Ohio; in California, Nebraska, and Washington. By the end of the nineteenth century, the laws had spread to cover nearly all the states of the U.S. West, where state legislators made it their business to name several racial groups, including Chinese, Japanese, Filipinos, American Indians, native Hawaiians, and South Asians as well as Blacks and Whites. By the 1920s, this multiracial pattern of white supremacy was being adopted by southern states like Georgia and Virginia.

Miscegenation law was, I argue, not just one of the various forms of race segregation practiced between 1880 and 1930 but the foundation for the larger racial projects of white supremacy and white purity. As such, it rested on three animating fictions—one constitutional, one scientific, and one popular—which together served as the obvious, seemingly natural foundation of white supremacy.

The constitutional fiction of miscegenation law held that laws punishing both partners in an interracial relationship were racially equal rather than racially discriminatory. This, for example, was the position the Alabama Supreme Court put forth in 1881 in *Pace v. State,* a case involving a White woman and Black man, when it ruled:

> The fact that a different punishment is affixed to the offense of adultery when committed between a negro and a white person, and when committed between two white persons or two negroes, does not constitute a discrimination against or in favor of either race. The discrimination is not directed against the person of any particular color or race, but against the offense, the nature of which is determined by the opposite color of the cohabiting parties. The punishment of each offending party, white and black, is precisely the same. There is obviously no difference or discrimination in the punishment. The evil tendency of the crime of living in adultery or fornication is greater when it is committed between persons of the two races than between persons of the same race.[9]

This was also the position the Oregon Supreme Court maintained a half century later when it ruled that its miscegenation law did not discriminate against Indians because it "applies alike to all persons, either white, negroes, Chinese, Kanaka, or Indians."[10]

The second fiction of miscegenation law, the scientific one, held that racial purity could and should be protected. Its roots were in the writings of race scientists, who posited a finite number of "pure" races and insisted that races needed to be protected from intermixture, which was deemed to be a catastrophic mistake. The scientific notion of racial purity, visible in the works of naturalists, ethnologists, and anthropologists across the course of the entire nineteenth century, would reach its pinnacle in the writings of eugenicists during the 1920s. Its impact on miscegenation law, however, was clear enough by 1869, when the Georgia Supreme Court proclaimed:

> The amalgamation of the races is not only unnatural, but is always productive of deplorable results. Our daily observation shows us, that the offspring of these unnatural connections are generally sickly and effeminate, and that they are inferior in physical development and strength, to the full-blood of either race.[11]

It is important to note the final phrase, "of either race," here, because it shows how badly judges wanted to reconcile the scientific goal of racial purity with the constitutional veneration of equality. The abstract ideal of racial purity, judges and legislators liked to imply, might apply to Blacks as well as to Whites, or, for that matter, to Chinese or Japanese.

The third, and still most enduring, fiction of miscegenation law was the popular notion that race actually existed, that it was a thing that could be measured, determined, gotten to the truth of. Lawmakers reflected this belief when they passed laws to define race, usually by blood quantum standards, as Oregon did when it declared that "it shall not be lawful within this state for any white person, male or female, to intermarry with any negro, Chinese, or any person having one fourth or more negro, Chinese, or kanaka blood, or any person having more than one half Indian blood."[12] Prosecutors reflected this belief when they charged defendants with being "white," "negro," "Mongolian," or "Indian." Marriage license clerks reflected this belief when they filled in the blanks for "race and color" on license forms. White husbands and wives often reflected it, too, when they asked courts to give them divorces from partners they claimed were "negroes."

Behind these three fictions lay a much more complex historical reality. Despite all the judicial rhetoric about equality, miscegenation law was clearly a project of white supremacy rooted in notions of white purity. Both the text and the structure of the laws were steeped in white supremacy. The laws were written to prohibit Whites from marrying Blacks, Asian Americans, and Indians but not to prohibit Blacks from marrying Asian Americans, or Asian Americans from marrying Indians. In this sense, the structure of the laws was an attempt to place non-Whites in structurally similar subordination to Whites, as if all non-Whites inhabited the same social world and embodied the same threat to whiteness.

Although the list of races named in each law varied, from state to state and law to law, every miscegenation law banned Whites from marrying Blacks. In this sense, white supremacy was built on a long history of the enslavement and segregation of African Americans. But here, too, there is more to the story, for by the end of the nineteenth century, miscegenation law had become a multiracial project in white supremacy; it often vibrated with the tension between the desire to separate Blacks from Whites and the desire to multiply the races subject to the law. So it is essential to examine the distinctive historical trajectories of each of the various communities affected by the laws, to examine which groups were and were not named in miscegenation law (and where and when), and to show how people reacted to—and resisted—such naming. And it is vitally important to recognize the racial triangulations that were central to both the construction and the demise of miscegenation law.

In practice, miscegenation law acted as a kind of legal factory for the defining, producing, and reproducing of the racial categories of the state. One form of the production of race was rooted in the text of miscegenation laws, which listed specific racial categories and often defined them by blood quantum. These categories were then applied in court cases, from criminal trials to inheritance disputes, in which the results hinged on the determination of an individual's race.[13] Such cases demonstrate how nonsensical it is to try to pin racial categories on particular individuals. Modern readers may recoil at the details of these cases and find it a considerable relief to know that the repeal of state miscegenation laws finally put an end to them. This is why the campaign against miscegenation law is so often called the last battle against segregation.

But, although it has so far attracted much less attention, there was also a second form of the production of race in miscegenation law: the lodging of race in the process of marriage licensing. As miscegenation laws began to take hold, marriage license applicants were required to state (and clerks to record or approve) their "race or color." During the twentieth century, marriage licensing was the most common, and surely the most effective, means of preventing interracial marriage and enforcing miscegenation laws. And it was a procedure that survived long after miscegenation laws themselves were repealed. Marriage license application forms in a number of states still ask applicants to record their race as a means of recording vital statistics.[14]

Recognizing the production of race in marriage licensing can help dislodge the notion, prevalent in nearly every history of miscegenation laws, that during the twentieth century the laws were in nearly constant decline and that it was only a matter of time until they would disappear completely. In fact, miscegenation law grew steadily more significant throughout the first half of the twentieth century, as marriage licensing helped weave race and white supremacy throughout the American racial state. The production of race in marriage licenses can also help explain why the collapse of miscegenation law did not lead to a colorblind utopia. Racial categories may be absent from the texts of most of today's statutory laws, but they continue to be reproduced by the American racial state in ways less than obvious, and all the more powerful for being so. Categorizing by race remains a central function of local, state, and federal governments. The U.S. Census Bureau and the Office of Management and Budget spend a great deal of time determining official racial categories, which play a role in everything from the dividing up of voting districts to the determination of university admissions to the tracking of civil rights goals.[15] In this sense, miscegenation law, like immigration law and railroad segregation law, was a key building block of the racial infrastructure of today's administrative state.[16]

From beginning to end, the racial projects of miscegenation law were inextricably tied to gender and sexuality. It can be easy to miss the significance of gender in the operation of miscegenation laws, for the terminology of the laws is decidedly misleading. All but a very few of the laws were technically gender-neutral, that is, they were written so as to apply to both men and women in all the racial groups listed. In Montana, for example, any "white person" was prohibited from marrying "any Chinese person," "any Japanese person," or "a negro, or a person of negro blood or in part negro."[17] In Indiana, the clause providing that "no negro man, mulatto, or any man having one-eighth of negro blood" could marry "any white woman" was immediately followed by its companion: "nor shall any white man be permitted to marry any black woman, mulatto, or any woman having one-eighth part or more of negro blood."[18]

Historians have tried to count the numbers of White and Black men and women prosecuted under miscegenation law and have reached inconsistent conclusions. Some believe that White women and Black men were much more likely to be targeted by state officials, and others insist that White men and Black women were nearly as likely to come under scrutiny.[19] As it turns out, though, neither terminology nor numbers tell the full story.

Like the claim that miscegenation laws applied equally to all races, the idea that miscegenation laws applied equally on the basis of gender is more fiction than reality. In actual practice, the legislators who enacted miscegenation laws and the judges who enforced them nearly always had particular race-and-gender pairs in mind when they did so. When those pairs included White women, the tendency to enact, enforce, and elaborate miscegenation laws was sharper, the tendency to resort to criminal law stronger. Images of White women and Black men often sparked the passage of miscegenation laws; criminal prosecutions often reflected the desire to protect white womanhood that buttressed white supremacy in many of its forms, including miscegenation laws as well as lynchings. During the 1870s and early 1880s, when judges used the claim that interracial marriage was unnatural to uphold the constitutionality of miscegenation laws, they did so in cases involving White women and Black men, but images of White women and Asian American men also set lawmakers rushing to defend the barricades of white supremacy. The naming of Asian Americans in miscegenation laws took place remarkably rapidly, and with little or no debate, in large part because it expressed successive waves of fear that Chinese, Japanese, and finally Filipino men might marry White women.

When the race-and-gender pairs in question included White men, the story was much different. Unlike the naming of Asian Americans, the naming of American Indians in miscegenation law sparked considerable debate, because nineteenth-century lawmakers considered it through the lens of the history of White men married to Indian women. Many of the miscegenation cases involving White men came to court not as criminal prosecutions at all but as struggles over the inheritance of the estates of White men after their deaths. Throughout the nineteenth century, bans on interracial marriage con flicted with long-standing conceptions of White men's sexual freedoms and civil rights, including the right to choose their own wives and control their own property.

By the 1890s, the outcome of this struggle was clear. The stronger white supremacy grew, the more likely it was that White men would be subject to the full range of the disabilities of miscegenation law: that grand juries would indict them, state officials would prosecute them, and judges would sentence them. Indeed, by 1900, White men were nearly as likely as White women and Black men to run afoul of the laws. But the targeting of White men remained the hardest won—and most unstable—achievement in the history of miscegenation law. Rhetoric about the rights of White men ran through the entire history of opposition to the laws, from the assaults on miscegenation law during Reconstruction to repeals enacted in western states in the 1950s to the media coverage of the U.S. Supreme Court case that finally overturned miscegenation laws.

There is one more way in which the experience of men and women was profoundly unequal under miscegenation law, and that is in the assumptions about gender that nineteenth-century Americans, from would-be husbands and wives all the way to Supreme Court justices, brought to the subject of marriage in the first place. As historian Nancy F. Cott has argued, "marriage has been a cardinal—arguably the cardinal—agent of gender formation and has institutionalized gender roles."[20] In nineteenth-century law, husbands and wives held distinct responsibilities, obligations, and privileges. Husbands served as economic providers and family heads, in return for which they enjoyed sexual rights and represented the family to the state, as voters and jury members, and in the marketplace, as economic actors. Wives were expected to be sexually faithful and economically dependent; their rights came to them secondhand, via marriage.

In much the same way that miscegenation law was a kind of factory for the production of race, marriage was a kind of factory for the production of gender. Interracial marriage brought these two processes together, rooting race and gender in larger discussions of the rights of citizens. The independence of husbands and the dependence of wives were themes that appeared repeatedly in miscegenation law and the court cases it spawned: in the assumptions of all-male juries and state legislatures, in court cases over a widowed wife's right to inherit her husband's estate, in the fault line between illicit sex and marriage on which women's claims to respectability depended. Debates over the wisdom of miscegenation law often read like debates over the institution of manhood: during Reconstruction, when Black legislators struggled to limit the sexual access White men had long enjoyed to Black women; during the 1920s and 1930s, when Filipino men tried to insist on their right to choose White women for their wives.

The men who enacted miscegenation laws paid much more attention to interracial marriage than to interracial sex. As American history clearly shows, interracial sex was both commonplace and often ignored or tolerated by state and local authorities. The law was usually inclined to step in only when interracial couples began to claim the public respectability and the property and inheritance rights that went with marriage.

But sexuality is at least as important to this history as gender because the development of miscegenation law depended on judges drawing lines between legitimate marriage and illicit sex, then branding interracial relationships of all kinds *as* illicit sex. In this process, which I call the sexualization of miscegenation law, interracial couples, many of them long-standing deeply committed couples, were subjected to the powerful stigmas associated with immorality, illegitimacy, and vice. The sexualization of miscegenation law was a key element in the long survival of laws banning interracial marriage.

To write a history of miscegenation law is to be immersed in the ideas of white supremacy and the phrasing of race-making, to struggle almost endlessly with issues of terminology. It is difficult to choose words when all the available alternatives are clearly products of the process of race-making. Problems of terminology arise at every level: the words to describe the laws, the racial projects they sustained, and the groups and individuals—the supposed "races"—subject to them. Like anyone who has struggled with these problems, I have sometimes wished it were possible to abandon the terminology of race altogether. Yet even the briefest attempt to do that quickly proved impossible. I simply could not imagine a way to show how miscegenation law produced and reproduced notions of race without naming race as its product, and without naming the races produced, and reproduced, in the text of laws and indictments, in court trials, and in the process of marriage licensing.

In the end, I settled on four rhetorical strategies I hope will help me show the enormous power miscegenation laws held to produce race even as

I emphasize the arbitrariness of the categories created by these laws. First, I have decided to use the word "miscegenation," unpleasant though it is, rather than to adopt of any of the milder, seemingly less pejorative, alternatives. The invention of the term "miscegenation" marked a new and highly significant turn in the longer history of the regulation of interracial marriage. Between 1864 and 1967, lawmakers and their supporters routinely called laws that banned interracial sex and marriage "anti-miscegenation" laws; they did so in order to signal their belief that sex and marriage between people of different races was a distinctly different phenomenon than sex and marriage between people of the same race. In this book I will use the term "miscegenation" to mark that particular racist belief; that is, I will use "miscegenation" in much the same way that another historian might speak of "eugenics" or, for that matter, "racism."

Second, I have decided to use the term "white supremacy" rather than the term "racial caste," which so often appears in other histories of miscegenation law. "White supremacy" has the malleability to reveal the several different layers of racial domination (structure, ideology, and aspiration) and the relations between them more effectively than "racial caste," a term borrowed from mid-twentieth-century social science and, in the United States at least, most closely associated with the legal segregation of Whites from Blacks. By using the term "white supremacy," I hope to suggest that the concept of whiteness carried vexed meaning, not just for Whites and Blacks but for all the groups, including recent Southern European immigrants, Mexican Americans, Filipinos, and Asian Americans, who lived their lives at its edges, despite wide differences in their individual racial formations and specific structures of oppression.

Third, I have tried to show just how commanding a force miscegenation law was in the production of race and racial categories. These laws did much more than reflect racial identities or terminologies borrowed from the surrounding society. A prosecutor who charged a "Negro man" with marrying a "white woman" engaged in a very powerful act of naming, categorizing, and defining. When I put a racial term in quotation marks, I do so to show that it is the exact terminology used in the legal records, right down to the punctuation and capitalization. My goal is to keep this process of racial naming, and its distance from the lived experience of individuals, right before the reader. A miscegenation law that listed the category "Mongolian" set in motion a whole host of processes, in and out of courtrooms, designed to fit particular living individuals into the category thus named. Neither "Negro" nor "Mongolian" would be used today, and neither should be taken to map neatly onto the categories, such as African American or Asian American, that might seem to have replaced them. Even in their own day, these categories often carried little correlation to the self-identities or observable characteristics of the individuals to whom they were applied.

Finally, to show the pervasiveness of racial categories then and now, I have departed from the usual grammatical practice and decided to capitalize the words "Black" and "White" as well as more routinely capitalized words such as "Japanese," "Chinese," and "Filipino." My hope here is to show "Black" Americans as a group of men and women with a wide variety of skin colors and backgrounds rather than to let the word "black" slide into physical description. And by capitalizing "White," I hope to help mark the category that so often remains unmarked, and taken for the norm, when the fact is that, in American history, to be "White" is often an aspiration as well as an entitlement.[21]

This book sets out to prove, then, that miscegenation law was a national—and multiracial—project, that it laid the foundation for the projects of white supremacy and white purity in bureaucratic practice as well as in courts and state legislatures, that it was inextricably tied to gender and sexuality, and that it was a key arena for the production of race in everything from language to criminal prosecution to the structuring of families. As the title, *What Comes Naturally,* suggests, it also has a loftier goal: to raise questions about what is and is not really natural or unnatural and to expose the powerfully pernicious effects these labels have had in America's past—and in America's present.

Part I

Miscegenation Law and Constitutional Equality, 1863–1900

Chapter One

ENGENDERING MISCEGENATION

"Be it further enacted, That it shall not be lawful for any person of European blood or their descendants, to intermarry with Africans, or the descendants of Africans; and should any person as aforesaid violate the provisions of this section such marriage shall be null and void."

—*Republic of Texas Laws, 1837*

FORT BEND COUNTY, TEXAS

Alfred Foster never told anyone that Leah Foster was his wife. Perhaps he never believed it himself. Certainly he kept his family out of public view. The reason was simple: Alfred Foster was a "white" man and a slaveowner; Leah Foster was a "coloured" woman and his slave.

Sometime in the 1820s or 1830s, Alfred Foster, then an aspiring Mississippi planter, purchased a slave woman named Leah. Soon after, he started sleeping with her. Between 1837 and the 1850s, Leah had five children. Unlike Foster's other slaves, Leah and her children took the Foster name. In 1847, they accompanied Alfred to Cincinnati, Ohio, where he emancipated them, claiming in the deed of manumission that "motives of benevolence and humanity" led him to do so. Then Leah and the children followed Alfred back to the South, where they gathered the slaves he had left behind and moved again, this time to Fort Bend County, Texas.[1]

A few decades earlier, when East Texas was under Mexican rule, interracial couples had often found refuge there.[2] But by the time Alfred and Leah arrived, Fort Bend County was dominated by transplanted American southerners determined to make their new home a bastion of slavery and white supremacy. Under these circumstances, White men who slept with Black women took care to avoid their neighbors' disapproval. On the Foster plantation, Leah slept with Alfred, but she and the children lived in their own quarters outside the big house. Foster's slaves thought that Alfred treated Leah and the children like family, but the census taker counted them as slaves, and neighboring White men who visited Alfred called Leah a servant. Neighboring White women seem to have steered clear of the Foster household.[3]

In 1867, Alfred Foster died. In his will, written the year before, he left the bulk of his estate, "my farm, or plantation . . . together with all the appurtenances and improvements thereon," to "Leah a coloured woman formily owned by me but now free and her five children, namely Fields, George, Isaac, Margaret and Monroe." Under its terms, Foster's house and the three hundred acres of land surrounding it would have gone to Leah and the children "to have and to hold the same during their natural lives and after their deaths to go to their children." In this legal document signed before White witnesses, Foster once again stopped short of calling Leah his wife. He did not, however, hesitate to invoke a standard husbandly privilege: "It is my will," he declared, "that should the freedwoman Leah at any time after my Death marry she thereby relinquishes all her interest in my estate."[4]

By the time Alfred Foster said his last good-byes, the Civil War was over, and slavery had died along with it. Fort Bend County's newly freed Blacks dreamed of owning land. Alfred's will promised Leah and her children a farm larger than those most Texas Blacks were in any position to acquire.[5] But holding on to it meant, as so much else in Leah Foster's life had, depending on a White man.

Alfred Foster had named Leah and their eldest son, thirty-year-old Fields Foster, as two of the three coexecutors of his estate, but neither of them could secure the $15,000 bond required by the court to be appointed administrator, so control of the estate fell to the third coexecutor, a White merchant aptly named Benjamin Bonds.[6] It is possible, even likely, that Alfred Foster chose Bonds because he expected him to look after Leah and the children. If so, he underestimated the greed for land—and the White panic over Black property ownership—that swept through East Texas during Reconstruction.

While Leah and her younger children waited for Bonds to settle the estate and give them their inheritance, her older sons Fields, George, and Isaac farmed the Foster land. They obtained the supplies they needed, including a wagon and some oxen, by promising to pay Bonds a "rent" of $430 in gold at the end of the year. When the end of that year rolled around, Bonds set the "rent" for the next year at $700, and this time he took a lien on the crop as security. In November 1868, nearly two years after Alfred Foster had died, Benjamin Bonds finished his accounting, declared that the Foster estate was deeply in debt to another White man, a merchant named Elisha Ryon, and asked the county judge to put the land up for auction. At the auction, Ryon bought the property for $2,775, an amount suspiciously close to the sum he claimed to be owed by the Foster estate, and a bargain price for land that had been valued at $4,635 in the county's 1864 tax rolls.[7]

Leah Foster refused to accept the loss of her promised inheritance. Charging that Bonds and Ryon had acted "in utter disregard" of her "rights," she went to court to ask the judge to invalidate the land sale. As part of her case, Leah Foster made the public declaration of marriage that Alfred had always avoided. Calling herself "the surviving widow" of Alfred Foster, she claimed the wifely privilege of exempting her homestead, which according to Texas law would amount to two hundred of the three hundred acres of the Foster property, from the reach of creditors like Bonds and Ryon. On November 21, 1871, Judge Livingston Lindsay of Fort Bend County, Texas, heard Leah's case and reopened a question the Texas legislature thought it had settled three decades earlier by passing a law forbidding "any person of European blood or their descendants, to intermarry with Africans, or the descendants of Africans."[8]

Were Alfred and Leah Foster married? Answering this question requires moving from a local property dispute to a provocative issue for Reconstruction-era courts and into a larger history of the relationships between race, sex, and gender in American marriage law. This is a story that focuses, on one level, on women like Leah Foster, whose futures rested on the outcome of court cases defining marriage. On another level, it traces the history of an American legal system in which traditionally powerful groups— state legislators, lawyers, judges—used notions of gender and sexuality to enact, enforce, and reproduce categories of race. In the end, though, it shows the interaction between these two levels, that is, the way that people shape and are shaped by categories that are both arbitrary and extremely powerful. To understand Alfred and Leah Foster's relationship in the 1860s, it is important to begin by recognizing that laws against interracial sex and marriage had their origins two centuries earlier.

Slavery, Race, and Laws against Interracial Marriage

America's earliest laws against interracial sex and marriage were spawned by slavery. The first such law, designed to prevent marriages between "freeborne English women" and "Negro Slaues [*sic*]," was passed in Maryland in 1664 as part of the act that authorized lifelong slavery in that colony.[9] As Barbara Fields insightfully notes, it "shows society in the act of inventing race" in order to fortify slavery.[10] A similar determination to draw racial dividing lines can be seen in the laws of neighboring Virginia. In 1662, Virginia legislators resolved "doubts [that had] arisen whether children got by any Englishman upon a negro woman should be slave or free" by passing a law that defined slavery as a condition inherited from mothers and prohibited fornication between "any christian . . . with a negro man or woman." By 1691, Virginia legislators had decided to prohibit marriage and bastardy between any "English or other white man or woman" and any "negroe, mulatto, or Indian man or woman bond or free."[11] Other colonies soon followed. During the colonial period, laws against interracial marriage were passed in the British colonies of Massachusetts (1705), North Carolina (1715), Pennsylvania (1726), and Georgia (1750) and, by decree of Louis XV, in the French colony of Louisiana (1724).[12]

These early laws, which, like slavery, existed in northern as well as southern colonies, had two central characteristics.[13] First, they covered interracial sexual behavior such as adultery, fornication, and bastardy as well as marriage. Indeed, three colonies—Dutch New Netherland (1638) and British South Carolina (1717) and Delaware (1726–36)—passed laws that covered only sexual behavior.[14] Second, they placed special emphasis on controlling the sexual and reproductive behavior of White women. This focus was evident not only in the naming of "freeborne English women" in the Maryland statute of 1664 but also in the detailed punishments meted out to White women offenders. According to the Virginia law of 1691, for example, any "English woman being free" who had a "bastard child by any negro or mulatto" man was subject to a fine of fifteen pounds or five years in service; if she was already a servant, her term of service would be extended by five years. The child would be bound out until age thirty.[15]

Colonial laws against interracial sex and marriage relied on the withdrawal of freedom, fines, and corporal punishment; they worked in concert with laws that defined the children of slave mothers as slaves. Beginning in 1750, a new element was added to this mix, when Georgia passed the first law nullifying interracial marriages. Setting a pattern that would be used much more widely in the nineteenth century, Georgia declared marriages between "white People" and "Negroes or Blacks" "unlawful . . . and . . . absolutely null and void."[16]

After the American Revolution, laws against interracial marriage grew new roots in both the North and the South, while laws against interracial sex languished. Bans on marriage between Whites and Blacks helped the emerging

American republic draw racial dividing lines. In southern states, where slavery became even more deeply entrenched, laws against interracial marriage continued to serve as props for the racial system of slavery, as one more way to distinguish free Whites from slaves. In northern states, where lawmakers could no longer rely on the categories of "master" and "slave," they named and tried to define racial categories per se.[17] The racial categories set forth in northern laws against interracial marriage strengthened the fiction that race distinctions could be maintained and laid the legal framework of white supremacy in so-called free states.

Although Pennsylvania repealed its colonial law in 1780, the process of American state-making frequently involved the passage of laws against interracial marriage.[18] Between the formation of the American republic and the outbreak of the Civil War, twenty-eight American states relied on these laws.[19] The colonial law remained in effect in Maryland, and new versions of older laws against interracial marriage were passed in Massachusetts (1786), Virginia (1792), Delaware (1807), Louisiana (1808), and North Carolina (1830).[20] Alfred Foster's home state of Mississippi did not have a law explicitly prohibiting the marriage of Whites and Blacks, but its 1822 marriage law provided that marriages could only be solemnized "between any free white persons within this state."[21] When Alfred Foster purchased Leah, laws that prohibited the marriage of Blacks and Whites had spread to Kentucky (1792), Rhode Island (1798), the District of Columbia (1801), Indiana (1818), Maine (1821), Tennessee (1822), and Illinois (1829).[22] By the time Leah Foster was emancipated, the list included Florida (1832), Missouri (1835), Texas (1837), Arkansas (1838), Michigan (1838), and Iowa (1840).[23] In 1852, Alabama passed a law against interracial marriage, and both Georgia and Utah passed laws prohibiting interracial sex.[24] Before the Civil War broke out, laws against interracial marriage had spread to many midwestern states and territories as well, including California (1850), Kansas (1855), Nebraska (1855), Washington (1855), New Mexico (1857), and Ohio (1861).[25]

American Indian nations also banned marriage to Blacks. This pattern was most pronounced among the Five Civilized Nations, whose leaders, like their White southern counterparts, were slaveholders. Thus, in 1824, the Cherokee National Committee and Council passed a law that banned "intermarriages between negro slaves, and Indians, or Whites," set fines for slaveholders who allowed the marriages, and threatened "any male Indian or white man marrying a negro woman slave" with "fifty-nine stripes on the bare back," and "any Indian or white woman, marrying a negro male slave" with "twenty-five stripes on her or their bare back." The Creek Nation linked its concern about intermarriage directly to property. In 1825, it passed two laws. The first required "white" men who fathered children with "Indian" women to leave their property for the children's support if they subsequently left the Nation. The second, however, provided that "any of our children" who "take a Negro as a husband or wife" would forfeit all right to property from their parents, "as it is a disgrace to our Nation for our people to marry a Negro." In 1839, the Cherokee Nation broadened its initial ban to prohibit marriage "between a free male or female citizen with any person of color."[26] Nearly twenty years later, in 1858, the Chickasaw Nation forbade "all persons other than a negro . . . from cohabiting with a negro or negroes," on penalty of a fine of twenty-five to fifty dollars, "one half . . . to go to the informer."[27]

Gender and the Properties of Marriage

Laws against interracial marriage did more than separate and enforce social categories of race. By using marriage to delineate race, lawmakers wrapped race in and around the gender differences that stood at the heart of nineteenth-century marriage, which, in turn, stood at the heart of the American state.[28] Nineteenth-century Americans liked to think of their marriages as the product of romantic love, far removed from older understandings of marriage as a propertied agreement between families. Legal commentators echoed the ideal of romantic mutuality by promulgating a legal fiction of marital unity in which husbands and wives were said to become one with each other.[29] But when it came to the day-to-day workings of the law, the notion of marital unity was a fiction in every sense of the word, for even the most romantic of marriages was encased in a set of legal provisions that granted considerable powers to husbands and considerable disadvantages to wives. As legal historian Hendrik Hartog aptly concludes, to be married was to be "joined in a permanent relationship of power and submission."[30]

In Alfred Foster's America, marriage was built around the gendered privileges and responsibilities of husbands and wives. The marital powers of husbands were integrally related to notions of property. As husbands and fathers, men were thought to have certain property rights *in* their wives and children. One such power was the father's "paramount" right to custody of his children, which remained the norm through the first half of the nineteenth century. Another, even more basic, example was the notion of conjugal rights expressed in laws that gave husbands de facto property rights in their wives' sexuality by exempting husbands from prosecution for rape within marriage.[31]

Nineteenth-century American husbands also controlled property *for* their wives. As historian Linda Kerber puts it, the basis of marriage law was a system of coverture that "transferred a woman's civil identity to her husband at marriage, giving him use and direction of her property throughout the marriage."[32] The economic power of husbands was a long-standing tradition that took on new significance in the early nineteenth century as middle-class women began to mark their own status by withdrawing from work for wages outside the home and cloaking their work inside the home with an aura of mystical domesticity. In a world that offered women few opportunities for supporting themselves, marriage offered them incorporation in the proper-tied order. Because wives became the financial beneficiaries as well as the financial dependents of their husbands, nineteenth-century women had an economic as well as a social and emotional investment in the institution of marriage.[33]

The many functions of marriage—the gendered molding of husbands and wives, the containment of sexuality, the raising of children, the linking of the private family to the political and economic figure of the male householder, the orderly handing down of property from generation to generation—made it an institution of singular importance to the state. Fledgling American states strongly encouraged marriage. As mid-nineteenth-century lawyer Joel Bishop asserted, marriage was "cherished by the government, as the first and choic-est object of its regard." Because American lawmakers believed that marriage should be a civil status chosen by the partners rather than a religious ritual, they defined marriage as a contract between two persons and placed that con-tract firmly under state control. The possibility "that any government could, consistently with the general weal, permit this institution to become merely [a] matter of bargain between men and women, and not regulate it by its own power," was, Bishop asserted, "too absurd to require a word of refutation."[34]

In early nineteenth-century America, states used their power to make marriage as easy to contract as possible. In hopes of encouraging marriage, state legislatures passed laws that sanctioned civil and religious ceremonies of many different kinds. State officials tried to smooth potential conflicts between the laws of various states by extending the legal courtesy of comity, or routine recognition, to marriages performed and recognized in other states.[35] As the new nation pushed beyond its Atlantic coast origins, states claimed authority over newly incorporated residents partly by legitimating marriages made according to other forms, such as Spanish law or Indian custom. Ameri-can judges even developed a unique form of marriage with no ceremony at all, the so-called common-law marriage, which quickly became a popular feature of many state law codes.[36]

In Texas, Alfred and Leah Foster's neighbors made good use of this wide variety of forms of marriage. Fort Bend County's earliest settlers had improvised an informal process of marriage "by bond" to satisfy Mexican officials. After Texas wrested its independence from Mexico and joined the United States, the state legislature retroactively legitimized all marriages by bond as well as marriages previously entered into "agreeably to the custom of the times," that is, under Spanish law. Then, in an awkward attempt to force its Spanish legal heritage into Anglo channels, Texas adopted the common law, and with it the American institution of common-law marriage. Texas also recognized yet another form of nonceremonial marriage, called putative marriage.[37]

The institution of marriage was deemed so important that American courts developed a formal presumption of marriage, which, in the absence of absolute proof to the contrary, shielded couples from most challenges to the validity of their marriages. In the words of Joel Bishop, "every court, in considering questions not clearly settled or defined in the law, should lean toward this institution of marriage; holding, consequently, all persons to be married, who, living in the way of husband and wife, may accordingly be presumed to have intended entering into the relation, unless the rule of law which is set up to prevent this conclusion is distinct and absolute, or some impediment of nature intervenes."[38]

Legitimate Marriage and Illicit Sex

Couples like Alfred and Leah Foster, however, stood outside this presumption of marriage. They were, in effect, stuck at the spot where the state's determination to foster marriage ran up against the state's determination to draw racial dividing lines. To understand what happened when these forces collided requires exploring how gender and race were intertwined with the divide between legitimate marriage and illicit sex in a legal system built around the propertied privileges of husbands.

As propertied White men of substance, slaveholders like Alfred Foster stood at the pinnacle of the systems of gender, sex, and racial authority of their day. They expected, and enjoyed, considerable liberty to do as they wished, inside and outside the law. For many masters, Foster among them, one of these liberties was having sex with slaves, a practice that was widespread despite the laws against interracial sex and marriage that had been in effect since the 1660s. During the antebellum period, some states abandoned their laws against interracial sex, substituting stronger bans on interracial marriage instead. The remaining laws were simply unenforced—indeed, when it came to White men, at least, unenforceable— since neither slaves nor free Blacks could testify against Whites. Under these circumstances, plantation masters could indulge their sexual desires with slave women with little fear of legal penalty. Sex with slaves provided a particularly intimate demonstration of the privileges of White manhood, of absolute power over both the slave women who were its immediate targets and the slave men who were held powerless to prevent it. At the same time, it presented few risks for slave masters. Because children born of these unions were defined as slaves, they added to the masters' wealth. And though the White wives of slave masters generally resented the practice, their own economic dependence on their husbands discouraged them from protesting.

Another of the privileges White male slaveowners enjoyed was the right to control their households and distribute their property as they saw fit, during their lifetime and after their death. Consider, for example, the major mechanism of inheritance, the "will." Like other privileges available to free White men of the day, wills were associated with power and property. Nineteenth-century legal expert Isaac Redfield quoted John Buchanan, the chief justice of the Maryland Court of Appeals, to explain the general rule. "A testator," Buchanan opined, "should enjoy full liberty and freedom, in the making of his will, and possess the power to withstand all contradiction and control." In contrast to English courts, Redfield asserted, "American courts, in determining the construction of wills, have almost universally been governed by a leading reference to the intent of the testator."[39] When American probate courts upheld the wills of White men, they reproduced a system devoted to maximizing opportunities for economic advancement. When Alfred Foster declared that it was his "will" that his farm should go to Leah as long as she did not marry another man, he used a phrase that was both comfortably familiar and legally forceful; it signaled both his freedom to dispose of his property as he wished and his expectation that his will as household head would be upheld.

Neither slaves nor women enjoyed anything like the wide range of liberties that White male slaveholders took as their due. All of the freedoms that free White men enjoyed—to own and bequeath property, to make contracts, to marry—were deliberately denied to slaves. As part of the general denial of property rights, slaves were deemed incapable of entering into a legal marriage. So, although most masters encouraged (and some forced) their slaves to pair up with each other, courts refused to grant these relationships any formal validity. As a North Carolina judge explained in 1858, "Marriage is based upon contract; consequently the relation of 'man and wife' cannot exist among slaves. It is excluded, both on account of their incapacity to contract, and of the paramount right of ownership in them, as property."[40]

For slaves and for women, too, the status of marriage, which was associated with the privileges of citizenship, took shape in contrast to the seeming alternative of illicit sex, which lived in the shadowy netherworld of immorality evoked in phrases like "adultery and fornication" or "illicit cohabitation." Judges who refused to recognize slave marriages were, in effect, assigning all relationships between slaves to the disreputable category of illicit sex.

The legal and social fault line between legitimate marriage and illicit sex loomed especially large for women, who were expected to remain sexually chaste until marriage and faithful within it. Unable or unwilling to prevent men from exercising sexual license, Americans condemned as immoral in women the kind of behavior they pretended not to notice in men.

As an ex-slave and as a woman, Leah Foster's fortunes would hinge on the distinction between legitimate marriage and illicit sex. In the nineteenth-century legal world, husbands were expected to provide their wives with support and maintenance, and the law worked to extend these protections to their widows. The specific laws that protected widows varied from state to state: some states held on to colonial notions of a wife's "dower" right in her husband's estate; others spelled out a widow's "thirds"; still others, like Alfred Foster's Texas, passed homestead laws. All of these shielded wives and widows from being disinherited, being left in the lurch by husbands who died without wills, or having to pay the claims of their husbands' creditors; their goal was to reduce the number of impoverished widows who might become dependent on state support.[41]

But there was a catch: only a legal, legitimate wife could claim the protections built into marriage and inheritance law. Men carried no economic responsibility at all for women who were sexual partners outside of legitimate marriage. A man might—or might not—leave money or property to his paramour; if he did not, the courts would do nothing to protect her. Women in illicit relationships were not considered legal wives; they could not claim family property by inheritance; and their children were categorized as illegitimate bastards. Women in this situation were at the mercy of legally legitimate relatives, who might accuse them of exerting undue influence over the wills of men who tried to leave them money or property. For women, then, the distinction between marriage and illicit sex was crucial.[42]

In determining just where to draw the line between legitimate marriage and illicit sex, judges were faced with overlapping and contradictory legal traditions. The expansive history of nineteenth-century marriage law and the legal presumption of marriage clashed with the moral impulse to condemn women for indulging in illicit sexual behavior, all within the context of a legal system designed to protect the prerogatives of White male citizens. When it came to interracial marriage, though, the privileges of free White men reached one of their pre–Civil War limits. Marriage was so strongly associated with whiteness, freedom, property, and propriety that interracial marriage threatened slavery in a way that interracial sex did not. Southern legislators used laws against interracial marriage to build a barricade, which judges then enforced, right at the point where a sexual relationship might turn into a marriage.

It was to this end that antebellum states passed so many laws declaring interracial marriages "illegal and void," setting misdemeanor punishments for officials who solemnized the marriages and often, but not always, setting punishments for the men and women who tried to marry as well. In slave states, the penalties for participants fell mostly on the White partners to the marriages. In Tennessee, for example, any "white" person who would "presume to live with any negro, mustee, or mulatto man or woman as man and wife" was subject to criminal conviction and a fine of $500 payable "to any person who will sue for the same."[43] An additional fine could be levied on any official who issued the license for such a marriage and anyone who performed the ceremony. In free states, both marriage partners were subject to penalties, and so were the officials involved. Thus in Illinois both partners to an interracial marriage were subject to fines, public whippings, and/or one-year prison sentences; those who issued the license or performed the ceremony were fined not less than $200 and made ineligible to hold public office.[44]

Before the Civil War, then, the long history of sexual license on the part of slave masters, the denial of marriage rights to slaves, and laws against interracial marriage shaped the sexual parameters of slaveholders' racial authority. To put it in other words, laws against interracial marriage didn't prevent masters from having sex with slave women or having mixed-race children, both of which were common occurrences. Rather, they prevented masters from turning slaves they slept with into respectable wives who might claim freedom, demand citizenship rights, or inherit family property, and so undermine the foundations of racialized slavery.

Engendering Miscegenation

Before the Civil War, laws against interracial marriage were widely accepted as a necessary adjunct to slavery in the South and a means of drawing lines between Whites and Blacks in the North. It was not until the Civil War threw the future of slavery into doubt that lawyers, legislators, and judges began to develop the elaborate justifications that signified the emergence of miscegenation law and made restrictions on interracial marriage the foundation of post–Civil War white supremacy.

The first step in this process was the invention of the term "miscegenation," which conveniently marks the moment when the topic of interracial marriage first captured the national political spotlight. In happened in 1863, and began, so the story goes, as a joke. At the height of the hard-fought presidential election of 1864, two Democratic pamphleteers working in New York published a thinly disguised parody, *Miscegenation: The Theory of the Blending of the Races, Applied to the American White Man and Negro,* in which they pretended to argue that science, religion, common sense, and the Republican Party all agreed that "the intermarriage of diverse races is indispensable to a progressive humanity." Hoping to persuade unwary readers to vote against Abraham Lincoln, the pamphlet built up to an argument that when Lincoln "proclaimed Emancipation he proclaimed also the mingling of the races. The one follows the other as surely as noonday follows sunrise."[45]

The pamphlet opened with an elaborate defense of the term "miscegenation," which the authors had coined and which they used to refer to race mixtures in a mock-scientific style. The pamphleteers were soon exposed for the cynical partisans they really were, but Americans adopted the term "miscegenation," with such alacrity that it would frame public debate over race, sex, and marriage for the next century. As David Roediger has suggested, the term itself shows the rise of the issue to national prominence: it links "misceg," or the mixing of genus/family/race, with "nation."[46]

The birth of the term "miscegenation" occurred in a very particular, and revealing, setting. The pamphlet's parody relied on turning the supposedly natural separation of the races upside down by insisting that "miscegenation" would soon become the new "law of nature." Reaching for an analogy that could ground their point, the pamphleteers fastened on the "natural" attraction between men and women, then claimed that the joining of two races in marriage was every bit as natural as the joining of two sexes. "We love our opposites," they declared. "It is in the nature of things that we should do so, and where nature has free course, men like those we have indicated, whether anti-slavery or pro-slavery, conservative or radical, democrat or republican, will marry and be given in marriage to the most perfect specimens of the colored race."[47] It was by analogy to the "natural" difference of sex that "miscegenation" became so deeply grounded in the "natural" difference of race.

During and immediately after the Civil War, growing public fears about the possibility of "miscegenation" were reflected in an unprecedented outburst

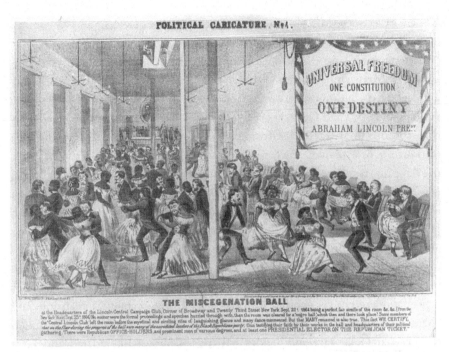

Political Caricature No. 4, The Miscegenation Ball. One of many attempts to use the newly minted word "miscegenation" to embarrass the Republican Party during the presidential election of 1864, this purports to be a drawing of "The Miscegenation Ball and the Headquarters of the Lincoln Central Campaign Club, Corner of Broadway and Twenty Third Street New York Sept 22d. 1864." (Prints and Photographs Division, Library of Congress)

of state laws. Concern stretched across the country, as new laws were passed in the far western states and territories of Nevada (1861), Oregon (1862), Idaho (1864), and Arizona (1865).[48] In the South, old laws against interracial marriage, which remained in effect in Arkansas, Delaware, Louisiana, Tennessee, Texas, and Virginia, were joined by new ones.[49] Midway through the Civil War, when West Virginia broke away from Virginia to become a state, it refused to join the Confederacy, but it held on to Virginia's law against interracial marriage.[50] As the war drew to a close in 1865, Mississippi and South Carolina, the only two slave states that had failed to ban interracial marriage before the war, passed miscegenation laws.[51] In 1866, Georgia replaced its previous law against interracial sex with one that prohibited interracial marriage; in 1867, Maryland adjusted its prewar law against interracial marriage by removing the possibility of enslavement as punishment.[52] Postwar laws were passed in Alabama (1866), Florida (1866),

Kentucky (1866), Missouri (1866), North Carolina (1866), and Wyoming (1869).[53] These laws, passed in the spirit of the contemporary uproar over "miscegenation," were considerably harsher than their antebellum predecessors. The Mississippi law, for example, declared interracial marriage a felony and declared that violators would be subject to life in prison.[54] Two states, Alabama (1865) and Georgia (1865), went so far as to put these provisions directly into their state constitutions.[55]

During this period, then, miscegenation law was engendered in three overlapping respects. It was engendered in the sense of being born; that is, the use of the term "miscegenation" helped transform the prewar skeleton of laws against interracial marriage into a postwar body of miscegenation law that emerged from the shadow of slavery to stand on its own. It was also engendered in the sense that both its proponents and its opponents used assumptions about sex and gender in marriage already woven through the American legal system to restructure American race relations. And it was engendered in yet another way, too, for the enforcement, expansion, and entrenchment of miscegenation laws was selectively, and powerfully, linked to very particular race-and-gender pairings. Couples like Alfred and Leah Foster, made up of White men and Black women, would figure very differently in the development of miscegenation law than couples made up of White women and Black men.

The Reconstruction of Male Privilege

By November 1871, when fifty-nine-year-old Leah Foster appeared in Judge Livingston Lindsay's court, the Civil War had stripped the South of both its foundational institution, slavery, and its symbolic center, the White male slaveowner. Reconstruction, the short-lived effort to extend civil and political rights to freed slaves, was in full swing, visible in laws and constitutional amendments that raised the possibility of racial equality. In 1866, the U.S. Congress had passed a Civil Rights Act that declared that citizens of "every race and color" held the right "to make and enforce contracts, to sue, be parties, and give evidence, to inherit, purchase, lease, sell, hold, and convey real and personal property" and to enjoy the "full and equal benefit of all laws and proceedings for the security of person and property, as is enjoyed by white citizens." Later that year, Congress raised these specific protections to the broader level of constitutional privilege by proposing the Fourteenth Amendment to the U.S. Constitution. Ratified in 1868, the Fourteenth Amendment promised to protect the "privileges and immunities of citizens of the United States" by offering "equal protection of the laws."[56]

Across the South, newly freed slaves struggled to link these abstract concepts of citizenship to everyday privileges of race, gender, and sex. Because marriage encoded so many manly privileges—such as household authority, sexual privileges, economic rights, and political standing—and because marriage involved obligations that tied households to the state, marriage proved a particularly productive site for reformulating the privileges and responsibilities of men and women, Black and White.[57]

One such reformulation was the passage of post–Civil War laws legalizing the marriages of freed slaves. One of the first demands freed slaves made was for the legal recognition of their marriages, in part because they longed to remove Black women from the sexual and economic reach of White men. Although many southern Whites regarded the marriage of ex-slaves as a contradiction in terms, they had forged such a long-standing association between freedom, marriage, and morality that they were hard-pressed to resist these demands. Even the most recalcitrant of southern legislatures, those that passed the infamous black codes, also passed laws giving freed slaves the legal right to marry.[58]

The passage of laws legitimizing the marriages of ex-slaves reflected nineteenth-century understandings of the dual nature of the privileges and obligations of marriage. In demanding the right to marry, freed slaves emphasized the privileges of marriage, especially its connections to property and citizenship rights. But in granting the right to marry, state and federal officials emphasized the obligations of marriage. Federal Reconstruction officials and Christian reformers applauded laws that provided for the marriage of freed slaves because of their potential to mold freedmen and women into models of moral respectability, while southern legislators hoped to transfer legal and economic responsibility for former slaves from White masters to Black fathers and husbands. In much the same way that the expansion of antebellum marriage law forged links of privilege and obligation between White male husbands and the states of the early American republic, postwar laws forged links of privilege and obligation between Black male husbands and the American nation-state.[59]

Freed slaves vociferously demanded the right to marry, but they did not generally call for the legalization of interracial marriage. During Reconstruction, a number of Black men sat in state and federal legislatures and constitutional conventions, and many more in conventions of "colored men." These men, who were well aware that any demand for the right to interracial marriage that came from a body of Black men might endanger both their tenuous coalitions with White Republicans and their claims to a host of other civil and political privileges, avoided discussing the issue of interracial marriage. None of the two dozen conventions of "colored men" held in the years between 1865 and 1868 called for the repeal of laws against interracial marriage.[60] When state legislatures and constitutional conventions debated the passage of new miscegenation laws, most Black representatives considered them so insulting that they voted against them, but some tried to defuse the issue by insisting they and their brethren had so little interest in marrying White women that they had no objection to passage of the laws.[61]

Rather than challenge existing laws, Black politicians preferred to change the subject from interracial marriage, a topic that raised public fears of predatory Black men, to interracial sex, a topic that raised suspicions of predatory White men. In so doing, Black men tried to use their knowledge of the history of sexual oppression that had accompanied slavery to stop White men from having sex with Black women. Thus Arkansas constitutional convention delegate James T. White charged that "the white men of the South have been for years indulging in illicit intercourse with colored women, and in the dark days of slavery this intercourse was in a great majority of cases forced upon the innocent victims; and I think the time has come when such a course should end." His colleague William H. Grey argued that if a miscegenation provision was to be placed in the Arkansas constitution, it should include a section providing that "if any white man shall be found cohabiting with a negro woman, the penalty shall be death."[62]

These attempts to punish White men for their sexual behavior with Black women went down in defeat, but the arguments were nonetheless significant. They served the rhetorical purpose of trying to consolidate the gains promised by laws legitimizing the marriage of freed slaves by aligning Black men on the legitimate side of the traditional split between marriage and illicit sex. By daring White men to marry rather than just consort with Black women, Black leaders tried to brand White men with the moral stigma of illicit sex, and to elevate the moral stature of Black men by comparison to the immoral behavior of White men. These proposals were also, and not incidentally, part of an attempt by Black men to claim Black women for themselves, free from competition and interference on the part of White men, so that Black men could enforce their newly gained privileges as household heads. As Black minister Henry Turner explained in an 1866 speech to celebrate the anniversary of Emancipation, "All we ask of the white man is to let our ladies alone, and they need not fear us. The difficulty has heretofore been our ladies were not always at our disposal."[63]

While Black politicians tried to tar White men with the brush of illicit sex, White officials stepped up the criminal prosecution of interracial couples. During Reconstruction, southern appellate courts heard a handful of cases involving couples prosecuted by local authorities for "fornication" or "cohabiting as man and wife." Angry that they had been convicted despite offering to prove that they had been married in formal legal ceremonies, the couples argued that under the guarantees of equality provided by the Civil Rights Act of 1866 and the Fourteenth Amendment, they now had the legal right to marry. In two cases involving "white" women and "colored" or "negro" men, North Carolina and Tennessee judges emphatically rejected these claims. In two Georgia cases, courts denied similar claims of marriage made by "white" men and "colored" women.[64]

But as critical race feminist Adrienne Davis has argued, cases like these, brought under the criminal law of illicit sex, are only part of the story.[65] Understanding the full range of White men's privileges as household heads—and how deeply embedded they were in the law (and in the minds of southern judges)—requires taking a look at civil cases, involving matters such as probate and inheritance, too. And civil cases show that even as interracial couples were being prosecuted in criminal courts, some interracial marriages were being upheld in civil courts.

One example is Leah Foster, whose claim to be the wife of Alfred Foster appeared before Judge Livingston Lindsay in November 1871.[66] In Fort Bend County, Texas, the Civil War and Reconstruction had turned traditional politics upside down. Before the Civil War, the county had been a stronghold of slaveholding; in 1860, its 260 slaveholders owned a total of 4,127 slaves. After the war, these once proud planters were reduced to counting the dead and wounded, surveying their wasted property, and lamenting the loss of their labor force. Unable to prevent Reconstruction officials from granting suffrage to freedmen, they found themselves dependent on the political will of their former slaves. African Americans accounted for 67 percent of Fort Bend County's population in 1860, 77 percent in 1870, and 80 percent in 1880, so newly enfranchised Black male voters were in a position to determine the outcome of local elections. Long-term patronage networks collapsed as a tenuous coalition of White Republicans and newly elected Black officials swept into office. The county judge who had ordered the auction of the Foster land was removed from office, and the district court, too, changed hands. When the new district court judge, Livingston Lindsay, ordered the summons and subpoenas for Leah Foster's case, they were served by the authority of a Black man and former slave, the newly elected county sheriff Walter Burton Moses.[67]

Even in these changed circumstances, Leah Foster's claim to legal marriage was not, at least at first glance, likely to succeed. The state's Reconstruction legislature had, reluctantly, passed a law providing for the marriage of ex-slaves, but both of the Texas laws against interracial marriage remained on the books: the 1837 civil ban on marriages between "any person of European blood or their descendants" and "Africans, or the descendants of Africans" and the 1858 criminal statute that set prison sentences of two to five years for "any white person" who married any "negro, or a person of mixed blood, descended from negro ancestry, to the third generation inclusive."[68] Even if these laws hadn't stood in the way, Leah Foster's claim of marriage had very slim evidentiary backing. None of the many witnesses ever contended that there had been a marriage ceremony of any kind, and they all agreed that while he was alive, Alfred Foster had never referred to Leah as his wife. If Alfred Foster had died even two years earlier, the case would never have been heard.

But Leah Foster's case was heard, by a White southern judge, and argued by White southern lawyers who, it turned out, disagreed sharply over how to reconstruct race and gender hierarchies in a postwar southern legal system. Because American law had always measured the rights of White citizens in terms of the privileges of White men, the Reconstruction-era debate over Black citizenship had quickly been cast in terms of the privileges of Black men. As southern Black men began to claim the rights of citizens, however, southern White men, Republicans and Democrats alike, began to focus on what seemed to them a more pressing question. In a world without slavery, they wondered, where would the privileges and responsibilities of free White men begin and end?[69]

Leah Foster's lawyers rested their case on the civil law of marriage, with its emphasis on the privileges and responsibilities of White men as husbands. Recognizing that proving a marriage often came down to showing the intentions of the man within it, Leah's lawyers tried to establish three facts: that Alfred Foster publicly recognized the Foster children as his own, that he had supported Leah and the children ever since he emancipated them, and that Alfred and Leah Foster had lived together "as man and wife."

To do so, they relied on the testimony of Leah Foster's children and Alfred Foster's former slaves. Lawyers called Leah and Alfred's son Fields to the witness stand to testify that Alfred and Leah "bedded together every night or two" and that Alfred "claimed me and treated me as his son—same with the other children—Leah is my Mother." Foster's former slaves Jere and Abbie Nelson offered additional details. Jere Nelson testified that "Leah & [Alfred] Foster lived in separate houses, but he bedded with her, and got children by her." He went on, "Foster treated Leahs children as his own. He acted towards them as his own, but I never heard him say, they were his children." Abbie Nelson had evidently been in a position to see and hear more than her husband. She testified that "both [Leah and Alfred Foster] have told me that Leah's children were got by him." Using the kind of detail that a woman who was a longtime intimate and occasional rival of Leah Foster might notice, she commented that "he treated her children different from other negroes" and gave her money. It was Abbie who provided the words that the lawyers hoped would be the icing on the cake: "Leah & A.H. Foster lived same as man & wife."[70]

Leah's lawyers wrapped up their case by turning to Alfred Foster himself. They placed in evidence the deed of manumission Foster had executed freeing Leah and the children in 1847 and Foster's will, calling a neighbor—their only White witness—to testify to the validity of Foster's signature on them. After putting several additional probate documents on the record, they rested their case. Leah's case, then, hinged on the contention that Alfred Foster's behavior in sleeping with Leah, emancipating her and the children, admitting paternity, and supporting them was enough to add up to the legal presumption of marriage.[71]

For their part, Leah Foster's opponents, Benjamin Bonds and Elisha Ryon, relied on the equally familiar tradition of the law of criminal morality to argue that the relationship between Alfred and Leah was nothing more than illicit sex. If so, neither Leah nor her children would hold any property rights the court was bound to respect. The lawyers tried to get Leah's witnesses to characterize the Foster relationship in terms that were less familial and more illicit. Under cross-examination, they pushed Foster's former slave Jere Nelson to admit that "I never heard him [Alfred Foster] say they were married." Abbie Nelson, who started out by insisting to the lawyers that "A.H. Foster was as good to Leah as a man to his wife" ended up admitting that "I never heard them, or ether [sic] of them, or any one say Leah & Mr. Foster were married. He lived with her as many white men used to live with colored women. He bought her as his slave." Walter Andrus, the White neighbor who had validated Foster's signature on the deed of manumission, told cross-examining lawyers that Alfred Foster's "reputation in the County was that he was an old bachelor & kept a negro woman by whom he had mulatto children."[72]

Most of the White citizens of Fort Bend County stood firmly behind Bonds and Ryon. Unsettled by a world in which Black witnesses were allowed to testify in court cases involving Whites, they were determined to hold on to the stigmatizing power of moral judgment reflected in the slave-era association between blackness and illicit sex. The half-dozen witnesses the lawyers for Bonds and Ryon called were White men who used racialized moral gradations to claim the right to determine the reputation of the relationship in the larger community. As one explained: "I always knew [Alfred Foster] . . . as a single man . . . he was generally reputed a bachelor. I never met any one at his house as his wife he never introduced any one to me at his house (or elsewhere) as his wife. I never saw any person at his house acting as his wife." Another went even further. "There was no reputation in the community that he was a married man," he testified. "I have seen Leah at his house, she was treated by him as a servant. I have dined with him she never sat at table. I have stayed all night with him—he slept in his house—Leah did not."[73]

Both sides waived a jury trial, perhaps because jury composition was a touchy issue in a county with a newly registered majority of Black voters and a Black sheriff in charge of calling citizens for jury service. As a result, the decision fell to Judge Livingston Lindsay. Like most other Reconstruction appointees, Judge Lindsay was a Republican. He was also, however, a southern slaveowner, born and educated in Virginia, who had practiced law in Kentucky and Texas, then served three years on the Texas Supreme Court between before ending his career as a district judge in Fort Bend County.[74]

Judge Lindsay listened carefully to the case against Leah Foster, which relied on legal patterns set during slavery, when lawyers easily conflated illicit sex with blackness and contrasted both to respectable marriage and whiteness. Now that slave law had been consigned to the dustbin and former slaves had been granted the right to marry, it was no longer obvious that the Foster relationship should be categorized as illicit sex rather than legitimate marriage. Freed from the restrictions of slavery law, Lindsay was in a position to see the *Foster* case as a matter of respecting the will and intentions of a propertied White man like Alfred Foster. If such a man wanted to marry and leave property to a Black woman, Lindsay was no longer willing to stand in his way.

So, surprising though it may seem, Leah Foster won her case. Judge Lindsay ruled that because Alfred and Leah had conducted themselves as man and wife and Alfred had acknowledged their children as his own, the Fosters' relationship fit the legal definition of marriage. Accordingly, he declared that Leah was indeed Alfred's widow and her children his legitimate heirs. As a wife and widow, Leah Foster was entitled to protect her homestead from creditors, so Lindsay ordered Bonds and Ryon to return to Leah her homestead claim of two hundred acres of the three-hundred-acre Foster tract, all the miscellaneous pieces of Foster property (from kitchen utensils to horses),

Judge Livingston Lindsay. (Tarleton Law Library, Jamail
Center for Legal Research, University of Texas School
of Law)

the "rents" they had charged Fields and his brothers to work the land, and all
associated profits.[75]

Lindsay's decision enraged Bonds and Ryon, who immediately appealed
to the Texas Supreme Court. The brief they submitted offered a competing vision of postwar society, one built on the sexual privileges traditionally
enjoyed by White men.[76] The property rights that mattered to Bonds and
Ryon were those of White men like themselves, who were scrambling to
establish a system of racialized economic subordination that might replace
the one rooted in slavery.

Like all the White residents of Fort Bend County, Bonds and Ryon had
benefited from slavery. Unlike many of their fellow citizens, though, they
had decided early on that their futures lay in more indirect forms of racial

control. After his arrival in Texas in 1850, Benjamin Bonds had worked as a plantation overseer for a year or so, but as soon as he had enough money to purchase his own land, he had set himself up as a stock-raiser and, eventually, a merchant. Elisha Ryon arrived later in the decade but had been even more successful at cultivating business interests. By the time of the Civil War, Ryon operated the local ferry, a necessity for farmers who hoped to market their crops. Since neither man was among the county's major slaveholders, both had survived the postwar loss of slave property, so devastating to their planter neighbors, in good enough shape that they were in a prime position to expand their landholdings.[77]

Bonds and Ryon seem to have assumed that even in the postwar world, Black laborers might work the land, but Whites should own it.[78] As they told the story of the Foster estate, they interpreted every economic relationship so as to mark the power of Whites and subordination of Blacks. The Fosters, they insisted, had lived on the land as "tenants" who paid "rent" rather than as heirs-to-be. The payments that Bonds had given to Leah Foster and her children while he settled the estate were only wages for "servant hire."[79] (What Leah and her children understood these payments to be is, of course, another matter. Accustomed to being supported by a White man who was their master, husband, and father, they may well have expected financial support from the man who was acting as his executor.)

Bonds and Ryon showed their strongest indignation in the section of their brief where, in prose studded with heavy underlining, they drew distinctions between legitimate marriage and illicit sex. Clearly appalled that Judge Lindsay had chosen to extend the presumption of marriage, with all its links to community legitimacy and property, to the Fosters, Bonds and Ryon used every argument they could think of to push Leah Foster back outside the parameters of social and legal respectability. They began by asking whether a marriage "without license & ceremony" could be legal. Given the well-established presumption of marriage in American law, the answer to this question was clearly yes; even Bonds and Ryon had to admit that "evidence of marriage from cohabitation, acknowledgment, reputation &c is receivable in nearly all civil cases." But they insisted that the evidence they provided from White witnesses so sullied the reputation of the Fosters that the presumption of marriage could never apply to them. "*Cohabitation*" that leads to marriage, they argued, "does not mean *Copulation*, but has a special meaning viz. living together as *man & wife*, and so appearing to the world or those around." This definition of marriage could not fit Alfred Foster, for "the *Reputation* was that Foster was a *bachelor* and 'kept' a negro woman by whom he had mulatto children, that he was reputed never to have been married." Bonds and Ryon's case ultimately depended on the operation of the Texas laws against interracial marriage. "Even if a formal marriage had been had," they insisted, "it would have been null & void, because between one of African descent & a white person. . . . Foster could not have *legally* married Leah had he openly tried to do so."[80]

The three justices of the Texas Supreme Court, however, rejected all these claims. They offered their own interpretation of the relationship between the privileges of race, gender, and freedom, assembling new models from old elements. Like Judge Lindsay in the lower court, they believed that the Civil War and Reconstruction spelled a decisive break with the past, and they, too, resigned laws against interracial marriage to the past. If, during slavery, these laws had placed acceptable limits on White men's liberty, after the war, those limits could no longer stand. According to the Texas Supreme Court, the Fourteenth Amendment to the U.S. Constitution, which prohibited states from passing laws that limited "the privileges or immunities of citizens of the United States" or denied "to any person within its jurisdiction the equal protection of the laws," had "abrogated" the Texas law against interracial marriage. Once the Texas law was pushed out of the picture, the court declared that the Foster relationship should be regarded as a legitimate marriage rather than illicit sex because "[a] marriage might then be presumed in the State of Texas upon the same state of facts, which would raise a similar presumption in Indiana or Ohio."[81]

The decision in the *Foster* case challenged established patterns of southern lawmaking on a number of points, by asserting the power of the federal constitution over state laws, by distancing southern state courts from slavery, and by dismissing the Texas law against interracial marriage. Yet in one respect, this seemingly novel decision was quite traditional: it was rooted in the tendency to see every legal issue through the lens of the wills and rights of White male actors. It is revealing that the court's decision covered the Fourteenth Amendment in less than a sentence but lingered over Alfred Foster's intentions toward Leah as shown in his will. "That Foster himself regarded this woman and her family in the light of a wife and children, cannot be doubted . . . ," the court wrote. "He not only devises his property mainly to this woman and children, but he provides by a clause (often found in the testaments of jealous husbands) that if Leah shall marry, she is to forfeit all her right and interest in his estate. We confess it is somewhat difficult to account for this inhibition of a second marriage in any case, but it would be still more difficult to find a reason for this kind of embargo upon marital commerce in the will of one who had not been the husband."[82]

Like Lindsay's district court, then, the Texas Supreme Court issued a decision upholding the marriage of Alfred and Leah Foster. By bringing Leah Foster within the coverage of homestead provisions, they offered her the same kind of support a White wife might have expected, tying her economic fortunes to those of her husband. Such a decision was in keeping with the original aims of homestead legislation, which had since been reinforced by widespread postwar sympathy for the plight of widows. The court's decision also reflected the well-known preference for assigning husbands, living or dead, responsibility for the well-being of their wives rather than face the possibility of providing state support to indigent women. But the *Foster* decision did something else as well. It offered postwar White men shaken by the loss of slavery some reason to believe that their rights would continue to be the lodestone of the southern legal system. Now that judges were no longer able to enforce the system of social control embodied in slave law, which guarded the rights and responsibilities of White men as slaveowners, they fell back on the system of social control embodied in marriage law, which guarded the rights and responsibilities of White men as husbands.

White Men, Black Men, and the Promise of Reconstruction

The *Foster* case was only one of many cracks in the wall of antebellum laws against interracial marriage. The first of these had appeared in 1843, when, under pressure from abolitionists, the Massachusetts state legislature had repealed its law against interracial marriage.[83] During the 1850s, two more states—Iowa and Kansas—let their laws lapse.[84] After the Civil War, many lawmakers, in and outside the former Confederacy, concluded that the combination of the end of slavery and the passage of Reconstruction civil rights legislation would render the remaining laws inoperable. During this period, five states repealed their laws: New Mexico (1866), Louisiana (1868), South Carolina (1868), Washington (1868), and Mississippi (1870).[85] In the early 1870s, three more, Arkansas, Illinois, and Florida, omitted their laws from state code compilations.[86] As legislative repeals gathered momentum, laws against interracial marriage were increasingly challenged in the courts. In Alabama and in Texas, courts declared state laws unconstitutional.[87] In Louisiana, Mississippi, and even, in one case, North Carolina, courts issued decisions that upheld the validity of individual interracial marriages.[88]

The sum total of this activity was impressive, especially in southern states. Altogether, in seven of the eleven former Confederate States, miscegenation laws were repealed, removed from state law codes, or declared unconstitutional.[89] The cumulative effect was significant enough that when James Schouler surveyed the field of marriage law in 1870, he confidently explained that "by local statutes in some of the United States, intermarriage has been discouraged between persons of the negro, Indian, and white races. With the recent extinction of slavery, many of these laws have passed into oblivion, together with such as refused to allow to persons held in bondage the rights of husband and wife."[90]

On one level, of course, these challenges to miscegenation law reflected the political fortunes of Reconstruction. In this period, when radical Republicans pushed for the federal assertion of power over southern states, many southerners feared that the Democrats' prediction that Republicans intended to make miscegenation the law of the land might really come true. While some southerners reacted to this possibility with horrified determination to prevent such a presumed calamity, others reacted, as they had to the demise of slavery, with something more like resignation. In 1872, for example, Florida removed its ban on interracial marriages from the state code. "The various provisions of the statutes in relation to marriages between white and colored persons are omitted," the code compiler explained in a footnote, "out of deference to the opinion of those who think that they are opposed to our Constitution and to the legislation of Congress."[91] Still other southerners, including the judges of the Texas Supreme Court, and those the Florida lawmakers mentioned, developed significant postwar doubts about the constitutionality of miscegenation laws, doubts that ultimately rested on the connections between marriage, civil rights, and political equality in nineteenth-century thinking about the rights of free White men.

These themes ran through a variety of civil court cases about interracial marriages heard during Reconstruction. Each of these cases rested on a particular change in post–Civil War law. While the *Foster* decision turned on the Fourteenth Amendment, other judges relied on postwar state laws designed to recognize the marriages of ex-slaves. In 1873, for example, just a year after the *Foster* decision, the Texas Supreme Court recognized a "mulatto" woman as the widow and legitimate heir of a wealthy "white" man, and the Mississippi Supreme Court upheld a marriage between "a white man and a colored woman" in another case involving a substantial estate.[92] In both cases, judges held that state laws legitimizing the marriages of freed slaves were broad enough to protect marriages between ex-slaves and their masters. In 1874, the Louisiana Supreme Court upheld the marriage of a "White" man who had, after years of living in concubinage, married the "colored" woman who was the mother of his children. In this case, the court declared that the Civil Rights Act of 1866 covered the contract of marriage as well as economic contracts.[93]

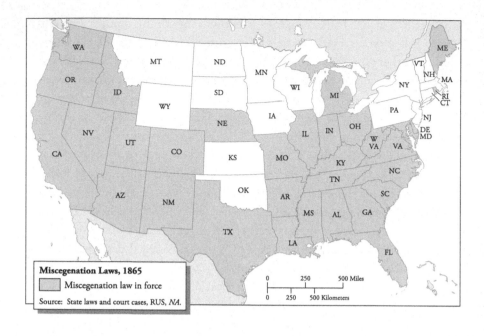

Miscegenation Laws, 1865

Miscegenation law in force

Source: State laws and court cases, RUS, *NA*.

Whether the legal basis for these rulings came from state laws legalizing the marriage of former slaves, from the federal Civil Rights Act of 1866, or from the Fourteenth Amendment, these state supreme court decisions had two things in common. First, each of them involved the race-and-gender pairing of a White man and a Black woman. Second, in making their decisions, judges relied on links between marriage, citizenship, and equality forged in the antebellum South and echoed in Reconstruction laws. The irony seems inescapable: in civil miscegenation cases, appellate courts used laws intended to secure civil rights for Blacks to buttress the propertied powers of White male citizens. To put it another way, southern judges tried to reconstruct White male privilege in a world without slavery. Before the Civil War, prohibitions on marriages between White men and Black women had been regarded as necessary—if sometimes uncomfortable—restraints on the rights of White men. But in a postwar world in which Black as well as White men claimed the privilege of marriage, prohibitions on the rights of White men to marry Black women took on a new cast. No longer justifiable as a necessary part of the system of slavery, they were increasingly vulnerable to challenge as unjustifiable restrictions on the rights of White men.

The seeds of this argument could be seen as early as 1871, when the Tennessee attorney general won a criminal conviction against a "negro" man accused of interracial marriage by offering a striking interpretation of the Civil Rights Act of 1866. That act, he maintained, provided Blacks with

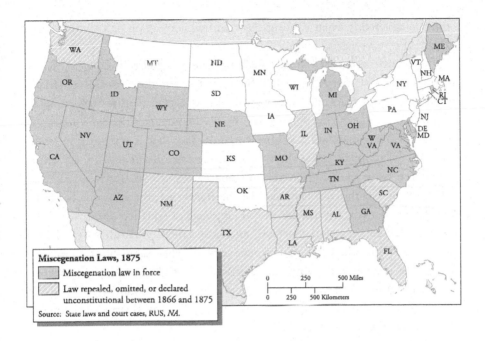

Miscegenation Laws, 1875

Miscegenation law in force

Law repealed, omitted, or declared
unconstitutional between 1866 and 1875

Source: State laws and court cases, RUS, *NA*.

"the *same* rights to contract with each other that the whites have with each other" and "the *same* [rights] to contract with the whites that the whites have with the blacks," but it did *not* provide "a *superior* right of a negro to marry a white woman, when a white man *can not* marry a negro." In this way, he rejected the Black man's claim that the state miscegenation law was discriminatory by shifting the focus from the rights and privileges of Black men to the rights and privileges of White men. As he put it, rather sarcastically, "If the males of one race [that is, Black men] had the right to appropriate the females of the other, while that right was denied to the males of the other race [that is, White men], there might be some *foundation* for the charge of discrimination."[94]

Two years later, in a Mississippi case, lawyers offered opposing views of the Mississippi law that legalized the marriage of freed slaves. One side claimed that the law should be "applied to negroes *alone*." The other side claimed that "*all* rights belong to *all*. . . . Indeed it might [even] be argued, that [the law recognizing the marriages of freed slaves] was intended to apply more especially to *whites* than *blacks*." The justices of the Mississippi Supreme Court agreed, using civil rights rhetoric to uphold the marriage of "a white man and a colored woman" by declaring that the law "was intended to apply to *all* classes, 'without regard to race, color or previous condition of servitude.'"[95] By 1877, the notion that miscegenation laws victimized White men was sufficiently well developed in civil cases that at least one court considered it when voiding the criminal conviction of a "white" man arrested for marrying a "negro."[96]

If Reconstruction courts used the language of equality to uphold White men's interracial marriages, what happened when they considered Black men's interracial marriages? Answering this question requires returning to criminal cases, for during these years, no civil court ever upheld a marriage between a Black man and a White woman, a fact that is revealing in itself. Even in the criminal cases, there is only one case, *Burns v. State,* in which a southern court used Reconstruction guarantees of equality in a case that involved the rights of a Black man. In the *Burns* case, the Alabama Supreme Court offered a ringing defense of the language of equality. "Marriage," the court explained, "is a civil contract," and under the Civil Rights Act, Blacks as well as Whites had the right to contract it. "The same right to make a contract as is enjoyed by white citizens *means* the right to make any contract which a white citizen may make." There could be no doubt, continued the court, this "cardinal principle" was protected "by the Fourteenth Amendment to the Federal constitution."[97]

With this language, the Alabama Supreme Court appeared entirely willing to use civil rights laws to protect the marriage of Thomas Woods, a "negro" man, and Echie Bunch, a "white" woman. It is, however, worth noting that this case, too, reinforced patterns of White male privilege. In order not to leave the impression that women, White or Black, held the same rights as men, the court took care to explain that "many citizens are debarred from rights and privileges allowed to others, as is the case with married women and children." Even more revealing, though, is the fact that the defendant—that is, the man who was on trial in the *Burns* case—was not the "negro" man whose marriage was in question but a "white" man, the justice of the peace who had performed the marriage ceremony. So the most direct outcome of the *Burns* case was that a White justice of the peace, Thomas A. Burns, was saved from the fines and jail sentence he faced had he been convicted of the crime of "solemnizing the rites of matrimony between a white person and a negro."[98]

The two other cases that involved the race-and-gender pairing of Black men and White women suggest just how unusual the *Burns* decision was. The first was decided by the North Carolina Supreme Court, which, after a long debate, agreed to recognize one particular relationship between a "negro" man and a "white" woman as a legal marriage. Although the majority opinion in this criminal case was quite detailed, it made no reference whatsoever to civil rights acts or constitutional guarantees of equal citizenship; instead, it hinged on a technical argument about the recognition of marriages performed in other jurisdictions.[99]

The significance of this omission becomes apparent when this case is juxtaposed to another that took place at about the same time in another southern state. This case, too, was a criminal appeals case, but the appellant was a "white" woman convicted of breaking the Texas state miscegenation law. In this case, the judge relied heavily on the Reconstruction rhetoric of equality; he declared that the Texas law was "unfair and unequal in its operation" because it fixed a "prohibition based solely upon color." But the inequality the judge had in mind was that the law "would visit a heavy penalty upon a white citizen, and none whatever upon a colored citizen, for doing a certain act."[100] So on the grounds that the law discriminated against *Whites,* the judge declared it in conflict with the Civil Rights Act of 1866 and the Fourteenth and Fifteenth Amendments to the U.S. Constitution.

Taken together, these examples—the state legislative repeals of laws against interracial marriage, the civil court cases upholding the marriages of White men to Black women, and the clear judicial reluctance to protect Black men accused of marrying White women—reveal a little-known but fundamental aspect of the emergence of miscegenation law. On the simplest level, these examples refute the usual portrait of nearly universal White southern opposition to interracial marriage. They show postwar southern judges, lawyers, and legislators debating whether and when to prohibit interracial marriage. They may even reveal a moment when it might have been possible to remove racial dividing lines from American marriage law. But these cases also show that Reconstruction-era challenges to the emergence of miscegenation law were rooted at least as deeply in attempts to reconstruct White male privilege as in attempts to guarantee civil rights to Black men.

——

To show that Reconstruction-era judges who upheld marriages between White men and Black women saw the issue of interracial marriage through the eyes of White men is not, however, to argue that their decisions were irrelevant to the handful of Black women who benefited from these decisions. While southern courts toyed with the possibility that the postwar privileges of White men might extend to interracial marriage, Leah Foster and her children lived out their lives on the land she had won in Livingston Lindsay's court.

For nearly a decade, Leah steadfastly paid the required taxes on her property. After her death in the early 1880s, the land passed to her sons. In 1883, the tax rolls contained a proud listing for "Fields Foster and Bros.," a venture that claimed two hundred acres of land, one wagon, eight horses, twenty-five cattle, and five dollars in miscellaneous wealth. A few years later, its assets had been divided among Leah's surviving sons, Fields, George, and Monroe, and Leah's daughter Margaret's husband, John Milton. Each took title to fifty acres of land, and each held on to it. When Fields Foster died near the end of the first decade of the twentieth century, he left an estate valued at $800.[101]

Though none of the Foster children did as well as their planter father Alfred, Leah Foster's homestead made the difference between indigence and self-sufficiency. This was an achievement all the more remarkable because it endured through the years when irate Texas Democrats threw Texas Republicans and their Reconstruction government out of office, when White Texas landowners and managers reduced most of the rural Blacks around them to debt peonage, and when Fort Bend County erupted in violence that ended only when a political party created, as its founders declared, "by the white people, for the white people, and of the white people" captured control of county government.[102]

Meanwhile, in and outside of Texas, the emergence of miscegenation law provided the postwar foundation for the growth and reproduction of white supremacy. This depended in part on overruling, denying, and finally forgetting that a "coloured" woman like Leah Foster had ever been successful in having her marriage to a "white" man declared legitimate. During the next decade, the Reconstruction-era decisions upholding interracial marriages were first overruled and then abandoned. By the 1890s, they were all but forgotten, and judges and lawyers would routinely rattle off a supposedly unbroken string of court precedents upholding miscegenation laws. The legal momentum for this process came from another line of court cases decided in the post–Civil War period, one that was every bit as gendered as the Reconstruction-era challenges to miscegenation law. The decisions reached in these cases, which involved Black men and White women, would eventually place all interracial relationships back on the "illicit sex" side of the dividing line between sex and marriage.

Chapter Two

SEXUALIZING MISCEGENATION LAW

"No person having one eighth part or more of negro blood shall be permitted to marry any white woman of this state, nor shall any white man be permitted to marry any negro woman, or any woman having one eighth part or more of negro blood, and every person who shall knowingly marry in violation of the provisions of this section, shall upon conviction thereof, be imprisoned in the state's prison not less than one, nor more than ten years, and be fined not less than one thousand nor more than five thousand dollars."

—Indiana Statutes, 1870

EVANSVILLE, INDIANA

Unlike Alfred Foster, Thomas Gibson never tried to keep his marriage a secret. On April 13, 1870, Gibson, a sixty-year-old laborer "having one eighth part of negro blood," and Jennie Williams, a twenty-six-year-old "white" woman, went to the Reverend Green McFarland, the Black pastor of the Evansville Liberty Baptist Church, to be married. McFarland performed the ceremony, which was licensed by the county clerk, recorded by county officials, and listed alongside other marriages in the local newspaper, the *Evansville Journal*. Ten days later, the Evansville grand jury indicted Gibson for "unlawfully and feloniously" marrying Jennie Williams, "a white woman of the State of Indiana."[1]

While Gibson was awaiting his trial, Reverend McFarland performed another Evansville marriage, between Peter van der Mede, a "white" man, and

Lucy Ann Bolen, a "negro" woman. This time, all three participants—van der Mede, Bolen, and Pastor McFarland—were arrested. In court, all three were represented by a Republican lawyer who asked the judge to dismiss the charges. His argument was simple. Marriage was "a civil contract." Because the federal Civil Rights Act of 1866 had given "colored people" the right to "make and enforce contracts," it "nullified" the thirty-year-old Indiana law against interracial marriage. Accepting this argument, justice of the peace James T. Walker, a Democrat, ruled that Indiana's law against interracial marriage was unconstitutional and ordered all three prisoners released from custody.[2]

The Gibsons and the van der Medes were only two of dozens, more likely hundreds, of interracial couples who married during Reconstruction, many of them relying on the precedents set in recent court decisions to do so. In Texas, where the case of Alfred and Leah Foster had paved the way, Charles Frasher, a "white" man, married "negro" Lettuce Howell; then Emile Francois, "who was alleged to be of the white race," married "a colored female who was of the African race" whose name is not listed in the record. Isaac and Mag Kennedy, a "negro" man and a "white" woman, left their native North Carolina to marry in neighboring South Carolina, which had recently repealed its miscegenation law, then returned to live in North Carolina. On July 4, 1872, J. P. Bell and M. A., a "white" man and a "woman of color," traveled from Tennessee to Mississippi, where the legislature had repealed the state miscegenation law, to celebrate their marriage. In 1874, Virginians Andrew Kinney and Mahala Miller, a "negro" man and a "white" woman, went to Washington, D.C., which had abandoned its law against interracial marriage after the Civil War, to get married, then returned to Virginia to set up housekeeping. Four years later, Virginians Edmund Kinney and Mary Hall, a "negro" man and a "white" woman, did the same.[3]

Other couples used loopholes in the remaining state laws to press the possibilities of Reconstruction rhetoric about equality. In Georgia, for example, the 1865 state constitutional ban on interracial marriages had been reinforced by an 1866 state miscegenation law, but in 1868, a new state constitution omitted the previous ban and added a provision that "the social status of the citizen shall never be the subject of legislation." Relying on this provision, Leopold Daniels, a "white" man, and Charlotte Scott, a "woman of color," persuaded a Black preacher in Macon, Georgia, to marry them. Two years later, William Hobbs, a "white" man, decided to marry Martha A. Johnson, a "colored" woman. Hobbs went to a local official in Fulton County, Georgia, who issued him a marriage license that authorized a ceremony "provided there is no lawful cause to obstruct the same, according to the constitution and laws of this state." Using this license, Hobbs and Johnson were married in Georgia in September 1870.[4]

A few couples even managed to find local officials willing to marry them in southern states that had miscegenation laws firmly in force. In December 1868, Alexander Reinhardt, a "person of color," and Alice Love, a "white" woman, were married "in due form of law by a licensed minister of the Gospel" in North Carolina. A year or so later, Doc Lonas, a "negro" man, and Rebecca Teaster, a "white" woman, were married in Tennessee.[5]

All of these couples ended up in court trying to defend their marriages. Unlike the cases discussed in the previous chapter, most of which were heard in civil courts and centered around inheritance and property claims made in the wills of White men, these cases were heard in criminal courts after couples were arrested and prosecuted on charges that ranged from "adultery and fornication" to "cohabiting, as man and wife" to "unlawful" or "felonious" marriage. Rooted in an old, familiar practice of using local courts to enforce community morals, criminal prosecutions like these were carried to new heights during the 1860s and 1870s as community officials reacted to the social and legal dislocations of the post–Civil War world by trying to clamp down on the practice they now labeled "miscegenation." In and outside of the South, when local prosecutors brought these couples to court, they discovered that laws against interracial marriage faced significant new obstacles, including the assumption that laws against interracial marriage were an outdated relic of slavery, the belief that marriage was a contractual right of free citizens, and the possibility that the Fourteenth Amendment really did guarantee equal protection of the laws.

The Racial Authority of Free States

In November 1870, when Thomas Gibson came to trial in the Evansville Criminal Court, the judicial scales seemed likely to tip against miscegenation law in Indiana. Judge Walker's decision in the *van der Mede* case made it possible to believe that the Indiana law might be overturned, and Gibson's lawyer, Andrew L. Robinson, came to his client's defense with a fierce determination born of politics, religion, and moral principle. Robinson had been a fervent Democrat in his younger years, but during a particularly grim battle in the Mexican-American War, he found religion and became a reformer with a special passion for the anti-slavery cause. In 1852, he ran a largely symbolic campaign for governor on the Free Soil ticket. After losing by an embarrassingly wide margin, Robinson became a judge of the Evansville Court of Conciliation, where he was noted for his lenience toward runaway slaves who appeared in his courtroom. By the 1860s, he had become a Radical Republican whose principled support of civil rights for Blacks set him well apart from most White Indianans. A proud member of Evansville's First Baptist Church, Robinson had helped establish its Black offshoot, Liberty Baptist, where the Reverend Green McFarland served as pastor.[6]

Robinson knew that Indiana judges and juries often imposed harsh penalties on Black men accused of relationships with White women. In 1867, when an Indianapolis court considered the case of a Black man charged with marrying a White woman, the judge refused to use the Civil Rights Act of 1866 to uphold the marriage and punished the defendant with a two-year prison sentence and a fine of $5,000. Two years later a Black man convicted of having sex with a White woman was fined $300 and sentenced to three months in prison.[7]

But Robinson was used to championing unpopular causes, and he believed that Thomas Gibson had as much right to marry a White woman as Peter van der Mede did to marry a Black woman. When Gibson came to trial, Robinson asked Judge Charles Butterfield to quash the indictment before the trial even began. Butterfield, a man whose heroic service as a Union officer had vaulted him into the judgeship at the youthful age of thirty-six, granted Robinson's motion. Whether he did so because of the *van der Mede* precedent, because he was determined to make headway against his court's daunting caseload, or out of deference to the sixty-two-year-old Robinson, who had recently stepped down from the criminal court bench Butterfield now occupied, is impossible to say. Whatever the reason, though, Judge Butterfield freed Thomas Gibson. Two months later, the U.S. census taker reported that Gibson, his wife, and her two-year-old daughter were living together in a residential Evansville neighborhood.[8]

Thomas Gibson's trials were not yet over. Lawyers on both sides of his case agreed to submit an appeal to the Indiana Supreme Court.[9] Both sides thought they had much to gain. The state prosecutor hoped that, in addition to punishing Gibson, the state supreme court would endorse the Indiana law against marriage between "whites" and "negroes," which had been in effect for three decades. Gibson's lawyer, Andrew Robinson, hoped that the court would declare the law against interracial marriage unconstitutional with a ruling broad enough to cover all African Americans in Indiana.

On both sides the stakes were high. The decision in the *Gibson* case would indeed prove fateful for the development of postwar miscegenation law all over the country. Why was it so significant? Because it offered judges across the nation a template for using state police power to sidestep federal guarantees of civil rights, using the race-and-gender pairing of White women and Black men to invoke notions of White women's supposed racial purity so as to chart a path from antebellum free-state race law to postwar white supremacy.[10]

These developments were rooted in three aspects of Indiana history. Indiana was, first of all, a free state with a long tradition of race law. Second, its officials displayed a pronounced tendency to use the purity of White women as a political symbol. Third and finally, the Indiana law against interracial marriage was an exceptionally punitive criminal statute.

The Northwest Ordinance of 1787 had prohibited slavery in Indiana and the surrounding territories, so Indiana had been a free state from its inception. But if the state was free of slavery, it was by no means free of racism. Like other northern states, Indiana quickly developed a tradition of race law that privileged Whites and disadvantaged Blacks. In 1818 and again in 1821, the state legislature passed short-lived laws against interracial sex and marriage. In 1831, it required all Blacks entering the state to register and post a $500 bond with county officials. In 1840, it passed a new and more enduring law against interracial marriage, one that laid the foundation for a number of other restrictions. During the 1840s and 1850s, White Indianans made it illegal for Black Indianans to attend public schools, vote, serve in the militia, or testify in court cases involving Whites.[11]

In 1851, when Indiana wrote a new constitution, it tried to exclude Blacks from the state altogether. Article 13 of the new state constitution contained clauses providing that "no Negro or mulatto shall come into, or settle in the state" and that "all contracts made with any negro or mulatto coming into the state contrary to [this article] . . . shall be void."[12] Under these provisions, anyone who either employed or encouraged Blacks to remain in the state would be subject to a fine, the proceeds of which would be used to promote the colonization of Indiana Blacks to Liberia.

In 1856, state officials showed how far they would go to enforce these clauses. Arthur Barkshire, a Black man who lived on the Indiana side of the border with Ohio, married Elizabeth Keith, a Black woman who lived on the Ohio side. Barkshire was promptly arrested and fined ten dollars for the crime of "bringing a Negro woman into this state." When Barkshire appealed this decision, the Indiana Supreme Court upheld his conviction, then suggested that Elizabeth be prosecuted, too. The court's reasoning linked Indiana's black code to contract theories of marriage. "The policy of the state . . . ," the court asserted, "is to exclude any further ingress of negroes, and to remove those among us as speedily as possible." Under this policy, Arthur Barkshire was subject to arrest as a person "who encouraged the negro woman Elizabeth to remain in the state," and Elizabeth was subject to arrest as a person "coming into the state or settling here." The justices held that the Barkshire marriage "must be regarded as void." As the court explained: "Marriage, in this state, is but a civil contract. As such it is clearly embraced in the constitutional provision . . . which declares all contracts made with negroes and mulattoes coming into the state contrary to the provisions . . . void."[13]

Indiana's tradition of race law took on special significance in the post–Civil War period. While southern jurists considered the likelihood that laws against interracial marriage would have to be discarded as relics of slavery, Indiana stood as an example of the possibility that laws forbidding Whites to marry Blacks were entirely consistent with the legal traditions of free states. As such, it offered judges eager to justify miscegenation laws a template that was ostensibly distinct from the discredited institution of slavery—and the political winds of Reconstruction then sweeping through the South.

Before and after the Civil War, Indiana's devotion to race law was nurtured by the tendency to use White women's purity as a symbol of the body politic. It was just such a moral panic that had prompted the passage of the Indiana law against interracial marriage at stake in the *Gibson* case. The law dated back to 1840, and to a public scandal involving Sophia Spears, a "white" woman in Indianapolis. On his deathbed, Sophia Spears's father had asked John Wilson, a "nearly white" but part "colored" man who was a trusted family servant, to care for his widow and daughters. When John Wilson asked Sophia to marry him, her mother and sister both approved of the match, but news of the marriage sparked fierce opposition from Indianapolis residents. On the night of the wedding, a mob that was led, according to one account, by two "respectable physicians" acting "in the capacity of surgeons," assembled and marched to the house where the couple was staying. John fled; the mob, unable to catch him, shamed Sophia by riding her around the city streets on a rail.[14]

Legislators eager to quash this scandal were appalled to learn that Sophia Spears and John Wilson had not broken any law, since Indiana's first and second laws against interracial marriage, passed in 1818 and 1821, had been repealed in 1824. Indiana legislators immediately started debating a third act "to prohibit the amalgamation of whites and blacks." Dismissing a suggestion that they find some way to control mobs such as the one that had captured Sophia Wilson, legislators quickly agreed that "whites and blacks" who tried to marry should be subject to criminal punishments. The bill the legislature passed in February 1840 not only made interracial marriage a crime but also set penalties that applied to all potential participants, including marriage partners, state officials, ministers, and anyone who "shall aid, counsel, abet, or in any manner be known to assist in any such marriage."[15]

In successive decades, Indiana politicians sharpened their skills at using the mere possibility of White women's involvement with Black men as a political brickbat. In the state's 1856 election, Democrats staved off the emerging Republican Party with political parades featuring companies of young White women with signs that read, "Fathers, save us from nigger husbands." In 1860, Indiana Republicans won precarious control of state government only after they labeled Democrats the *real* amalgamationists and claimed that Republicans were the true "white man's party." Not until the end of the Civil War and the growing national power of Radical Reconstruction forced them to do so did Indiana officials reconsider their by then decades-old hostility to African Americans. When pressed, Republican judges declared the Black exclusion clause of the state constitution unconstitutional, and Republican legislators reluctantly acquiesced in Black suffrage and passed laws conceding that Black citizens could testify in courts and attend public schools, though they also made provisions for school segregation.[16]

Meanwhile, Indiana Democrats recaptured the state's legislature and supreme court in 1870 and the governorship in 1872. Thereafter state elections hinged on a few thousand swing votes, a situation that encouraged each party to try to outdo the other in appealing to popular prejudices.[17] In such a context, the tactic of using White women as symbols of the purity of the body politic became even more deeply entrenched. The Indiana Supreme Court had only to identify the Gibsons as a "negro" man and a "white" woman to invoke this tendency. And in their focus on White women, as well as in the production of laws targeting free Blacks, Indiana politicians were pioneers whose antebellum rhetoric anticipated the defense of white womanhood that would eventually saturate late nineteenth-century southern politics.

In Indiana, this pattern was clearly apparent in 1840, when the state passed a law that set some of the strongest criminal penalties in the United States for interracial marriage. In 1840, three southern states had not yet passed any laws at all forbidding interracial marriage, and five other states maintained civil bans on the marriages but set no criminal penalties.[18] Of the thirteen states that did criminalize interracial marriage, three states fined the officials who performed the marriages but not the couples who married, and ten states subjected both the couples and the officials who married them to criminal punishments, mostly at the misdemeanor or "high misdemeanor" level.[19]

Indiana, however, pushed beyond them all, becoming the first American state to make interracial marriage a felony. Reflecting the frenzy of the Sophia Spears scandal, the penalties were harsh. Under the 1840 law, "every person who shall knowingly counsel, or assist in any manner, in any [such] marriage" faced fines of $100 to $1,000 for ordinary citizens, $1,000 to $10,000 for ministers, and $500 to $5,000 for marriage license clerks and other state officials, plus the loss of office. The stiffest punishment of all was saved for the marriage partners, who were subject to fines of $1,000 to $5,000 *and* prison sentences of ten to twenty years. Calmer Indiana legislators repealed these penalties in 1841, then in 1842 passed what they considered a more moderate bill. Under its terms, ministers and state officials escaped special punishment, but any Indianan who encouraged interracial marriage continued to be subject to fines of $100 to $1,000, and partners in interracial marriages could expect fines of $1,000 to $5,000 along with prison sentences of one to ten years.[20]

By 1840, then, Indiana's criminal punishments had eclipsed its civil prohibitions on interracial marriage. This tendency toward criminalization was only reinforced after the Civil War, when freed slaves began to flee from former slave states into border towns like Evansville, where Thomas and Jennie Gibson were married. By the 1860s, Evansville, a growing industrial town located on the banks of the Ohio River, had become the second largest city in Indiana. After the Civil War, its relative prosperity, its urban amenities, and its potential employment base attracted substantial numbers of freed slaves from nearby southern states. In 1860, the town had only 96 Black residents, but by 1870, the Black population had increased nearly fifteen-fold, to 1,408, out of a total city population of 21,830.[21]

Some, perhaps most, Evansville Whites reacted to the arrival of free Blacks as if it were a criminal invasion. In the summer of 1865, a White mob lynched two Black men accused of robbing and assaulting a White woman, then followed up their crime with a citywide riot targeting local Blacks. The prejudices of native-born Indiana Whites were matched—by some accounts, exceeded—by those of Evansville's growing population of German immigrants, working-class men and women eager to grasp and defend their own rung on the ladder of success. In this volatile situation, local judges scrambled to keep up with a dramatic increase of criminal complaints levied in the immediate postwar years. In 1869, the Indiana legislature established special courts to hear criminal cases. For the next decade, White Indianans used the newly established Evansville Criminal Court, which heard the *Gibson* case, to exert control over the state's burgeoning Black population.[22]

These traditions of free-state race law, concern about White women's racial purity, and reliance on state criminal police power formed the background as the Indiana Supreme Court heard arguments in the case of Thomas Gibson. In that court, Robinson tried to defend Thomas Gibson, a Black man, with much the same argument that another lawyer had used so successfully to defend Peter van der Mede, a White man, only a few months earlier. "All the laws of this State prohibiting the marrying of blacks and whites," Robinson told the state supreme court justices, "are abrogated by the Fourteenth amendment to the constitution of the United States and the [Civil Rights Act of 1866] . . . which in express terms confers upon colored people the power of making contracts." Robinson went on to explain, "Marriage by the laws of Indiana being only a civil contract, it follows that the marriage specified in this indictment was lawful."[23]

In Indiana, Robinson's argument that marriage was a civil contract protected by the contract clause of the Civil Rights Act of 1866 would seem to have been especially good law. In 1856, after all, the state supreme court had used the claim that marriage was "but a civil contract" to invalidate the marriage of Arthur Barkshire. But the justices who sat on the bench of the Indiana Supreme Court in 1870 were absolutely unwilling to uphold the marriage of a "negro" man to a "white" woman. So, although the decision in the *Gibson* case was written by a judge who would, just a few years later, advise Indiana lawyers that "the point to be considered in a majority of cases is, not what the law ought to be, but how has the law on the given point been settled," it did not even mention the *Barkshire* precedent.[24]

Instead, Indiana Supreme Court Justice Samuel H. Buskirk wove a powerful postwar defense of miscegenation law. "The magnitude and importance of the question . . . ," Buskirk wrote, speaking for the three-man court, "cannot be overestimated, and we have given it our best and most thoughtful consideration." Buskirk then pushed Reconstruction-era civil rights legislation, and the increased federal power that might have accompanied it, firmly out of the way. The Civil Rights Act of 1866, Buskirk admitted, gave "persons of the African race the right to make and enforce contracts," but it applied only to the District of Columbia and "other places where the federal government has exclusive jurisdiction [that is, territories and the reconstructed states of the South]." The Fourteenth Amendment was designed only to "confer the right of citizenship upon persons of the African race, who had previously not been citizens." Buskirk insisted, "We deny the power and the authority of Congress to determine who shall make contracts or the manner of enforcing them in the several states. . . . [and] we utterly deny the power of Congress to regulate, control, or in any manner to interfere with the states in determining what shall constitute crimes against the laws of the state, or the manner or extent of the punishment of persons charged and convicted with the violation of the criminal laws of a sovereign state."[25]

In this manner, Buskirk made Indiana state criminal law seem more important to the outcome of the *Gibson* case than the federal provisions of the Civil Rights Act or the Fourteenth Amendment. But since Indiana state judges had themselves treated marriage as a contract, Buskirk did not stop there. His second justification for miscegenation law tied the defense of Indiana's "internal police power" to a definition of marriage broad enough to supersede analogies to contracts altogether. "In this State," Buskirk intoned, "marriage is treated as a civil contract, but it is more than a mere civil contract. It is a public institution established by God himself, is recognized in all Christian and civilized nations, and is essential to the peace, happiness, and well-being of society. . . . The right, in the states, to regulate and control, to guard, protect, and preserve this God-given, civilizing, and Christianizing institution is of inestimable importance, and cannot be surrendered." Using these justifications to uphold the constitutionality of the Indiana law against interracial marriage, the Indiana Supreme Court reversed the decision of the Evansville Criminal Court and ordered that the lower court once again "place [Thomas Gibson] upon his trial for the crime charged."[26]

Sexualizing Miscegenation

Shortly after the *Gibson* decision, Thomas and Jennie Gibson disappeared from the historical record. Perhaps they did so deliberately, fleeing the state to avoid another prosecution. But whatever happened to the Gibsons after their marriage was judged a criminal offense, the *Gibson* decision took on a life of its own, gathering legitimacy and authority with each passing year. Issued at a key time and place in post–Civil War race relations, the *Gibson* decision carved the foundation for the emerging judicial consensus in favor of miscegenation law. With an authority that only a northern state free of the taint of secession could muster, the *Gibson* decision established the principle that marriage was a state rather than a federal matter, and so could be held apart from federal guarantees and civil rights protections. And it demonstrated that by transforming the traditional American understanding of the contract of marriage, states could use their police powers to criminalize as well as to prohibit interracial marriage. Because it was issued at a moment when the future of miscegenation law in southern states seemed in doubt, the *Gibson* decision offered a lifeline to those White southerners who were most determined to make miscegenation law the foundation of postwar racial structures.

During the 1870s, southern state officials dusted off their prewar denunciations of interracial sexuality as necessarily illicit and attached them to the arguments put forth in the *Gibson* case. The sexualization of miscegenation law was already at work in Alabama, where a bitter debate over the future of miscegenation law raged for nearly a decade.

When it came to laws against interracial marriage, the state of Alabama had been a latecomer. Its first law on the subject was not passed until 1852, and that was a relatively mild statute that made it a finable misdemeanor for any state official to solemnize an interracial marriage but set no penalties for the partners to such a marriage. After the Civil War, though, Alabama made up for its past lenience with a vengeance. The state's 1866 constitution directed the General Assembly to "enact laws prohibiting the intermarriages of white persons with negroes, or with persons of mixed blood, declaring such marriages null and void *ab initio,* and making the parties to any such marriage subject to criminal prosecutions." In 1866, the Alabama legislature did just that, passing a classic postwar miscegenation law. Under the 1866 law, any such couple bold enough to "intermarry, or live in adultery or fornication with each other" faced felony convictions that carried prison sentences of two to seven years. The penalty for officials who performed interracial marriages covered marriage license clerks as well as justices of the peace and ministers; it was increased to a fine of $100 to $1,000, with a possible additional jail sentence of six months.[27]

Once this law was on the books, Alabama prosecutors matched the fervor of the Alabama state legislature in trying to enforce it. Between 1868 and 1877, Alabama prosecutors charged so many defendants with violating Alabama miscegenation law that the issue came before the Alabama Supreme Court on five separate occasions. In all five of these trials, the same man, John W. A. Sanford, a die-hard states' rights Democrat who served as state attorney general, defended the state of Alabama.[28]

The first two of these trials, held in 1868 and 1872, showed how difficult the task of defending miscegenation law could be: in the first, Sanford stumbled short of his goal; in the second, he fell flat on his face. In the 1868 trial, a "negro" man and a "white" woman had been convicted of the illicit sex crime of "living in fornication" and sentenced to pay a fine. On its face, the case was unremarkable. Throughout the antebellum period, local prosecutors had charged couples who flouted community morals with "living in fornication" and punished them in local courts. This practice, which reflected a long tradition of criminal prosecutions for illicit sex, applied to same-race as well as interracial couples. In this particular case, the fine imposed by the judge was, in fact, the same punishment that was ordinarily handed down to same-race couples convicted on fornication charges. But the arrest had occurred after the passage of the 1866 Alabama miscegenation law and the rise of Reconstruction, developments that left the Alabama Supreme Court caught between the impulse to uphold the strict new law and the fear that it might be unconstitutional. Mindful of both these possibilities, the justices of the Alabama Supreme Court tried to chart a middle ground. They started by criticizing the lower-court judge for punishing the couple with the fines appropriate for same-race fornication rather than the prison sentences recently mandated for interracial fornication, making it clear that they considered differential punishments for same-race and interracial fornication entirely appropriate. If, the justices said, the lower-court judge had assumed that the Civil Rights Act of 1866 invalidated the state miscegenation law on this point, he must have been mistaken. But to Attorney General Sanford's dismay, the Alabama Supreme Court stopped right there. Its judges not only refused to rule on the constitutionality of Alabama's ban on interracial marriage but took care to note that "we wish . . . not to be understood. . . . to affirm its validity."[29]

In the second case, heard in 1872, the Alabama Supreme Court *did* consider the constitutionality of the ban on interracial marriage, and this time Attorney General John Sanford lost on every count. As chapter 1 explained, the *Burns* decision cleared justice of the peace T. J. Burns, a White man, of criminal charges for performing an interracial marriage. In it, the Alabama Supreme Court declared the Alabama miscegenation law unconstitutional on the ground that it was in direct opposition to the "cardinal principle" of the Civil Rights Act of 1866 and the Fourteenth Amendment guarantee of equal protection. The *Burns* case was rendered in language so sweeping that to some observers, at least, it seemed to show that equal protection might apply to Black men as well as White men. Robert Hoover was willing to bet that it did. In 1875, Hoover, a "negro," went to the local probate judge to ask for formal permission to marry Betsy Litsey, a "white" woman. Constrained by the *Burns* precedent, the judge admitted that the Alabama Supreme Court had declared "the law forbidding such marriage to be unconstitutional." He gave Hoover written authorization to marry Litsey, after which the couple celebrated their marriage and set up housekeeping in Talladega, Alabama. A year later, Alabamans Aaron Green and Julia Atkinson, a "negro" man and a "white" woman, celebrated their marriage, too, apparently without asking for any special permission.[30]

Meanwhile, Attorney General Sanford, stung by his defeat in the *Burns* case, struggled to come up with a new and more persuasive defense of miscegenation law, one strong enough to reinstate the now discarded Alabama statute. Sanford needed to find a way to pull judicial attention away from civil rights, equal protection, and the right to contract a marriage, considerations that state supreme courts in Alabama and Texas had used to invalidate miscegenation laws. One possibility was to shift the focus of miscegenation cases from marriage, which implied contract, citizenship, and property rights, to illicit sex, which implied criminal immorality. This strategy seemed promising, since the 1868 and 1872 cases suggested that although the Alabama

Supreme Court would no longer countenance laws against interracial marriage, it would support racially differential punishments for interracial sex.

Sanford could take heart from the fact that in other southern states prosecutors had recently persuaded judges to convict interracial couples on criminal charges of illicit sex, largely by pushing the possibility of interracial marriage out of the picture. In Georgia, for example, Charlotte Scott had married Leopold Daniels only to find herself indicted for being a "colored" woman "cohabiting and having sexual intercourse with" a "white" man. During the trial, the judge refused to allow the jury to hear testimony that the Danielses had been legally married, and then rejected a request to instruct the jury that if Scott was married to Daniels, she must be acquitted of the cohabitation charge. In a last-ditch attempt to show the validity of their marriage to the jury, Scott's lawyer grandstanded, telling the judge the couple was willing to remarry right then and there if the judge would only perform the ceremony. The judge's sarcastic response—he told the couple "they might go out and get some one to perform it, if they could find any one who would"—suggests both the willingness to transfer traditional condemnations of illicit sex to interracial couples and the relative ease of doing so in a criminal case when the defendant, whose rights were at stake, was a Black woman. In 1868, the Georgia Supreme Court upheld Charlotte Scott's conviction in a decision marked by a particularly vicious language of racialized immorality.[31]

A year later, the North Carolina Supreme Court considered the case of Wesley Hairston, a "colored" man, and Puss Williams, a "white" woman. Like Charlotte Scott, the Hairstons had been indicted for the illicit sex crime of fornication. The Hairstons also claimed to be married, and both sides admitted that, as the court reporter explained, "the facts established a marriage, if such relation could exist between parties, one of whom is colored and the other white." Nonetheless, at the end of their trial, the judge instructed the jury that "by the law of the State the alleged marriage in this case was a nullity." Working on this premise, the jury found the couple guilty, and the North Carolina Supreme Court upheld their convictions.[32]

Decisions like these appeared to depend on drawing a sharp line between illicit sex and legitimate marriage, but actually they revealed the links between the two. The prosecution of interracial couples on illicit sex charges would prove effective only if interracial couples were denied access to the strategy that many same-race couples accused of fornication used to avoid conviction, which was to turn an illicit relationship into a legitimate one by marrying. In other words, the arrests would stick only if judges were persuaded to uphold laws against interracial marriage.

This is where Indiana's *Gibson* case proved so important, because it offered a way to push aside equal protection, civil rights, and the right to contract marriage in cases involving interracial marriage as well as in cases involving interracial sex. Accordingly, when the next miscegenation case came before the Alabama Supreme Court, John Sanford tried a double-pronged strategy. On the one hand, he emphasized the supposedly illicit nature of interracial sex, and on the other, he urged the court to use the *Gibson* decision from Indiana to uphold prohibitions on interracial marriage. This case involved a "white" man and a "negro" woman who had been charged under Alabama's 1866 miscegenation law with "living in adultery or fornication," convicted, and given a two-year prison sentence. Their lawyer appealed their conviction on the grounds that "the legislature had no power to make an act which when committed by persons of the same race is only a misdemeanor, a felony when committed by persons of different races." Fortunately for Sanford, this couple never intended to marry and did not claim marriage as part of their defense. Their silence on this issue let Sanford raise the question of marriage without fear of challenge, and he urged the court to reinstate the constitutionality of Alabama's law against both interracial sex *and* interracial marriage by using the *Gibson* precedent to overrule the *Burns* decision on interracial marriage. He succeeded, however, only on the issue of sex. In 1875, the Alabama Supreme Court was perfectly willing to conflate interracial couples with illicit sex, but it still distinguished between the criminal offense of illicit sex and the civil status of marriage. "Living in adultery is offensive to all laws human and divine, and human laws must impose punishments adequate to the enormity of the offence and its insult to public decency," said the court, but "marriage may be a natural and civil right, pertaining to all persons."[33]

John Sanford was not content to leave it at that. Two years later, he was still trying to get the Alabama Supreme Court to pay attention to the *Gibson* precedent on interracial marriage. He got his chance in 1877, when the last of these five cases, that of Julia Green, came before the court. Green, a "white" woman, had been sentenced to two years in prison after being convicted of marrying Aaron Green, a "negro" man. Once again, Sanford urged the court to overrule the 1872 *Burns* decision. Once again, he pleaded with the court to read the *Gibson* decision, "a very exhaustive discussion of the question," and to overrule *Burns*, which, he insisted, was "not supported by reason or authority."[34]

This time, the Alabama Supreme Court took Sanford's advice. It issued a decision that combined the free-state example of Indiana with the slave-state condemnation of interracial sex to make bans on interracial marriage seem entirely consistent with civil rights laws. Praising the Indiana Supreme

Court for its "able and emphatic" decision in *Gibson,* the Alabama Supreme Court relied on it to argue that southern states had no obligation to tolerate marriages that northern states like Indiana would not. Combining the *Gibson* contention that marriage was more than a civil contract with sexualized rhetoric about the natural differences between the races and the "discord, shame [and] disruption" that interracial unions must "must naturally cause," the justices explained that civil-rights-based objections to miscegenation laws now seemed to them "a very narrow and an illogical view of the subject." As the court explained, "What the law declares to be a punishable offense is marriage between a white person and a negro. And it no more tolerates it in one of the parties than the other—in a white person than in a negro or mulatto," because "each of them is punishable for the offense prohibited, in precisely the same manner and to the same extent." Seen from this vantage point, the Alabama miscegenation law of 1866 appeared to be a necessary, even equitable, law. "Surely," the court opined, "there can not be any tyranny or injustice in requiring both alike, to form this union with those of their own race only, whom God hath joined together by indelible peculiarities, which declare that He has made the two races distinct."[35] So saying, the Alabama Supreme Court granted John Sanford's wish, overruled the *Burns* decision, and declared Alabama's 1866 miscegenation law once again constitutional.

In Texas, too, the strategy of using the slave-era stigma of interracial sex to push for the postwar prohibition of interracial marriage allowed judges to cast off lingering doubts about the constitutionality of miscegenation laws. Three years after upholding the marriage of Leah and Alfred Foster, the Texas Supreme Court heard another civil case involving the property of a "white" man who lived with a "mulatto" woman. This time, however, the court refused to grant any rights or benefits to the woman who claimed to be a legal wife. The court dismissed her argument that a provision of the state constitution that extended the legal presumption of marriage to couples who had been denied it because of slavery could and should be applied to a former slave woman involved with a free White man. "It is not," the court commented tartly, "the letter of the Constitution, nor is it believed to be its intention, to confer on any parties, white or black, whose intercourse was illegal and immoral, the rights and benefits of lawful wedlock."[36]

At about the same time, the Texas Court of Appeals upheld the Texas law against interracial marriage. The Court of Appeals, a new body created by the post-Reconstruction Texas legislature to take jurisdiction in criminal cases away from the Texas Supreme Court, issued its ruling in the case of Charles Frasher, a "white" man who had been sentenced to four years in the state penitentiary for marrying "a negro." Frasher's lawyers relied on the same arguments that had persuaded earlier Texas courts to consider White men the husbands of Black women; they contended that the 1858 Texas law against interracial marriage was "in conflict with the 14th and 15th amendments of the Constitution of the United States and the 1st section of the Civil Rights Bill; that [it] . . . was passed in the interest of slavery, before that institution was abolished, and when the negro was not a citizen of the United States; and that it cannot be enforced, because it prescribes a penalty to be inflicted upon the white person alone." But the judges on the Texas Court of Appeals refused to accept any of these arguments. Judge Matthew Ector's opinion included a lengthy discussion of state and federal constitutional questions, but in the end, it, like the *Green* ruling in Alabama, placed heavy reliance on the *Gibson* precedent, which Ector explained the Texas court was "fully indorsing." Ector concluded, "Marriage is not a contract protected by the Constitution of the United States, or within the meaning of the Civil Rights Bill. Marriage is more than a contract within the meaning of the act. It is a civil *status*, left solely by the Federal Constitution and the laws to the discretion of the states, under their general power to regulate their domestic affairs."[37]

In this fashion, southern state courts linked the association between interracial and illicit sex born in slavery to the authority of state police powers upheld in *Gibson* to forge a powerfully persuasive rationale for miscegenation law. In so doing, they gathered the various strands of the relatively loose antebellum condemnation of illicit sexuality into a much stronger weave of late nineteenth-century prosecutions for illicit sex, a development that, in turn, strengthened the power of criminal law in miscegenation cases. By the 1880s, the sexualization of miscegenation law led judges into a neatly constructed white supremacist tautology. Judges began by using the traditional divide between illicit sex and illegitimate marriage to describe all interracial relationships as being, *by definition*, illicit sex. Their next step, which was to refuse to allow interracial couples to legitimize their sexual relationships by marrying, took them into another, even more tightly wound circle, in which every attempt to legalize an interracial marriage could be interpreted as illicit interracial sex. By this means, defenders of miscegenation law not only condemned interracial sex in its casual and illicit forms but also turned long-term settled relationships, some entered into with official approval, into illicit sex, thus in effect *producing* as well as condemning illicit sex.

Built on the foundation of the attack on interracial marriage in *Gibson,* the sexualization of miscegenation law turned into a legal formula powerful enough to produce and reproduce miscegenation law from the 1880s through the middle of the twentieth century. Its power was quickly apparent in state legislatures and constitutional conventions. After courts in Alabama

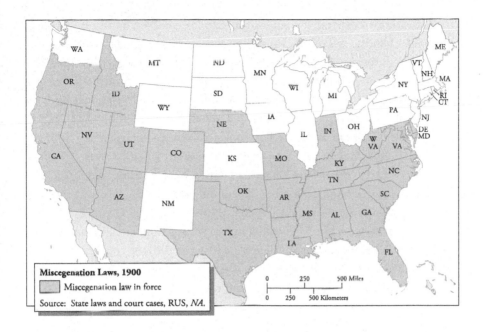

Miscegenation Laws, 1900

Miscegenation law in force

Source: State laws and court cases, RUS, *NA.*

and Texas issued new rulings upholding miscegenation laws, all of the five southern states whose legislatures had repealed them—Louisiana, Mississippi, South Carolina, Arkansas, and Florida—reinstated them between 1879 and 1894.[38] In 1877, the Virginia state legislature increased its punishment for miscegenation to two to five years in prison; in 1879, Missouri raised its penalty to two years in prison.[39] In 1884, the Maryland legislature redefined miscegenation as an "infamous crime" punishable by prison sentences.[40] Bans on marriage to Blacks also continued to appear in Indian nations. In 1888, for example, the Choctaw General Council declared that "if a Choctaw man or Choctaw woman should marry a negro man or negro woman he or she shall be deemed guilty of a felony."[41] Five states—North Carolina in 1876, Florida in 1885, Mississippi in 1890, South Carolina in 1895, and Alabama in 1901— put bans on interracial marriage directly into their state constitutions.[42]

Sexualizing Equal Protection

Perhaps it was predictable that in cases that pitted state miscegenation laws against federal guarantees of civil rights, state supreme courts would emphasize illicit sex and marriage, two legal arenas that were widely acknowledged to fall under state control. Perhaps federal courts would take federal civil rights legislation more seriously.

Yet during the 1870s, few interracial couples gambled on this possibility, and only a handful succeeded in getting federal district courts to hear their pleas. The outcome of their cases demonstrates just how much power the connection between marriage and states' rights could muster. In all but one of them, federal judges solved the conflict between state miscegenation laws and federal civil rights laws by adopting states' rights arguments. In 1871, for example, William and Martha Hobbs, a "white" man and a "colored" woman, asked a federal district judge in Georgia to issue a writ of habeas corpus and release them from the jail where they were being held after their conviction for marrying each other. The judge granted the writ but rejected the couple's argument for their freedom. Noting that the Georgia Supreme Court had already declared that the state's miscegenation law did not conflict with Georgia's state constitution, he ruled that it did not conflict with federal law either. As this judge saw it, neither the Civil Rights Act of 1866 nor the Fourteenth Amendment could accommodate the Hobbs marriage.[43]

In Texas, federal district judge Thomas Duval at first seemed to disagree. In an 1877 case involving a "white" woman, Duval decided that because the 1858 version of the Texas law against interracial marriage punished only the White partner, it was "unfair," "unequal," and in violation of the Fourteenth Amendment. Two years later, however, when Duval heard a case involving a "white" man, he came to the opposite conclusion. In the meantime, he explained, he had realized that because marriage was "exclusively under the control of each state," state legislatures had the power to pass laws that might otherwise seem to be discriminatory. So although he still considered the law unwise and unfair, he now held that its deficiencies stopped short of unconstitutionality.[44]

In 1879, Edmund Kinney tried a slightly different argument. Kinney, a Virginia "negro," used a writ of habeas corpus to ask a federal judge to relieve him of the five-year-prison sentence he faced for marrying Mary Hall, a "white" woman, by arguing that a marriage legal in the District of Columbia ought to be legal anywhere in the United States. The district court judge who heard Kinney's case cited a Virginia Supreme Court decision rejecting a similar argument, then ruled that the Virginia miscegenation law did not conflict with the Fourteenth Amendment. "There is," the court asserted, "nothing in the national constitution expressly forbidding a state from abridging the right of marrying, or indeed any right but that of voting, on account of race or color."[45]

By echoing state court arguments on these points, federal district courts lent their authority to the argument, put forth so forcefully in *Gibson,* that marriage was a matter of state rather than federal control. In effect, they allowed state courts to remove the contract of marriage from the reach of civil rights laws. By 1880, both assumptions—that marriage was a matter for state control and was immune to federal civil rights laws—had become routine in state and federal court cases involving interracial couples who tried to make formal marriages. By the time that the U.S. Supreme Court was finally brought into the mix, its justices were easily able to bypass the issue of interracial marriage; they would not, in fact, agree to address that question until 1967.

In the meantime, though, the U.S. Supreme Court did something that was even more important: it lent its considerable weight to the sexualization of miscegenation law. In 1880, the Court agreed to hear a criminal case involving charges of illicit sex, which focused on a "negro" man and a "white" woman and took place in Alabama, a state where laws against interracial marriage had been subjected to sharp and, as we have seen, sometimes successful challenge.[46]

The case had originated in the tiny town of Grove Hill, Alabama. In 1881, the local grand jury indicted Tony Pace, a "negro," for "living in fornication and adultery" with Mary Jane Cox, "a white woman." In separate trials, both Pace and Cox were convicted under the Alabama law that state attorney general John Sanford had revived in 1877, which punished interracial couples convicted of fornication much more heavily than same-race couples. At Tony Pace's trial, the court wasted little time debating the evidence, which consisted mostly of testimony from White neighbors and property holders. Pace's lawyer asked the judge to tell the jury that unless the state could prove that Pace and Cox were living together rather than having occasional illicit sex, Pace was innocent of the charge, but the judge refused to do so. After the jury found him guilty, Tony Pace was sentenced to two years in the penitentiary.[47]

The *Pace* trial might have ended right there were it not for the fact that on that day John Tompkins, a lawyer from the relatively cosmopolitan city of Mobile, happened to be in the courtroom. After watching Pace's conviction, Tompkins, who later explained that "I did not think him under the evidence guilty," offered to handle an appeal. Tompkins took the case despite the fact that he knew Pace had no money to pay him. Convinced that Pace "was suffering an illegal penalty in our state penitentiary," he also believed that the "question involved" was "one of great interest to the criminal courts of Ala. and other states."[48]

Tompkins first went to the Alabama Supreme Court, where he argued that the Alabama miscegenation law violated both the privileges and immunities and the equal protection clauses of the Fourteenth Amendment. By this time, however, the Alabama Supreme Court was quite skilled at deflecting these arguments. In language that encapsulated the sexualization of miscegenation law, the court dismissed Tompkins's equal protection claim. There was, the court insisted, "no difference or discrimination" because "the punishment of each offending party, white and black, is precisely the same." It made no difference that Alabama's law punished interracial couples more harshly than same-race couples, since judges simply folded these racial distinctions into condemnations of illicit sex. "The evil tendency of the crime of living in adultery or fornication," they declared, "is greater when it is committed between persons of the two races than between persons of the same race." Using this argument and citing the *Gibson* case from Indiana as well as recent decisions from North Carolina, Virginia, and Texas, the Alabama Supreme Court upheld Tony Pace's conviction.[49]

Tompkins, who had expected to lose at the state level, then set about finding a way to bring the case to the U.S. Supreme Court. He wrote to the only person he knew with legal contacts in Washington, D.C., inquiring whether the Supreme Court might hear the case of Tony Pace, a "colored and *poor*" man, without requiring the payment of court fees and asking whether his contact knew of any "colored societies" that might help fund his appeal. Evidently nothing came of this request, for in the end, Tompkins wrote and published his appeal brief at his own expense. When it was finished, he sent a copy to the Grove Hill newspaper, which politely acknowledged receiving it but declined to print it. A copy remains, however, in the U.S. Supreme Court files, and it shows Tompkins's reasoning.[50]

Like so many of his southern White legal brethren, Tompkins drew a sharp distinction between marriage and illicit sex; unlike them, however, he tried to use it to the advantage of a Black man. From the outset, he admitted that the state of Alabama had the power to prohibit interracial marriage, a concession that shows how influential the argument presented in *Gibson* had become in the decade since it had been issued. For Tompkins, though, distinguishing between interracial marriage and interracial sex served another purpose: it allowed him to remove Tony Pace from the state-controlled realm of marriage law and plead his case in the realm of criminal law. When it came to criminal rights, Tompkins argued, the Fourteenth Amendment guarantee of equal protection should trump state law. "Legislative power may regulate how the lawful institution of marriage may be celebrated . . . ," he wrote, "but legislative power may not say how crimes, in themselves penal, may be discriminately punished (where all are equal before the law) according to the caste of the individual who invades them."[51]

In what is perhaps the most revealing passage of his brief, Tompkins reached for an example that might make his point. Rather than comparing a Black man like his client to a White man, he chose to compare two White men. In wording that replicated decades of southern White male sexual privilege, Tompkins asked the justices to note that under Alabama's miscegenation law, which prohibited sex only between "any white person and any negro," a man "of the Saxon race" who "becomes enamored of an octoroon" would be guilty of a felony, while his brother who "grovels in lowest licentiousness with the most degraded of Indian squaws" would be guilty only of a misdemeanor. "Is this," he asked, "equality before the law?"[52]

Tompkins's brief was carefully designed to appeal to U.S. Supreme Court Justice Stephen J. Field, a man known for his opposition to "class legislation" and his willingness to take the words "equal protection" seriously. In two California cases, Field had taken a strong stand on these issues. In the first, which involved immigrant women from China who were threatened with deportation under a law authorizing immigration inspectors to detain "lewd and debauched" women, Field had argued that even when it came to noncitizens like immigrant women, the Fourteenth Amendment prohibited "discriminating and partial legislation, favoring particular persons, or against particular persons of the same class." In the second, which involved an ordinance allowing San Francisco city jailers to cut off the queues of Chinese immigrant men serving jail sentences for violating a city ordinance, Field reiterated his interpretation of the Fourteenth Amendment's equal protection clause and added:

> When we take our seats on the bench we are not struck with blindness, and forbidden to know as judges what we see as men; and where an ordinance, though general in its terms, only operates upon a special race, sect or class, it being universally understood that it is to be enforced only against that race, sect or class, we may justly conclude that it was the intention of the body adopting it that it should only have such operation, and treat it accordingly.

In his brief to the Supreme Court in the *Pace* case, Tompkins cited both these cases and inveighed against "that legislative monstrosity condemned of all enlightened governments commonly known as 'class legislation.'"[53]

Tompkins had counted on Field to recognize race discrimination when he saw it, but he was to be sorely disappointed. When the Supreme Court issued its decision in *Pace v. Alabama*, Justice Field spoke for the Court, and in this case involving the race-and-gender pairing of a Black man and a White woman, Field's devotion to equal protection took a new and different turn. Field began by repeating his general position on the issue. "Equality of protection under the laws," he wrote, "implies not only accessibility by each one, whatever his race, on the same terms with others to the courts of the country for the security of his person and property, but that in the administration of criminal justice he shall not be subjected, for the same offence, to any greater or different punishment." Then, by adopting the rhetoric of racial symmetry advanced in

Supreme Court Justice Stephen J. Field in 1875. (Prints and Photographs Division, Library of Congress)

the Alabama Supreme Court, Field took the fateful step that American courts would follow for the next four generations. "The defect in the argument of counsel," he opined, "consists in his assumption that any discrimination is made by the laws of Alabama in the punishment provided for the offence for which . . . [Tony Pace] was indicted when committed by a person of the African race and when committed by a white person." He continued:

> The two sections of the code cited [prohibiting same-race and interracial fornication] are entirely consistent. The one prescribes, generally, a punishment for an offence committed between persons of different sexes; the other prescribes a punishment for an offence which can only be committed where the two sexes are of different races. . . . Whatever discrimination is made . . . is directed against the offence designated and not against the person of any particular color or race. The punishment of each offending person, whether white or black, is the same.

So saying, the U.S. Supreme Court unanimously rejected the appeal of Tony Pace. A dismayed Tompkins summed it all up. "The Supreme Court," he wrote in a private letter, "'has knocked the stuffing' out of Justice Field's California decisions, and *poor Tony* remains a convict and worse than a pauper."[54]

The *Pace* decision crowned the Supreme Court's endorsement of the post-war judicial defense of miscegenation law. Beginning with the *Gibson* case in Indiana, judges had found one way after another to avoid potential conflicts between miscegenation law and the promises of racial equality generated by Reconstruction. By defining marriage as a social status and an institution that was "much more" than a "mere" contract, they placed interracial marriage outside of the contract rights guaranteed to Blacks "on the same terms as whites" in the Civil Rights Acts of 1866 and 1875. By taking miscegenation law out from under federal guarantees of civil rights and placing it in the bailiwick of state police power, they enabled the criminalization of interracial sex and marriage and encouraged lawyers and judges to place heavy reliance on rhetorical condemnation of illicit sex. Once interracial marriage had been both delegitimized and sexualized, state and local officials frequently, and often successfully, prosecuted White men and Black women as well as White women and Black men for interracial illicit sex crimes. It is nonetheless significant that in the three key cases that forged the judicial defense of miscegenation law, *Gibson, Green,* and *Pace,* judicial avoidance of civil rights claims was made easier by the fact that it was Black men and White women— two groups whose claims to the privileges of contract, citizenship, and property were tenuous at best—who stood before the court.

By asserting that interracial illicit sex was a different offense than same-race illicit sex, the *Pace* decision embedded race distinctions within the "offence" itself in a manner that made felony punishments for interracial couples seem compatible with guarantees of equal protection. In this way, it expanded the sexualization of miscegenation law developed in state courts into the sexualization of equal protection that shielded miscegenation law in federal courts. By so doing, it fueled the perception that "miscegenation" was something real, definable, and punishable. And finally, it offered an illusion of equal protection that made miscegenation laws seem so natural that they weren't racially discriminatory at all.

"God and Nature Seem to Forbid Them"

In *Pace,* the U.S. Supreme Court declared that there was no race discrimination in making race difference central to the definition of a crime. Such a ruling might well seem to be the product of an Alice-in-Wonderland world in which nothing appears to be what it really is. This is hardly unusual in the world of law, where distinctions can be piled on distinctions until they reach a logic that seems skewed, even entirely inverted, to an ordinary person. Late nineteenth-century judges are generally believed to have enjoyed escaping into this rarefied realm of legal niceties. When it came to miscegenation law, however, judges worked hard to link law to society and to embed their judgments in the world outside their courtrooms.

To justify miscegenation law, judges fired all the cannons of the Victorian rhetorical arsenal: religion, science, history, democracy, and above all, nature. Miscegenation law emerged in a cultural moment when nature was a key reference point in many forms of public discourse. Clergymen linked nature to religion by invoking "God and Nature" or describing Nature as God's handmaiden. Scientists, who were experts at explaining "the laws of nature" that governed the physical world, were beginning to promulgate newer, even more powerful laws of "natural selection." Political thinkers imagined civil society as rising out of a "state of nature" that grounded "the natural and inalienable rights of man," which governments were obligated to protect. Judges assumed the "natural" affection of family members and frequently invoked the "natural" dependence of women and the "natural" differences between the races.[55]

The sheer multiplicity of these references—and the frequent contradictions within them—can help us understand why judicial rhetoric about nature was such an effective means of naturalizing miscegenation law. The key point is that in the last half of the nineteenth century, nature was conceived of as *both* an inherited, innate, predetermined essence *and* an all-powerful social and historical force. It was the relationship between the two, that is, between nature as a powerful religious or scientific force, expressed in phrases like "the God of Nature" and "the laws of nature," and nature as a predetermined essence, expressed in phrases like "natural" affections or "natural" rights or "natural" differences, that helped miscegenation law push its roots so deeply into the American legal system and twist its branches through American culture and society.

After the Civil War, judges used interracial sex and marriage as a foundational example of the supposed links between the God-given "natural law" and the "natural separation of the races" both inside and outside miscegenation law. One especially influential example came from a Pennsylvania court in 1867, where a judge struggled to explain why he felt it necessary to uphold segregation in railroads. In language studded with references to nature, he declared:

> Why the Creator made one black and the other white, we know not;
> but the fact is apparent, and the races distinct, each producing its

own kind, and following the peculiar law of its constitution. Conceding equality, with natures as perfect and rights as sacred, yet God has made them dissimilar, with those natural instincts and feelings which He always imparts to His creatures, when He intends that they shall not overstep the natural boundaries He has assigned to them. The natural law which forbids their intermarriage and that social amalgamation which leads to a corruption of races, is as clearly divine as that which imparted to them different natures. The tendency of intimate social intermixture is to amalgamation, contrary to the law of races. The separation of the white and black races upon the surface of the globe is a fact equally apparent. Why this is so, it is not necessary to speculate; but the fact of a distribution of men by race and color is as visible in the providential arrangement of the earth as that of heat and cold. The natural separation of the races is therefore an undeniable fact, and all social organizations which lead to their amalgamation are repugnant to the law of nature. From social amalgamation it is but a step to illicit intercourse, and but another to intermarriage.[56]

In cases involving interracial marriage, judges often quoted this passage, then raised the stakes by replacing their admiration for the natural with their clear repugnance for the unnatural.[57] On the unnaturality of miscegenation, judges formed a virtual chorus. In Georgia: "The amalgamation of the races is not only unnatural, but is always productive of deplorable results." In Texas: "For such unnatural marriages, the whites are mainly to blame." In Tennessee, marriage was made "of natural as well as municipal law," but interracial marriage was "revolting" and "unnatural." At its most expansive, this rhetoric blended natural and religious authority with claims to civilization. This is how the Virginia Supreme Court put it: "The purity of public morals, the moral and physical development of both races, and the highest advancement of our cherished southern civilization, under which two distinct races are to work out and accomplish the destiny to which the Almighty has assigned them on this continent—all require that they should be kept distinct and separate, and that connections and alliances so unnatural that God and nature seem to forbid them, should be prohibited by positive law, and be subject to no evasion."[58]

In a world where the term "natural" implied religious, moral, and political merit, the term "unnatural" was a many-sided stigma. At the level of common usage, "unnatural" signaled that something was monstrous, wicked, or contrary to the "laws of nature." The labeling of interracial relationships as unnatural in this sense was not an entirely new phenomenon. The term can be found as far back as the colonial period, and it occasionally appeared in antebellum court decisions as well. In the post–Civil War period, however, the force and frequency of the reliance on the rhetoric of unnaturality expanded alongside the range of connections references to unnaturality allowed judges to make.

Within the law itself, one of the most frequent uses of the term "unnatural" was to critique intolerable behavior on the part of a family member, whether a father who left his property to a stranger rather than to his children, a mother who agreed to a separation from a child, or a child who refused to defer to a parent; in other words, to contrast bad behavior to the supposed familial norm. In this respect, labeling a relationship unnatural helped widen the gap between interracial relationships, seen as illegitimate and immoral, and marriage and family life, seen as both legitimate and virtuous.

Labeling a relationship unnatural also helped judges analogize miscegenation to other supposed crimes against nature and civilization. The most striking of these, another of miscegenation's rhetorical tricks, was a comparison between interracial marriage and incest. Family members were prohibited from marrying each other in even more American states than interracial couples were, but with this shared illegality the logical comparisons between the two ended. The fact that judges could analogize relationships between people who were, biologically speaking, supposedly too close together with those between people who were, biologically speaking, supposedly too far apart speaks volumes about the power of the rhetoric of nature: it allowed for seemingly opposite kinds of relationships to appear to be the same. The comparison seemed to make sense even to legal commentators who were otherwise doubtful about the validity of race segregation, including Ernst Freund, a northern judge who wrote the standard work on police powers in 1904. "Marriage," Freund explained, "is clearly a matter in which race difference has a natural and specific operation . . . and the prohibition is at least as reasonable as that of marriages between first cousins."[59]

Another such analogy, between interracial marriage and polygamy, helped judges underline the sexualization of miscegenation law. In the late nineteenth-century mind, polygamy was associated with Mormon patriarchs and Turkish harems, both of which stood as unrestrained symbols of sexual lust. When a judge in Tennessee argued that "the Turk or Mohammedan, with his numerous wives" and "harem," was no "more revolting, more to be avoided, or more unnatural" than the miscegenation case he was then considering, he relied on both sets of associations.[60]

Buttressed by the breadth of these analogies, and reaching deeply into popular notions of the true nature of things, claims about unnaturality allowed courts to mask the novelty of postwar miscegenation law. In time-honored fashion, courts linked postwar miscegenation law to judicial precedent and political principle by positing a supposedly unbroken history of American opposition to interracial sex and marriage. Pushing Reconstruction-era challenges to miscegenation law (like the *Foster* and *Burns* cases) into obscurity and hiding historical contingency behind the certainties of political principle, judges routinely exaggerated the continuities between pre–Civil War laws against interracial marriage and postwar miscegenation law. Thus, a North Carolina judge dismissed the impact of Reconstruction on miscegenation law by asserting that "late events, and the emancipation of the slaves, have made no alteration in our policy, or in the sentiments of our people." In Texas, when the Court of Appeals issued a decision that reinstated the Texas miscegenation law, its judges simply pretended that the question had never been open for debate. "It has always been the policy of this state," the judges opined, "to maintain separate marital relations between the whites and the blacks. It is useless for us to cite the different statutes on this subject, enacted from time to time, showing that the people of Texas are now, and have ever been, opposed to the intermixture of these races."[61]

This rhetoric sometimes reached extraordinary heights. As one judge in Tennessee put it, prohibitions on interracial marriage were "the policy of our own legislation, as to bond and free, fifty years ago. . . . Such, also, were the laws of the British Colonies in this country, reenacted after the separation by the thirteen States . . . and such, indeed, we believe was the law of every State." Carrying this already overstated rhetoric to its logical, if also wildly inaccurate, conclusion, he insisted that "the right to regulate the institution of marriage, to classify the parties and persons who may lawfully marry, to dissolve the relation by divorce, and to impose such restraints upon the relation as the laws of God and the laws of propriety demand, has been exercised by all governments, and in all ages of the world. The discrimination as to race and people, in this most important institution, has been observed, even from the days of the patriarchs, and even as to different people of the same race."[62]

While some judges used judicial precedent to emphasize the historical depth of miscegenation laws, others relied on democratic political principle to emphasize the breadth of the consensus that supposedly sustained the laws. In the *Gibson* case, Chief Justice Buskirk of the Indiana Supreme Court proclaimed that "the people of this State have declared that they are opposed to the intermixture of races and all amalgamation." In this vein, southern state court judges soon grew fond of citing northern refusals to extend rights to free Blacks in justification of continued southern unwillingness to do so. Both Alabama and Texas judges used this argument to reinstate miscegenation laws. "If not in every State of the Union," an Alabama judge claimed, "in all of them in which any considerable numbers of the negro race resided, statutes have been enacted prohibiting marriages between them and persons of the white race."[63]

Some judges even fashioned a democratic consensus that appeared to reflect postwar change by claiming Black as well as White support for miscegenation laws. Some jurists pointed out that during Reconstruction both Blacks and Whites attended state constitutional conventions and sat in state legislatures, implying that Black presence in these arenas meant Black approval for the laws. Others simply asserted that miscegenation laws were "in the best interests" of both groups. "Manifestly," wrote the judge in Alabama's *Green* case, "it is for the peace and happiness of the black race, as well as of the white, that such laws should exist."[64]

By invoking religion, science, history, and democracy, judges stitched the seams of the emerging justification for miscegenation law, tailoring technical discussions of the provisions and coverage of federal civil rights legislation to fit assertions about the natural separation of the races and the unnaturality of miscegenation. This judicial consensus reached well beyond court cases involving interracial couples to nurture race segregation in other arenas as well. Favorable references to the constitutionality of miscegenation laws ran through court cases on libel, testimony and property rights, and school, railroad, and streetcar segregation.[65] In 1896, when the U.S. Supreme Court issued the decision that became the most significant of all the segregation cases, *Plessy v. Ferguson*, it used the example of miscegenation law, and the *Gibson* case in Indiana, as precedents for upholding railroad segregation. In a single sentence, the justices summarized what had become the accepted wisdom about the constitutionality of miscegenation laws: "Laws forbidding the intermarriage of the two races may be said in a technical sense to interfere with the freedom of contract, and yet have been universally recognized as within the police power of the State."[66]

Once this consensus about the unnaturalness of interracial marriage, and the rewriting of history that accompanied it, were in place, they paid continual dividends for supporters of miscegenation laws. Engendered, sexualized, and built on criminal prosecutions that featured Black men and White women, the framework of miscegenation laws had grown so strong that its constitutionality was assured and its naturalness assumed. Building on this base, it would soon extend to cover a larger number of states than ever before—and to encompass a larger number of "races" as well.

Part II

MISCEGENATION LAW AND RACE CLASSIFICATION, 1860–1948

Chapter Three

CONFIGURING RACE IN THE AMERICAN WEST

"Hereafter it shall not be lawful within this state for any white person, male or female, to intermarry with any negro, Chinese, or any person having one fourth or more negro, Chinese, or kanaka blood, or any person having more than one half Indian blood; and all such marriages, or attempted marriages, shall be absolutely null and void."

—*Oregon Laws, 1866*

SALEM, OREGON

Oregon already had a law prohibiting marriage between "a white person" and "a negro," but State Representative James Gingles thought that wasn't enough. In October 1866, Gingles introduced a bill to "prohibit Amalgamation and the Intermarriage of the races" by punishing "any white person" who married "any negro, Chinese, kanaka or Indian" in the Oregon House of Representatives.[1] To Gingles, and to other nineteenth-century legislators in western states and territories, the passage of a miscegenation law was an ordinary exercise in state-making, one of many actions they took to secure the rights of White men like themselves. Men like Gingles proved every bit as eager as their southern counterparts to build new structures of white supremacy from the tumbling bricks of older racial hierarchies. But their western version of white supremacy reached beyond the baseline obsession with categories of White and Black, to build a longer list of non-White races that were then targeted in miscegenation laws.

From the 1860s, and especially after 1882, when the U.S. Supreme Court issued its ruling in *Pace v. Alabama*, the channeling of constitutional equality took a backseat to the multiplication of racial categories, which then became the central theme of miscegenation law. This chapter traces the development of the multiracial miscegenation laws passed in the West from the 1860s to the 1930s, exploring the manner in which these laws, like those in the South, were gendered, sexualized, and shaped around the symbolism of particular race-and-gender pairs. It starts with a look at the development of white supremacy in Oregon, then examines the racialization of Asian Americans, which was built on the race-and-gender pairing of White women and Asian American men and was designed to protect white supremacy by advocating the protection of white womanhood. Then it turns to the racialization of American Indians, which was built around the race-and-gender pairing of White men and Indian women and was designed to protect white supremacy by protecting white property.

White Supremacy, Oregon Style

The list of races featured in the Gingles bill—"negro, Chinese, kanaka or Indian"—was a racialized distillation of the history of Oregon's development from a frontier province into a territory and, finally, a state. As soon as American settlers arrived in Oregon in the 1830s, they started trying to turn a polyglot province peopled by Pacific Coast Indians, French and British fur traders, and native Hawaiian laborers into a White body politic. They began by preempting as much land as they could, then sought government protection for their self-proclaimed titles. The Oregon Donation Land Act, passed by the U.S. Congress in 1850, invited "all white male citizens of the United States, or persons who shall have made a declaration of intention to become such" to participate in a land bonanza. White American men already living in Oregon could claim 320 acres of land for themselves and another 320 acres in the name of their wives; settlers who later moved there could claim half as much. These unusually generous land grants, from which British nationals, native Hawaiians, and African Americans were excluded, enticed men like James Gingles, a native Pennsylvanian, to move to Oregon.[2]

Once settled on donation land claims, Gingles and his peers built a legal and economic structure that privileged the White farmers, merchants, and miners who were soon streaming into the territory. While Gingles served as one of the first jurors in Benton County and ran for the Board of County Commissioners, Oregon's territorial government fought vicious wars against

Indians, refused to allow Hawaiian laborers to petition for U.S. citizenship, and enacted a mining tax on "Chinamen." In 1859, Oregon's state constitution denied every "Negro, Chinaman, or Mulatto" the right to vote and directed the legislature to find a way to ensure that "No Chinaman . . . [entering the state] shall ever hold any real estate, or mining claim, or work any mining claim therein." The formation of Oregon's state legislature only upped the racial ante, as lawmakers promptly enacted a poll tax that applied to every "negro, Chinaman, Kanaka, or mulatto" in the state.[3]

By the mid-1860s, then, a composite list of non-White groups—"Indians," "Chinamen," "Kanakas," "Negroes and mulattoes"—had surfaced in a variety of proposals to limit the privileges of citizenship to Whites, including an unsuccessful 1864 attempt to pass a bill that would reserve the right to testify in court to Whites.[4] In 1865, in a special legislative session called to ratify the Thirteenth Amendment ban on slavery, Representative G. W. Lawson proposed to "prohibit amalgamation by intermarriage of races" by punishing "white[s]" for marrying "negroes, mulattoes, chinese, kanakas, etc."[5] That bill never became law, but a year later, James Gingles proposed an even more elaborate miscegenation law.

The 1866 session of the Oregon legislature was one of the most contentious in the state's history, but legislators who fought a pitched battle over the ratification of the Fourteenth Amendment reached a near-unanimous consensus on the Gingles bill. Before approving the bill, Oregon Democrats did some posturing, facetiously suggesting that men like Gingles, who was a member of the Civil War–time Union Party and a supporter of the Fourteenth Amendment, should logically favor rather than oppose interracial marriage. But Oregon's Union Party leader, W. W. Upton, left no room for doubt on his party's position. The very idea, Upton proclaimed, "that there is any party in the State which favors amalgamation of the races" was simply "too absurd to demand attention." Although there was some discussion about which groups should be named in the law, the final vote left no doubt that both of Oregon's political parties, Democrats and Unionists, endorsed "a bill to prohibit the amalgamation and intermarriage of the races." The bill passed the House by a vote of 32–4, the Senate by a vote of 15–4, and was signed into law by the governor a week later.[6]

The Oregon miscegenation law of 1866 reflected the particularities of Oregon history, but it was also part of a larger pattern. It was, in fact, one of five miscegenation laws passed by western legislatures in the 1860s, all of which named more than Whites and Blacks. Nevada's 1861 law prohibited "whites" from marrying "any black person, mulatto, Indian, or Chinese." Idaho's 1864 law forbade "whites" to marry "any person of African descent,

Indian or Chinese." Arizona's 1865 law set "white[s]" against "negroes, mulattoes, Indians, or mongolians." Wyoming's 1869 law prohibited any "person belonging to the caucasian or white race" from marrying any person of "negro, asiatic, or mongolian blood."[7]

The wording of these laws grouped African Americans, Asian Americans, Indians, and native Hawaiians together in a manner that suggested equivalence between them, as if they were parallel threats to the virtuous White families who stood at the symbolic center of the imagined community of post–Civil War America. Yet expanding the list of races subject to miscegenation law and building the appearance of parallelism within the law required a great deal of cultural work. Supporters of miscegenation laws not only had to believe in the existence of discrete races, and in their own ability to distinguish between them, but they also had to squeeze peoples with vastly different historical experiences into structurally similar subordination to white supremacy. Over the long period between 1860 and 1939, when the last western miscegenation law was enacted, a wide variety of westerners, beginning with legislators like James Gingles, and eventually including a whole host of citizens, newspaper reporters, and officials, from county clerks and police officers to district attorneys and judges, worked to do just that.

The Racialization of Asian Americans

The most notable aspect of the Oregon miscegenation law of 1866 was its targeting of "Chinese" and "Kanakas." Oregon was the first—and would remain the only—state to mark "Kanakas," or native Hawaiians, in this way, but the targeting of "Chinese" was part of a larger pattern, the racialization of Asian Americans in miscegenation law.[8] In the decade of the 1860s, the first step in this direction was taken by the legislatures of Nevada, Idaho, Arizona, and Wyoming as well as Oregon.

These laws grew out of the anti-Chinese movement of the 1860s, which followed the trail of gold and silver mining rushes of these years, leapfrogging from Nevada's Comstock Lode to Idaho's Owyhee District, then to Jacksonville, Oregon, and Prescott, Arizona. American prospectors who rushed to these strikes enacted a version of the "possessive investment in whiteness" akin to that played out in the Oregon land grant bonanza of the 1850s. They started by trying to exclude Chinese immigrants altogether. In the famous Gold Hill district of Nevada, for example, miners didn't even wait for the formation of a territorial government to proclaim that "no Chinaman shall

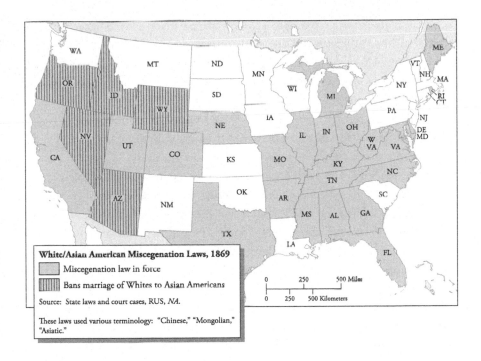

White/Asian American Miscegenation Laws, 1869

▨ Miscegenation law in force

▥ Bans marriage of Whites to Asian Americans

Source: State laws and court cases, RUS, *NA*.

These laws used various terminology: "Chinese," "Mongolian," "Asiatic."

hold a claim in this district"; similar measures dotted the district "laws" passed by miners in Idaho and Oregon.[9]

Before long, though, territorial legislatures replaced these early, and largely ineffective, attempts at excluding Chinese newcomers with a patchwork of legal restrictions on Chinese residents. Chinese immigrants were subjected to a wide variety of taxes, including, in different locations, foreign miner's taxes, head or capitation taxes, poll taxes, and business license taxes, the revenue from which was then used to support governments that sharply restricted their political rights. The specific mix of measures varied from place to place, but lawmakers selected from a wish list that included denying Chinese the right to vote, to testify in court or serve on juries, and to marry Whites. The first miscegenation law that named "Chinese" was enacted by the Nevada territorial legislature in 1861. It was proposed by Dr. John S. Pugh, a physician from the mining town of Aurora, who followed it up a year later with an apparently unsuccessful proposal to impose a capitation tax on every Chinese resident in Nevada. In Oregon, James Gingles proposed his 1866 miscegenation law after the previous legislature buried his earlier proposal to limit the right to testify in court to Whites.[10]

All the major political parties of the 1860s played a part in adding "Chinese" to miscegenation laws. Nevada's law was proposed and passed by a legislature dominated by the Union Party; Oregon's came from a legislature in which Unionists claimed only a slim majority. Idaho's law emerged from a legislature that was heavily Democratic; Arizona's from one that was largely Republican. Wyoming's law was proposed and passed by an entirely Democratic legislature over the veto of a Republican governor who objected because the bill failed to include "Indians."[11]

Lawmakers seem to have regarded the addition of "Chinese" to miscegenation laws as such a clear necessity that it required little or no justification. In western legislatures, laws forbidding "whites" to marry "Chinese" passed by higher margins, and with fewer objections, than other anti-Chinese measures. If the paucity of discussion is any indication, the addition of "Chinese" to miscegenation laws was less controversial than the addition of "Indians" among legislators and, apparently, among the public at large. Local newspapers mentioned these laws, if they mentioned them at all, only in passing, as part of their routine coverage of legislative actions.

As the taken-for-granted quality of this process suggests, a powerful set of cultural assumptions was at work, rooted in lawmakers' presumption that the marriages prevented by the laws were those involving Chinese men and White women. From the outset, images of Chinese immigrants had been highly gendered. In the 1860s and 1870s, lawmakers repeatedly referred to "China*men*" rather than "Chinese" when describing the threat supposedly posed to White men, a subject that initially garnered more attention than any threat "Chinamen" may have posed to White women. Western legislators tried to cut off competition from Chinese men in all the prerogatives of citizenship—economic, political, and familial—enjoyed by White men. Like post–Civil War southern politicians unsettled by the need to recognize the marriages of freed slaves, western politicians considered access to marriage and family formation an index of American liberty and citizenship rights. Like legislators all across America, they conflated the families of White citizens with the American national family.[12]

These ideas, which were taken for granted by legislators who named "Chinese" in miscegenation laws of the 1860s, framed public debate during the next, and even more virulent, wave of anti-Chinese sentiment, which erupted in the late 1870s. In California, for example, the anti-Chinese workingmen's movement of the 1870s found common cause with White businessmen by pleading for the protection of liberty-loving White families. During the constitutional convention of 1878, San Francisco businessman S. M. Miller, chairman of the convention's Committee on Chinese, explained:

> If the Chinaman comes and occupies the fields of labor now open to the white man, it operates in restraint of marriage among the whites,

and stops white immigration. Increase of white population is thereby stopped, for the prudent, intelligent, sympathetic white man . . . will not marry unless he can see a reasonable chance of maintaining wife as well as children. . . . If we must have immigration, let us choose it from the Anglo-Saxon race, or kindred varieties of men—men who will build homes and love liberty; who appreciate republican institutions and the grandeur of western civilization, and whose intelligence and loyalty to the principles of our government render them worthy of the great privilege of American citizenship.

In anti-Chinese rhetoric, the supposedly virtuous homes and families built by Anglo-Saxon men were contrasted to alarming possibilities that echoed the distinction between legitimate marriage and illicit sex. A few of these images focused on the possibility of interracial marriage. When, for example, the transcontinental railroad was completed in 1869, the popular magazine *Harper's Weekly* illustrated its completion with a lithograph of a middle-class White woman standing arm in arm with a Chinese man in front of the "Church of St. Confucius."

By 1878, however, California constitutional convention delegates who bemoaned the absence of "real homes" among the Chinese did so with images steeped in sexuality rather than by envisioning marriage of any sort. One set of these sexualized images depicted all Chinese immigrant women as prostitutes. Another portrayed Chinese men as reducing wages to levels so low that virtuous White working girls had to turn to prostitution in order to support themselves.[13]

In popular culture and in politics, the sexualization of the Chinese took different forms than the sexualization of African Americans, which was occurring in these same years. Many images linked Chinese men to White women, sometimes directly, as in the *Harper's* illustration of interracial marriage, but more often indirectly, as in the rhetoric about labor competition reducing White working women to prostitution. Unlike Black men, Chinese immigrant men were rarely depicted as direct sexual dangers to White women. Rather, images of fraudulent marriages, rampant prostitution, and commercial vice fostered the impression that Chinese immigrants were contagious purveyors of "deviant heterosexuality," to use the evocative phrase coined by scholar Jennifer Ting. Yet the differences between these two forms of sexualization mattered little to the development of miscegenation law. Images of deviant heterosexuality proved just as potent as images of sexual danger in fueling the sexualization of miscegenation law, since both served to associate interracial relationships with illicit sex and to distinguish them from legitimate marriage.[14]

PACIFIC RAILROAD COMPLETE.

"The Pacific Railroad Complete," *Harper's Weekly,* June 12, 1869, p. 384. (University of Oregon Library)

The political effects of bringing the Chinese within the sexualization of miscegenation law were soon visible in California. In 1878, a delegate to the California constitutional convention proposed a ban on "intermarriage of white persons with Chinese." Two years later, in 1880, the California legislature amended the state's 1850 law prohibiting marriage between "whites" and "negroes" or "mulattoes" by adding a provision forbidding the issuance of marriage licenses to "whites" and "Mongolians." Because California was home to more Chinese immigrants than any other western state or territory, this law tipped the balance of western miscegenation laws.[15]

California's use of the term "Mongolian," chosen as an all-purpose alternative to the more specific "Chinese" and the more indefinite "aliens ineligible for citizenship," marked the next step in the racialization of Asian Americans in miscegenation law.[16] Most California lawmakers seem to have considered the term "Mongolian" roughly synonymous with "Chinese," but a few clearly understood it as a kind of collective racial category. As one delegate to the state constitutional convention explained, "The term Mongolians does not apply exclusively to the Chinese. It is a generic type of the human family, and some of the leading authorities on ethnology have divided the species into three classes—Mongolian, Caucasian, and Negro."[17] Placing the Chinese in the context of seemingly comprehensive race classification schemes like this one produced an appearance of racial parallelism much like that soon to be employed in the *Pace* decision—that is, the notion that all races were being treated equally—even as miscegenation laws structured white supremacy by grouping all non-White races in opposition to Whites.

Miscegenation Law and the Protection
of White Womanhood

During the last two decades of the nineteenth century, the circle of analogies enabled by the racialization and sexualization of Asian Americans drew "Mongolians" steadily closer to "Negroes" in the minds of American white supremacists, until the two became standard companions in western miscegenation laws. In 1888, Utah's first law prohibiting interracial marriage targeted both "Mongolian[s]" and "negroe[s]." In 1892, the western pattern began to move into the South, when Mississippi revised its miscegenation law to add a ban on marriage to "Mongolians" to its existing ban on "the marriage of a white person and a negro or mulatto." In 1893, the Oregon legislature added insult to injury by adding a civil prohibition on marriages "when either of the parties is a white person and the other a negro, or Mongolian, or a person of one fourth or more of negro of Mongolian blood" to its existing criminal punishments for marriage between "any white person [and any] negro, chinese, kanaka, or Indian."[18]

Once implanted in the language of miscegenation laws, the supposed parallels between "Mongolians" and "Negroes" were brought to life in the social practices built up around the laws. By the turn of the century, miscegenation laws served as a commonsense method of policing the racial borders of white supremacy. One of the forms this took was miscegenation dramas provoked by newspaper stories about interracial couples. Scandalous stories incited angry citizens to express moral indignation, which then required stern public officials to ride to the rescue, embodying the moral of the story: the preservation of white purity through the protection of white womanhood. The formative miscegenation dramas, such as the Sophia Spears scandal that had spurred passage of Indiana's 1840 law against interracial marriage, appeared before the Civil War and directed the embryonic public defense of white womanhood against free Black men. During the Civil War and Reconstruction, calls for the protection of White families were channeled into restrictions on the political and economic rights of Black and Chinese men as well as into the passage of postwar miscegenation laws in both the South and the West. It was not, however, until the 1880s, when the sexualization of miscegenation law linked calls for the protection of white womanhood to sensational images of sexual danger, that the stage was set for the mass production of miscegenation dramas.

By the turn of the century, calls for the protection of white womanhood were ubiquitous, made by progressive reformers who favored women's suffrage or prohibition as well as by the most conservative of evolutionary scientists, by judges who upheld protective labor legislation for women as well as by lynch mobs that targeted Black men. As many historians have noted, lynchings and "white slavery" campaigns relied on images of interracial sex that linked sexual desire to physical violence (in images of rape) or money (in images of the degrading economic "slavery" of prostitution).[19] The images that animated miscegenation dramas were also highly sexualized, but their special power to provoke turned on the notion that interracial sex might lead not to rape or prostitution but to marriage. In this sense, miscegenation dramas functioned by endangering marriage—and the respectability, property, and civilized values that were attached to it—using the race-and-gender pairing of White women with non-White men as lightning rods for the entire social order.

As calls for the protection of white womanhood became clichéd, the most thrilling—and productive—miscegenation dramas lingered over enticing images of forbidden behavior before concluding with the inevitable moral strictures for young White women. They proved to be an especially fruitful discourse for turn-of-the-century newspapers, which had been goaded by cutthroat competition into pushing the limits of cultural sensibilities while appearing to uphold civilized society.

In much of the country, miscegenation dramas focused on White women and Black men. The most famous example is the Chicago marriage of boxer Jack Johnson and Lucille Cameron, which set off a wave of attempts to pass miscegenation laws in 1913. In the West, however, miscegenation dramas increasingly featured Japanese men. After 1900, when Japanese immigrants began to replace the now-excluded Chinese immigrants as laborers, complaints about the dangers Japanese "aliens" posed to the American national family combined with sexual sensationalism in a pairing that newspaper reporters found irresistible.[20] Whenever and wherever reporters could find Japanese men who wanted to marry White women, they told scandalous stories of interracial love and drew social and legal morals.

One such miscegenation drama, the case of Helen Emery and Gunjiro Aoki, was splashed across the front pages of newspapers up and down the West Coast in 1909. The first report of the case, issued on the front page of the *San Francisco Chronicle*, was a relatively restrained notice of the engagement of Helen Emery, the daughter of respected California Episcopal archdeacon John A. Emery, to Gunjiro Aoki, a Japanese student of "noble" lineage and Christian leanings introduced to the Emery family by his brother, who served as pastor of a local Japanese Episcopal church. In no time at all, however, reporters were depicting the Emery family as a virtuous White family in peril. The first sign of trouble was that Bishop Emery, who opposed the marriage, quarreled with his wife, who supported her daughter. Before long, the bishop moved out, leaving Helen and her mother alone in the family's country house at Corte Madera.[21]

In the meantime, reporters tracked down Aoki's elder brother, a businessman, who raised the specter of heterosexual deviance by describing Gunjiro as an uneducated farm boy who amused himself by wasting money and being "a trouble maker among women, Japanese and white." These intimations of sexual danger provoked a group of young men in Corte Madera to threaten to "run the Japanese out" of town; in language that echoed that of white supremacists in the South, they spoke of tarring and feathering Aoki. While the young men tried, and failed, to capture Aoki, friends and associates of both families joined the chorus of public disapproval. A local Japanese community organization was said to have offered Aoki $1,000 to give up his fiancée. The Episcopal Ladies Guild insisted that Mrs. Emery leave her position as local president, and both Bishop Emery and Reverend Aoki were asked to resign from their posts, too. Helen Emery and Gunjiro Aoki drew the obvious conclusion that if they wanted to be married, they would have to leave California.[22]

So Helen Emery and her mother traveled up the Pacific Coast in search of a less poisonous venue, surrounded by crowds and hounded by newspaper

Friend of Emery Family Seeks Medical Advice as to Whether Hypnotism Can Explain Girl's Wild Infatuation for Japanese

GUNGIRO AOKI

J. AOKI

MRS JOHN A EMERY

HELEN GLADYS EMERY

Miss Helen Gladys Emery and Gungiro Aoki, Whose Engagement Has Startled Society on Two Sides of the Bay; Mrs. John A. Emery, Who Approves of Her Daughter's Choice, and J. Aoki, Who Declares He Will Send His Brother Out of the Country if Necessary to Prevent the Match.

reporters who speculated endlessly on where and how the young couple might try to hold a marriage ceremony. The public spotlight shifted from California, where the state miscegenation law had named "Mongolians" since 1880, to Oregon, which had added the term "Mongolian" to its law in 1893. In both states, the term "Mongolian" had been adopted with Chinese immigrants in mind, yet local officials quickly stretched it to cover Gunjiro Aoki, a Japanese immigrant. Before the couple even arrived in the state of Oregon, Portland's county clerk issued orders to his staff to "not only refuse them a license, but if they attempt to argue the matter, throw them out of the office." Portland's district attorney threatened to have them arrested as a "public nuisance." "If they think," he said, "that the people of Portland will accord them any better treatment than they got in San Francisco they are mistaken." Although the *Oregonian* dutifully noted that "the Japanese disclaim being Mongols," it reassured its readers that the "foolish and unnatural" wedding would never take place in Oregon, because "at any case the County Clerk and District Attorney will place their own construction on that law, and they are agreed that a Jap and a Mongolian are one and the same."[23]

As these details suggest, the enforcement of miscegenation law relied heavily on local officials, including county clerks, who issued marriage licenses; justices of the peace, who performed marriage ceremonies; and district attorneys, who prosecuted sex crimes. All of them closed ranks against interracial marriage. By the time Helen Emery and her mother entered Washington state, they had learned to expect trouble from every local official they encountered. But there officials ran into an awkward problem. Washington's territorial miscegenation law, passed in 1855, had never named "Chinese," "Japanese," or "Mongolians" and had, in any case, been repealed in 1868.[24] The Vancouver, Washington, city attorney tried to hold the line anyway, announcing that "while there is no legal impediment to such a marriage in this state, I should do all I can to prevent such a union." Not until the procession reached Tacoma was a public official, the mayor, willing to concede that his personal opposition to the marriage would not translate into legal interference, no matter how much he wanted it to. Faced with this wall of hostility, Helen Emery's father, who had belatedly come to his daughter's defense, tried to persuade the couple to hold their ceremony in Canada, but Helen, who had heard reports of vicious anti-Japanese riots in Vancouver, British Columbia,

Opposite: Part of the sensational coverage of Helen Emery's engagement to Gunjiro Aoki, this article appeared on the front page of the *San Francisco Chronicle* on March 12, 1909. (Proquest; University of Oregon Library)

a few years earlier, chose the disdain of public officials over the lawlessness of mobs. The couple was married in Seattle on March 27, 1909.[25]

Although the Aokis had succeeded in marrying—indeed, partly *because* they succeeded in marrying—their case nonetheless furthered the racialization and sexualization of Asian Americans in miscegenation law. For months afterward, California and Nevada newspapers carried stories about White women who married Japanese men in Washington state, always with a reference to the Aoki case.[26] In Nevada, reporters honed in on three couples made up of Japanese American men and White women, each of which traveled from California to Nevada, apparently hoping that Nevada law, which prohibited "whites" from marrying "Chinese" but did not name either "Mongolians" or "Japanese," would permit them to marry.[27]

From the moment these couples tried to obtain licenses, they ran into trouble. When the first couple arrived in Goldfield, Nevada, in March 1910, the county clerk refused to grant them a marriage license without first consulting the district attorney. After the district attorney confessed that he was legally powerless to stop the marriage, a local clergyman refused to perform the ceremony. The justice of the peace the couple approached as a last resort insisted that the twenty-four-year-old bride telegraph her mother for permission before he reluctantly agreed to officiate. The second couple ran into even stiffer resistance. Turned down by several clergymen, they tried a justice of the peace, who demanded that they go before a district court judge to ask for a writ of mandamus allowing the ceremony to proceed. The district court judge refused to issue the writ, declaring that the Japanese American groom would be covered under the state's prohibition on marriages between "whites" and "Chinese." "My American blood revolts against such a union," the judge told a reporter, "and I am glad the law permits me to exercise my discretion against it," adding that if the category "Chinese" didn't apply, "I would say a Jap was black in the interests of morality and charity." In this case, judicial resistance foiled the marriage: a deputy clerk "forced" the couple to accept a refund of their license fee, the young woman collapsed in tears, and local officials escorted the pair out of town. The third couple, too, met immediate resistance. The justice of the peace they approached refused to help them, saying, "Really, I don't know of anything in the statutes forbidding me to perform the ceremony, but I certainly deem it to be contrary to the laws of nature." They were married only after their lawyer finally managed to locate the only local minister who would agree to perform the ceremony.[28]

Newspaper coverage of all these cases fueled the sexualization of miscegenation law by circulating images of White women as deluded victims and

Japanese American men as sexual dangers. Although Helen Emery repeatedly stated her love for Gunjiro Aoki and her pride in her proposed marriage, reporters characterized her either as the victim of a hypnotic trance that induced her "wild infatuation" for Aoki or as a shy, unpopular girl led by a domineering mother; one even labeled both mother and daughter "religious and social perverts, who enjoy this notoriety." The moral of other stories was made clear in headlines such as "Romance of a Seattle Girl Is Quickly Shattered After Wedding," about a "Seattle girl" who sought a divorce from her "Japanese serving man" husband, claiming that he "sought to drive her into a life of [sexual] slavery" within a month of their wedding. In Nevada, the editor of the *Reno Gazette* summed up his response to these marriages in no uncertain terms: "Intelligent, Christian, refined civilization should shudder at the spectacle of such miscegenation."[29]

When newspaper reporters exposed interracial couples, titillated readers may have lingered over the salacious details, but they still expected local officials to enforce the moral of the story. Western legislators quickly turned these and other dramas into miscegenation laws that targeted the Japanese, usually relying on the catchall category "Mongolian" rather than the more specific category of "Japanese" to do so. Between 1909 and 1921, Missouri, South Dakota, Wyoming, and Idaho named "Mongolians" in their miscegenation laws, reflecting the growing preference for terms that were expansively racial rather than specifically national.[30] Indeed, the term "Mongolian" proved so popular that even though eleven states eventually prohibited marriages between Whites and Japanese Americans, only two, Montana (1909) and Nebraska (1913), did so by placing the specific term "Japanese" in their miscegenation laws.[31]

Meanwhile, Nevada showed just how expansive the racial categories of miscegenation law could become by trying to make its law racially comprehensive. In the wake of the highly publicized Nevada cases of 1910 and 1911, Nevada legislators decided to replace their state's longtime prohibition on the marriages of "whites" to "Chinese" with broader language. In 1911, two Republicans got the ball rolling by introducing bills that would have added "Japanese" to Nevada's miscegenation law. Nevada legislators, however, rejected these proposals in favor of a Democratic plan to make the law so broad-based that no future amendments would ever be necessary. Under this Democratic plan, "any person of the Caucasian or white race" was prohibited from marrying "any person of the Ethiopian or black race, Malay or brown race, Mongolian or yellow race, or the American Indian or red race." Calling the proposal "an emergency measure," the Nevada legislature adopted it by a vote of 32–2 in the House and 16–0 in the Senate.[32]

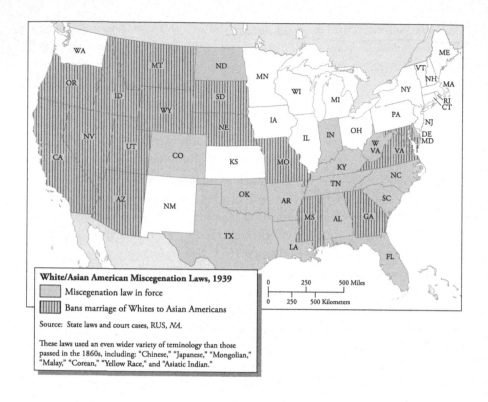

White/Asian American Miscegenation Laws, 1939

Miscegenation law in force

Bans marriage of Whites to Asian Americans

Source: State laws and court cases, RUS, *NA*.

These laws used an even wider variety of terminology than those
passed in the 1860s, including: "Chinese," "Japanese," "Mongolian,"
"Malay," "Corean," "Yellow Race," and "Asiatic Indian."

Nevada's reference to "Malays," or Filipinos, marked another "first" in miscegenation law, and the next stage in its racialization of Asian Americans. In 1905, when reports of a handful of Filipino students flirting with White women had resulted in discussion of an anti-Filipino miscegenation law in the Indiana legislature, the legislature had quickly rejected the proposal. But after Nevada took the lead, two more western states quickly followed. In 1913, South Dakota amended its 1909 law, which had banned marriage between "persons belonging to the African race" and persons "belonging to the Caucasian race," so as to prohibit marriages between "the Caucasian or White Race" and "the African, Corean, Malayan, or Mongolian Race." In the same year, Wyoming passed a law preventing "white persons" from marrying "Negroes, Mulattoes, Mongolians, or Malays." The fact that these laws were passed despite the then-tiny numbers of Filipinos in all three states reflects both the multiplication of racial classifications and the extent to which western legislators had come to rely on miscegenation laws rooted in concern about the race-and-gender pairing of White women and Asian American men as preemptive actions against Asian American immigrants.[33]

During the decade that followed, Filipinos began to arrive in considerably larger numbers, and West Coast nativists, fresh from their success at excluding Chinese and Japanese immigrants, quickly turned their attention to this new "peril." After nativists discovered, much to their distress, that Filipinos had become American nationals as a result of the American occupation of the Philippines, they built their campaign to turn Filipinos back into "aliens" around the use of miscegenation dramas. In 1928 and 1929, for example, the small California communities of Dinuba, Exeter, and Watsonville erupted in violence ignited by sensational images of Filipino men and White women. In Exeter, where a Filipino labor camp was burned "to the ground," newspapers concluded that "the insistence of Filipinos that they be treated as equals by white girls has been the chief cause of friction between the races here." The Watsonville riot was sparked by the opening of a taxi-dance hall that employed White women and was patronized by Filipino men. Newspaper narratives of the conflict relied heavily on the words of an outspoken local judge, D. W. Rohrback. In a successful attempt to get the Northern Monterey County Chamber of Commerce to pass his anti-Filipino resolution, Judge Rohrback used multiple images of Filipino men and White women. In an interview with the local paper, Rohrback claimed that "The worst part of his [any Filipino man] being here is his mixing with young white girls from thirteen to seventeen. He gives them silk underwear and makes them pregnant and crowds whites out of jobs in the bargain." Rohrback's resolution made a slightly different, but no less incendiary, claim: "If the present state of affairs continues there will be 40,000 half-breeds in California before ten years have passed." These dramas encouraged the passage of yet another round of miscegenation laws naming "Malays" in Arizona (1931), California (1933), and Utah (1939).[34]

As these stories suggest, miscegenation dramas multiplied after the turn of the century, gathering force and becoming more productive as they were expanded to include Japanese and Filipino men. No doubt these dramas captivated readers partly for the enticing lure of the forbidden, the new and exotic possibilities they pitted against traditional morality. But no matter how many readers might have fantasized about choosing interracial romance over legal propriety, there was no mistaking the moral of these stories—or their political effects. By reinforcing the impression that the function of miscegenation laws was to preserve the purity of white womanhood, miscegenation dramas closed off avenues of change. By showing young White women that their protection depended on loyalty to their race, and by encouraging officials to pass and enforce miscegenation laws, miscegenation dramas served white supremacy by racializing and sexualizing Asian American men in relation to White women.

The protection of white womanhood was not, however, the only aspect of white supremacy, and White women and Asian American men were not the only race-and-gender pairing that attracted attention from western lawmakers. In the 1860s, four western legislatures added American Indians to their laws at the same time they named the Chinese. The racialization of Indians in miscegenation law was figured around, and often against, the race-and-gender pairing of White men and Indian women; once in place, it served white supremacy by protecting white property.

In miscegenation law, the naming of Asian Americans had followed closely on the heels of Chinese, Japanese, and Filipino immigration, but the racialization of American Indians developed slowly and haltingly, over the course of three centuries of American history.[35] Laws prohibiting Whites from marrying Indians had been in existence nearly as long as laws prohibiting Whites from marrying Blacks, but they had traditionally played a very small role in the history of laws against interracial marriage.[36] Only two colonies, Virginia (1691) and North Carolina (1715), enacted laws forbidding "whites" to marry "Indians."[37] The racial project of slavery, which provided the grounding for colonial laws against interracial marriage, soon came to focus on Blacks rather than on Indians. And, in any case, marriages between British colonists and American Indians were rare occurrences.[38]

After the American Revolution, though, some Americans began to welcome the prospect of marriage between the self-consciously "white" citizens of the new United States and the Indians whose land (quite literally) grounded the emerging nation. As fur traders and trappers ventured farther and farther into the vast American continent, they relied on relationships with Indian women for trade as well for sexual and domestic comfort.[39] As long as Indians retained effective control of land Whites wanted, and as long as Whites considered them formidable rivals, intermarriage offered a powerful symbol of the creation of a uniquely "American" body politic and a seemingly peaceful alternative to outright conquest. Accordingly, a handful of early American leaders, including Thomas Jefferson, Patrick Henry, and William H. Crawford, endorsed "amalgamation" between "whites" and "Indians." In 1784, for example, Henry introduced a bill in the Virginia legislature "for the encouragement of marriages with the Indians" that offered financial incentives to "free white" men and women who married "Indians" and guaranteed citizenship to their children.[40] Henry's bill, however, failed to pass, and over the next thirty-five years Massachusetts (1786), Rhode Island (1798), and Maine (1821) moved in the opposite direction, encouraging racial separation by passing laws prohibiting "whites" from marrying "Indians."[41]

Nonetheless, individual White men continued to forge connections to Indian peoples by setting up households with Indian women. Both as metaphor and in practice, the pairing of White men and Indian women helped American officials reach their goal of rendering the continent safe for White settlement. In theory, marriage offered republican America one of its most powerful metaphors because, as legal historian Amy Dru Stanley has shown, it linked the rhetoric of consent and contract to the substance of subordination.[42] In practice, when these relationships lasted long enough to function as marriages, they facilitated the passage of land from Indians to Whites. White men who married into Indian tribes drew Indians into trade networks that paved the way for future encroachment on Indian land. White men who lived with Indian women established land claims that the U.S. government helped defend by moving Indians to reservations. After the formation of Indian reservations, White men and women claimed the land then "opened up" to settlement.

Marriage between White men and Indian women was so intimately linked to American land settlement that it was never far from the minds of legislators. As a result, when it came to Whites and Indians, lawmakers curbed their usual impulse to deny legal recognition to intermarried couples. Nearly all of the states that passed antebellum laws against marriage between Whites and Blacks stopped short of enacting legal prohibitions on marriage between Whites and Indians. During the first half of the nineteenth century, in fact, only one of the interior states ever adopted such a law, and that state, Tennessee, repealed it in 1822.[43]

By then, the racialization of Indians in miscegenation law had ground to a halt. In the absence of specific laws prohibiting marriage to Indians, nineteenth-century judges developed a policy of recognizing—and upholding—what they referred to as "Indian custom" marriages, whether they took place between Indian men and Indian women or between White men and Indian women.[44] Labeling these relationships marriages rather than illicit sex served a variety of purposes. When both the partners to an "Indian custom" marriage were Indians, recognizing the marriage allowed federal officials to maintain the fiction that Indians retained full power over their "domestic relations," which, in turn, avoided conflict between the federal government, which was assigned responsibility for Indian policy, and state legislatures, which regulated marriage among White citizens. But when the partners to an "Indian custom" marriage were a White man and an Indian woman, recognizing the marriage slowly but surely brought couples under the jurisdiction of

American state laws, which vested the right to economic authority and land ownership in husbands and channeled property and inheritance along familial lines. These decisions, then, used marriage to confirm the land and property rights of White husbands.

This happened in Oregon when courts confirmed the land titles of some of the first men to file claims under the Oregon Donation Land Act. Passed in 1850, the Oregon Land Act had gone into effect a full five years before the U.S. government succeeded in negotiating the treaties under which Indians would cede the land it opened to settlement.[45] In the meantime, the existing practice of cross-cultural marriage, which was common among early White male settlers, and the instability of settlers' claims to property combined to make white purity a luxury lawmakers simply could not afford. The formal provisions of the Oregon Land Act, which was designed to foster settlement by "white" men, allowed only one other group of men to file land claims, "American half-breeds," who were envisioned as the sons of White men.[46] In practice, however, the law also confirmed titles to land held in the names of Indian women married to White men. Under the terms of the law, a married man might claim twice as much land as a single man, half of which would be set aside in the name of his wife.[47] In some districts, many of these double-sized donation claims went to White men married to Indian women whose tribes had long been resident in the area. After these initial claims had been made, a second, more impatient, group of White settlers "jumped" the portion of the claims held in the names of Indian wives. The original claim holders promptly protested, and in the 1854 case of *Vandolf v. Otis,* the Oregon Territorial Supreme Court was forced to decide whether Indian women married to White men should be allowed to hold land that Congress had supposedly set aside for White settlement.[48]

In the *Vandolf* case, the Oregon Territorial Supreme Court was caught between the land claims of first-round settlers, whose relationships with Indian women had proved so conducive to establishing White settlement, and the land claims of White newcomers, who sought to draw a much sharper racial line around "Indians." With a cautious eye on the fact that none of the land in question had yet been ceded by Indians, the court resolved this dilemma by turning Indian women into wives. Since in American law wives were the economic dependents of husbands, this move allowed judges to emphasize the propertied rights of White husbands. So when the Oregon Territorial Supreme Court posed the rhetorical question "Is not an Indian woman, married to a white male citizen of the United States, a wife in every sense of the law?" it answered with a resounding "Yes," then justified its decision in terms of the rights of White husbands. "When the donation act was passed,"

White supremacy fuelled further and native land taken even when marrying native women.

the justices wrote, "Congress must have known that many of the early settlers of Oregon had married Indian women; and if it was not intended to place men so married upon the same footing with other married men, why did not Congress say so?" Then the court made clear that the equality it envisioned between White husbands would extend neither to Indian husbands nor to Indian or White wives. "No other Indians," the court explained, "can take as settlers, under said act; but married women, let it be remembered, take as 'wives' and not as 'settlers.'"[49]

The *Vandolf* case is an especially revealing example because it occurred at a moment when White land rights in Oregon were so precarious. It was by no means an anomaly, for in the mid-nineteenth century, courts across the nation made Indian women into "wives" by upholding marriages between White men and Indian women. Judges offered a variety of rationales for recognizing intermarriages, making analogies to foreign marriages, proclaiming their roots in Indian custom, or sheltering them under the American-made legal umbrella of common-law marriage. In 1844, the Tennessee Supreme Court explained that "our courts of justice recognize as valid all marriages of a foreign country if made in pursuance of the forms and usages of that country; and there is no reason why a marriage made and consummated in an Indian Nation should be subject to a different rule of action." In 1860, the Missouri Supreme Court noted that "the contract [of marriage] is a natural, civil or religious one, or embraces all these elements, according to the condition of society in which it occurs. . . . It is well settled, as a general proposition, that a marriage, valid according to the law or custom of the place where it is contracted, is valid everywhere." These cases placed relationships between White men and Indian women on the "marriage" side of the divide between marriage and illicit sex. And they protected White husbands' property rights by bringing Indian women and mixed-raced children within the circle of familial inheritance rights.[50]

In 1877, the U.S. Supreme Court capped this tradition by upholding the popular American practice of common-law marriage. The case, *Meister v. Moore*, centered on the marriage of a White man, William A. Mowry, of Saginaw, Michigan, to "the daughter of the Indian Pero," which the court treated exactly as if the common-law relationship had involved a White man and a White woman. All the parties agreed that the marriage had not been presided over by the clergyman or magistrate required by Michigan state law, but the Court decided that the letter of the law need not have been followed because it was, after all, "merely directory." "Marriage," said the Court, "is a thing of common right . . . it is the policy of the State to encourage it, and . . . any other construction would compel holding illegitimate the offspring of many parents conscious of no violation of law." For all these reasons, and "in view of the adjudications made in this country, from its earliest settlement to the present day," there should be "no doubt," the justices ruled, that the Mowry relationship "constitutes a marriage at common law."[51]

In order to uphold these marriages, though, judges from the Oregon Territorial Supreme Court all the way to the U.S. Supreme Court had to overlook mounting popular opposition. During the early years of far western settlement, when White men's marriages to Indian women helped keep local relations peaceful and Indian labor plentiful, some intermarried men had become known as respected community pioneers, and a few were honored as community founders. But as White settlers continued to pour into the West, newcomers disparaged "squaw men" as riff-raff who needed to be shunted aside in order for a truly respectable White polity to form.[52]

Both groups of settlers—those who honored pioneers married to Indians and those who criticized "squaw men"—phrased their arguments in the rhetoric of White male property rights and citizenship privileges. In the Pacific Northwest, for example, this conflict was visible in the very claims-jumping that had produced Oregon's 1854 *Vandolf* case. In commenting on the decision in that case, an editor at the *Oregon Statesman* tried to please both sides by praising the territorial supreme court for issuing a decision that benefited "lawful settlers" and their "Indian wives" but also explained, respectfully, that many other settlers "would prefer that the lands held by these Indian wives should pass into the hands of white settlers, and believe it would be to the advantage of the community and country that they should do so."[53] Two months later, neighboring Washington territory, which had also been settled under the Oregon Donation Land Act, opted for the quicker route to whitening its land ownership base. In January 1855, the Washington legislature passed "the Color Act," a miscegenation law that named "Indians" as well as "negroes."[54]

With the passage of the Color Act, Washington's legislature became the first to name "Indians" in a miscegenation law in more than three decades; this law revitalized the racialization of Indians in marriage law. Over the next decade, Nevada (1861), Idaho (1864), Arizona (1865), and Oregon (1866) added "Indians" to miscegenation laws at the same time they added "Chinese."[55] But when western legislators discussed the case of Indians, they showed little of the consensus they had reached so easily in the case of the Chinese. The entanglement of land claims with White men's marriages to Indian women made it so difficult to push White men's property and citizenship rights out of the picture that lawmakers raised questions about proposals to name "Indians" in miscegenation laws.[56] In Oregon, these misgivings were serious enough to result in a special provision of the

Gingles miscegenation law. James Gingles's original proposal would have prohibited "whites" from marrying "Indians" on exactly the same terms as "negroes," "Chinese" and "kanakas," measuring all these groups by a standard of "one-fourth or more of negro, Chinese, kanaka or Indian blood."[57] But the committee that considered the bill recommended loosening this standard, and the final bill was amended to include a special "one-half" standard for Indians. Committee members justified this provision by explaining that they wanted to be "more liberal to that class of our citizens who, coming here at an early day, married Indian women and have raised families by them."[58] During the discussion, two legislators objected that this "liberal" standard was still too tightly drawn. As one explained, he "did not like the idea of making the law apply to persons of light Indian blood. There are a great many people in the State of this class, who are persons of talent and respectability—some of them educated and highly accomplished. This would be a direct insult to them."[59]

These hesitations did not, in the end, prevent western legislatures from passing laws banning marriage between Whites and Indians. Yet even after the laws had been enacted, the racialization of Indians in western miscegenation laws continued to be sporadic and conflicted, marked by repeals and reenactments, and subject to judicial overrule. In Washington territory, for example, lawmakers passed the Color Act in 1855, amended it in 1866, then repealed it in 1868.[60] After the repeal took effect, local prosecutors charged

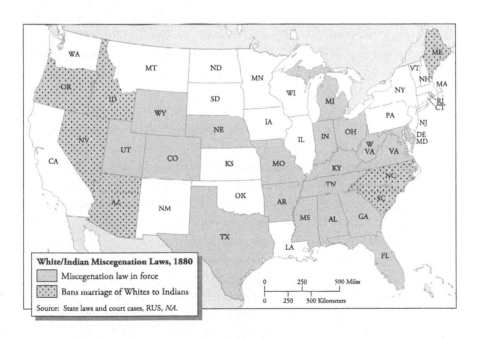

White/Indian Miscegenation Laws, 1880

■ Miscegenation law in force

▨ Bans marriage of Whites to Indians

Source: State laws and court cases, RUS, *NA*.

0   250   500 Miles
0   250   500 Kilometers

several batches of White men who lived with Indian women with the sex crime of fornication and adultery. The prosecutions were designed to force these men into either formalizing or abandoning their relationships with Indian women; in other words, they relied on the distinction between legitimate marriage and illicit sex to pressure White men into changing their behavior. But without the racialization of Indians in miscegenation law to give it muscle, the distinction between legitimate marriage and illicit sex failed to hold. In 1879, after nine men indicted in Washington's Whatcom County contested the prosecutions, a judge ruled that the relationships were legally protected as common-law marriages; in this case and nearly all the others, the charges were eventually dropped.[61]

So despite the passage of the western miscegenation laws naming Indians in the 1860s, marriages between White men and Indian women continued to be sheltered by two contradictions. The first, and most obvious, was the contradiction between the handful of western laws forbidding the marriages and the national network of court decisions upholding them. The second contradiction centered on the issue of legal jurisdiction over Indians. Under the American system of federalism, the federal government claimed control over most aspects of Indian policy, including the "domestic relation" of marriage, making it difficult for states, which were ordinarily assigned control over criminal prosecutions for illicit sex and the marriage of local citizens, to exert control over intermarried couples. With no one entirely sure who held ultimate authority, intermarriages continued to take place, especially in areas near reservations, where federal Indian officials often relied on interracial couples as cultural and political allies. In Oregon, for example, the number of marriages between Whites and Indians appears to have increased in the decade after passage of the state's 1866 miscegenation law.[62] As late as 1891, the Oregon Supreme Court resolved the jurisdictional contradiction by simply ignoring the state's miscegenation law when it issued a decision upholding the validity of one such marriage, which had been performed by a federal Indian agent on the reservation, noting that "we confidently assert that no well-considered case can be found in the books where the courts in a civil case have declared such a marriage void."[63]

Cases involving White men married to Indian women did, however, continue to arrive in courts. In contrast to the publicly scandalous miscegenation dramas that brought White women and Asian American men into public view, cases involving White men and Indian women generally came to court over matters of property and inheritance. Rather than requiring county officials to use miscegenation law to stop interracial couples from marrying in the first place, these cases required probate judges to sort out the affairs of couples who had managed for much of their lives to ignore, avoid, or escape existing laws against interracial marriage. Instead of serving white supremacy by protecting white womanhood, these cases were designed to reinforce white supremacy by protecting white property.

In order to do so, though, courts would first have to turn their backs on the well-established policy of recognizing the marriages of White men and Indian women and subject couples to the power of the miscegenation laws passed by western legislatures in the 1860s. In the 1890s, judges came under increasing pressure to do just that, when cases involving White men and Indian women in Arizona, Missouri, and Washington became battlegrounds for jurisdiction over Indians as well as the racialization of Indians in miscegenation law.

In Arizona, territorial officials had long demanded that the federal government allow them more control over Indians. In 1887, their hand was strengthened by the adoption of federal allotment policy, which sought to break up reservations and turn individual Indians into tax-paying U.S. citizens who would then logically be subject to territorial laws. Cases involving Indian women married to White men served as entering wedges for the expansion of local jurisdiction. In this vein, one Arizona attorney sought to invalidate one such marriage by insisting that Arizona territorial laws must be extended over Indian reservations. "The law," he insisted, "does reach white men who are citizens of Arizona, or those who come within her borders, and prohibits them from marriages with Indians," repeating, for emphasis, that "the laws of the territory reach into the reservation."[64]

Claims of local jurisdiction over Indians were accompanied, indeed enabled, by attempts to bring relationships between White men and Indian women inside the sexualization of miscegenation law. In Missouri, for example, lawyers tried to protect one intermarried couple's marriage by combining the familiar and long-accepted maxim that "state laws have no force whatever over Indians maintaining tribal relations" with "ample" evidence to prove "a valid marriage between William Banks and the Indian woman, according to the Indian custom, and according to nature and the common law." The Missouri Supreme Court had issued a long string of decisions upholding similar marriages. This time, though, it decided in favor of opposing lawyers, who had quickly and sarcastically responded that "one swallow does not constitute a spring—neither does the ferrying of a single squaw across the Missouri constitute a 'tribal relation.' . . . An adulterous connection however long continued never ripens into marriage."[65]

In Whatcom County, Washington, local judge Henry McBride found another way to place intermarried couples within the sexualization of miscegenation law. After hearing an 1893 case involving the marriage of a local White man to an Indian woman, he issued a decision that placed the case "away back in 1867, when many of the towns, not ambitious of county seat honors, were as yet unknown." In it, he waxed eloquent about the "dusky maiden of the forest" and "sable enchantress" who had first rejected but then, inevitably, accepted the "amorous swain," the White man in question, as her husband. The local newspaper printed the opinion in full, calling it "quite an original romance" and headlining "some of the most spicy facts ever published."[66]

The sexualized language put forth in these cases reflected a variety of contemporary concerns, which, in turn, helped change the context in which relationships between White men and Indian women were understood. Pushing them into the distant past helped western town boosters uphold the values of "civilized morality" even as they distinguished their modern cities-in-the-making from their enticingly disreputable frontier past. The censuring of commercial sex resonated and responded to urban reformers, who pressured state and local officials to clamp down on prostitution. Critiques of common-law marriage reflected a broader campaign among reformers determined to strengthen the institution of marriage by making it harder to enter, harder to exit, and more ceremonial. One of its first indications of success was the increased willingness of western judges to abandon common-law marriage as legal protection for White men married to Indian women.[67]

When the Arizona, Missouri, and Washington cases reached appellate courts, judges in all three states reversed the long-standing tradition of upholding marriages between White men and Indian women. Arizona's supreme court declared that Arizona's miscegenation law now trumped all other considerations. Marriage, the judges opined, "could not be consummated at the time this was alleged to have taken place, in Arizona, between a Pima Indian squaw and a white man, either by ceremony . . . by the customs of said Indian tribe, cohabitation, or any other method."[68] In this case the marriage in question had been made on the Pima reservation in 1871 and lasted until the man's death in 1891, so the court had to overlook the inconvenient fact that Arizona had removed "Indians" from its miscegenation law in 1887. In Missouri, "Indians" had never been named in the state's miscegenation law, but in 1899 the state supreme court reversed course after three decades of decisions upholding intermarriages with language that sexualized the relationships. Considering one such relationship, the Missouri Supreme Court now held that "the arrangement was clearly illicit in the beginning and the proofs did not show any change in the subsequent relations of the parties, but on the contrary confirmed the view that it was a mere commercial arrangement without any of the sanctity or permanence of marriage."[69]

Perhaps the most striking example came in Washington. Washington's Color Act, passed in 1855, had been repealed in 1868, so Washington had had no miscegenation law of any kind in force for nearly twenty-five years. Yet in 1893, the Washington Supreme Court not only endorsed the ban on marriages between "whites" and "Indians" originally contained in the Color Act but went out of its way to do so. The court invalidated a marriage between a "white" man and an "Indian" woman that had been made according to the "custom of the country" by condemning the entire notion of Indian custom marriage. "It is clearly apparent that white men had no difficulty in obtaining Indian women to live with them by paying money to their relatives, and that the practice was a somewhat common one in the earlier history of the territory," the court noted, in language dripping with disdain. "Such arrangements could hardly amount to marriages under any law."[70]

By 1900, then, western judges had abandoned, one by one, the series of justifications their mid-nineteenth-century predecessors had used to validate marriages between White men and Indian women. Where once such a marriage might have been upheld as meeting the standards for an Indian custom marriage, as a case of common-law marriage, or as confirmation of a White man's common right to marriage, it might now be dismissed as cohabitation or a commercial arrangement rather than marriage; it might even be invalidated on the basis of a law long since repealed. In this manner, judges pushed marriages between White men and Indian women over the legal boundary that separated legitimate marriage from illicit sex.

The most interesting thing about these cases is their timing. Between the midcentury decisions, which brought Indian women and mixed-race children inside the circle of familial property rights, and the decisions of the 1890s, which cast them out, judges subordinated their concern with the property rights of White husbands to the seeming imperative of serving white supremacy by channeling of property along racial dividing lines. Yet before these racial dividing lines could serve white supremacy, two historical conditions had to be met. First, as in cases involving White men and Black women, judges had to be willing to let miscegenation laws overrule the presumption that White male citizens had every right to choose their own wives. Second, and especially important in the case of Indians, property had to be concentrated in the hands of Whites in the first place. During most of the nineteenth century, when marriage between White men and Indian women was one of many processes, including wars and treaty negotiations, that facilitated the transfer of Indian land to Whites, judges routinely upheld marriages between White men and Indian women. Only in the 1890s, when White control of land seemed beyond further dispute, did western courts begin to subject these marriages to the patterns established two decades earlier in cases involving White men and Black women.

Miscegenation Law and the Protection of White Property

One Oregon case, *In re Paquet,* telescopes the racialization and sexualization of Indians in miscegenation law into a single relationship, showing the fully developed use of miscegenation law to serve white supremacy by protecting white property. Like most miscegenation court cases involving Indians, this one centered on the estate of a White man. The man in question, Fred Paquet, died in 1919, survived by his sixty-three-year-old Tillamook wife, Ophelia. The Paquet estate included twenty-two acres of land, some farm animals, tools, and a buggy, altogether worth perhaps $2,500. Like many relationships between White men and Indian women, Fred and Ophelia's had lasted a long time. It had begun in the 1880s, when Fred visited Ophelia frequently and openly enough that he had become one of many targets of a local grand jury that periodically threatened to indict White men who lived with Indian women. Seeking to formalize the relationship—and, presumably, to end this harassment—Fred consulted a lawyer, who advised him to hold a ceremony that would meet the legal requirements for an Indian custom marriage. Accordingly, in 1889, Fred not only reached the customary agreement with Ophelia's Tillamook relatives, paying them fifty dollars in gifts, but also sought the formal sanction of Tillamook tribal chief Betsy Fuller (who was herself married to a White man); Fuller arranged for a tribal council to consider and confirm the Paquet marriage. Afterward Fred and Ophelia lived together until his death, for more than thirty years. Over the course of their relationship, then, Fred and Ophelia had managed to ignore the Oregon miscegenation law of 1866, elude the grand jury crackdowns of the 1880s, and win recognition as a couple from many of those around them.[71]

They would not, however, ultimately escape the links miscegenation law forged between white supremacy and the transmission of property. Fred Paquet clearly considered Ophelia his wife, and his neighbors, too, recognized their relationship, but because Fred died without leaving a will, administration of the estate was subject to state laws that provided for the distribution of property to surviving family members. After Fred Paquet's death, the county court recognized Ophelia as his widow and promptly appointed her administrator of the estate. Because the couple had no children, all the property, including the land, which Ophelia lived on and the Paquets had owned for more than two decades, would ordinarily have gone to her as the surviving widow. Two days later, though, Fred's brother John came forward to contest Ophelia for control of the property. John Paquet had little to recommend him to the court. Some of his neighbors accused him of raping Indian women, and he had such an unsavory reputation in the community that at one point the county judge declared him "a man of immoral habits ... incompetent to transact ordinary business affairs and generally untrustworthy." He was, however, a "white" man, and that was enough to ensure that he won his case against Ophelia, an "Indian" woman.[72]

The case eventually ended up in the Oregon Supreme Court. In making its decision, the court focused on the issue of whether or not to recognize Fred and Ophelia's marriage, which violated Oregon's miscegenation law. The stakes in this case were much like those in the Alfred and Leah Foster case fifty years earlier: if the court recognized Ophelia Paquet as the legitimate wife of Fred Paquet, she would inherit his estate; if the court did not, Ophelia would, in effect, be moved from the category of legitimate wife to the category of illicit sexual partner and would no longer be entitled to inherit anything at all from her "alleged" husband. When the court heard the case, Ophelia's lawyers offered arguments that would have prevailed in many a nineteenth-century case involving a White man married to an Indian woman. They asserted that Fred and Ophelia had entered an Indian custom marriage and that the marriage should have been recognized as valid out of routine courtesy to the authority of a foreign jurisdiction (that of the Tillamook tribe).

But in 1921, the Oregon Supreme Court would have none of this. Declaring that Fred and Ophelia's marriage was void because it violated Oregon's miscegenation law, the court ordered that the estate and all its property be transferred to "the only relative in the state," John Paquet, to be distributed among him, his siblings and their heirs.[73] In this manner, miscegenation law kept the Paquet land within White racial boundaries by invalidating the marriage of a "white" man to an "Indian" woman at the request of an ancillary White relative.

In a legal system that took the protection of property rights as one of its central functions, property, so often described in legal sources as simple economic assets like land and capital, was actually a much more expansive phenomenon, one that took various forms and structured crucial relationships. By the time the Paquet case was heard, notions of property in slaves, which had sustained slavery and conquest, had all but disappeared from the legal landscape. Yet the ability of the legal system to structure myriad forms of property was not only alive and well but heavily implicated newer forms of white supremacy. These newer forms can be seen by tracing three of the property relations visible in the Paquet case.

The first sense in which property entered into the Paquet case was rooted in the etymological connection between the words "property" and "propriety."[74] Miscegenation law played on this connection by drawing a sharp line between legitimate marriage on the one hand and illicit sex on the other, then defining all interracial relationships as illicit sex. Conditioned by stereotypes that associated women of color with hypersexuality, judges routinely branded long-term settled relationships as "mere" sex rather than marriage. Lawyers played to these assumptions by associating interracial sex with prostitution.

As Indian women were encompassed by the sexualization of miscegenation law, it became more and more difficult for them to escape the legacy of these associations. Describing the relationship between Fred and Ophelia Paquet, for example, John Paquet's lawyers claimed that "the alleged 'marriage' was a mere commercial affair" that did not deserve legal recognition because "the relations were entirely meretricious from their inception."[75] Ophelia Paquet's lawyers tried to find a way out by changing the subject. Rather than refuting the association between Indian women and illicit sexuality, they highlighted its flip side, the supposed connection between White women and legitimate marriage. Ophelia Paquet, they told the court, "had been to the man as good a wife as any white woman could have been."[76] In its final decision, the Oregon Supreme Court came close to accepting this line of argument. Admitting that "the record is conclusive that [Ophelia] lived with [Fred] as a good and faithful wife for more than 30 years," the justices agreed that they felt some sympathy for Ophelia, enough to recommend—but not require—that John Paquet offer her what they called "a fair and reasonable settlement."[77] But in the Paquet case, as in other miscegenation cases, sexual morality, important as it was, was subordinate to channeling the transmission of property along racial dividing lines. Ophelia got a judicial pat on the head for good behavior, but John and his siblings got the property.

The second property relationship structured by miscegenation law is suggested by the work of critical race theorists, who argue that in the American legal system, race is in and of itself a kind of property.[78] In the *Paquet* case, for example, the victorious John Paquet had turned his whiteness (the best—and perhaps the only—asset he had) into property, and did so at Ophelia's expense. This transformation happened not once but repeatedly. One instance occurred shortly after the county judge had branded John Paquet immoral and unreliable. Dismissing these charges as the opinions of "a few skalawags and Garibaldi Indians," John Paquet's lawyers rallied enough White witnesses who would speak in his defense to mount an appeal that convinced a circuit court judge to declare him competent to administer the estate.[79] Another example came when the Oregon Supreme Court ruled that Ophelia Paquet's Indian-ness disqualified her from legal marriage to a "white" man; with Ophelia out of the way, John and his siblings won the right to inherit the property.

The third, and often least visible, form of property relationship structured by miscegenation laws—and, for that matter, marriage laws in general—was women's economic dependence on men. Here the problems started long before the final decision gave John Paquet control of the Paquet estate. One of the most intriguing facts about the *Paquet* case is that everyone acted as if the estate in question belonged solely to Fred Paquet. Such a conclusion was, of course, an outgrowth of the long history of intermarriage between White men and Indian women, and the accumulation of court decisions that placed control over property in the hands of White husbands. In actual fact, though, throughout the Paquet marriage, Fred had whiled away most of his time; it was Ophelia's basket-making, fruit-picking, milk-selling, and wage work that had provided the income they needed to sustain themselves. Although the deed to their land was made out in Fred Paquet's name, the couple had used Ophelia's earnings, combined with her proceeds from government pay-ments to Tillamook tribal members, to purchase the property and to pay the yearly taxes on it. It is significant that, although lawyers on both sides of the case knew this, neither they nor the Oregon Supreme Court considered it a key issue at the trial in which Ophelia lost all legal right to what the courts considered Fred's estate.

Indeed, Ophelia's economic contribution might never have been taken into account if it were not for the fact that after the Oregon Supreme Court issued its decision, federal Indian officials found themselves responsible for the care of the now impoverished Ophelia. Apparently hoping both to pro-tect Ophelia and to relieve themselves of the burden of her support, they sued John Paquet on Ophelia's behalf. Working through the federal courts that covered Indian relations and equity claims, rather than the state courts that enforced miscegenation laws, they eventually won a partial settlement. Yet their argument, too, reflected the assumption that men were better suited than women to the ownership of what the legal system referred to as "real" property. Although their brief claimed that "Fred Paquet had practically no income aside from the income he received through the labor and efforts of the said Ophelia Paquet," they asked the court to grant Ophelia the right to only half of the Paquet land. In the end, the court ordered that Ophelia should receive a cash settlement (the amount was figured at half the value of the land), but only if she agreed to make her award contingent on its sale.

To get any settlement at all, Ophelia Paquet had to relinquish all claims to actual ownership of the land, although such a claim might have given her legal grounds to prevent its sale and so allow her to spend her final years on the property. It is not clear that she ever received payment on the settlement ordered by the court.[80]

———

By the time the *Paquet* decision was issued in 1921, it was legally unremarkable. Built on the string of western cases from the 1890s that shaped family formation and property transmission along racial dividing lines by taking property away from Indian women who had been married to White men, it reflected the aura of judicial legitimacy that multiracial versions of white supremacy had acquired in the West since the passage of miscegenation laws in the 1860s. When Ophelia Paquet's lawyers argued that the Oregon miscegenation law was an unconstitutional discrimination against Indians, the court replied in language that echoed the judicial common sense established forty years earlier in *Pace v. Alabama* even as it confirmed its widening racial range. Oregon's miscegenation law did not, the court ruled, discriminate against Indians because it "applies alike to all persons, either white, negroes, Chinese, Kanaka, or Indians."[81]

But the Oregon Supreme Court's statement that its miscegenation law applied "to all persons" was both powerfully persuasive and deeply deceptive. In this sense, it encapsulates the achievements of western miscegenation laws. Between the 1860s and the 1930s, western legislatures pioneered in the multiplication of racial categories that gave the impression of racial parallelism and steered miscegenation law in the direction of racial comprehensiveness. The western racial projects of miscegenation law were carved out in highly gendered ways that functioned to sustain the system of white supremacy, whether by protecting white womanhood or by protecting white property. Yet during the century in which the linkage established in *Pace v. Alabama* between miscegenation law and equal protection held sway, each new race classification was described as parallel to all the others mentioned in the laws, so that the laws might be said to apply to everyone, and so to fall within the much-vaunted notion of American constitutional equality.

As long as the illusion of racially parallel treatment survived, the constitutionality of miscegenation laws was taken for granted, so supporters and opponents of the laws devoted themselves to arguing over which racial categories should or should not be named in the laws and which individuals fit into each named category. Here is where the story gets even more intriguing, for the assumption that races were discrete, identifiable, and obvious was as much an illusion as the assumption that miscegenation laws were racially parallel.

Chapter Four

THE FACTS OF RACE IN THE COURTROOM

"All marriages of persons of Caucasian blood, or their descendants, with negroes, Mongolians or Indians, and their descendants, shall be null and void."

—*Arizona Revised Statutes, 1913*

TUCSON, ARIZONA

On March 21, 1921, Joe Kirby took his wife, Mayellen, to court. The Kirbys had been married for seven years, and Joe wanted out. Ignoring the usual option of divorce, he asked for an annulment, charging that his marriage had been invalid from its very beginning because Arizona law prohibited marriages between "persons of Caucasian blood, or their descendants" and "negroes, Mongolians or Indians, and their descendants." Specifically, Joe Kirby claimed that while he was "a person of the Caucasian blood," his wife, Mayellen, was "a person of negro blood."[1]

The *Kirby* case quickly disintegrated into a definitional dispute that bordered on the ridiculous. The first witness was Joe's mother, Tula Kirby, who gave her testimony in Spanish through an interpreter. Joe's lawyer laid out the case by asking Tula Kirby a few seemingly simple questions:

Q. To what race do you belong?

A. Mexican.

Q. Are you white or have you Indian blood?

A. I have no Indian blood. . . .

Q. Do you know the defendant [Mayellen] Kirby?

A. Yes.

Q. To what race does she belong?

A. Negro.

Then the cross-examination began.

Q. Who was your father? [Mayellen's lawyer asked Tula Kirby.]

A. Jose Romero.

Q. Was he a Spaniard?

A. Yes, a Mexican. . . .

Q. Was [your mother] a Spaniard?

A. She was on her father's side.

Q. And what on her mother's side?

A. Mexican.

Q. What do you mean by Mexican [do you mean] Indian, a native [?]

A. I don't know what is meant by Mexican. . . .

Q. Who was your grandfather on your [mother's] father's side?

A. He was a Spaniard. . . .

Q. Where was he born?

A. That I don't know. He was my grandfather.

Q. How do you know he was a [Spaniard] then?

A. Because he told me ever since I had knowledge that he was a Spaniard. . . .

Q. Then, as a matter of fact, you don't know what your blood is at all?

A. I do know that my mother is Mexican and my father is Mexican, half Spaniard.

Next the questioning turned to Tula's opinion about Mayellen. Joe's lawyer asked Tula:

Q. You said Mrs. [Mayellen] Kirby was a negress. What do you know about Mrs. Kirby's family?

She answered:

A. I distinguish her by her color and the hair; that is all I do know.[2]

The second witness in the trial was Joe Kirby himself, and by the time he took the stand, everyone in the courtroom knew they were in murky waters. When Joe's lawyer opened with the question "What race do *you* belong to?" Joe answered "Well . . . ," and paused, while Mayellen's lawyer objected to the question on the ground that it called for a conclusion of the witness. "Oh, no," said the judge, breaking into the proceedings, "it is a matter of pedigree." Eventually allowed to answer the question, Joe said, "I belong to the white race I suppose." Under cross-examination, he described his father as having been of the "Irish race," although he admitted that "I never knew any one of his people."[3]

Hesitant to go any deeper into this morass, Joe's lawyer rested his case. He told the judge he had established that Joe was "Caucasian." Mayellen's lawyer scoffed, claiming that Joe had "failed utterly to prove his case" and arguing that "[Joe's] mother has admitted that. She has [testified] that she only claims a quarter Spanish blood; the rest of it is native blood." At this point the court intervened again. "I know," said the judge, "but that does not signify anything."[4]

Know It When You See It

Most Americans are sure they know race when they see it, but very few can offer a definition of the term.[5] The question of what race signifies and what signifies race bedeviled the creators and enforcers of miscegenation law—from the state legislators who enacted the laws to the judges who tried to carry them out to the marriage license clerks required by law to turn some, but not other, interracial couples away.

Miscegenation law made race classification seem to be imperative—that is, in order to determine who could and couldn't marry, it was first necessary to identify every person's race quickly and correctly. The more imperative it seemed to assign people to racial categories, and the harder officials tried to pin down race, the more arbitrary—and less logical—the categories became. The next two chapters will trace this contradiction, between the imperative of race classification on the one hand and the unreliability of race categories on the other, as it emerged in two key arenas of miscegenation law enforcement: the courtroom and the marriage license bureau.

The imperative of race classification depended on an illusion of certainty that was reflected in the enactment of state laws defining race as well as in the confident pronouncements of scientists who made it their business to define and categorize the races. During the 1920s, when Joe Kirby went to court, race was a central element of state policy-making, visible in everything from miscegenation law to school segregation, from railroads to the rules for immigration and naturalization. The white supremacist conviction that race was a compellingly significant factor in culture, history, and the development of civilization was everywhere on display, even, sometimes, among those who tried to challenge the presumptions of white supremacy in the name of racialized groups. But no matter how deeply people believed in the significance of race, or how often they linked race to power and resistance in everyday life, they had a devil of a time defining it. Despite its enormous social power, race was neither a natural essence nor a scientific reality, and pinning it down was often a logical impossibility.

This was nowhere more apparent than in the courtroom, where plaintiffs, defendants, lawyers, judges, and juries repeatedly puzzled over how to categorize by race. For every prosecutor who worked to translate the lists of races named by state legislators into identifiable, provable categories, there was a defense lawyer ready to poke holes in the kinds of evidence used to prove race. For every judge determined to enforce the most reliable categories he could find, there was a defendant ready to argue that his or her race had been misconstrued. And for every scientist who offered one answer to a problem of race classification, there was another scientist with a different answer.

These doubts were apparent to all concerned. But, as this chapter will show by exploring the history of race-making in law, science, and the courtroom, the perceived need to determine the legal "fact" of race survived despite repeated criticisms of the contradictions, gaps, and logical deficiencies of the process of race classification. Indeed, it was a measure of the power of miscegenation law in this period that, although many people recognized the arbitrary nature of race classifications and some individuals succeeded in persuading courts they had been misclassified, no one succeeded in dislodging the imperative of race classification, which remained at the very heart of miscegenation law.

Making Race in the Courtroom

In the courtroom, the imperative of race classification made its appearance early and often. The primary form it took was that of a logical, practical task: in order to enforce miscegenation law, it was necessary to classify individuals by race. Yet the process of determining race in a courtroom was anything but precise. It began at the local level, where, as historian Ariela Gross has shown in a fine study of southern courts, trials were structured by racial inequalities that were more personal and performative than mathematical.[6] Local juries cared little about the technicalities of legal standards of definition, but they cared a great deal about the White community's need to identify and place individuals in the local racial hierarchy. White male judges and juries sat in judgment on the race of local residents in a society in which White people were so deeply invested in supremacy that the mere charge that a person might be Black was considered humiliating. If the community was small enough, jurors might know some of the lawyers, litigants, or witnesses personally; in any case, they were likely to be participants in local knowledge and gossip networks about racial reputations.

The strategies lawyers used for determining race in miscegenation trials were formulated in cases involving charges of blackness and in circumstances that enabled juries to apply the nebulous definitions of race popular among White southerners without much concern for the niceties of legal definitions or scientific authority. Whenever they could, lawyers relied on the jury's visual scrutiny to determine the race of the plaintiff or defendant who appeared in the courtroom before them. Since lawyers, judges, and juries believed that the race of a person was usually obvious, visible in skin color and physical characteristics, this technique had the considerable advantage of appearing to rest on the common sense of jurors rather than legal strategy and thus appearing to be no technique at all. In other words, the visual scrutiny technique made it seem as if judges and juries were merely recognizing or identifying preexisting race rather than producing and enforcing race classifications.

But the technique of visual scrutiny worked better in some cases than in others. In so-called borderline cases, where the supposedly natural fact of skin color either was not so obvious or did not fit the social roles it was presumed to match, lawyers had to produce more explicit evidence. Some of these cases showed just how deep the belief that one could see the race of a person written on his or her body really ran. In the hope that race would surely become evident if juries were only allowed to see enough physical markers, judges sometimes allowed juries to see parts of the body that would not ordinarily have been visible in the courtroom. One woman was asked to display her fingernails and remove her shoes, another to partially disrobe before a jury in an attempt to uncover supposedly persuasive physical evidence of race.[7]

Yet very few lawyers were content to let borderline cases rest solely on a jury's impression of physical markers of race. In order to ensure that the jury saw the same race they wanted them to see, lawyers also called witnesses to offer additional opinions. Judges routinely allowed lawyers to ask, and witnesses to testify, about a person's ancestry, associates, and reputation in the community; they even allowed testimony about the very physical characteristics that were supposed to be on obvious display in the courtroom. In one Alabama case, for example, when a woman indicted for miscegenation denied the charge that she was "a negro or a descendant of a negro," witnesses testified that "you can tell by her looks she is a negro," that "I know she has negro associates," and that "I saw negro women in the house all the time, and she has been on the streets with negroes."[8]

Family members were often asked to testify about the physical characteristics of their ancestors. So were local people with some claim to authority, such as physicians and midwives, police officers, court bailiffs, and the "colored" pastor of a local Black church. The most common witnesses, however, were friends and neighbors, called by both sides on the assumption that they had, as the Supreme Court of North Carolina put it, "had opportunities of observation."[9] In court, lawyers quizzed them for their observations about everything from a person's skin color to a person's racial reputation in the community to a person's links to segregated churches and schools.

Because race was believed to be a natural fact determinable by ordinary observation, nineteenth-century courts saw little need for expert witnesses, and lawyers made few references to scientific classifications of race. As the Supreme Court of North Carolina again explained, "It was not necessary that the witness should be an expert to testify to a matter which is simply one of common observation."[10] In local courts, judges allowed juries to hear a wide range of evidence, from unspoken observation of physical characteristics to testimony about friends and associations, then held that the race of the defendant was ultimately "an issue of fact" for the jury (or, in cases without a jury, for the judge) to decide.[11] In other words, in borderline trials judges and juries produced a legal fact of race that would, presumably, mirror the natural fact of race they also presumed must exist, even, and perhaps especially, in cases where race appeared to be much less than obvious.

Throughout the nineteenth century, lawyers who sought to challenge racial evidence found it very hard going. The appellate courts that considered local verdicts routinely upheld all sorts of evidence of race. Their decisions make for grim reading. "There was no error," the Supreme Court of Alabama insisted, "in allowing the State to make profert of [show] the person of John Blue to the jury, in order that they might determine by inspection whether he was a negro, as charged in the indictment." The Texas Court of Criminal Appeals upheld the use of a person's reputation for being of a particular race: "The fact that her first husband was a white man was a circumstance that might go to show that appellant was known and recognized as a white woman." The Supreme Court of North Carolina agreed, seeing "no force" in objections "to the witness testifying that Anne Booth was a colored person and reputed to be such" and also upholding "the testimony of the witness who knew her and had had opportunities of observation, that in his opinion said Anne was of mixed blood."[12]

During the 1880s and 1890s, when the judicial consensus on the constitutionality of miscegenation law was relatively new and fragile, appellate courts routinely upheld convictions in miscegenation court cases. But the more the constitutionality of miscegenation law could be taken for granted, the more room there was for judges' doubts about racial proof to grow. Obliged to pay attention to the laws passed by state legislatures, appellate judges were sometimes receptive to defense lawyers who exposed the gaps between the vagaries of local race-making practices and the specific definitions enshrined in state law. As these doubts grew, appellate court decisions began to diverge from local court judgments. One reason for this gap was that since individual litigants rarely appeared in person in appellate courts, appellate judges were often unable to rely on the visual scrutiny that lower-court judges and juries took for granted. Without the evidence of their own eyes to persuade them of what they were seeing, appellate judges were in a position to notice the discrepancies and contradictions that marked race making in local courts. Thus the Court of Appeals of Alabama overturned one man's conviction, after noting that a lower-court judge's belief that the defendant was "of Indian and Spanish origin" conflicted with a jury verdict that he was "of African origin." In such a case, the justices concluded, "one cannot help asking how the trial judge made this ascertainment," which was "in no wise evidence in the case." Appellate judges were also in a position to notice just how far local prosecutors stretched the commonplace custom of calling witnesses to testify to skin color or other physical characteristics. The Criminal Court of Appeals of Oklahoma, for example, freed one couple that had been indicted for fornication on racial evidence the court dismissed as the "unscientific opinions of ignorant men who worked for a livelihood in and around the territorial courts."[13]

The Illusion of Certainty

When judges who were charged with enforcing miscegenation laws had questions about racial categories, there were two obvious places to look for answers: the precise wording of the race definition laws passed by state legislatures and the authoritative expertise of race science.

Laws that tried to define race were a product of the difficulties southern and border states had long encountered in setting racial boundaries. The first such laws supported slavery by preventing free Blacks from voting, testifying, serving on juries, or attending public schools. After the Civil War, when miscegenation law inherited from slavery the task of defining race in the law, many states placed definitions of race directly in the text of their miscegenation laws. These definitions took one of two forms. The first, used by a handful of southern states, measured race by the yardstick of ancestry. Thus Alabama prohibited Whites from marrying "any negro, or the descendant of any negro, to the third generation, inclusive, though one ancestor of each generation was a white person." The second, and far more common, form, used by most southern states and a handful of border and western states as well, measured race by a mathematical fraction of racial blood, a so-called blood-quantum standard. Thus, Indiana voided marriages between "any white woman" or "any white man" and any person "having one-eighth part or more of negro blood." The vast majority of statutory definitions of race used the terms "Negro" or "colored," as Indiana did, to refer to African Americans, but a couple of western states applied blood-quantum standards to other racial groups as well. Oregon, for example, forbade "any white person, male or female" from marrying "any negro, Chinese, or any person having one-fourth or more negro, Chinese, or Kanaka blood, or any person having more than one-half Indian blood." The specific fractions used in blood-quantum laws varied a bit from state to state (and sometimes, as in Oregon, from group to group), but during the nineteenth century, most states settled on a one-eighth standard.[14]

Both definitions—ancestry and blood quantum—framed the imperative of race classification in ways that made charges of non-Whiteness hard to refute. Under the terms of most ancestry definitions, a person with seven White great-grandparents and one Black great-grandparent would be categorized as a "negro." Similarly, blood-quantum definitions translated one-eighth "negro blood" into the category "Negro" and one-fourth "Kanaka blood" into the category "Kanaka." The notion of racial blood was, of course, a fiction: there are no racial differences in blood, and therefore no way to measure them. In the final analysis, blood-quantum definitions, too, relied on ancestry. But no matter what statutory standard was adopted, or what it was called, a relatively small percentage of Black or Asian American or Indian blood or ancestry took on greater importance than a seemingly larger percentage of White blood or ancestry.

If race definition laws were one place judges could look for the illusion of certainty, another was to the pronouncements of race scientists. Since the early 1800s, white supremacy and race science had been largely interdependent enterprises. A century-long parade of experts—beginning, in the nineteenth century, with naturalists, physicians, ethnologists, and physical anthropologists and ending, after the turn of the twentieth century, with eugenicists—had claimed scientific authority over the study of race, and all had lent their authority to various forms of white supremacy one after another. These scientists are often described as biological determinists, but that description is more than a little misleading. Physical difference was the indicator race scientists used to refine their classification schemes, but physical difference was not, in their eyes, the essence of race. In their formulations, racial essence stretched seamlessly from physical shape to character, morality, psychology, social organization, even, in the more elaborate schemes, to language. In other words, race scientists invested the term "race" with all the explanatory power we now associate with the term "culture."[15]

Race scientists convinced themselves and many others of the significance of race, but their expertise rested on decidedly shaky foundations. While racialists agreed that race signified a great deal, they did not—and they knew they did not—even agree on such a seemingly simply matter as how many races there were. Early estimates were low: in the first decades of the nineteenth century, for example, natural historians debated whether there were three, four, or five major races. Most of these groupings corresponded with geography or skin color, and when they didn't, no matter. When scientists found an area of the world, such as the Pacific Archipelago, that showed substantial intermarriage, they took it as a challenge to separate the mixtures into their supposedly pure original categories.

And when scientists ran into difficulty classifying races, they tried to straighten out their confusion by subdividing their classification schemes into more and more categories. As a result, the number of scientifically recognized races increased steadily over the course of the nineteenth century. The more links Americans had drawn between race and public policy, the more attention they had given to listing and identifying races, and the harder they had looked for scientific systems to ground their classifications. Yet even among scientists, there was an enormous gap between the perceived necessity to classify the races and the ability to agree about who fit into which one. For much of the nineteenth century, ethnologists and physical anthropologists had stood as the authoritative experts on scientific race classification, but despite their supposed expertise, they disagreed—often sharply—over the number and variety of races. Rather than give up the project of racial classification entirely, though, ethnologists solved their disagreements (and retained their professional authority) by either adding more categories or rearranging the ones already at hand into major and minor groups. By the time the United

States Immigration Commission published the *Dictionary of Races and Peoples* it designed to enforce its racially based National Origins immigration policy, the dictionary listed forty-five different races or peoples and spoke of grand racial divisions with multiple subdivisions. By the 1920s, some ethnologists, like eugenicists, were shifting the focus of racial definition schemes by building on distinctions that T. H. Huxley, a nineteenth-century ethnologist, had drawn between so-called Xanthochroi, or "fair whites," of northern Europe and Melanochroi, or "dark whites," of Southern Europe.[16]

As racial categories multiplied, in science as well as in the law, the map of miscegenation laws grew increasingly complex. More than a dozen states added new groups to their lists of the races prohibited from marrying Whites. Montana (1909) and Nebraska (1913) added "Japanese" and "Chinese."[17] Missouri (1909) and Idaho (1921) added "Mongolians"; and Nevada (1911), Wyoming (1913), California (1933), and Maryland (1935) added "Malays."[18] South Dakota added "Corean, Malayan, or Mongolian" to its state law in 1913, and Arizona added "Malays" and "Hindus" in 1931.[19] In some states, the lists of named races grew longer with each successive revision. Georgia's 1927 law named "West Indian, Asiatic Indian, Malay, Japanese, or Chinese"; Arizona's 1931 law named "Negroes, Hindus, Mongolians, members of the Malay race, or Indians, and their descendants"; Utah's 1939 law used the phrase "Mongolian, member of the malay race or a mulatto, quadroon, or octoroon."[20] And,

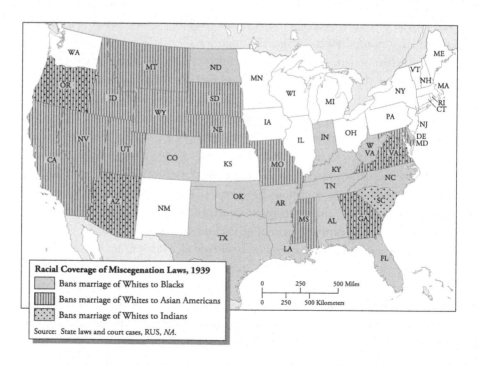

Racial Coverage of Miscegenation Laws, 1939

- Bans marriage of Whites to Blacks
- Bans marriage of Whites to Asian Americans
- Bans marriage of Whites to Indians

Source: State laws and court cases, RUS, *NA*.

under the influence of race scientists' constant search for racial purity, several states, including Oklahoma (1907), Arkansas (1911), Tennessee (1917), Virginia (1924), Alabama (1927), and Georgia (1927), adopted one-drop standards of white purity.[21]

By end of the 1930s, the list of races named in miscegenation law was so complex and convoluted that its logic was apparent to no one. In one state or another, all of the following groups were prohibited from marrying Whites: Negroes, Mulattoes, Quadroons, Octoroons, Blacks, Persons of African Descent, Ethiopians, Persons of Color, Indians, Mestizos, Half-Breeds, Mongolians, Chinese, Japanese, Malays, Kanakas, Coreans, Asiatic Indians, West Indians, and Hindus. In judicial rhetoric, the presumption that race classifications were natural and obvious buttressed the claim that interracial marriage was unnatural. In practice, though, the obvious illogic of these race classifications stretched this conceit close to the breaking point.

So Little Certainty to Offer

Faced with puzzles like that of Joe and Mayellen Kirby while trying to enforce the sprawling, ungainly state-by-state network of increasingly complicated miscegenation laws, it is no wonder that judges longed for clearer definitions of race and more consistent lists of categories. Judges who lived in states like Arizona, which had no race definition law on its books, might have longed for such a blood-quantum statute, though those in states that had such laws soon learned that their seemingly mathematical precision of blood quantum was also an illusion. Others, like the Oklahoma judge who had dismissed the opinions of casual acquaintances as "unscientific," seemed to yearn for the authority of scientific expertise. But if, at first glance, race science seemed to provide a handy solution to these problems—and it did, indeed, offer the authority of widely acknowledged expertise—it soon became clear that expertise only compounded the problem. Science had so little certainty to offer that resorting to scientists only made the problem worse.

Judges who ventured into the writings of race scientists came back appalled by the seemingly limitless lists they encountered there. In California, for example, one judge discovered that if the latest writings of ethnologists were taken as the basis of race classification, Californians who had prohibited "whites" from marrying "Mongolians" would have been targeting more groups than just Chinese, Japanese, Koreans, and Filipinos. This judge had learned, much to his consternation, that "Laplanders, Hawaiians, Estonians, Huns, Finns, Turks, Eskimos, American Indians, native Peruvians, Native

Mexicans and many other peoples . . . are included within the present-day scientist's classification of 'Mongolian.'" The more race scientists had to say about Europeans, the more uncomfortable even the staunchest defenders of white purity seemed to become. In 1935, for example, when a Washington state legislator proposed a miscegenation law that would have defined Whites so as to exclude "those of eastern and southeastern Europe embracing the Balkan peninsula or states, and Russia as now delineated," protests from the Slavic-American Federation helped ensure that the bill went down to defeat.[22]

Resorting to race science pushed defenders of miscegenation law into one logical contortion after another. Consider, for example, the logical inconsistency between the scientific concept of racial purity and the legal structure of white supremacy. Whether the scientist in question was an eighteenth-century naturalist, a nineteenth-century ethnologist, or a twentieth-century eugenicist, the project of race science was ultimately based on a belief that it was scientifically possible to identify, and politically desirable to maintain, a particular number of "pure" races.

Miscegenation law, however, depended on playing fast and loose with the logic of maintaining several pure races; it translated a theoretical commitment to racial purity into an actual commitment to white supremacy by using the legislative and administrative race-defining powers of the state to protect only the racial purity of Whites. So even as judges clung to the constitutional fiction that miscegenation laws "applied to all races alike," miscegenation laws actually prohibited Whites from marrying other groups, like "Negroes," "Mongolians," or "Malays," without prohibiting "Negroes," "Mongolians," or "Malays" from marrying each other. In California, for example, Blacks were prohibited from marrying Whites, but they could, and did, marry Indians and Asian Americans. Likewise, the addition of "Malays" to California's miscegenation law meant that Filipinos could no longer marry Whites, but they could, and did, continue to marry Blacks and Indians.

Like California, most states tried to grasp both sides of this contradiction—the "white purity" structure of miscegenation law on the one hand and the "equal application" rationale on the other—at one and the same time. But as the white supremacist drive for purity increased the pressure to segregate not only Whites and Blacks but also those who were neither Whites nor Blacks, a few states began to experiment with miscegenation laws that applied solely to groups labeled "non-White." North Carolina and Louisiana, for example, passed laws that prohibited Indians from marrying Blacks. North Carolina's list of the specific Indians forbidden to marry "Negroes" evidently required a good deal of fine-tuning. In 1887, the state prohibited "Negroes" from

marrying "Croatan Indians," and in 1911 it revised that provision to co
marriages to "Indians of Robeson County," but in 1913, it revised this ca.
egory again to cover "Cherokee Indians of Robeson County."[23] Louisiana's
law, passed in 1920, prohibited all "persons of the Indian race" from marrying "persons of the colored and black race."[24] Maryland passed a 1935 law
banning marriages between "a negro and a member or the Malay race, or
between a person of negro descent, to the third generation, inclusive, and a
member of the Malay race."[25] These laws were awkward attempts to smooth
the jagged edges of southern race classifications by reconciling the movement
for one-drop white purity with the history of marriages between Whites and
Indians or the presence of groups, like Filipinos, that were considered both
non-White and non-Black.

The ragged edges of western race classifications were on display in Oklahoma, where lawmakers also struggled to cut the trend toward one-drop standards of white purity to fit the history of a place where Indians, who had a
long history of marriage with Blacks, still held a little political power and
quite a lot of land. In a transparent effort to avoid offending the Indians of the
Five Civilized Nations, whose political support Oklahoma lawmakers needed
and whose land Oklahoma boosters coveted, Oklahoma lawmakers concocted
a unique legal definition of race. Oklahoma's state constitution, adopted in
1907, defined the terms "colored" and "negro race" to include "all persons of
African descent" and the phrase "white race" to "include all other persons,"
bringing Indians within the "white" classification.[26] After the constitution was
ratified, Oklahomans made the implications of this definition perfectly clear.
Boosters celebrated statehood with the symbolic marriage of a White man
and a Cherokee woman, but the state's first legislature prohibited "any person of African descent" from marrying "any person not of African descent."[27]
From its passage in 1907 until the late 1960s, Oklahoma courts interpreted
this law so as to allow White men to marry and inherit property from Indian
women while preventing Black men from doing the very same thing.[28]

The classification problems that applied to supposedly distinct racial
groups, like "whites," "negroes," "Indians," or "Malays," grew even more convoluted when it came to groups that scientists considered "mixed race." Here
again, scientists were very little help. Take, for example, the case of Mexican Americans. In the history of miscegenation law, the experience of Mexican
Americans is studded with contradictions.[29] On the one hand, no American
state ever explicitly named Mexican Americans, or any other Latino group,
in a state miscegenation law, and Mexican Americans had a long and well-
documented history of intermarriage.[30] Marriages between Spanish/Mexicans
and Anglos had taken place ever since the early nineteenth century, when much

of the Southwest was under first Spanish, then Mexican control. During this period, White men who married Spanish/Mexican women gained entrance into local trade networks and circles of landholding, and the practice was no more controversial than marriages between White men and Indian women. But after the American conquest, the treatment of Mexican Americans hinged on the contradiction between treaties that guaranteed that Mexican citizens who remained in the now-American territory would enjoy the legal privileges of White citizens and the stubborn determination of growing numbers of white supremacists to racialize "Mexicans" in every way they possibly could.[31] Race scientists, whose goal was to link their classifications to original, supposedly pure races, considered Mexicans such an irredeemably mixed-race population that they never produced a racial term for "Mexican" that carried the same aura of scientific authority as terms like "Mongolian" or "Malay."

Their absence from miscegenation laws did not mean, however, that Mexican Americans were unaffected by them. As the move toward one-drop definitions of white purity put pressure on mixed-race peoples of all kinds, courts began to distinguish between mixed-race peoples whose origins could be traced to "Spanish" (and therefore White) roots, and those whose origins could be traced to Indian or African (and therefore non-White) roots. So although a "Mexican Indian" man or woman might legally marry a White in states like California and Texas, which did not name either "Indians" or "Mexicans" in its miscegenation law, they could not necessarily have done so in states like Arizona, Oregon, or North Carolina, which did name "Indians" in their miscegenation laws, or in Virginia, where the state registrar of vital statistics voided marriages between "whites" and "Mexicans" in the belief that "Mexicans" were a mixture of "Spanish or Portuguese, Indian and negro."[32] In practice, the treatment of Mexican Americans depended a great deal on local officials' perceptions of individual ancestry and skin color. Anecdotal evidence shows a good deal of confusion on the part of licensing clerks, who sometimes considered Mexicans too "white" to marry partners from groups clerks assumed were non-White, like Punjabi Indians, and other times considered Mexicans too "dark" to marry Whites.[33] It was uncertainties like this that Mayellen Kirby's lawyer hoped to raise by suggesting that if Joe Kirby had a "Mexican" mother, he could not be a "white" man. In the end, then, despite their official absence from the text of miscegenation laws, Mexican Americans were subjected to them in an especially bewildering, and often unpredictable, manner. Indeed, for the rest of the twentieth century, the racial categorization of Mexican Americans would befuddle bureaucrats, lawyers, and judges alike.[34]

Yet in order for miscegenation law to survive, judges had to push these edges into alignment, conflating racial purity with white supremacy, bridging gaps between the races listed in the miscegenation laws of different states, and borrowing what authority they could from race science without allowing its labyrinthine subclassifications to make enforcing the laws seem impossible.

The Imperative of Race Classification

The needs of judges differed, however, from the needs of lawyers, who quickly realized that they might be able to turn the slippery borderlines of race classification to the advantage of mixed-race clients. If a lawyer could persuade a judge that his client's race classification was in error, his client might prevail. So lawyers raised questions that troubled judges, who then had to struggle through the sorts of questions raised in the *Kirby* case. To judges and juries who believed that setting racial boundaries was crucial to the maintenance of ordered society, the criteria used to determine who fit in which category were more notable for their malleability than their logical consistency. Genealogy, appearance, claims to identity, or that mystical quality, "blood"—any of these would do, and they might be mixed and matched with (il)logical abandon.

In Arizona, Judge Samuel L. Pattee demonstrated this malleability in deciding the *Kirby* case. Although Mayellen Kirby's lawyer later maintained that Joe Kirby "appeared" to be an Indian, the judge insisted that parentage, not appearance, was the key to Joe's racial classification. "Mexicans," the judge said, "are classed as of the Caucasian Race. They are descendants, supposed to be, at least, of the Spanish conquerors of that country, and unless it can be shown that they are mixed up with some other races, why the presumption is that they are descendants of the Caucasian race."[35]

Yet at the same time that the judge decided that ancestry determined that Joe Kirby was a "Caucasian" man, he simply assumed that Mayellen Kirby was a "Negro" woman. Mayellen Kirby sat silently through the entire trial; she was spoken about and spoken for but never allowed to speak herself. There was no testimony about her ancestry; her race was assumed to rest in her physical characteristics. Neither of the lawyers bothered to argue over Mayellen's racial designation. As Joe's lawyer would later explain, "The learned and discriminating judge . . . had the opportunity to gaze upon the dusky countenance of the appellant [Mayellen Kirby] and could not and did not fail to observe the distinguishing characteristics of the African race and blood."[36]

In the end, the judge accepted the claim that Joe Kirby was "Caucasian" and Mayellen Kirby "a Negro" and held that the marriage violated Arizona miscegenation law; he granted Joe Kirby his annulment. By granting Joe

Kirby an annulment rather than a divorce, the judge not only avoided recognizing the validity of the marriage while it had lasted but also excused
Joe Kirby from his obligation to provide economic support to a divorced
wife. In so doing, the judge resolved the miscegenation drama by adding
a patriarchal moral to the white supremacist plot. In this case and others
like it, White men involved with non-White women were able to avoid the
social and economic responsibilities they would have been expected to carry
in legally sanctioned marriages with White women.

For her part, Mayellen Kirby had nothing left to lose. She and her lawyer
appealed to the Arizona Supreme Court. This time they threw caution to the
winds, moving beyond their limited argument about Joe's individual racial
classification to challenge the entire racial logic of miscegenation law. The
Arizona statute provided a tempting target for their attack, for under its
"descendants" provision, a person of "mixed blood" could not legally marry
anyone. Pointing this out, Mayellen Kirby's lawyer argued that the law must
therefore be unconstitutional. He failed to convince the court. Relying on
an individual exception of its own, the court brushed aside these objections.
The argument that the law was unconstitutional, the court held, "is an
attack . . . [Mayellen Kirby] is not entitled to make for the reason that there
is no evidence that she is other than of the black race. . . . It will be time
enough to pass on the question she raises . . . when it is presented by
some one whose rights are involved or affected."[37]

Mixed-race clients were subjected to the imperative of race classification
even in cases where their lawyers tried to offset the seeming certainties of
race science by asking for help from a pioneering group of modern social scientists who were willing to challenge the authority of race science head-on.
Led by cultural anthropologist Franz Boas, these new scientists believed that
human difference and human history were much better understood in terms
of cultural imperatives than racial ones. Because they interpreted character,
morality, and social organization as cultural rather than racial phenomena,
they are perhaps best described as culturalists, as opposed to the racialists
whose compulsion to classify by race was so deeply embedded in the structure
of miscegenation law.

Two of the arguments made by culturalists caught the attention of defense
lawyers in miscegenation cases. The first of these was the argument that the
key notion of race science—race itself—made no biological sense. In their
most dramatic mode, culturalists went so far as to insist that physical indicators were completely unreliable indicators of race; in biological terms, they
insisted, race must be considered indeterminable. Thus, in an influential
encyclopedia article on race, Boas insisted that "it is not possible to assign

with certainty any one individual to a definite group." Perhaps the strongest statement of this kind came from Julian Huxley and A. C. Haddon, British scientists who maintained that "the term *race* as applied to human groups should be dropped from the vocabulary of science." In this and other forms, the culturalist argument that race was biologically indeterminable captured the attention of both contemporaries and later historians.[38]

The second argument that culturalists put forth started from the other end of the spectrum, maintaining not that there was no such thing as biological race but that race was nothing more than biology. Since biology was a phenomenon culturalists considered to be of remarkably little importance, consigning race to the realm of biology pushed it out of the picture. Thus Boas ended his article on race by concluding that although it remained "likely" enough that scientific study of the "anatomical differences between the races" might reveal biological influences on the formation of personality, "the study of cultural forms shows that such differences are altogether irrelevant as compared with the powerful influence of the cultural environment in which the group lives."[39]

Following this logic, contrasts between important and wide-reaching culture and unimportant (but biological) race stood as the cornerstone of many culturalist arguments. Thus cultural anthropologist Ruth Benedict began her widely influential pamphlets *Race: Science and Politics* and *The Races of Mankind* with an analysis of "what race is *not*," including language, customs, intelligence, character, and civilization. Real "racial differences," Benedict maintained, occurred only in "nonessentials such as texture of head hair, amount of body hair, shape of the nose or head, or color of the eyes and the skin." Following these distinctions, Benedict could argue that, while race was a scientific "fact," racism, which she saw as "the dogma that the hope of civilization depends upon eliminating some races and keeping others pure," was no more than a "modern superstition."[40]

Culturalists set these two seemingly contradictory depictions of race—the argument that biological race was nonsense and the argument that race was merely biology—right beside each other. The contradiction mattered little to them. Used either alone or in conjunction with each other, these arguments appeared to take a giant step away from popular common sense on the issue of race. Recognizing—even at times celebrating—this gap between themselves and the public, culturalists devoted a good deal of their work to dislodging popular racial assumptions. Seeing the public as lamentably behind the times and sadly prone to race prejudice, they used their academic credentials to emphasize the gulf between expert and ordinary opinion, insisting that racial categories not only did not rest on common sense but made little sense at all.

This, of course, was just what lawyers challenging miscegenation laws wanted to hear. Because culturalist social scientists could offer their arguments with an air of scientific and academic authority that might prove persuasive to judges, attorneys began to invite them to appear as expert witnesses. But when culturalists appeared in court, they entered an arena where their argument for the biological indeterminacy of race ran headlong into the imperative of race classification, which shaped trial outcomes in ways neither social scientists nor the lawyers who recruited them could control.

Take, for example, the *Monks* trial, held in the Superior Court of San Diego County in 1939. By all accounts, Marie Antoinette Monks was a woman with a clear eye for her main chance. In the early 1930s, she had entranced and married a man named Allan Monks, potential heir to a Boston fortune. Shortly after their marriage, which took place in Arizona, Allan Monks declined into insanity. Whether his mental condition resulted from injuries sustained in a motorcycle crash or from drugs administered by Marie Antoinette, the court

Marie Antoinette Monks, in a photograph taken by the *Los Angeles Examiner* in 1932. (Courtesy of University of Southern California, on behalf of the USC Special Collections)

would debate at great length. In any case, Allan Monks died. He left two wills, an old one in favor of a friend named Ida Lee and a newer one in favor of his wife. Ida Lee submitted her version of the will for probate; Marie Antoinette challenged her claim, and Lee fought back. Lee's lawyers rested their hopes on their contention that the Monks marriage was illegal. They charged that Marie Antoinette Monks, who had told her husband she was a French countess, was actually "a Negro," and therefore prohibited by Arizona law from marrying Allan Monks, whom the court presumed to be "Caucasian."[41]

Much of the six-week trial was devoted to determining the race of Marie Antoinette Monks. To prove that she was "a Negro," her opponents called five people to the witness stand: a disgruntled friend of her husband, a local labor commissioner, and three expert witnesses, all of whom offered arguments that emphasized biological indicators of race. The first so-called expert, Monks's hairdresser, claimed that she could tell that Monks was of mixed blood from looking at the size of the moons of her fingernails, the color of the "ring" around the palms of her hands, and her "kinky" hair. The second, a physical anthropologist from the nearby San Diego Museum, claimed to be able to tell that Monks was "at least one-eighth negroid" from the shape of her face, the color of her hands, and her "protruding heels," all of which he had observed casually while a spectator in the courtroom. The third expert witness, a surgeon, had grown up and practiced medicine in the South and later served at a Southern Baptist mission in Africa. Having once walked alongside Monks when entering the courthouse (at which time he tried, he said, to make a close observation of her), he testified that he could tell that she was of "one-eighth negro blood" from the contour of her calves and heels, the "peculiar pallor" on the back of her neck, the shape of her face, and the wave of her hair.[42]

To defend Monks, her lawyers called a friend, a relative, and two expert witnesses of their own, one anthropologist and one biologist. Her experts started out by testifying to the culturalist position that it was impossible to tell a person's race from physical characteristics, especially if that person was, as they put it, "of mixed blood." This was the argument culturalists used whenever they were cornered into talking about biology, a phenomenon they tended to regard as so insignificant a factor in social life that they preferred to avoid talking about it at all.

But this argument did not play very well in the *Monks* courtroom. Seeking to find the definitiveness they needed to offset the experts who had already testified, Monks's lawyers paraded their client in front of the witness stand, asking her to show the anthropologist her fingernails and to remove her shoes so that he could see her heels. They lingered over the biologist's testimony that Monks's physical features resembled those of the people of southern

France. In the end, Monks's lawyers backed both experts into a corner; when pressed repeatedly for a definite answer, both reluctantly admitted that it was their opinion that Monks was a "white" woman.[43]

The experts' dilemma reveals the limitations of the argument for racial indeterminacy in the courtroom. Faced with a conflict between one set of experts, the culturalists, who offered uncertainty and indeterminacy, and their opponents, who offered concrete biological answers to racial questions, judges were predisposed to favor the latter. To judges, culturalists appeared to be frustratingly vague and uncooperative (in other words, to be lousy witnesses), while their opponents seemed to be good witnesses willing to answer direct questions.

In the *Monks* case, the judge admitted that his own "inexpert" opinion that Marie Antoinette "did have many characteristics that I would say . . . [showed] mixed negro and some other blood" was not enough to justify a ruling. Turning to the experts before him, he dismissed the hairdresser (whose experience he was willing to grant, but whose scientific credentials he considered dubious), and he dismissed the two anthropologists, whose testimony, he said, more or less canceled each other out. The only expert the judge was willing to rely on was the surgeon, because, as he put it, the surgeon "seemed to me to hold a very unique and peculiar position as an expert on the question involved from his work in life."[44]

Relying on the surgeon's testimony, the judge declared that Marie Antoinette Monks was "the descendant of a negro" who had "one-eighth negro blood . . . and 7/8 caucasian blood"; he said that her race prohibited her from marrying Allan Monks or from inheriting his estate. Marie Antoinette's race invalidated the marriage, both because it made the marriage impermissible under Arizona miscegenation law and because, in telling her husband-to-be that she was French, she had committed a fraud serious enough to render the marriage legally void. The court's decision that she had also exerted undue influence over Monks was hardly necessary to the outcome.[45]

The Rule Born of Necessity

In both the *Kirby* and *Monks* cases, lawyers tried to build on the doubts that appellate judges had expressed about questions of racial proof in the early twentieth century. In *Kirby,* the challenge relied on the illogicality of tying race to ancestry; in *Monks,* it relied on the emerging authority of a group of culturalist scientists eager to oust their racialist predecessors. Both challenges were thoughtful, logical, strategic attempts to take advantage of well-known weaknesses in the structure and enforcement of miscegenation laws, but both fell well short of their mark. By the end of the 1930s, the imperative of race classification was more deeply embedded in miscegenation law than ever before.[46]

It is not that these, and other, challenges had no effect at all. Compared to the 1890s, judges of the 1930s were less likely to regard the racial "facts" produced and enforced in courts as indications of the fundamentally different "natures" of the races. Rather than waxing eloquent about "unnatural connections" and illicit sex, courts increasingly focused on the relatively narrow, and seemingly more objective, task of determining the supposedly simple biological "fact" of race. In so doing, they constructed a version of race that mediated between the language of white supremacists and their allies in race science, who believed that the very "future of the white race" rested on maintaining one-drop standards of white purity, and modern social scientists, who described biological markers of race as nonessential foils to the all-important phenomenon of culture.[47]

The more race seemed like a biological fact, the less it seemed, to judges at least, like a moral or political judgment, and the easier it was to believe that recognizing race was exercising common sense. As early as 1924, courts in some states were ready to close the door on the doubts early twentieth century appellate judges had expressed about the uncertainties of race classification in miscegenation law. In *Wilson v. State,* the Alabama Court of Appeals capped two decades of dispute about standards of racial proof in Alabama with a decision that showed the limits of the challenges it would henceforth tolerate from lawyers. The case involved a mixed-race woman whose lawyer had tried to defend his client by insisting that it was "necessary and incumbent upon the state to fully trace the antecedents of a defendant in order to establish the race of an accused." The court rejected that claim, explaining:

> A rule of that kind, where the inquiry is material, might, and no doubt would, often defeat the ends of justice, because of the impossibility clearly apparent in making such proof. We think that, if for no other reason, the rule born of necessity should and does permit a witness, if he knows such to be the fact, to testify that a person is a negro, or is a white person, or that he is a man, or that she is a woman; for courts are not supposed to be ignorant of what everybody else is presumed to know, and in this jurisdiction certainly every person possessed of any degree of intelligence knows a negro.[48]

Here, in a nutshell, was the imperative of race classification that grounded miscegenation law. To the appellate judges who held the last word on the facts of race in the courtroom, the legal requirement of proving the fact of race appeared to be a "rule born of necessity" that served "the ends of justice." Although they were aware of "the impossibility clearly apparent" in pinning race down, the transformation of competing, disputed, and partial proofs of physical characteristics, ancestry, associations, and reputation offered by witnesses and recorded on documents into the legal "fact" of race was simply too important to be derailed for long by logical objections from lawyers. In order to enforce miscegenation law, lawyers and local officials were required to place individuals in racial categories, and judges were required to justify doing so.

Buried in the language of the Alabama court's decision in *Wilson v. State* was a phrase that might have given the judges pause. The rule born of necessity, the judges had intoned, allowed witnesses "to testify that a person is a negro, or is a white person, or that he is a man, or that she is a woman." From its earliest stages, the development of miscegenation law, and before that, laws against interracial marriage, had depended on hierarchies of sex and gender as well as on hierarchies of race. In order to make an interracial marriage, a couple had to cross both racial dividing lines (to be interracial) and sexual dividing lines (to be a legal marriage), so criminal trials for miscegenation might well have required proving both the race and the sex of the partners on trial. Before leaving the topic of the imperative of race classification behind, it is worth noting that although lawyers, judges, and juries spent an enormous amount of energy debating the race classification of the partners to a marriage, the issue of sex classification only rarely entered their minds.[49] This, too, shows the extent to which the imperative of race classification had come to structure the enforcement of miscegenation law.

Chapter Five

SEEING LIKE A RACIAL STATE

"All persons about to be joined in marriage must first obtain a license therefor, from the county clerk of the county in which the marriage is to be celebrated. . . . No license must be issued authorizing the marriage of a white person with a negro, mulatto, or mongolian."

—*California Code,* 1920

LOS ANGELES, CALIFORNIA

Leon Lampton couldn't make up his mind. As clerk of Los Angeles County, Lampton was in charge of the county's marriage license bureau, which, in turn, was required to carry out California's miscegenation law. Bureau officials declared, with more than a hint of pride, that it was part of their job to "be able to distinguish races and detect those who, because of youth or race, are not entitled to obtain a license to marry."[1] Its employees were accustomed to turning away Black, Chinese, and Japanese applicants who planned to marry Whites, but neither Lampton nor California's other county clerks knew what they should do in the case of Filipinos. To do his job, Lampton had to know whether Filipinos were "Mongolians" or not.[2]

No one Lampton consulted could answer to this seemingly simple "yes" or "no" question. In 1921, the LA County counsel advised Lampton that Filipinos were not "Mongolians," but a few years later the California attorney general insisted that they were.[3] The question came before judges of the Los Angeles Superior Court on five separate occasions, and they, too, failed to agree. Two judges voided marriages between Filipino men and White women on the basis of the racially expansive logic that, as one of them put it, "a Filipino is a Malay and a Malay is a Mongolian."[4] But two other judges used a kind of racial strict construction to permit marriages between Filipino men and White women on the grounds that Filipinos were *not* "Mongolians."[5] The fifth judge sidestepped the issue by holding that whatever effect California's miscegenation law might have on the marriages of Filipino men and White women, it would not prevent a Filipino man from marrying the "Mexican Indian" woman in the case he had heard.[6]

Meanwhile, the number of Filipinos in California, which had been negligible at the turn of the century, grew to thirty thousand, and anti-Filipino forces began pressuring Leon Lampton to support their growing campaign for exclusion.[7] In 1929, after San Francisco's influential Commonwealth Club conducted an investigation of Filipino immigration with an exclusionary bent, it demanded that the state legislature "*expressly* prohibit marriages between Filipinos and members of the white races."[8] Sensational rumors about Filipino men and White women soon sparked a riot in Exeter, California. A few months later, there was another, even bigger, riot in Watsonville.

Through it all, a small but growing line of Filipino men appeared at the offices of California county clerks asking for licenses to marry. The ranks of Filipino immigrants contained far more men than women, and few of these men had found Filipina partners. Roughly half proposed to marry White women, and the others to marry Black, Indian, Japanese, Chinese, or Mexican immigrant women. Until 1930, the clerks of several southern California counties allowed their deputies to issue marriage licenses in all of these cases. "When they [Filipinos] first began coming to the United States," one clerk explained in phrasing steeped in white supremacy, "we thought they were as good as we were and had a right to marry anybody." Under this policy, Leon Lampton's Los Angeles office had issued more than a hundred marriage licenses to Filipino men and White women.[9]

But after one Los Angeles mother persuaded a sympathetic judge to stop Lampton from issuing a license to the Filipino man her White daughter wanted to marry, Lampton ordered his deputy clerks to begin rejecting all applications from Filipino men and White women. His abrupt change in policy infuriated Filipino leaders, who responded by going to court. Raising funds through community organizations like the Filipino Home Club, they hired lawyers who asked local judges to issue writs of mandamus that would force the county clerk's office to grant individual licenses. In 1931, after winning one of these cases, Filipino leader Pablo Manlapit asked Leon Lampton to reinstate his old policy of issuing licenses. In public Lampton refused, but in private he consulted the county counsel's office, which confessed, in a letter to Manlapit, that county clerks like Lampton, who had to operate by racial "guess work," longed for a more definitive interpretation of the California law.[10] By 1932, both Lampton and the Filipino community had come to pin their hopes on the outcome of yet another court case, one that both sides hoped would settle the issue once and for all. It was the case of Salvador Roldan, a Filipino man, and his fiancée, Marjorie Rogers, a White woman from Great Britain, whose courtship, which had begun on a Pasadena tennis court, ran into trouble at the Los Angeles County Marriage License Bureau.

Seeing Like a Racial State

Lawyers, judges, and interracial couples were not the only ones who had to face the contradiction between the imperative of race classification and the instability of race categories. In every state with a miscegenation law in force, there were officials like Leon Lampton, whose job it was to fit the men and women who came into county offices asking for marriage licenses into the categories listed in state miscegenation laws, accepting some and rejecting others. When marriage license clerks appeared in miscegenation dramas, they were usually bit players, with interracial couples, prosecutors, and judges playing the leads. But it was precisely because marriage license clerks operated at one remove from the center of attention—that is, they carried out their tasks as a matter of bureaucratic routine rather than criminal enforcement, in quiet county offices rather than dramatic courtrooms—that they would come to be so crucial to the enforcement of miscegenation law. They were a fine example of the ways in which state officials worked quietly, persistently, and as comprehensively as possible to make individuals "legible" to the state through processes of government that seemed too ordinary to merit comment or challenge even as they imposed considerable control over individual lives.[11] In much the same way that a seemingly natural biological "fact" of race was produced in courtrooms, a seemingly natural documentary "fact" of race was produced in marriage license bureaus.

After a Los Angeles marriage license clerk told Salvador Roldan that he couldn't marry Marjorie Rogers, Roldan hired a lawyer and took his case to court. When he named county clerk Leon Lampton as the defendant, he revealed the rising involvement of local bureaucracies in determining and enforcing race classifications in miscegenation law. This chapter will start with an overview of the various means of enforcing miscegenation law, then

move to an examination of the reasons why marriage licensing became such
an important form of enforcement during the early twentieth century. In
1924, the growing authority of the marriage licensing process, and behind
it the modern administrative state, was epitomized in the passage of the Virginia Racial Integrity Act. But whether the focus is on Virginia's especially
harsh law or on California's relatively lax one, the imperative of race classification remained firmly in place, easily able to absorb challenges like those
posed by Salvador Roldan.

The Enforcement of Miscegenation Law

From the 1890s through the 1920s, as the movement for white supremacy
spread its tentacles through American society, the guardians of white purity
began to ask for new and even tougher miscegenation laws. Accustomed to
seeing bans on interracial marriage as the foundation on which all things
racial rested, and worried about the doubts appellate judges had begun to
show about how to classify by race, they demanded that miscegenation laws
cover more groups and that their race definition clauses meet new and ever-
tighter standards of white purity. These efforts to put one-drop standards of
"white" into the laws built on what had been, until then, some rather idiosyncratic language in the miscegenation laws of nineteenth-century western
states, most of which had avoided adopting the fractional blood-quantum
standards so common in southern states. As early as 1837, Texas had decided
to void marriages between persons "of European blood or their descendants"
and "Africans, or the descendants of Africans." In 1887, Arizona echoed this
language in a law that prohibited "marriages of persons of Caucasian blood
or their descendants with Africans or Mongolians and their descendants."
In 1894, Louisiana, which had a large and prominent mixed-race population, prohibited marriages between "white persons" and "persons of color";
in 1910, state courts defined "colored" as "a person of negro blood pure or
mixed," noting that "the term applies no matter what may be the propor-
tions of the admixture, so long as the negro blood is traceable." By the turn
of the century, this trend was rapidly becoming the norm. Oklahoma's 1907
miscegenation law relied on its state constitution to target every "person of
African descent"; in 1909, Montana passed a law that specified "Negro or a
person of Negro Blood or in part Negro" without any fractional quantum.[12]
    In addition to calling for the passage of new and stricter laws, white
supremacists became increasingly critical of the two most common methods of enforcing miscegenation law in the courts: the criminal arrest and

imprisonment of interracial couples and the voiding of interracial marriages in civil court cases. Both of these methods were capable of wreaking havoc on the lives of individual couples, but neither of them reached enough interracial couples, soon enough, to satisfy the Progressive-era push for white purity.

White supremacists were heartily in favor of criminal sanctions for interracial sex and marriage, but they recognized, and lamented, the undeniable gaps in applying these penalties. Many, though not all, of the states with miscegenation laws set criminal penalties that applied to interracial couples who tried to marry. In the 1920s, the penalties for interracial marriage ranged from the relatively mild sanctions in states like Colorado, which relied on a $50 to $500 fine and/or three months to two years in prison, to the harsher penalties of states like Maryland, which called for eighteen months to ten years in the state penitentiary. Only a handful of states, like Alabama, had miscegenation laws that set specific penalties for interracial sex as well as marriage. Under the provisions of Alabama's law, an interracial couple could be indicted for living in adultery and fornication, as well as for marriage, both of which carried a punishment of two to seven years in prison.[13]

Yet states did not always, or even often, rely on the criminal penalties placed in miscegenation law to prosecute interracial couples. In actual practice, most criminal prosecutions embodied the sexualization of miscegenation law by subjecting interracial couples to generic laws against illicit sex. So although interracial couples were occasionally arrested for attempting to marry, the more common practice was to arrest them for adultery or fornication or other illicit sex crimes. Both interracial and same-race couples were arrested for these crimes, but once in court, the two groups were subject to different treatment. Same-race couples could avoid convictions on these charges by marrying, but interracial couples were denied the right to decide to marry and the right to claim an existing marriage in their defense. Moreover, in some states, like Alabama, the laws set higher criminal penalties for illicit sex for interracial couples than for same-race couples.[14]

Arrests were by no means uncommon. In Alabama, the attorney general pressed charges of miscegenation against 343 men and women between 1883 and 1938.[15] In most other states, statistics are harder to come by. In North Carolina, for example, statistics on the arrests of interracial couples were folded, invisibly, into the larger category of arrests for adultery and fornication. During the 1920s, North Carolina police arrested more than two hundred couples a year on charges of adultery and fornication, but the records did not differentiate between same-race and interracial couples.[16] A great deal of anecdotal evidence suggests that in practice police enforced miscegenation laws, like adultery and fornication laws, rather sporadically, overlooking a good deal of illicit sexuality, both interracial and same-race, that occurred in private. In the end, the criminal enforcement of miscegenation laws depended heavily on public complaints. In general, arrests were used to make examples of particular couples rather than to capture every supposed offender. Only when a relationship became visible enough to threaten public order or raise community eyebrows—when, in other words, couples might be accused of the "crime" of coming too close to claiming the status of marriage and family life—were police likely to intervene.

The second major means of enforcing miscegenation laws, the voiding of interracial marriages in civil court proceedings, was even less reliable than criminal prosecutions. Civil enforcement of miscegenation laws rested on provisions that labeled interracial marriages "illegal," "unlawful," "prohibited," or "null and void." These provisions placed all interracial couples, even those who lived quietly enough to escape the notice of police or vindictive neighbors, outside the protective cover of the legal presumption of marriage. This, in turn, opened their relationships to challenge in a courtroom. As the Supreme Court of Montana put it, considering the 1942 case of a "white" woman widowed by a "Japanese" man, a marriage that is "void and ineffectual for any lawful purpose in this state . . . is open to collateral attack in any proceeding wherein the question of its validity may be raised, whether before or after the death of either or both of the parties."[17]

Inheritance disputes and probate courts were the most common examples. In inheritance cases, miscegenation law offered disgruntled relatives, state officials, and creditors a powerful tool for taking property away from Black and Indian women widowed by White men, and sometimes from mixed-race children as well. In the absence of comprehensive statistics about how frequently probate judges voided interracial marriages, the best estimate is that inheritance disputes formed a significant number—perhaps as many as one-third—of all the instances in which miscegenation law arose in state appellate courts. In at least two states, Louisiana and Oklahoma, they were the basis for a steady stream of judicial interpretations of miscegenation laws.[18]

Interracial marriages were attacked in other kinds of civil cases as well. An unhappy husband or wife could, and sometimes did, use miscegenation law to seek annulment or divorce by claiming that a marriage had been void from its inception, or that a spouse had lied about his or her race before marriage. On at least one occasion, the sensational *Rhinelander* case, which was front-page news in New York and much of the rest of the country in 1925, an unhappy husband tried to use his wife's racial status to annul his marriage even though his state had no miscegenation law on its books. The case was brought by well-heeled Leonard Rhinelander, a "white" man who charged that his wife's failure to tell him that she was a "negro" before they married made the marriage a fraud.[19]

Miscegenation law could also be used to attack interracial marriages in civil disputes over pensions and benefits. In the 1940s, for example, the Indiana Supreme Court considered a case in which a company challenged a widow's claim to her husband's workmen's compensation. In that case, the Indiana Court of Appeals upheld the state's Industrial Board, which had granted the widow's claim, over the objections of the Inland Steel Company, which had claimed the marriage was void under the state miscegenation law. If the wife had been "a Negro" and the husband "a white," the court explained, the company would have been right and the marriage voided, but in this case the wife was "a Negro" and the husband "a Mexican" who could not, therefore, be assumed to be "white."[20]

The effects of the civil voiding of marriages even found their way into otherwise unrelated criminal cases. One example is that of Frank Pass, a "man of half Indian blood," who went on trial for murder in Arizona in 1942. The major witness in the Pass trial was Frank's wife, Ruby, "a woman of Spanish and French descent," who had testified at the local trial without her husband's consent and over his objections. Frank's lawyers tried to persuade an appellate court to exclude her testimony on the ground that a wife could not testify against her husband without his consent, but the court relied on Arizona's miscegenation law to declare the marriage void, allow the testimony, and uphold the conviction.[21]

The mere possibility that miscegenation law might become an issue in any given court case, and in such a wide variety of situations, gave interracial couples reason to fear even the most routine appearance in court. Whenever this happened, it had a powerful impact on the couples themselves and ripple effects on those who read the scandalous details in newspapers. Yet it was by no means certain that miscegenation law might become an issue in any particular case. Take, for example, probate courts. In order for a probate judge to void an interracial marriage, one of the parties to an inheritance dispute had to raise the issue, and doing so required both a hard-edged lawyer and a litigant who was willing to suffer some public embarrassment. In the end, the complaining party might receive some property for his or her trouble, but inheritance cases, which got to court only after one of the partners had already died, were decidedly ex post facto means of enforcing miscegenation laws. For those who were eager to prevent the formation of interracial relationships in the first place, probate cases were just too little, too late.

The Significance of Marriage Licenses

A third method of enforcing miscegenation law, the exercise of state control over the issuance of marriage licenses, reached more couples, sooner, than either criminal prosecutions or civil court cases. There was nothing particularly new about marriage licenses, and the officials who issued them had always been required to observe the provisions of state marriage laws, which included age limits, restrictions on various kinds of kin marriage, and prohibitions on incest, bigamy, and polygamy as well as bans on interracial marriage. Before the Civil War, common-law and other unlicensed forms of marriage were so popular that licensing provisions carried little bite. By 1900, though, marriage reformers were on the verge of turning marriage licenses into the sole gateway to legal marriage and making them, as such, "the society's first line of defense against unwanted marriages." By 1931, every American state had a licensing law that required applicants to state that they were legally competent to marry, and every state designated officials to administer the process of determining a couple's fitness to marry. Because these officials were ordinarily located in county government agencies, their numbers were impressive, and their increasing control over marriage attracted considerable attention on the part of reformers.[22]

During the first three decades of the twentieth century, eugenicists, vital statisticians, and white supremacists threw themselves into the development of marriage license procedures, from somewhat different perspectives but with remarkably similar results. Displaying considerable faith in the modern administrative state, they assigned marriage license officials the task of sorting applicants into a wide, and increasing, number of categories, some racial, others physical or mental. Eugenicists, for example, set out to strengthen state control over the marriages of the physically and mentally unfit, with stunning success. By the 1930s, forty-one states would use eugenic categories to restrict the marriage of "lunatics," "imbeciles," "idiots," and the "feebleminded," and twenty-six states would restrict the marriages of those infected with syphilis and gonorrhea; by midcentury, prenuptial blood tests had become a standard legal requirement for marriage partners.[23]

While eugenicists developed the potential of marriage licensing as a form of law enforcement, bureaucrats collected information about America's vital statistics and, in the process, developed the potential of marriage licensing as a means of tracking race. Building on the racialist belief that culture, morality, and intelligence were best understood in terms of race and on the assumption that races had lives of their own, vital statisticians measured races against each other in a competition for status and survival reflected in comparative birth, death, and marriage rates. Administrative procedures race classification in marriage licenses were grafted onto earlier efforts tracking race on birth and death certificates. By the turn of the century, a growing number of state governments had established bureaus of vital statistics, which claimed supervisory power over the local officials who issued marriage licenses. In 1911, when the first National Uniform Marriage and Marriage Licensing Act was proposed, it included "color" in the list of information that should be required on every marriage license.[24] By 1931, the use of marriage licenses to track race had become so commonplace that even states such as Michigan, New York, Rhode Island, Wisconsin, and Vermont, none of which had miscegenation laws, required all marriage applicants to list their "race" or "color" on licensing forms.[25]

By the 1920s, all this activity had turned marriage license clerks into the gatekeepers of white supremacy. During that decade, there were 6,070 marriage license issuers spread across the United States, a virtual army of bureaucrats perfectly positioned to enforce state miscegenation laws.[26] The issuance of marriage licenses was, on the one hand, a seemingly minor, almost invisible, process carried out by local officials who ordinarily attracted little public attention. On the other hand, it reached deeply into the lives of ordinary citizens. The process of licensing applied to every couple who wished to marry, shepherded couples through the public ritual of obeying the law, and provided the state with the perfect opportunity to emphasize the contrast between couples who could—and could not—claim the privilege of marriage. Perhaps just as important, marriage licensing took place relatively early in a relationship, at the moment when a couple first claimed the public, consensual status of marriage.

In all these respects, marriage licensing offered a relatively comprehensive, routine means of enforcing a prohibition thought to be natural in any case, and did so well outside the glare of publicity that surrounded sensational miscegenation dramas in the public press. Moreover, if local officials did their work well, they would foster the social invisibility of interracial sex and marriage by, in effect, erasing interracial couples from national marriage statistics, reinforcing the common impression that, with or without laws to prevent them, interracial marriages were extreme rarities. As these administrative procedures began to take hold, the process of issuing marriage licenses would provide first a functional complement to and then, increasingly, a functional substitute for the rhetoric of naturality and unnaturality that had supported miscegenation law in the late nineteenth century.

In the mid-1920s, all these developments—the call for one-drop definitions of white purity, the rising popularity of eugenics, and the vital statistics campaign to track race in marriage licenses—converged in the passage of Virginia's Racial Integrity Act, which raised marriage license enforcement to new, and draconian, levels.

The Virginia Racial Integrity Act

The Virginia Racial Integrity Act owed a great deal of its impact to Walter Plecker, the state's first registrar of vital statistics.[27] A physician by training, Plecker had started a second career as a bureaucrat in 1912, when the newly formed Bureau of Vital Statistics was assigned responsibility for carrying out a vital statistics law that required, among other things, that race be recorded on every birth and death certificate issued in Virginia. The results, Plecker discovered, to his "greatest surprise and shock," revealed "the great amount of racial intermixture going on quietly and steadily, apparently unknown to the public generally and without producing any evidence of alarm to our people."[28]

In 1918, when the state legislature added marriage records to the purview of the Bureau of Vital Statistics, Plecker quickly turned his attention to enforcing Virginia's miscegenation law, which prohibited "any white person" from marrying "a colored person." He started by using the racial information recorded on birth certificates to report interracial couples to commonwealth attorneys. This practice, however, quickly ran up against the traditional gaps in the criminal enforcement of miscegenation law. As Plecker complained, little was accomplished because "none of these officers . . . had brought these cases into court." Exasperated by the foot-dragging of local police, Plecker was also unhappy that Virginia's miscegenation law, like its vital statistics law, was dependent on another state law that defined "colored" according to a blood quantum standard of one-sixteenth "negro." Plecker, who feared that it was "the deliberate purpose of persons of colored descent to be registered, if possible, as white" so as to achieve "their supreme ambition, of marrying into the white race," regarded this standard as dangerously loose.[29]

Plecker's obsession with drawing racial lines around sex and marriage linked the politics of white purity to the rising scientific authority of eugenics, which was then attracting considerable interest among modern reformers, bureaucrats, and public health advocates.[30] His pronouncements were laced with popular eugenics references to "hybrids," "inbreeding," "reversion," and "race suicide." "The variation in races," he explained in a pamphlet for high school students distributed by the Bureau of Vital Statistics, "is not simply a matter of color of skin, eyes, and hair and facial and bodily contour, but goes through every cell of the body." Eugenicists had shown that racial differences were "hereditary, carried in the germ plasm," and that in humankind as well as in the animal kingdom "the offspring of greatly different breeds are inferior to either parent." The laws of eugenics were "unquestionable scientific fact," but, Plecker warned his fellow Virginians, too many White women, some of whom were "depraved" and others "feeble-minded," were "giving birth to mulatto children." "The future of the white race and its civilization in America, and the welfare of our children," he proclaimed, "are in the keeping of this generation. Shall we rise to the situation and save our country from the terrible calamity which awaits us if we are indifferent?"[31]

Plecker was confident that Virginia's existing miscegenation law was strong enough to prevent intermarriage between "whites" and "negroes" whose physical characteristics rendered them visibly non-White. The real danger lay in the possibility that racial differences, however real and scientific they may have been, were not always visible. On every possible occasion, Plecker regaled his audiences with stories of "near-whites" who fooled their marital partners, eluded the scrutiny of county officials, or lulled or threatened their neighbors into recognizing them as "white." To Plecker's way of thinking, "near-whites" epitomized the urgency of placing a one-drop standard of white purity in Virginia's miscegenation law, for without this standard, "Many thousands of white Negroes . . . were quietly and persistently passing over the line."[32]

Determined to expose these racial imposters, Plecker developed a fiendishly bureaucratic solution to the perennial problem of proving race. He built his method on the documentary records of the state. Virginia had plenty of records at hand. During the last half of the nineteenth century, state officials had classified citizens as "white" or "colored" on birth and death certificates; the state's commissioner of revenue had kept lists of "white" and "free negro" taxpayers, and various other government agencies, including the U.S. Census Bureau and the Confederate War Department, had also collected racial data. Plecker used his position as state registrar of vital statistics to gather this precious "store of valuable information" under his control.[33]

Despite Plecker's belief in their validity, these records were far from definitive. For most of the nineteenth century, Virginia had defined "colored" according to a one-quarter blood-quantum standard that made no attempt to differentiate Indians from African Americans, making it impossible to distinguish between the two groups. Moreover, the races recorded in official records often contradicted each other, within family units as well as between different agencies. And even if the records could be believed, there had been significant gaps in the collection of racial information.[34] None of these problems stopped Plecker. His commitment to eugenics, with its emphasis on ancestry, led him to believe that the documentary record offered the possibility of ensuring white purity by pinning down even the smallest trace of non-White ancestry, freezing it in time, and carrying it forward into the present. Hoping to stave off "the evil day when this is no longer a white man's country," Plecker honed his skills at researching the old records, making himself into Virginia's official expert on the documentary tracking of race.[35]

In February 1924, the Anglo-Saxon Clubs of America, a Virginia-based white supremacist group led by Plecker's lifelong friend John Powell, offered the state legislature a proposal to tighten Virginia's miscegenation law, and Plecker threw himself into the campaign to pass the bill. The measure, which had been called "an act to preserve the integrity of the White Race" until someone with more cautious political instincts retitled it "an act to preserve Racial Integrity," was a miscegenation law with a one-drop definition of white purity. It put forth the state's first legal definition of the term "white" as a person "who has no trace whatsoever of any blood other than Caucasian" and then made it "unlawful for any white person in this State to marry any save a white person." Plecker, who hoped this definition would provide the tool he needed to thwart "negroid aspirants for admission to the white race," supported this proposal wholeheartedly. He and the Anglo-Saxon Clubs allowed for only one exception to the rule, a provision that "persons who have less than one sixty-fourth of the blood of an American Indian and have no other non-Caucasic blood shall be deemed to be white persons."[36]

The Virginia state legislature was, however, reluctant to ratchet its laws up to these standards. The legislature was caught between two forces. On the one hand, there was the growing desire of white supremacists like Plecker and the Anglo-Saxon Clubs to legislate one-drop standards of white purity. On the other, there was the long-term, undeniable history of marriage between Whites and Indians in Virginia. Virginians knew their family histories, and several of Virginia's first families proudly claimed descent from the most famous of these marriages, between John Rolfe and Pocahontas. Even Walter Plecker could see that interests as politically powerful as these would have to be accommodated, but he hoped to draw the line as narrowly as possible, at the "one-sixty-fourth of the blood of an American Indian" limit proposed in the draft bill. Much to his disappointment, however, a more cautious legislature insisted on loosening this so-called Pocahontas exception to a one-sixteenth blood quantum standard.[37]

Virginia legislators objected even more strongly to the second provision of the bill, a mandatory system of registration, under which every resident of the state would be required to file a form certifying his or her race or racial mixtures. Misrepresenting one's race on these forms, which Virginians would be required to present when applying for marriage licenses, would have been a felony offense. This plan ran into immediate trouble in the legislature, and with the public, too. A Norfolk newspaper seems to have captured the flavor of the objections. Its editor supported miscegenation laws in general, and one-drop racial standards in particular, but he complained about systematizing race in such "a bureaucratic, meddlesome way," which would "force the whole population . . . to take out passports attesting their racial composition, in order that a documentary check may be had on the 1 or 2 percent of the population so indefinitely blooded and pigmented as to need registration."[38] Walter Plecker's Bureau of Vital Statistics would have been responsible for administering this racial registration program, but Plecker seems to have shared these reservations. He was, it seems, "never at all enthusiastic" about stretching his already inadequate budget to track the racial roots of "white" as well as "colored" Virginians. The whole bill was on the edge of defeat when Plecker, who hoped to save the one-drop definition of whiteness he regarded as its "chief feature," suggested making racial registration voluntary. The compromise he engineered made it possible for the Virginia state legislature to pass the final version, known as the Virginia Racial Integrity Act, in March 1924.[39]

Administering White Purity in Virginia

Even with the Pocahontas exception and the voluntary racial registration scheme, the Virginia Racial Integrity Act was the toughest miscegenation law in the nation. The Bureau of Vital Statistics held far-reaching power to enforce it, and Walter Plecker dedicated the rest of his long professional life to doing so. He immediately set out to make the new Virginia law a model for the rest of the country. Lecturing before conventions of physicians and circulating copies of his speeches to anyone who would take them, he tried to build a network of lawmakers and public health officials who would ensure that the Virginia model "would quickly spread throughout the South and eventually throughout the northern states."[40] As part of this effort, Virginia's governor sent copies of the Virginia law to the governors of every state in the union, and Plecker tried to persuade everyone who replied that they should follow Virginia's lead. It was slow going. The U.S. Congress declined to pass the miscegenation bill Plecker recommended for Washington, D.C., and Plecker's prodding of officials in Massachusetts, Ohio, Maryland, Mississippi, Arkansas, Tennessee, and North and South Carolina produced few concrete results.[41] But in 1927, Alabama legislators, who were also influenced by eugenics, revised their miscegenation law to include a one-drop standard, and Georgia legislators agreed to a law that combined a one-drop standard with a mandatory system of racial registration.[42] To Plecker's delight, the Georgia law, which defined a "white" person as one who has "no ascertainable trace of either Negro, African, West Indian, Asiatic Indian, Mongolian, Japanese, or Chinese blood in their veins," allowed for no exceptions, and it, too, lodged considerable race definition power in the state Bureau of Vital Statistics by providing that "no person shall be deemed to be a white person any one of whose ancestors has been duly registered with the State Bureau of Vital Statistics as a colored person or person of color."[43]

Plecker's most significant impact on the history of miscegenation law came, however, not from lobbying for laws but from designing the administrative procedures to carry them out.[44] In Virginia's Bureau of Vital Statistics, Plecker was in his element. As he boasted to an Ohio congressman, "The enforcement of this law naturally falls upon our Bureau, as we have the supervision of the registration of births, deaths, marriages and divorces

Walter Plecker, head of the Virginia Bureau of Vital Statistics, and his clerks at work on Virginia's birth, marriage, and death records in 1935. (*Richmond Times-Dispatch*)

and have the legal supervision over the 6,000 midwives who have to report births; 2500 physicians, 2500 undertakers and 1300 local registrars are also under our direction."[45] Situated at the junction of miscegenation law, race definition, and the administrative state, Plecker's bureau invited, directed, and occasionally threatened all these constituencies to enforce the new law.

Plecker's enforcement campaign rested on the Vital Statistics Bureau's oversight of two key aspects of the Virginia Racial Integrity Act. The first was the law's definition of "white," which set "whites" apart from a long list of "non-Caucasic" groups, and which applied to birth and death certificates as well as marriage licenses, all of which were under the bureau's supervision. The second was the law's granting of broad, quasi-judicial powers of race classification to officials who issued marriage licenses, so that they could enforce the provision that it was "unlawful for any white person . . . to marry any save a white person." These powers were spelled out in the fourth section of the act, which provided:

> No marriage license shall be granted until the clerk or deputy clerk has reasonable assurance that the statements as to color of both man and woman are correct. If there is reasonable cause to disbelieve that applicants are of pure white race, when that fact is stated, the clerk or deputy clerk shall withhold the granting of the license until satisfactory proof is produced that both applicants are "white persons" as provided for in this act.[46]

As soon as the law went into effect, Plecker instructed marriage license clerks to take full advantage of these powers and to make "every effort to prevent the marriage of white persons with those of colored origin." His instructions brought marriage license clerks right into the thick of administrative race classification, trying to set "Negroes, Mongolians, American Indians, Asiatic Indians, Malays, and any mixture thereof" apart from "whites" while keeping the Pocahontas exception in mind.[47]

Plecker did not, however, stop there. Building on the fact that "all of our vital statistics work in registering births, deaths, marriages and divorces is based upon the color of the individuals registered," he began checking these various records against each other and "correcting" what he considered errors in racial reporting. He then circulated lists of suspicious families, arranged by surname, to county officials, warning them "to watch that they are not counted as whites."[48]

Consider, for example, the letter that Plecker sent to Mrs. Robert S. Cheatham. Cheatham was a White woman whose midwife had filled out a birth certificate listing her newborn child as "white," only to have this record

SURNAMES, BY COUNTIES AND CITIES, OF MIXED NEGROID VIRGINIA
FAMILIES STRIVING TO PASS AS "INDIAN" OR WHITE.

Albemarle:	Moon, Powell, Kidd, Pumphrey.
Amherst: (Migrants to Alleghany and Campbell)	Adcock (Adcox), Beverly (this family is now trying to evade the situation by adopting the name of Burch or Birch, which was the name of the white mother of the present adult generation), Branham, Duff, Floyd, Hamilton, Hartless, Hicks, Johns, Lawless, Nuckles (Knuckles), Painter, Ramsey, Redcross, Roberts, Southards (Suthards, Southerds, Southers), Sorrells, Terry, Tyree, Willis, Clark, Cash, Wood.
Bedford:	McVey, Maxey, Branham, Burley. (See Amherst County)
Rockbridge: (Migrants to Augusta)	Cash, Clark, Coleman, Duff, Floyd, Hartless, Hicks, Mason, Mayse (Mays), Painters, Pults, Ramsey, Southerds (Southers, Southards, Suthards), Sorrells, Terry, Tyree, Wood, Johns.
Charles City:	Collins, Dennis, Bradby, Howell, Langston, Stewart, Wynn, Adkins.
King William:	Collins, Dennis, Bradby, Howell, Langston, Stewart, Wynn, Custalow (Custaloe), Dungee, Holmes, Miles, Page, Allmond, Adams, Hawkes, Spurlock, Doggett.
New Kent:	Collins, Bradby, Stewart, Wynn, Adkins, Langston.
Henrico and Richmond City:	See Charles City, New Kent, and King William.
Caroline:	Byrd, Fortune, Nelson. (See Essex)
Essex and King and Queen:	Nelson, Fortune, Byrd, Cooper, Tate, Hammond, Brooks, Boughton, Prince, Mitchell, Robinson.
Elizabeth City & Newport News:	Stewart (descendants of Charles City families).
Halifax:	Epps (Eppes), Stewart (Stuart), Coleman, Johnson, Martin, Talley, Sheppard (Shepard), Young.
Norfolk County & Portsmouth:	Sawyer, Bass, Weaver, Locklear (Locklair), King, Bright, Porter, Ingram.
Westmoreland:	Sorrells, Worlds (or Worrell), Atwells, Gutridge, Oliff.
Greene:	Shifflett, Shiflet.
Prince William:	Tyson, Segar. (See Fauquier)
Fauquier:	Hoffman (Huffman), Riley, Colvin, Phillips. (See Prince William)
Lancaster:	Dorsey (Dawson).
Washington:	Beverly, Barlow, Thomas, Hughes, Lethcoe, Worley.
Roanoke County:	Beverly. (See Washington)
Lee and Smyth:	Collins, Gibson (Gipson), Moore, Goins, Ramsey, Delph, Bunch, Freeman, Mise, Barlow, Bolden (Bolin), Mullins, Hawkins. – Chiefly Tennessee "Melungeons."
Scott:	Dingus. (See Lee County)
Russell:	Keith, Castell, Stillwell, Meade, Proffitt. (See Lee & Tazewell)
Tazewell:	Hammed, Duncan. (See Russell)
Wise:	See Lee, Smyth, Scott, and Russell Counties.

corrected by the city health department because its clerks, who reported to Plecker, believed that "the father of the child is a negro." The point of his letter, Plecker told Cheatham, was "to give you a warning that this is a mulatto child and you cannot pass it off as white." Backed by the authority of a "new law passed by the last legislature" that "says that if a child has one drop of negro blood in it, it cannot be counted as white," Plecker spelled out the implications: "You will have to do something about this matter and see that the child is not allowed to mix with white children. It cannot go to white schools and can never marry a white person in Virginia." The next letter Plecker wrote went to Cheatham's midwife, informing her that it was "a penitentiary offense to willfully state that a child is white when it is colored" and demanding an explanation for her behavior.[49]

No matter how many employees he supervised, how many documents he corrected, or how much authority he had or was willing to claim, it was never enough to satisfy Plecker, who kept poking away at the gaps in his ability to pin down race and prevent interracial marriage. Much to his irritation, he could not seem to stop couples who married in states with looser laws from moving to Virginia. He was also exasperated that the state attorney general refused him permission to enforce the Virginia Racial Integrity Act retroactively against Virginia couples who had married before its passage.

Plecker's worst frustration, however, came when he tried to use the new law's voluntary race registration system to plug some of the holes in his documentary records. Charged with establishing the system, Plecker had mounted a campaign to persuade Virginia citizens, especially those who had been born in the period before Virginia began documenting race on birth certificates, to volunteer to register their race. A few thousand Virginians actually responded to this call, but many who volunteered were precisely the people Plecker did not want to see register. They came from communities of Virginia Indians, including the Monacan Indians of Amherst and Rockbridge counties, which had a long history of intermarriage with Whites, and at least an occasional instance of intermarriage with Blacks. And they had a racial agenda of their own, one that built on Virginia's long history of using blood-quantum laws to define both Blacks and Indians as "colored." Making astute use of the

Opposite: A list of surnames circulated by Walter Plecker in 1943 and sent to Local Registrars, Physicians, Health Officers, Nurses, School Superintendents, and Clerks of the Courts. "Please report all known or suspicious cases to the Bureau of Vital Statistics," Plecker wrote in an accompanying letter, "giving names, ages, parents, and as much other information as possible." (Papers of John Powell, MSS 7284, Special Collections, University of Virginia Library)

one-sixteenth blood-quantum definition that had been placed in the Pocahontas exception clause, they registered neither as "Indians" nor as "Negroes" but as "whites."

The actions of these "near-whites" infuriated Plecker. Fearing that as long as the Pocahontas exception was still in effect, the registration system might actually be more "dangerous" than helpful to the goal of enforcing white purity, Plecker searched through his documentary records to prove that even if there was a "slight Indian mixture" in the history of the Monacans, it had "long since been lost in the black-white tide." He soon satisfied himself that the new registrants were actually "negroes" trying to become "white" by "the 'Indian' route." Swinging his networks into action, he directed local registrars, court clerks, doctors, and midwives to "see that all persons of mixed descent in Amherst and Rockbridge Counties are correctly reported and that they be not reported as white," taking special care to remind court clerks "to use every precaution not to issue [a] marriage license for one of these people to intermarry with a person of known pure white blood."[50]

Plecker's rigidity soon met with resistance. Two couples whose applications for marriage licenses had been rejected by the Rockbridge County clerk asked a judge to overrule the clerk's decision. Both cases involved White men and women who claimed to be White and Indian, in percentages small enough to fall within the Pocahontas exception clause. Worried that the fate of his whole project might hinge on the outcome of these two cases, Plecker jumped at this chance to make an example of couples he hoped would illustrate his bold claim that "there are *no* native Virginia Indians unmixed with negro blood." Plecker traveled across the state to testify at both trials, resting his testimony on nineteenth-century state documents that listed distant ancestors of the applicants as "colored."[51]

Both trials were heard in the western Virginia county of Rockbridge by circuit court judge Henry Holt, who made it clear that he was in "cordial sympathy with the general purpose" of the Virginia Racial Integrity Act. Yet before he knew it, Holt was, as one of Virginia's Black newspapers reported with barely restrained glee, "more deeply entangled than Alice in Wonderland" trying to figure out how to enforce it. For more than two centuries, Virginia judges had subjected Blacks and Indians to blood-quantum definitions of "colored" that made no more logical sense than the white purity standards at work in this law, but Judge Holt recoiled from the possibility that White Virginians might now have to prove their claims to racial purity. Holt's reaction suggests that this possibility came too close for comfort. "In twenty-five generations," Holt protested, "one has thirty-two millions of grandfathers not to speak of grandmothers, assuming there is no intermarriage. Half the men who fought at Hastings were my grandfathers. Some of them were probably hanged and some knighted, who can tell? Certainly in some instances th was alien strain. Beyond peradventure, I cannot prove that there was not."[52]

Judge Holt's growing awareness of the impossibility of proving one-drop racial purity led him to try to limit Plecker's authority to determine race by bureaucratic fiat. In the first of the two cases, Holt expressed some reservations about the enforcement provisions of the Virginia Racial Integrity Act, but by and large he accepted Walter Plecker's documentary evidence as proof of race, and on that basis upheld the court clerk's refusal to issue a license to the couple in question. But in the second case, an even more doubtful one, Holt dug in his heels, rejected Plecker's documents, and overturned the clerk's decision to refuse the license. In his decision, he complained that the new law allowed clerks to refuse marriage licenses without taking any evidence or holding any hearings, then saddled the few couples who were bold enough to go to court for "relief" from such arbitrary decisions with the impossible burden of proving that they had "no trace whatsoever of any blood other than Caucasian, excepting those who have one sixteenth or less blood of American Indians." When a furious Walter Plecker threatened an appeal, Judge Holt made it known that he was prepared to declare the Virginia Racial Integrity Act unconstitutional if necessary, and Plecker reluctantly backed down.[53]

Judge Holt won that battle, but Walter Plecker would win the war. Both men were, in effect, playing small roles in a bigger production, the state's gradual transfer of responsibility for race classification away from the legislative and judicial branches of government and into the hands of bureaucrats. Today this power rests in the U.S. Office of Management and Budget, where it comes into public view largely in connection with recurrent debates over the racial categories used in each U.S. census. In the early twentieth century, however, the census was only one of many state projects, including the issuance of marriage licenses, the enforcement of segregation in schools and on trains, the development of immigration exclusion and deportation policies, the establishment of vital statistics bureaus, and the passage of miscegenation laws, that developed the capacity of the modern administrative state for race classification.[54] It would be decades before this process was complete, but Walter Plecker had positioned himself at the cusp of a movement that linked county bureaucrats to state and, eventually, national reporting systems.

Plecker believed that the Virginia Racial Integrity Act gave his office "the necessity of acting in a judicial, as well as in a clerical capacity, in numerous instances when the color became a question of dispute," and he had no intention of letting a local judge in a far-off county interfere. Defying Judge Holt, he issued a statement to the press that "any offspring of any member of this group will be considered negroid in the bureau of vital statistics whatever they are considered in Rockbridge county." For the next twenty years, until he retired in 1946, Walter Plecker used miscegenation law to carry out a policy that one of Virginia's later directors admitted amounted to "documentary genocide" against the Monacan Indians.[55] By then, the bureaucratic grooves of one-drop white purity were so well worn that they rarely attracted much attention. In the end, it would take until 1967—and then it would require a decision from the U.S. Supreme Court—to make Virginia relinquish its Racial Integrity Act.

Walter Plecker provides a frightening example of the extent to which a state official might go in attempting to pin down race. In bureaucratic hands like his, a one-drop definition of "white," the race science of eugenics, and the administrative state came together in ways that were all the more powerful because the procedures used to carry them out came to be taken for granted. Although there are, as yet, few studies of this phenomenon, there is reason to believe that at least a few other states developed similar procedures. In Louisiana, for example, vital statistics officials used procedures much like Plecker's well into the 1950s and 1960s. After Louisiana judges ruled that the state's miscegenation law defined the category "colored" according to a "one-drop" standard of "traceable" Negro blood, the Louisiana Bureau of Vital Statistics enforced this standard by keeping "race lists," red-flagging certain surnames, and "correcting" birth and death certificates to reflect even the smallest traces of "colored" blood.[56] Until more records of marriage license bureaus can be located, it is impossible to tell how many state and local officials tried to match Walter Plecker's zealous defense of white purity. In every state with a miscegenation law in force in this period, though, marriage license officials faced the problem of classifying applicants by race.

Just Part of the Job

If Virginia had one of the strictest miscegenation laws in the country, California had one of the mildest. Unlike Virginia, which mandated felony penalties for interracial couples who tried to marry, California's law had no criminal provisions.[57] Unlike Virginia, which specifically prohibited its residents from evading the state law by marrying in another state, California courts routinely recognized marriages that its residents made in other jurisdictions, such as Washington state or Mexico. And unlike Virginia's Racial Integrity Act, which set a one-drop standard and aimed to set Whites apart from as many other racial groups as possible, California's miscegenation law was a piecemeal statute that set no specific standard of race definition and registered some aspects of the state's structure of white supremacy while entirely ignoring others. Under its terms, California officials were forbidden to issue marriage licenses to "whites" coupled with "negroes, mulattoes, or mongolians."[58] The California legislature had, however, never bothered to name Indians in its miscegenation law, perhaps because they made up such a tiny proportion of the state's population. The law also did not mention a much larger group that was also a consistent target of western race-making venom, Mexican immigrants.

Yet California, like Virginia and every other state with a miscegenation law, required its marriage license officials to make and enforce race distinctions. In Los Angeles, where Salvador Roldan applied for his marriage license in July 1931, Leon Lampton's marriage license bureau faced racial dilemmas of its own. Los Angeles County had a population larger than many entire states, and the Los Angeles County employees who issued marriage licenses had gradually become on-the-ground experts at race classification. Beginning in 1858, California had required that "color" be recorded on every birth and death certificate issued in the state, but the formal recording of race on marriage licenses developed more slowly. From the 1870s through the turn of the century, county clerks had enforced California's miscegenation law more or less by sight, making their own determination of whether a couple did or didn't fit within the prescribed racial categories. Then, in 1907, the California state legislature, enticed by eugenics and drawn into a campaign for Japanese exclusion, amended its licensing law to forbid the issuance of marriage licenses "when either of the parties . . . is an imbecile, or insane" or "under the influence of any intoxicating liquor, or narcotic drug" and to require that the race of each applicant be recorded on every marriage license.[59]

The task of translating the racial categories entered on marriage license forms into the enforcement of miscegenation law required clerks to bring the racial power of the state into sharp, and selective, focus. During the 1920s and 1930s, the population of Los Angeles was predominantly White, but it also included a wide—and growing—range of ethnic and racial groups, among them Blacks, Indians, and immigrants from China, Japan, the Philippines, India, and Mexico. At one time or another, all these groups had been targeted by California's white supremacists, and all these groups—and more—appeared among the "races" that clerks typed in on marriage license application forms. Clerks were, however, only expected to prevent "whites" from marrying "negroes, mulattoes and mongolians." The fact that California's miscegenation law set these groups apart from all the others gives us an opportunity to see the racializing powers of California marriage license clerks in action.

Between 1924 and 1933, the Los Angeles County clerk's office issued 170,636 marriage licenses. In the early 1940s, sociologist Constantine Panunzio conducted a study of interracial marriages that examined every one of these licenses, using the races recorded on the application forms to track patterns of interracial marriage. Panunzio found that four licenses were issued to White/Black couples, one to a White/Chinese couple, and seven to White/Japanese couples. He struggled to explain how even a dozen couples "got by the license clerks," remarking that all four Blacks who married Whites had been born outside the United States and hypothesizing that the handful of Asian Americans who married Whites may have been able to do so because "in some remote part of the county a clerk may not have been informed of the law and [so] granted the license. "Whatever may have happened in those cases, though, the fact remains that marriage license clerks had followed the letter of the law in all but 12 of 170,636 cases.[60]

The range and significance of marriage license enforcement becomes even clearer if we look at Panunzio's statistics for marriages to Whites by Indians and Mexican Americans, two groups that were not mentioned in California's miscegenation law. During these same years, Los Angeles marriage license clerks issued licenses to 4,338 "white" and "Mexican" couples and 34 "white" and "American Indian" couples. If these raw numbers are rendered in a form that corrects for the population differences between groups, the gap between these two groups and those listed in California's miscegenation law is even clearer. Of every thousand marriages recorded for Los Angeles "Mexicans," 393 were marriages to "whites"; for Los Angeles "Indians," the rate of marriage to "whites" was 333 per thousand. But of every thousand marriages recorded for Los Angeles "Chinese," only 10 were with "whites"; for Los Angeles "Japanese," only 6 were with "whites," and for Los Angeles "Negroes," the rate declined even further, to .8 marriages with "whites" per thousand marriages. Each of these rates was undoubtedly the product of a whole host of factors, but their overall correspondence with California's miscegenation law seems unmistakable.[61]

These numbers can help explain what happened when Filipino men like Salvador Roldan began coming to the LA County clerk's office asking for marriage licenses. At first, during the 1920s, officials issued licenses to Filipinos without much question.[62] In the absence of systematic intervention by marriage license officials, the recorded rate of marriages between Filipinos and Whites in Los Angeles was very nearly the same as the rates of Indians and Mexican Americans with Whites. Before long, though, California nativists, appalled by this relatively high rate of intermarriage, used images of Filipino men marrying White women to exploit the rhetoric of the protection of white womanhood that had long fostered the racialization of Asian Americans in western state miscegenation laws. They argued that Filipinos, like Chinese and Japanese before them, fell under the generic category of "Mongolians." By 1930, pressure from nativists and decisions from local judges pushed Leon Lampton into rescinding his policy of allowing Filipinos to obtain licenses for marriages to Whites.[63] Lampton's change of heart prompted marriage license clerks to turn the full power of the state's racial scrutiny on Filipinos.

When Salvador Roldan went to obtain a license to marry Marjorie Rogers, the clerk put him through these racial paces. "I asked for an application blank required by law," Roldan testified, "and they asked me whether I was a Filipino and . . . also whether I was white, or yellow, or brown, or red." After Roldan told the deputy clerks that "I am a Filipino," the questioning focused on his fiancée, Marjorie Rogers, who was not present. "They asked me also whether she was an American," Roldan remembered, "and I told them that she was an English girl." The questioning continued: "They did ask me if she was white and I said 'yes.' Then they told me that I could not have a license." The end of this sad encounter shows the kind of power marriage license clerks held over applicants. "They did not tell me why," Roldan remembered, "and I didn't ask them. They merely denied me the license and I walked away."[64]

For the overwhelming number of the 170,636 couples who married in Los Angeles between 1924 and 1933, obtaining a marriage license was a minor bureaucratic procedure. But as Roldan's account suggests, for interracial couples, the denial of a license operated as a kind of public shaming ritual performed by state and local officials. In California, some of these officials went beyond the legal requirements, paying more attention to their own perceptions of skin color than to the letter of the law. In February 1930, for example, Orange County clerk J. M. Backs refused a license to Piare S. Dail, "a swarthy-skinned keen-featured son of an Indian ruler," because "the would-be bridegroom was not a member of the white race, while his proposed bride was." Although Dail and his fiancée returned to the office "reinforced by friends" who spoke on their behalf, Backs turned the couple away twice in less than a week. Orange County Santa Ana clerks also refused to issue the license for a Filipino man to marry "a girl who said she was a Filipino, but whose father was born in Illinois" on the ground that "the bride failed to bring proper proof that she was a Filipino, to prove the proposed wedding would not break the State law forbidding the intermarriage of races." On a slow news day, stories like these would make the pages of the *Los Angeles Times,* which kept an eye on marriage licensing in other states as well. For example, the *Times* carried a story about Antonio Biggs, a "negro," Cecil

Robinson, a "white girl," and Spokane, Washington's acting county auditor, a Mr. Glover, who refused them a marriage license. Washington had no miscegenation law, but Glover claimed that "[I have] the right to ascertain whether the mentality of applicants for marriage licenses is sound, and I can but question the acts of a white woman that will marry a negro."[65]

There were ways to avoid this kind of humiliation. Applicants could, of course, claim to be whatever race the law required. Although the Orange County "girl who said she was Filipino" failed to pass muster with the clerk she encountered, some of these claims were accepted by local officials. Couples with enough resources could, and often did, travel to states with less stringent miscegenation laws, or no laws at all, in search of officials who would place fewer roadblocks in their way. Antonio Biggs, for example, described Glover's refusal to issue him a marriage license "an outrage" and vowed to go to another county for a license.[66] But both of these strategies required more knowledge, resources, and preparation than most young couples could muster, and even those who succeeded in evading the laws learned, through the process of doing so, that their home states were determined to prevent them from marrying.

In states with miscegenation laws on the books, interracial couples who appeared at their local marriage license offices faced reactions that were, no doubt, as various as the clerks themselves. Like Virginia's Walter Plecker, some officials welcomed every opportunity to deliver a lecture on the dire consequences of interracial marriage, while others may have been nearly as uncomfortable and embarrassed as the applicants they faced. But whatever the clerks might think, their job required them to reject ineligible applicants, and that was exactly what happened to Salvador Roldan.

Racial Rights

In many cases, perhaps most, the incident would have ended right there. But Los Angeles Filipinos had for nearly a decade been allowed to marry White women, and Filipino men, like their white supremacist opponents, regarded the racial distinctions drawn in marriage licenses as a litmus test of their rights. Salvador Roldan may not have argued with the marriage license clerks, but he did consult a lawyer. The lawyer he selected, a White woman named Gladys Towles Root, was fresh out of law school and had been in practice for less than a year, but she, too, was aware that the issue of intermarriage resonated very deeply among Filipinos in Los Angeles. A few months earlier, Filipino leader Pablo Manlapit had persuaded her to defend another Filipino man,

Gavino Visco, whose plan to marry Ruth Salas had also run into roadblocks in the county clerk's office. That trial, which Root won by persuading a superior court judge that Salas was a "Mexican Indian" woman rather than a "white" woman, had attracted considerable attention in the local Filipino press.[67]

By the time the *Roldan* case was heard in court, all parties regarded it as an important test case, from the couple, Salvador Roldan and Marjorie Rogers, to their lawyer Gladys Root and their supporter Pablo Manlapit to Los Angeles County clerk Leon Lampton, Los Angeles deputy county counsel S.V.O. Prichard, and State Attorney General U.S. Webb.[68] In accordance with the imperative of race classification developed in the courts, both sides agreed that the *Roldan* case hinged on the single question of whether Filipinos fit into the racial category of "Mongolian," and both sides professed to regard finding the proper race classification as a question of fact rather than a matter of law. Of course, the process of determining the fact of race in a courtroom left plenty of room for argument.

Gladys Towles Root had just begun to build what would turn out to be one of California's more spectacular criminal defense practices. An inch short of six feet tall and splashily self-confident, Root was eager to challenge the hidebound prejudice of public opinion by bringing the facts of scientific and social scientific research to bear on her cases. In the *Roldan* case, which was heard without a jury in both the local and appellate courts, she used these skills to persuade California judges that "a Filipino is *not* ethnologically, historically or legally a Mongolian."[69]

Root knew that she faced tough opposition from California's guardians of white purity, whose campaign for Filipino exclusion was headline news in California. Worried that judges, like other officials, might give in to their demands, Root looked for something a court could hold on to. She found it by reaching deep into the realm of race science. Eschewing the modern science of eugenics, which was nearly as popular in California as in Virginia, Root chose a form of race science with an aura of longtime legitimacy she hoped would stiffen the spines of judges as well as allow her to defend Filipinos. Accordingly, she based her case on eighteenth-century German naturalist Johannes Blumenbach's widely influential division of the races of man into five pure varieties, "Caucasian, Ethiopian, American, Mongolian, and Malay." In Blumenbach's scheme, Japanese and Chinese were classified as "Mongolians," but Filipinos were classified as "Malays." Root argued that the California state legislators who had inserted the term "Mongolian" into the state's miscegenation law in 1880 would have been familiar with Blumenbach's five-part classification and would have used the term "Mongolian" to mean only Chinese and Japanese. If they had wanted to include Filipinos

Lawyer Gladys Towles Root in 1932. (*Herald Examiner* Collection, Los Angeles Public Library)

within the ban on marriage to Whites, she insisted, they would have used the term "Malay" to do so. In this manner, Root substituted the positive assertion that Filipinos were "Malays" for the negative assertion that Filipinos were *not* "Mongolians," offering judges a chance to reject what she called the contemporary "propaganda" of anti-Filipino "labor leaders and agitators" by buttressing legislative intent with the authority of race science.[70]

In so doing, however, Root had opened the Pandora's box of scientific race classification. The ongoing multiplication of scientific classifications and subclassifications of race allowed Root's opponents, the lawyers for Los Angeles County, plenty of room to build an equally scientific defense for county clerk Leon Lampton. Well aware that for more than a century, race science had nurtured white supremacy, Lampton's defenders welcomed Root's reliance on race science as a source of authority. They quarreled with her, and with each other, only about which race scientist to choose. Claiming that Blumenbach's system of race classification had long since been surpassed by newer, better alternatives, Los Angeles County rested its case on ethnologist T H. Huxley, who had gathered "Malays" under the classificatory umbrella of something called the "Mongoloid" group. County lawyers, explaining to the court that the category "Mongoloid" referred to a general set of physical features that characterized a number of subgroups, including those of "Malays," argued that "the word 'Mongolian' was used in a generic sense and is equivalent to 'Mongoloid.'" So county lawyers insisted that the California legislators who put the term "Mongolian" in the state miscegenation law meant that "no person having the physical and racial characteristics of a Mongolian shall marry a white whether he is a Mongolian in a strict ethnological sense or not." The state attorney general, Ulysses S. Webb, a proud architect of California's anti-Japanese laws, agreed with this conclusion. He, however, rested his case on yet another ethnologist, Ales Hrdlicka, whom he described as "probably the best known and ablest anthropologist in the United States," citing Hrdlicka's 1922 testimony to Congress to the effect that Filipinos, Malays, Chinese, Koreans, Japanese, Mongols, and Siberians "all belong to the yellow-brown or *mongoloid* race."[71]

With all sides citing their own race scientist, each with his own system of classification, the briefs quickly turned into a debate about which scientist had been most influential, when, and to whom. Which classification did California state legislators rely on in 1880, at the height of California's anti-Chinese crusade, when they had added the word "Mongolian" to California's miscegenation law? Which classification did legislators rely on in 1905, at the height of California's anti-Japanese crusade, when they had added the word "Mongolian" to another section of the miscegenation law? Which classification might legislators have learned in California schoolbooks, or found if they looked for guidance in dictionaries, or encyclopedias, and, again, when? As the California attorney general would later ruefully note, "a court may find much in the evidence adduced in support of either contention to justify whatever conclusion it may reach."[72]

In the end, though, Gladys Root won her case. In April 1932, superior court judge Henry Gates ruled that Salvador Roldan was a "Malay," not a "Mongolian," and ordered Leon Lampton to issue him a license to marry Marjorie Rogers. On January 27, 1933, Justice Thomas Archbald sustained Gates when he issued the unanimous decision of the three justices of the California District Court of Appeal. Archbald agreed with Root that of all the classifications offered to the court, Blumenbach's had been the most influential. Still, he, too, had glimpsed the Pandora's box of possibilities race science had to offer, and he tried to close the lid on it by shifting the basis for the court's decision from scientific authority to popular race-making of the sort that had sustained the expansion of miscegenation law for the last half century. Courts, Archbald asserted, should pay less attention to "scientific thought" than to "the common use of the word 'Mongolian' in California at the time of the enactment of the legislation." Working his way through the debates of the notoriously anti-Chinese constitutional convention held in California in 1878 and other similar documents, Archbald concluded that when legislative leaders of that period used "the terms 'Asiatics,' 'Coolies' and 'Mongolians,'" they meant "Chinese."[73]

Meanwhile, in the 1920s and 1930s, the Los Angeles Filipinos who supported Salvador Roldan were indulging in some race-making of their own. As part of their campaign to challenge white supremacy, they displayed considerable, and evidently heartfelt, pride in the notion that Filipinos were, indeed, "Malays." The *Roldan* case marked the fourth time in three years that the racial classification of Filipinos had been an issue in Los Angeles superior courts, and by the time it got to court, the Filipino newspaper *The Three Stars* had concluded that the dispute was about much more than "the aspect of whether Filipinos can marry American girls." Rather, it was about "racial right." If Salvador Roldan did not succeed in marrying Marjorie Rogers, its readers were told, "Filipinos are apt to lose their identity as Malay or brown race." Ratcheting up its rhetoric, its editor introduced his readers to race scientists who stated that Filipinos had been "their own distinct race for centuries," then declared that "they cherish it—they have been developed and identified with it—fought and died for it. They are—if you please, A MALAY or BROWN RACE and PROUD OF IT."[74]

The decision in the *Roldan* case endorsed their claims that Filipinos were "Malays" and that, as "Malays," Filipinos could not be subjected to the provisions of a miscegenation law that targeted "Mongolians." Salvador Roldan was able to return to the county clerk's office, secure a license, and marry Marjorie Rogers on April 10, 1933. The couple, who eventually had three children, lived together until Roldan's death in 1975. Gladys Root moved on to defending clients charged with other forms of "unnatural" behavior, using psychiatric evidence to defend men accused of homosexuality and defending clients accused of sex crimes such as rape and prostitution, until she could claim to have "fought and won more sex cases than any lawyer in the United States." Regarding it as the most significant victory of her long career, she believed, to her dying day, that the *Roldan* case had made it possible for Filipinos to marry Whites in California.[75]

But there was more to the story than that, for Gladys Root's seeming victory played right into the dynamics that had structured the development and expansion of miscegenation laws from the 1880s through the 1930s.

Once Filipinos had been legally classified as "Malays," California legislators could add this new classification to the state's miscegenation law, and that is just what they did.[76] In January 1933, a few days before Justice Archbald issued his decision in the *Roldan* case, State Senator H. C. Jones introduced two bills designed to add "Malays" to California's miscegenation law.[77] On March 27, a deeply divided California Supreme Court refused, twice, to hear the county's appeal to the *Roldan* decision.[78] Three days later, the California legislature passed both bills, and the governor signed them soon after.[79] The first declared all marriages celebrated in California between "white persons" and "members of the Malay race," presumably including the Roldan marriage, "illegal and void."[80] The second specifically forbade California county clerks from issuing marriage licenses to "white persons" and "a member of the Malay race."[81] So in this convoluted but nonetheless powerful manner, Leon Lampton's confusion was cleared up, and the imperative of race classification stood firm. Salvador Roldan had won his case, gotten his license, and held his ceremony, but in the eyes of the law, his marriage was "illegal and void" and would remain so as long as California's newest miscegenation law remained on the books.

Part III

Miscegenation Law and Its Opponents, 1913–1967

Chapter Six

BETWEEN A ROCK AND A HARD PLACE

"This winter will see a determined attempt to insult and degrade us by such non-intermarriage laws. We must kill them, not because we are anxious to marry white men's sisters, but because we are determined that white men shall let our sisters alone."

—*W.E.B. Du Bois, 1913*

NEW YORK CITY, NEW YORK

From its headquarters in New York City, the National Association for the Advancement of Colored People (NAACP) kept a wary eye on the progress of miscegenation law. As the laws began to blanket western states, each passing year brought new cause for concern. In 1909, the year the NAACP was founded, Montana, North Dakota, and South Dakota enacted their first miscegenation laws and Missouri added "Mongolians" to its existing statute. In 1911, Nevada replaced a law from the Civil War era with a broader prohibition on the marriage of "any person of the Caucasian or white race" with "any person of the Ethiopian or black race, Malay or brown race, Mongolian or yellow race, or the American Indian or red race."[1]

And it was not only western states that worried the NAACP. In Illinois and Michigan, legislators had proposed banning marriages between "Whites or Caucasians" and any "African, Chinese or Japanese."[2] Even New York, which had not prohibited interracial marriage since the Dutch colonial period, considered a law that would have declared marriages between "a white or Caucasian person and person of the negro or black race" to be "incestuous and void."[3] Fortunately for the NAACP, none of these plans attracted much support, not, that is, until Jack Johnson married Lucille Cameron and all hell broke loose.

Prizefighter Jack Johnson was a Black man, and not just any Black man. In July 1910, Johnson had beaten White boxer Jim Jeffries, the so-called Great White Hope, in a heavyweight title bout billed as a national contest for racial superiority. Johnson's victory, which touched off riots in several cities, made him, overnight, the nation's most powerful symbol of black manhood.[4] Idolized by triumphant Blacks and reviled by crestfallen Whites, Jack Johnson soon became as notorious for his escapades with White women as for his audacity in the boxing ring. In 1911, he married White society woman Etta Duryea and settled in Chicago, where he opened an interracial nightclub he called the Café de Champion. The marriage was not a happy one. Johnson continued to see other women, and Etta grew depressed and complained that she was treated like a "social outcast."[5] On occasion Johnson resorted to his famous fists, once beating Etta so badly that she was admitted to the hospital. The finale came in September 1912, when a despondent Etta shot herself in the head. Newspapers used Etta's suicide to pontificate on the folly of interracial marriage; the *New York Times,* for example, sniffed that Johnson's "venture in miscegenation has come to an end [only] a little more dreadful than was confidently to be expected from such a violation of the social proprieties."[6] Etta made the point more directly. "All of my misery," reporters quoted her as telling a close friend shortly before she died, "comes through marrying a black man."[7]

Even before Etta's suicide, Johnson had become involved with another White woman, eighteen-year-old Lucille Cameron. The teenaged Cameron made her living as a prostitute. Originally from Minneapolis, she had relocated to Chicago, where two of the "sporting women" who kept Johnson supplied with female companions introduced her to the boxing champion. Cameron claimed that she fell in love with Johnson at first sight, and for a few months, the romance proceeded smoothly enough. But when Lucille's mother, Mrs. Cameron-Falconet, learned of the match, she and her lawyer raced to Chicago to put a stop to it. "I would," Mrs. Cameron-Falconet told reporters, "rather see my daughter spend the rest of her life in an insane asylum than see her the plaything of a nigger."[8] Lucille flatly refused to give up her lover, so Cameron-Falconet went to the police, who arrested Johnson and charged him with abduction. As Chicago was in the midst of a moral panic over "white slavery," these charges fell on receptive ears. Accustomed to the clichés of miscegenation dramas, journalists paid little attention to the facts of the story; they quickly cast Jack Johnson as a symbol of dangerously predatory black male sexuality and Lucille Cameron as the picture of innocent white womanhood. Angry Whites followed Johnson around Chicago, threatening to lynch him, while Black newspaper editors lamented the seemingly indefensible behavior of a man they had once admired. Even the NAACP's magazine, the *Crisis*, understood that "the Southern white press has quite lost its head on the matter, and . . . many colored people have joined in the hue and cry."[9]

Zealous prosecutors, itching for a chance to make a public example of a man they despised, laid plans to charge Jack Johnson with additional offenses under the Mann Act, a federal law designed to eradicate "white slavery" by punishing men who took women across state lines for immoral purposes. The only thing that stood in their way was Lucille Cameron, who insisted that Jack Johnson had never taken her anywhere, or done anything, against her will. The story Lucille told was simple and consistent: as one investigator told his frustrated superior, she declared "in every breath that she loved [Jack Johnson], wanted to marry him, and would do so immediately on being given the opportunity."[10] The people holding Lucille against her will were government investigators, who placed her in custody after she declined to testify along the lines they set out for her. Lucille's refusal to cooperate left the abduction case in tatters and threatened to sink the Mann Act trial, too. Unable to shake her story, federal agents scoured the region for a White woman more willing to testify. Eventually they located another of Johnson's paramours, Belle Schreiber, who agreed to tell her story before a Chicago grand jury. Once Schreiber was in their corner, federal agents released Lucille Cameron, who went straight to Jack Johnson. Less than three months had elapsed since Etta Johnson had committed suicide, and the boxing legend was out on bail awaiting trial on the Schreiber charges. Yet Johnson, who had always been the kind of man who threw caution to the winds, announced to a *New York Times* reporter that "he would marry Miss Lucille Cameron before the end of the week."[11]

Jack Johnson and Lucille Cameron were married on December 4, 1912, at Johnson's mother's Chicago home, before a group of Black and White guests. Outside, police kept a thousand or so sensation seekers at bay; in truth, the whole country was watching.[12] In the barrage of nationwide publicity that ensued, the Johnson scandal was dissected by Black newspaper editors as well as angry white supremacists, by men on the street as well as members of the U.S. Congress.

Furious federal prosecutors made no bones about their opinion of the happy couple. As one of them later explained, Jack Johnson had become the nation's "foremost example of the evil in permitting the intermarriage of whites and blacks."[13] When news of the marriage broke, a nationwide

The wedding of Jack Johnson and Lucille Cameron. Johnson's mother, Tiny, stands at the far right. (No. 164211, Record Group 60, Records of the Department of Justice, NARA, College Park, Maryland)

conference of state governors was meeting in Richmond, Virginia; their condemnation of Johnson was immediate and wide-ranging. Governor Cole Blease of South Carolina bragged that "the boasted hero of the black race, who claims to be the superior of the white man in the ring, could not disgrace South Carolina by having himself united to a white woman within its borders," then defended lynching as the best method of dealing with "black brutes."[14] Most of the assembled governors recoiled at Blease's advocacy of lynching, but they agreed with him on the necessity of miscegenation laws. "The Johnson marriage would never have been allowed in Maryland," that state's governor declared. "We protect our white girls." The governor of Utah referred to interracial marriage as "one of the most disgraceful crimes of modern times." Not to be outdone, the governors of New York, Ohio, Connecticut, Massachusetts, and Pennsylvania, northern states with no miscegenation laws on their books, proclaimed their willingness to enact them. As Governor John Tener of Pennsylvania declared, "Any law to prevent the mixture of races of different colors has my hearty approval."[15]

Back at NAACP headquarters, W.E.B. Du Bois, the group's most promi-nent Black official and the editor of the *Crisis*, tried to put a damper on the growing scandal. Worried that Cole Blease and Jack Johnson had become "the two most talked of persons in the United States," Du Bois reminded the readers of the *Crisis* that "no matter how bad a man Johnson may be—and he is bad undoubtedly . . . he is entitled to his rights under laws impar-tially administered."[16] But by this time, the scandal had spread to the U.S. House of Representatives, where Georgia congressman Seaborn Roddenbery introduced a constitutional amendment providing that marriage between "negroes or persons of color and Caucasians" would be "forever prohibited" anywhere in the "United States or any territory under their jurisdiction."[17] A constitutional amendment was needed, Roddenbery insisted, so that errant northern states like Jack Johnson's Illinois could be pressed into line with the rest of the country. "No brutality, no infamy, no degradation in all the years of southern slavery," Roddenbery fumed, "possessed such villainous character and such atrocious qualities as the provision of the laws of Illinois, New York, Massachusetts and other States which allow the marriage of the negro, Jack Johnson, to a woman of the Caucasian strain."[18]

While the Roddenbery amendment awaited action by the House Commit-tee on the Judiciary, Congress took up a miscegenation law that would have covered Washington, D.C., a city that was regarded as something of a national bellwether and was also home to the largest urban population of Blacks in the United States. White supremacists had often complained that the District of Columbia, which was governed by Congress, fell between the cracks of mis-cegenation laws in the surrounding states of Maryland and Virginia, and they made the most of the furor over the Johnson-Cameron wedding. In February 1913, the D.C. proposal passed the House of Representatives, without debate, by a vote of 90–8.[19]

By then, state legislatures were in session, and NAACP officials could see the full extent of the damage. In addition to the D.C. bill and Roddenbery's constitutional amendment, miscegenation laws had been introduced in eleven of the last nineteen states without such laws in effect. Proposals had appeared in far western states like Washington, Wyoming, and Kansas as well as in midwestern states like Minnesota, Wisconsin, Michigan, and Iowa. Most ominous of all were the laws proposed in Ohio, Illinois, Pennsylvania, and New York, the four northern states with the largest Black populations.[20]

In February 1913, the NAACP was only three years old. Despite its ambi-tious plans to launch its New York base into a national program, it had only just begun to recruit members, build branches, and choose priorities.[21] But the Jack Johnson scandal—and the rash of miscegenation laws introduced in

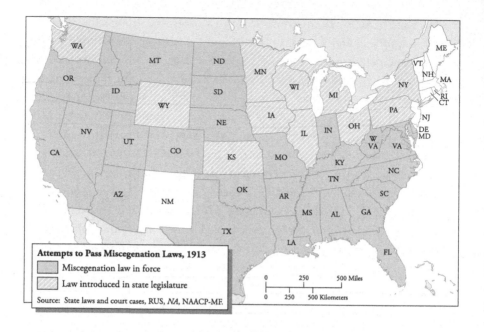

Attempts to Pass Miscegenation Laws, 1913

Miscegenation law in force

Law introduced in state legislature

Source: State laws and court cases, RUS, *NA*, NAACP-MF.

its wake—made this a defining moment: Could the NAACP stop this legislative juggernaut? And should it?

Drawing the Line

For African Americans, interracial sex and marriage were, as David Levering Lewis has so aptly put it, "deadly delicate" issues. In public, at least, no one defended interracial sex, and most Blacks found plenty of reason to avoid the subject of interracial marriage. The right to marry across racial lines rarely seemed as important as challenging racial discrimination in jobs, housing, or political rights. Consciously or unconsciously, most Blacks preferred to marry among themselves. Like Whites, many Blacks, including NAACP spokesman Kelley Miller, assumed that in-group marriage was "the natural course of things." Even those who did not take in-group marriage for granted might see it as necessary to ensuring the future of African America. In any case, the question was largely out of their hands, for in most of the nation miscegenation law reigned supreme, and just behind the law hovered the vicious specter of lynching. For all these reasons, southern Black leaders like Booker T. Washington had long since concluded that progress for Blacks depended on denying that they had any interest in what was euphemistically referred to as "social equality."[22]

The NAACP, however, was the brainchild of an interracial group of activists who regarded Booker T. Washington's reluctance to push the boundaries of equality as an unacceptable accommodation to the forces of segregation. As W.E.B. Du Bois saw it, a cautious approach to "social equality" was one of the evils the NAACP existed to overcome. As early as 1910, Du Bois made his opposition to miscegenation laws crystal clear. "I believe," he wrote in an article published in the reform journal *The Independent*, "that the mingling of blood between white and black and yellow races is neither 'unnatural' or physical deleterious. . . . I believe that all so-called 'laws against intermarriage' are simply wicked devices to make the seduction of women easy and without penalty, and should be forthwith repealed."[23]

Yet the NAACP had reasons of its own to avoid the subject of interracial marriage. In its early years, the NAACP's national committee was dominated and financed by White reformers whose plans for advancing racial equality depended on catering to the social sensibilities of relatively conservative White donors. And its long-term plans for building a mass membership depended on appealing to middle-class and professional people, Black and White, whose claims to respectability required distancing themselves from the stigma of immorality and illegitimacy produced by the sexualization of miscegenation law. During the first few years of its existence, then, the NAACP treated Du Bois's outburst as a statement of individual opinion; the organization itself was careful to say as little as possible about interracial marriage. If the NAACP had been left to its own devices, there is no telling how long it might have soft-pedaled the issue.[24]

But the Jack Johnson scandal left the NAACP between a rock and hard place: if it maintained the cautious silence most of its officers and members would have preferred, it might soon find the nation's capital—and two-thirds of the North—under the reign of miscegenation law. That would have been a catastrophe for the NAACP, which planned to build its political future on the slippery legal rights Black voters had struggled to secure in northern states.[25] The fact that most northern states had no miscegenation laws was itself a testament to decades of lobbying by African Americans. During the half century between the Civil War and the Progressive era, when miscegenation laws had marched across the rest of the nation, African Americans in several states of the Old Northwest had gradually persuaded their legislatures to shelve laws against interracial marriages passed before the Civil War.[26] Illinois had repealed its law in 1874, and Michigan had done so in 1883.[27] In Ohio, repeal took most of a decade to secure: the first attempt was sponsored by a Black legislator in 1880, and there was a second failed attempt in 1884, before another Black legislator introduced the bill that finally repealed the statute in 1887.[28]

By 1890, miscegenation law had, it seemed, become a thing of the past New England and the Old Northwest, too, except for the state of Indiana. ....iana Blacks had tried four times, in 1873, 1875, 1885, and 1895, to repeal their state statute, but the law remained on the books.[29] And in 1913, it seemed possible that Indiana might be joined by Illinois, Iowa, Michigan, Minnesota, New York, Ohio, Pennsylvania, and Wisconsin.

So when the Jack Johnson scandal made equivocation seem nearly as risky as speaking out, the NAACP drew a line in the sand. Gathering together a list of reasons, "physical, social, and moral," why miscegenation laws should be opposed, W.E.B. Du Bois called his troops into battle. "Note these arguments, my brothers and sisters," he commanded in an editorial in the *Crisis,* "and watch your State legislatures. This winter will see a determined attempt to insult and degrade us by such non-intermarriage laws. We must kill them, not because we are anxious to marry white men's sisters, but because we are determined that white men shall let our sisters alone."[30]

Carrying this banner, NAACP branches rallied to the cause, scrambling to defeat miscegenation laws in state legislatures. In Topeka, Kansas, a

W.E.B. Du Bois in the *Crisis* office. (Photographs and Prints Division, Schomburg Center for Research in Black Culture, The New York Public Library, Astor, Lenox and Tilden Foundations)

brand-new branch began lobbying against the "obnoxious Kansas Separate Marriage Bill" before it even elected its first officers. "Its passage in Kansas we fear would have been followed by a like disaster throughout the nation," the branch secretary reported to the national office in New York. "It was to avert such a national calamity that we put forth our most strenuous efforts."[31] In Detroit, Michigan, too, the NAACP branch took credit for having "killed" a bill to prohibit the marriage of "Whites or Caucasians" and any "African, Chinese, or Japanese."[32] In New York, the proposed law contained an especially vicious clause that listed "sterilization" among the possible range of punishments for convicted defendants.[33] To kill that bill, New York NAACPers enlisted, among others, the Cosmopolitan Club, a radically interracial social group, which fired off a "vigorous protest" on behalf of "marital freedom of choice" to Democratic state senator Franklin Delano Roosevelt, who quietly assured them that "this is not a matter of sufficient practical importance in this State to warrant legislation of this kind."[34] The toughest battle came in Ohio, where a bill that would have covered the marriage and cohabitation of "white persons with Negroes, mulattos . . . or Chinamen" had passed the Ohio house on second reading.[35] It took the combined efforts of the local NAACP, working through attorneys Harry Davis and Charles Chesnutt, the Douglass Men's Club, and the Cleveland Association of Colored Men, along with a local Catholic newspaper editor and the mayor of Cleveland, to defeat to defeat the Ohio bill on its third and final vote.[36]

The NAACP was so determined to defeat miscegenation laws that it even interceded in states where it had, as yet, no functioning branches. When the NAACP's New York City headquarters heard that California, which already had a miscegenation law on its books, was considering passing yet another one, they fired off an official protest to the state legislature. In Wisconsin, where the Booker T. Washington Men's League of Milwaukee had already united behind a Black former state legislator to oppose that state's bill, one league member "got his feelings hurt because he thought that organization was not receiving sufficient credit" after the national NAACP insisted on distributing copies of Du Bois's *Crisis* editorial and lodging their own protest against the bill. When Washington state lawmakers rejected one of the nine miscegenation laws that body considered between 1911 and 1939, NAACP officers congratulated the attorney they believed was responsible for its defeat, then tutored him on the "position of the National Association in this matter." The letter explained that "in states where such a law exists, its only result is to degrade the women of the defenseless colored race. . . . The passage of such a law invariably means the introduction of other measures designed to reduce the colored man to a condition of caste inferiority which is in many respects more galling and unbearable than the slavery which this country attempted to abolish fifty years ago."[37]

The NAACP's assault on miscegenation law was remarkably brave, its scale entirely unprecedented. At the end of the 1913 legislative season, the NAACP declared the campaign a success, and, although this claim proved premature, the results had, in fact, far exceeded expectations. At the outset, several of the NAACP's White leaders, like Joel Springarn, had counseled caution, warning that "too much publicity might crystallize unconscious desires that had never been self-conscious before, and then *the deluge!*" But in the end, the NAACP had a perfect scorecard: none of the miscegenation laws it lobbied against, not even the D.C. bill that had initially received so many votes in the House of Representatives, was enacted. Skeptics might claim that the failure of these bills owed less to the efforts of the NAACP than to the relatively small numbers of African Americans in northern states. Certainly the small size of the northern Black population helped sympathetic legislators like Franklin Roosevelt conclude that interracial marriages were too infrequent to register as any kind of social problem. But the NAACP knew that when it came to interracial marriage, all it took to ignite a national scandal was one case like Jack Johnson's. Executive Secretary May Childs Nerney was sure the results spoke for themselves. As she boasted to NAACP correspondents, "This Association had much to do with killing all the anti-intermarriage bills which came up immediately after the Jack Johnson episode."[38]

And the NAACP was not done yet, for these bills refused to stay dead. From 1913 through 1929, wave after wave of proposals for miscegenation laws swept through northern states and the District of Columbia. The NAACP met every attempt with firm resistance, mounting at least twenty-nine separate campaigns in northern state legislatures, and lobbying against fourteen proposals for laws designed to cover Washington, D.C. In 1916, when five separate D.C. bills were introduced in Congress, the NAACP managed to obtain a public hearing before the House Committee on the District of Columbia. The hearing was nearly a fiasco. Most of the southern congressmen on the committee boycotted the event, and the one who did show up stayed only long enough to complain about the presence of "a lot of niggers and mongrels" before walking out. By the time the testimony began, only one committee member, George Holden Tinkham of Massachusetts, remained. Yet even under these humiliating conditions, the NAACP delegation, which included Archibald Grimké, Kelley Miller, George W. Cook, Whitfield McKinley, and James A. Cobb, took a valiant stand against miscegenation law.[39]

In the end, it took nearly two decades for the NAACP to defeat enough miscegenation laws to feel able to relax its vigilance. By 1930, however, it had succeeded in bringing the introduction of new miscegenation laws in northern states to a virtual halt. Except for Indiana, which kept its law on the books until 1965, the North would remain outside the regime of miscegenation law.

Opposing the Laws Without Endorsing the Practice

The success of the NAACP's campaign owed a great deal to the political savvy of the NAACP officials who developed the arguments the group presented, over and over again, to state and federal legislators. In building their case, they borrowed from earlier attempts to defeat miscegenation laws. They quoted antebellum abolitionists in Massachusetts, developed lines of reasoning set forth by Black and White Reconstruction-era radicals, and recycled the statements of late nineteenth-century Black lobbyists in northern state legislatures. In retooling these arguments to fit new conditions, NAACP officials made the first sustained attempt to develop an ideological toolkit that might be used to oppose and, eventually, to dismantle miscegenation laws.

This toolkit had three rhetorical hammers: an attack on the "nature" of Black racial inferiority; a plea for marital freedom of choice, and a critique of the sexualization of miscegenation law. The first of these arguments, the critique of biological racial inferiority, was the simplest. In 1913, when W.E.B. Du Bois wrote his first *Crisis* editorial about racial intermarriage, he tried to state this point as clearly as possible: the very existence of miscegenation laws, he asserted, suggested "that black blood is a physical taint—a thing that no decent, self-respecting black man can be asked to admit." In hopes of discrediting these naturalized notions of Black inferiority, Du Bois kept a close eye on the progress of race science, ridiculing the presumptions of old-fashioned racialists and newfangled eugenicists while publicizing the emerging ideas of culturalists. Thus the second issue of the *Crisis,* issued in December 1910, opened with Franz Boas's article on "The Real Race Problem," which defended "mulattoes" from charges of biological inferiority and argued that racial differences were "differences in kind, not in value." A few months later, Du Bois used a report on the First Universal Congress of the Races to emphasize two key principles of the emerging culturalist consensus. First, Du Bois insisted, "It is not legitimate to argue from differences in physical characteristics to differences in mental characteristics," and, second, "The civilization of a people or race at any particular moment of time offers no index to its innate or inherited capacities."[40]

The NAACP occasionally pushed this argument far enough to claim that race was, ultimately, an illusion. In 1912, for example, the *Crisis* reported on a "recent" scientific "pronouncement on racial intermixture": "If you were to take a hundred men of half a dozen different races," it announced gleefully, "shave their heads and color them all dead black, it would be impossible even for an expert to pick them out correctly. In 75 per cent of the cases you could not tell to what race they belonged." In tracking "The Vagaries of Prejudice," the *Crisis* reported on cases of White men who sought to annul their marriages to women they accused having "Negro blood" and on a Kentucky contractor who "married a colored woman" but later learned "that he is white." The *Crisis* also ridiculed White officials who believed they could pin down even the smallest "trace" of "black blood." Yet the NAACP generally stopped short of rejecting the idea of race even as it rejected the structures of racism. To men and women who lived race as a daily identity, the notion that race was nothing more than an illusion was personally disconcerting; it was also politically perilous, because, as historian Mia Bay explains, "it called into question the very basis of black unity."[41]

This did not, however, prevent the NAACP from attacking the notion of "natural" race inferiority. In the hope that legislators would be swayed by the expertise of academic authorities, the NAACP took care to include social scientists in the delegations they sent to persuade lawmakers to reject miscegenation laws. One of the featured speakers at the 1916 congressional hearings on a law for the District of Columbia was Black sociologist Kelley Miller, who was well known for his critiques of racialist ethnology. In 1925, when Ohio attorney Harry Davis put together a coalition to defeat a proposed law in that state, he included a local professor of sociology and his students. By 1939, the lines of communication between the NAACP and social scientists were so well-established that when White anthropologist Melville Jacobs learned that a miscegenation law had been introduced in the Washington state legislature, he contacted the NAACP, which promptly provided him with all the information he needed to make a case against the measure.[42]

The NAACP's second argument against miscegenation laws—that they restricted marital freedom of choice—was, as it turned out, harder to use effectively with legislators. This may seem odd, for the notion that marriage should be considered an individual choice, one associated with the liberties of free men and the privileges of citizenship, had a long and influential history. Freedom of choice had long been a staple of White men's political discourse, and it had been applied to the issue of interracial marriage as early as 1843, when White abolitionist William Lloyd Garrison of Massachusetts used it in the first successful campaign to repeal a state law prohibiting interracial marriage. Furthermore, the concept of choice undoubtedly appealed to NAACP, which often argued that freedom, choice, and civil rights sh apply to Black citizens on a whole range of issues.[43]

But when it came to opposing miscegenation laws, the argument for marital freedom of choice ran headlong into the sexual sensationalism that surrounded the race-and-gender pairing of Black men and White women. In making this argument, the NAACP was hamstrung by two very awkward facts. First, in all the northern cities for which figures are available, the statistical reality was that many more Black men married White women than White men married Black women.[44] Second, the delegations of Black voters the NAACP used to lobby White legislators were made up, overwhelmingly, of Black men. And in 1913, Black men could not argue for marital freedom of choice without reminding White legislators of Jack Johnson. It did not help that Johnson himself defended his marriages to Etta Duryea and Lucille Cameron on these grounds. After newspapers began reporting that Johnson had boasted that he could "get as many white women" as he liked, a group of prominent Chicago Blacks arranged a meeting at the Appomattox Club to quiz Johnson about the truth of this damaging report. Although Johnson attended the meeting and denied making that particular statement, he flatly refused to back down on the question of his desire to marry White women. "I am not a slave," he said. "I have the right to choose who my mate shall be without the dictation of any man. I have eyes and I have a heart, and when they fail to tell me who I shall have for mine I want to be put away in a lunatic asylum."[45]

Jack Johnson's defense of his "right to choose who my mate shall be" was much more direct than the convoluted statements William Lloyd Garrison had offered the Massachusetts legislature in the 1840s. "It is not the province," Garrison had said, "and does not belong to the power of any legislative assembly, in a republican government, to decide on the complexional affinity of those who choose to be united together in wedlock."[46] Yet the danger of raising the specter of Jack Johnson was so marked that when the NAACP offered the freedom of choice argument to the California state legislature in 1913 and the Wisconsin legislature in 1917, it used Garrison's awkward phrasing to do so.[47] It was not until the mid-1920s, when Jack Johnson, who by then had been convicted and imprisoned, and had lost his heavyweight title to a White male fighter, had faded from public view, that the NAACP was able to offer an argument for marital freedom of choice in the voices of twentieth-century Black men rather than those of nineteenth-century White abolitionists. And even then it was consistently overshadowed by the sexualization of miscegenation law, which had long since driven a wedge between interracial marriage and other civil rights, especially for the race-and-gender pairing of Black men and White women.

This is why the NAACP's third and most complex argument, its critique of the sexualization of miscegenation law, was always the most important. The line of reasoning the NAACP offered on nearly every occasion, it was designed to counter objections from Blacks as well as Whites. Conditioned by the accumulated effects of half a century of miscegenation laws, most Blacks and Whites believed that interracial marriages were unwise, if not downright dangerous.[48] Where they disagreed was on the source of the danger: while white supremacists obsessed over the perils of racial intermixture, Black leaders worried about the lynching of Black men. Under these circumstances, challenging miscegenation laws required physical courage as well as steely determination. It also required steering a careful path between the political clout of white supremacists, who defended miscegenation laws as the natural foundation of the entire framework of racial segregation, and the reluctance of the NAACP's own Black constituency to raise the subject of interracial marriage.

Hoping to marshal Black support while disarming White critics, the NAACP linked its firm opposition to miscegenation law to a cautious refusal to endorse the practice of interracial marriage. Even W.E.B. Du Bois routinely wrapped his opposition to the laws inside denials that either he or the NAACP intended to endorse interracial marriage. "So far as the present advisability of intermarrying between white and colored people is concerned," Du Bois maintained, "both races are practically in complete agreement. Colored folk marry colored folk and white marry white, and the exceptions are very few."[49]

This strategy put the NAACP in the awkward, almost contradictory, position of wholeheartedly opposing laws that banned a practice it refused to defend. Yet this awkwardness was based on astute political calculations. Interracial marriage, NAACP spokesmen insisted, was a statistically negligible phenomenon, especially in those northern states where it was perfectly legal. The point of this argument, which displayed Progressive-era enthusiasm for race-tracking statistics like those on marriage licenses, was, of course, to downplay the existence of marriages between Black men and White women. W.E.B. Du Bois, for example, used the language of statistics to claim, without accompanying evidence, that "999 black men out of every thousand" married Black women. "The statistics of intermarriage in those States where it is permitted," the NAACP assured the California state legislature in 1913, "show this happens so infrequently as to make the whole matter of legislation unnecessary." In 1916, Kelley Miller used a similar argument to fend off passage of a miscegenation law for the District of Columbia. "I have I here for thirty years," Miller testified, "and I know from daily observati/ what is going on in the marriage clerk's office in the courthouse that ... are very few cases of intermarriage; not enough to be of any social importance whatsoever. The races would not blend in 50,000 years according to the number of intermarriages between the races that we have now."[50]

The NAACP then compared the rarity of interracial marriage in northern states and the District of Columbia, where there were no miscegenation laws, to the prevalence of interracial sex in southern states, where miscegenation laws reigned supreme. Pointing to census statistics on the number of "mulattoes" in southern states as evidence of the prevalence of race-mixing there, they painted the South as a cesspool of illicit sex. "The real peril of an admixture of the races in the South," Archibald Grimké explained, "lies not in intermarriage," which was prohibited by law in every southern state, "but in concubinage." It "lies through that secret door which connects the races, the key to which is in the hands of the white men of the South. It is they who first opened it, and it is they who continue to keep it open." In the postslavery world, NAACP spokesmen argued, miscegenation laws protected White men from having to take social and economic responsibility for their continuing sexual activity with Black women. Thus the problem with miscegenation laws was that they provided incentives for race-mixing by promoting illicit sex. As usual, Du Bois put it most succinctly. "'Jim Crow' legislation," he asserted, "is an open bribe to amalgamation." "Such laws," the NAACP told the California legislature in 1913, "leave the colored girl absolutely helpless before the lust of the white man, without the power to compel the seducer to marry."[51]

At the heart of this analysis was a critique of the fundamental inequality in the treatment of Black and White men who engaged in illicit sex. The commonplace assumption that miscegenation laws applied equally to Blacks and Whites was, as the NAACP's Wendell P. Dabney explained in 1924, "camouflage, pure and simple," not only in the southern states that led the way in interracial sex but also in northern states like Dabney's Ohio. "The police in all cities," Dabney explained, "have combined to prevent colored men from lingering in loving dalliance with white women—but they are deaf, dumb and blind, relative to illicit relations between white men and colored women."[52] In southern states, Black men linked to White women could be, and often were, arrested for sexual assault or rape—a capital crime, punishable by death—or, worse, lynched. In northern states, Black men linked to White women could be arrested, as Jack Johnson had been, for abduction, violations of the Mann Act, or a variety of other sex crimes or offenses against public order.[53] For Black men, then, miscegenation laws were just one among many legal and extralegal means of keeping Black men away from White women. When it came to White men, though, miscegenation laws functioned much differently. Because White men could and did debauch Black women with little or no fear of prosecution, laws against interracial marriage merely helped them hide their abuse of Black women and escape from economic responsibility for the children they fathered. On the basis of this analysis, NAACP spokesmen repeatedly asserted that both Blacks and Whites naturally preferred to marry "their own kind" but flatly rejected the notion that miscegenation laws applied equally to Blacks and Whites.

By shifting the blame for race-mixing from interracial marriage to interracial sex, the NAACP turned the logic of the sexualization of miscegenation law against itself. "These anti-intermarriage bills," James Weldon Johnson fumed in an NAACP press release in 1927, "are nothing short of a magna charta [sic] of concubinage and bastardy. They deprive colored women of the protection of matrimony and of the legal recourse and protection where white men are concerned, that are due all women of whatever race. They constitute an attempt to fasten the Southern slavery conception of race relations upon the entire nation."[54] In this manner NAACP spokesmen framed their campaign against miscegenation as a defense of marriage and a plea for the protection of womanhood, aligning themselves with two of the most popular, and powerful, shibboleths of Victorian and Progressive-era America.

The NAACP frequently phrased its opposition to miscegenation laws as a defense of marriage.[55] Archibald Grimké, for example, maintained that the best way to stop illicit sex would be to legalize interracial marriage. "When it comes to a [White] man marrying a colored woman," Grimké maintained, "he does not want to do it, and he is not going to do it." If "everybody" were forced "into the open," there would be "a great deal less" race-mixing.[56] Once again, W.E.B. Du Bois pushed further than most of his peers, couching his version of the controversial argument for marital freedom of choice as a defense of marriage. "If two full-grown responsible human beings of any race and color propose to live together as man and wife," Du Bois declared, "it is only social decency not simply to allow, but to compel them to marry." Recognizing that Jack Johnson's marriage to Lucille Cameron had offended many Blacks, Du Bois tried to persuade readers of the *Crisis* that they should defend Johnson despite their distaste for his actions. "Granted," he wrote, "that Johnson and Miss Cameron proposed to live together, was it better for them to be legally married or not? We know," he continued, "what the answer of the Bourbon South is. We know that they would rather uproot the foundations of decent society than to call the consorts of their brothers, sons and fathers their legal wives. We infinitely prefer the methods of Jack Johnson."[57]

The NAACP's opposition to miscegenation laws was also phrased, repeatedly and vehemently, as an argument for the protection of black womanhood. Like the argument for the defense of marriage, the argument for the protection of black womanhood was cleverly designed to hold white supremacists, whose arguments for the protection of white womanhood had been so powerfully productive of the entire structure of miscegenation laws, to the moral standards they claimed to espouse. "The black woman of America," Archibald Grimké insisted, "must be as sacredly guarded by law and public opinion against the sexual passion and pursuit of the white man as is the white woman." In the mid-1920s, when Black women began to appear among those testifying against miscegenation bills, they, too, offered this argument. Thus, when the Iowa state legislature was considering a miscegenation bill, Mrs. S. Joe Brown testified "in behalf of the Black women of the State" that "they were opposed to the bill on the ground that it tended to degrade the Black women." Reporting on the NAACP's campaign against a similar law in Michigan, the Louisville, Kentucky, *News* summed it up: "Whenever colored people oppose anti-intermarriage laws . . . the claim is made they want 'social equality,' whatever that is. But the truth is colored men want to see their women protected."[58]

Of all the arguments the NAACP put forward, its critique of the sexualization of miscegenation law had the most political potential, especially for NAACP lobbyists in northern states. Brushing right over the fact that African Americans were only a tiny fraction of the northern population, it emphasized the negligible number of interracial marriages in the North, highlighted the history of interracial sex in the South, and echoed notions about the nature of sex and gender that were conventional enough to make Victorians proud. In the world that NAACP lobbyists described, White men's tendency to sexual license had to be restrained by institutions like marriage in order to protect civilized morality. Tapping into the moralist temper of Progressive reform, they positioned themselves as protectors of Black women, proponents of ingroup marriage, and opponents of illicit interracial sex. Unlike the critique of biological racial inferiority, which challenged conventional notions of race, this argument operated to uphold conventional notions of sex and gender. And unlike the argument for marital freedom of choice, which raised inflammatory images of White women paired with Black men, the critique of the sexualization of miscegenation law claimed to protect Black women *from* White men.

Made to order for downplaying scandals, the NAACP's case against miscegenation law harnessed the energy of Progressive campaigns against vice,

public outcries about "white slavery" into racially inclusive cam-
the protection of Black as well as White women.[59] Once in place,
remained much the same for the next half century.

Race Purity and the Politics of Black Solidarity

By the mid-1920s, the NAACP had fought off so many attempts to pass miscegenation laws that its strategies had been reduced to marching orders. Local
branches were given a three-point list of arguments to offer and directed to
carry out a seven-point plan of action, which began with such small steps as
sending telegrams to legislators and securing resolutions from local churches
and ended with the suggestion, to be used only "if the situation becomes acute
and there seems any likelihood of passage of the bill," of holding mass protest meetings. Repeating these arguments until they became formulaic, the
NAACP regarded opposition to miscegenation laws as a kind of litmus test
"of the courage and sincerity of those who profess to stand for racial justice."
But while the NAACP launched rhetorical grenades shaped by the moral and
political imperatives of Progressive-era campaigns against vice, the forces of
racial purity gained ground among Blacks as well as Whites.[60]

During the 1920s, the NAACP engaged in a fierce battle with the new and
revitalized Ku Klux Klan. This version of the Klan, which had been spurred
by the 1915 release of the virulently racist depictions of black male sexuality and white female victimhood in D. W. Griffith's famous film *The Birth
of Nation*, enjoyed phenomenal growth in the 1920s, in America's heartland
as well as in the South. Unlike its Reconstruction-era predecessor, the Klan
of the 1920s targeted Catholics, Jews, and immigrant aliens in addition to
African Americans; it also stoutly resisted such supposedly modern habits as
drinking, indecency, and illicit sex. By 1925, the revitalized Klan numbered
nearly five million members, many of them in midwestern and western states
such as Indiana, Colorado, and Oregon, and it was determined to spread its
influence through the legislatures of as many states as possible. Translating its ideals of white racial purity into frightening images of Black men as
sexual predators, the Klan whipped white supremacists and their allies into a
moral frenzy of racial vigilance.[61]

Proposals for miscegenation laws soon popped up in midwestern states
with growing numbers of Blacks and significant Klan influence; in 1925, for
example, they appeared in Indiana, Ohio, Michigan, and Iowa. As it had for
more than a decade, the NAACP immediately organized against their passage. In Iowa, where a bill had passed the house of representatives and had

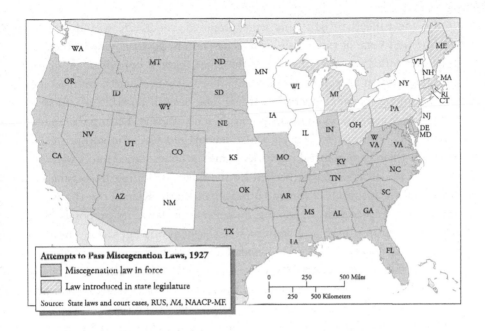

Attempts to Pass Miscegenation Laws, 1927

▨ Miscegenation law in force

▨ Law introduced in state legislature

Source: State laws and court cases, RUS, *NA*, NAACP-MF.

been sent on to the senate, the NAACP pushed the judiciary committee into holding a hearing, where it was represented by two attorneys, a newspaper editor, and a representative of the state federation of Black women's clubs, who reported that a "large delegation of Black people from all walks of life was present" to hear their arguments. An even bigger hearing in Ohio protested a one-drop, racially comprehensive bill. In Michigan, a bill to stop "any person of negro blood" from marrying "any white person" was tabled by the judiciary committee before it ever got to a vote, but it took the "adjournment of the session" to assure "Michigan Colored people" that they had won "another victory over the large Klan element in the State."[62]

The NAACP's opposition spurred the Klan to redouble its efforts. In 1927, eight more miscegenation laws were introduced, this time reaching as far as the New England states of Connecticut, Maine, and Rhode Island. Once again the NAACP rallied against a "conspiracy by the Ku Klux Klan to introduce anti-intermarriage bills throughout the Northern States." In Connecticut, NAACP officials urged branches to "get busy and smash this [bill] before it can gain any general support." In Michigan, the NAACP was facing the fourth legislative session in a row where a miscegenation bill had been introduced. This time, their fast action persuaded a handful of "fair-minded men" on the judiciary committee to scuttle a proposal to ban marriage between "a white person and one of one-eighth or more Negro, Japanese, Chinese or Turkish blood," despite repeated petitions "from Klan-infested districts."[63]

By the time the 1927 bills were proposed, the KKK was already in decline, and none of these bills even came close to passage. One of the reasons they failed was that the rise of the Klan sparked opposition from the Catholic Church as well as the NAACP. The Catholic Church counted few Blacks among its parishioners, but it had long been disposed to regard state control over marriage as an incursion on church authority. During the 1920s, when Klan attempts to ban parochial schools led Catholic authorities to mobilize their local political networks, some Catholics joined forces with the NAACP to defeat proposals backed by the Klan, including miscegenation laws.[64] Partly as a result of this and other alliances, the Klan of the 1920s was remarkably unsuccessful at passing miscegenation laws: its proposals were superfluous in southern and western states, where miscegenation laws had long been in effect, and they were fended off in northern states.

Nonetheless, the NAACP's focus on the Ku Klux Klan left it ill-prepared to notice the extent to which the leadership of campaigns for white supremacy was shifting, quietly but decisively, away from the Ku Klux Klan and toward men like Walter Plecker, who disdained mob spectacles and preferred to reach the goal of white purity through bureaucratic rather than violent means.[65] In 1924, when Walter Plecker championed the Virginia Racial Integrity Act, the NAACP was too busy fighting Klan proposals for miscegenation laws in northern states to pay much attention. It was only after James Weldon Johnson, the first Black executive secretary of the NAACP, came across one of Plecker's pamphlets for Virginia schoolchildren, which he called "the most insulting and virulent attack upon the colored people of the United States that could be imagined," that the NAACP belatedly tried to make up the ground it had lost. Johnson proposed an NAACP campaign to remove Plecker from his post as Virginia's registrar of vital statistics, but when he was unable to find any Virginian, Black or White, who would agree to lead this charge, he reluctantly concluded that "our demand that [Walter Plecker] . . . be dismissed would make many friends for him in that State." In the end, the most Johnson could manage was to persuade the U.S. secretary of labor to relieve Plecker of a largely honorary post as an advisor to the Children's Bureau. From then on, though, the NAACP kept a much closer eye on the bureaucratic administration of white purity.[66]

Meanwhile, the NAACP began to run into trouble from people it assumed would be its allies. Take, for example, Arthur Capper, a White member of the NAACP's board of directors. In 1923, Capper, as a U.S. senator from Kansas, brought to Congress a bill that was the proud product of more than two decades of reformers' hopes for the enactment of a uniform national marriage and divorce code. Since at least the 1890s, reform-minded African Americans had entertained the unlikely, but nonetheless appealing, possibility that such a bill might present an opportunity to eradicate miscegenation laws in one fell swoop. So when a copy of the Capper bill arrived at NAACP headquarters, James Weldon Johnson was appalled to discover that it contained a clause that would have established a nationwide ban on marriages "between members of the white and black or of the white and yellow races." Johnson demanded an explanation from Capper, who shamefacedly admitted that he had introduced the bill at the behest of the General Federation of Women's Clubs without even noticing this provision. Capper promised to remove the offending clause before the bill emerged from committee, and he did so, but the clubwomen's proposal provided a haunting reminder of how many White Americans took the existence of miscegenation laws for granted.[67]

The NAACP increasingly had to worry about Black Americans, too. The group was well aware that many, perhaps most, Blacks opposed interracial marriage, and it had expected they would be reluctant to take a public stand against miscegenation laws. It was, however, entirely unprepared for the possibility that Blacks might actually support miscegenation laws. Yet this was the prospect that arose in the mid-1920s, when a growing number of African Americans responded to the surging political power of calls for white racial purity by advancing an offsetting program of black racial purity.

This position found its champion in Marcus Garvey, whose Universal Negro Improvement Association (UNIA) caught on like wildfire among working-class Blacks, and who was determined to turn Blacks' distaste for interracial marriage into support for miscegenation laws.[68] Like Walter Plecker, who sneeringly referred to the NAACP as "a New York organization of Mulattoes," Marcus Garvey railed against the NAACP, which he called a "Miscegenationist organization," and which he used as his rhetorical punching bag.[69] Garvey's name-calling was rooted partly in his heartfelt belief that black racial purity was the foundation for potential black nationhood, and partly in his determination to discredit the NAACP, which he held responsible for his 1923 arrest and conviction on charges of mail fraud.[70] In a series of pronouncements issued from his Atlanta prison cell, Garvey declared that "the Universal Negro Improvement Association stands in opposition to this association [the NAACP] on the miscegenation question, because we believe in the racial purity of both the Negro and white races." The UNIA, Garvey insisted, would "save the negro race from extinction through miscegenation" while "W.E.B. Du Bois and his National Association for the 'Advancement' of 'Colored' people . . . advocate racial amalgamation or general miscegenation with the hope of creating a new type of colored race by wiping out both black and white. . . . Slave masters," Garvey raged, "were able to abuse our slave mothers and thereby create a hybrid bastardy," but "we ourselves, at this time of freedom and culture, should not perpetuate the crime of nature."[71]

Garvey's belief in racial purity soon translated into concrete support for miscegenation laws. In June 1925, he wrote to Walter Plecker's idol Earnest Sevier Cox, author of the virulently racist tract *White America* and a strong supporter of the Virginia Racial Integrity Act, to say that he hoped Cox and his white supremacist colleagues would get Georgia "to bring about a similar law as exists in Virginia." Then, in August 1925, Garvey's wife, who represented him during his stint in prison, set out on an errand that led to one of the most bizarre moments in the history of miscegenation law. On a hot summer day in Virginia, Amy Jacques Garvey, trailed by reporters, stopped by Plecker's office at the Virginia Bureau of Vital Statistics. According to the *Richmond Daily Times-Dispatch,* Plecker was "out of the city," but Garvey nonetheless assured "officials" in the office that "Virginia's racial integrity law has the support of millions of negroes throughout the country." Adding insult to injury, Garvey continued, "The National Association for the Advancement of Colored People wants us all to become white by amalgamation, but they are not honest enough to come out with the truth. We of the Universal Negro Improvement Association do not want to become white."[72]

The Garveys' devotion to black racial purity stemmed from different sources than Plecker's devotion to white racial purity—the Garveys hoped to tear down the structure of white supremacy that Plecker was determined to uphold—yet both made their case by contrasting the supposedly noble ideal of racial purity to the dangers of race-mixing, and both regarded the NAACP as the penultimate symbol of race mixture.[73] After W.E.B. Du Bois realized the extent of the threat the UNIA posed to the NAACP, he traded insults with Garvey for most of the 1920s. Calling Garvey the "most dangerous enemy of the Negro race in America and in the world," Du Bois declared that he was "either a lunatic or a traitor." Garvey returned the favor by accusing Du Bois of "racial treachery and disloyalty," then upped the ante, calling Du Bois an "'unfortunate mulatto' who bewails every day the drop of Negro blood in his veins" who had "taken upon himself the responsibility of criticizing and condemning other people while holding himself up as . . . the great 'I AM' of the Negro race." Telling his followers that Du Bois "likes to dance with white people and dine with them and sometimes sleep with them," Garvey persuaded the UNIA to pass a resolution that declared Du Bois should be "ostracized from the Negro race . . . [and] henceforth be regarded as an enemy of the black people of the world."[74]

No one knows how many UNIA members shared Garvey's support for miscegenation laws, but surely far fewer than the millions Amy Jacques

Garvey claimed. Still, UNIA rhetoric on black racial purity was undeniably influential. During the mid-1920s, when the Virginia Racial Integrity Act was adopted, Virginia boasted no fewer than forty-eight local branches of the UNIA. Virginia Blacks knew better than to believe anything Walter Plecker or the Anglo-Saxon Clubs of America had to say about the good of "true negroes," but they voiced public objections to the act only after its passage, and then in language that owed as much to Garvey's program of racial purity as the NAACP's championing of civil rights. Thus in 1928, the Black newspaper the *Richmond Planet* published an editorial, "Negroes Want Racial Integrity, Too." "It is apparent to us," wrote the *Planet*'s editor, "that the Racial Integrity Bill . . . is in plain violation of the Fourteenth Amendment to the Constitution of the United States, in that it alleges to protect the racial integrity of the white person and affords no protection to the racial integrity of the Negro."[75]

What Comes Naturally: Race, Sex and Nature in Modern America

While Marcus Garvey tried to shame the NAACP into protecting "the racial integrity of the Negro" by supporting miscegenation laws, other Black spokesmen pushed in the opposite direction; they tried to push the NAACP into offering a positive defense of interracial marriage.

The argument that there was nothing unnatural about interracial marriage was only a small logical step beyond the position already taken by the NAACP; moreover, it was an argument that some NAACP leaders would have accepted, at least in private. Yet it was also an argument the NAACP steadfastly avoided making in public. When, in 1913, the group told the California legislature that "no man-made law can stop the union of the races," they quickly added that "its prevention is best left to public opinion and to Nature, which wreaks its own fearful punishments on those who transgress its laws and sin against it."[76] In subsequent campaigns, NAACP spokesmen occasionally described interracial sex as a force that operated according to the supposedly inevitable laws of nature rather than the artificial laws of the state, but they stopped short of the claim that there was anything natural about interracial marriage.

It is easy enough to see why. Defending interracial marriage on any basis required a certain freedom from the need to calculate immediate political costs, a luxury that the NAACP, which spent so much time lobbying legislators, could rarely afford. Arguing that interracial marriage was natural required something more: a willingness to entertain the idea that people should be true to their own sexual natures rather than subordinate their natural desires to the demands of civilized morality.[77] This belief would eventually become one of the foundations of modern thought, but adopting it required discarding not only conventional notions of the nature of race but also conventional notions of the nature of sex and gender. And here was the rub, for the NAACP's campaign against miscegenation law, especially its critique of the sexualization of miscegenation law, was built on much different assumptions. The NAACP's most successful arguments worked in tandem with conventional morality, strengthening the power of marriage by cracking down on illicit sex; in effect, NAACP lobbyists offset their controversial challenges to the nature of race by adopting entirely conventional notions of sex and gender.

NAACP stalwarts like Du Bois, Grimké, and Miller had been schooled in and would remain influenced by the middle-class conventions of Victorian morality, so the argument for the naturalness of interracial sex and marriage would be developed by Black spokesmen a generation younger. The lives of George Schuyler and J. A. Rogers, the most prominent advocates of this position, were marked by their relative political independence as journalists, and by their own movement in and out of the interracial bohemian circles produced by post–World War I migration of Blacks to northern cities. Schuyler and Rogers were not necessarily any more supportive of the abstract rights of women than W.E.B. Du Bois, but they were more in tune with the emerging rhythms of modern America. Among these was the emergence of the sex and gender formations that were, by the 1920s, making both American women and American marriage seem decidedly more modern and decidedly less Victorian.[78] Du Bois and his peers prided themselves on embodying the public canons of middle-class respectability, which rested on notions of women's sexual purity and sharp contrasts between legitimate marriage and illicit sex.[79] But modern men like Schuyler and Rogers valued what they idealized as authentic romance and rooted their conception of marriage in a franker recognition of female sexual desire. They prided themselves on facing the sometimes gritty, but always undeniable, facts of human sexuality, as they were understood in a soon-to-be-Freudian world.

George Schuyler and his wife, Josephine, made their marriage a public template for interracial marriage. Josephine Cogdell Schuyler was, in many respects, the epitome of a modern woman. A White woman born in Texas, she moved to San Francisco as a young woman, where she studied modern dance with Ruth St. Denis, modeled as a Mack Sennett bathing beauty, and wrote occasional articles for A. Philip Randolph's socialist journal, the

George and Josephine Schuyler (bottom row, far left and far right), at the birthday party of their six year old daughter, Philippa, who sits on the lap of J. A. Rogers. (Photographs by Morgan and Marvin Smith; Schomburg Center for Research in Black Culture, New York Public Library, Astor, Lenox and Tilden Foundations)

Messenger, before meeting George Schuyler, the *Messenger*'s assistant editor, on a trip to New York City. In an autobiographical article published in 1946, she presented her interracial marriage as a natural outgrowth of her Texas girlhood. As a child, she wrote, "the activities of the Negroes fascinated me"; "they were always doing something interesting" on her father's ranch. Even as a girl, Josephine knew that "interracial love" ran in her family, "with my father drawing no color line in his love life and my eldest brother, publicly thought to be childless," having "a colored daughter attending school out of the state." Josephine's mother complained, with more than a bit of bite, that her husband "never knew what class or color he was," but Josephine regarded her father's behavior as more enticing than immoral. Years later, when she met George Schuyler, "the fact that he was dark and I fair gave an added fillip to our association."[80]

Six months after they married, George Schuyler embarked on what he believed was the first serious study of the topic of interracial marriage. Convinced by his own experience that the actual number of interracial marriages far exceeded the totals recorded on marriage licenses or by the Census Bureau, Schuyler dismissed all the available statistics as unreliable and set out to make his own count. Using contacts he had developed as a journalist, he sent a detailed questionnaire to "editors, physicians, social workers, students and labor leaders in about 100 communities." He used the replies, which provided plenty of evidence that interracial marriage was far more common than anyone had yet claimed, to write an article on "Racial Intermarriage in America" originally published in the *American Parade* and reissued in pamphlet form a year later.[81]

In typically combative fashion, Schuyler framed his article as a head-on attack on what he called the four "greatest myths" about interracial marriages: that they were unnatural, infrequent, low class, and invariably tragic. "The color problem in the United States," Schuyler insisted, was "basically sexual," and when it came to sex, there was no such thing as "natural aversion" between Whites and Blacks. "Not only," he asserted, "is it not true that there is any aversion or repugnance between the two extreme races, but on the contrary the researches of scientists prove that there is a great deal of attraction between them."[82]

Understanding interracial marriage was, Schuyler maintained, simply a matter of facing the facts. It was true enough that interracial couples encountered obstacles ranging from the disdain of their neighbors to rejection by marriage license clerks or the criminal sanctions of miscegenation laws. Yet they were, by and large, quiet, respectable members of their communities with exemplary marriages. And they were by no means uncommon. By Schuyler's estimate, there were "close to 10,000" married "black and tan" couples in the United States.[83]

Over the next two decades, as Schuyler made his name as the New York editor of the nation's second-largest Black newspaper, he continued to develop his defense of interracial marriage. From the outset, he paid special attention to White women and Black men, the race-and-gender pairing that provided the focus of his satirical novel *Black No More,* published in 1931, as well as his journalistic accounts of interracial marriages. In 1930, he told readers of the *American Mercury* that "today at least three-quarters of the mixed marriages in the United States are of the white-women-black-man class." By 1944, in a piece about "The Caucasian Problem," written for Rayford Logan's collection *What the Negro Wants*, Schuyler estimated the number of interracial marriages at fifteen thousand and advocated "the rescinding of all racial pollution laws barring marriage because of so-called race" as well as the "end of gathering population statistics by race." At various moments, Schuyler argued that Blacks and Whites were "two peoples who are actually one people" and claimed to look forward to the day when "a full-blooded American negro may be rare enough to get a job in a museum, and . . . our American social leaders may be as tanned naturally as they are now striving to become artificially."[84]

While George Schuyler defended interracial marriage, his close friend and fellow newspaper columnist J. A. Rogers argued that there was a natural sexual attraction between Whites and Blacks. Beginning in 1919, with the publication of his first book on race-mixing, *As Nature Leads,* which was followed by a massive three-volume compilation, *Sex and Race* (1940–44), and *Nature Knows No Color-Line* (1952), Rogers, a self-taught historian, set himself the task of persuading a decidedly doubtful public that "sex relations between so-called whites and Blacks go back to prehistorical times and on all the continents." Whatever jurists, politicians, clergymen, and racialist scientists might say about the unnaturality of interracial sex and marriage, Rogers was sure that nature was on the side of race-mixing. "Races have always mixed," he insisted, "and will continue to mix; if not in accordance with man-made laws, then against them."[85]

Like Schuyler's defense of interracial marriage, Rogers's defense of interracial sex reflected his familiarity with the multiracial urban districts of New York and Chicago. "I have seen so much race-mixing in America," Rogers told his readers in *Sex and Race,* "that I now regard it as commonplace which it certainly would be for all others if the mixed couples were to appear on the street," adding that "the individual experiences of anyone in this respect can be multiplied by the hundreds of thousands." Those who believed that either sex or marriage between Blacks and Whites was uncommon simply didn't know what they were talking about. "For a real knowledge of race-mixing in America," he explained, "one must go not to the colleges and libraries but to Negro bell-boys, taxi-drivers, bootleggers, Pullman porters, barbers, maids, musicians, cabaret employees, doctors, lawyers, news reporters and others."[86]

Rogers argued that, contrary to popular opinion, White women felt considerable sexual desire for Black men. "Take the case of Jack Johnson," he said. "The impression that newspapers gave was that Johnson was running after white women, while the truth was, as I personally know, that he had to do far more running from them than toward them. White women of all grades of society used to pester him." Rogers believed that "it is nearly always the white woman who makes the advance to the Negro." To prove this point, he collected clippings and published letters from White women who expressed desire for Black men. He was especially pleased by a letter from two White women who had written to a Black newspaper in response to an article about the formation of a New York organization of interracial couples called the enguin Club. "Please keep up this good work," the two young women had portedly written, "which will eventually ameliorate the sad and unnecessary barriers which now exist between colored and white girls and boys who otherwise would freely carry out Nature's true law—'opposites attract' by meeting and marrying."[87]

Rogers's belief in the "cosmic" significance of interracial sex ran so deep that he found it in subconscious as well as conscious desires, among White women who hated Blacks as well as among those who sought them out. "A great deal of the hate of Negroes," he maintained, "really is a reflex of the desire for sexual contact with them." He claimed that Whites were so fascinated by reports of the sexual prowess of Blacks that White women who feared rape by Blacks were only indulging in a kind of wishful thinking spurred by "an ungratified desire for intimacy with Negroes." The prudish American notion that race mixture, a "perfectly natural process," could and should be outlawed had only made things worse. "Whatever is forbidden, most of all sex and drink," he explained, "becomes at once a great temptation, a joy that we feel others would snatch from us. . . . And so curiosity was aroused until 'black' sex became an obsession."[88]

Although Rogers placed more emphasis on interracial desire than any other Black spokesman, there was nothing new about the argument that there was a sexual component to the structures of white supremacy. As early as 1904, Archibald Grimké had labeled interracial sex "The Heart of the Race Problem"; and W.E.B. Du Bois insisted that "the race question is at bottom simply a matter of the ownership of women; white men want the right to own and use all women, colored and white, and they resent any intrusion of colored men into this domain."[89] There was, however, a considerable distance between the NAACP's argument that Black women, like White women, should use marriage as a protection against male sexual license and Rogers's argument that interracial sex was everywhere and could be avoided only at the cost of unhealthy repression of human nature.

Schuyler and Rogers's insistence on the fundamental naturality of interracial desire put them in a position to turn the existing discourse about miscegenation upside down. White supremacists saw miscegenation laws as the civilized embodiment of the "natural aversion between the races," and NAACP spokesmen softened their objections to miscegenation law with assurances that most Blacks always had and always would prefer to marry other Blacks. Schuyler and Rogers, however, took direct aim at laws they regarded as perverse obstacles to the fulfillment of natural sexual desires. In their view it was miscegenation law, not interracial sex or marriage, that was unnatural. "It is no exaggeration," Rogers opined, "to say that in their freakishness and the mix-ups they have caused, especially in the inheritance of property, [miscegenation laws] could very well have been composed by a congress of prize lunatics in the heart of a madhouse at the craziest season of the year." Virginia's Racial Integrity Act was, he claimed, "as fantastic as the distorting mirror of a dime museum."[90]

But even as Schuyler and Rogers upended traditional wisdom by labeling miscegenation laws unnatural, their advocacy of interracial sex and marriage reinforced other, overlapping notions of nature. By labeling interracial sex and marriage natural, they made interracial sexual desire appear as enticing as it was forbidden. But, as the emphasis they placed on discussions of White women's sexual desire for Black men suggested, it was not just sexual desire, or even interracial sexual desire, that appeared to be natural in this formulation; it was heterosexual desire in particular. In this respect, Schuyler and Rogers played a role in producing a modern culture that increasingly assigned its fears of unnaturality to homosexuality rather than to race mixture. It would be decades before the implications of this development were fully understood.

Geographies of Evasion

Meanwhile, more civil rights groups were beginning to take note of miscegenation laws. After the NAACP, the first, and eventually the most important, organization to go on record against them was the American Civil Liberties Union (ACLU), founded in 1919 and also based in New York City. In its early years, the ACLU focused on protecting free speech, but by 1930, it had expanded its surveys of "State Laws Restricting Civil Liberty" to include laws "prohibiting intermarriage of blacks and whites." The ACLU illustrated its newfound interest in civil rights with a map of restrictions on "Negroes' Rights," which tracked state laws restricting voting, school attendance, and marriage on the basis of race. In 1931, when the ACLU published its first *Black Justice* report, it took the occasion to announce its opposition to miscegenation laws. From that point on, and for the next thirty-five years, the ACLU repeated arguments first developed by the NAACP, placing special emphasis on the issue of individual rights in order to emphasize what it called "the right to marry according to choice."[91]

The ACLU's map offers a useful schematic of the regional arrangement of miscegenation law as it existed in 1930. If this arrangement reflected the impact of the NAACP's lobbying campaigns on northern states, it also shows the limits of NAACP and ACLU influence in the South and West.

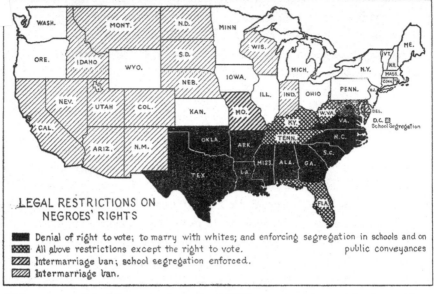

LEGAL RESTRICTIONS ON
NEGROES' RIGHTS

▮ Denial of right to vote; to marry with whites; and enforcing segregation in schools and on
▦ All above restrictions except the right to vote.   public conveyances
▨ Intermarriage ban; school segregation enforced.
▧ Intermarriage ban.

This map, published in 1930, shows the ACLU's emerging interest in the problem of miscegenation laws. (American Civil Liberties Union)

Every southern state had a miscegenation law on its books, and even as northern public opinion turned against the laws, southern public opinion tightened around them. By 1944, when social scientist Gunnar Myrdal codified "the white man's rank order of discriminations" and reported, accurately, that in the minds of Whites "the ban on intermarriage and other sex relations involving white women and colored men takes precedence before everything else," miscegenation laws had become politically untouchable in the South.[92]

In the West, where miscegenation laws were nearly as common and frequently covered more racial categories, the situation was a little different. In these states, the sheer inconsistency of the laws, which set white supremacy against a multiracial field, led to continual sparring matches over the terms of the laws, especially in states like California, where, despite the best efforts of white supremacists, the laws failed to keep pace with the rapidly changing racial formations of a multiracial population.

Between 1930 and 1948, miscegenation law remained stuck in this regional impasse. Neither the NAACP nor the ACLU was able to develop constituencies with enough local clout to persuade state legislatures to repeal any of the laws in the West and the South. Court challenges could only have been made in states with miscegenation laws already in force, where judges were long since accustomed to their racial imperatives. The chances of success were so low that during the 1930s and 1940s neither the ACLU, which deferred to the NAACP's legal expertise on issues it described as "Negroes' rights," nor the NAACP, which was uncomfortably aware that the question of interracial marriage deeply divided the Black population it claimed to represent, tried to take a case to court.[93]

In the absence of organized attempts to repeal the laws or court tests of their constitutionality, the best way to trace the midcentury networks of opposition to miscegenation laws is to follow the strategies used by individual interracial couples. In western and southern states, interracial couples faced a bewildering structure of laws that named different racial groups in different states and struggled to find ways to evade them. Until World War II, when the most persistent managed to persuade civil rights organizations to support them, many couples negotiated their way through this morass by taking advantage of the state-by-state gaps between the laws, charting geographies of evasion that challenged the laws in a variety of indirect, but sometimes effective, ways.

For interracial couples, the differences between individual states were more significant than the differences between regions. For some, securing a marriage license was just a matter of driving across the nearest state boundary. Because Squire Granville Wilkerson knew that a Black man couldn't marry a White woman in Los Angeles, California, he persuaded his eighteen-year-old girlfriend, Virginia Meyers, to go across the border to Tijuana, Mexico, where the couple had their wedding performed. Sometimes, though, it was a much more complicated process. Stan Henshall and Mary Ban, for example, knew that they would have to leave their home state of Arizona in order to avoid its ban on the marriages of Whites and Asian Americans, so they loaded their two children from previous marriages into their car and set out for Nevada. But, as Mary Ban explained, they soon found out that "Nevada, the state where we thought anything goes, would not issue us a license," so the couple drove on to Idaho, when they once again met rejection, eventually they secured a license in College Place, Washington. By the time the Henshalls returned to their home in Clarkdale, Arizona, they had traveled 2,800 miles.[94]

Regardless of whether the actual distance was long or short, geographies of evasion hinged on the hope that a marriage certificate from another state (or country) would be recognized as valid in a couple's home state. Yet a continuing stream of court cases showed that no one could be sure whether a marriage that violated one state's miscegenation law could or would be honored by another state, and for what purposes. If a woman "who had one-eighth or more of negro blood" left her home state of Florida to marry a "white" man in Kansas, then remained in Kansas until she died, should the property she owned in Florida descend to her husband in Kansas or to her mother in Florida? What should happen to the property of a "Japanese" man from Montana who took his "white" fiancée to Spokane, Washington, to marry? After he died, could his wife inherit his estate, or could the state of Montana use its miscegenation law to establish its own claim to the property? If a "white" woman from California married a "Filipino" man in New Mexico, a state with no miscegenation law, could she expect a California judge to annul her marriage on the grounds that her husband had committed a "fraud" by telling her he was "Spanish Castilian" instead of "Filipino"?[95]

Even in a system that assigned control of marriage law to individual states rather than the federal government, the answers to these questions need not have been difficult. Americans were a notoriously mobile people, and conflicts between state laws were a familiar feature of nearly every aspect of marriage law. Courts had long since agreed on the general principle that a marriage valid under the laws of one state would be recognized in any other state; indeed, many state law codes said as much. When it came to the issue of the recognition of marriages made in another state, then, interracial couples might have had this principle of reciprocal recognition on their side.

Yet states repeatedly tried to crack down on interracial couples whose marriages had taken place outside state boundaries. As early as 1878, Virginia judges had complained that miscegenation laws "would be futile and a dead letter if in fraud of these salutary enactments, both races might, by stepping across an imaginary line, bid defiance to the law, by immediately returning and insisting that the marriage celebrated in another state or country, should be recognized as lawful."[96] Some states passed laws that specifically prohibited residents from "evading" the laws in their own states by marrying elsewhere.[97] In 1912 and 1913, when the Jack Johnson scandal was front-page news, even states like Vermont and Massachusetts, which had no miscegenation laws of their own, passed laws preventing out-of-state couples from marrying in either state if their marriage was considered illegal in their home state.[98] As late as 1942, the Montana Supreme Court held that "it is the policy of our law that there shall be no marriage between white persons and Japanese. To make that policy effective such marriage within the state is forbidden; and our own residents are not permitted to circumvent the law by marriage outside the state."[99]

Judges developed four overlapping rationales for removing interracial marriage from the controlling principle of reciprocal recognition. The first, and surely the most interesting, of these rationales drew an analogy between "miscegenous" marriage and incestuous or polygamous marriages, since both incest and polygamy were already regarded as exceptions to the general principle of reciprocal recognition.[100] The second distinguished between marriages that deserved reciprocal recognition and marriages that were prohibited by the positive public policy of a particular state, as shown by the existence of a state miscegenation law.[101] The third distinguished between reciprocal recognition of the "forms" of a marriage, which included such supposedly minor details as minimum ages and waiting periods, and the "essentials," which included such supposedly significant elements as the "capacity to contract marriage," which was then measured by race.[102] North Carolina, for example, considered its prohibition on marriages between "whites" and "negroes" to be "a personal incapacity which follows the parties wherever they go."[103]

By the 1940s, very few of the states that prohibited interracial marriages were clearly willing to recognize marriages made in states that allowed them. One of these states was Nebraska, which recognized the out-of-state marriages of interracial couples, even those who deliberately sought to evade Nebraska's miscegenation law. The most visible example, however, was California, which maintained both a broad-based, multiracial miscegenation law and a seemingly contradictory policy of recognizing the marriages of California couples, interracial or otherwise, who married in other states or, as in the case of Squire Wilkerson, other countries.[104]

For these reasons, the geography of evasion grew particularly deep roots in California, frustrating state officials, who were never able to persuade judges to set interracial marriages apart from other out-of-state marriages. Stymied by the courts, California officials forged alternate methods of cracking down on geographies of evasion, such as asking legislators in nearby states to make their laws conform to California's. In 1938, for example, California state legislators, who had been inflamed by a rash of publicity about Filipinos marrying White women in Utah, passed a resolution asking the Utah legislature to "stop the practice whereby citizens of the State of California and members of [a] non-assimilable alien race have been defeating California marriage laws by resorting to a subterfuge of transient residence in the State of Utah"; a year later, Utah responded by adding "malay" to its state miscegenation law.[105]

Despite these repeated attempts to crack down on out-of-state marriages, interracial couples continued to slip through the cracks in the state-by-state coverage of miscegenation law. During World War II, these geographies of evasion bloomed on an unprecedented scale in a wide variety of settings. One such arena was the U.S. military. Partly because it plucked so many young men and women out of the familiar networks of friends and family and resettled them on military bases in and outside the United States, the military found itself at the center of the tug-of war between interracial couples, who now brought a sense of life-and-death urgency to their decisions about marriage, and the conflicted and confusing marriage laws of forty-eight states, thirty of which prohibited some form of interracial marriage, and eighteen of which did not.[106]

Take, for instance, the case of Iris and Manuel Buaken.[107] Iris, a White woman originally from Wyoming, and Manuel, a Filipino who came to the United States in 1927, met and fell in love in Los Angeles, where they were legally forbidden to marry. They were committed Methodists who were embarrassed not to be married, but they were also a young couple struggling to make ends meet on the Depression-era wages Manuel earned as a "houseboy" for a Los Angeles physician. Too poor to travel, they put off making what Iris called "the desperate sacrifice required to get to a state where we could be 'married.'"[108] Shortly after the United States entered World War II, however, Manuel Buaken was drafted into the U.S. Army, and promptly sent to join an all-Filipino unit based at Camp Roberts, California.

It was ironic that Filipinos, who had never been granted the rights of U.S. citizens, were eligible for the draft, and unjust that they were placed in racially segregated units under the command of White officers.[109] Yet because segregation brought together so many Filipino men like Manuel Buaken, who lived with White women they were legally forbidden to marry, it also brought their situation to the attention of their commanding officers, who knew that without legal marriages, the wives and children of these soldiers would be ineligible for the family allowances that other soldiers received as a matter of course. Because this problem affected troop morale, the unit's Catholic chaplain, Father Noury, and its commanding officer, a White man who had been chosen partly because he had previous experience living in the Philippines, set out to solve it.

With the commanding officer's tacit approval, Father Noury tried to find a way for Filipino soldiers to legalize their marriages. He started by enlisting help from the Red Cross, which he talked into taking advantage of California's unusual willingness to recognize out-of-state marriages. Under Noury's first plan, the Red Cross offered a handful of couples, including the Buakens, emergency loans to travel to New Mexico or Washington to have legal marriages performed. Noury's next plan, which, like the first, was a stopgap measure, relied on a handful of Catholic priests who pressed the church's claims of religious authority over marriage by issuing church marriage licenses for individual couples and performing quasi-legal ceremonies.

Buoyed by these successes, Noury began to nourish the hope that the U.S. military might use the power of the federal government to trump California's

Company 1 of the First Filipino Infantry during World War II. Shortly after this picture was taken, the soldiers were sent to fight against the Japanese in the Philippines. (Shades of L.A. Archives, Los Angeles Public Library)

miscegenation law. Accordingly, he took his case to the War Department, which dashed his hopes by insisting that the marriages of individual soldiers must comply with the laws of their home states. So Noury wrote an open letter to the governor of California, asking "as a favor the abrogation of the marriage laws against the Filipinos." In language that reflected both the growing notion of the naturalness of interracial marriages and Catholic resistance to state rather than church control over marriage, Noury described California's law as being "against the law of nature, against the law of God and contrary to the spirit of the Constitution of the United States."[110]

The response, noted a disappointed Iris Buaken, who watched Noury's bold campaign with considerable interest, was "some flag waving and tongue-chewing democracy, but no action."[111] By this time, though, the soldiers were about to ship out, and many of their families were still without the allowances. Unable to wait any longer, Noury arranged for a mass trip to New Mexico, enabled by "emergency furloughs" granted by the commanding officer and paid for by loans from both the Red Cross and the unit itself.

By the time Buaken and his fellow soldiers shipped out in April 1944, the wives and children they left behind would receive their family allowances.

If this remarkable incident shows how far a few determined advocates might stretch the boundaries of the military's policies on soldier marriage, the situation of Black soldiers stationed in Europe shows another side of the story. During and after World War II any U.S. soldier who wanted to marry a woman he met in France, England, or Italy had to get permission from his commanding officer before doing so. Black men, however, had so much difficulty getting permission that the NAACP often received letters from disappointed soldiers, and sometimes from their relatives or lovers, "reporting that American Army officers have refused permission to these individuals to marry." Their pleas for help spurred the NAACP to protest to military officials, whose responses showed that the U.S. military had, in effect, erected a series of rhetorical firewalls around its practice of discouraging as many interracial marriages as possible. After the NAACP dismissed the Army's insistence that "all rules and regulations which govern the marriage of military personnel in overseas areas are applicable to all members of the Army, regardless of race, creed or color" as patently inaccurate, the Army fell back on the argument that the laws of a soldier's home state should determine whether a Black soldier could marry a White woman, even if that woman was from England, France, or Italy. If that failed, officers refused permission for interracial marriages on other grounds. Thus one officer refused a Black soldier's repeated appeals with the simple statement, typed neatly across the bottom of the appeal form, that such marriages were "considered to be against the best interests of the parties concerned and of the service."[112]

Unable to make much headway changing military policy, the NAACP turned to helping soldiers construct geographies of evasion. As one soldier who wrote to the NAACP put it, "The Army's alibi for not let colored marry because their State don't allow it [but] A man does not have to live where he once lived especially if he want to be happy and see her happy." The group provided much-needed information. In 1946, a French woman wrote to the NAACP asking:

> Is marriage between a colored man and a white woman forbidden in certain American states? Could you tell me if such a marriage in the state of California would have any validity? In Los Angeles, for example? Could you also tell me how much it would cost in dollars for a railroad ticket from New York to Los Angeles?

In response, the NAACP's Julia Baster broke the bad news that "California does not permit marriage between Negroes and whites to take place within its borders" but then added, "However, the state of New York permits marriages between persons of different races. You will probably be interested in knowing that it is possible to marry in a state permitting interracial marriage and live in the state of California."[113]

By the end of World War II, the NAACP had begun to enlist sympathetic military authorities in its efforts to ease the problems that Black soldiers married to White women would face on their return from Europe. In a series of letters, the NAACP approached Army authorities on behalf of intermarried Black soldiers who had been assigned postwar duties in southern states like Florida, where miscegenation laws prohibited the couples from living together within the state. Telling the Army that these men were caught between the desire to obey state laws and the duty to support their wives, the NAACP succeeded in getting several men reassigned to bases in northern states. Before long, they were telling those who approached them for help that "the present policy of the Department [of the Army] calls for the arrangements of such transfers in situations like yours."[114]

As the Allied victory in World War II was succeeded by American military occupation in Japan, yet another civil rights organization, the Japanese American Citizens League (JACL), was drawn into the defense of interracial couples. The JACL's initial interest had little to do with interracial marriage; rather, it hoped to help Nisei (or second-generation Japanese American) soldiers who wanted to marry women they met in Japan negotiate a variety of obstacles that had been placed in their way. Japanese war brides had been deliberately excluded from the war brides programs that provided immigration assistance to European and even Chinese women married to American soldiers. Acting on behalf of Nisei veterans, the JACL repeatedly urged the Congress to solve this problem by passing a bill it called the "First Japanese Soldier Brides Act."[115]

But though the JACL continued to foreground marriages of Nisei men and Japanese women, marriages between White or Black men and Japanese women made up a substantial number, according to some estimates as many as three-quarters, of the war bride marriages in Japan. After its Soldier Brides bill was passed, the JACL's Anti-Discrimination Committee reported that it had "been flooded with inquiries about the law, and personal appeals from servicemen and veterans, both Nisei and Caucasian." In private, they complained that these letters came "mostly from non-Japanese," and they could not help noticing that "the only contributions which have been enclosed to help us with our work have been from these non-Japanese." Over the next decade, as Japanese war brides became a steadily increasing segment of the Japanese American population, the JACL was pulled into helping interracial couples navigate the state-by-state geography of miscegenation laws they faced on their arrival in the United States. Like the NAACP, the Red Cross, and Father Noury, the JACL quickly became intimately familiar with the structure of American miscegenation laws.[116]

The Paradox of Postwar Possibility

By the end of World War II, the NAACP, which in 1913 had been the only significant organization willing to oppose miscegenation laws, no longer stood alone. Interracial couples once relegated to lonely isolation were increasingly able to request help from a growing range of organizations familiar with details of the state-by-state fabric of miscegenation law. The federal government had begun, for the first time, to claim that American democracy should be free of racial bias. And if this promise, like the Army's flatly inaccurate assurance that its policies on soldier marriage were carried out without regard to race, was often more rhetoric than reality, the power of that rhetoric was growing. In the postwar period, retrospective horror at the policies of Hitler's Germany made arguments that race prejudice had to go and that race purity was not only a scientific illusion but also a dangerous and decidedly undemocratic political program considerably more persuasive.

By the end of World War II, then, opponents of miscegenation laws could elaborate on nearly every line of argument the NAACP had put forth during the past thirty years, wrapping the whole with an aura of urgency and stark comparisons between the potential of democracy and the reality of racism. In the late 1930s, the Black press had begun to compare miscegenation laws to the political program of the Nazis; by the end of the war, this analogy carried substantial impact. In articles describing the plight of Whites married to Filipinos, Iris Buaken could rail against the "unnatural law" that prohibited her marriage in California, complain that "thousands of men have been denied the right to marry and told to resort to prostitution," and paint an angry picture of lives "lived under the shadow of one of the senseless race taboos that have been a prime factor in creating this hell the world now suffers."[117]

Postwar legal commentators wrote in more restrained tones, but they, too, had begun to consider miscegenation laws an embarrassing contradiction to the notion of American democracy. A prime example was California, where World War II quadrupled the state's prewar population of African Americans, labeled Japanese Americans as enemies, and turned Filipinos and Chinese into national allies, recasting the state's existing racial formations and pushing and pulling against a miscegenation law that was the product of earlier attempts to legislate white supremacy. For World War II–era White liberal lawyers, taking a close look at miscegenation law in California was something like turning over a rock—all sorts of worms were ready to crawl out. In 1944, the *California Law Review* published Walter Tragen's study of California miscegenation law. Although Tragen admitted that "the constitutionality of the miscegenation statute is apparently well-settled," his article offered a laundry list of problems with the law, which, he pointed out, rested on vague and indefinable definitions of race, clouded the legal status of a couple's children as well as their property holdings and inheritances, contradicted the state's own policy of recognizing the out-of-state marriages of interracial couples, and, in any case, was largely ineffective in preventing interracial mixture. Tragen emphasized the gap between the abstract racial language of the law and the "very human" problems encountered by "the men, women, and children whose lives have become enmeshed in the miscegenation statute," but he ended on a milder note, by simply questioning "whether the statute accomplishes anything more than public opinion and individual preferences without it do." A year later, the *Southern California Law Review* published an article by Eugene Marias, who noted that courts had consistently upheld miscegenation laws on both contractual and equal protection grounds, then listed the arguments that might be used in challenging the laws, noting that the common law had never prohibited interracial marriage, that the laws were rooted primarily in prejudice, and that they were "in contradiction to the American concept of equality." In 1948, after NAACP lawyers won a U.S. Supreme Court ruling against racially restrictive housing covenants, the legitimacy of miscegenation law once again came under question. Later that year, the *Southern California Law Review* published Harry Gershon's prediction that the Supreme Court's housing decision had, in effect, paved the way for challenges to the constitutionality of miscegenation laws on equal protection grounds "in the face of the indisputable fact that a discrimination between the races is the backbone of the statute."[118]

No one would seem to have been better prepared to mount a Supreme Court challenge to miscegenation laws than the NAACP. During the 1940s, the NAACP became a mass organization, and its Legal Defense Fund (LDF) had grown from a tiny volunteer operation into the nation's leading force in civil rights litigation. The LDF, which had evolved out of the NAACP's in-house legal department, could count a growing number of victories, among them *Smith v. Allwright,* a 1944 case involving Black voting rights, and *Shelley v. Kraemer,* the housing case decided in 1948. Its stellar legal team, led by Thurgood Marshall, had identified the eradication of segregation as its goal and become adept at identifying promising areas of attack, then building on each successive victory. In 1950, it won two key education cases, *Sweatt v. Painter* and *McLaurin vs. Oklahoma State Regents,* which would, in 1954, lead to the U.S. Supreme Court's historic *Brown v. Board of Education* decision outlawing racial segregation in public schools.[119]

But every victory the LDF won led it to exert additional care when picking and choosing court cases that seemed to offer "a possibility of establishing a precedent that would advance the due process or equal protection rights of black people." By 1950, the LDF took on dozens of cases each year. A majority of these cases reflected its campaign against segregation in education; they challenged discrimination in such arenas as funding for elementary schools, admission to graduate schools, and teachers' salaries. But the NAACP's caseload always ranged well beyond its educational center: the LDF frequently took civil cases on voting rights and on racial discrimination in housing, transportation, and recreation facilities; in the criminal arena, it took rape and sexual assault cases as well as courts-martial.[120]

Noticeably absent from the LDF's list, however, were cases challenging miscegenation law. In 1939, when the LDF was approached by the editor of one of the nation's most prominent Black newspapers, the *Baltimore Afro-American,* on behalf of a Black man arrested for violating a state miscegenation law, LDF staffers checked their files but said that they could find "nothing at all on the legal side of the issue."[121] By 1944, however, LDF lawyers could clearly glimpse the potential that the World War II climate offered for challenges to miscegenation law. When Oklahoma lawyer A. L. Emery asked for help with a case involving the inheritance rights of a "Creek Freedman" who was "of African descent" and a "full-blood Creek Indian" woman, Thurgood Marshall initially responded with enthusiasm, telling Emery that "this is most certainly the type of case we are vitally interested in" and assuring him that "we are anxious to cooperate in every way possible in getting the issue before the Supreme Court."[122] Marshall persuaded the LDF to agree to post a bond for some of Emery's expenses in mounting the projected appeal. But when the LDF's National Legal Committee considered the case, doubts set in. In a memo examining the case, Marshall's assistant Milton Konvitz emphasized the twin dangers posed by the long string of Oklahoma Supreme Court decisions upholding the state's miscegenation law and the U.S. Supreme Court's ruling in the 1882 case of *Pace v. Alabama,* then weighed these prospects against the NAACP's other challenges to segregation. "The problem of miscegenation from the legislative and legal standpoint naturally is in our great interest," Konvitz told Emery, but "we are afraid of raising the issue in an Appellate Court in a case such as this case at the present time" because "our conclusion is that there is a great likelihood and danger of creating an unfavorable Appellate Court precedent."[123] By 1946, this conclusion had become the NAACP's accepted wisdom on the question of miscegenation law. When Montana lawyer Lewis B. Stewart asked the NAACP for help with a case he planned to bring in that state, Special Counsel Robert Carter responded, truthfully, that the NAACP "has not, as yet, handled a case similar to the one which you have brought to our attention" and once again declined to help.[124]

The NAACP's refusal to mount a court challenge to miscegenation law reflected a complicated set of historical developments. By the end of World War II, three decades had passed since the NAACP first considered whether and how to challenge laws against interracial marriage. Many of the problems it had encountered were problems no longer. The uproar over Jack Johnson was a distant memory, and Marcus Garvey, who had been deported in 1927, had died in 1940. Garvey's program of black racial purity was clearly on the wane, and the NAACP, which had long since consolidated its status as the primary advocacy group for Black Americans, had enjoyed an enormous spike in membership during World War II. Even the argument that interracial marriage was entirely natural, which had once reached so far beyond accepted wisdom, could now be heard with increasing frequency, especially after the defeat of Adolf Hitler turned White liberals decisively against the notions of racial purity that had once been commonplace. The NAACP's legal campaign against racial segregation was on the verge of making historic breakthroughs.

But these successes generated problems of their own. The closer the NAACP came to eradicating the principle of separate but equal in education, the more southern intransigents defended race segregation in the schools as necessary in order to stave off interracial sex and marriage. As Jack Greenberg, the newest addition to the NAACP legal team, recognized, "the White South was insane on the issue—Northern attitudes weren't very rational either." When LDF lawyers prepared the arguments they would use before the U.S. Supreme Court in the education cases of *Sweatt* and *McLaurin*, their discussion of this potentially "explosive" issue raised nothing but problems. Greenberg summarized the possibilities—and the solution they chose:

> To assert that laws prohibiting miscegenation or interracial sex were unconstitutional would bring down a firestorm of criticism and possibly intimidate the Court or some of its justices. But to deny that those laws were unconstitutional would be wrong and lack credibility. Moreover, some blacks would view such a position as craven. The thing to do would be to duck, artfully, if possible.[125]

In the 1940s and 1950s, the NAACP did just that. Thurgood Marshall, the LDF's chief legal strategist, believed, as had NAACP officials ever since the Jack Johnson scandal had first put their backs to the wall, that miscegenation laws were fundamentally wrongheaded. But Marshall was increasingly worried that every attempt to raise the question of interracial marriage would endanger the LDF's entire campaign against segregation just as it was finally coming to fruition.

When it came to miscegenation law, then, the NAACP was still between a rock and a hard place. It had, for decades, been the most experienced, most thoughtful, and most determined critic of miscegenation laws. But when it had finally begun to attract allies among other civil rights organizations and to create the context it needed to challenge the laws, it had, ironically enough, become the organization that was least likely to mount that challenge. If the postwar period provided new possibilities for challenging miscegenation law, someone else would have to lead the way.

Chapter Seven

INTERRACIAL MARRIAGE AS A NATURAL RIGHT

"The statute here attacked is an interference with their natural right to marry the person of their choice and a prevention of their full participation in the sacramental life of the religion of their conscience."

—*California lawyer Dan Marshall, 1947*

LOS ANGELES, CALIFORNIA

When Andrea Pérez told her family she wanted to marry Sylvester Davis, her father stopped speaking to her. And that was only the beginning. Before Andrea and Sylvester finally wed, they had to face a long line of obstacles. They had to find a lawyer to help them challenge the racial roadblocks they ran into at the marriage license bureau. They had to steel themselves against the hate mail that arrived after they took their case to court. And then they had to endure the two long years of legal wrangling that followed. During the reign of miscegenation law, interracial couples often faced opposition, and even interference, from their families, friends, and neighbors. They were stalked by the possibility of scandal, and they risked a range of legal problems that ran from criminal charges all the way to inheritance troubles. At first glance, then, Andrea and Sylvester's situation might seem much like that of interracial couples in earlier periods.[1]

But Andrea and Sylvester had fallen in love in the 1940s, when the way Americans conceived of the relationship between race and American democracy was beginning to change. So although they knew that other interracial couples in California had traveled to Mexico, or New Mexico, to get married,

Andrea and Sylvester decided to stand their ground.[2] For legal advice, they turned to Dan Marshall, a man they knew well enough to approach with a problem. When Andrea was in high school, Dan and his wife, Dorothy, had hired her to babysit their children. The Marshalls, like the Davises, were members of St. Patrick's Catholic Church, where Dan Marshall presided over a small but very determined Catholic Interracial Council.[3] And as it happened, Dan Marshall was no ordinary lawyer. Acting on behalf of Andrea Pérez and Sylvester Davis, Marshall succeeded where generations of other lawyers had failed. In the case of *Perez v. Sharp,* Marshall persuaded the California Supreme Court to become the first court in the twentieth century to declare a miscegenation law unconstitutional. In the process, he jump-started the post–World War II campaign to eliminate the laws once and for all.

In the history of miscegenation law, Dan Marshall's 1948 victory in *Perez v. Sharp* stands as a clear turning point. Before *Perez,* the lawyers who defended interracial couples were likely to be lone voices pleading for individual exceptions to well-established laws; after *Perez,* they were likely to be working in concert with, or directly for, civil rights organizations. Before *Perez,* both lawyers and judges routinely consigned miscegenation cases to the domain of state law; after *Perez,* they conducted their cases with the U.S. Supreme Court in mind. Before *Perez,* lawyers had little choice but to operate on the assumption that miscegenation laws were unambiguously constitutional because they applied to all races "equally." After *Perez,* though, lawyers set their sights on upending the "equal application" rationale.

Between 1949 and 1963, however, the campaign against miscegenation law proceeded by fits and starts, as a handful of civil rights organizations, including the ACLU and the JACL—but notably not the NAACP—tried to expand Dan Marshall's victory in *Perez* to cover the rest of the country. In 1955, the ACLU and the JACL struck right at the southern core of miscegenation law, in a Virginia case called *Naim v. Naim.* But the U.S. Supreme Court rebuffed this challenge, and both groups shifted their focus back to the U.S. West, where they searched for the perfect test case while persuading a dozen state legislatures to repeal their miscegenation laws.

Measured against the high hopes unleashed by *Perez,* these developments seem cautious, even unimpressive. Each knocked a brick or two off the tower of miscegenation law; none shook its foundation. But seen in the context of opinion polls that showed that during the 1950s more than 92 percent of White Americans opposed interracial marriage (in the South, the number exceeded 99 percent), they illustrate the formidable odds that midcentury opponents of miscegenation laws had to face.[4] And they show the rise of arguments that interracial marriage was a natural (if not yet a civil) right, that the right to marry a person of one's own choice trumped the state's investment in the maintenance of white purity, and finally, and most important of all, that miscegenation laws violated the Fourteenth Amendment's guarantee of equal protection.

The "Natural and Constitutional Right" to Marry: Perez v. Sharp

In the long and tortuous history of miscegenation law, no case shows the presumptive power—and the powerful arbitrariness—of racial categories better than *Perez v. Sharp*. The *Perez* case is curious in many respects, beginning with the racial logic (or illogic) by which Andrea Pérez, a Mexican American woman, and Sylvester Davis, an African American man, ever became subject to California's miscegenation law in the first place.

Both Pérez and Davis were lifelong Californians. Their families had lived in Los Angeles since the 1920s, hers in a mostly Mexican neighborhood called Dogtown and his on the multiracial edge of the mostly Black Central Avenue district. After the hard years of the Great Depression, when California mobilized for World War II, they grabbed at the new opportunities the war provided for Black and women workers. In 1941, Sylvester Davis was one of the first Black men hired to work on the assembly line at Lockheed Aircraft's Burbank plant. A year or so later, when Lockheed started hiring women war workers, Andrea Pérez took a job there, too. One of the first people she met at work was Sylvester Davis, who volunteered to show her the ropes. The two hit it off, and Sylvester began driving Andrea to and from work, getting to know her without raising too many eyebrows among their friends and families. The budding romance was interrupted when Sylvester was drafted, but when he returned to Los Angeles after a year of fighting in France, the young couple began seeing each other in earnest. In 1947, they decided to marry.[5]

In some states, a match between a Mexican American woman and a Black man might have slipped beneath the radar of state officials assigned to enforce white supremacy. In Los Angeles, however, Andrea Pérez and Sylvester Davis knew they would run into more trouble than the adamant opposition of Andrea's family. Both Andrea and Sylvester were over twenty-one, old enough to marry without parental permission. But before they could obtain a marriage license, they would have to run the racial gauntlet maintained by Rosamond Rice, the head of Los Angeles County's marriage license bureau. Rice's determination to do her job was so deeply ingrained that on one occasion, she horrified a reporter from a local Black newspaper by explaining that she took

Andrea Pérez, shown here in her sixties, when she
worked as a teacher's aide at Morningside Elementary
School in San Fernando, California. (Dara Orenstein;
Helen Rosas; University of Oregon Library)

great pride in recording the "color or race" of each marriage license applicant,
using a "sixth sense" she had developed for following the letter of the law.
In the case of Andrea Pérez, the bureaucratic mandate for categorization led
to unlikely results. The races entered on each marriage license form had to
be approved by license clerks, who, in order to reconcile the forms with the
categories listed in California miscegenation law ("white persons," "negroes,
Mongolians, members of the Malay race, or mulattoes"), routinely categorized
Mexican American applicants as "white." Under this system, Andrea Pérez
counted as a "white" woman who wanted to marry a "negro" man, a marriage
that would violate California's miscegenation law.[6]

This process of bureaucratic racial alchemy made no sense to Andrea's
fiancé, Sylvester Davis, who years later still insisted "that's horse manure,
that she was white."[7] It did, however, make sense to Andrea's father, Fermín

Pérez, who was appalled that his daughter wanted to marry a Black man.[8] Fermín Pérez was hardly alone in this attitude. In mid-twentieth-century Los Angeles, most Mexican Americans married other Mexican Americans, and although quite a few married Whites and some married Filipinos or East Indians, very few married Blacks.[9] California's Mexican Americans enjoyed some of the same rights as Whites, but they lived their lives on the racial precipice that divided Whites from "non-Whites." In nearby Orange County, for example, Mexican American children had been placed in separate schools; in San Bernardino, they had been refused access to public parks and swimming pools.[10] These alarming signs underlined the importance of staying on the "white" side of the legal line whenever possible. As Andrea Pérez's brother later recalled, "on forms we went by Caucasian."[11]

Caught in this racial bind, Andrea and Sylvester put off going to the marriage license bureau while they sought advice from Sylvester's parents, from the parish priest at St. Patrick's Catholic Church, and from Dorothy Marshall, who took their questions to her lawyer husband. Dan Marshall probably agreed to defend the beleaguered young couple partly as a personal favor. But he also did so because he saw Andrea and Sylvester's predicament as the perfect opportunity to strike a blow for racial equality.[12]

Dan Marshall believed in racial equality with an urgency that only the most liberal of White Californians could match. In 1944, he put his beliefs into action when he and a handful of like-minded Catholics, including his college roommate, journalist Ted LeBerthon, formed the Catholic Interracial Council of Los Angeles (LACIC). The LACIC started with a Black and White membership base but soon stretched its analysis of race and racism to include Chinese, Filipinos, and Mexican Americans. In a matter of months, the fledgling civil rights organization had adopted what LeBerthon described as an "adamant platform calling for integration as against segregation; free and uncondescending social mingling as against friendship for non-Caucasians at a safe distance; and the cleaning of our own houses by some of us white Catholics before we start ridding others of racism."[13]

The LACIC's initial demands were much like those of the other civil rights groups that proliferated in World War II–era Los Angeles.[14] As LACIC president, Dan Marshall called for the immediate return of Japanese Americans from relocation camps and demanded a permanent Fair Employment Practices Commission; he campaigned against racially restrictive housing covenants and pressured the Los Angeles Bar Association to admit Black lawyers. Working out of the multiracial parish of St. Patrick's Church, the group also prodded Catholic schools to admit Black students and demanded that Catholic hospitals hire Black doctors. These projects—and the urgency

Lawyer Dan Marshall in 1952. (Courtesy of University
of Southern California, on behalf of the USC Special
Collections)

that Dan Marshall brought to each of them—gave him a reputation for, as
Ted LeBerthon put it, "virtually terrifying the excessively prudent," especially the Catholic Church's Los Angeles Diocese, which found the LACIC
a constant thorn in its side.[15] Before much longer, diocesan officials would
decide they had had enough; in early 1950, they shut the group down.[16]

In the meantime, though, the LACIC reached well beyond the comfort
zone of other civil rights organizations to raise the potentially explosive issue
of interracial marriage. Dan Marshall's discussions with Andrea Pérez and Sylvester Davis quickly turned into LACIC plans to mount a test case. In April
1947, the group issued a press release announcing its plan to launch a frontal
"attack" on California's miscegenation law in the California Supreme Court.
The plan went into operation on August 1, 1947, when Dan Marshall sent

Pérez and Davis to the county clerk's office to apply for a marriage license. As everyone expected, officials refused to issue it, and a week later, Marshall filed suit against the county clerk of Los Angeles County, asking for a writ of mandate that would force the county to issue the marriage license. Skipping right over the lower courts, Marshall filed directly with the California Supreme Court, which agreed to hear the case.[17]

The sheer arbitrariness of California's system of race classification was clearly apparent in the *Perez* case, which turned on the state's flimsy premise that because its marriage license bureau (unlike some of its school and park administrators) defined Mexican Americans as White, a marriage between a Mexican American woman and a Black man was a threat to white supremacy. Yet—and this is the second curious thing about the *Perez* case—Dan Marshall made no effort to challenge the racial labels the county applied to his clients. Perhaps he felt that too many lawyers had fallen on these rocks before, even when all they were trying to do was to win an individual exception to the general rule. Certainly Marshall had no intention of settling for so little: he wanted to pull California's miscegenation law out by its roots. In order to mount a credible test case, Marshall had to present the court with a couple whose marriage fit the categories listed in California's miscegenation law. In other words, if one partner to the marriage was Black, the other had to be White. The layers of unlikeliness lined up like ducks in a row: Marshall's reliance on the racial categories in the law corresponded with the county clerk's bureaucratic classification of Mexican Americans as "white," which corresponded with the Pérez family practice of recording themselves as "Caucasian." As a result, the *Perez* case went forward with all sides in agreement that Sylvester Davis was "a Negro male" and Andrea Pérez was "a white female."[18]

By treating these racial "facts" as unremarkable, Dan Marshall laid the basis for the most curious of all the aspects of the *Perez* case, his determination to rest his case against miscegenation law on the claim of religious freedom, a claim that was novel, indeed virtually unheard of, in court cases on interracial marriage. In a nutshell, the argument went like this. Both Pérez and Davis were members of the Catholic Church. The Catholic Church, which considered marriage a sacrament, did not prohibit interracial marriage. Because California miscegenation law prevented Pérez and Davis from exercising their right "to participate fully in the sacramental life of the religion in which they believe," it was an unconstitutional restraint on their freedom of religion.[19]

In making this argument, Dan Marshall brought his Catholic convictions to bear on his experience as a civil rights advocate and a legal strategist. His ideas were shaped by the work of three Catholic thinkers he particularly admired. The first, Father John LaFarge, was the founder of the New York Catholic Interracial Council and Marshall's inspiration for founding the LACIC. LaFarge was known for his books on Catholic racial doctrine, in which he offered a cautious, and carefully qualified, claim that nothing in Catholic doctrine actually prohibited interracial marriage, a claim that Marshall optimistically stretched into a full-blown, official church policy.[20] Marshall's second inspiration, George Dunne, a classmate at Los Angeles' Jesuit-run Loyola Law School in the 1920s and a friend ever since, was a man no one ever regarded as cautious. Dunne was in the process of publishing an article, "The Sin of Segregation," in which he labeled the segregationist argument that "elimination of racial segregation will mean miscegenation on a grand scale" as "the grand-daddy of all red herrings," a falsehood whose "roots lie in a pride of race and blood that belongs properly to the nazi, not to the Christian, philosophy of life."[21] Marshall's third, and even more radical, inspiration was Denver priest John Markoe, who insisted that when it came to interracial marriage "it is time to explode the bomb of Catholic truth, and let the chips fall where they may."[22]

As a legal strategy, Marshall's freedom of religion argument was an attempt to break the impasse between the California Supreme Court and budding civil rights organizations eager to press the postwar promise of wartime rhetoric about democracy and equality. Marshall had experienced this impasse firsthand when he joined with several ACLU attorneys to submit an amicus brief in a case that challenged California's notorious anti-Japanese alien land laws. In a decision issued just a few months before Marshall took the *Perez* case, the California Supreme Court upheld the hated alien land laws. State lawmakers, the court ruled, were entitled to use race classifications, like those in the alien land laws, as long as they could show a "rational basis" for doing so. Alien land laws, the court insisted, did not affect fundamental civil liberties, such as freedom of speech, press, assembly, and worship, which, the California court admitted, the U.S. Supreme Court had decided could not be limited by a state unless there was a "grave and immediate danger to interests which the state may lawfully protect."[23]

Dan Marshall built his arguments in *Perez* around the lessons he had learned in the alien land law case. By raising the freedom of religion issue, he tried to wrench the California Supreme Court out of its habitual deference to the racial imperatives of miscegenation law (and its resistance to claims for civil rights) by getting the court to see interracial marriage as a matter of civil liberties. In doing so, he hoped to trigger a higher standard of proof. Once in the realm of civil liberties, the state would no longer be able to settle for providing a merely "rational" basis for miscegenation laws; instead, it would have to show the court that interracial marriage posed a "grave and immediate danger."

To this end, Marshall's opening petition in *Perez* was studded with claims of religious, constitutional, and natural rights forged in the rhetorical irons of civil liberties law. Charging that California's miscegenation law denied Andrea Pérez and Sylvester Davis "the natural and constitutional right . . . to intermarry," Marshall claimed that it was "an interference with their natural right to marry the person of their choice and a prevention of their full participation in the sacramental life of the religion of their conscience." There was, he told the California Supreme Court, "nothing licentious nor inconsistent with the peace and safety of the state in these petitioners exercising their right of religious freedom, and natural right, to intermarry."[24]

Of all the things Marshall brought to the *Perez* case, the most significant may have been his argument that interracial marriage was a natural right, contradicting the "unnatural" label that had been a mainstay of miscegenation law ever since the 1880s. Outside the courtroom, this notion had come under increasing challenge. In the 1920s, modern cultural critics like George Schuyler had argued that interracial sex and marriage were more natural than unnatural; by the end of World War II, these ideas had gained a good deal of credence in liberal and intellectual circles. Yet they had so far made little impact on the courts, which had, by the 1940s, settled into the routine administrative enforcement of racial imperatives that judges took more or less for granted. It seems likely that some judges regarded the assertion that interracial marriage was unnatural as more than a little shopworn. Yet they always refrained from saying so—until, that is, Dan Marshall's claim that interracial marriage was a natural right forced them to face the question of just what kind of right interracial marriage might be.

Dan Marshall's argument that marriage was a natural right had religious roots and strategic legal implications. To Catholic thinkers, the concept of natural rights carried special significance because it referred to a sphere of human activity above and beyond the control of the state, and over which the church, rather than the state, could claim authority.[25] Within the American legal system, the notion of natural rights was also a familiar one; it referred to those rights individuals possessed prior to and outside of (though not necessarily in opposition to) the state.[26]

Discussions of marriage as a natural right had long since been banished from the realm of miscegenation law, but the idea itself was familiar to judges, who occasionally invoked it in other kinds of cases. Dan Marshall's search for precedents turned up two promising, if also rather obscure, examples: a California Supreme Court case from the 1890s, involving a couple who had been married at sea, and *Meyer v. Nebraska,* a U.S. Supreme Court case from 1923. The *Meyer* case was about an entirely different subject—the teaching of German language in public schools—but in justifying their decision, the justices had thrown in a lofty rhetorical statement that the personal "liberty" guaranteed by the Fourteenth Amendment included the "right of the individual . . . to marry, establish a home and bring up children, to worship God according to the dictates of his own conscience, and generally to enjoy those privileges, long recognized at common law as essential to the orderly pursuit of happiness by free men."[27] By hitching a traditionally Catholic notion of natural rights to *Meyer v. Nebraska*'s rhetoric about personal liberty, Dan Marshall opened a legal channel through which modern convictions about the naturality of interracial marriage could flow back into judicial consideration of miscegenation laws.

First, however, Marshall would have to win the *Perez* case. He faced formidable odds with precious little support. Outside Marshall's own LACIC, the religious freedom argument fell almost entirely flat. Most observers regarded the claim that interracial marriage denied freedom of religion as idiosyncratic, controversial, even foolhardy. The sheer riskiness of Marshall's strategy seems to have precluded Los Angeles' other civil rights groups from coming to his aid. Although he had worked with several of these groups on previous occasions, none of them expressed any public support for the *Perez* case—not the NAACP, the JACL, or even the ACLU, which briefly contemplated, but in the end failed to produce, an amicus brief in *Perez*.[28] (Afterward, the liberal magazine *The Nation* would account for their absence by reporting that "most of the civil-rights organizations failed or refused to participate in the case on the assumption that miscegenation statutes could not be successfully challenged in the courts.")[29]

At the Los Angeles Diocese, Catholic officials were appalled that Marshall had put the Catholic Church in the position of seeming to endorse interracial marriage. When Marshall wrote to ask Auxiliary Bishop Joseph McGucken, a onetime LACIC supporter, to testify in the *Perez* case, he received an immediate, and visceral, refusal. "I cannot think of any point in existing race relationships that will stir up more passion and prejudice," McGucken fumed. "I want to make very clear that I am not at all willing to be pulled into a controversy of this kind."[30]

In the courtroom, too, the odds seemed to be stacked against Marshall. As his critics had predicted, lawyers for Los Angeles County made short work of his religious freedom claims. The Catholic Church, they insisted, was no supporter of interracial marriage, and even Marshall's idol, fellow Catholic interracialist Father John LaFarge, had said so. In his book *The Race Question and the Negro,* LaFarge had ended a largely favorable discussion of interracial marriage with the comment that "where such intermarriages are prohibited by law, as they are in several States of the Union, the Church bids her ministers to respect these laws, and to do all that is in their power to dissuade persons from entering into such unions." Moreover, as county lawyers also pointed out, the U.S. Supreme Court had repeatedly rejected claims that freedom of religion might protect polygamy, another kind of marriage often described as unnatural.[31]

Los Angeles County was confident that California courts would reject Marshall's religious freedom claim, and Marshall's decision not to challenge the race classification of his clients seemed only to have made the county's job that much easier. When it came to the constitutionality of miscegenation laws, county lawyers had at their fingertips a long list of judicial precedents in and outside of California, so all they needed to do was offer the court a presentable justification for California's law. Assuming that the court would reject Dan Marshall's "clear and present danger" standard, the county offered two distinct but overlapping arguments that there was a "rational" basis for the law. The first argument, a "biological" one, rested on eugenics-era notions of black inferiority, including claims that Blacks suffered higher mortality rates, had shorter life expectancies, and were more likely than Whites to suffer from diseases like sickle-cell anemia, and on assertions that birth rates were declining among "hybrids."[32] The second, a "sociological" argument, was designed to cover the potentially awkward fact that biological arguments like these were increasingly out of fashion, at least in academic circles. In this vein, the county argued that intermarriage resulted in dangerous "social evils." Quoting Father LaFarge as well as several well-known social scientists, lawyers for Los Angeles County asserted that "there is ample evidence of sociological conditions which exist and are becoming increasingly acute in California which would justify a finding that marriages between Negroes and Whites would result in such a strain upon the marriage bond and in such a strain upon the family relations of the parties to such a marriage and in such unfortunate social conditions for the offspring of such a marriage as to justify the legal prohibition of such marriages." Then, playing their trump card, they proclaimed: "The sociologists and scientists agree that there is widespread public opinion throughout the United States against interracial marriages."[33]

"A Fundamental Right of Free Men"

Here matters stood when the California Supreme Court assembled in Los Angeles to hear oral arguments in *Perez*. Dan Marshall spoke first. "No rational person," he said in an opening attempt to label California's miscegenation law as arbitrary and unreasonable, "can subscribe to the dogma that it is imperative at all costs to preserve the purity of the blood."[34] Then he laid out his argument that Andrea Pérez and Sylvester Davis had a natural right to marry, a right protected by fundamental constitutional guarantees of religious liberty.[35] The justices listened politely, and silently, to Marshall's presentation. But as soon as Charles Stanley, who represented Los Angeles County, began to challenge Marshall's religious freedom argument, one of the court's junior justices, Roger Traynor, impatiently interrupted, steering the proceedings in an altogether different direction. Wasn't, Traynor asked, this case really about equal protection of the law? And what about race classification?

> MR. JUSTICE TRAYNOR: . . . it might help to explain the statute, what it means. What is a negro?
>
> MR. STANLEY: We have not the benefit of any judicial interpretation. The statute states that a negro [this is evidently an error; Stanley clearly meant to say, as the law did, "a white"] cannot marry a negro, which can be construed to mean a full-blooded negro, since the statute also says mulatto, Mongolian, or Malay.
>
> MR. JUSTICE TRAYNOR: What is a mulatto? One-sixteenth blood?
>
> MR. STANLEY: Certainly certain states have seen fit to state what a mulatto is.
>
> MR. JUSTICE TRAYNOR: If there is 1/8 blood, can they marry? If you can marry with 1/8, why not with 1/16, 1/32, 1/64? And then don't you get in the ridiculous position where a negro cannot marry anybody? If he is white, he cannot marry black, or if he is black, he cannot marry white.
>
> MR. STANLEY: I agree that it would be better for the Legislature to lay down an exact amount of blood, but I do not think that the statute should be declared unconstitutional as indefinite on this ground.
>
> MR. JUSTICE TRAYNOR: That is something anthropologists have not been able to furnish, although they say generally that there is no such thing as race.
>
> MR. STANLEY: I would not say that anthropologists have said that generally, except such statements for sensational purposes.
>
> MR. JUSTICE TRAYNOR: Would you say that Professor Wooten of Harvard was a sensationalist? The crucial question is how can a county clerk determine who are negroes and who are whites?[36]

It was no accident that these questions came from Roger Traynor, a justice with two qualities that set him apart from his peers. One was the breadth of Traynor's educational background. The holder of a Ph.D. in political science as well as a law degree, Traynor had spent several years as a professor at UC Berkeley's Boalt Hall before being appointed to the California Supreme Court in 1940, largely on the basis of his academic expertise. Determined to show his skeptical fellow justices that, as he would later put it, "the mind counts," Traynor kept abreast of developments in modern social science. The other quality was Traynor's willingness to jettison what he called "bad" precedents. "Who among us," he grew fond of asking lawyers in his later years, "has not known a precedent that should never have been born. . . . [or] a precedent that has had a good life in its day but whose day is over?" A "bad precedent is doubly evil," he wrote on another occasion, "because it has not only wrought hardship but threatens to continue wreaking it."[37]

Traynor's questions caught Stanley off guard, all the more so when Traynor began to press Stanley on the academic merits of the outdated biological arguments the county had offered. Backed into a corner, Stanley reached for a generalization he could defend. "I do not like to say it," Stanley blurted, "or to tie myself in with *Mein Kampf,* but it has been shown that the white race is superior physically and mentally to the black race, and the intermarriage of these races results in a lessening of physical vitality and mentality in their offspring." "Are there," an incredulous Traynor shot back, "medical men in this country today who say such a thing?" Now thoroughly shaken, Stanley tried to shift from biological to sociological justifications for the laws, only to end up arguing that "people who enter into miscegenous marriages are usually from the lower walks of both races . . . generally people who are lost to shame."[38]

Reporters from Los Angeles's Black newspapers hung on Stanley's every word. "To the spectators in the court," the *California Eagle* told its readers, "the scene seemed to shift from 'democratic' America to Nazi Germany as Marshall sat down and Deputy County Counsel Charles C. Stanley proceeded to justify the racist statute." The *Los Angeles Sentinel* tracked down a copy of Stanley's brief, which contained, its editor said, "statements that 'pure' Negroes are inferior mentally and physically to whites, that mulattoes are close to the very dregs of society, apt to be moral and physical degenerates afflicted with some of the most repulsive diseases known to man and a drain upon society. . . . The brief and argument alike," the editor seethed, "were filled with cheap appeals to racial prejudice and with citations from discredited and long discarded text books reminiscent of the trash used by Hitler to justify the Nuremburg laws." After the *Sentinel* demanded an investigation, the Los Angeles Board of Supervisors went so far as to order Stanley to explain his actions to the board before quietly shelving the *Sentinel*'s protest.[39]

Justice Traynor's questions, however, did more than put Charles Stanley on the defensive. They also gave Dan Marshall the kind of gift no lawyer had ever before received in a miscegenation case: judicial willingness to question the entire enterprise of race classification. While Stanley was busy fending off criticisms, Dan Marshall took advantage of the foothold Traynor had offered, making sure that his next brief highlighted the deeply illogical nature of race and race classification. In it, he asserted that experts had determined that "race, as popularly understood, is a myth"; he played on the gap between expert opinion and "irrational" laws based on "prejudice" rooted in "myth, folk belief and superstition"; and he dismissed his opponents' reliance on the "hallucination of race" and the "grotesque reasoning of eugenicists," comparing their statements to excerpts from Hitler's *Mein Kampf*.[40]

It took nearly a year for the California Supreme Court to issue its decision in the *Perez* case. When it did, on October 1, 1948, it was clear that the seven justices on the court were in no more agreement than Dan Marshall and Charles Stanley. By a razor-thin 4–3 margin, they declared California's miscegenation law unconstitutional.[41]

Three of the four justices in the majority ruled that California's miscegenation law was unconstitutional because it violated the Fourteenth Amendment's guarantee of equal protection of the laws. Roger Traynor, who wrote the opinion that laid out this argument, took Dan Marshall's reliance on *Meyer v. Nebraska* much more seriously than either his religious freedom argument or his "clear and present danger" standard. In effect, Traynor transformed Marshall's argument that marriage was a "natural" right into a ruling that marriage was "a fundamental right of free men." As a fundamental right, marriage could not, under the equal protection clause, be limited on the basis of race. Traynor acknowledged that the U.S. Supreme Court had upheld segregation in schools and public transportation, but he insisted that marriage was a different matter. "The right to marry," Traynor declared, "is the right of individuals, not of racial groups," adding, a bit later, that "the essence of the right to marry is freedom to join in marriage with the person of one's choice." California's miscegenation law, he explained, restricted "the right of Negroes, mulattoes, Mongolians, and Malays to marry," and the right of "Caucasians," too. "A member of any of these races," Traynor declared, "may find himself barred by law from marrying the person of his choice and that person to him may be irreplaceable. Human beings are bereft of worth and dignity by a doctrine that would make them as interchangeable as trains."[42]

When it came to the issue of race classification, though, these three judges divided into two different camps. With the backing of the court's chief justice, Phil Gibson, Roger Traynor developed a critique of the entire enterprise of race classification. Citing a virtual "who's who" of culturalist social scientists, from Franz Boas to Gunnar Myrdal, Traynor took the step that judges in miscegenation cases had, until *Perez*, consistently refused to take—he moved beyond the race classification of a particular individual to consider race classification as a general practice. In this vein, Traynor insisted that the California law, which, he pointed out, "does not include 'Indians' or 'Hindus' . . . nor does it set up 'Mexicans' as a separate category," was irrational not only for the inconsistency of the groups mentioned in the law but also because none of the usual dividing lines—skin color, ancestry, or blood—offered a reliable way of distinguishing between them, especially in a world where "the fact is overwhelming that there has been a steady increase in the number of people in this country who belong to more than one race." Traynor and Gibson declared California's racial classifications "too vague and uncertain to be enforceable regulations of a fundamental right."[43]

The third justice, Stephen Carter, staked out broader grounds. "It is my position," Carter declared, in language that could only be described as wishful thinking, "that the statutes before us *never* were constitutional." Reaching for authority for this position, Carter cited the Declaration of Independence, the Bill of Rights, the Fourteenth Amendment, and the charter of the recently formed United Nations. Carter's ideological foundation was U.S. Supreme Court Justice John Marshall Harlan's powerful dissent in the 1896 case of *Plessy v. Ferguson,* the judicial rock on which segregation had depended ever since. "Our Constitution," Harlan had written, "is color-blind, and neither knows nor tolerates classes among citizens. . . . The law regards man as man, and takes no account of his surroundings or of his color when his civil rights as guaranteed by the supreme law of the land are involved."[44]

On the other side of the court, the three justices who wanted to uphold California's miscegenation law issued an opinion heavy with the accumulated weight of historical justification. Insisting that "the attitude of the church has no particular bearing," they flatly rejected Dan Marshall's claim that interracial marriage was a natural right protected by religious freedom. As they saw it, "the right of the state to exercise extensive control over the marriage contract has always been recognized," in prohibitions on polygamy and incest as well as prohibitions on interracial marriage. Quoting extensively from previous court decisions, they recycled judicial condemnations of interracial marriage ("Connections and alliances so unnatural should be prohibited by positive law and subject to no evasion"), judicial endorsement of miscegenation laws ("Civilized society has the power of self-preservation"), and judicial adherence to the equal application rationale ("The punishment of each offending person, whether white or black, is the same"). They dismissed Roger Traynor's critique of race classification as "more theoretical than real" and quoted eugenicists as proof that there was "not only some but a great deal" of evidence to show both the biological and sociological dangers posed by interracial marriage. Claiming that they had the U.S. Constitution, the legislatures of thirty states, and "an unbroken line of judicial support, both state and federal," on their side, they posed the challenge that would soon haunt judges in the other twenty-nine states with miscegenation laws. "It is difficult," they declared, "to see why such laws, valid when enacted and constitutionally enforceable in this state for nearly 100 years and elsewhere for a much longer period of time, are now unconstitutional."[45]

Neither the three justices who supported California's miscegenation law nor the three who criticized it on equal protection grounds were sufficient to provide the four-vote majority needed to decide the *Perez* case. So it mattered a great deal that the final—and deciding—vote was cast by Justice Douglas Edmonds, who was, as it turned out, the only one of the seven justices to accept Dan Marshall's religious freedom argument. In a separate opinion, Edmonds agreed with Roger Traynor that marriage was "a fundamental right of free men" but insisted that it was a right "grounded in the fundamental principles of Christianity" and "protected by the constitutional guarantee of religious freedom." Because he based his decision on this religious freedom claim and the "clear and present danger" standard that went with it, Edmonds deemed it unnecessary to discuss the issue of equal protection and refused even to consider whether miscegenation laws were, as Traynor had claimed, "discriminatory and irrational."[46]

Perez's 4–3 margin of victory fell far short of establishing a judicial consensus on the unconstitutionality of miscegenation laws, but the outcome of the case led journalists to jump to the conclusion that there had indeed been a judicial sea change, which they hurried to explain to their readers. The mainstream press catalogued the various rationales for overruling the law, including religious freedom as well as equal protection, illustrating these positions with pithy quotes about laws rooted in "ignorance, prejudice and intolerance" being toppled by "the fundamental right of free men to marry" and "the right to marry the person of one's choice."[47] The liberal and ethnic press celebrated a decision that was, as one writer in the liberal Catholic journal *America* claimed, "absolutely unique in American history.[48] The *Los Angeles Sentinel,* an African American paper, told its readers that "this is the first time in more than a hundred years of litigation that a successful attack has been made upon this prohibition in the United States."[49] Dan Marshall, elated at his victory over daunting odds, told the *Korean Independence* that it was "a magnificent decision" that "sets a tremendous precedent for the entire nation."[50] The *Nation* agreed, calling the case a "personal triumph" for Marshall, in "some respects . . . the most important civil-rights victory that racial minorities have yet won in American courts."[51]

The possibility that miscegenation laws, which had seemed invulnerable to constitutional attack since the 1880s, might soon succumb was heady stuff indeed. Civil rights groups across the country took note of the fact that Dan Marshall's dogged persistence had proved that it was possible to win such a case. In the *Pittsburgh Courier,* one of the nation's leading Black newspapers, columnist Marjorie McKenzie offered extensive analysis of the "heroic" decision, which, she explained, came "as a shock because it has not been a part of the [NAACP's] official fight, the grand strategy."[52] The JACL also noted the "historic" decision, and the ACLU, which already regretted its failure to file an amicus brief in Marshall's support, started looking for ways to make the leap from the California Supreme Court to the U.S. Supreme Court.[53]

For a while it looked as if they might get their chance. Back at the marriage license bureau, Rosamond Rice tried to fend off the changes, announcing that she would continue to refuse licenses to interracial couples until she received official notice from county counsel Harold Kennedy "to do otherwise."[54] Kennedy asked the California Supreme Court to reconsider the case, but when he was turned down by the same 4–3 margin, he directed the marriage license bureau to begin issuing licenses to interracial couples.[55] Rosamond Rice complied with obvious reluctance, continuing to record the race of each applicant in the hope that it might still prove possible to overturn the decision.[56] She had some basis for her hopes; in early December, a deputy county counsel announced that his office intended to appeal the case to the U.S. Supreme Court.[57] The prospect of an appeal pleased Dan Marshall, who predicted victory there, too, and it delighted the ACLU, whose national officials quickly assured Al Wirin of the Southern California branch that this time they would "by all means" offer their support.[58] In the end, though, for reasons that were never made clear, Los Angeles County decided not to pursue the appeal.

On December 13, 1948, Andrea Pérez and Sylvester Davis applied for, and finally received, their marriage license. Still trying to avoid publicity, they waited several more months before holding their ceremony. The wedding finally took place on May 7, 1949, at St. Patrick's Church, without Andrea's parents present. Andrea and Sylvester lived

Marriage License and Certificate of Andrea Pérez and Sylvester Davis. (County Clerk/Recorder, Los Angeles County; University of Oregon Library)

for a while with Sylvester's family, and then used Sylvester's benefits under the GI Bill to move to the newly opened Joe Louis housing tract in Pacoima, where they raised three children. After the birth of their first daughter, Andrea's parents slowly reconciled themselves to the marriage, which lasted until Andrea's death in 2000. During their more than fifty happy years of marriage, the Davises said as little as possible about their role in the case that was the first in the twentieth century to overturn a state miscegenation law.[59]

By proving that miscegenation laws could be successfully challenged in court, Dan Marshall had paved the way for Andrea Pérez to marry Sylvester Davis, and in the process raised new—and as yet unanswered—questions about the future of miscegenation law. Was the *Perez* decision, which was, as the *Wyoming Law Journal* quickly noted, "contra to 'well-settled law,'" a legal anomaly or a portent of things to come?[60] Would other state courts, in the West or the South, follow the example of California? How soon might a miscegenation case reach the U.S. Supreme Court?

With all these possibilities in play, everyone struggled to assess a new (and only shortly before unimaginable) landscape of opportunities—and risks. Lawyers who wanted to follow in Dan Marshall's footsteps debated which of the many legal avenues laid out in *Perez* would prove the most effective in overturning miscegenation laws. Some insisted that *Perez* proved the power of equal protection arguments, while others cautioned against abandoning the religious freedom claim that had provided Marshall's narrow margin of victory. The desire to launch a full-out assault on the rationality of race categorization jostled with claims for colorblind models, which relied on the deliberate nonrecognition of race. Faced with all these alternatives, those judges who came to believe that miscegenation laws were, in fact, "bad" precedent struggled to find a position of principled decisiveness strong enough to mold the judicial consensus that was strikingly absent from *Perez*.

On the other side of the issue, defenders of miscegenation laws dug in their heels, invoking the specter of interracial marriage whenever and wherever the subject of civil rights was raised. Among Whites, opposition to interracial marriage was so nearly unanimous that the issue provided a deeply emotional touchstone. By pressing this point, white supremacists further narrowed the already limited political maneuverability of the NAACP. Miscegenation law had always been one of the toughest issues the NAACP faced, and the difficulty was especially pronounced during the decade that followed *Perez*. Six months before *Perez*, the NAACP had won a key U.S. Supreme Court ruling in a housing discrimination case; it was inching closer and closer to persuading the nation's highest court to use the equal protection clause of the Fourteenth Amendment to declare an end to racial segregation in public schools.[61] It had taken the organization's Legal Defense Fund decades of careful strategizing to get this far. And now, standing on the brink of success, the NAACP feared that any attempt to raise the volatile issue of interracial marriage might derail the campaign against segregation in the schools.

The Art of Judicial Ducking

After *Perez* made the overturning of miscegenation laws seem a realistic possibility for the first time since Reconstruction, the chance of U.S. Supreme Court review began to hover over every miscegenation court case. Since the 1880s, responsibility for miscegenation laws had been left almost entirely to state rather than federal courts, but Roger Traynor's equal protection argument rested heavily on the Fourteenth Amendment to the U.S. Constitution, a matter for U.S. Supreme Court interpretation. In the South, where miscegenation law was an article of faith, the prospect of U.S. Supreme Court review quickly began to shape the strategies and the outcomes of what might otherwise have been run-of-the-mill state-level court cases.

One such case took place in Mississippi, where, just a few months before the *Perez* ruling, a grand jury had indicted Davis Knight, a light-skinned man who considered himself White but was descended from a mixed-race grandmother, for marrying a White woman. Like many a pre-*Perez* attorney, Knight's lawyer, Quitman Ross, had opted to argue that his client had been racially miscategorized rather than challenge the constitutionality of Mississippi's miscegenation law head-on. And like many such lawyers, Ross lost. In December 1948, the Jones County Circuit Court convicted Davis Knight of criminal miscegenation and sentenced him to five years in the state penitentiary. By this time, however, the *Perez* ruling had been issued, and lawyers, judges, and prosecutors, too, started to factor the possibility of U.S. Supreme Court review into their strategies.[62]

So when Quitman Ross appealed Knight's conviction to the Mississippi Supreme Court, he received unexpected assistance from the unlikeliest of quarters—the lawyer charged with defending the state of Mississippi. Southern prosecutors were acknowledged experts at chaining mixed-race men and women to the legal walls of race definition, but Mississippi's assistant attorney general decided that it would be better to let Davis Knight slip through the cracks than to risk triggering U.S. Supreme Court review. So he took the remarkable step of telling the Mississippi Supreme Court that he agreed with Quitman Ross that Knight had been unjustly convicted. "The evidence is overwhelming . . . ," he told the court, "that the appellant has less than one-eighth Negro blood, if he had any Negro blood." With both sides seemingly in agreement, the court overturned Davis's conviction, citing the state's own "admission . . . that the proof in this case does not establish beyond every reasonable doubt that the defendant had one-eighth or more Negro blood." As historian Victoria Bynum concluded, the Mississippi Supreme Court held "that Davis Knight was legally white in order to sidestep the more volatile question of whether antimiscegenation laws were constitutional."[63]

From their national offices in New York City, the Catholic Interracial Council, the ACLU, and the NAACP followed the *Knight* case closely, trying to calculate the opportunities and the risks it might offer. But while the state of Mississippi worried that the U.S. Supreme Court might declare its miscegenation law unconstitutional, Quitman Ross worried that support from civil rights organizations would provoke the Mississippi Supreme Court into upholding his client's conviction. Like most midcentury southern lawyers, Ross was determined to keep that danger at arm's length. As he explained to a friend, "Various domestic organizations having to do with the Negro race sought to inject themselves into the matter but their offers of assistance were courteously and firmly declined."[64]

Five years later, when Alabama lawyer E. B. Haltom defended Linnie Jackson against an indictment for criminal miscegenation, he, too, avoided contact with civil rights organizations. Yet when Haltom took the *Jackson* case to court, he made the most of the critiques of miscegenation law that were beginning to surface in southern legal circles, launching a direct assault on the constitutionality of the Alabama miscegenation law. Haltom told the Court of Appeals of Alabama that Alabama's law violated both the Fifth and Fourteenth Amendment restraints on "arbitrary and unreasonable discrimination" and the Fourteenth Amendment protection of "the privileges and immunities" of citizens. And when the Alabama Supreme Court refused to hear his appeal of the Court of Appeals decision, Haltom became the first southern lawyer since John Tompkins had taken Tony Pace's case in 1882 to appeal a miscegenation conviction to the U.S. Supreme Court.[65]

When the *Jackson* case reached the U.S. Supreme Court, the futility of trying to separate challenges to miscegenation law from campaigns for civil rights quickly became apparent. Six months earlier, in May 1954, the Court had issued its famous decision *Brown v. Board of Education,* in which, after much urging from the LDF, the justices held that legally mandated race segregation violated the Fourteenth Amendment's guarantee of equal protection. White and Black liberals, who were delighted by the decision, celebrated what they considered a long-overdue step toward racial equality, but die-hard White racists, who were horrified by *Brown,* organized themselves to resist, issuing incendiary pronouncements that integration in the schools was only the first step on the road to a world of miscegenation run amok. "White and Negro children in the same schools will lead to miscegenation," the Jackson, Mississippi, *Daily News* insisted in response to *Brown.*

"Miscegenation leads to mixed marriages and mixed marriages lead to mongrelization of the human race."[66]

The *Jackson* case reached the U.S. Supreme Court six months after *Brown,* in a period when the South seemed poised between acquiescence and resistance. Everyone at the Court, even the law clerks, regarded the case as political dynamite, likely to add fuel to the fires of resistance. Three justices voted to hear the case anyway, but the rest were content to dispose of the matter by simply refusing, as the Court can (and often does, in responding to petitions for certiorari like that offered in *Jackson*), to grant the petition for review. As a result, *Jackson,* the boldest statement of southern liberalism to appear on the question of miscegenation law in three-quarters of a century, was consigned to the status of a footnote in the history of miscegenation law.[67]

Only a few months later, however, another lawyer, thirty-six-year-old David Carliner, thought he had found a way to overcome the U.S. Supreme Court's reluctance to face the question of interracial marriage. Carliner's case, *Naim v. Naim,* had arisen in a rather roundabout fashion. It started in early 1954, when one of Carliner's clients, Ham Say Naim, a "Chinese" seaman from Portsmouth, Virginia, came to Carliner with an immigration problem. Naim wanted to become a U.S. citizen, but his wife, a "white" woman named Ruby, planned to dissolve their marriage, either by divorce or annulment; if she succeeded, Naim's application for an extension of his visa would be rejected. Carliner practiced immigration law in Washington, D.C., but as a graduate of the University of Virginia's law school, he was familiar with the Racial Integrity Act that Ruby Naim relied on in her plea for annulment. Even as a student, Carliner had believed that the Racial Integrity Act was unconstitutional, and in the stirring days just before the U.S. Supreme Court issued its ruling in *Brown v. Board of Education,* he found it easy to imagine that a Supreme Court bold enough to oppose segregation in public schools would be bold enough oppose to miscegenation laws, too. What better place to do so than in a case involving the strictest miscegenation law in the country? With this goal in mind, Carliner took Naim's case to Portsmouth City Court in Virginia.[68]

In February 1954, the Portsmouth City Court ruled against Ham Say Naim, and Carliner, who had taken the case without pay, began to look for the financial backing he needed to mount an appeal.[69] He started by approaching the ACLU, a logical choice for three reasons: first, the NAACP's withdrawal from the field had left the ACLU as the most visible public critic of miscegenation laws; second, the ACLU was beginning to pile up Supreme Court victories in civil liberties cases; third, Carliner was personally acquainted with some of the men in the ACLU's Washington, D.C., office. In a two-page memo, Carliner laid out an embryonic challenge to the constitutionality of miscegenation laws, then asked for money and organizational support. "The Virginia law," Carliner explained in an accompanying letter, "is so broad that not even ostensibly white persons can tell whether their marriages are legal. . . . This statute is offensive and behind that there seems little question that it is unconstitutional. . . . It is a challenging case and will offer an opportunity to throw out the southern miscegenation statutes." Primed by *Perez,* the ACLU required little persuading. It quickly agreed to finance the appeal and assigned its general counsel, Herbert Levy, at the group's New York headquarters, to advise Carliner every step of the way.[70]

Over the next two years, as the *Naim* case appeared and reappeared in courts at a variety of levels, Carliner and Levy shaped their case for U.S. Supreme Court review. To this end, Carliner jettisoned lines of argument he had tried in lower courts but now feared might distract Supreme Court justices from the key constitutional issues of due process and equal protection. He started by shedding his contention that Virginia's miscegenation law conflicted with U.S. treaties with China. Then, on Levy's advice, he discarded his argument that Virginia's provision prohibiting interracial couples in Virginia from marrying in other states violated the "full faith and credit" clause of the U.S. Constitution. In May 1954, when the Supreme Court issued its decision in *Brown v. Board of Education,* its emphasis on equal protection seemed to confirm the wisdom of this pared-down strategy. In September, Carliner proudly reported to Levy that "the sole issues before the Court now are (1) Whether the 14th Amendment limits the jurisdiction of the trial court to grant annulment decrees based solely upon racial ineligibility to marry and (2) Whether the racial ineligibility statute violates the equal protection and due process clauses."[71]

Not until Carliner had exhausted all his appeals in Virginia and was ready to bring the *Naim* case to the U.S. Supreme Court did he learn that the Court had refused to hear the *Jackson* case from Alabama. Neither Carliner nor Levy had been aware of the case, and both were stunned by the refusal. "Frankly," Levy told Carliner, "I can't imagine the Supreme Court denying review of a miscegenation decision unless there were some defect in the record." But Carliner's search for a procedural error came up short. "I have read the petition," he explained, "and although it was not drafted as forcefully as it might have been, it properly raised the constitutional issues." Carliner's contacts suggested another explanation. "I have learned from quite an authoritative source," he told Levy in February 1955, "that the Supreme Court *did* deny certiorari in the Alabama miscegenation case because it came too soon after the school cases."[72]

Yet Carliner managed to persuade himself that the court's refusal to hear *Jackson* did not necessarily "foreclose" *Naim*. He did so by fastening on a procedural difference in the ways cases arrive at the U.S. Supreme Court. Rather than asking the Court to grant a writ of certiorari, a petition that the justices can accept, or refuse, for any reason, Carliner decided to send *Naim* to the Court directly on appeal, gambling that it would be more difficult for the Court, which was required to hear direct appeals, to reject the case without ruling on its merits. The direct appeal plan was, however, a risky strategy, for in forcing the Court to hear the case, Carliner dramatically increased the chances that the justices might sacrifice interracial marriage on the altar of school desegregation.[73]

To offset this risk, Carliner and Levy decided to try one of the strategies the NAACP had used so successfully in *Brown v. Board of Education*: building a coalition of civil rights groups to support their case. One such organization, the American Jewish Congress, had already volunteered to participate in *Naim,* and Carliner soon began to approach others, starting with groups that represented "non-Caucasians" and then expanding to religious organizations, too. By the time *Naim* reached the U.S. Supreme Court, representatives of the JACL, the Association of Immigration and Nationality Lawyers, the Association on American Indian Affairs, and the American Jewish Congress had all signed on to the ACLU brief.[74]

Yet almost as interesting as the list of organizations that supported the ACLU in *Naim* was the list of organizations that either ignored or dismissed Carliner's appeal. The Chinese-American Citizens' Alliance, the Filipino Federation of America, and the Korean National Association were all on this list.[75] By far the most important, though, was the NAACP. Carliner and Levy contacted the NAACP early on in their case, and at least one Black newspaper, the *Baltimore Afro-American,* urged the NAACP to take advantage of the opportunity. "We hope the NAACP, which for years has been seeking a test case in this field, will join the Naims in an amicus curaie brief before the United States Supreme Court," the paper editorialized optimistically. "They're bound to win."[76] Levy's approach to the NAACP was, however, clumsy at best; insulting is probably a better word. "Though it is a miscegenation case," Levy told Thurgood Marshall in an April 1954 letter describing *Naim,* which was then in its early stages, "we feel that since it does not involve a Negro, the NAACP is not the logical organization to openly back it." Levy didn't want the NAACP's endorsement, but he did want the group's money. "I think any public statement by you on the case would probably not be helpful, but might be harmful," Levy lectured. "However, we could use the money! Could you let me know?"[77] By the time the Supreme

Court briefs for *Naim* were in preparation, all sides were tiptoeing around the subject of NAACP participation. As the JACL's Mike Masaoka reported to the JACL board, "The policy question as to whether the NAACP will be invited to join in the brief has not yet been settled; there is a feeling that perhaps, public relations-wise, it might be better to leave this group officially out of this particular picture."[18]

Even if an invitation had been forthcoming, it would have made no difference, for neither the NAACP nor its Legal Defense Fund wanted anything to do with *Naim*. In 1955, NAACP executive director Roy Wilkins issued a "statement on interracial marriage" that all but denied the group's long tradition of opposing miscegenation laws. "Marriage is a personal matter on which the NAACP takes no position," Wilkins insisted, adding, "The only kind of a marriage we are for is the happy marriage, the success of which depends upon the two individuals involved." Thurgood Marshall chose the course of silence, simply refusing to respond to Carliner and Levy's overtures.[79]

Other civil rights groups, however, issued explicit warnings of the dire consequences that might ensue if Carliner backed the U.S. Supreme Court into a corner. In July 1955, for example, Carliner tried to persuade the U.S. Department of Justice, which had written an amicus brief on the side of the NAACP in *Brown*, to enter the *Naim* case as well. Carliner's request was rejected, and emphatically, too. As he reported to Levy, Justice "wants no part of this case because it is too hot"; moreover, Carliner's contact at the Justice Department told him that "all the people with whom he has spoken" expected the Supreme Court to "deny the appeal." In August 1955, the Anti-Defamation League (ADL), a prominent Jewish civil rights organization, tried to talk the ACLU out of bringing the case at all. "Our friends in Washington believe," the ADL explained, that the uproar over *Brown* showed "that this is not the time to push the Supreme Court for a decision on the validity of miscegenation statutes." The ADL regarded Carliner's decision to bring the case on appeal as especially risky because the possibility of creating "even more furor in the South" might actually provoke the Court into upholding miscegenation laws.[80]

All these predictions fell on deaf ears. Carliner remained optimistic that the Supreme Court could and would overturn miscegenation laws. As he told Levy shortly after being turned down by the Justice Department, he was "inclined to believe that the effects on the school segregation problem are much exaggerated." Levy, who had more experience in these matters than his younger colleague, was less sanguine but no more concerned. "I could not share the alarm of others about this case," Levy later remembered, "for I felt that the court would find a way to postponing its decision."[81]

When *Naim* reached the U.S. Supreme Court, it caused even more distress among the justices than it had among civil rights organizations. As the law clerks who first read the case immediately recognized, Carliner's strategy had put the Court in a real bind. "I do not see how the question can be said to be insubstantial," wrote one clerk, "and that appears to be the only method available to avoid decision." Another clerk agreed. "The problem is of real importance," he wrote, concluding that the Court would have to hear the case regardless of its effect on the issue of school segregation. "I simply see no alternative."[82]

Justice Felix Frankfurter was, however, determined to find one. When the Court first discussed the *Naim* case, on November 4, 1955, Frankfurter came prepared with a lengthy memo to his colleagues. In order to avoid "thwarting or seriously handicapping the enforcement of . . . the [school] segregation cases," Frankfurter argued, the Court had to find a way to avoid ruling on *Naim*. Because interracial marriage "involved such a momentum of history, deep feeling, moral and psychological presuppositions," Frankfurter thought it might be possible to claim "that the issue has not reached that compelling demand for consideration which precludes refusal to consider it."[83] In order for the Court to hear *Naim*, four justices would have to vote to do so. Justices Earl Warren, Hugo Black, Stanley Reed, and William O. Douglas did, but Frankfurter's proposal had raised enough questions in their minds that they granted a request by Justice Tom Clark to wait a week before making their decision final.[84]

In the meantime, Clark and Frankfurter worried their way through several drafts of a per curiam opinion that would offer language vague enough to allow the Court to avoid taking a case that even Frankfurter admitted was "of a seriousness that cannot be rejected as frivolous."[85] When the justices met again on November 11, Frankfurter and Clark persuaded their colleagues to adopt their draft by a vote of 7 to 2.[86] Some years earlier, the Court had declared its preference for cases that presented "constitutional issues in clean-cut and concrete form, unclouded by any serious problem of construction."[87] Now it pretended that the constitutional issues in *Naim* were too "clouded" to allow for a decision. Citing "the inadequacy of the record as to the relationship of the parties to the Commonwealth of Virginia at the time of the marriage in North Carolina and upon their return to Virginia," they remanded *Naim* to the Virginia Court of Appeals "in order that the case may be returned to the Circuit Court of the City of Portsmouth for action not inconsistent with this opinion."[88] As an observer from the Justice Department later commented, "the Court wanted to duck [the case]. And if the Supreme Court wants to duck, nothing can stop them from ducking."[89]

Carliner and Levy were mystified by this (non)decision and astonished by what happened next.[90] Rather than following the U.S. Supreme Court's instructions, the Virginia Supreme Court took the extraordinary step of refusing to send the case back to the lower court. Insisting that in its opinion "the record . . . was adequate for decision of the issues presented" and claiming that its procedures prevented it from remanding the case, the Virginia court reaffirmed its decision upholding Virginia's miscegenation law, and in effect dared the Supreme Court to call its bluff.[91] Hoping that Virginia's intransigence would finally spur the U.S. Supreme Court into action, Carliner asked the Court to reconsider its ruling.

Carliner's second petition split the justices again, at first even more sharply.[92] But in the end, the U.S. Supreme Court simply had no stomach for this battle.[93] It rejected Carliner's final appeal with a seemingly unanimous per curiam ruling and the craven statement that "the decision of the [Virginia] Supreme Court . . . leaves the case devoid of a properly presented federal question."[94] Chief Justice Earl Warren, who believed that the Court had no choice but to hear the case, drafted—and then, at the last minute, withdrew—a stinging dissent chiding his colleagues for a decision he regarded as "completely impermissible in view of this Court's obligatory jurisdiction."[95] David Carliner was bitterly disappointed. "Just how the Virginia Court's last decision divests this case of the federal question under the Fourteenth Amendment," he complained to the ACLU, "I am unable to say."[96] One thing, however, was entirely clear. If *Perez* had raised high hopes among opponents of miscegenation law, *Naim* had shown how elusive those hopes could be.

The Search for the Perfect Test Case

Inspired by the victory in *Perez* and haunted by the lost opportunities in *Naim,* both the ACLU and the JACL redoubled their opposition to miscegenation laws during the late 1950s and early 1960s. Both groups continued to believe that a decision from the U.S. Supreme Court would provide the most authoritative, the most efficient, and the most economical method of overturning miscegenation laws. "Our overall philosophy . . . ," Masao Satow of the JACL explained to a colleague in 1964, "has been to look for a suitable case for U.S. Supreme Court review. We feel it would be better to rid all the States of such statutes at one time."[97]

Persuading Supreme Court justices to weigh in on the issue seemed, however, to require bringing the Court a case that avoided *Naim*'s pitfalls: the conflict with *Brown v. Board of Education,* the fear that Court approval of interracial marriage would produce a backlash against other civil rights campaigns, and the conspicuous absence of the NAACP. In hopes of finding a better test case, the ACLU began to take seriously some of the suggestions David Carliner had dismissed when the Anti-Defamation League had tried to talk him out of taking *Naim* to the U.S. Supreme Court. *Naim,* the ADL had insisted, had been a bad case from the very beginning. "A civil proceeding in which a white woman is escaping from a marriage to a Chinese man," the ADL complained to Carliner, "was hardly likely to excite public sympathy for the defendant-appellant." A "much better case," the ADL maintained, "would be one in which one of our returning veterans, who married a Japanese or Korean bride, is prosecuted and threatened with a jail sentence."[98]

In the late 1950s, both the ACLU and the JACL compiled lists of their criteria for a test case that might prove good enough to tip the balance in the Supreme Court. In 1959, the ACLU's new staff counsel, Rowland Watts, circulated the ACLU's criteria to hundreds of cooperating lawyers, asking them to keep an eye out for promising possibilities. With a careful eye to the political implications, Watts noted the benefits to be wrung from race-and-gender pairings involving White men, in whose cases it seemed easier to make an appeal for citizenship rights. Watts told his lawyer lookouts that a case from a western state would be better than a case from the South, a criminal case better than a civil one, a case involving "a white-Indian or a white-Oriental combination . . . better than a white-Negro combination," and a "white husband and non-white combination . . . better than vice versa."[99] The JACL reached largely similar conclusions. "We have always felt," the JACL explained to its officials in a confidential memo written in 1963, "that a 'good case' would involve an American serviceman, preferably a decorated combat veteran, who married a Japanese woman in Japan while on duty there and who has been returned to the states and assigned to one of the eight states that specifically prohibits persons of the white race to marry 'Mongolians' or 'Japanese.'"[100]

In accordance with these criteria, both the ACLU and the JACL embarked on a rather quixotic search for the perfect test case. By turning their attention back to the West and focusing their search on White men and Asian women, they hoped to sidestep both the issue of school segregation and the problem of NAACP participation while taking advantage of the political dynamics and racial reformations then taking place in the western United States. Two of these developments had already been visible in *Perez*: the emergence of clusters of liberal lawyers like Dan Marshall, who were willing to challenge legal systems of white supremacy, and the rising prominence of judges like Roger Traynor, who were eager to develop the necessary judicial rationales.

A third development was the postwar changes in the racial status of Asian Americans. At the end of World War II, when victorious U.S. troops occupied a defeated Japan, American opinion makers—journalists, government officials, even movie studios—recast the racial terms of the relationship between Asia and America in ways that allowed for the possibility of marriages between American soldiers and Japanese women. During and immediately after the war, the ingrained opposition of U.S. military commanders had kept the number of soldiers who married Japanese women to a minimum.[101] But over the next several years, as the United States set the terms for an ongoing political and economic relationship between the two countries, new pieces of legislation, beginning with the Soldier Brides Act of 1947 and ending with the Walter-McCarran Act of 1952, paved the way for military officials to begin to countenance the unions.[102] By 1952, U.S. officials admitted that ten thousand American soldiers, three-quarters of them White men, had made Japanese women their "war brides."[103]

By the mid-1950s, the pairing of White men with Japanese women had begun to carry powerful political resonance. As the number of actual marriages rose, feeding the media's interest and providing reporters with plenty of ready examples, Japanese war brides came to be seen as compliant and sexually erotic helpmeets who embodied the ideal of good wifely behavior. In the hands of sympathetic reporters, stories about soldier marriages played on public admiration for heroic veterans who had made the United States the world's strongest military, political, and economic power; softened the sharp edges of American victory and Japanese defeat by symbolically bringing two peoples into intimate contact; and figured a form of marriage that was both modern, in the sense of being powerfully sexual at its core, and traditional, in the sense of reinforcing husbands' authority over wives.[104]

In a manner reminiscent of mid-nineteenth-century White men who married Indian women, mid-twentieth-century White men who married Japanese women stirred rhetoric about White men's citizenship rights, including White men's right to choose their own marriage partners. With this rhetoric paving the way, White soldiers and their Japanese brides came to be seen as brave challengers of lamentable, and increasingly outdated, structures of American racism.

Both the JACL and the ACLU tried to take advantage of these changes. In its newsletter, the *Pacific Citizen,* for example, the JACL began to report on the reasons why White—and sometimes Black—soldiers preferred Japanese wives, using the marriages, which often took place over the objections of Japanese as well as American parents, as evidence that "nature is taking her course" and "love conquers all." "I married an Oriental girl," the *Pacific Citizen* quoted one White soldier as saying. "I had previously married an American girl [but now] I place myself on record that Oriental wives are superior in many respects, as any Caucasian husband of an Oriental girl will admit." Commenting on this phenomenon, reporter Larry Nakatsuka quoted educator Dr. Jesse Steiner, who opined that "inter-marriage is nature's way of solving racial problems."[105] By linking assumptions about White men's right to choose their marital partners to claims about the naturality of interracial sex and marriage, the JACL used the orientalization of Asian war brides to challenge the miscegenation laws that they considered a long-standing insult to Asian American communities in western states.

Yet the search for the perfect test case constantly fell short of expectations. The ACLU and the JACL both wanted a case involving a White solider and a Japanese war bride, but none of the cases their network of lookouts turned up actually fit this image. Most soldier marriages took place on or near military bases in Japan, where couples were subject to the whims of their commanding officers but did not have to face the marriage license officials who served as the primary means of enforcing miscegenation laws in western U.S. states. In the South, where criminal arrests were most likely to occur, their targets tended to be Whites involved with Blacks. As William Marutani, a Philadelphia lawyer for the JACL, once confided to one of his associates, in language that both reflected and mocked the orientalization of Asian women in this period, it was "unlikely . . . that one of these Southern states is going to prosecute a highly-decorated war veteran married to a demure, sloe-eyed Japanese war bride."[106] By 1964, the JACL had concluded that it might never find the test case it really wanted.

There was, however, no shortage of cases involving Whites and Asian Americans. During the 1950s and early 1960s, several cases came to the attention of the ACLU and the JACL, most of which revealed a growing gap between the needs and desires of interracial couples and the expectations of civil rights lawyers. Lawyers who planned to uproot state laws needed to find couples who were willing to endure the time-consuming process required to reach a U.S. Supreme Court decision, but few couples with their hearts set on marriage were willing to tolerate even the briefest of delays. In 1964, for example, the Intermountain and Plains chapter of the JACL grew particularly excited over a case in Wyoming that involved a "white boy" and a "Nisei girl," but before they could even try to talk the couple into challenging the law, the youngsters had traveled to a nearby state to be married.[107]

This case, and several others, collapsed because young couples eager to marry were constantly subject to the temptation to take the faster and easier route of slipping over the nearest state boundary to marry.

A high tolerance for delay was not the only thing lawyers required of their clients; they also needed couples willing to endure a good deal of embarrassing publicity. In 1961, for example, the ACLU learned of a sixteen-year-old Japanese American boy in Salt Lake City, Utah, who wanted to marry a sixteen-year-old White girl. The couple was eager to marry, partly because the girl was pregnant, but they had been unable to obtain a marriage license from the Salt Lake County clerk's office. The local branch of the ACLU tried to talk the couple into challenging Utah's miscegenation law, but the lawyer they dispatched could not persuade the couple to brave the publicity they knew would upset the boy's father. "The family would have been willing to go along with the suit," he explained, "providing there would be no publicity so that the father would never hear about it. Of course," he added, "in a miscegenation case that is impossible."[108]

When such a couple finally did challenge the constitutionality of miscegenation laws in a western state, the issue arose too quickly and unexpectedly for either the ACLU or the JACL to get involved in the case. In December 1958, San Francisco labor leader Harry Bridges, a White man, brought his fiancée, Noriko Sawada, a Japanese American legal secretary, to Reno, Nevada, to get married.[109] Having been red-baited throughout the 1950s, Bridges was a well-known lightning rod for the California press; in Reno, he hoped to hold a quick, quiet marriage ceremony, without any reporters in attendance and without the hassle of California's three-day waiting period for obtaining a marriage license. Instead, he found Nevada newspapermen camped outside his hotel room and his marriage blocked by the only factor he hadn't taken into account: Nevada's miscegenation law. With the help of one of the lawyers at Sawada's San Francisco law firm, Bridges retained a local lawyer, Sam Francovich, then proceeded to the county clerk's office, where he and Sawada endured the humiliation of having their application for a marriage license rejected by license clerk Viola Givens.[110] "Are you black, white, brown, red or yellow?" Givens asked Sawada. "Under those categories, I must be yellow," Sawada, who preferred to emphasize her American birth, reluctantly replied. "It's not where you were born," said Givens. "It's blood that counts."[111]

When Francovich was also unable to persuade either Givens or her boss, county clerk Harry K. Brown, to change their minds, Bridges, Sawada, and the trail of reporters trooped off to court, where Francovich asked district judge Taylor Wines to issue a writ of mandate ordering the clerk to issue the

Reno marriage license clerk Viola Givens refuses to issue a marriage license to Harry Bridges and Noriko Sawada. (Labor Archives and Research Center, San Francisco State University)

marriage license. Prepped by lawyers from Sawada's California firm, Francovich played on the power of the *Perez* precedent, telling Judge Wines that Nevada's law was every bit as unconstitutional as California's, while the local district attorney insisted that miscegenation laws were routinely upheld in all the states that had them *except* California. Judge Wines cast his lot with California and ordered the clerk to issue the license, explaining to the packed courtroom, in words that echoed California's Justice Roger Traynor, that "a right to marry is the right of the individual, not of the race." Bridges and Sawada were married later that afternoon.[112]

Press coverage of this episode showed that few reporters had anything positive to say about the Nevada miscegenation law—or about Harry Bridges, who was cast as "a man with an extremely unsavory reputation" in reports that made sure to mention his history as a labor and political radical, his two previous marriages, and the fact that he was twenty-three years older than Sawada. It was surely unfortunate, one editor explained, "that a man the government tried to deport as a communist brought the matter to a head." County clerks treated Judge Wines's decision as if it applied only to a single marriage, so Nevada's miscegenation law remained intact amid rumors that the Reno district attorney would appeal the case to the Nevada Supreme Court.[113]

Meanwhile, however, the Arizona branch of the ACLU had finally found a couple it was eager to represent in court. Henry Oyama, a thirty-three-year-old Japanese American man, was a lifelong resident of Tucson. During his teenage years, he had been imprisoned in one of the internment camps for Japanese Americans, but had later gone on to serve in the U.S. Army and become a high school teacher of American history. Mary Ann Jordan, a twenty-eight-year-old White woman, was an employee of American Airlines. Unlike many younger, and more impetuous, couples, Oyama and Jordan displayed what their lawyers called "rare courage and patience" throughout their legal ordeal.[114]

The ACLU lawyers who took Henry Oyama's case to court tried much the same strategy that had worked in Nevada: they tried to build on the *Perez* precedent. In a move that harked back to Dan Marshall's example, they brought their case directly to the Arizona Supreme Court, which, however, refused to hear it until a decision had been issued at the lower-court level.[115] Banished to the Pima County Superior Court, the ACLU argued that Arizona's miscegenation law violated the First and Fourteenth Amendments to the U.S. Constitution, and two additional provisions of the Arizona State Constitution.[116] Taking note of the fact that Oyama and Jordan, like Andrea Pérez and Sylvester Davis, were Roman Catholics, superior court judge Herbert Krucker declared Arizona's miscegenation law "unconstitutional and void" and "commanded" the county clerk "to issue a marriage license."[117] The Oyamas were married on December 28, 1959.[118] But in Arizona, as in Nevada, Judge Krucker's decision carried little or no weight outside the local jurisdiction in which it had been issued. So while Arizona ACLU officials proudly touted their "terrific" victory, the ACLU's staff counsel, Roland Watts, based in New York, hoped "that the case will be appealed, so that it will have more persuasive weight in other jurisdictions."[119]

In January 1960, Pima County clerk Grayce O'Neill granted Watts's wish by appealing Judge Krucker's decision to the Arizona Supreme Court.[120] Pima County insisted that religious freedom was entirely beside the point, that "the right to marry as a basic, or fundamental right" was an argument that had "less to recommend it" than the traditional power of the state to control marriage "upon any rational basis," and that *Perez* was a "divergent" and "unsupported" exception to the rule.[121] The ACLU took its stand with *Perez*, reiterating the key aspects of Roger Traynor's ruling by claiming that Arizona's miscegenation law not only violated Oyama and Jordan's religious freedom but also denied them equal protection and due process of the law. "What are involved here," the ACLU insisted, "are not the rights of a class or a race, as such, but the right of two individuals to marry as they choose."[122] But the ACLU's hopes that the Arizona Supreme Court might become the second state supreme court in the twentieth century to overturn a miscegenation law proved premature. Before the Arizona Supreme Court got around to making its decision, the Arizona state legislature repealed Arizona's miscegenation law.

"A Mistake to Simmer the Question Down to White and Black"

Although it distressed the legal strategists in the ACLU and the JACL to admit it, court cases were not the only—nor, in these years, the most effective—means of doing away with miscegenation laws. The other major possibility, legislative repeal of the statutes, had, however, traditionally attracted little support and enjoyed even less success. Compared to winning a ruling from the U.S. Supreme Court, mounting state-by-state legislative repeals was a costly and time-consuming process. Moreover, persuading state legislators to take a public stand against miscegenation laws had proven so difficult—even more difficult than persuading judges to overturn convictions—that the last state legislature to repeal a miscegenation law had been Ohio in 1887.[123] Yet in the period between 1948, the year of the *Perez* decision, and 1964, when the NAACP entered the ranks of those willing to challenge miscegenation laws in court, most of the progress against miscegenation laws came in the form of legislative repeals.

All of these took place in western states. The potential of the repeal strategy was first demonstrated in 1951, when Oregon became the first state since Ohio to repeal its miscegenation law. The Oregon repeal had been inadvertently set in motion the year before, when the state's Republican governor, Douglas McKay, had scheduled a state Conference on Indian Affairs. In the context of discussions of the impending termination of government responsibility for tribal affairs, Indian delegates demanded progress on a number of civil rights issues, including the repeal of Oregon's miscegenation law, which Boyd Jackson of the Klamath tribe described as a particularly humiliating example of the state's entrenched history of race discrimination. After the conference, McKay asked the state's attorney general to take a look at the law. The attorney general did so, and predicted that if Oregon's miscegenation law were ever challenged in court, Oregon judges were likely to follow the example of Roger Traynor in the *Perez* case and declare it unconstitutional. With the Council on Indian Affairs, the governor, and the attorney general all in agreement that Oregon's miscegenation law had to go, a bill to repeal it was submitted to the state legislature. Its primary supporter was Senator Philip Hitchcock, who called the law "a disgrace to the state of Oregon" and "an insult to the other races."[124]

It soon became clear, though, that legislators were more worried about insulting some races than others. Democratic senator Thomas R. Mahoney, who came from Portland, the home to the vast majority of Oregon's Blacks, immediately objected to the bill, telling reporters that "he is not opposed to marriage between whites and Indians, but objects to Negro and white marriages," which he described as a "crime to unborn children." Insisting that Oregon's miscegenation law was "just as discriminatory against whites as against colored persons," Mahoney claimed that repeal was "the kind of legislation Negroes do not want," that it would "set civil rights back 20 years," and that it "might agitate matters." There is some reason to believe that when it came to Whites marrying Blacks, a majority of Oregonians would have agreed with Mahoney, for only six months earlier, Portland voters had rejected a civil rights ordinance by a vote of 77,084 to 60,969. Building on this base, Mahoney initially managed to persuade the senate law committee to kill the repeal bill, by a one-vote margin.[125]

Then, however, supporters of repeal forced the committee to reconsider. Unlike Mahoney, who spoke in terms of Whites and Blacks, the senators who supported repeal spoke in the language of equal protection and religious liberty and illustrated their claims of race discrimination with examples of Whites married to Indians and Asian Americans. Building on the *Perez* example, Hitchcock got the ball rolling by insisting that Oregon's miscegenation law violated "fundamental concepts of the constitution of the United States and of the law of God." Then other legislators worked to shift the racial focus of the debate away from Blacks. Warren Gill, of Lebanon, expressed "sympathy for the stand of Oregon Indians," whose complaints that the law was discriminatory became the leitmotif of newspaper coverage of the repeal. The example of White men married to Indian women had long been a familiar one in Oregon, but in the years since World War II, legislators had begun to focus on another example as well, White soldiers who had served in Japan and Korea and now wished to bring their "war brides" to the States. As legislator Marie Wilcox explained to reporters, "Several veterans, who have married girls overseas who belong to races other than white, had asked her to support the bill so they could bring their wives home." In the end, it was supporters like Wilcox, who insisted that it was a "mistake to simmer the question down to white and black," who carried the day. The Oregon Senate passed the repeal bill by a vote of 21–7, the Oregon House followed suit by an even larger margin, and Governor Douglas McKay signed the bill on May 8, 1951.[126]

Over the next dozen years, the ACLU and the JACL developed the patterns that had emerged in Oregon—using arguments about personal choice and equal protection taken from Roger Traynor's decision in *Perez* and focusing as much attention as possible on Whites and Asian Americans—into a flexible and effective blueprint for legislative repeal of miscegenation laws. Sometimes, as in Arizona, they used the threat of legal action as a spur to legislative action. Although the JACL had discussed repealing Arizona's law as early as 1955, it was the ACLU's 1958 decision to take the *Oyama* case to court, which had generated a burst of publicity about the denial of a marriage license to a Japanese American man and a White woman, that provided the catalyst for Arizona's repeal. When the Arizona Supreme Court took its time issuing a decision in the case, the state branch of the ACLU grew impatient with the courtroom strategy and used the *Oyama* example as a rallying point to get Arizona legislators to consider repealing the law. "Vigorously supported" by the Arizona ACLU, a repeal bill, which eventually received bipartisan support from legislators, was enacted in March 1962.[127]

In several cases, repeal campaigns were supported by state and local officials who had grown uneasy with their traditional role as the gatekeepers of white supremacy. In Salt Lake City, for example, the ACLU lawyer who tried—and failed—to talk a sixteen-year-old Nisei and his White fiancée into challenging Utah's miscegenation law in court found local officials more receptive than his prospective clients. As he reported to the national office of the ACLU, "The County Attorney's office would like to see us win such a case," and "the County Clerk thinks we ought to win and anyway he would like to see the law tested." After the case fell apart, the county clerk not only promised to keep "his eye out for another miscegenation case. . . . [and] send it over to us" but was also "prepared to help us repeal the miscegenation statute through the legislature." There were, however, limits to the county clerk's enthusiasm. "He felt," the ACLU correspondent reported, that while "we could easily repeal the provision outlawing marriages between white people on one hand and oriental and malays on the other . . . we could not change the law forbidding marriages between white people and negroes." Concluding that he was "probably right," the local chapter of the ACLU moved on to other issues, but the Utah JACL pushed hard for legislative repeal of Utah's law, which took place in 1963.[128]

Although the ACLU and the JACL often provided the catalyst for the repeal of miscegenation laws in western states, repeal campaigns attracted support from a range of community groups. The Wyoming repeal epitomized several of the developments that came together in western states. First, it was sparked by a case involving a White man and a Nisei woman who had tried, unsuccessfully, to obtain a marriage license (in the town of Worland). Second, it was led by the JACL, which, as the group's local correspondent informed national officials, began by mobilizing its network of personal contacts, which included Speaker of the House Walter B. Phelan, "other key individuals in Cheyenne," and a former local judge in Cheyenne named Tosh Suyematsu, who was "married to Ellen Crowley, who is the daughter of a former Attorney General in Wyoming." Third, it depended on drawing in a number of allies, including the Mountain States Anti-Defamation League, the Council of Churches, and the AFL-CIO, which mobilized its oil workers' unions. The final, and most significant, element of the Wyoming coalition against miscegenation laws was the NAACP, whose regional chairman, Jesse Johnson, not only joined the coalition but threw a scare into JACL organizers in the bargain. As the JACL local reported to its national office, Johnson "was all for driving to Cheyenne to stage a demonstration" until "we put a stop to that."[129]

As Johnson's threatened demonstration suggests, while the ACLU and the JACL were busy running a campaign against miscegenation law that tried to win concessions for all races by foregrounding marriages between Whites and Asian Americans and implicitly, and sometimes explicitly, avoiding the question of marriage between Whites and Blacks, state and local branches of the NAACP were slowly becoming involved in western state campaigns to repeal miscegenation laws. They understood the reasons why the national NAACP and its Legal Defense Fund had refused to participate in miscegenation court cases, but some local and regional NAACP leaders wanted to press the point anyway. When NAACP chapters in western states asked themselves the old, familiar question of whether progress on interracial marriage would endanger other civil rights campaigns, they slowly but surely began to come up with a new answer.

The first signs of change occurred in San Francisco, where the NAACP had established a West Coast Regional Branch Office, which tracked the performance of the California legislature on a number of civil rights issues. When it came to miscegenation law, the California legislature's record was particularly dismal. Despite the *Perez* decision, and despite three subsequent attempts to repeal California's miscegenation law—one in 1949 and two more in 1951—the legislature had steadfastly refused, and the law, though unconstitutional and unenforceable, remained on the books, a conspicuous insult to non-White Californians.[130] Beginning in 1954, under the leadership of Regional Secretary Franklin Williams, the NAACP listed the repeal of miscegenation law as one of its legislative goals. Noting that California's inaction was particularly galling in light of the fact that "Oregon repealed its miscegenation statute recently," the regional office promised to "press for the repeal of such laws" not only in California but "in all other states" as well. "Such laws are a heritage of slavery," it declared in a publicity pamphlet. "They impute inferiority to the proscribed groups and they interfere with the right of the citizen to contract freely as to his own personal affairs." For the next five years, the West Coast Regional NAACP pressed these arguments with the California state legislature.[131] In 1959, after it urged Los Angeles Assemblyman Edward Elliott to introduce a repeal bill, the California legislature finally repealed the law.[132]

In other western states, too, the NAACP played an increasingly visible role in repeal campaigns. During the rash of publicity that followed Harry Bridges's 1958 court challenge to Nevada's miscegenation law, local NAACP chapters at first kept quiet; as the president of the Reno-Sparks chapter of the NAACP told a local historian, he "feared the issue would create a backlash among lawmakers, jeopardizing such measures as fair housing, equal employment opportunity, educational reform, and public service, all pending for consideration in Carson City." But by 1959, when the Nevada state legislature finally repealed its miscegenation law, NAACP regional secretary Williams was able to cite "the able leadership of the NAACP forces in Nevada" as a key factor in the repeal effort. And in 1959, when the Idaho state legislature repealed its miscegenation law (in a campaign for which the JACL also claimed credit), Field Secretary Everett P. Brandon claimed that "since this was the only NAACP legislative program in Idaho this action represents a hundred percent success this year for the Association."[133]

All this state-by-state activity slowly began to add up to substantial gains. Between 1951 and 1963, eleven western states repealed their miscegenation

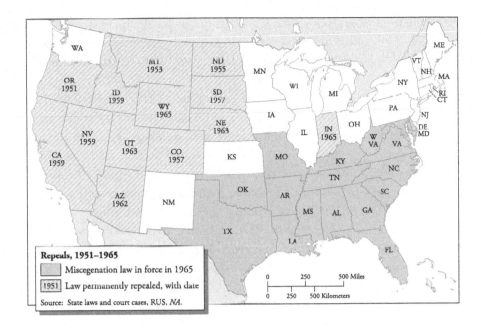

Repeals, 1951–1965

⬜ Miscegenation law in force in 1965

1951 Law permanently repealed, with date

Source: State laws and court cases, RUS, *NA*.

laws, including Oregon, Idaho, California, Utah, Montana, Arizona, Nevada, Colorado, Nebraska, and North and South Dakota.[134] In 1965, both Wyoming and Indiana would follow, leaving only two western states—Texas and Oklahoma—where miscegenation laws remained in force.[135]

In 1948, when Roger Traynor issued his precedent-shattering decision in *Perez v. Sharp*, it was hard to tell whether his ideas would prove to be prophetic or if they were, as critics suggested, hopelessly unrealistic. Over the next decade and a half, the campaign against miscegenation law veered from the utopian enthusiasm of *Perez* to the dashed hopes of *Naim* and, finally, to the cautious optimism that marked the steady stream of western state repeals. These repeals, and the search for the perfect test case, had been carefully crafted to fit the dominant political rhetorics of the 1950s. By drawing poignant portraits of innocent young couples victimized by a cruel state bent on denying respectable young people the right to choose their own marriage partners, opponents of miscegenation law developed the argument that marriage was a "fundamental right of free men." By spotlighting the marriages of Whites and Indians and Asian Americans and insisting that it was "a mistake to simmer the question down to white and black," they found political leverage in western states where the racial status of Asian Americans was changing so rapidly. By choosing arguments that emphasized dominant notions of marriage, individualism, and democracy, they attracted allies to the cause.

Growing from these 1950s roots, the legal campaign against miscegenation laws led to a politics of racial respectability that described marriage as a "right" and spoke in terms of the "fundamentals" of American liberty and democracy.

In some respects, this politics of respectability proved effective. The emphasis on Whites married to Indians and Asian Americans, for example, allowed legislators in states with relatively small numbers of African Americans to override the objections of those who wanted to continue to ban marriages between Whites and Blacks. As one Oregon editor explained, "Mixed marriage appears to present no problem in Oregon, and the matter can well be left to the individual judgment of the parties concerned."[136]

Yet the politics of respectability had its limits, and it should also be seen as a politics of avoidance. The emphasis on Whites married to Asian Americans, for example, avoided facing the extent to which miscegenation laws continued to be grounded in ideas about blackness and bound up in public approval of and resistance to campaigns for civil rights for Blacks. Opponents of miscegenation law had argued that marriage was a natural right and managed to persuade courts that it was a fundamental right of free men, but they had not yet persuaded judges that interracial marriage was a civil right, and they had done little or nothing to develop Roger Traynor's ambitious attack on the underlying logic of the entire enterprise of race classification. It is significant that Texas and Oklahoma, the two western states that failed to repeal their miscegenation laws in this period, were also the only two western states where Blacks made up more than 6 percent of the population.[137]

And it is revealing that the JACL, which was, as we have seen, eager to lead campaigns against miscegenation laws in western states like Utah and Wyoming, hesitated to do so in states like Missouri, where the population of Blacks registered in the hundred thousands rather than just the hundreds. In 1959, when the leaders of the Missouri chapter of the JACL proposed a campaign to repeal that state's miscegenation law, which was, they said, causing problems for the children of Japanese Americans married to Whites, the JACL's Washington representative, Mike Masaoka, talked them out of it. "Missouri," Masaoka explained to the disappointed local chapter, "is a border state and is not concerned so much with Japanese and other Orientals as it is with Negroes." In this context, Masaoka continued, any attempt to raise the issue of miscegenation law "might well boomerang against us" and "result in greater discrimination and persecution of the Negroes, and possibly of the Japanese, because of this effort." As Masaoka's comments showed, the political collisions that plagued the *Naim* case continued to cast a long shadow over the campaign to eliminate miscegenation laws. "You may know," he told his correspondent, "that when JACL joined in a Virginia case to have the United States Supreme Court declare this type of law unconstitutional, a number of Negro and Jewish organizations frowned upon our effort as jeopardizing their fight for public school desegregation." Chastened by these warnings, the Missouri chapter abandoned its campaign. Three years later, in 1962, when it made the same request again, it received much the same answer.[138]

In yet another way the campaigns of the 1950s were a politics of avoidance: they sidestepped the conflation of interracial marriage with illicit sex that formed the criminal underbelly of miscegenation law. During the 1940s and 1950s, the LACIC, the ACLU, and the JACL all tried to distance their arguments on behalf of the "right" of interracial marriage from the smoldering stigmas that surrounded interracial sex. "There is," Dan Marshall had argued in *Perez*, "nothing licentious nor inconsistent with the peace and safety of the state in these petitioners exercising their right of religious freedom, and natural right, to intermarry."[139] This position was, of course, politically expedient, but it was also politically possible only outside the South, where the specter of interracial sex remained firmly tied to both the rhetoric about interracial marriage and the enforcement of miscegenation law. It is hardly surprising, then, that the civil rights organization that took these links most seriously was the NAACP, which had never enjoyed the luxury of being able to separate interracial sex from interracial marriage.

Fifteen years after the *Perez* decision, an increasing number of couples—and civil rights organizations—had entered the campaign against miscegenation law, and a steady stream of western state legislatures had repealed their laws. Yet before the campaign to eliminate miscegenation laws would be able to build the judicial consensus that had been so obviously lacking in *Perez*, its advocates would have to confront each of these problems—the continuing significance of notions of blackness, the contradictions between the imperative of race classification and the indefinability of race, and the links between illicit sex and interracial marriage that sustained criminal miscegenation law enforcement. And despite all the time and energy the LACIC, the ACLU, and the JACL had devoted to the midcentury campaign against miscegenation law, the organization that was by far the best equipped to do this was the NAACP.

Chapter Eight

INTERRACIAL MARRIAGE AS A CIVIL RIGHT

"The time has come to remove this stigma from the fabric of American law."

—*NAACP LDF lawyer Louis H. Pollak, 1964*

MIAMI BEACH, FLORIDA

When Connie Hoffman was arrested, she simply didn't believe it. Her outrage barely under control, she told the detectives that she had "never heard of any law that a Negro and a white woman couldn't live together." But unfortunately for Connie Hoffman, her landlady, Dora Goodnick, had. And in February 1962, when Dora Goodnick reported Hoffman and her lover, Dewey McLaughlin, to the Miami Beach Police Department, the officer on duty listened with interest as Goodnick poured out her story.[1]

Dewey McLaughlin had been living with Connie Hoffman and her five-year-old son for several weeks when landlady Goodnick, who was outside one night hanging up her wash, caught a glimpse of him standing naked in her apartment. Goodnick indignantly confronted Connie Hoffman, who offered the hasty explanation that McLaughlin, a Honduran immigrant, was "Spanish," not "colored"; he was, she said, her husband. Goodnick would have none of it. "You can't stay one more minute," she told Hoffman. "I want you to move out." But, as Goodnick told the police, Hoffman refused to leave.[2]

Two Miami Beach detectives were promptly dispatched to Hoffman's apartment. Their task, they said, was to investigate "information that we had had a Negro and a white woman living together with the added information that a child was being neglected." When the policemen pounded on the door of Hoffman's ground-floor efficiency apartment, Dewey McLaughlin, who was the only one home, tried to duck out the back door. He didn't succeed. One of the officers blocked his exit, then brought him back into the apartment, where the detectives noticed that McLaughlin's shirts were hanging in the closet. It was McLaughlin's bad luck that one of the detectives was fluent in Spanish; soon both were quizzing him, in Spanish and in English, about his relationship with Hoffman. The officers were initially unsure which of Florida's several laws against interracial sex and marriage might apply to the case, so they arrested Dewey McLaughlin on a technicality. Under a local ordinance, the mostly Black workers who staffed Miami Beach's resort hotels were required to carry official identification cards, and although McLaughlin, who worked as a hotel porter, had such a card, it had expired a month earlier. Later that day, Connie Hoffman was arrested, too, on charges of contributing to the delinquency of a minor. Both were quickly released, but as it turned out, their ordeal was just beginning.[3]

Five days later, the police arrested Connie Hoffman and Dewey McLaughlin again, this time charging them both with violating a little-known Florida law that made it a crime for any "negro man and white woman, or any white man and negro woman" to "habitually live in and occupy in the nighttime the same room."[4] This was not the only law Miami Beach police might have invoked Florida also prohibited "whites" and "negroes" from marrying each other and from living in adultery and fornication—but it was the easiest to prosecute, for under the cohabitation provision, no evidence of a marriage, or even a sexual relationship, was necessary to obtain a conviction.[5] And although the "crimes" of interracial marriage, adultery, and fornication carried stiffer penalties, the cohabitation law was no slap on the wrist: Hoffman and McLaughlin both faced a $500 fine and up to a year in jail. There was more to come: while Hoffman was busy fighting criminal charges, Dora Goodnick locked her out of her apartment and the State Welfare Board took custody of her son.[6] Connie Hoffman needed help, fast, so she called for a lawyer—from the NAACP.[7]

In deciding to defend Connie Hoffman and Dewey McLaughlin, the NAACP and its Legal Defense Fund cast off their midcentury reluctance to challenge miscegenation laws in court and put their best efforts into eliminating them once and for all. In the process, they wrenched the campaign against miscegenation law, which had, until then, been focused on applying the "natural" or "fundamental" right to marry to interracial couples, into alignment with the NAACP's legal campaign for civil rights and racial integration. With the NAACP on board, the LDF succeeded where other organizations had failed. First, it persuaded the U.S. Supreme Court to overcome its aversion to the touchy subject of interracial sex and marriage. Second, it used the Fourteenth Amendment's equal protection clause to overturn the equal application argument that had shaped the outcome of miscegenation court cases ever since the 1880s. And finally, by bringing miscegenation law under the umbrella of a newly expansive understanding of the equal protection clause, the LDF precipitated the Supreme Court's emerging consensus that miscegenation laws would have to be declared unconstitutional.

The development of this consensus would require not one but two U.S. Supreme Court decisions—one issued in 1964 in the case of Connie Hoffman and Dewey McLaughlin, which became known as *McLaughlin v. Florida,* and another issued in 1967 in the much more famous case of *Loving v. Virginia*. In *McLaughlin v. Florida,* the LDF set the sexualization of miscegenation law on a collision course with the equal protection clause, prompting the Supreme Court to overturn Florida's interracial cohabitation law and, along with it, the 1882 case of *Pace v. Alabama*. In *Loving v. Virginia,* the Supreme Court combined the arguments about equal protection offered in *McLaughlin* with the arguments about personal liberty and the "fundamental" right of marriage from the 1940s and 1950s and used them to declare state bans on interracial marriage unconstitutional. "Marriage," Chief Justice Earl Warren declared in *Loving,* giving new and deeper meaning to an old, familiar phrase, "is one of the 'basic civil rights of man.'"[8]

In the decades since, *Loving v. Virginia* has been memorialized in legal textbooks as "the" case on interracial marriage, the story told and retold in compelling detail in newspapers, docudramas, and scholarly accounts. But any truly historical account of the U.S. Supreme Court's ultimate encounter with miscegenation law in *Loving v. Virginia* needs to begin by paying careful attention to *McLaughlin v. Florida,* the case that paved the legal path the Supreme Court would follow.[9]

Pace v. Alabama Revisited

Of all the things the NAACP LDF hoped to accomplish in *McLaughlin v. Florida,* the most important was to persuade the U.S. Supreme Court to overrule *Pace v. Alabama*. Issued in 1882, *Pace* still stood as the Supreme Court's only substantive opinion on the subject of interracial sex or marriage. In it, Supreme Court Justice Stephen J. Field had tied a Gordian knot between the stigma of illicit sex, the imperative of race classification, and the denial of equal protection. And *Pace* enshrined the logic of equal application, or the argument that miscegenation laws were not discriminatory because they applied to Whites as well as Blacks.[10]

Over the years, Field's logic in *Pace* had proved influential in cases involving interracial marriage as well as interracial sex. The state courts that heard cases on interracial marriage adopted Field's equal application argument so wholeheartedly that they soon came to think of it as their very own. Moreover, by giving racially differential punishment for illicit sex the stamp of legal legitimacy, *Pace* allowed courts to construct a definitional circle in which all interracial relationships were defined *as* illicit sex. Thus, in 1942, when the Colorado Supreme Court upheld the conviction of a Black man and a White woman under its state miscegenation laws, it started by explaining that "there is here no question of race discrimination [because] the statute applies to both white and black." Under these circumstances, the court declared, redefining the marriage as illicit sex, the "defendants could not, either ceremonially or by common law, be married" so "they were, if living together, leading 'an immoral course of life.'"[11]

During and after World War II, judges who heard cases about interracial marriage continued to take refuge in *Pace*'s equal application rationale. In 1944, in one of the cases in which the NAACP's Thurgood Marshall had declined to participate, a federal district court cited *Pace* in its decision upholding Oklahoma's miscegenation law. "The statute," the court declared, "does not merely forbid a person of African descent to intermarry with a person of other race or descent. It equally forbids a person of other race or descent to intermarry with a person of African descent. . . . There is no discrimination against the colored race." In 1955, when the Supreme Court of Virginia upheld Virginia's miscegenation law in the *Naim* case, one of the pillars it rested on was *Pace v. Alabama*.[12]

And yet, over the course of the twentieth century, the *Pace* decision stood on increasingly shaky ground, as the commonsense conflations that sustained Justice Field's reasoning slowly eroded. The first civil rights groups to challenge miscegenation laws in court—the LACIC, the ACLU, and the JACL—were eager to protect their clients from the sexual stigmas that surrounded interracial couples, but they were only dimly aware of the crucial role that *Pace* had played in defining interracial relationships as illicit sex in the first place. Their attempts to establish a natural or fundamental right to interracial marriage proceeded according to a politics of respectability in which marriage and marriage law stood as the absolute opposite of illicit sex and sex crime prosecution. By presenting their clients as innocent young couples eager to enter the respectable state of marriage, they placed their cases on one side of this divide and *Pace* on the other. *Pace*, they claimed, was a sex crime prosecution, so it had little or no bearing on civil cases in which interracial couples fought for the right to marry.

In the 1948 *Perez* case, for example, Dan Marshall made just this claim. His opponent, Los Angeles County Attorney Charles Stanley, had followed generations of state prosecutors in telling the justices of the California Supreme Court that *Pace* applied to interracial marriage as well as interracial sex. The U.S. Supreme Court, Stanley insisted, had ruled that miscegenation laws "are not discriminatory." In response, Marshall protested that *Pace* had nothing to do with marriage and was therefore "pointless" as precedent. After listening to both sides, Justice Roger Traynor broke yet another judicial tradition by agreeing with Dan Marshall. *Pace* didn't apply, Traynor wrote in his *Perez* ruling, because "adultery and non-marital intercourse are not, like marriage, a basic right, but are offenses subject to various degrees of punishment."[13] After Traynor's ruling offered opponents of miscegenation laws the hope that wishing might make it so, the ACLU and JACL tried to slide past *Pace* with much the same argument.[14]

The NAACP LDF, however, found it impossible to believe that *Pace* could be contained in this manner. To its way of thinking, consigning *Pace* to the realm of illicit sex was nearly as dangerous as raising the subject of interracial marriage in court in the first place. LACIC lawyers might draw neat distinctions between illicit sex and marriage, but the LDF had extensive experience with the cultural circuits that linked the stigma of interracial sex to interracial marriage, and both to each and every campaign for civil rights. As a result, its attorneys treated *Pace* as if it were a rattlesnake coiled to strike— a deeply powerful judicial precedent that could easily be used to justify the entire edifice of racial segregation.

So although the LDF was determined to challenge such bulwarks of racial segregation as the Supreme Court's 1896 decision in *Plessy v. Ferguson,* it repeatedly shied away from challenging *Pace v. Alabama*. In 1946, for example, when a lawyer in Montana asked for help in challenging a miscegenation law in that state, the LDF demurred, explaining to its disappointed correspondent that *Pace* "had already foreclosed" the question.[15] During the 1950s, when the NAACP devoted most of its legal resources to attacking racial segregation in public schools, the risks seemed even higher to LDF lawyers, who believed that the success of their efforts depended on keeping the potentially explosive subjects of interracial sex and marriage as far away as possible from the minds of the justices of the U.S. Supreme Court. In a period when southern conservatives insisted that *Brown v. Board of Education* was only the first step toward "mongrelization" and Whites in every region of the country stood in nearly unanimous opposition to interracial marriage, the last thing the NAACP wanted anyone to do was to remind the Supreme Court of its seventy-year-old decision in *Pace.*

What the LDF did want to do, however, was to persuade the U.S. Supreme Court to adopt a new and dramatically different interpretation of the Fourteenth Amendment's guarantee of equal protection, one that would spell the end of the old principle of "separate but equal." And even as NAACP lawyers focused more and more of their attention on school segregation, it was clear that if they succeeded, there would be broader implications. As one of them, Jack Greenberg, put it, the LDF "had an agenda: to abolish Jim Crow" by getting the Supreme Court to adopt an interpretation of equal protection that would be broad enough to outlaw racial segregation of any kind.[16] In this way, the LDF's campaign against school segregation placed its own kind of pressure on the *Pace* precedent—indirectly, to be sure, but in the end even more effectively than other civil rights organizations.

After the *Brown* decision gave the LDF's broad interpretation of equal protection the stamp of legal legitimacy, the NAACP began to expand the range of its demands. In 1959, for example, the Florida state branch of the NAACP had committed itself to a campaign for "complete racial desegregation in voting, schools, housing, government, and industry in Florida by 1963." In 1960, when the LDF stood at the epicenter of American civil rights law, it began to apply the U.S. Supreme Court's new and expanded understanding of equal protection to the sit-ins and freedom rides that were engendering a bold civil rights movement among students. Then, in 1962, when the LDF had amassed such a long list of Supreme Court precedents in equal protection cases that it was finally ready to confront *Pace* head-on, the Miami Beach chapter of the NAACP agreed to defend Connie Hoffman and Dewey McLaughlin.[17]

No NAACP lawyer could have made such a decision lightly, not in Florida, where violence against Black men had repeatedly sliced through the heart of the state, much of it justified in the name of protecting White women. Florida's NAACP tracked much of its early history as a string of responses to violence against Black men—the 1944 death (by drowning) of fifteen-year-old Willie James Howard, who had flouted local custom by sending a White girl a Christmas card; the 1945 death (by multiple gunshots) of Jesse James Payne, a sharecropper who had quarreled with his White landlord over money only to find himself accused of raping the landlord's daughter; the 1946 disappearance of Leroy Bradwell, who was accused of asking a White woman for a date. For the better part of a decade, Florida NAACP organizer Harry T. Moore had worked, with little success, to expose the White men responsible for these and other killings, but on Christmas Day 1951, Moore was killed when a bomb blew up his house.[18]

When the number of lynchings per capita was measured according to each state's Black population, Florida led the list by a considerable margin.

Lynching lingered longer in Florida than in most other states, and when it finally began to decline, Black men found themselves at the mercy of a justice system enforced by police officers who could be nearly as vicious as the lynchers had been. In 1951, the LDF's Jack Greenberg saw this dynamic firsthand when he volunteered to defend two Black men who had been accused of raping a White woman in Groveland. Greenberg's clients never made it to court for their hearing; one was killed and the other seriously wounded by gunshots from the sheriff who had been assigned to transport them (the sheriff's implausible claim was that the handcuffed prisoners had attacked him after he got out of his car to fix a flat tire).[19]

During the 1950s, segregation was the rule in Florida, in jobs and housing as well as on the state's fabled beaches and golf courses, and officials did everything they could to minimize the impact of the Supreme Court's rulings against segregation in the schools. But by the end of the decade, these patterns had begun to change. The Sunshine State's postwar economy was increasingly dependent on tourism, and boosters and developers realized that attracting tourists required putting an end to the brutal episodes of racial violence that marred their state's history. For Florida civil rights organizations, the new economy provided an opening to play on the sympathies of those White Floridians, many of them recent migrants to the state, who were willing to jettison segregation in order to establish the appearance of racial harmony. In a series of public protests, civil rights organizations pitted the determination of Florida's Black citizens against the recalcitrance of Florida's state officials by challenging segregation on Florida's beaches, at its drugstore soda fountains and swimming pools, and on its golf courses. They had begun to win these battles, one by one, by the time Miami Beach police arrested Connie Hoffman and Dewey McLaughlin in 1962.[20]

By then, *Pace* was vulnerable for yet another reason: the gradual withering away of most criminal prosecutions for adultery and fornication. Florida's chapter of adultery and fornication law shows the wide range of conduct that a state might prohibit under this rubric. An amalgam of individual laws passed between 1868 and 1892, it listed five ostensibly different, but often overlapping, "crimes." The first three—"living in open adultery," "lewd and lascivious behavior," and "fornication"—covered "any man and woman" who engaged in these practices, regardless of race.[21] There was nothing unusual about these provisions. Most American states had laws covering similar crimes, sometimes under slightly different names, such as "illicit cohabitation," the crime that covered couples who lived together outside marriage.[22] Most prosecutions of interracial couples proceeded under these ostensibly race-neutral illicit sex laws, which worked in tandem with prohibitions on interracial marriages. When prosecutors charged interracial couples with illicit sex crimes, courts denied them the chance to avoid conviction by claiming marriage as a defense.

If there was anything unusual about Florida's adultery and fornication law, it was its last two provisions, which applied only to "white persons and negroes," who were specifically forbidden to "live in adultery or fornication with each other" or to "habitually live in and occupy in the nighttime the same room."[23] Among the dozens of states with laws that prohibited interracial marriage, only a handful had gone so far as to pass provisions like these, aimed specifically at interracial illicit sex. All of these laws, including Florida's, subjected interracial couples to different penalties than those applied to same-race couples for similar behavior, and all targeted ongoing relationships (living in adultery or fornication, cohabitation, or habitually occupying the same room) rather than individual acts of interracial sex.[24] The definitive example was, of course, Alabama, whose prohibition on living in interracial adultery and fornication had been upheld by the U.S. Supreme Court in *Pace*.

In the 1880s, when Tony Pace's case had come before the Supreme Court, charges of adultery and fornication had been a commonplace, though certainly selective, means of enforcing community disapproval of extramarital sex. Both same-race and interracial couples were frequently arrested on these charges, and the racial breadth of the arrests helped hide the harassment of interracial couples behind what appeared to be an across-the-board insistence on punishing sex outside marriage. Arrests for adultery and fornication continued to occur more or less frequently through the 1920s, but as middle-class Americans began to adopt modern sexual mores, enforcement grew less and less appealing to judges, prosecutors, and the public at large. By 1950, when New York judge Morris Ploscowe published his influential survey *Sex and the Law*, enforcement had fallen to the point where Ploscowe declared that laws against adultery and fornication were virtually "dead letters."[25]

There were, however, exceptions to this generalization, and one of them was interracial couples. Given the striking decline in overall enforcement of sex laws, the harassment of interracial couples became that much more apparent. With each passing decade, the notion that the private sexual relationships of adult men and women could or should be subject to criminal prosecution faded a little further, until by 1962 the idea of putting someone on trial for adultery or fornication seemed old-fashioned. Most White Floridians lived in comfortable ignorance of these "dead letter" laws. Yet, as Connie Hoffman's arrest demonstrated, interracial couples continued to be caught in their legal net, because laws against illicit sex continued to provide prosecutors with a useful means of responding to complaints about interracial relationships in states where the vast majority of Whites were determined to prevent what the Florida Supreme Court would, in the case of Hoffman and McLaughlin, sneeringly refer to as the "right to engage in integrated illicit cohabitation."[26]

The continued use of adultery and fornication laws against interracial couples was one of many reasons that legal experts began recommending that these laws be repealed altogether. In 1955, for example, when the reform-minded American Law Institute was developing its Model Penal Code, its members held a lengthy discussion about laws prohibiting "illicit cohabitation or intercourse." The conversation started with the commonplace observation that such laws were "generally unenforced" but then turned to an examination of those occasions on which the laws *were,* in fact, enforced. "Like other dead letter statutes . . . ," the members assigned to report on this topic explained, these laws "lend themselves to abuse [and] may be invoked only in special circumstances, such as relations between different races." Partly for this reason, the Institute decided against including any punishments for adultery and fornication in its model code.[27]

In liberal legal circles, calls for the repeal of adultery and fornication laws helped detach the stigma of illicit sex from the "fundamental right" of marriage; when combined with the application of a broad-based conception of equal protection to a growing range of civil rights, they added up to a strong case against miscegenation law. As early as 1957, NAACP board member Andrew Weinberger, a New York lawyer, published an article in which he argued that, given the recent history of Supreme Court decisions on equal protection, interracial marriage should be considered a "civil right" protected by the Fourteenth Amendment. Weinberger took care to distinguish his personal views from the policy of the NAACP, but two years later, in 1959, when Jack Greenberg published *Race Relations and American Law,* he took Weinberger's analysis as a given. "There is no doubt," Greenberg wrote, that laws prohibiting interracial marriage "are unconstitutional. . . . The reasoning in every segregation case in the Supreme Court of the past decade points the other way." In 1961, when Gerhard Mueller published his survey *Legal Regulation of Sexual Conduct,* he left miscegenation laws out of his book on the grounds that they were "bound to disappear from the statute books in a very short time."[28]

In public discourse, too, challenges to miscegenation law soon began to be expressed as defenses of civil rights and equality (with accompanying condemnations of race discrimination). In November 1963, for example, *U.S. News and World Report* interviewed a number of "leading authorities" about "Intermarriage and the Race Problem." Of the seven experts included in the article, only one defended miscegenation laws, on the ground that "racial mixing is undesirable in this country and could be catastrophic." Anthropologist Margaret Mead, who disagreed, dismissed this argument out of hand. "We've always had interracial breeding in this country . . . ," Mead insisted. "The difference between interbreeding and intermarriage is that, with intermarriage, you treat the women of both races with equal courtesy and consideration." Swedish social scientist Gunnar Myrdal offered a similar critique. "I do believe," Myrdal opined, "that every Negro and every good American must be against these laws because they are obviously discriminating. . . . From a scientific point of view," Myrdal added, "there is no reason why people shouldn't marry as they please." "In my opinion," sociologist Brewton Berry told the interviewer, "nature doesn't care—one way or another—about the mixing of races."[29]

Black leaders, too, were increasingly likely to see miscegenation laws as a civil rights issue that demanded their attention. During the 1950s, most Black leaders seem to have placed interracial marriage at the absolute bottom of their list of priorities. But by 1963, when *U.S. News and World Report* reported on the comments of NAACP Executive Director Roy Wilkins, a new attitude was clearly in evidence. During a television interview in New York City, Wilkins, who had been asked about the NAACP's stance on interracial marriage, shed the group's customary caution. "Well, we've moved into that area some time ago," Wilkins told his interviewer, and went on to credit the NAACP for the "repeal of a number of laws that formerly existed" in western states. Although Wilkins was careful to mention that the NAACP had many other, often higher, priorities, he returned to the subject long enough to make his position entirely clear. "Our basic feeling," he said, "is that there must be no legal interference with two persons who wish to get married, and especially there ought to be no interference on the basis of race and color."[30]

As Wilkins spoke these words, the LDF was preparing to put them into practice by defending Connie Hoffman and Dewey McLaughlin. But before the LDF could end legal "interference on the basis of race and color" in marriage, it would have to move beyond the northern states where civil rights organizations like the NAACP and the ACLU were based, and beyond the western states where legislatures had begun to repeal prohibitions on interracial marriage. They would have to confront miscegenation law in the South, where White public opinion still stood overwhelmingly in favor of miscegenation laws, where judges had upheld them again and again in decisions that still deferred to *Pace*. When the Miami chapter of the NAACP decided to take Hoffman and McLaughlin's case, it jettisoned the politics of respectability that had marked the ACLU and JACL's earlier attempts to establish a fundamental right of marriage and the politics of avoidance that had marked its own midcentury reluctance to challenge miscegenation laws in court. Then, in trying to defend them, it entered the realm of criminal law and waded hip-deep in the messy underbelly of the sexualization of miscegenation law in order to challenge the commonsense imperative of race classification that stood at its very core.

In the Belly of the Beast

In June 1961, when Connie Hoffman and Dewey McLaughlin went on trial, their case offered a stark illustration of the on-the-ground realities in southern courts. Their lawyer, Grattan E. Graves Jr., knew only too well what he was up against. One of a handful of Black lawyers in Miami, Florida, Graves had grown up in Washington, D.C., and obtained his law degree in 1943 from Howard University, the school that was, in the words of historian J. Clay Smith, "the center of modern civil rights methodology." In 1946, Graves moved to Miami, where he began his work as a civil rights lawyer by serving as attorney for the Miami branch of the NAACP. During the 1950s, Graves sued to desegregate Miami's public schools, buses, civic auditoriums, golf courses, and swimming pools; by 1960, he was defending the Black and White college students who had been arrested for holding sit-ins at drugstore lunch counters and swim-ins on Florida's beaches. In city and state courts, where Florida judges seemed determined to defend segregation, Graves lost nearly every one of his cases, including four in a row before the Florida Supreme Court. But when he appealed these losses in federal courts, his arguments on the basis of equal protection resulted in a string of victories for the civil rights cause—and a good deal of embarrassment for the Florida judges overruled by federal courts.[31]

When Graves tried to defend Connie Hoffman and Dewey McLaughlin in Miami's Dade County Criminal Court, he got nowhere fast.[32] Even before the trial, Judge Gene Williams had rejected Graves's broad-based motion to quash the information (or indictment) against his clients on the grounds that Florida's interracial cohabitation law violated both the due process and equal protection clauses of the U.S. Constitution, that the detectives' search of Hoffman's apartment violated the couple's right to privacy, and that Florida's race definition statute was too "vague, indefinite, and uncertain" to be enforceable. During the trial, Graves tried to force the state to prove both of the key elements of the crime as charged: that Hoffman and McLaughlin were a "white

Civil rights lawyers meet to plan strategy in Florida. Grattan E. Graves is at the far right; second from the left is Thurgood Marshall, general counsel of the NAACP Legal Defense Fund from 1940 to 1961. (State Archives of Florida)

woman" and a "negro man," as defined by Florida law, and that they were "not married to each other." On both counts, he failed hands down.[33]

Graves put the bulk of his energy into insisting that the state prove that his clients were a "negro" man and a "white" woman. To do so, he pointed a finger at Florida's statutory definition of race. Placed at the very beginning of *Florida Statutes of 1959* (title 1, chapter 1, section 1), it provided that "the words 'negro,' 'colored,' 'colored persons,' 'mulatto' or 'persons of color' . . . include every person having one-eighth or more of African or negro blood." Blood-quantum laws like this one, which remained on the books in most southern states, reflected the kind of thinking that had been ridiculed by culturalists ever since the 1920s, the kind of thinking that had, in 1948, led Roger Traynor to declare that the racial categories in California's miscegenation laws were "too vague and uncertain to be enforceable."[34]

Graves believed that Florida's race definition law was every bit as vague as California's, and he hoped to make the illogic of its blood-quantum definition apparent by insisting on two points: first, that in order to convict his clients, Florida had to prove their race beyond a reasonable doubt; and second, that there was no reliable way to prove *anyone's* race. His opening gambit, a truly striking strategy, was an attempt to prevent the jury from ever seeing his clients, and by so doing, to make the state prove their race without relying on jurors' impressions of their skin colors to do so. To this end, Graves filed a motion to let the trial proceed without the defendants present in the courtroom. "In this case," he explained to the surprised judge, "the question of identification is very important, and . . . the defendants' presence before the jury could, and would, constitute self-incriminatory evidence." Judge Williams denied this motion, so Graves tried to find another way to make the same point. When prosecutors called a Miami police detective to the witness stand, Graves tried to persuade the judge not to let the policeman use the word "negro" to refer to Dewey McLaughlin. When, Graves argued, the detective "refers to 'negro' he is going to create the impression in the minds of the jurors that this is actually a negro, which is not necessarily a fact," at least not until the state had shown that McLaughlin fit the statutory definition of one-eighth "negro blood," which, of course, it could not do.[35]

Annoyed by all these interruptions, the prosecutor tried to stop them by insisting that race was "solely a question of fact" and maintaining that "any person can be in a position to give an opinion as to what he feels," while Graves argued that race was a "mixed question of law and fact" that required formal statutory proof. Hoping to settle the issue once and for all, the judge sent the jury out of the courtroom, then engaged in a remarkable—and revealing—colloquy:

> [G. E. GRAVES]: If the State is not prepared to prove a percentage of blood in keeping with the Statute, then I think we even at this juncture are entitled to a directed verdict. . . . We have argued this statute is indefinite and vague . . . I see no test set forth that the jury can use to set forth whether one of these persons is white and one colored unless some person testifies they tested the blood of each of them and found eight percent colored blood in one and 7/8ths per cent is white in the other.

> THE COURT [JUDGE WILLIAMS]: The last time I declared a Statute unconstitutional and indefinite they reversed me and said anybody with common sense would know, and I am afraid that is the way that is going to be, especially when another Judge has already ruled that it is constitutional and definite enough. I will have to take the same attitude and think about common sense. . . .

> MR. GRAVES: . . . I submit there is no such thing as Negro or white-blood.

THE COURT: That being so, they must have meant something else.

MR. GRAVES: What else could they have meant?

THE COURT: They meant anyone whose blood is 1/8th from a Negro ancestor.

MR. GRAVES: If we are going to interpret the word "blood" as meaning ancestor, then there has been no demonstration about whose ancestors belong to whom.

THE COURT: Then we come back to the appearance again.[36]

And come back to appearance they did. The judge offered Graves a small victory or two along the way; he refused, for example, to admit some of the documentary evidence of race that prosecutors hoped to put before the jury, including forms on which clerks had recorded Dewey McLaughlin's race without even bothering to ask him for the information. But over the course of the trial two police detectives, landlady Goodnick, and the welfare worker who had interviewed Connie Hoffman all referred to Dewey McLaughlin as a "colored" or "negro" man and to Hoffman as a "white" woman; indeed, the welfare worker said that Connie Hoffman used these terms herself. Prosecutors made no attempt to pin down the blood or ancestry of either defendant.[37]

Graves's other major defense strategy was to raise the possibility that Hoffman and McLaughlin might have had a common-law marriage to each other. In so doing, he tried to take advantage of the fact that Florida was one of a dwindling minority of states that still allowed common-law marriage, a status that Connie Hoffman, at least, was eager to claim. In an attempt to get her landlady to leave her alone, Hoffman had told Goodnick that Dewey McLaughlin was her husband and had "signed [him] in" as such on Goodnick's rental records.[38] In legal terms, Graves's argument about common-law marriage was both unlikely and insightful. It was unlikely because, during the long history of miscegenation law, courts had excluded White/Black couples from the protections of common-law marriage so consistently that most lawyers had stopped even bothering to make the claim. It was insightful, though, in that it recognized—and confronted—the pivotal role that denying the status of marriage to interracial couples played in the sexualization of miscegenation law by defining interracial relationships as illicit sex.

But Graves's attempts to raise the jury's consciousness on this issue were repeatedly stymied, first by the prosecution, and then by the judge. Relying on the very sexualization that Graves was trying to resist, the prosecution began by impugning Connie Hoffman's morals. One of their witnesses, the welfare worker assigned to quiz Hoffman about her five-year-old son, Ralph, testified that Dewey McLaughlin was Connie Hoffman's third live-in boy-friend in the past six years, replacing Fred Hoffman, a White mechanic who did contract work for the Miami Beach Police Department, and before him Robert Gonzalez, Ralph's father. Having painted Connie Hoffman's entire life as one episode of illicit sex after another, they then shifted their atten-tion to Dewey McLaughlin, who, they insisted, was in no position to marry anyone. As proof, they called the city clerk who had filled out the expired registration card that led to McLaughlin's first arrest, who testified that when Dewey McLaughlin had applied for the card, he said he was separated from his wife, Willie May McLaughlin.[39]

Where the prosecution left off, the judge took over. At the end of the trial, Graves asked the judge to tell the jury that Florida recognized common-law marriages, and the judge agreed to do so. But any impact this instruction might have had was offset immediately afterward, when the judge gave the jury the added instruction that because the state of Florida banned marriage between "whites" and "negroes," any such marriage was absolutely invalid. This last instruction trumped Graves's claim of common-law marriage, but for reasons that are still unclear, Graves listened to it without raising any objection, an error that would come back to haunt the *McLaughlin* case.[40]

Graves had no better luck with his claim of racial indeterminacy. At the close of the trial, the judge went through the motions of instructing the jury that the state had to prove beyond a reasonable doubt that "one defen-dant in this case has at least one-eighth Negro blood, and that the other defendant has more than seven-eighths white blood." Yet the members of the jury seemed no more concerned about meeting this requirement than the lawyers for the state of Florida had been. They listened to the witnesses, looked at the defendants, and drew their own conclusions. After deliberat-ing for all of twenty-four minutes, they found both defendants guilty, and Judge Williams sentenced each of them to thirty days in the county jail and a $150 fine.[41] In the end, Graves's argument about the "vagueness" of race had proved even less effective than his argument about common-law marriage. As this outcome made clear, southern judges and juries remained deeply committed to notions of race, which they continued to justify in the name of a common sense so deeply embedded in the minds of its proponents that no logical arguments seemed capable of dislodging it.

Graves immediately appealed his clients' conviction to the Florida Supreme Court in Tallahassee. This time around, he downplayed the vague-ness of race and emphasized his argument about common-law marriage. In his appeal brief, Graves argued that Judge Williams's instructions to the jury had, in effect, denied Connie Hoffman and Dewey McLaughlin the right to claim a common-law marriage in their defense, and so violated their right to both due process and equal protection. In doing so, Graves built on claims that had emerged from the fight to establish a natural or fundamental right to interracial marriage in the 1940s and 1950s. In language that echoed Roger Traynor, Graves declared that the "essence of the right to marry is a freedom to join in marriage with the person of one's own choice" and insisted that Florida had failed to prove that "any valid governmental purpose is furthered by depriving individuals of the privacy of their homes and a marital relationship solely because the mate they have chosen is of a different race."[42]

The rest of Graves's brief attacked Florida's interracial cohabitation law, using arguments that had emerged from the LDF's campaign to ensure civil rights for African Americans. By punishing interracial "cohabitation" more severely than simple "fornication," Graves argued, Florida denied Hoffman and McLaughlin equal protection of the laws. In making this argument, Graves used the strategy that had succeeded in so many of his other civil rights cases. Pointedly ignoring Florida jurisprudence, he lectured Florida's supreme court justices about federal civil rights laws. The U.S. Supreme Court, Graves declared, "has often held that race is 'constitutionally an irrelevance,'" illustrating this point with a list of federal court cases decided on equal protection grounds. The only exception worth noting was the Supreme Court's decision in *Pace,* which, Graves had to admit, "upheld a statute similar to that involved in this case." But that, he insisted, should no longer matter, because "the *Pace* case, decided some 80 years ago, is squarely in conflict with all presently existing interpretations of the equal protection clause."[43]

Florida's attorney general, however, had no intention of letting Graves slip so lightly over this issue. His brief to the Florida Supreme Court put *Pace* front and center, then built the state's argument around it. He opened with a summary of *Pace,* in which, he argued, the U.S. Supreme Court had ruled that "the discrimination involved in a statute which prohibited interracial cohabitation was directed against the offense and not against the person of any particular color or race."[44] Since the "punishment of each offending person, whether white or black, was found to be the same," there was "no discrimination against a particular race." The conviction of Connie Hoffman and Dewey McLaughlin was, the Florida brief claimed, exactly the same thing. Noting that *Pace* had been upheld as recently as 1944, in an Oklahoma decision involving a law banning interracial marriage, it insisted that the only way the Florida Supreme Court could rule in Hoffman and McLaughlin's favor would be to "directly overrule" *Pace,* something that the state's attorney general conveniently insisted only the U.S. Supreme Court could do.[45]

Offered a choice between *Pace* on the one hand and the U.S. Supreme Court's recent decisions in equal protection cases on the other, the Florida Supreme Court chose *Pace*. The court's unanimous decision was written by Justice Millard F. Caldwell, a former governor, a segregationist, and a long-time foe of the NAACP.[46] Obviously offended at seeing Graves treat his court as if it were "a mere way station on the route to the United States Supreme Court," Caldwell nonetheless clung to the U.S. Supreme Court's decision in *Pace,* the only federal precedent that offered southern prosecutors any reassurance on the subject of interracial sex and marriage. "This Court is obligated . . . ," he wrote, by "the precedent of the well written decision in *Pace. . . .* The Federal Constitution," Caldwell declared, "as it was when construed by the United States Supreme Court in that case, is quite adequate but if the new-found concept of 'social justice' has out-dated 'the law of the land' as therein announced and, by way of consequence, some new law is necessary, it must be enacted by legislative process or some other court must write it."[47]

From Equal Application to Invidious Discrimination

After the Florida Supreme Court issued its decision, G. E. Graves handed the *McLaughlin* case over to the New York office of the LDF, where the next move fell to Jack Greenberg, who had succeeded Thurgood Marshall as general counsel. The LDF had been keeping an eye on *McLaughlin* since its early stages, but Greenberg was aware of its shortcomings, which by now included Graves's initial failure to object to the trial court judge's instruction about interracial marriage and his subsequent failure to raise the issue of Florida's race definition law before the Florida Supreme Court, either of which might hand the U.S. Supreme Court an excuse for dismissing these lines of argument—or, given the Court's reluctance to consider the subjects of interracial sex and marriage, the case itself. So before Greenberg agreed to go any further, he asked two of the LDF's longtime board members, William T. Coleman, a Black lawyer who worked for an eminent firm in Philadelphia, and Louis Pollak, a White lawyer who was then dean of Yale Law School, for their advice. Both men had begun their careers by clerking for U.S. Supreme Court justices and since gone on to argue dozens of cases before that court. Both told Greenberg that they were eager to see the LDF appeal the case, so eager, in fact, that they offered to argue it themselves.[48]

Like G. E. Graves in Florida, Coleman and Pollak wanted to link Florida's law prohibiting interracial cohabitation to its law prohibiting interracial marriage. Their strategy marked a significant departure from the politics of respectability pursued in the 1940s and 1950s, when the LACIC, the ACLU and the JACL had tried to build a legal retaining wall between the question of interracial marriage and the stigma of illicit sex. Indeed, the JACL still wanted to do so. When the JACL's General Counsel, William Marutani, heard that the LDF had decided to take *McLaughlin* to the U.S. Supreme Court, he asked Jack Greenberg for details about the case, evidently in anticipation of adding JACL support. But the more the JACL learned about *McLaughlin*, the less it liked the case. In a memo to the JACL's inner circle, Marutani concluded that *McLaughlin* was both legally risky and socially distasteful; as he put it, the "facts of this case itself do not lend themselves readily to stirring social sympathy." Marutani had little interest in challenging laws against adultery and fornication, interracial or otherwise, and he worried that the Supreme Court was not very likely to decide to invalidate laws against interracial marriage in a case where one of the supposed marital partners was, it appeared, already married to another woman. On his recommendation, the JACL turned its back on *McLaughlin* in order to keep looking for a "clean" case, one in which the issue of interracial marriage could be isolated from the stigma of illicit sex.[49]

But this, of course, was the problem. Ever since the 1880s, the sexualization of miscegenation law had ensured that any such isolation was only an illusion. Ending the regime of miscegenation law would ultimately require breaking the definitional circle in which states used laws that prohibited interracial marriage to define interracial relationships *as* illicit sex. Moreover, as long as states were able to use adultery and fornication laws to prosecute interracial couples for illicit sex crimes, and to rely on *Pace* and its equal application rationale for doing so, they would be able to justify their prohibitions on interracial marriage.

So when the LDF brought the *McLaughlin* case to the U.S. Supreme Court, it threw its considerable legal weight behind an argument broad enough to attack three of Florida's laws at once: Florida's ban on interracial cohabitation, its ban on interracial marriage, and its race definition law, too. Wielding the broad-based conception of equal protection the LDF had done so much to establish in cases like *Brown v. Board of Education*, Coleman and Pollak hammered the Florida Supreme Court for relying on *Pace*. "*Pace*," their brief declared, "stands as an isolated vestige of the 'separate but equal' era inconsistent with the entire development of the law" since 1917, when the NAACP had won its first Supreme Court victory in a housing discrimination case. "It ought," they told the Court, "to be overruled."[50]

On the question of interracial marriage, they made much the same argument that G. E. Graves had advanced, that if it weren't for Florida's miscegenation law, Connie Hoffman and Dewey McLaughlin would have been able to claim common-law marriage in their defense. By denying them the right to do this, the lower-court judge had harmed the couple, since "the evidence taken in its most favorable light tends to establish that appellants had contracted a common law marriage." Once this rather tenuous basis had been laid, the brief launched a full-blown assault on laws against interracial marriage, linking the fight against segregation (an equal protection issue) to the fight for personal liberty (a due process issue). "Miscegenation laws are 'relics of slavery'" ultimately based on notions "of Negro inferiority," Coleman and Pollak told the Court; like other segregation laws, "their enforcement by the states violates the Fourteenth Amendment." Because "the right to choose one's own husband or wife is clearly a right going to the very heart of personal liberty and freedom. . . . The due process and equal protection clauses surely prevent the states from engaging in irrational discriminations in this vital area of personal liberty." Marriage, they told the Court, "is a protected liberty under the Fourteenth Amendment; it is one of the 'basic civil rights of man.'"[51]

When it came to the question of Florida's race definition law, Coleman and Pollak offered the Court two overlapping but alternative arguments. One of these, the claim that Florida's race definition was too vague to pass due process muster, also echoed the arguments Graves had made in the lower court. Florida prosecutors, they told the Supreme Court, had "made no pretense of proving race" in the lower-court trial, either according to the statutory requirement of one-eighth "Negro" blood or on the basis of ancestry. "The appearance test upon which Florida ultimately relies . . . ," they complained, "based on witnesses' and jurors' opinions of a person's race, depends on their shifting and subjective perceptions influenced by stereotypes and conditioned by their differing personal appearances. In the 'never-never-land' of the appearance test," they continued, "a person's race is not an objective fact at all, but depends entirely on other persons' views of him. . . . This standard," they insisted, "obviously leaves the jurors to their own devices in determining race on any basis they choose." Their conclusion was bitingly clear: "To make a man conduct himself on the basis of a preliminary guess as to what his race will be in the opinion of some future unknown witnesses and jurors who will use no precise standards places liberty on a slippery surface unworthy of a civilized system of criminal law."[52]

But claiming that Florida's race definition was too vague was not the only way the LDF tried to persuade the Supreme Court to derail the imperative of race classification. In keeping with its philosophy of offering the Supreme Court as many rationales as possible with which to reach their desired result, the LDF offered the Court another alternative, one that side-stepped the seemingly counterintuitive argument that there was no such thing as race in favor of the simpler argument that the equal protection clause flatly forbade a state from classifying by race. "On their face," the LDF maintained, miscegenation laws "run counter to the 'color-blindness' of the Constitution."[53] Race, they claimed, citing Graves's argument to Florida and the U.S. Supreme Court's own language in another earlier case, "is constitutionally an irrelevance."[54]

On October 13–14, 1964, the Supreme Court held oral arguments in the *McLaughlin* case. Coleman and Pollak stood ready to persuade the justices to see this case as one more battle in the Supreme Court's decade-long war between equal protection and race segregation. Coleman, who spoke first, insisted that Florida's laws defining "negroes" and prohibiting interracial marriage were every bit as much at stake in the case as Florida's interracial cohabitation law. All three had to be overturned, Coleman argued, because under the Fourteenth Amendment's "spacious" language about equal protection, race had to be considered "constitutionally irrelevant." That, he explained, had been the principle the Court had used in deciding its famous school segregation cases, and it should be the principle here, too. In an argument that was all the more remarkable for coming out of the mouth of an LDF lawyer, Coleman went so far as to tell the justices that choice in marriage was more important than choice in schools, so *McLaughlin* should be an "easier" case for the Supreme Court to decide than *Brown v. Board of Education*. When it was his turn, Louis Pollak declared nineteenth-century decisions like *Pace* outmoded and inappropriate under what he called the "Twentieth-Century Fourteenth Amendment." "The time has come," Pollak told the justices, "to remove this stigma from the fabric of American law."[55]

If there was a stumbling point in this presentation, it came when Chief Justice Earl Warren asked Coleman if Hoffman and McLaughlin were married. When Coleman said they were, Warren asked why there was no marriage certificate in evidence. Coleman knew the answer: in a state where interracial marriage was punishable by a ten-year prison sentence but occupying the same room was punishable by a one-year prison sentence, any lawyer who tried to prove that Hoffman and McLaughlin were married would only have gotten them in deeper trouble. But when he couldn't find the details of the applicable prison sentences quickly enough to include them in his answer, he deflected the question, missing, he later lamented, another chance to insist that the court strike down Florida's ban on interracial marriage as well as its cohabitation law. Nonetheless, the LDF case was a tight, confident presentation, offered by lawyers who were at the top of their game. The arguments had been pretested before an audience of lawyers that included, among others, David Carliner, who had brought the *Naim* case before the U.S. Supreme Court nearly a decade earlier, and they were offered to a Court the LDF had reason to expect would be sympathetic.[56]

James Mahorner, the twenty-seven-year-old assistant district attorney general who argued the case for the state of Florida, enjoyed none of these advantages, but he tried hard not to let it show. Making cunning use of the stigmas that made illicit sex so symbolically powerful, Mahorner responded to the LDF's jurisdictional statement by insisting that all Florida was trying to do was to uphold "basic concepts of sexual decency." In Mahorner's view, Florida's treatment of Connie Hoffman and Dewey McLaughlin had nothing to do with race prejudice. From the moment the Miami Beach police had arrested the couple, they had treated them with admirable restraint. Miami Beach detectives were accustomed to working "in an area the citizens of which are metropolitan, sophisticated, and possessed of a diversified cultural background," a place "generally conducive to racial tolerance," and, as a result, its jury had given the couple a light sentence. It was sex, he insisted, not race, that stood at the heart of the case.[57]

Mahorner's objective was to limit the Court's consideration solely to Florida's cohabitation law, placing Florida's race definition law and its ban on interracial marriage out of bounds. If there was no race prejudice in the case, Florida's race definition law held no valence one way or the other. The LDF's charge that Florida's blood-quantum definition of race was unconstitutionally vague hardly applied, for "the sin of such sections, if anything, is over-exactness; it is not ambiguity." In keeping with generations of southern prosecutors before him, Mahorner insisted that race classification was little more than simple common sense. "The court," he claimed, "can take judicial knowledge of the fact that there exists a race known as the Negro race."[58]

And if the case was all about illicit sex, Florida's law against interracial marriage should also be considered beside the point. "This court," Mahorner declared, "should not be led by opposing argument into ruling on a constitutional question of such import as miscegenation in a case the style of which records for eternal history the fact that the parties were not married." There was, he insisted, no actual marriage anywhere in the *McLaughlin* case, and there was "much evidence which indicates that the defendants were not married to each other." Even if they had been married, Mahorner maintained, the LDF could not raise this issue now, because G. E. Graves's failure to object during the lower-court trial put the issue out of consideration at the appellate level.[59]

Yet even as Mahorner tried to remove Florida's law against interracial marriage from consideration, he returned, again and again, to its importance.

In his oral argument before the Supreme Court, Mahorner admitted that Florida regarded its ban on interracial marriage as the "most important" of all the laws raised in the case. Mahorner was so sure that Florida had the power to prohibit interracial marriage that at one point in his brief, he offered that power as the ultimate justification for the state's power to punish interracial sex. "Clearly," he declared, "if the state may prohibit interracial marriage, it may as a corollary thereto prohibit interracial cohabitation."[60]

Unable to decouple Florida's ban on interracial cohabitation from its ban on interracial marriage, Mahorner instead tried to distinguish interracial cohabitation *and* interracial marriage from other civil rights. Here his argument reached deep into the history of the Fourteenth Amendment, whose origins, Mahorner claimed, could be found in the intentions of the congressmen who supported its predecessor, the Civil Rights Act of 1866. Neither the 1866 act nor the 1868 amendment, Mahorner insisted, had anything to do with prohibitions on interracial marriage, as both state and federal courts of that period and since had demonstrated by repeatedly sustaining miscegenation laws under the Fourteenth Amendment. His definitive example was, of course, *Pace v. Alabama*.[61]

In *McLaughlin*, then, the U.S. Supreme Court faced much the same choice as the Florida Supreme Court below it: between *Pace* on the one hand and its recent string of equal protection cases on the other. It was no contest: *Pace* would have to go, and Florida's ban on interracial cohabitation along with it. Beyond that, though, nothing was entirely clear. The justices were especially worried over what to do about Florida's ban on interracial marriage. Both the LDF and the state of Florida had, in different ways, shown that the links between Florida's ban on interracial cohabitation and its ban on interracial marriage were all but inescapable. The LDF had painstakingly designed its arguments to bring the Supreme Court right to the brink of overturning Florida's ban on interracial marriage, and, with a little help from its opponent, it had succeeded in doing just that. When James Mahorner told the Court that the equal application rationale offered in *Pace* applied to interracial marriage as well as interracial sex, he had, quite unintentionally, offered the Court all the excuse it really needed to strike down laws prohibiting interracial marriage.

Chief Justice Earl Warren was ready to do so. He had, in fact, been ready to do so a decade earlier—in 1954, when he and two other justices had voted to issue a writ of certiorari in the *Jackson* case from Alabama, only to be outvoted by their fellow justices, and again in 1955, when the Supreme Court's decision to duck the *Naim* case left him, according to one of his clerks, "furious" at the "total bullshit" of the Court's rejection. But, as Justice William O. Douglas's private notes reveal, this was not what happened. When the justices met in conference to discuss their decision in *McLaughlin,* Warren opened the discussion by urging his colleagues to issue a decision broad enough to overturn Florida's prohibition on interracial marriage as well as its cohabitation law. He couldn't, he said, "see any justification for denying common law marriage to those of different races and granting it to others." Justice Hugo Black agreed with Warren that it was hard to see "how the question can be decided without deciding marriage questions."[62]

But then the caution the Court had displayed, repeatedly, on the subject of interracial marriage set in, spurred in part by James Mahorner's assertion that Connie Hoffman and Dewey McLaughlin could not have established a persuasive claim to common-law marriage even if the defense had been open to them. Justice Black had no sooner expressed his interest in a broad decision than he began to worry that "this is a bad case to reach the issue." Justice Douglas, who was deeply disappointed to discover that "no marriage is involved," confessed that he "thought there was when he voted to grant certiorari." Their doubts struck a chord with Justice John Marshall Harlan, who had taken Mahorner's argument about Fourteenth Amendment history seriously enough to send his clerks scouring through the historical evidence. ("The heart of [the issue] . . . does not appear," his clerk had eventually concluded in a summary memo, "until someone reads the history, concludes as I have done that the framers of the 14th amendment did not intend it to wipe out antimiscegenation statutes, and then says 'so what'?") Justice Douglas wondered aloud whether the case ought to be dismissed, and Justice William Brennan raised the possibility of ruling on the issue of racial "vagueness" rather than on equal protection grounds. But neither of these suggestions attracted enough support to make a difference, so the justices returned to the question of Florida's ban on interracial marriage. In the end, although most of them seemed well aware that, as Justice Potter Stewart put it, "our decisions over the last ten years require us to reverse both this [the cohabitation statute] and the miscegenation act," they settled for the lowest common denominator, a ruling that would overturn the cohabitation provision without reaching Florida's law prohibiting interracial marriage.[63]

The decision the Court issued in *McLaughlin* opened with an adamant rejection of the equal application logic put forth in *Pace v. Alabama.* "Pace," Justice Byron White wrote for the Court, "represents a limited view of the Equal Protection Clause which has not withstood analysis in the subsequent decisions of this Court. . . . Judicial inquiry under the Equal Protection Clause . . . ," White ruled, "does not end with a showing of equal application among the members of the class defined by the legislation." Rather, it required an examination of the construction of the class itself, "in this case, whether there is an arbitrary or invidious discrimination between those classes covered by Florida's cohabitation law and those excluded. That question," he intoned, "is what *Pace* ignored and which must be faced here." Noting that race classifications required particularly strong justification, and all the more so in criminal laws, White ruled that "without such justification the racial classification contained in [Florida's cohabitation law] . . . is reduced to an invidious discrimination forbidden by the Equal Protection Clause."[64]

In this manner, *McLaughlin v. Florida* accomplished two things. First, by resting its decision on "the single issue of equal protection" and relying on the concept of invidious discrimination, it reoriented the debate about race classification, replacing older arguments about racial vagueness as a violation of due process with an equal protection rationale that was much closer to colorblindness, the belief, which had been urged on it by the LDF, that the best way to end racism was to banish racial categories from the law altogether.[65] In so doing, it found a way to derail the imperative of race classification that had sustained miscegenation law ever since the 1880s.

Second, by overruling *Pace*, *McLaughlin* deprived the South of the equal application argument that had been the strongest support not only for laws prohibiting interracial cohabitation but also for laws prohibiting interracial marriage. In the decade since *Brown v. Board of Education*, *Pace* had offered southern state courts their best hope—perhaps their only hope—of offsetting the equal protection analysis that was emerging from the Supreme Court's other decisions. Every southern court that upheld its state miscegenation law—the Supreme Court of Virginia in 1955, the Supreme Court of Louisiana in 1959, and the Supreme Court of Florida in 1963—had cited *Pace* in doing so.[66] Its loss could hardly have been more significant.

But these accomplishments were encased in a decision—indeed, three separate decisions—that showed how far the Supreme Court still had to go to reach a judicial consensus that miscegenation laws were unconstitutional. The majority decision, written by Justice Byron White, was hedged with qualifications at every turn. It was "unnecessary," White insisted, for the Court to consider either the LDF's arguments about due process or Florida's arguments about the history of the Fourteenth Amendment. White was not, he insisted, "expressing any views about the State's prohibition of interracial marriage," and, in passages that seem almost to contradict his initial statements about invidious discrimination, he took Florida's claim that its adultery and fornication law was based on "a general and strong state policy against promiscuous conduct" at face value. Justice Harlan, who would have preferred to see the outcome determined by the First rather than the

Fourteenth Amendment, insisted on writing his own separate concurrence. Justices Stewart and Douglas were so impatient with what they regarded as White's overly cautious understanding of the equal protection clause that they offered a tart critique in yet another concurring opinion. "The Court implies," Stewart complained on behalf of both of them, "that a criminal law of the kind here involved might be constitutionally valid if a State could show 'some overriding statutory purpose.' This," he insisted, "is an implication in which I cannot join, because I cannot conceive of a valid legislative purpose under our Constitution for a state law which makes the color of a person's skin the test of whether his conduct is a criminal offense."[67]

McLaughlin was, in the end, too hesitant a ruling even to do what Justice White insisted it was designed to do: remove race categories from the criminal enforcement of laws against illicit sex. In the eighty years since *Pace* had originally been issued, the links between laws prohibiting illicit sex and those prohibiting interracial marriage had grown deeply entangled with each other. Though the LDF had done its best to confront them all, the decision in *McLaughlin* barely scratched the surface of the sexualization of miscegenation law. Florida police could no longer arrest couples for the interracial "crime" of occupying the same room. They could, however, still arrest interracial couples for violating Florida's ostensibly race-neutral ban on fornication or on lewd and lascivious behavior, and because Florida's law prohibiting racial intermarriages remained in force, these couples would still be denied the right to claim marriage in their defense, and their relationships would still be defined as illicit sex rather than marriage. As long as the Court allowed laws prohibiting interracial marriage to remain standing, the invidious discriminations embedded in those laws would continue to ground deep-seated historical links between illicit sex, interracial marriage, and race classification. In refusing to rule on the issue of interracial marriage, the Supreme Court had left behind an enormous piece of unfinished business.

Unfinished Business

When the Supreme Court issued its decision in *McLaughlin,* laws prohibiting and punishing interracial marriage remained in effect in nineteen states, stretching from Virginia north to Indiana, west to Oklahoma, south to Texas, and back east again to Florida.[68] Challenges to these laws continued to reach state supreme courts, and continued to be rebuffed. In 1965, for example, the Supreme Court of Oklahoma upheld the constitutionality of its state miscegenation law; a year later, the Court of Appeal of Louisiana upheld its law, too.[69] No state, however, held on to its prohibition on interracial marriage with more tenacity than Virginia.

By 1950, Virginia's miscegenation law contained ten interlocking provisions. In 1955, the Virginia Supreme Court issued a lengthy decision upholding the law, in the process handing David Carliner the second of his many losses in *Naim*. Buttressing its authority with equal application rhetoric and citations to *Pace,* the Virginia court ruled that states held complete control over interracial marriage and offered a revealing—and smugly approving—description of the state's purpose in passing these laws. The Fourteenth Amendment posed no obstacle to a state that was, as Virginia was, determined "to preserve the racial integrity of its citizens" and "regulate the marriage relation so that it shall not have a mongrel breed of citizens." As the justices wrote, "We find . . . no requirement that the State shall not legislate to prevent the obliteration of racial pride. . . . Both sacred and secular history," they concluded, "teach that nations and races have better advanced in human progress when they cultivated their own distinctive characteristics and culture and developed their own peculiar genius."[70] David Carliner appealed this decision to the U.S. Supreme Court, but when it ducked the case, the Virginia decision was left standing, and Virginia chose to interpret the Supreme Court's retreat as an endorsement of its claim that interracial marriage was a question for state rather than federal courts.

Two years later, when Richard Loving, a "white" man, decided to marry Mildred Jeter, a "colored" woman, he knew he had no hope of getting a license at the county courthouse in Bowling Green, Virginia. Richard and Mildred had grown up in nearby Central Point, a town so tiny that no one was a stranger to anyone else. As Simeon Booker reported in *Ebony* magazine, Central Point's Whites, Blacks, and Indians had been mixing for decades, until many of its "colored" residents were too light-skinned to be easily distinguishable from "whites." Outsiders whispered that Central Point was "the passing capital of America"; on a day-to-day basis, it was a place where racial labels were frequently ignored and residents felt a keen desire to guard their privacy.[71]

Richard's father, a "white" man, was a truck driver who worked for twenty-three years for a well-off "Negro" farmer; Richard's childhood friends were "Negroes" of a wide variety of skin colors. Mildred's family reflected the racial mixes often collapsed into the southern label "colored"; she was, as she would later tell lawyers and reporters, "part negro and part Indian." The labels "white" and "colored" carried enough weight that Richard and Mildred belonged to different churches and attended different schools. Still, they knew each other even before they met at a local dance and started dating and, under the watchful, if not always approving, eyes of both their families, kept company for seven years. When Richard was twenty-four and Mildred eighteen, they decided to get married, pinning their hopes on the belief that their marriage was no one's business but their own.[72]

In June 1958, Richard and Mildred traveled to Washington, D.C., where they obtained a license and held their ceremony, returning with an official copy of their marriage certificate, which they framed and placed proudly on a wall of the home they shared with Mildred's parents. Most of their Central Point neighbors paid little attention to the marriage, but someone told Caroline County officials, who quickly determined to put a stop to it. The newlyweds had lived together for a little more than a month when they were awakened in the middle of the night by the county sheriff and two deputies, who had walked through the unlocked front door of the house and right into their bedroom to arrest them for violating Virginia's miscegenation law. They were taken to the county jail in Bowling Green, where Mildred remained for several days after her husband had been released, while Richard's attempts to bail her out were rebuffed by local officials. Once both had been allowed to post $1,000 in bail, they lived apart, each staying with parents while they awaited trial.[73]

Their trial, which took place in January 1959, was held before Judge Leon Bazile, whose career as a Virginia public official spanned the entire history of Virginia's Racial Integrity Act. In 1924, the year that law was enacted, Bazile was a young assistant attorney general in Richmond, where he had a front-row seat for the flurry of local court cases that arose when Walter Plecker started enforcing Virginia's one-drop racial definitions. Bazile had even played a bit part in this drama by persuading John Powell and Walter Plecker that the survival of the entire Racial Integrity Act might depend on refraining from appealing the adverse rulings issued by Judge Henry Holt in the Rockbridge County Court. "The law seems to be working all right outside of Judge Holt's circuit," Bazile had told them in November 1924, and "we would run the risk of losing a great deal on the chance of reversing him in one case." Three and a half decades later, sixty-eight-year-old Bazile had spent seventeen years as the judge of Caroline County's circuit court and developed a reputation as a staunch defender of states' rights.[74]

The fate of the Lovings rested entirely in Bazile's hands, since they had waived their right to a jury trial, assuming, probably correctly, that they would find no more sympathy from Caroline County jurors than from its judge. The prosecutor had no trouble persuading Judge Bazile that the Lovings were guilty as charged. They had, he showed, violated the Virginia code, which punished "any white person and colored person" who "shall go out of this State, for the purpose of being married, and with the intention of returning, and be married out of it, and afterwards return to and reside in it, cohabiting as man and wife." Under its terms, any such marriage "shall be governed by the same law as if it had been solemnized in this State," which meant that the marriage itself was "absolutely void" and the marriage partners were subject to felony-level punishments of one to five years in the state penitentiary.[75]

Judge Bazile was determined to enforce Virginia's miscegenation law, and to do so without provoking outside review of his actions. The result was something like a plea bargain, in which the Lovings changed their earlier pleas of "not guilty" to "guilty" and Bazile suspended the one-year prison sentences he had imposed. To the frightened young couple's immense relief, they would not have to go to prison. But there was a catch, for Bazile added the condition that "both accused leave Caroline County and the state of Virginia at once and do not return together or at the same time to said county and state for a period of twenty-five years."[76] As extraordinary as Bazile's disposition of the case now seems, the idea of enforcing state miscegenation laws by banishing interracial couples from the state seems to have been used by a handful of judges in other southern states during this same period, who were, like Bazile, caught between the desire to enforce the state's disapproval of interracial marriage on the one hand and the fear that the growing opposition to miscegenation law might provoke federal oversight on the other.[77] Rather than go to prison, the Lovings moved to Washington, D.C., where they lived for the next four years, raising three children, missing their friends and families, and making as many surreptitious visits back home as they dared.[78]

In the summer of 1963, when the LDF was trying to persuade the U.S. Supreme Court to hear the *McLaughlin* case, Mildred Loving, who had grown increasingly miserable living in Washington, took a cousin's advice and wrote to Attorney General Robert F. Kennedy, asking if the civil rights bill that was then being debated in Congress would lift the twenty-five-year restriction on visiting—much less living in—Virginia with her husband. Kennedy sent her letter to the ACLU, which asked a young lawyer from Alexandria, Virginia, Bernard Cohen, to look into the case. A few months before the Supreme Court was scheduled to hear *McLaughlin*, the Lovings moved quietly back into Virginia, where they remained while they pursued their appeals. Their position could hardly have been more precarious. The sheriff from a neighboring county threatened the Lovings with arrest if he found them in his jurisdiction; their lawyer was harassed by locals who put sugar in his gas tank. Then the momentum of the case ground to a halt when Cohen's attempt to get Judge Bazile to reconsider the matter led to what seemed like endless delays. By this time, another young lawyer, Phil Hirschkop, had entered the case, and at his urging, the lawyers decided to spur federal intervention by filing a class-action suit in federal court, which eventually placed enough

Richard and Mildred Loving talking with their lawyer in 1963, with their daughter, Peggy, in the background. (Getty Images)

pressure on Bazile to get him to issue the written opinion they had requested as part of a reconsideration of his 1959 sentence.[79]

In January 1965, a little more than a month after the U.S. Supreme Court had issued its decision in *McLaughlin,* Bazile finally released his written decision. A few months away from retirement, Bazile was as determined as ever to hold the line against illegitimate federal incursion in matters of states' rights. Refusing to change any aspect of the sentence he had imposed on the

Lovings, he offered a ringing defense of Virginia's racial purity statute. Harking back to the kind of language that had, when he was a young lawyer, been garden-variety judicial justification for miscegenation laws, but which few southern jurists were still willing to risk putting in writing, Bazile quoted earlier Virginia decisions in which interracial marriages were referred to as "unnatural alliances," cited the recently overruled decision in *Pace,* and finished with a flourish by parading his own belief that

> Almighty God created the races white, black, yellow, malay and red, and he placed them on separate continents. And but for the interference with his arrangement there would be no cause for such marriages. The fact that he separated the races shows that he did not intend for the races to mix.[80]

The Lovings appealed to the Virginia Supreme Court. Its justices dutifully slapped Judge Bazile's hand for attaching what they called an "unreasonable" condition to the suspended sentences, but in every other respect, the Virginia Supreme Court held firm. Its decision, like Bazile's, rested on the belief that, despite "numerous federal decisions in the civil rights field," from *Brown v. Board of Education* to *McLaughlin,* the state of Virginia had every right to prohibit interracial marriage. Citing "a legal truth which had always been recognized—that there is an overriding state interest in the institution of marriage," there was, the justices ruled in a unanimous decision, "no sound judicial reason . . . to depart from our holding in the *Naim* case." Showing, however, that they were more politic than Judge Bazile, they declined to mention the basis for that holding.[81]

The Virginia Supreme Court's decision in *Loving v. Commonwealth* showed in a nutshell how much—and how little—difference *McLaughlin* had made. Unable to rely on either *Pace* or its equal application argument, which the Supreme Court had rejected in *McLaughlin,* Virginia shifted its emphasis to states' traditional control over marriage and omitted the rhetoric about racial purity that it had trumpeted less than a decade earlier. But *McLaughlin* or no *McLaughlin,* the Virginia Supreme Court had no intention of changing its mind about interracial marriage.

The "Basic Civil Rights of Man"

The Virginia Supreme Court's decision in *Loving v. Commonwealth* offered the ACLU the opportunity it had long sought to take the issue of interracial marriage back to the U.S. Supreme Court. A team of lawyers, beginning with Phil

Hirschkop and Bernard Cohen in Virginia, was soon assembled to plan the case, including Melvin Wulf, the ACLU's legal director in New York City; William Zabel, a New York lawyer invited by Wulf; Arthur Berney, a Boston law professor invited by Hirschkop; and David Carliner.[82] Thanks to the LDF, they started from a strong position, for *McLaughlin* had cleared *Pace* out of the way and offered a preview of the Court's willingness to overturn criminal penalties on interracial couples on equal protection grounds. And they had, they thought, an unusually sympathetic case, one that seemed to center on the figure of a White man whose choices were being restricted by the law, one that presented the issue of interracial marriage in a manner that would seem to have been inescapable.[83]

But the ACLU had seen the Supreme Court slip out of similar situations before, and its lawyers worried that the Court might choose the narrowest possible path in *Loving,* too. The Court might, for example, issue a decision overturning only the two criminal provisions of Virginia law under which the Lovings had been tried and convicted, leaving the state's civil bans on interracial marriage still standing. Or it might issue a decision limited solely to Virginia rather than one applying to all the southern states that still had miscegenation laws on their books. To secure the broad ruling it dreamed of in *Loving,* the ACLU would have to find a way to push the Court past the caution that had set in on each and every previous occasion that it had considered the issue.

So the brief the ACLU submitted in the case was designed to argue for breadth at every opportunity. Like the LDF in *McLaughlin,* the ACLU lawyers asked for a decision that reached beyond the two specific clauses that had been used to convict their clients, the provision on evasion and the accompanying criminal penalty, to strike down "the entire Virginia statutory scheme prohibiting interracial marriage," all of which stood "at issue in this case." They illustrated this point with a chillingly concise list of the "outrageous civil effects" of Virginia's ban on interracial marriage. Unless the Supreme Court declared the civil as well as the criminal provisions of Virginia's miscegenation law unconstitutional, they told the Court, the Lovings "would not be able to inherit from each other; their three children would be deemed illegitimate; they could lose Social Security benefits, the right to file joint income tax returns and even rights to workmen's compensation benefits—all of which are contingent upon a valid marital relationship." They pleaded with the Court not to issue "a holding that the evasion statute is invalid, on some limited ground, without reaching the basic question of the validity of Virginia's bans on miscegenetic marriages." To do so, they insisted, would not only "seem disingenuous and incorrect" but "would not do justice to appellants."[84]

Echoing the phrase LDF lawyer Louis Pollak had used in *McLaughlin,* the ACLU attorneys told the Supreme Court that the "time had come" to bring the long history of miscegenation laws to an end. "The history of the Virginia anti-miscegenation laws," they said, "shows that they are relics of slavery and expressions of racism." As early as the seventeenth century, "with the establishment of Negro slavery," Virginia had begun to prohibit interracial marriage and, for "economic reasons," to forbid slaves from marrying each other and to punish Whites who tried to live with or marry blacks. Then, with "the end of slavery . . . new motivations arose which were purely racist and based on the theory that Negroes and other non-whites are members of inferior races." In the 1870s, the state had raised its punishments for miscegenation to felony levels, applied them to Blacks as well as Whites, and passed the "evasion" provision. But it was in the 1920s, during "a period of intolerance and racial animosity expressed in the spread of all forms of hate groups and super-patriotic orders with dogmas of 'yellow peril,' 'mongrelization of the white race' and 'un-Americanism,'" that the modern form of racism, with its close ties to eugenics, spurred the passage of Virginia's Racial Integrity Act of 1924, with provisions—including the one that defined a "white" person as one "who has no trace whatsoever of any other blood than Caucasian"—that now "remind one of the laws of Nazi Germany."[85]

Then the ACLU lawyers dug even deeper into the history of miscegenation law. "There is," they continued, "still another history to be told," one that "lurks beneath the surface of the 'written' history we have examined." This, they said, "is the story of what these laws have done to our entire peo ple . . . the familiar chronicle of race relations in our nation." Taking a page from the arguments the NAACP had offered in its 1913 campaigns to halt the spread of miscegenation law, they placed special emphasis on "the history of illicit sex relationships," which "conditions . . . the entire pattern of American race relations" and was, they charged, the "socio-psychological tap-root of American racial prejudice." Because Virginia's miscegenation laws "do not simply bar interracial marriage, they perpetuate and foster illicit exploitative sex relationships," they "stand as a present day incarnation of an ancient evil." They had to go, because "the ultimate evil of these laws is that they constitute an infliction of indignity upon every person cast among others as not good enough to marry a 'White person.'"[86]

The ACLU built its constitutional argument on two pillars—equal protection and due process. The stronger of these—and the one all the lawyers agreed on—was the equal protection argument. To make it, they needed to do little more than repeat the arguments the LDF had already laid out, and the Supreme Court had accepted, in the *McLaughlin* case. "Statutory distinctions based on race alone," they told the Court, "have been struck down in many cases involving rights much less substantial than the right to marry." Like William Coleman in *McLaughlin,* they cited the Court's historic decision in *Brown v. Board of Education,* then argued that "miscegenation laws seem more clearly unconstitutional than school segregation" because marriage was a "more fundamental" right than school attendance and because "both parties to an interracial marriage [already] wish to associate or join together." In *McLaughlin,* they argued, the Court had abandoned the equal application argument once enshrined in the now-overruled *Pace* and labeled race classifications "constitutionally suspect" and "in most circumstances irrelevant." Right next to this quote from Justice White's opinion in *McLaughlin,* they placed the stronger language offered by Justices Stewart and Douglas, who had said they could not imagine "a valid legislative purpose under our Constitution for a state law which makes the color of a person's skin the test of whether his conduct is a criminal offense."[87]

The due process argument, which was included at Bernard Cohen's insistence, and over the objections of others, developed the case for protecting the right to marry as a civil liberty that was also protected by the Fourteenth Amendment. Here the ACLU consolidated a line of judicial precedents about the right to marry that stretched from the era of substantive due process in the 1920s through the right to privacy promulgated in the mid-1960s. The oldest, *Meyer v. Nebraska,* a U.S. Supreme Court decision from the 1920s, had been cited by Dan Marshall in the *Perez* case in support of the position that marriage was a fundamental right rooted in natural law. The next, *Skinner v. Oklahoma,* a U.S. Supreme Court decision from 1942, was the source of two crucial phrases. Its strictures on "invidious discrimination" had given Byron White the basis of his decision in *McLaughlin,* and its assertion that marriage and reproduction were among "the basic civil rights of man" had been echoed by California Supreme Court Justice Roger Traynor in *Perez* and urged on the Court by William Coleman and the LDF in *McLaughlin.* The last case, however, *Griswold v. Connecticut,* was new. Issued in 1965, it was the culmination of decades of attempts to establish a constitutional right of privacy, and the ACLU cited it to prove that "the privacy of the marital relationship is a constitutionally protected freedom . . . protected from arbitrary governmental interference by the basic guarantees of our Constitution. . . . [and] part of a broader constitutional freedom of association."[88]

The ACLU's brief in *Loving* was complemented by amicus briefs volunteered by several other groups, which offered arguments—the case for religious freedom, the attack on scientific racism, an appeal for across-the-board colorblindness—that the ACLU seems to have regarded as too risky to serve as the core of its case.[89] The religious freedom argument was offered by a loose constellation of Catholic bishops and lay action organizations, who also claimed that miscegenation law violated the Lovings' right to have children.[90] The JACL, which summarized the now familiar attacks on the illogical and irrational nature of race classification, the idea of pure races, and the notion of natural biological inferiority, tried to align nature and biology with rather than against interracial marriage. The right to marry, the JACL told the Court, in language that paraphrased *Skinner v. Oklahoma,* is "one of the most basic and fundamental rights of the individual, rooted, indeed, in one of man's biological drives." The NAACP submitted a brief that echoed the JACL's attack on scientific racism and called the right to marry "a civil right" lodged "within the purview of the equal protection clause of the Fourteenth Amendment." The LDF, which submitted a separate brief, complained that the Virginia Supreme Court was thumbing its nose at the entire list of "cases involving the civil rights of Negroes" from *Brown v. Board of Education* to *McLaughlin* and tried to get the entire Court to adopt the position Justices Stewart and Douglas had pronounced in *McLaughlin.* "We urge," the LDF brief said, "that racially discriminatory state laws are no longer only 'constitutionally suspect' and merely subject to 'rigid scrutiny.'" Rather, "the decisions which have invalidated every state segregation law or practice to come before this Court establish that there can be no justification for such laws and that they are all invalid *per se.*"[91]

While the ACLU was assembling a case that was every bit as broad as the decision it hoped the Supreme Court would eventually issue, the state of Virginia, which was well aware it was fighting a losing battle, tried to limit the damage. Its brief recapitulated the strategies the state of Florida had tried in *McLaughlin,* minus, of course, the linchpin of *Pace.* It opened by insisting that the Lovings could challenge only the two provisions of Virginia's miscegenation law under which they had been arrested and convicted (the evasion provision with its associated criminal penalty). The couple, it insisted, did not have the standing to challenge the remaining provisions of Virginia's law, which prohibited the issuance of marriage licenses to interracial couples in Virginia, declared interracial marriages void, and limited Whites to marrying only other Whites.[92]

Within these narrow parameters, Virginia argued that history and judicial precedent were entirely on its side. Virginia's historical case rested almost word for word on the argument that Florida's James Mahorner had used in *McLaughlin,* that the history of the Civil Rights Act of 1866 proved that the framers of the Fourteenth Amendment had no intention of allowing interracial marriage. So did its invocation of "the virtually uninterrupted line of judicial decisions, both Federal and State," upholding the constitutionality of miscegenation laws. These arguments about history and judicial precedent were, the Virginia brief insisted, more than sufficient to prove that "the Fourteenth Amendment . . . does not circumscribe, to any degree, the power of the States to prevent interracial marriages." It was, Virginia argued, "the exclusive province of the legislature of each State to make the determination for its citizens as to the desirability, character and scope of a policy of permitting or preventing such alliances—a province which the judiciary may not, under well-settled constitutional doctrine, invade."[93]

Virginia's final point—the one that filled the void left by the absence of *Pace*—was an exceedingly awkward argument about the "wisdom of statutory policy." Because Justice Byron White had raised this consideration in *McLaughlin,* Virginia could hardly afford to ignore the issue. Obviously fearful that the Supreme Court might reject its attempt to warn it away from making "any judicial inquiry into the wisdom of the anti-miscegenation policy reflected in the statutes under attack, or any analysis of scientific treaties or texts," Virginia gathered together as many examples as it could find of scientists and social scientists who were still willing to censure interracial marriage. Most of its examples were secondhand quotes from the same race scientists cited two decades earlier by dissenting California justices in *Perez,* but the final pages of the argument relied very heavily on *Intermarriage— Interfaith, Interracial, Interethnic,* a book published by Albert I. Gordon in 1964, which contained several statements about the social inadvisability of interracial marriage.[94]

The only support Virginia enjoyed came from the state of North Carolina, whose attorney general also filed an amicus brief in the case. In a scant six pages, he echoed two of the three main aspects of Virginia's argument. "The great weight of judicial authority," he told the Court, "supports the constitutional validity of a state's anti-miscegenation statute," and "neither the Virginia statutes nor the North Carolina statutes violate any provisions of the Fourteenth Amendment." North Carolina's attorney general was, however, unable to bring himself to use the "so-called scientific argument" Virginia had offered the Court, which rested on the kind of sociological evidence southern leaders had been condemning the U.S. Supreme Court for relying on ever since it issued its decision in *Brown v. Board of Education.* "We do not," he told the Court, "enter into the scientific realm on this question. . . . This field is like expert witnesses in that you pay your money and take your choice." The key to the issue, he insisted, was not science but states' rights. "If a state feels like the life of its people is better protected by a policy of racial integrity as to both races, or for any race for that matter," he concluded, "then it has the right to legislate in that field."[95]

The gap between the breadth of the ACLU's argument and the narrowness of Virginia's was perfectly clear when the Supreme Court heard oral arguments in the case on April 10, 1967. The ACLU was represented by Phil Hirschkop and Bernard Cohen. Both men were making their first appearance before the U.S. Supreme Court, but they argued their cases with clarity and confidence before a largely sympathetic bench. Hirschkop covered the issue of equal protection. Secure in the knowledge that the Supreme Court's understanding of the Fourteenth Amendment overlapped with his own, he focused on placing the case in the context of the larger history he said was necessary to understanding the laws. "These are slavery laws, pure and simple," he told the Court. "These laws rob the Negro race of their dignity" in ways that extended well beyond the outrageous criminal punishment that Judge Bazile had imposed on the Lovings. "We ask that the Court consider the full spectrum of these laws," he concluded "and not just the criminality, because it's more than the criminality that's at point here. It's the legitimacy of children, the right to inherit land, and many, many rights, and in reaching a decision we ask you to reach it on that basis."[96]

Cohen, who gave the due process argument, also urged the Court to reach beyond the individual case of the Lovings. Going over territory Roger Traynor had traveled before him, Cohen offered the Court multiple definitions of due process, including the "right to be free from racial discrimination," "the right to be free from infringement of basic values implicit in ordered liberty," and "the right to be free from arbitrary and capricious denials of Fourteenth Amendment liberty." All of these rights and freedoms, he said, could and should be applied to the Lovings on the ground that "marriage is a fundamental right or liberty." Harnessing the symbolic power of the image of a White man denied his legal right to marriage, the image that had haunted miscegenation law ever since its inception, Cohen had a last word for the justices. "No one," he told the Court, "could articulate it better than Richard Loving, when he said to me: 'Mr. Cohen, tell the Court I love my wife, and it is just unfair that I can't live with her in Virginia.'"[97]

Hirschkop and Cohen were followed by William Marutani of the JACL, who had been granted a "special leave of Court" to appear at the oral argument. Marutani was the first Nisei lawyer to appear before the Supreme Court in a civil rights case, and as such carried the symbolic weight of representing all the other non-Whites affected by Virginia's miscegenation law. He targeted the provisions that defined racial categories. Since it was, he said impossible for any White person to prove that he had "no trace whatever of any blood other than Caucasian," these laws epitomized "vagueness in its grossest sense." Scientists had, he said, shown that there was no such thing as a pure race, and even if there were, Virginia was interested in protecting "the white race only"; its law was not designed so much to ensure race purity as it was to ensure "white supremacy."[98]

The case for Virginia was made by Robert McIlwaine, the state's senior assistant attorney general. McIlwaine had been before the Supreme Court on several occasions, most notably trying, unsuccessfully, to defend Virginia's attempts to avoid integrating its public schools.[99] From the outset, he struggled to find some ground on which to stand. Virginia lawyers knew only too well that, over the course of the twentieth century, the scientific foundations of the eugenic biological argument in favor of miscegenation laws had crumbled and that their argument about the "sociological and psychological evils which attend interracial marriage" was suspect at best.[100] Even when it came to the turf they regarded as their strongest—their arguments from judicial precedent and legislative history—McIlwaine had to steer a careful path around the boulders that had been strewn in his path. The long string of precedents upholding restrictions on interracial marriage had been broken by the *Perez* decision. In a series of civil rights cases, the Supreme Court had made the state's power to classify by race so deeply suspect that federal courts no longer felt obliged to defer to the state's traditional power to regulate marriage. In some of these very same cases, the Court had rejected the contention that the nineteenth-century framers of the Fourteenth Amendment never intended to provide for either integration of the schools or voting rights for Blacks. And then, in *McLaughlin,* the Supreme Court had overruled *Pace,* the cornerstone of the equal application argument so many states had relied on to justify miscegenation laws, and an argument that McIlwaine proved unable to jettison.

McIlwaine started his oral argument, as he had his brief, by trying to limit the Court's consideration to the two sections of Virginia's miscegenation law he thought he could defend, then launched into an argument that the framers of the Fourteenth Amendment had never intended to allow interracial marriage.[101] But the justices peppered him with questions about all the things he had left out of his brief. What about the Court's decision in *McLaughlin?* Hadn't that decision overruled *Pace* and the whole idea of equal application? If the Court limited its decision to the two sections of the law that McIlwaine claimed were the only ones at issue, wouldn't the Lovings still be subject to prosecution for "illicit cohabitation"? Weren't the states that still had miscegenation laws in force the same states that used to have racial segregation in the schools? Wasn't "a man who belongs to this race that is forbidden to marry into the other race . . . bound to feel that he's not given the equal protection of the laws"? Did the state's definition of "colored" include American Indians? Did its law apply to Japanese Americans?[102]

Four days later, when the Supreme Court justices met in conference to discuss the *Loving* case, they were finally ready to forge a judicial consensus to declare miscegenation laws unconstitutional. "The Fourteenth Amendment," Chief Justice Earl Warren said in leading off the discussion, "was intended to wipe out discrimination on the basis of race. Miscegenation statutes maintain white supremacy. They should all go down the drain." One by one, the other justices agreed. As he had done in *Brown v. Board of Education*, and would do with other key cases as well, Warren assigned himself the task of writing the opinion, which was drafted by his law clerk, Benno Schmidt. Schmidt remembers that his first draft elicited "two kinds of reactions" among the justices. "Justice [Hugo] Black blew up because we were referring to the right to marry, which is nowhere mentioned in the Constitution . . . and a couple of the other Justices . . . felt that something much stronger ought to be said about the race classification." Warren, who was eager to get all nine justices to speak with one voice, immediately put his superb consensus-building skills to work. By agreeing to tone down—but not to eliminate—the language about the right to marry, he got Justice Black to agree to sign on, and he also persuaded Justice William O. Douglas, one of the other outliers, to join in. He was, however, less successful with Justice Potter Stewart, who issued a one-sentence concurrence that echoed the point he had made three years earlier in *McLaughlin*. "It is simply not possible," Stewart reiterated, "for a state law to be valid under our Constitution which makes the criminality of an act depend upon the race of the actor."[103]

On behalf of eight of the nine justices, Earl Warren issued a decision in *Loving v. Virginia* that both reflected and contributed to a new commonsense consensus about race. The foundational premise for this consensus was the rejection of the older notion of equal application. Revisiting the territory the Court had covered in *McLaughlin*, Warren reiterated the Court's repudiation of *Pace*. "The mere equal application of a statute containing racial classifications," Warren wrote, was not "enough to remove the classifications from the Fourteenth Amendment's proscription of all invidious racial discriminations."[104]

All that was left to do was to make two seemingly simple points. According to Warren, Virginia's miscegenation laws violated the Fourteenth Amendment in two overlapping respects. The first, and most important, was that they violated the guarantee of equal protection of the laws. Rejecting the historical claims the state of Virginia had made concerning the intentions of the framers of the Fourteenth Amendment, Warren made liberal use of those the ACLU had offered instead. He traced Virginia's miscegenation laws from their roots "as an incident to slavery," emphasized their expansion "during the period of extreme nativism which followed the end of the First World War," and labeled the state's defense of them "obviously an endorsement of the doctrine of White supremacy." In this connection, *Loving* fit right into a line of civil rights decisions issued by the Warren Court. "There can," he insisted, "be no doubt that restricting the freedom to marry solely because of racial classifications violates the central meaning of the Equal Protection Clause."[105]

The second, and final, way in which Virginia's miscegenation laws violated the Fourteenth Amendment was by denying liberty to marry under the due process clause. Here Warren reached back to the line of cases that had established the freedom to marry as a fundamental right, decisions that had, when they were originally issued, little or nothing to do with questions of race but that now seemed especially apt. Marriage, the Court had said in one of these cases, "is one of the 'basic civil rights of man' . . . fundamental to our very existence and survival." Warren declared that "to deny this fundamental freedom on so unsupportable a basis as the racial classifications embodied in these statutes, classifications so directly subversive of the principle of equality at the heart of the Fourteenth Amendment, is surely to deprive all the State's citizens of liberty without due process of law. . . . Under our Constitution," he concluded, "the freedom to marry, or not marry, a person of another race resides with the individual and cannot be infringed by the State."[106]

Part IV

THE POLITICS
OF COLORBLINDNESS,
1967–2000

Chapter Nine

LIONIZING *LOVING*

"As legal barriers fall and society adopts a more tolerant attitude, young people of all races will see marriage as an expression of confidence in the future, not of revolt against the past. Love will then be truly color blind."

—*New York Times, June 20, 1967*

WASHINGTON, D.C.

The word "colorblind" does not appear in the U.S. Supreme Court's decision in the case of *Loving v. Virginia*. Its absence was no accident. According to Benno Schmidt, the law clerk who revised several drafts of the opinion to fit Chief Justice Earl Warren's specifications, Warren deliberately "shied away" from issuing an across-the-board ban on race classifications. He "didn't want to say that racial classification in the law can never be constitutional," Schmidt remembered; he wanted to show that Virginia's miscegenation law was an "invidious discrimination" rather than to rule "in broad terms that any discrimination is bad." So where Schmidt had written that Virginia's race classifications were "arbitrary," Warren substituted the word "unsupportable" and instructed Schmidt to be sure to link Virginia's race classifications directly to the state's goal of ensuring "white supremacy." As Schmidt explained, he "wanted the opinion to make it clear that this Virginia statute was designed to stigmatize blacks."[1]

Yet a tendency to regard the *Loving* decision as proof positive of Justice John Marshall Harlan's famous 1896 assertion that "our constitution is colorblind" was already in the making.[2] The dream of colorblindness appealed to Richard Loving, who once told a reporter that "everybody looked alike to me." It appealed to the NAACP's Legal Defense Fund, which had quoted Harlan's comments on colorblindness to the U.S. Supreme Court in *McLaughlin* and had hoped, in *Loving,* to get the Supreme Court to rule that all race classifications were "invalid *per se.*" It appealed to the *New York Times,* which greeted the *Loving* decision with an editorial that longed for the day when love would be "truly color blind."[3]

That day has yet to come, but the years between 1967 and 2000 saw three truly remarkable developments. The first was the dismantling and discrediting of American's deeply embedded structure of miscegenation law. The second was the ascendance of *Loving v. Virginia* into an icon of equality, a symbol so powerful that it was claimed in support of a wide variety of political causes. By the end of the twentieth century, Americans who tried to establish a "multiracial" category on the U.S. Census took *Loving* as a lodestone, but so did lesbian and gay activists who argued for the right to same-sex marriage—and so did opponents of affirmative action. The third development, the tendency to link *Loving* to the pursuit of colorblindness, put *Loving* at the center of a fierce struggle between U.S. Supreme Court justices over the meaning of race, equality, and the U.S. Constitution.

The Collapse of Miscegenation Law

The pursuit of colorblindness could hardly get off the ground until miscegenation law was dismantled. The first step was for southern states to swallow their long-standing distaste for federal power and accept the Supreme Court's ruling in *Loving v. Virginia.* The example of Florida shows the reluctance with which southern states did so. Ever since the 1964 case of Dewey McLaughlin and Connie Hoffman, Florida officials had been expecting—and trying to fend off—a ruling like *Loving.* In 1965, when the U.S. Supreme Court sent the *McLaughlin* case back to the Florida Supreme Court, Florida's Chief Justice Millard F. Caldwell had reversed himself with obvious irritation. Unable to resist repeating the equal application argument he and his Florida court had tried so hard to uphold, Caldwell complained about the U.S. Supreme Court's decision to "reduce" race classifications "to an invidious discrimination." Under this "new and contrary construction of the Constitution," he groused, the Florida Supreme Court was "required, perforce" to abandon its earlier judgment and obey "the new Law of the Land."[4] There was only one thing the Florida Supreme Court liked about the *McLaughlin* decision: that in it the U.S. Supreme Court had left Florida's ban on interracial marriages alone.

After the *McLaughlin* decision, indeed even after the U.S. Supreme Court's ruling in *Loving,* Florida continued to refuse marriage licenses to interracial couples. Two months after *Loving,* when James Van Hook and Liane Peters applied for a marriage license in Miami, they were turned away by county judge Harold Blanton on the ground that Van Hook was a "Negro male" and Peters a "white female." Like Dewey McLaughlin and Connie Hoffman before them, Van Hook and Peters asked the NAACP LDF for help, and the LDF came to their defense. When their case came before the Florida Supreme Court, Florida's attorney general insisted that the U.S. Supreme Court's *McLaughlin* decision left Florida's ban on interracial marriage still in force, impervious to anything short of repeal by the Florida state legislature. The LDF, however, maintained that the *McLaughlin* ruling had led the way to *Loving,* which applied to miscegenation laws all across the country. When push finally came to shove, five of Florida's seven supreme court justices felt they had no choice but to agree. Chief Justice Caldwell, however, was not among them. He and another justice dissented, refusing, to the bitter end, to change their minds on the rock-bottom issue of interracial marriage.[5]

Most southern states were as reluctant as Florida to accept the *Loving* ruling, so interracial couples often had to appeal to federal courts for help in overcoming state and local resistance. In Delaware, Louisiana, and Arkansas, federal judges quickly issued decisions insisting that state officials adhere to *Loving.*[6] In 1970, when a die-hard segregationist group persuaded a Mississippi state judge to issue an injunction prohibiting one interracial marriage in that state, another round of federal court cases ensued.[7] In 1970 and 1971, the federal government itself brought suit on behalf of soldiers stationed in Alabama and Georgia after their requests for marriage licenses had been blocked by local officials.[8] Four years after the *Loving* decision, then, some state officials still needed to be told, as the judge in the Alabama case intoned, that "the unconstitutionality of these miscegenation laws cannot be seriously questioned by any trained in the law."[9]

As the legal authority of *Loving* took hold, marriage license clerks gradually began to change their practices. The county clerk of Columbia, South Carolina, issued his first license for an interracial marriage two days after the *Loving* decision had been handed down, but elsewhere, the dust took longer to settle. In Memphis, Tennessee, one county clerk tried to juggle deference for state officials with obedience to the U.S. Supreme Court. "Our attorneys recommend that we wait until the Virginia couple has filed for a rehearing of their case (in a Virginia court) . . . and until we get a copy of the U.S. Supreme Court ruling," he explained to a reporter from *Jet* magazine, adding the reassurance that "there is no move here to circumvent this ruling and we do expect to get requests for marriage licenses from interracial couples." In Virginia, county clerks issued marriage licenses to couples who requested them but continued to pass out pamphlets telling applicants that interracial marriage was illegal, a practice that persisted until Phil Hirschkop, one of the lawyers who had defended the Lovings, asked the state's attorney general to issue a formal opinion confirming the U.S. Supreme Court's ruling in *Loving*. In Virginia and the rest of the South, most local officials waited until state attorney generals or federal district courts issued definitive rulings.[10]

Once set in motion, though, the changes were highly significant. For generations, marriage license clerks had served as the front lines of white supremacy, but now, in county courthouses all across the South, they were obliged to abandon that role and issue marriage licenses to interracial couples on demand. The reversal attracted the attention of the *New York Times,* which responded with a series of triumphant stories chronicling the "first" interracial marriages on record in each southern state. "A license for an interracial marriage was issued today to James Edward Todd, a white sailor, and Floria Marquita Mayhorn, a Negro," the *Times* reported in January 1968, adding that "Tennessee has issued only one other license for an interracial marriage since Reconstruction." Nearly two years later, in August 1970, the *Times* announced the most dramatic first of all, under the headline "Mississippi Allows a Mixed Marriage." "A 24-year-old white civil rights law clerk and a young black woman from a poor rural south Mississippi county were married here today," the story read, "toppling a legal barrier against interracial marriage that had been on the books for more than 100 years. It was believed to be the first such wedding in Mississippi."[11]

One by one, southern state legislatures repealed miscegenation laws they could no longer enforce. Maryland, the first southern state to do so, had repealed its law shortly before the Supreme Court issued its decision in *Loving*; Virginia did so shortly afterward.[12] Two years later, in 1969, Florida, Missouri, Oklahoma, and Texas did, too.[13] Then, however, foot-dragging ensued, as legislators in the remaining states decided they were in no great hurry to record their votes on a matter they knew spurred such strong feelings among their White constituents, many of whom remained adamantly opposed to interracial marriage. Repeals in Alabama, Arkansas, Georgia, Kentucky, Louisiana, Mississippi, North and South Carolina, and Tennessee stretched over the decade of the 1970s, with Delaware, the last state to repeal a miscegenation statute, bringing up the rear in 1986.[14]

Southern states were well aware of the ideological implications of these repeals. The Florida state legislature, for example, went out of its way to show that it could adapt to what its reluctant chief justice had once dismissed as the "new Law of the Land." In June 1969, it passed a bill that repealed all the remaining race classifications in Florida's statutory law—the state's race definition law, its bans on interracial cohabitation and adultery and fornication, its ban on interracial marriage, and also its laws on race segregation in railroads and schools, all of which had remained on the books as long as the question of interracial marriage remained in doubt. These laws, the legislature explained, "apply discriminately to the citizens of this state on the basis of race, color, creed, or national origin." They were not only "in violation of the Bill of Rights of the Constitution of the United States and the Declaration of Rights of the Constitution of the State of Florida" but also "immoral and an affront to the American sense of justice." "It is fundamental to democratic principles," the resolution proclaimed, "that all statutes should be uniform in their application to all citizens."[15]

The last prop of the regime of miscegenation law was the bans on interracial marriage in several southern state constitutions, which also came under challenge. The process of removing these provisions started smoothly enough. Florida, which was in the midst of revising its state constitution, quietly dropped its constitutional ban in 1968. In the rest of the states, however, the passage of constitutional amendments required both legislative action, which was subject to the familiar foot-dragging of state legislators, and popular votes, which, given the strength of anti-miscegenation sentiment among southern Whites, posed an even more daunting obstacle. As a result, although North Carolina and Tennessee amended their constitutions in the 1970s, and Mississippi did so in 1987, bans on interracial marriage remained a part of the constitutions of South Carolina and Alabama.[16]

Forgetting Miscegenation Law

As historian Benedict Anderson once noted, "profound changes in consciousness, by their very nature, bring with them characteristic amnesias."[17] The three decades after *Loving v. Virginia* provide a revealing example. Despite— or perhaps even because of lingering southern opposition to interracial marriage, the collapse of miscegenation law was accompanied by a concerted, and surprisingly successful, effort to push the three-century-long history of bans on interracial marriage out of public memory. In little more than a generation, most White Americans somehow managed to forget how fundamental they had once believed these bans to be and, moreover, managed to persuade themselves that they, and their government, had always been firmly committed to civil rights and racial equality. This was a profoundly important development in American political ideology, one that would eventually transform the ideology of political conservatives, who had long been the backbone of resistance to civil rights legislation of all kinds.[18]

Forgetting the history of miscegenation law would not, however, be easy. At the time the U.S. Supreme Court issued its decision in *Loving,* Americans remained deeply divided about miscegenation laws and overwhelmingly opposed to interracial marriage. An opinion poll conducted in 1965, at a point when every state in the North and all but two states in the West had already repealed their legal bans, showed that more Americans approved of the laws (48 percent of those polled, in fact) than disapproved of them (46 percent). In the South, where the laws were still in force, fully 72 percent approved of them.[19] Opposition to interracial marriage in general (as opposed to legal bans in particular) was even more pronounced, especially among Whites. According to a poll taken in 1968, 75 percent of Whites disapproved of interracial marriages, while only 17 percent claimed to approve of them.[20]

Before most Americans could begin to accord the links between civil rights, constitutional equality, and colorblindness the commonsense status so often claimed for them today, key aspects of America's racist past would have to be buried, denied, or pushed aside, and new articles of political faith established. In this ideological conversion experience, the newly faithful turned once-radical critiques of miscegenation law into mainstream orthodoxy, building a body of beliefs that would eventually stretch across the political spectrum.

The first of these beliefs was that the demise of miscegenation law had been inevitable. This idea had originated in the wishful thinking of a handful of early critics of the laws, who had cultivated it at every possible opportunity, so that by the beginning of the 1960s, liberal legal opinion was laced with predictions of the laws' imminent downfall. "Eventually, we predict, our Supreme Court will declare miscegenation laws unconstitutional," two lawyers wrote in *Dicta,* a Colorado legal journal, in 1961. "We remain," they concluded "—only waiting for the word, only hoping for the time." By 1964, even Alexander Bickel, a relatively conservative lawyer who had wholeheartedly approved of the U.S. Supreme Court's decision to duck the issue of interracial marriage in the 1950s, had come to agree. In a piece about the Court's upcoming decision in the *McLaughlin* case, Bickel noted that if the Court decided to rule on Florida's bans on cohabitation and interracial marriage, it "could scarcely do anything *but* hold them unconstitutional."[21]

A second and closely related belief was that miscegenation laws were outdated remnants of a long-distant past. Lawyers who challenged miscegenation laws in the 1960s peppered their briefs with descriptions of the laws as outdated "relics" or "remnants" of slavery, and so did the press coverage of court cases.[22] Based on "outmoded and unscientific genetical conclusions," bans on interracial marriage were labeled "the *last* remnants of legalized slavery," the "*last* . . . racial laws with any sort of claim to viability," "the *last* group of segregation laws to remain standing," "the *last* real legal bastion of segregation."[23] As lawyer Bernard Cohen put it at the press conference immediately after the *Loving* ruling was issued, "We hope we have put to rest the last vestiges of racial discrimination that were supported by the law in Virginia and all over the country."[24] After the *Loving* decision, the cumulative power of this language of "lasts" helped bury the memory of miscegenation law and encourage the belief that racism had died along with it.

The third belief, that marriage should be considered a private matter of individual choice, was then substituted for the once heartfelt conviction that marriage was a public symbol of white racial purity that should be enforced by the state. This, too, was a development that had been decades in the making. "The right to marry according to choice" had been an ACLU rallying cry ever since the 1930s; it had also been a key part of the rationale California Supreme Court Justice Roger Traynor offered in the 1948 *Perez* case. "The essence of the right to marry," Traynor had written, is "the freedom to join in marriage with the person of one's choice."[25] During the 1950s and early 1960s, Black leaders, for whom opposition to miscegenation laws was not only controversial but also dangerous, often insisted that intermarriage was a private decision of little or no public significance. After 1967, when the U.S. Supreme Court rejected, once and for all, the notion that white supremacy was an acceptable public policy, the notion that marriage was a private choice was in the ascendance.

The adoption of the fourth belief, that race classification in the law was deeply un-American, required an even bigger leap of faith—and an even sharper denial of the actual historical record. Chief Justice Earl Warren, who devoted much of his time on the U.S. Supreme Court to creating a new, and newly egalitarian, American public consensus on race, took instilling this conviction as a personal challenge. When the Warren court issued its historic 1954 decision in *Brown v. Board of Education,* everyone recognized that the Court was setting out in a new—and sharply different—direction. But by 1967, the Supreme Court had issued several anti-segregation rulings, and Chief Justice Warren, who considered the *Loving* case the culmination of his judicial campaign against racism in the law, was eager to leave the impression that the court was, and always had been, opposed to race discrimination. "Over the years," Warren wrote in *Loving,* the Supreme Court had "consistently repudiated" the use of race; he cited a 1943 case in which the Court had described "distinctions between citizens solely because of their ancestry" as "odious to a free people whose institutions are founded upon the doctrine of equality."[26] His words not only flew in the face of the Supreme Court's long history of countenancing segregation, they also ignored the outcome of the very 1943 case he cited, which had upheld a curfew imposed on Japanese Americans during World War II. That Warren could make such a statement, and do so with every indication of believing his own rhetoric, suggests the depth of his desire to dislodge all trace of the Court's longtime support for race discrimination. Like America's three-century-long history of laws against interracial marriage, the country's history of race discrimination had become too embarrassing to admit.

After the *Loving* decision, each of these beliefs—that the collapse of miscegenation law had been inevitable, that opposition to interracial marriage belonged to the distant past, that marriage was a private matter of individual choice, that the American government had always opposed race discrimination—seeped into the consciousness of ordinary White Americans. The effect of the *Loving* decision was almost immediately apparent in opinion polls; overall support for miscegenation laws dipped from 48 percent in 1965 to 35 percent by 1970. A closer look at the polling data on interracial marriage shows two things: a considerable gap between the opinions of Whites and Blacks, and a slow but steady transformation in White attitudes. In 1968, when 75 percent of Whites disapproved of interracial marriage, and only 17 percent approved, 33 percent of Blacks disapproved of interracial marriage, while 56 percent approved. Thereafter, however, White approval rose inch by inch, year by year, until by 2003, 70 percent of "non-Hispanic whites," 77 percent of "Hispanics," and 80 percent of "non-Hispanic blacks" said they approved of interracial marriages. Disapproval of interracial marriage remained higher among Whites than among Blacks and Hispanics (27 percent to 16 percent to 15 percent, respectively), but these figures nonetheless mapped an extraordinary reversal of White public opinion.[27] And each rise in the percentage of Americans who claimed to approve of interracial marriage marked another step on the road to purging American public memory of miscegenation laws.

This public process of forgetting was reinforced by the interests of many interracial couples, who were understandably eager to put their painful encounters with the pre-*Loving* legal system behind them. During the regime of miscegenation law, interracial couples had, of necessity, learned how to fly below the legal radar, covering their lives with a defensive curtain of privacy, holding their weddings in other states and saying little about them to their friends and neighbors. Richard and Mildred Loving were no exception to this rule, displaying such a fierce determination to protect their privacy that they did not even attend the Supreme Court arguments in their case. Like many a couple who had run afoul of miscegenation laws, the Lovings were eager to keep the details of an experience that Richard Loving once called "right rough" away from their three children.[28]

As the ideological conversion that followed *Loving* took hold, the public officials who had once enforced and defended the laws found that they, too, had reason to bury the memory of miscegenation law. There were, to be sure, some Whites who refused to adopt the new articles of political faith, as *New York Times* legal correspondent David Margolick discovered in 1992, when he tracked down several of the participants in the *Loving* case in preparation for an article on the twenty-fifth anniversary of the decision. Garnett Brooks, the sheriff who had arrested the Lovings back in 1958, remained proud of his actions. "I was acting according to the law at the time," Brooks told Margolick, "and I still think it should be on the books. I don't think a white person should marry a black person," he continued, "I'm from the old school."[29] Brooks had some company; during the 1990s, opinion polls suggested that as many as 16 percent of Whites and 4 percent of Blacks, most of them, like Brooks, of older generations, continued to believe that interracial marriage should be illegal.[30] But much more revealing—and much more typical—was the response of Robert McIlwaine, who had represented Virginia in the *Loving* case. Unlike Sheriff Brooks, McIlwaine was determined to consign the case to the distant past. Telling Margolick that "he had thought little about the case since it was handed down," McIlwaine claimed that it wasn't all that important. "Nobody," he insisted, "even remembers it."[31]

As legal barriers fell and White opposition declined, both the number and the percentage of interracial marriages increased, slowly at first, then picking up speed as the sordid history of miscegenation law faded from public memory. By the year 2000, the overall rate of interracial marriage had risen from .7 to 5.4 percent of all American marriages, and the total number of interracial marriages from 300,000 to 3.1 million. Within this larger whole, though, the figures varied considerably from one group to another. By the year 2000, 3 percent of Whites, 7 percent of Blacks, 16 percent of Asian Americans, 46 percent of native Hawaiians, and 56 percent of American Indians and those who listed themselves as being of "more than one race" would marry across racial lines. (Government statistics are careful to name "Hispanics" as an "ethnic" rather than a "racial" category; a quarter of all U.S. "Hispanics" marry "non-Hispanics," too.)[32]

Marriages between Whites and Blacks remain the most infrequent, but they, too, are increasing in number. In 1960, the U.S. Census reported that the number of marriages between Whites and Blacks stood at 51,000. By

1970, it had increased slightly, to 65,000. But by 1980 it stood at 167,000; by 1990, 211,000; by 2000, 363,000; and by 2003, 416,000. The rise was even more dramatic among younger Americans. According to social scientists, Black and White Americans under the age of thirty are nearly five times more likely to be married to each other than those over the age of sixty.[33]

There were limits to these changes. The collapse of legal barriers did not, by itself, prevent friends and families from objecting to their sons' or daughters' choices, and it did not prevent strangers from staring at interracial couples on the street. Interracial marriage is still statistically unusual, and marriage between Blacks and Whites remains the most uncommon of all.

But it is nonetheless true that, in what must be regarded as one of the most dramatic shifts in public opinion in American history, the overwhelming majority of Whites had come to believe that laws against interracial marriage were clearly, irrevocably wrong. One statistic might make the point. In 1958, 91 percent of southern Whites and 79 percent of northern Whites told pollsters that "Negroes and white marrying" would "hurt in solving the Negro-white problem."[34] By 1999, however, 65 percent of all Americans had come to believe that "interracial marriages are good because they help break down racial barriers."[35] With each year that passed, the dwindling minority of mostly older Americans who continued to disapprove of interracial marriage found it harder to make a public case for their views. And by the end of the twentieth century, they were rapidly being displaced by an entire generation of young Americans who found it difficult to believe that interracial marriage had *ever* been illegal.

Remembering Loving *in the Multiracial Movement*

The less Americans remembered about the history of miscegenation law, the easier it was to link the U.S. Supreme Court's decision in *Loving v. Virginia* to a variety of social movements and political causes. One of these was the multiracial movement, which emerged in 1979, with the formation of Interracial Intercultural Pride, or I-Pride, one of what would soon be several dozen support groups for interracial couples and families. Many of their members were interracial couples who had married right around the time of the *Loving* decision. Well aware of the difference legal legitimacy could make, they wanted to ensure that their mixed-race children enjoyed its full benefits. They were soon joined by other groups of interracial families, most notably those being formed by transracial adoption. By 1988, the leaders of several of these budding organizations formed an umbrella group, the Association of MultiEthnic Americans (AMEA), and the multiracial movement mushroomed, with the addition of highly visible new groups such as Eurasian Nation and the Hapa Issues Forum, the publication of magazines such as the *Multiracial Activist, Interrace,* and *Mavin,* and the emergence of youth-oriented groups located on college campuses.[36]

Older activists frequently invoked the Supreme Court's decision in *Loving,* as an explanation for the timing of their movement, as a touchstone for the legal legitimacy of their cause, and as a harbinger of the increase in the multiracial population they linked to the post-*Loving* rise in the number of interracial marriages. Small wonder, then, that in 1992, when the AMEA and the Interracial Family Circle of Washington, D.C., had grown large enough to cohost a national convention, they timed it to coincide with the twenty-fifth anniversary of *Loving.* Dubbed "the Loving Conference," the entire event was built around a celebration of the *Loving* decision; it featured a keynote address from *Loving* lawyer Bernard Cohen, as well as a rare public appearance by "mixed race" Mildred Loving, who was presented with a "Magic of Change" mug. The symbolism struck a deep chord among the AMEA's member organizations, most of which traced their origins to *Loving,* a lineage that was routinely cited by newspaper reporters who profiled the multiracial movement.[37]

Younger activists initially stood in a somewhat different relation to *Loving.* Those born after the mid-1970s came of age during the post-*Loving* burial of the history of miscegenation law. "Having a multiracial family does not guarantee you knowledge of multiracial issues," Ken Tanabe, one such young man, explained. "Despite having an interracial couple as parents, and despite the fact that they were married just after it became legal nationwide, I was never told by my parents that marriage was once restricted by race." It was not until Tanabe was in his twenties that he learned of the *Loving* decision, a discovery he called "surprising, shocking, and completely accidental." Appalled by the fact that "I have not met a single person of my generation who has heard of [miscegenation laws] . . . in the context of America's history," Tanabe set out to remedy what he considered a major gap in his education. A Web site designer by profession, he turned his passion for remembrance into an Internet-based call for an annual Loving Day celebration, complete with an elaborate Web site designed to inform eighteen- to thirty-four-year-olds about the history of miscegenation laws. Loving Day celebrations quickly became commonplace among multiracial support groups, in West Coast cities as well as on East Coast college campuses.[38]

Among multiracialists, though, the celebration of *Loving* did not necessarily lead to the end of race classification. During the 1990s, the central political goal of the multiracial movement was the inclusion of a "multiracial"

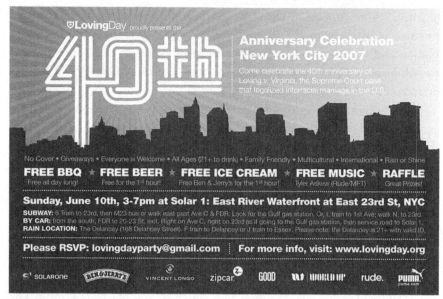

This poster shows the growing popularity, and the growing commercialization, of annual Loving Day celebrations. More than a thousand people attended this New York City event, which commemorated the fortieth anniversary of the U.S. Supreme Court's decision in *Loving v. Virginia*. (LovingDay.org)

category in the 2000 census. Such a category was necessary, its proponents argued, because interracial children were being overlooked and often discriminated against because they stood outside the traditional race classifications. In a world where everything from scientific research on medical conditions to voting districts was computed on the basis of the outmoded "single-race" classifications of the census, the costs of misclassification loomed large. When activists succeeded in persuading census officials to allow every respondent to check off more than one racial box, they counted it as a victory that marked the formal emergence of a now-measurable mixed-race community.[39]

Remembering Loving *in the Campaign to Legalize Same-Sex Marriage*

While multiracial activists were proposing changes to the census, lawyers were trying to use *Loving* as a kind of solvent against other forms of discrimination. In court cases involving sex and race discrimination, the rights of immigrants and the rights of prisoners, obscenity, maternity leave, and a host of other issues, lawyers cited *Loving* as a precedent for expanding the freedoms of clients in these and other situations. Often they succeeded. Using *Loving* as precedent, the U.S. Supreme Court upheld the right of marriage for divorced men who owed child support payments and for prison inmates, declared a grandmother and two cousin grandsons a family eligible for public housing, upheld a biological mother's right to appeal a decision revoking her parental rights, and exempted welfare recipients from having to pay filing fees for divorces.[40]

Gay and lesbian activists at first seemed among the least likely candidates to become beneficiaries of the *Loving* decision. Over the course of the twentieth century, the stigma of unnaturality, which had, for so long, haunted interracial couples, had come to surround gays and lesbians, too. When a pioneering handful of gay and lesbian couples sued state officials for the right to marry, their lawyers offered arguments much like those in the *Loving* case: that state laws that defined marriage as a "contract between persons" were not specific enough to justify denying committed couples the fundamental right to marry; that allowing George to marry Sally, but forbidding Linda to do the same thing, was sex discrimination; that sex discrimination, like race discrimination, was a violation of the constitutional guarantee of equal protection and as such entitled to "strict scrutiny" by the courts.[41]

But the judges who heard these cases had a hard time tempering their incredulity at what they regarded as the nonsensical contention that same-sex couples might have any such right. "In commonsense and in a constitutional sense," the Minnesota Supreme Court ruled, dismissing the arguments of two men who had tried to obtain a marriage license in 1971, "there is a clear distinction between a marital restriction based merely upon race and one based upon the fundamental difference in sex." Three years later, the judges on the Washington state Court of Appeals tried to explain the reasons they, too, rejected the analogy between the *Loving* case and the question of same-sex marriage. First, they declared the analogy between race discrimination and sex discrimination legally inoperative; then, using language ironically reminiscent of miscegenation cases, they agreed with Washington state's prosecuting attorney that when it came to sex discrimination "there is no violation of the [state's Equal Rights Amendment] as long as marriage licenses are denied equally to both male and female pairs." As the judges explained, in a remarkably convoluted passage, "laws which differentiate between the sexes are permissible so long as they are based upon the unique physical characteristics of a particular sex, rather than upon a person's membership in a particular sex per se."[42]

During the 1980s, judges held the line against same-sex marriage with such tenacity that most gay rights leaders concluded that raising the issue in the courts was a strategy doomed to fail. It was not until the 1990s, by which time the notion that miscegenation laws were irrevocably wrong had become an article of public faith and the *Loving* decision had become an icon of equality, that judges began to realize the logical force of the analogy between prohibitions on same-sex marriage and prohibitions on interracial marriage.[43]

The turning point came in 1993, when the Hawaii Supreme Court ruled that under the equal protection clause of Hawaii's state constitution, denying same-sex couples the right to marry was unconstitutional sex discrimination, in a decision shot through with references to *Loving v. Virginia*. The majority justices began by quoting *Loving* on the crucial significance of marriage. "So 'fundamental' does the United States Supreme Court consider the institution of marriage," the court explained, "that it has deemed marriage to be 'one of the 'basic civil rights.'" Comparing judges who had rejected the idea of same-sex marriage in the 1970s to judges who had once upheld miscegenation laws, the ruling exposed the logical fallacies in all the previous decisions on the subject. "Virginia courts," the Hawaii court noted, had "declared that interracial marriage simply could not exist because the Deity had deemed such a union intrinsically unnatural, and, in effect, because it had theretofore never been the 'custom' of the state to recognize mixed marriages, marriage 'always' having been construed to presuppose a different configuration." This claim, the court insisted, could no longer pass muster, and neither could the argument that restricting marriages to opposite-sex couples "treats everyone alike and applies equally to both sexes," which the U.S. Supreme Court had "expressly considered and rejected" in *Loving*. "As *Loving* amply demonstrates," the Hawaii court declared, "constitutional law may mandate, like it or not, that customs change with an evolving social order."[44]

After the Hawaii ruling, both the energy of the campaign to legalize same-sex marriage and the number of court cases that accompanied it grew by leaps and bounds. Over the next decade, several judges issued rulings overturning state bans, and they used the parallel to *Loving v. Virginia* to do so. In the 2003 decision that made the state of Massachusetts the first in the nation to allow same-sex couples the full legal right to marry, for example, the Supreme Judicial Court of Massachusetts made frequent references to both *Loving v. Virginia* and *Perez v. Sharp*. "As both *Perez* and *Loving* make clear," the Massachusetts court declared, "the right to marry means little if it does not include the right to marry the person of one's choice." In the case at hand, they explained, "as in *Perez* and *Loving*, a statute deprives individuals of access to an institution of fundamental legal, personal, and social significance—the institution of marriage—because of a single trait: skin color in *Perez* and *Loving*, sexual orientation here." And "as it did in *Perez* and *Loving*, history must yield to a more fully developed understanding of the invidious quality of the discrimination."[45]

Reconstituting Colorblindness

The legacy of *Loving* has proved equally important to a third, and perhaps even more unlikely, group: opponents of affirmative action. Their story shows the convoluted history of the fifth and final belief that is commonly described as a product of *Loving*: the notion that the demise of miscegenation law would lead to the triumph of colorblindness.

In the half century before *Loving,* the argument that the American state should be colorblind was generally advanced by racial liberals, Black and White, who had used it as a hopeful weapon in the fight for racial justice. Because segregation had rested in large part on state identification and enforcement of race classifications, they considered the erasure of race classifications from the law a necessary first step on the road to integration.[46] For liberal proponents of colorblindness, there was no more powerful symbolic moment than the overturning of miscegenation laws. White opposition to interracial marriage had long seemed the most fundamental of all the color lines, and once miscegenation laws had been declared unconstitutional, it seemed only a short step to the conclusion that all race classifications were now beyond the legal pale.

During the 1960s and 1970s, each step the U.S. Congress or U.S. Supreme Court took toward ensuring civil rights and equal protection of the law seemed to move colorblindness one step further from the oppositional sidelines and one step closer to the symbolic center of American life and law. As the language of civil rights slowly became the public face of American hopes, the sound-bite simplicity and obvious political appeal of colorblindness cut a wide swath through middle America. By the mid-1980s, mainstream Americans who revered Martin Luther King Jr. as the hero of the civil rights movement described his achievements largely in terms of his famous dream of being judged not by the color of his skin but by the content of his character.

As colorblindness came to occupy the political center, both the left and right redefined their relationship to it. Civil rights organizations, Black newspapers, and the liberal left in general had greeted the *Loving* decision with enthusiasm. As long-suffering proponents of the ideal of colorblindness, they welcomed the removal of the stigma of "miscegenation" from the law and hoped it would begin to dissolve the fierce opposition White Americans had shown to interracial marriage. But then, in a development that echoed the belief that miscegenation law was the last form of racial segregation, the leaders of the integration movement began to retire from the scene, their major victories behind them. The generation of civil rights leaders who replaced them had to walk a fine line between the old liberal commitment to individual civil rights, which emphasized racial integration, and the burgeoning radicalism of the black power and black nationalist movements, which emphasized race solidarity.[47]

So at the very same moment that Whites started to abandon their opposition to interracial marriage, critiques of interracial marriage began to swirl with a new openness through Black communities. For black nationalists, who were immersed in the project of fostering a proud, strong, all-Black nation, the specter of "out"-marriage quickly came to carry connotations of racial disloyalty. Inspired by Malcolm X, who voiced these objections early and often ("We do oppose intermarriage," he told an interviewer in 1964. "We are as much against intermarriage as we are against all of the other injustices that our people have encountered"), advocates of black power ridiculed inter-married Black leaders they accused of "Talking Black and Sleeping White." These arguments caused considerable discomfort for interracial couples in activist circles, but they had relatively little effect on either the overall number of interracial marriages or the opinions Blacks expressed in opinion polls, which continued to show that Blacks were much less likely than Whites to object to interracial marriages.[48]

But black nationalists did strike a chord among Blacks, and many Whites as well, by indicting the suspicious haste with which some Whites turned hopeful visions of a colorblind society into defensive claims that racism was a thing of the past. Frustrated by the slow pace of progress, civil rights leaders confronted a yawning gap between the lofty rhetoric of colorblind civil rights and the daily reality of color-coded racism. They began to argue that for the purposes of civil rights enforcement, race classifications were too important to jettison, and to recommend "race-conscious" remedies as practical solutions to ongoing discrimination.[49]

During the 1970s, race-conscious remedies attracted considerable support on the political left and were widely adopted in government as well. Affirmative action programs were adopted by state and municipal officials responsible for hiring police and firefighters, by federal officials who oversaw government contracts, and by colleges and universities. After the National Association of Black Social Workers issued a sharp critique of the placement of Black babies in White adoptive families, most adoption agencies established policies designed to give Black adoptive parents first preference in adopting

Black children. Similarly, in an attempt to reduce the remarkably high rate of placement of Indian children in White families, the U.S. Congress passed a bill designed to give Indian parents and their tribal governments more control over the adoption of Indian children.[50]

As civil rights leaders and the liberal left grew more committed to race-conscious remedies, the conservative right grew more committed to color-blindness. They built, in part, on complaints from White families whose bids to adopt Black children were rejected by adoption agencies, White students unable to get into medical or law schools, and White employees who failed to win promotions, all of whom were quick to identify race-conscious remedies as the source of their problems. These complaints allowed conservatives to wrap themselves in the mantle of colorblind equality, and in the process throw off the political liability of their opposition to civil rights. As they told the story, the colorblind spirit of the civil rights revolution, embodied by Martin Luther King Jr., had been betrayed by King's civil rights successors, who, they charged, had followed a path toward race consciousness and special privilege that was a rank denial of the true meaning of civil rights in American society. [51]

An embodiment of the rise of colorblind conservatism can be seen in Ward Connerly, a highly visible Black conservative who attracted national public attention during the 1990s when, as a member of the University of California's board of regents, he sponsored two initiatives he hoped would put colorblindness at the center of the conservative political agenda. The first was Proposition 209, a plan to kill affirmative action programs by forbidding California government agencies, including colleges and universities, from taking race into account in determining college and university admissions, financial aid, and other government benefits. Much to the distress of the major civil rights organizations, all of which opposed it, Connerly called his proposition the "California Civil Rights Initiative." Before Proposition 209, Connerly later admitted, conservatives "had embraced color blindness somewhat tardily" and "pessimistically," but, he claimed, "their pessimism" was "dispelled overnight" when 56 percent of California voters approved Proposition 209 in November 1996.[52] In an attempt to capitalize on this momentum, Connerly then offered a second proposal, the "Racial Privacy Initiative," which was designed to forbid the state of California from using race classifications in any kind of government record-keeping. It, too, was opposed by nearly every civil rights organization, and eventually went down to defeat at the polls in 2002. But by this time, colorblind conservatism was an identifiable political movement with a well-defined ideology and legal agenda.

As a colorblind conservative and also as an opponent of affirmative action, Connerly looked to the Supreme Court's decision in *Loving v. Virginia* as a historical landmark. His comments on the subject carried the authority of his personal history as a Black man who had married a White woman in 1962, five years before the *Loving* decision spurred the changes he celebrated in his speeches and writings. "My own personal experience," Connerly explained in his autobiography, *Creating Equal*, "tells me that the passageway to that place where all racial division ends goes directly through the human heart." "A successful interracial marriage," he wrote in another passage, "is by its nature an exercise in color blindness." In "Loving America," a guest editorial written in 2000 to celebrate the publication of his autobiography, Connerly maintained that "1967 marks a turning point in America's race relations, a turning point as important as the Three-Fifths Compromise, the Emancipation Proclamation or King's 'Dream.'" The significance of the ruling in *Loving*, he wrote, "cannot be overstated." In its wake, he claimed, "people began to ignore the government's racial lines," with interracial couples dating, marrying, and having children. "Love has become colorblind," Connerly insisted, in another piece introducing his Racial Privacy Initiative, so the "time has come for America to fulfill the promise of equal justice before the law and for the nation to renounce racial classifications."[53]

Loving *in the Courts*

By the end of the twentieth century, the conservative reconstitution of colorblindness was taking hold in the courts as well as in the political arena. In the thirty years since it had been issued, the *Loving* decision had grown deep roots in the American judicial system. Between 1967 and 2005, the U.S. Supreme Court had cited *Loving* as precedent in 78 different cases, and federal district courts had done so in 362 more, crafting a judicial legacy that both liberals and conservatives were eager to claim.[54]

Judges were in general agreement on cases that involved interracial couples. They overturned state laws that explicitly prohibited transracial adoptions, overruled judges who denied divorced White women who married Black men custody of their children, and upheld an IRS decision to revoke the tax-exempt status of Bob Jones University, a private religious school that banned interracial dating and marriage.[55] They also extended "the right to marry" in a variety of situations.[56]

On more controversial topics, however, courts debated how *Loving* should be remembered, and liberal and conservative judges alike sought to claim its legacy as their own. Some of these cases involved the right to privacy, abortion, and sodomy.[57] For the purposes of this book, though, the most important of them involved the Fourteenth Amendment's guarantee of equal protection and its relation to race classifications. In the legal arena of equal protection, *Loving* had, in effect, put the finishing touches on an interpretation that the Supreme Court had been developing for more than two decades, in which race classifications had come to be seen as "suspect" classifications that required "compelling" justification in order to survive "strict scrutiny" by the courts. In the years immediately before and after the *Loving* decision, liberal lawyers and judges were prone to assume that "strict scrutiny" by the courts was the same thing as an absolute ban on race classification. As long as the cases that came before the court involved race classifications designed to promote white supremacy, like those that structured segregation in schools, transportation, and marriage, strict scrutiny and colorblind laws seemed to walk in perfect harmony.

By the mid-1970s, however, many of the race classifications that came before the Court, including those used in affirmative action programs and voter redistricting plans, were designed to overturn rather than to promote white supremacy. In several highly controversial cases on these issues, references to *Loving* lined both sides of a deep judicial divide.

In affirmative action cases, liberal justices returned to the position Earl Warren had originally taken in *Loving*, and began to insist that when it came to race classifications, purpose really did matter. Race classifications, they acknowledged, might be "odious to a free people," but their use was not absolutely prohibited. "Our cases have always implied," Justice William Brennan insisted in 1978, citing both *Loving* and *McLaughlin* as authority, "that an 'overriding statutory purpose' could be found that would justify racial classifications."[58] "Race," Justice John Paul Stevens wrote in a 1986 case, "is not always irrelevant to sound governmental decisionmaking."[59] The use of race classifications embedded in affirmative action law was a practical necessity, Justice Ruth Bader Ginsburg explained in 1995, in order to fight the "lingering effects of racial discrimination against minority groups in this country."[60]

Conservative justices, however, insisted on treating the race classifications in affirmative action programs as if they were exact parallels to the race classifications in segregation law. *Loving,* they insisted, had banished both. Their version of why race classifications were "odious to a free people" emphasized the danger of "invidious discrimination," even when those claims of discrimination were raised by White plaintiffs who used them to roll back hard-won civil rights programs for African Americans. In 1978, Justice Lewis Powell took this position, citing *Loving* as authority for the claim that "preferring members of any one group for no reason other than race or ethnic origin is discrimination for its own sake."[61] Two years later, Justices Potter Stewart and William H. Rehnquist said *Loving* showed "the hostility of the Constitution to racial classifications" and had established that "racial discrimination is by definition invidious discrimination."[62] Throughout the 1990s, as the Court grew more and more conservative, it extended this interpretation of *Loving* to a wide variety of arenas, insisting that the "central mandate" of the Fourteenth Amendment was absolute "racial neutrality in governmental decisionmaking."[63]

There is no clearer indication of *Loving*'s status as an icon of equality than the fact that both sides of this judicial divide fought so hard to control its legacy. But as the use of *Loving* in affirmative action cases also shows, responsibility for the evolving ideology of colorblindness was gradually switching hands, in the courts as well as in the political arena. Arguments that the American state should be colorblind had once been the province of liberals, who sought to fight white supremacy by attacking the use of race classifications in the law. But by the 1980s, colorblindness was rapidly becoming the province of the Court's most conservative justices, who had learned to adapt the attack on race classification to a much different purpose, constructing a version of equal protection law that reinforced, rather than challenged, white privilege.

———

By the end of the twentieth century, the celebration of *Loving v. Virginia* and the self-conscious pursuit of colorblindness were both highly visible aspects of American public life. Organizations of multiracial Americans held annual Loving Day celebrations, victims of discrimination cited *Loving* in defense of a wide variety of social causes, and both liberal and conservative politicians touted the case as evidence that colorblindness was a bedrock American virtue. Yet, as Earl Warren's reservations suggest, the links between the *Loving* decision and the dream of colorblindness are by no means obvious. They had, in fact, to be forged out of a circuitous process of historical forgetting and remembering that repositioned *Loving* from the last vestige of the old racial past to the brave beginning of a new (and ostensibly nonracial) regime, then harnessed its symbolic power to a wide variety of personal and political causes. As a part of this process, colorblindness was reconstituted from an oppositional weapon in the fight for racial justice to a conservative statement of American values, while opposition to interracial marriage, which had once stood at the symbolic center of the entire system of white supremacy, came to be regarded as a mere ghost of America's troubled racial past.

Conclusion: The Ghost of the Past

WHEN THE LAST ACT in the historical drama of miscegenation law finally took place, it reflected a half century of transformation in the links between civil rights and constitutional equality, shaped by old and new debates about race discrimination, colorblindness, and same-sex marriage. In 1999, Curtis Inabinett, a Black legislator in South Carolina, sent legislative aides searching for remnants of racism in South Carolina law, and he was appalled to learn that the state constitution still contained a provision, enacted in 1895, that "the marriage of a white person with a negro or mulatto, or person who shall have one-eighth or more negro blood, shall be unlawful and void." Inabinett, a sixty-six-year old Democrat, vowed to "expunge the constitution of the language" of this "extremely offensive" provision.[1] In nearby Alabama, his contemporary Alvin Holmes was every bit as angry, though Holmes, who had built a career in electoral politics on his history of arrests in early civil rights demonstrations, was not at all surprised. Holmes and the Alabama chapter of the NAACP had already tried to get Alabama to repeal the section of its state constitution providing that "the legislature shall never pass any law to authorize or legalize any marriage between any white person and a negro, or descendant of a negro."[2] Holmes's 1998 attempt to do so had died in the state's judiciary committee, but in 1999, he tried once again.

Inabinett and Holmes regarded these constitutional provisions, neither of which had been enforced since 1970, as evidence of the stubborn persistence of white supremacy. "It's like when the Confederate flag was flying over the Capitol," said Holmes, who had fought that battle, too. "There were people who said it wasn't bothering anybody. But it's a symbol of racism. For this to be in the Alabama Constitution is a symbol of racism." "These kinds of things," he declared on another occasion, "represent oppression and slavery and discrimination against black people."[3]

Their supporters reached into the bag of beliefs that had grown up around the *Loving* decision, labeling the provisions remnants of a now-discredited past that simply defied common sense. "It makes no sense," South Carolina law professor James Underwood told a newspaper reporter, "to keep this anachronistic, old provision in the state constitution when the U.S. Supreme Court says it's improper." Alabama's attorney general, a White Republican who was notably conservative on most political issues, called his state's "embarrassing and obsolete" provision "the kind of deadwood in the constitution that ought to be removed."[4]

These arguments proved persuasive to the legislatures of Alabama and South Carolina. Neither held any debate on the measures, and the votes ranged from lopsided to unanimous. In the South Carolina house, for example, the tally was 99 in favor of repeal and only 4 against. The vote attracted considerable attention in and outside the state. The *Multiracial Activist* put a "hit list" of offending South Carolina legislators up on its Web site. "The following members of the South Carolina Legislature," the *Activist* informed its readers, "voted AGAINST the amendment to overturn the State's embarrassing, unconstitutional ban on interracial marriage or abstained from voting on the amendment. With these views," it concluded, "they clearly have NO business legislating." Especially sharp observers soon noticed that twenty South Carolina House members had failed to vote at all.[5]

When reporters contacted the South Carolina legislators who had missed the vote, they began to turn up disturbing hints of the extent of opposition to interracial marriage. "I just believe in the sanctity of the white race," Representative Olin Phillips, a White Democrat, told the reporter who interviewed him, adding, "I just can't condone interracial marriage." "We need some basic laws," Representative Lanny Littlejohn, a White Republican, explained. "That's not the way God meant it. He does create races of people, and He did that for a reason. From the beginning, He set the races apart." Representative Yancy McGill agreed. "As an elected official," McGill said, "we have to take a stand for the future. I just don't think, biblically, that's part of God's plan."[6] As these comments suggest, most of the lawmakers offered religious justifications that echoed notions about God and Nature that had once been endorsed by courts and legislatures, notions that had been fundamental to the post–Civil War naturalization of miscegenation law.

Supporters of repeal were quick to point out that in the post-*Loving* world, the claim that God was on the side of miscegenation law could no longer operate in constitutional circles. "If you can say people can't marry in a constitutional structure," Representative Fletcher Smith, a Black Democrat, told a newspaper reporter during the South Carolina campaign, "it is a race issue. It can't be anything other than a race issue." Religious opposition to interracial marriage, Smith continued, "is a racist religious belief." Even those legislators who opposed interracial marriage knew they had little to gain by saying so in public. Lanny Littlejohn, for example, was strongly opposed to interracial marriage. "I think God has a perfect plan," he explained, "and man has screwed it up time and again and this is just another example." But this, even Littlejohn acknowledged, was only his private religious opinion, since legal bans on interracial marriage "can't stay in the constitution now."[7]

When the South Carolina and Alabama measures went before voters, newspaper editors in both states did their best to encourage their fellow citizens to use the occasion to distance themselves once and for all from their white supremacist past. South Carolina's constitutional ban on interracial marriage "is an unsavory relic of the past," one editor told his readers. "The idea of telling people they are not permitted to marry because of their ancestry would be unthinkable today," he continued. "It is a stain on the constitution that needs to be removed." "It matters," the Birmingham News editorialized on the Alabama repeal, "because the ban is a remnant of the state's racist past that has no place, in this day and age, in a document that's supposed to protect rather than violate the rights of citizens. . . . How can we be open to business when we're not even open to the idea of mixed marriage? . . . Do we believe all people are created equal, or subscribe to the backward thinking in our archaic state constitution?"[8]

Most organizations, including the United Daughters of the Confederacy and the Sons of Confederate Veterans, refused to take a public stand on the issue, but the Confederate Heritage Political Action Committee, led by Michael Chappell, and the Alabama branch of the Southern Party both opposed the repeal. Chappell believed, as he told one reporter, that "interracial marriage is bad for our Southern culture." The repeal measure, the Southern Party declared, was "unnecessary and ridiculous" and was "being pushed to make Alabama look like a racist state."[9]

The results of the public votes suggested that if miscegenation law was a ghost of the past, it was a ghost with teeth. To be sure, both repeal bills were approved by voters. In South Carolina's election, which was held in November 1999, 62 percent of the state's electorate voted to repeal the ban, but 38 percent voted to leave it in the state constitution. In Alabama, 60 percent of voters were in favor of repeal and 40 percent opposed. In both states, more than a dozen counties voted to keep the ban intact, some by more than 70 percent.[10]

The Alabama campaign offered a revealing indication that some legislators saw future threats as well as past political battles in the repeal proposals. When Alvin Holmes had first suggested amending Alabama's constitution, he offered a proposal with two overlapping sections: the first removed the old language about miscegenation, and the second would have replaced it with a provision that "equal protection of the laws shall not intentionally be denied by any state, any county or city, or any official, agency, or instrumentality thereof, to any person on account of race, color, religion, national origin or sex." As Holmes explained, this language was designed to remedy two embarrassments at once, for Alabama was not only "the last state with a ban on interracial marriages" but also "the only state without an equal protection clause in our constitution."[11]

When Holmes took this proposal to the House committee assigned to hear the measure, he ran into trouble because, as the *Birmingham News* reported, some lawmakers worried that passage of the equal protection clause might "open the door for homosexuals to marry."[12] Perhaps because Holmes remembered that his 1998 repeal attempt had died in another House committee, reassurances on this point were offered immediately, and evidently persuasively, for this time the committee voted to go ahead with the repeal. But the version that reached voters included only the plan to remove the old language; somewhere along the way the equal protection language was quietly shelved. In November 2000, Alabama voters closed the final door on miscegenation law by repealing the provision banning interracial marriage, but the state constitution remains without an equal protection clause.

———

As the Alabama and South Carolina votes reveal, there are still places where opposition to interracial marriage had resolutely failed to fade into the mists of historical memory; in some locales, opposition to interracial marriage remains alive and well. Yet by the end of the twentieth century, *Loving v. Virginia* had been elevated to the status of political icon. With every year that had passed since the historic decision, it became easier to think of miscegenation law as a ghost of the past, to see interracial couples as valiant heroes who pitted romance against the power of the state, to believe that the *Loving* decision paved the way to colorblindness and that colorblindness would erase three centuries of white supremacy and bring racism to its knees.

The demise of miscegenation law was, by any measure, a very good thing. But it is nonetheless important to inject a measure of caution into the triumphal accounts of *Loving v. Virginia* that circulate today. These make it far too easy to celebrate the agency of individuals and thus understate the power of such larger forces as the political economy of marriage, the hegemonic power of the racial state, and the shape-shifting power of racism to emerge in new and different forms to meet new conditions.

In this book, I have tried to offer a fuller account of the history of miscegenation law than the popular lionization of *Loving* will allow. The forces were set in motion in the 1860s, when the invention of the term "miscegenation" brought the belief that interracial marriage was unnatural right into the heart of the American legal system. Built on taken-for-granted notions about the nature of sex and gender as well as the nature of race, miscegenation laws became the foundation for white supremacy across the nation, setting Whites apart from Chinese, Japanese, Filipinos, and Indians as well as Blacks. Enforced by marriage license clerks and in civil courts as well as by criminal prosecutors, miscegenation laws sustained nearly unanimous White opposition to interracial marriage, served as a legal factory for the production of race, and played a crucial, if rarely recognized, role in the development of the modern administrative state.

Over the course of the twentieth century, opposition to miscegenation laws cropped up again and again—when NAACP lobbyists took their case to northern state legislatures after the marriage of Jack Johnson to Lucille Cameron, when Filipino immigrant men went to court asking to be recognized as "Malays" rather than "Mongolians," when Dan Marshall argued that interracial marriage was a denial of the constitutional freedom of religion, when G. E. Graves defended Connie Hoffman and Dewey McLaughlin. By the time the ACLU accepted the case of Richard and Mildred Loving, it had all these examples to build on. Slowly but surely, critics managed to bury the belief that interracial marriage was unnatural, and though it would take them nearly a century to do it, they would eventually bring the reign of miscegenation law to an end.

Theirs was a fine achievement, but the rise and fall of miscegenation law should be remembered in its full complexity. It might be heartening to think of interracial couples as fierce opponents of wrongheaded laws determined to win the right of interracial marriage for everyone once and for all. But interracial couples should be relieved of the burden of having to stand as one-dimensional heroes and heroines. The history of miscegenation law includes men who insisted on racial equality in order to preserve the gender privileges of manhood, women who fought with other women over the spoils of White men's estates, and men and women who used the laws to try to free themselves from partners they decided they had mistakenly wed as well as men and women who linked their own marriages to the freedoms of others. In an era when it is fashionable to believe that marriage is all about romance, it is important to remember that economic and gender inequities and obligations to the state are still fundamental aspects of marriage.

In one sense or another, all the interracial couples featured in this book believed in their marriages, and many of those marriages lasted a very long time. Interracial couples often formed informal communities to help negotiate their way through the thicket of laws and regulations they confronted. Whenever they could find a loophole—during Reconstruction, for example—or when there were the makings of some kind of community support for interracial couples, as among Filipino men in Los Angeles in the 1930s, the numbers of interracial marriages swelled, and the voices of opposition grew sharper.

But most interracial couples entered the public arena only reluctantly, and made limited claims when they did so. They had plenty of reasons to keep a low profile: their neighbors or parents opposed the match, the bride-to-be was pregnant, they feared their lives would become the fodder of newspaper scandals. Most were aware that catching the public eye would only get them in more trouble; some even adopted the belief of the mid-twentieth-century NAACP: that any public support of interracial marriage would set off firestorms from opponents of civil rights. As a result, most litigants were reluctant to tell their stories to anyone but their closest friends and family; when they were forced into the public eye, they were usually careful to insist they were fighting for themselves and no one else.

On this point, Richard and Mildred Loving themselves can serve as an example. All they wanted, Richard Loving repeatedly told curious reporters, was to be left alone to raise their family in peace. The Lovings' case made it to the U.S. Supreme Court because when Mildred heard about the Civil Rights Act of 1964, she was spurred to reopen the case of her original arrest, which had taken place in 1958. But in public, and later to interviewers, Mildred Loving always insisted that she was no kind of civil rights pioneer, and she and her children did their best to honor Richard's insistence that they avoid the press. So many interracial couples shared this fierce—and perfectly understandable—desire to protect their privacy that by the mid-twentieth century, when lawyers had become eager to challenge miscegenation laws in court, they often had to talk reluctant clients into letting their individual legal troubles be turned into test cases. And like the Lovings, the couples themselves often knew very little of the legal machinations undertaken on their behalf.

In writing this book, I have tried to reconstruct the stories of many of the couples who were caught in the web of miscegenation laws, and to examine the backgrounds and motivations of their lawyers, too. The trail of clues has taken me well beyond the scanty details offered in the rulings of appellate court judges, into local tax and census records, legal society bulletins, and the records of county clerks' associations, through hundreds of newspaper articles, and into the handful of in-depth oral history interviews that have been conducted with lawyers and litigants. This research has allowed me to lift an edge of the veil of privacy that interracial couples tried to throw over their lives. Often, though, it falls short of answering the question that lies at their center of their stories: what was in the hearts of the men and women who were so determined to live together, marry, and maintain their relationships that they defied the law, and nearly unanimous White public opinion, in order to do so?

If it is wise to resist the tendency to romanticize the heroism of interracial couples, it may be even wiser to question the now commonplace beliefs that *Loving v. Virginia* removed the last roadblock on the road to colorblindness and that colorblindness means the end of racism and white supremacy. Colorblindness, or the powerfully persuasive belief that the eradication of racism depends on the deliberate nonrecognition of race, is one of today's foundational premises, taken for granted in much the same way that the unnaturalness of interracial marriage was a century earlier. The desire for a colorblind world was, in fact, a vision often urged by lawyers who challenged miscegenation laws, and although Chief Justice Earl Warren stopped short of accepting this premise in *Loving,* colorblindness has been more or less constantly identified with *Loving* ever since, as both liberals and conservatives use the case as a flashpoint in their battle for control over the forms colorblindness might take.

But American racial systems have always worked most effectively when they are taken so completely for granted that their structures are more or less invisible to Whites. Every successive American racial regime, beginning with slavery, but continuing with the taking of Indian lands, the establishment of segregation, and the development of American immigration restrictions, expended a great deal of energy making its racial notions appear so natural that they could not be comprehended as contradictions to a society ostensibly based on equality. The same point needs to be made about colorblindness, which needs to be seen not, as it is popularly constructed, as the celebrated end of racism but as a racial ideology of its own, one that can, like any racial project, be turned to the service of oppression.

So the conclusion I would draw is that if we should constantly be on guard against the charge that something is "unnatural" (whether it be interracial marriage in the 1890s or same-sex marriage in the 1990s), we should also be on guard against the belief that if white supremacy is the problem, then colorblindness must be the solution. Late-nineteenth-century white supremacists believed that there was no discrimination at all in racial hierarchies they took as a natural given; to their minds, miscegenation laws were perfectly compatible with American notions of equality. This history shows that equality, like nature, should never be taken for granted.

Acknowledgments

A S ANYONE WHO knows me can tell you, this book has taken me far too
long to write. That it is finished even now is a testament to the kindness of dozens of friends and colleagues who have helped me in a myriad of
ways, through good times and bad. For critiques, companionship, and endless encouragement, I want to thank Sue Armitage, Gabriella Arrendondo,
Margot Canaday, Sally Deutsch, Estelle Freedman, Matt Garcia, Bryna
Goodman, Ariela Gross, Dave Gutiérrez, Ramón Gutiérrez, Ellen Herman,
Yvette Huginnie, Patty Limerick, Ruthanne Lum McCunn, Colleen McDan-
nell, Valerie Matsumoto, Joanne Meyerowitz, Jim Mohr, Julie Novkov, Jeff
Ostler, Julee Raiskin, Renee Romano, Vicki Ruiz, Virginia Scharff, Martin
Summers, Anne Walthall, Barbara Welke, and Richard White.

The Departments of History and Ethnic Studies at the University of Oregon, and before that the Department of History at the University of Utah,
were delightfully welcoming intellectual homes while I was writing this
book, giving me colleagues to treasure. And I want to send a special thanks
to the co-editors and authors of the many books I worked on for the American Crossroads Series in Ethnic Studies at the University of California Press.
Their work taught me more than I can easily express, and fills me with hope
for all our disciplines.

Over the years, dozens of people sent me newspaper clippings and other
research leads. There were far more of these than I could use in this book,
but I am grateful for each and every one of them. I am especially obliged to
several people whose help I simply could not have done without. Quintard
Taylor turned my attention to Texas, showing me where to locate chapter 1;
Ellen Herman introduced me to the works of James Scott, transforming
my analysis in chapter 5. Nick Rosenthal and Veta Schlimgen did first-rate
research in newspapers and photographs on the California cases discussed in

several of the chapters. Michael Engh, Fay Botham, Mark Brilliant, and Dara Orenstein were wonderfully generous in sharing sources and unpublished writings on the Catholic Interracial Council and the case of *Perez v. Sharp.* I owe a particular debt to Dara Orenstein, for her marvelous research on *Perez,* which helped bring my discussion of that case to life in chapter 7, and for sending me a copy of the photograph of Andrea Pérez that appears in that chapter. Special thanks also to Georgie Michelson of Morningside Elementary School in San Fernando, California, for tracking down the copyright owner, and to Helen Rosas for graciously giving me permission to use it. I want to thank Linda España-Maram, who went out of her way to help me find the photo of the First Filipino Infantry, which also appears in chapter 7. Peter Wallenstein sent me important materials on the Virginia cases of *Naim v. Naim* and *Loving v. Virginia.* Nancy Cott kindly shared ideas and research materials while she was working on her brilliant book *Public Vows,* and Katherine Franke and Diana Williams sent me their books-in-progress, too.

County clerks, librarians, and archivists all across the country provided me with photocopies from countless court cases. At the head of this line stands the University of Oregon's long-suffering Interlibrary Loan staff, who cheerfully responded to dozens of difficult—and sometimes outright impossible—requests, even when I made them over and over again. The reference staff at the University of Oregon's John E. Jaqua Law Library, especially Mary Clayton, was remarkably helpful and efficient, and so were were Lesli Larson and Rick Gersbach of Image Services at the University of Oregon's Knight Library. Many wonderful graduate students served as my research assistants: Bonni Cermak, Sarah Hale, Torrie Hester, Taro Iwata, Bea McKenzie, Jessika Palmer, Nick Rosenthal, Veta Schlimgen, Angela Tone, and Camille Walsh.

For financial support, I am grateful to the National Endowment for the Humanities, for a fellowship in 1995–96, and to the Carrie C. Beekman Fund at the University of Oregon. I owe a special debt to John McCole, the chair of my history department at the University of Oregon, who helped me rearrange my teaching schedule several times during the last two years. I am much obliged to the journals and presses that granted me permission to use portions of articles and chapters previously published in somewhat different form by them: "Race, Gender, and Intercultural Relations: The Case of Interracial Marriage," *Frontiers: A Journal of Women Studies* 12, no. 1 (1991); "Miscegenation Law, Court Cases, and Ideologies of 'Race' in Twentieth-Century America," *Journal of American History* (June 1996); "Race, Gender, and the Privileges of Property: On the Significance of Miscegenation Law in the U.S. West," in *Over the Edge: Remapping the American West,* ed.

Valerie Matsumoto and Blake Allmendinger (University of California Press, 1999), "'A Mistake to Simmer the Question Down to Black and White': The History of Oregon's Miscegenation Law," in *Seeing Color: Indigenous Peoples and Racialized Minorities in Oregon,* ed. Jun Xing et al. (University Press of America, 2007); and "Sex, Gender, and Same-Sex Marriage," in *Is Academic Feminism Dead? Theory in Practice,* ed. Center for Advanced Feminist Studies, University of Minnesota (NYU Press, 2000).

My arguments were refined before audiences at several historical conferences and many more universities. I am grateful for all these invitations, and for the many questions that sent me back to my sources for another look. Two of the lawyers whose work is central to this book, Jack Greenberg and the late David Carliner, agreed to interviews, and I learned a good deal from speaking with them, too.

Estelle Freedman, Dave Gutiérrez, Ellen Herman, Dirk Hartog, Joe Lowndes, Valerie Matsumoto, Jim Mohr, Julie Novkov, Vicki Ruiz, Barbara Welke, and the faculty seminar of the University of Oregon's Center for Race, Ethnicity, and Sexuality Studies (CRESS) read part or all of the manuscript and offered wonderfully helpful suggestions. Julie Novkov's deep understanding of the history of miscegenation law in Alabama has influenced my entire approach to white supremacy and the administrative state. I owe a particularly deep debt to Barbara Welke, and not only for her detailed reading of the manuscript, which saved me from embarrassing errors and offered suggestions big and small. At a moment when my refusal to stop writing had begun to border on obsession, Barbara's offer to take it all off my hands broke the logjam; her persistence and generosity ensured that this book would get into print at all.

The last two and a half years of work on this project took place under especially difficult circumstances, while I struggled to recover from surgery and to adapt to an arduous regime of chemotherapy. I thank all the friends, family, and colleagues who sent cards, brought dinners, and drove me and my children where they needed to go. I also want to thank my oncologist, Peter Kovach, who adjusted my treatment schedule time and again to allow me to travel and write. Two longtime friends deserve special mention. Valerie Matsumoto has been a close friend ever since we were graduate students in the 1980s; her weekly efforts to raise my spirits have meant a great deal to me. A very long time ago, Estelle Freedman was my graduate school mentor; later, she became a good friend and the godmother to one of my daughters; these past two years, she has been, if it were possible, even more extraordinary, always anticipating whatever it is I need most, sometimes before I even know I need it.

My editor, Susan Ferber, waited far too many years for me to finish writing—and never once tried to make me feel guilty about it. From beginning to end, Susan showed why she has a reputation as every author's favorite editor. Her wonderfully incisive editing, pitch-perfect judgment, and all-around kindness made this a far better book. India Cooper provided superb copy editing, and Joellyn Ausanka deftly shepherded the manuscript through the production process. These and other consummate experts at Oxford University Press have knocked themselves out so that I can see this book in print; I deeply appreciate their efforts.

My partner, Linda Long, has lived with this project, and the demands it made on me and our family, for nearly two decades. If that wasn't enough, she cheerfully volunteered to help with the photographs (without her help, I would have missed that deadline, too). For more reasons than I will say here, and with enormous love and gratitude, this book is dedicated to her, and to our wonderful daughters, Ellie and Joie.

Abbreviations

ACLU   ACLU Archives, Seeley G. Mudd Manuscript Library, Princeton University, Princeton, New Jersey.

FBTX   Fort Bend County Tax Rolls, 1838–1910, Microfilm, A 157, Texas State Library/Archives, Austin.

EWP   Earl Warren Papers, Manuscript Division, Library of Congress, Washington, D.C.

FCF   Case File, Bonds v. Foster, Texas Supreme Court, M 6471, no. 859, Texas State Library/Archives, Austin.

FCP   Frank F. Chuman Papers, Japanese American Research Project Collection (Collection 2010), Department of Special Collections, Charles E. Young Research Library, University of California, Los Angeles.

FFP   Felix Frankfurter Papers, Manuscript Division, Library of Congress, Washington, D.C.

FPF   Probate File, Estate of Alfred H. Foster, Probate no. 653, Fort Bend County Clerk's Office, Richmond, Texas.

GCF   State of Indiana v. Thomas Gibson, Indiana Supreme Court Case File no. 2109, Indiana State Archives, Indianapolis.

HHBP   Harold H. Burton Papers, Manuscript Division, Library of Congress, Washington, D.C.

JPP   Papers of John Powell, MSS 7284, 7284-a, Special Collections, University of Virginia Library, Charlottesville.

KCF   Kirby v. Kirby, Arizona Supreme Court Record no. 1970, Arizona State Law Library, Phoenix.

LB	Philip B. Kurland and Gerhard Casper, eds., *Landmark Briefs and Arguments of the Supreme Court of the United States: Constitutional Law,* vol. 64. Arlington, Va.: University Publications of America, 1975.
LCF	Loving v. Virginia, Transcripts of Records and File Copies of Briefs, 1966, Case no. 395, U.S. Supreme Court Library, Washington, D.C.
McLCF	McLaughlin v. Florida, Transcripts of Records and File Copies of Briefs, 1964, Case no. 11, U.S. Supreme Court Library, Washington, D.C.
MCF	Estate of Monks, 4 Civ. 2835, Court of Appeal of California, California State Archives, Sacramento.
NA	David H. Fowler, *Northern Attitudes Towards Interracial Marriage: Legislation and Public Opinion in the Middle Atlantic and the States of the Old Northwest, 1780–1930.* 1963; New York: Garland Publishing, 1987.
NAACP-LC	Papers of the NAACP, Library of Congress, Washington, D.C.
NAACP-MF	Papers of the NAACP, Microfilm Edition.
NAACP-WC	Records of the NAACP, West Coast Region, Bancroft Library, University of California, Berkeley.
NARA	National Archives and Record Administration.
OCF	Oyama v. O'Neill, Arizona Supreme Court Case no. 7065, Arizona History and Archives Division, Arizona State Library, Phoenix.
PCF	Pace v. Alabama, no. 10291, Box 1536, Record Group 267, U.S. Supreme Court Appellate Case Files, NARA, Washington, D.C.
PaCF	Paquet v. Paquet, Oregon Supreme Court Case no. 10257, File no. 4268, Oregon State Archives, Salem.
PaPF	Estate of Fred Paquet, Tillamook County Probate File no. 605, Oregon State Archives, Salem.
PE	Chang Moon Sohn, "Principle and Expediency in Judicial Review: Miscegenation Cases in the Supreme Court," Ph.D. dissertation, Columbia University, 1970.
PeCF	Perez v. Sharp, California Supreme Court Case File L.A. 20305, California State Archives, Sacramento.
RCF	Roldan v. L.A. County, 2 Civ. 8455, District Court of Appeal of California, Second Appellate District, Division Two, California State Archives, Sacramento.

RUS Byron Curti Martyn, "Racism in the United States: A History of the Anti-Miscegenation Legislation and Litigation," Ph.D. dissertation, University of Southern California, 1979.

TCCP Tom C. Clark Papers, Tarleton Law Library, University of Texas, Austin.

WODP William O. Douglas Papers, Manuscript Division, Library of Congress, Washington, D.C.

NOTES

Introduction

1. *Miscegenation: The Theory of the Blending of the Races, Applied to the American White Man and Negro* (New York: Dexter, Hamilton, 1864), ii.

2. *Kinney v. Commonwealth*, 71 Va. 858, 869 (1878).

3. *Miscegenation*, 27–28. The first scholar to emphasize this aspect of the notorious pamphlet was Elise Lemire. See Elise Virginia Lemire, "Making Miscegenation: Discourses of Interracial Sex and Marriage in the United States, 1790–1865" (Ph.D. dissertation, Rutgers University, 1996), 229.

4. Peter Wallenstein, *Tell the Court I Love My Wife: Race, Marriage, and Law—An American History* (New York: Palgrave Macmillan, 2002); Randall Kennedy, *Interracial Intimacies: Sex, Marriage, Identity, and Adoption* (New York: Pantheon Books, 2003); David A. Hollinger, "Amalgamation and Hypodescent: The Question of Ethnoracial Mixture in the History of the United States," *American Historical Review* 108 (December 2003): 1363–90; Charles F. Robinson II, *Dangerous Liaisons: Sex and Love in the Segregated South* (Fayetteville: University of Arkansas Press, 2003); Phyl Newbeck, *Virginia Hasn't Always Been for Lovers: Interracial Marriage Bans and the Case of Richard and Mildred Loving* (Carbondale: Southern Illinois University Press, 2004). For older examples, see NA; PE; RUS; Robert J. Sickels, *Race, Marriage, and the Law* (Albuquerque: University of New Mexico Press, 1972); and James Hugo Johnston, *Race Relations in Virginia and Miscegenation in the South, 1776–1860* (1937; Amherst: University of Massachusetts Press, 1970).

5. Eva Saks, "Representing Miscegenation Law," *Raritan* 8 (Fall 1988): 39–69; Elise Lemire, *"Miscegenation": Making Race in America* (Philadelphia: University of Pennsylvania Press, 2002); Michelle Brattain, "Miscegenation and Competing Definitions of Race in Twentieth-Century Louisiana," *Journal of Southern History* 61 (August 2005): 621–58; Henry Yu, "Tiger Woods Is Not the End of History: or, Why Sex Across the Color Line Won't Save Us All," *American Historical Review* 108 (December 2003): 1406–14; Alex Lubin, *Romance and Rights: The Politics of Interracial Intimacy, 1945–1954* (Jackson: University Press of Mississippi, 2003). To this list should be added at least three studies of interracial cases that took place in states that had no miscegenation

laws: Earl Lewis and Heidi Ardizzone, *Love on Trial: An American Scandal in Black and White* (New York: W. W. Norton, 2001); Mary Ting Yu Lui, *The Chinatown Trunk Mystery: Murder, Miscegenation, and Other Dangerous Encounters in Turn-of-the-Century New York City* (Princeton: Princeton University Press, 2005); and Elizabeth Smith-Pryor, *Property Rites: The Protection of Whiteness and the Rhinelander Trial* (Chapel Hill: University of North Carolina Press, forthcoming).

6. Rachel F. Moran, *Interracial Intimacy: The Regulation of Race and Romance* (Chicago: University of Chicago Press, 2001), 28–36; Emily Field Van Tassel, "'Only the Law Would Rule Between Us': Antimiscegenation, the Moral Economy of Dependency, and the Debate over Rights After the Civil War," *Chicago-Kent Law Review* (1995): 873–926; Hannah Rosen, "The Rhetoric of Miscegenation and the Reconstruction of Race: Debating Marriage, Sex, and Citizenship in Postemancipation Arkansas," in *Gender and Slave Emancipation in the Atlantic World,* ed. Pamela Scully and Diana Paton (Durham: Duke University Press, 2005), 289–309; Fay Botham, "'Almighty God Created the Races': Theologies of Marriage and Race in Anti-Miscegenation Cases, 1865–1967" (Ph.D. dissertation, Claremont Graduate University, 2005); Diana Irene Williams, "'They Call It Marriage': The Interracial Louisiana Family and the Making of American Legitimacy" (Ph.D. dissertation, Harvard University, 2007); Karen M. Woods, "A 'Wicked and Mischievous Connection': The Origins and Development of Indian-White Miscegenation Law," *Legal Studies Forum* 23, nos. 1–2 (1999): 37–70; Leti Volpp, "American Mestizo: Filipinos and Antimiscegenation Laws in California," *UC Davis Law Review* 33 (1999–2000): 795–835; Susan Koshy, *Sexual Naturalization: Asian Americans and Miscegenation* (Stanford: Stanford University Press, 2004); Dara Orenstein, "Void for Vagueness: Mexicans and the Collapse of Miscegenation Law in California," *Pacific Historical Review* 74 (August 2005): 367–407.

7. Gregory Michael Dorr, "Principled Expedience: Eugenics, *Naim v. Naim,* and the Supreme Court," *American Journal of Legal History* 42, no. 2 (1998): 119–59; Renee C. Romano, *Race Mixing: Black-White Marriage in Postwar America* (Cambridge: Harvard University Press, 2003); Julie Novkov, *Racial Union: Law, Intimacy, and the White State in Alabama, 1865–1954* (Ann Arbor: University of Michigan Press, 2008).

8. *Miscegenation,* ii. On this point, too, see Lemire, *"Miscegenation,"* 213.

9. *Pace v. State,* 69 Ala. 231, 232 (1881).

10. *In re Paquet's Estate,* 200 P. 911, 913 (1921). The term "Kanaka" refers to Native Hawaiians.

11. *Scott v. Georgia,* 39 Ga. 321, 323 (1869).

12. An Act to Prohibit Amalgamation and the Intermarriage of Races, 1866 Or. Gen. Laws 10.

13. For more on "racial identity trials," see Ariela J. Gross, *What Blood Won't Tell: A History of Race on Trial in America* (Cambridge: Harvard University Press, 2008).

14. As late as 1994, it appears that thirty-three U.S. states still required prospective husbands and wives to list their "race" on marriage license applications. See "1994 Marriage Addendum to the 'Technical Appendix' of Vital Statistics of the United States, 1988, Volume III, Marriage and Divorce," http://www.nber.org/marrdivo/mar94ad.txt (accessed October 24, 2007).

15. Christopher A. Ford, "Administering Identity: The Determination of 'Race' in Race-Conscious Law," *California Law Review* 182 (1994): 1231–85; Michael Omi,

"Racial Identity and the State: The Dilemmas of Classification," *Law and Inequality* 15 (Winter 1997): 7–23.

16. Novkov, *Racial Union*; Lucy E. Salyer, *Laws Harsh as Tigers: Chinese Immigrants and the Shaping of Modern Immigration Law* (Chapel Hill: University of North Carolina Press, 1995); Erika Lee, *At America's Gates: Chinese Immigration During the Exclusion Era, 1882–1945* (Chapel Hill: University of North Carolina Press, 2003); Mae M. Ngai, *Impossible Subjects: Illegal Aliens and the Making of Modern America* (Princeton: Princeton University Press, 2004); Martha Mabie Gardner, *The Qualities of a Citizen: Women, Immigration, and Citizenship, 1870–1965* (Princeton: Princeton University Press, 2005); Barbara Young Welke, *Recasting American Liberty: Gender, Race, Law, and the Railroad Revolution, 1865–1920* (Cambridge: Cambridge University Press, 2001).

17. Montana Rev. Code, sec. 5701, 2 and 5700 (1935).

18. An Act to Prohibit the Amalgamation of Whites and Blacks, ch. 130, sec. 1, 1842, Indiana Gen. Laws 142.

19. Compare, for example, Robinson, *Dangerous Liaisons*, 67–68, and Mary Frances Berry, "Judging Morality: Sexual Behavior and Legal Consequences in the Late Nineteenth-Century South," *Journal of American History* 78 (December 1991): 839.

20. Nancy F. Cott, "Giving Character to Our Whole Civil Polity: Marriage and the Public Order in the Late Nineteenth Century," in *U.S. History as Women's History: New Feminist Essays*, ed. Linda K. Kerber, Alice Kessler-Harris, and Kathryn Kish Sklar (Chapel Hill: University of North Carolina Press, 1995), 111.

21. In the interests of readability, however, I have decided not to capitalize any of the following phrases, all of which seem to me to designate particular ideologies: whiteness, blackness, white supremacy, white purity, the protection of white womanhood, the protection of black womanhood, black inferiority.

Chapter 1

1. Transcript, 19–20, FCF; Deed of Manumission, August 25, 1847, FPF. On Fort Bend County, see Clarence R. Wharton, *History of Fort Bend County* (San Antonio: Naylor, 1939) and A. J. Sowell, *History of Fort Bend County* (Houston: W. H. Coyle, 1904).

2. Alwyn Barr, *Black Texans: A History of Negroes in Texas, 1528–1971* (Austin: Jenkins Publishing, 1973), 4–14.

3. Transcript, 19–21, 41, FCF; Population Schedules of the 8th Census of the United States, 1860: Slave Schedules, National Archives Microfilm Publications 635, Reel 1310, Fort Bend County, p. 7.

4. Last Will and Testament, February 1866, FPF.

5. James M. Smallwood, *Time of Hope, Time of Despair: Black Texans During Reconstruction* (Port Washington, N.Y.: National University Publications, 1981), 55, Donald G. Nieman, "African Americans and the Meaning of Freedom: Washington County, Texas, as a Case Study, 1865–1886," *Chicago-Kent Law Review* 70 (1994), 555–56.

6. Bonds's name is variously given in the sources as Bonds or Bond. I have used Bonds in the text since it was the version eventually used in published court records.

7. Bond of Fields Foster, February 26, 1867; Report of Renting Plantation, February 26, 1867; Report of Executor Renting Out Plantation, January 15, 1868, all in FPF; Transcript, 33–34, 38, FCF; Entry for A. H. Foster, 1864, FBTX. The calculation

of the price is mine, gained by multiplying the agreed-upon price of $9.25 an acre by 300 acres.

8. Transcript, 4, 1, FCF; An Act to Legalise Certain Marriages, sec. 9, 1837 Repub. Texas Laws 233.

9. An Act Concerning Negroes & Other Slaues (1664), in *Archives of Maryland,* vol. 1, ed. William H. Brown (Baltimore: Maryland Historical Society, 1883), 533.

10. Barbara J. Fields, "Slavery, Race, and Ideology in the United States of America," *New Left Review* 181 (May/June 1990): 107.

11. An Act for Suppressing Outlying Slaves (1726), in *Statutes at Large, Being a Collection of all the Laws of Virginia,* vol. 3, ed. William Waller Hening (Philadelphia, 1823), 86, 87.

12. An Act for the Better Preventing of a Spurious and Mixt Issue, Etc., ch. 6, 1705 Prov. Mass. Acts and Laws 151; An Act Concerning Servants and Slaves (1715), ch. 46, sec. 16, in *The State Records of North Carolina,* vol. 23, ed. Walter Clark (Goldsboro, N.C.: Nash Brothers, 1940), 62, 65; An Act for the Better Regulating of Negroes in this Province (1725–26), ch. 292, sec. 7–8, in *Statutes at Large of Pennsylvania from 1682 to 1801,* vol. 4 (Harrisburg: State Printer of Pennsylvania, 1896), 59, 62–63; An Act for Repealing an Act Intituled (An Act for Rendering the Colony of Georgia More Defensible by Prohibiting the Importation and Use of Black Slaves or Negroes into the Same) & for Permitting the Importation and Use of Them in the Colony Under Proper Restrictions and Regulations (1750), in *The Colonial Records of the State of Georgia,* vol. 1, ed. Allen D. Candler (Atlanta: Franklin Printing, 1904), 56, 59; Black Code (1724), art. 6, in Charles Gayarre, *History of Louisiana,* vol. 1 (New York: Redfield, 1854), 531.

13. On colonial laws, see Charles F. Robinson II, *Dangerous Liaisons: Sex and Love in the Segregated South* (Fayetteville: University of Arkansas Press, 2003), 2–8; Peter Wallenstein, *Tell the Court I Love My Wife: Race, Marriage, and Law—An American History* (New York: Palgrave Macmillan, 2002), 13–25; Kathleen M. Brown, *Good Wives, Nasty Wenches, and Anxious Patriarchs: Gender, Race, and Power in Colonial Virginia* (Chapel Hill: University of North Carolina Press, 1996), 195–211; Peter W. Bardaglio, *Reconstructing the Household: Families, Sex, and the Law in the Nineteenth-Century South* (Chapel Hill: University of North Carolina Press, 1995), 48–55; A. Leon Higginbotham and Barbara K. Kopytoff, "Racial Purity and Interracial Sex in the Law of Colonial and Antebellum Virginia," *Georgetown Law Journal* 77 (June 1989): 1967–2029; George M. Fredrickson, *White Supremacy: A Comparative Study in American and South African History* (New York: Oxford University Press, 1981), 99–108; James Hugo Johnston, *Race Relations in Virginia and Miscegenation in the South, 1776–1860* (1937; Amherst: University of Massachusetts Press, 1970), 165–90; and *NA,* 23–81.

14. *NA,* 402; An Act for the Better Governing and Regulating White Servants (1717), no. 383, sec. 21, in *The Statutes at Large of South Carolina,* vol. 3 (Columbia: A. S. Johnson, 1838), 20; *NA,* 351.

15. An Act for Suppressing Outlying Slaves, 87.

16. *NA,* 61–62; An Act for Repealing an Act Intituled..., 56, 59.

17. Johnston, *Race Relations,* 192–94.

18. An Act for the Gradual Abolition of Slavery, ch. 146, sec. 14, 1780 Pa. Acts 299.

19. On antebellum laws, see Nancy F. Cott, *Public Vows: A History of Marriage and the Nation* (Cambridge: Harvard University Press, 2000), 39–50; Robinson,

Dangerous Liaisons, 8–20; Wallenstein, *Tell the Court*, 39–50; Bardaglio, *Reconstructing the Household*, 55–64; Michael Grossberg, *Governing the Hearth: Law and the Family in Nineteenth-Century America* (Chapel Hill: University of North Carolina Press, 1985), 127–29; and *NA*, 82–220.

20. Virgil Maxcy, ed., *The Laws of Maryland*, vol. 1 (Baltimore: Philip H. Nicklin, 1811), ch. 13, sec. 6, 140, 141; An Act for the Orderly Solemnization of Marriages, ch. 3, 1786 Mass. Acts 437, 439; An Act to Regulate the Solemnization of Marriages, ch. 42, sec. 17–18, 1792 Va. Laws 130, 134–35; An Act for the Better Regulation of Free Negroes and Free Mulattoes, ch. 42, sec. 7–10 (1807) in *Laws of the State of Delaware, 1806–1813*, vol. 4 (Wilmington: M. Bradford and R. Porter, 1816), 112–13; *Digest of the Civil Laws Now in Force in the Territory of Orleans* (New Orleans: Bradford & Anderson, 1808), title 4, ch. 2, art. 8, 24; An Act to More Effectually Prevent Intermarriages Between Free Negroes or Free Persons of Colour and White Persons and Slaves, ch. 4, 1830–31 N.C. Sess. Laws 9.

21. An Act to Regulate the Solemnization of Marriages, ch. 75, sec. 1, 1822 Miss. Laws 560. According to Byron Curti Martyn, "As ambiguous as this statute was, nevertheless the racial implications were clear. Only marriages between whites would be solemnized as legally valid. All other attempted marriages, be they intra-racial Negro or Indian, or interracial of any combination, were illegal or extra-legal in nature and hence at best cohabitation." RUS, 324.

22. Ky. Const. of 1792, art. 8, sec. 6; An Act to Prevent Clandestine Marriages, sec. 5, 1798 R.I. Pub Laws 481, 483; An Act to Reduce into One Act, All the Acts and Parts of Acts Relative to Crime and Punishment, ch. 5, sec. 59, 1818 Ind. Laws 75, 94; An Act for Regulating Marriage, ch. 70, sec. 2 (1821), in Francis O. J. Smith, *Laws of the State of Maine* (Portland: Thomas Todd and Colman, Holden, 1834), 1:419, 420; An Act to Amend the Law Concerning Marriage, ch. 19, 1822 Tenn. Acts 22; An Act Respecting Free Negroes and Mulattoes, Servants and Slaves, part 3, sec. 3, Ill. Rev. Code (1829) 109. By an Act of February 27, 1801, Congress extended the laws of Maryland to cover the District of Columbia. For a brief history of D.C. code compilations, see *District of Columbia Code Encyclopedia* (St. Paul, Minn.: West Publishing, 1966), 2–3.

23. An Act to Amend the Act Entitled "An Act Concerning Marriage License," no. 3, 1832 Fla. Terr. Laws 4; An Act Regulating Marriages, sec. 3, in Mo. Rev. Stat. (1835), 401; An Act to Legalise Certain Marriages, sec. 9, 1837 Repub. Texas Laws 233; Ark. Dig. Stat., ch. 102, sec. 4, 9 (1838), in E. H. English, *A Digest of the Statutes of Arkansas... in Force... 1846* (Little Rock: Reardon & Garritt, 1848), 706; Mich. Rev. Stat. (1838), part 2, title 7, ch. 1, sec. 5, 334; An Act Regulating Marriages, ch. 25, sec. 13, 1839–49 Iowa Terr. Laws 39, 42.

24. Ala. Code (1852), title 5, ch. 1, art. 1, secs. 1946 and 1956, 376–77; An Act to Add an Additional Section to the Tenth Division of the Penal Code of this State, no. 161, 1851–52 Geo. Laws 262; Geo. Acts (1851–52), no. 161; An Act in Relation to Service, sec. 4, 1852 Utah Terr. Acts 80, 81.

25. An Act Regulating Marriages, ch. 140, sec. 3, 1850 Cal. Stat. 424; An Act Regulating Marriages, ch. 108, sec. 3, 1855 Kan. Terr. Stat. 487, 488; An Act Regulating Marriages, sec. 3, 1855 Neb. Terr. Laws 209; An Act to Amend an Act, Entitled "An Act to Regulate Marriage," 1854–55 Wash. Terr. Laws 33; An Act Concerning Free Negroes, sec. 3–4 (1857), in New Mexico Terr. Rev. Stat. (1865), art. 26, ch. 44,

456, 458; An Act to Prevent the Amalgamation of the White and Colored Races, 1861 Ohio Acts 6.

26. An Act to Prevent Amalgamation with Colored Persons, September 19, 1839, in *Laws of the Cherokee Nation, Passed During the Years 1839–1867, Compiled by Authority of the National Council* (St. Louis: Missouri Democrat Print, 1868), 22.

27. Act of November 11, 1824, in *Laws of the Cherokee Nation: Adopted by the Council at Various Periods* (Tahlequah, C.N.: Cherokee Advocate Office, 1852), 38; Law 19th and Law 20th (1825), in *Laws of the Creek Nation,* ed. Antonio J. Waring (Athens: University of Georgia Press, 1960), 20–21; An Act to Prevent Amalgamation with Colored Persons, September 19, 1839, in *Laws of the Cherokee Nation,* 22; An Act in Relation to Cohabiting with Negroes, March 16, 1858, in *Constitution and Laws of the Chickasaw Nation Together with the Treaties of 1831, 1833, 1834, 1837, 1852, and 1866,* ed. Davis A. Homer (1899; Wilmington: Scholarly Resources, 1973). For more on these laws, see Theda Perdue, *Slavery and the Evolution of Cherokee Society, 1540–1866* (Knoxville: University of Tennessee Press, 1979), 84–85; Daniel F. Littlefield Jr., *Africans and Creeks: From the Colonial Period to the Civil War* (Westport, Conn.: Greenwood Press, 1977), 85, 143, 257; Tiya Miles, *Ties That Bind: The Story of an Afro-Cherokee Family in Slavery and Freedom* (Berkeley: University of California Press, 2005), 168; Karen M. Woods, "A 'Wicked and Mischievous Connection': The Origins of Indian-White Miscegenation Law," *Legal Studies Forum* 23, nos. 1–2 (1999): 64–68; Fay Yarbrough, "Legislating Women's Sexuality: Cherokee Marriage Laws in the Nineteenth Century," *Journal of Social History* 38, no. 2 (2004): 389–95. Scholars, who have just begun to examine this aspect of the history of miscegenation law, have so far focused most of their attention on the written law codes of the five "civilized" tribes, but there are some indications that in later years other tribes, including the Pamunkey and Chickahominy of Virginia, also punished tribal members who married Blacks. See Phyl Newbeck, *Virginia Hasn't Always Been for Lovers: Interracial Marriage Bans and the Case of Richard and Mildred Loving* (Carbondale: Southern Illinois University Press, 2004), 32.

28. Brilliant analyses of the links between marriage, civil rights, and political equality can be found in Cott, *Public Vows*; Amy Dru Stanley, *From Bondage to Contract: Wage Labor, Marriage, and the Market in the Age of Slave Emancipation* (Cambridge: Cambridge University Press, 1998); and Laura F. Edwards, *Gendered Strife and Confusion: The Political Culture of Reconstruction* (Urbana: University of Illinois Press, 1997).

29. See the discussion of "The Doctrine of the Unity of Husband and Wife," in Joel Prentiss Bishop, *Commentaries on the Law of Married Women,* vol. 1 (Boston: Little, Brown, 1873), 19–21.

30. Hendrik Hartog, "Marital Exits and Marital Expectations in Nineteenth Century America," *Georgetown Law Journal* 30 (1991): 129.

31. Grossberg, *Governing the Hearth,* 233–57; Hendrik Hartog, *Man and Wife in America: A History* (Cambridge: Harvard University Press, 2000), 193–217; Rebecca M. Ryan, "The Sex Right: A Legal History of the Marital Rape Exemption," *Law and Social Inquiry* 20 (Fall 1995): 963–68. Although the father's right to custody eroded in the late nineteenth century as more and more people considered it inappropriate for a society that claimed to celebrate motherhood, the marital rape exemption lasted into the 1970s.

32. Linda K. Kerber, "The Paradox of Women's Citizenship in the Early Republic: The Case of *Martin v. Massachusetts, 1805,*" *American Historical Review* 97 (April 1992): 351. See also Bishop, *Married Women,* 22–25.

33. Bardaglio, *Reconstructing the Household,* 31–33; Cott, *Public Vows,* 52–53; Jeanne Boydston, *Home and Work: Housework, Wages and the Ideology of Labor in the Early Republic* (New York: Oxford University Press, 1990), 142–63.

34. Joel Prentiss Bishop, *Commentaries on the Law of Marriage and Divorce, and Evidence in Matrimonial Suits,* 3rd ed. (Boston: Little, Brown, 1859), 35; Cott, *Public Vows,* 5–7, 9–11, 14–15.

35. Bishop, *Marriage,* 117–26; James Schouler, *A Treatise on the Law of the Domestic Relations* (Boston: Little, Brown, 1870), 47–49.

36. Grossberg, *Governing the Hearth,* 69–85; Cott, *Public Vows,* 30–40.

37. Bennett Smith, *Marriage by Bond in Colonial Texas* (Fort Worth: privately printed, 1972), esp. 45–48; An Act to Legalise Certain Marriages, sec. 9, 1837 Repub. Texas Laws 233; Ocie Speer, *A Treatise on the Law of Marital Rights in Texas* (Rochester, N.Y.: Lawyers Co-operative Publishing, 1929), 12, 24–25, 32–58. Like marriage by bond, putative marriage offered a way to protect the property relationships established in marriages that did not fit official requirements; built on Spanish legal precedents, it covered people who entered into a marriage in good faith but later learned of a legal "impediment" to their union.

38. Bishop, *Marriage,* 36.

39. Isaac F. Redfield, *The Law of Wills,* 2nd ed. (Boston: Little, Brown, 1866–1870), 1:455 (citing Buchanan), 2:333.

40. *Howard v. Howard,* 51 N.C. 235, 236 (6 Jones) (1858); Margaret Burnham, "An Impossible Marriage: Slave Law and Family Law," *Law and Inequality* 5 (1987): 187–225; Cott, *Public Vows,* 32–35; Grossberg, *Governing the Hearth,* 129–32; Robert B. Shaw, *A Legal History of Slavery in the United States* (Potsdam, N.Y.: Northern Press, 1991), 165–66.

41. Alison D. Morantz, "There's No Place Like Home: Homestead Exemption and Judicial Construction of Family in Nineteenth-Century America," *Law and History Review* 24 (Summer 2006): 245–95; Suzanne D. Lebsock, "Radical Reconstruction and the Property Rights of Southern Women," *Journal of Southern History* 43, no. 2 (1977): 202–6; Carole Shammas, Marylynn Salmon, and Michel Dahlin, *Inheritance in America from Colonial Times to the Present* (New Brunswick: Rutgers University Press, 1987), 63–79, 83–101.

42. Tapping Reeve, *The Law of Baron and Femme,* 3rd ed. (Albany: William Gould, 1862), 404; Schouler, *Domestic Relations,* 408–13; Shammas et al., *Inheritance in America,* 71–72, 84–86; Redfield, *Law of Wills* (vol. 1, 1866), 465–67. The major exception to this pattern was Louisiana, where state law provided that a man could will 10 percent of his estate to a concubine. See Judith K. Schafer, "'Open and Notorious Concubinage': The Emancipation of Slave Mistresses by Will and the Supreme Court in Antebellum Louisiana," *Louisiana History* 28 (Spring 1987): 168–69.

43. An Act to Amend the Law Concerning Marriage, ch. 19, sec. 3, 1822 Tenn. Acts 22.

44. Ill. Rev. Stat. (1845), ch. 69, sec. 2, 353.

45. *Miscegenation: The Theory of the Blending of the Races, Applied to the American White Man and Negro* (New York: Dexter, Hamilton, 1864), 1, 49. For interpretation,

see Sidney Kaplan, "The Miscegenation Issue in the Election of 1864," *Journal of Negro History* 34 (1949): 274–343, and Elise Lemire, *"Miscegenation": Making Race in America* (Philadelphia: University of Pennsylvania Press, 2002), 116–44.

46. David R. Roediger, *The Wages of Whiteness: Race and the Making of the American Working Class* (London: Verso, 1991), 156.

47. *Miscegenation,* 28–29.

48. An Act to Prohibit Marriages and Cohabitation of Whites with Indians, Chinese, Mulattoes and Negroes, ch. 32, 1861 Nev. Terr. Stat. 93; An Act to Regulate Marriages, sec. 3, 1862 Or. Gen. Laws 85; An Act to Prohibit Marriages and Cohabitation of Whites with Indians, Chinese and Persons of African Descent, 1864 Idaho Terr. Laws 604; An Act Amendatory of Chapter Thirty, Thirty-one, and Thirty-two, Howell Code, ch. 30, 1865 Ariz. Terr. Sess. Laws 58.

49. An Act to Declare the Rights of Persons of African Descent, no. 35, sec. 2, 1867 Ark. Acts 99; Del. Rev. Stat., title 11, ch. 74, sec. 1 (1874); Article 95 of the Louisiana Civil Code, the language of which had been adopted in 1808, remained in force until it was repealed in 1868; Tenn. Comp. Laws (1873), title 4, ch. 1, art. 1, sec. 2437, 1097; An Act to Define and Declare the Rights of Persons Lately Known as Slaves, and Free Persons of Color, ch. 128, sec 2, 1866 Tex. Laws 131; Va. Code (1873), title 31, ch. 105, sec. 1 and title 54, ch. 192, sec. 8–9.

50. Va. Code (1860), ch. 109, sec. 1, 529; An Act to Repeal Certain Provisions of the Code of Virginia Concerning Slaves and Free Negroes [but not including miscegenation law], ch. 66, 1863 W. Va. Acts 62; W. Va. Code (1870), ch. 64, sec. 1, 3; ch. 149, sec. 4, 8, 9, pp. 440, 693–94.

51. An Act to Confer Civil Rights on Freedmen, and for Other Purposes, ch. 4, sec. 3, 1865 Miss. Laws 82; An Act to Establish and Regulate the Domestic Relations of Persons of Color, no. 4733, sec. 8, 1864–65 S.C. Acts 291.

52. An Act to Carry into Effect the Ninth Clause of the First Section of the Fifth Article of the Constitution, title 31, no. 254, 1865–66 Geo. Acts 241; An Act to Repeal...Sections of Article 30 of the Code of Public General Laws, Title "Crimes and Punishments," ch. 64, 1867 Md. Laws 93.

53. Ala. Penal Code (1866), ch. 5, sec. 61–62; An Act in Addition to an Act to Amend the Act Entitled an Act Concerning Marriage Licenses, ch. 1468, 1865–66 Fla. Acts 30; An Act in Relation to the Marriage of Negroes and Mulattoes, no. 37, sec. 3, in *A Digest of the General Laws of Kentucky* (Cincinnati: R. Clarke, 1866), 734, 735; Mo. Gen. Stat. (1866), ch. 113, sec. 2, 458; An Act Concerning Negroes and Persons of Color or of Mixed Blood, ch. 40, sec. 8, 1866 N.C. Laws 99, 101; An Act to Prevent Intermarriage between White Persons and Those of Negro, or Mongolian Blood, ch. 83, 1869 Wyo. Terr. Laws 706.

54. An Act to Confer Civil Rights on Freedmen, and for Other Purposes, ch. 4, sec. 3, 1865 Miss. Laws 82.

55. Ala. Const. of 1865, art. 4, sec. 31; Geo. Const. of 1865, art. 5, sec. 4988.

56. An Act to Protect all Persons in the United States in their Civil Rights, and Furnish the Means of their Vindication, ch. 31, 14 Stat. 27, 27 (1866); U.S. Const., amend. 14, sec. 1 (adopted 1868).

57. Hannah Rosen, "The Rhetoric of Miscegenation and the Reconstruction of Race: Debating Marriage, Sex, and Citizenship in Postemanicaption Arkansas," in *Gender and*

Slave Emancipation in the Atlantic World, ed. Pamela Scully and Diana Paton (Durham: Duke University Press, 2005), 289–309; Emily Field Van Tassel, "'Only the Law Would Rule Between Us': Antimiscegenation, the Moral Economy of Dependency, and the Debate over Rights After the Civil War," *Chicago-Kent Law Review* 70 (1995): 873–926.

58. See Theodore Brantner Wilson, *The Black Codes of the South* (University: University of Alabama Press, 1965), 73–74, 99, 103, 106.

59. Katherine M. Franke, "Emancipation Approximation," unpublished ms. circa 2007, ch. 5, passim; Cott, *Public Vows,* 82–89.

60. Philip S. Foner and George E. Walker, eds., *Proceedings of the Black National and State Conventions, 1865–1900* (Philadelphia: Temple University Press, 1986). By the end of the 1870s, however, African Americans in Texas had begun to protest the laws. One such protest arose at the Colored Conference held in 1879; another took place at the Texas Convention of Colored Men in 1883, where delegates complained that their state's miscegenation law punished intermarriage as a felony and cohabitation with a minor fine. They recommended that the legislature pass a law increasing the penalty for interracial sex in order to "stop the tide of immorality that now makes such inroads upon the morals of some of our most promising females." Robinson, *Dangerous Liaisons,* 47; *Proceedings of the State Convention of Colored Men of Texas* (Houston: Smallwood & Gray, 1883), 14.

61. Bardaglio, *Reconstructing the Household,* 178; Steven A. Bank, "Anti-Miscegenation Laws and the Dilemma of Symmetry: The Understanding of Equality in the Civil Rights Act of 1875," *University of Chicago Law School Roundtable* 2, no. 1 (1995): 315; Paul C. Palmer, "Miscegenation as an Issue in the Arkansas Constitutional Convention of 1868," *Arkansas Historical Quarterly* 24 (1965): 102–5.

62. Rosen, "Rhetoric of Miscegenation," 289–90, 302–4; John G. Price, ed., *Debates and Proceedings of the Convention... to Form a Constitution for the State of Arkansas* (Little Rock: J. G. Price, 1868), 501, 363.

63. Quoted in Herbert G. Gutman, *The Black Family in Slavery and Freedom, 1750–1925* (New York: Vintage Books, 1976), 388.

64. *State v. Hairston,* 63 N.C. 451, 453 (1869); *Lonas v. State,* 50 Tenn. 287, 311 (1871); *Scott v. Georgia,* 39 Ga. 321 (1869); *In re Hobbs,* 12 F. Cas. 262 (C.C.N.D. Ga. 1871) (No. 6550).

65. Adrienne D. Davis, "The Private Law of Race and Sex: An Antebellum Perspective," *Stanford Law Review* 51 (January 1999): 223–25.

66. Except for two short accounts in Robinson, *Dangerous Liaisons,* 31–32, and Wallenstein, *Tell the Court,* 86–88, the *Foster* case has received very little attention.

67. Slaveowner figures, County-Level Results, 1860, Historical Census Browser, Geospatial and Statistical Data Center, http://fisher.lib.virginia.edu/collections/stats/histcensus/ (accessed October 23, 2006); Black population figures, *Statistics of the Population of the United States at the Tenth Census* (June 1, 1880) (Washington: GPO, 1883), 79, 409; Wharton, *Fort Bend County,* 76, 178–82; Fort Bend County Probate Minutes and Records, 1868–78, vol. D, pp. 260, 420, Microfilm Reel 1007986, George Memorial Library, Richmond, Texas; Transcript, 7–8, FCF.

68. An Act to Legalise Certain Marriages, sec. 9, 1837 Repub. Texas Laws 233; Unlawful Marriage, title 12, ch. 1, 1858 Tex. Laws 164. The 1858 legislature had also passed a provision subjecting "every white person who shall live in adultery or fornication

with a negro, or a person of mixed blood, descended from negro ancestry, to the third generation inclusive" to fines of $100 to $1,000. Of Incest, Adultery and Fornication, title 12, ch. 2, 1858 Tex. Laws 165. The 1837 ban, which had originally been passed by the Republic of Texas, was carried into the state of Texas without interruption.

69. On the extent to which interracial marriage was seen as a threat to white manhood, see Rosen, "Rhetoric of Miscegenation," 291–300, and Van Tassel, "Only the Law," 896–98, 909, 918.

70. Transcript, 19–21, FCF.

71. Transcript, 22–25.

72. Transcript, 22.

73. Transcript, 40–41.

74. Walter Prescott Webb, ed., *The Handbook of Texas,* vol. 2 (Austin: Texas State Historical Association, 1952), 59; George E. Shelley, "The Semicolon Court of Texas," *Southwestern Historical Quarterly* 48 (April 1945): 450–51; Jewette Harbert Davenport, *History of the Supreme Court of the State of Texas, with Biographies of the Chief and Associate Justices* (Austin: Southern Law Book Publishers, 1917), 90–91.

75. Transcript, 47–51, FCF.

76. Transcript, 48–52.

77. Population Schedules of the 7th Census of the United States, 1850, NARA Microfilm M432, Reel 910, Fort Bend County, entry 114; Population Schedules of the 8th Census of the United States, 1860, NARA Microfilm M 653, Reel 1294, Fort Bend County, Richmond, entries 155 and 340; Population Schedules of the 9th Census of the United States, 1870, NARA Microfilm M593, Reel 1585, Texas, Fort Bend County, Richmond, p. 596 and entry 579; FBTX; Michael R. Moore, Director, Fort Bend Museum Association, to the author, September 10, 1996.

78. For descriptions of similar attitudes among Texas Whites, see Barry A. Crouch, *The Freedmen's Bureau and Black Texans* (Austin: University of Texas Press, 1992), 23–24, and Charles W. Ramsdell, *Reconstruction in Texas* (New York: Columbia University, 1910), 70–75.

79. Brief of Appellants, January 16, 1872, 5–6, FCF.

80. Brief of Appellants, 1–3.

81. U.S. Const., amend. 14, sec. 1 (adopted 1868); *Bonds v. Foster,* 36 Tex. 68, 69 (1872).

82. *Bonds,* 36 Tex. at 70.

83. An Act Relating to Marriages Between Individuals of Certain Races, ch. 5, 1843 Mass. Acts 4. For accounts of this fascinating episode, see Louis Ruchames, "Race, Marriage and Abolition in Massachusetts," *Journal of Negro History* 40 (July 1955), 250–73; *NA,* 149–53; Andrew Kull, *The Color-Blind Constitution* (Cambridge: Harvard University Press, 1992), 22–39.

84. Iowa Code (1851), title 17, ch. 85, 162; An Act in Relation to Marriage, ch. 49, 1858 Kan. Terr. Laws 325.

85. An Act to Repeal an Act Entitled "An Act Concerning Free Negroes," 1865–66 New Mex. Terr. Laws 90; An Act Relative to Marriages, no. 210, sec. 4, 1868 La. Acts 276, 277; S.C. Const. of 1868, art. 1, sec. 39; An Act to Amend an Act Entitled an Act to Regulate Marriages, January 23, 1868, in *Laws of Washington: A Publication of the Session Laws of Washington Territory* (Seattle: Tribune Printing, 1896),

2:431; An Act to Repeal Certain Laws Relating to Slaves, Free Negroes and Mulattoes and Freedmen, ch. 10, 1870 Miss. Laws 73.

86. See *A Digest of the Statues of Arkansas* (Little Rock: Little Rock Print. and Pub., 1874), ch. 92; Ill. Rev. Stat. (1874), ch. 89; Allen H. Bush, comp., *A Digest of the Statute Law of Florida of a General and Public Character, in Force Up to the First Day of January, 1872* (Tallahassee: C. W. Walton, 1872), ch. 117.

87. *Burns v. State*, 48 Ala. 195 (1872); *Bonds v. Foster*, 36 Tex. 68 (1872); *Honey v. Clark*, 37 Tex. 686 (1873); *State v. Webb* (1st Jud. Dist. Tex. 1877), 4 *Central Law Journal* 588; *Ex parte Lou Brown* (C.C.W.D. Tex. 1877), 5 *Central Law Journal* 149.

88. *Hart v. Hoss*, 26 La. Ann. 90 (1874); *Dickerson v. Brown*, 49 Miss. 357 (1873); *State v. Ross*, 76 N.C. 242 (1877).

89. Although its state supreme court upheld one particular interracial marriage, I have omitted North Carolina from this count because its court also issued decisions refusing to uphold such marriages. Peter Wallenstein was the first scholar to emphasize the breadth of Reconstruction-era changes; see his pathbreaking account in *Tell the Court*, 69–93.

90. Schouler, *Domestic Relations*, 29.

91. Footnote q, in Bush, *A Digest of the Statute Law of Florida*, p. 578; Bardaglio, *Reconstructing the Household*, 289, n. 19; Wallenstein, *Tell the Court*, 80.

92. *Honey v. Clark*, 37 Tex. 686 (1873); *Dickerson v. Brown*, 49 Miss. 357 (1873).

93. *Hart v. Hoss*, 26 La. Ann. 90 (1874).

94. *Lonas v. State*, 50 Tenn. 287, 298–99 (1871); my emphasis.

95. *Dickerson v. Brown*, 49 Miss. 357, 362, 375 (1873).

96. *State v. Webb* (1st Jud. Dist. Tex. 1877), 4 *Central Law Journal* 588.

97. *Burns v. State*, 48 Ala. 195, 197–98 (Alabama, 1872).

98. Entry for Thomas Wood and Echie Bunch, in Colored Marriage Index, January 13, 1872, Book 3, p. 463; Indictment, April 3, 1872, City Court Criminal Minute Book 9, p. 79, both in University Archives, University of South Alabama, Mobile; *Burns v. State*, 48 Ala. at 198, 196. Burns is identified as "white" in Population Schedules of the 9th Census of the United States, 1870, NARA Microfilm M593, Reel 31, p. 112, lines 38–40. Charges against Wood and Bunch were dismissed before the *Burns* trial. See City Court Criminal Minute Book 9, p. 125.

99. *State v. Ross*, 76 N.C. 242 (1877).

100. *Ex parte Lou Brown* (C.C.W.D. Tex. 1877), 5 *Central Law Journal* 149 at 149.

101. Entries for Leah Foster, Fields Foster and Bros., Field Foster, Monroe Foster, George Foster, and John Milton, FBTX.

102. On these developments, see Carl H. Moneyhon, *Republicanism in Reconstruction Texas* (Austin: University of Texas Press, 1980), 152–96; Rice, *Negro in Texas*, 113–39, 151–83; Barr, *Black Texans*, 70–111; Pitre, *Through Many Dangers*, 130–81; Wharton, *Fort Bend County*, 190–221; Sowell, *Fort Bend County*, 326–32.

Chapter 2

1. Vanderburgh County Marriage Records, vol. 6, July 12, 1867–May 21, 1870, p. 536, Reel 1479312, Church of Jesus Christ of Latter-day Saints Family History Center, Salt Lake City, Utah; *Evansville Journal*, April 16, 1870; Indictment, April 12,

1870, in Transcript of Record, 4–5, GCF; Population Schedules of the 9th Census of the United States, 1870, NARA Microfilm Publications M593, Reel 364, Indiana, Vanderburgh County, p. 468. The census, which recorded Gibson as "black" and his wife as "white," misnames Jennie Williams as "Nancy"; it identifies her two-year-old daughter, Rosellea, as a "white" female.

2. "The Miscegenation Case," *Evansville Courier,* July 12, 1870, 4; "Evansville," *Indianapolis Journal,* July 12, 1870, 1; Emma Lou Thornbrough, *The Negro in Indiana Before 1900: A Study of a Minority* (1957; Bloomington: Indiana University Press, 1993), 267.

3. *Frasher v. State,* 3 Tex. Ct. App. 263, 265 (Tex. Ct. App. 1877); *Ex parte Francois,* 9 F. Cas. 699, 700 (C.C.W.D. Tex. 1879) (No. 5047); *State v. Kennedy,* 76 N.C. 251, 251 (1877); *State v. Bell,* 66 Tenn. 9, 9 (1872); the date of the ceremony is in Transcript of Record, 4, Box 195, *State v. Bell,* Tennessee Supreme Court Cases, Tennessee State Library and Archives, Nashville; *Kinney v. Commonwealth,* 71 Va. 858, 859 (1879); *Compilation of the Laws in Force in the District of Columbia, April 1, 1868* (Washington: GPO, 1868), 159–61; *Ex parte Kinney,* 14 F. Cas. 602, 603 (C.C.E.D. Va. 1879) (No. 7825).

4. Geo. Const. of 1865, art. 5, sec. 4988; An Act to Carry into Effect the Ninth Clause of the First Section of the Fifth Article of the Constitution, title 31, no. 254, 1865–66 Geo. Acts 241; Geo. Const. of 1868, art. 1, sec. 11; *Scott v. Georgia,* 39 Ga. 321, 322 (1869); *In re Hobbs,* 12 F. Cas. 262, 262 (C.C.N.D. Ga. 1871) (No. 6550); Prosecutor's Charge, August 4, 1871, In re Hobbs, U.S. District Court File no. 1301, Box 4, Record Group 21, B 081/09/75, NARA, Southeast Region, Atlanta, Georgia.

5. *State v. Reinhardt,* 63 N.C. 547, 547 (1869); *Lonas v. State,* 50 Tenn. 287, 287, 300 (1871).

6. "Major A. L. Robinson," *Evansville Daily Journal,* February 28, 1883, 4; E. D. Eames to Wm. H. English, January 31, 1888, in William H. English Collection, M 98, Box 69, Folder 7, Indiana State Historical Society, Indianapolis; Frank M. Gilbert, *History of the City of Evansville and Vanderburg County, Indiana* (Chicago: Pioneer Publishing, 1910), 1:176; Gwen Crenshaw, *"Bury Me in a Free Land": The Abolitionist Movement in Indiana, 1816–1865* (Indianapolis: Indiana Historical Bureau, 1986), 26–27; *History of Vanderburgh County, Indiana, from the Earliest Times to the Present* (Madison, Wisc.: Brant & Fuller, 1889), 349–51, 384–85; Rebecca A. Shepherd, ed., *A Biographical Directory of the Indiana General Assembly* (Indianapolis: Indiana Historical Bureau, 1980–), 1:335.

7. Thornbrough, *The Negro in Indiana,* 267; Darrel E. Bigham, *We Ask Only a Fair Trial: A History of the Black Community of Evansville, Indiana* (Bloomington: Indiana University Press, 1987), 50.

8. Transcript of Record, 5, GCF; Edward White, *Evansville and Its Men of Mark* (Evansville: Historical Publishing, 1873), 100–101; *History of Vanderburgh County,* 374; Leander J. Monks, *Courts and Lawyers of Indiana* (Indianapolis: Federal Publishing, 1916), 3:1051–52; Population Schedules of the 9th Census of the United States, 1870, 468.

9. On the cover page of the Transcript of Record there is a handwritten note that the case was "submitted by agreement A. L. Robinson for appellee W. P. Hargrave Pros. Atty"; both men appear to have signed their names.

10. On the remarkably wide range of state police power in this period, see William J. Novak, *People's Welfare: Law and Regulation in Nineteenth-Century America* (Chapel Hill: University of North Carolina Press, 1996), esp. 13–17 and 235–37.

11. An Act to Reduce into One Act, All the Acts and Parts of Acts Relative to Crime and Punishment, ch. 5, sec. 59, 1818 Ind. Laws 75, 94; An Act to Repeal the Fourth Section of an Act to Amend an Act, Entitled an Act to Regulate Marriages, ch. 37, 1820–21 Ind. Laws 94; Thornbrough, *The Negro in Indiana*, 58, 119–28, 160–67; An Act to Prohibit the Amalgamation of Whites and Blacks, ch. 14, 1839–40 Ind. Laws 32; Bigham, *Fair Trial*, 4.

12. Ind. Const. of 1851, art. 13, sec. 1–2.

13. *Barkshire v. State*, 7 Ind. 309, 310–11 (1856); Thornbrough, *The Negro in Indiana*, 72–73.

14. Levi Coffin, *Reminiscences of Levi Coffin, the Reputed President of the Underground Railroad* (1898: New York: Arno Reprints, 1968), 155–60. Other accounts include "Miscegenation Again—Holloway's Indianapolis," *Indianapolis Sentinel*, January 20, 1872, 3; Jacob Piatt Dunn, *Greater Indianapolis: The History, the Industries, the Institutions, and the People of a City of Homes* (Chicago: Lewis Publishing, 1910), 1:240–41; Thornbrough, *The Negro in Indiana*, 125–27; and *NA*, 176–77.

15. An Act to Prohibit the Amalgamation of Whites and Blacks, ch. 14, sec. 4, 1839–40 Ind. Laws 32. All that remained was to find a way to void the marriage of Sophia Spears Wilson, which had taken place before the enactment of the bill. To this end, a delegation of leading citizens pressured her into petitioning the legislature for a divorce, which the legislature promptly granted. "Legislative," *Indiana Journal*, February 15, 1840, 3; see also *NA*, 177–82.

16. Emma Lou Thornbrough, *Indiana in the Civil War Era, 1850–1880* (Indianapolis: Indiana Historical Bureau, 1965), 75, 85–96; Henry Ellis Cheaney, "Attitudes of the Indiana Pulpit and Press Towards the Negro, 1860–1880" (Ph.D. dissertation, University of Chicago, 1961), 316–18; *Smith v. Moody*, 26 Ind. 299 (1866); Thornbrough, *The Negro in Indiana*, 231–54; Madison, *Indiana Way*, 205–7; Bigham, *Fair Trial*, 38.

17. Madison, *Indiana Way*, 205–9; Thornbrough, *Civil War Era*, 239–51.

18. As noted in chapter 1, Georgia and South Carolina had passed colonial-era laws, but they did not survive into statehood. Alabama and Georgia did not pass their first state laws against interracial marriage until 1852; South Carolina did not do so until 1865. *NA*, 339–439.

19. *NA*, 339–439.

20. An Act to Prohibit the Amalgamation of Whites and Blacks, ch. 14, 1839–40 Ind. Laws 32; An Act to Amend an Act Entitled an Act to Prohibit the Amalgamation of Whites and Blacks, ch. 46, 1840–41 Ind. Laws, 128; An Act to Prohibit the Amalgamation of Whites and Blacks, ch. 130, 1841–42 Ind. Laws 142.

21. Robert M. Taylor Jr., Errol Wayne Stevens, Mary Ann Ponder, and Paul Brockman, *Indiana: A New Historical Guide* (Indianapolis: Indiana Historical Society, 1989), 187–89; Bigham, *Fair Trial*, 22.

22. Thornbrough, *The Negro in Indiana*, 209–10; Bigham, *Fair Trial*, 38–39; Monks, *Courts and Lawyers* 1:348–49; Samuel H. Buskirk, *The Practice on Appeals to the Supreme Court of Indiana* (Indiana: Jay V. Olds, 1876), 3.

23. Appellee's Brief, 1, GCF.

24. *Barkshire,* 7 Ind. at 390; Buskirk, *Practice on Appeals,* 326.

25. *Gibson,* 36 Ind. at 390, 394, 402, 392, 402.

26. *Gibson,* 36 Ind. at 400–403, 405.

27. Ala. Code (1852), title 5, ch. 1, art. 1, sec. 1956, 377; Ala. Penal Code (1866), ch. 5, sec. 61–62.

28. For slightly different interpretations of these cases, and Sanford's involvement in them, see Peter Wallenstein, *Tell the Court I Love My Wife: Race, Marriage, and Law—An American History* (New York: Palgrave Macmillan, 2002), 71–80, and Julie Novkov, *Racial Union: Law, Intimacy, and the White State in Alabama, 1865–1954* (Ann Arbor: University of Michigan Press, 2008), 40–58.

29. *Ellis v. State,* 42 Ala. 525, 527 (1868).

30. *Burns v. State,* 48 Ala. 195, 198 (1872); *Hoover v. State,* 59 Ala. 57, 58 (1877); *Green v. State,* 58 Ala. 190, 191 (1877).

31. *Scott v. Georgia,* 39 Ga. 321, 322–23 (1869). "The amalgamation of the races," the court declared, "is not only unnatural, but is always productive of deplorable results. Our daily observation shows us, that the offspring of these unnatural connections are generally sickly and effeminate, and that they are inferior in physical development and strength, to the full-blood of either race." For especially insightful interpretations of the *Scott* case, see Charles F. Robinson II, *Dangerous Liaisons: Sex and Love in the Segregated South* (Fayetteville: University of Arkansas Press, 2003), 35–38, and Emily Field Van Tassel, "'Only the Law Would Rule Between Us': Antimiscegenation, the Moral Economy of Dependency, and the Debate over Rights After the Civil War," *Chicago-Kent Law Review* 70 (1995): 909–14.

32. *Hairston,* 63 N.C. at 451.

33. *Ford v. State,* 53 Ala. 150, 151 (1875).

34. *Green,* 58 Ala. at 191.

35. *Green,* 58 Ala. at 194, 192, 195.

36. *Clements v. Crawford,* 42 Tex. 601, 604 (1875).

37. *Frasher,* 3 Tex. Ct. App. at 265, 274, 276. But because Ector thought it possible that Frasher's wife, Lettuce Hall, had some "white blood in her," the court reversed Frasher's conviction and ordered a new trial.

38. An Act to Amend and Re-Enact Article 94 of the Revised Civil Code of Louisiana of 1870, no. 54, 1894 La. Acts 63; An Act in Relation to Marriage and Divorce, Miss. Rev. Stat. ch. 42, sec. 1147 (1880); An Act to Prevent and Punish the Intermarrying of Races, no. 5, 1879–80 S.C. Acts 3; ch. 103, sec. 4593 (1883), in *A Digest of the Statutes of Arkansas,* ed. W. W. Mansfield (Little Rock: Mitchell & Bettis, 1884), 911; An Act to Prevent the Improper Living Together of Certain Persons, ch. 3282, and An Act Relating to the Intermarriage of White Persons with Persons of Color, ch. 3283, 1881 Fla. Laws 85–86.

39. Of Offences Against Morality and Decency, ch. 7, sec. 8, 1876–77 Va. Acts 301, 302; Mo. Rev. Stat., ch. 24, art. 8, sec. 1540 (1879).

40. An Act to Amend Art. 30 of the Code of Public General Laws...by Adding Thereto an Additional Section Forbidding Marriages Between White Persons and Persons of Negro Descent to the Third Generation, ch. 264, 1884 Md. Laws 365.

41. Sec. 8, Inter-marriage Between Choctaws and Negroes, in *Constitution and Laws of the Choctaw Nation,* ed. A. R. Durant (1894; Wilmington: Scholarly Resources, 1973), 206.

42. N.C. Const. of 1868, art. 14, sec. 8 (amendment adopted in 1876), in *Amend-ments to the Constitution of North Carolina Proposed by the Constitutional Convention of 1875* (Raleigh: Josiah Turner, 1875), 65; John V. Orth, *The North Carolina State Constitu-tion: A Reference Guide* (Westport, Conn.: Greenwood Press, 1993), 177; Fla. Const. of 1885, art. 16, sec. 24; Miss. Const., art. 14, sec. 263 (enacted 1890, repealed 1987), in *Annotated Code of the General Statute Laws of the State of Mississippi*, ed. R. H. Thomp-son, George G. Dillard, and R. B. Campbell (Nashville: Marshall & Bruce, 1892), 86; S.C. Const, art. 2, sec. 6 (amended so as to remove "miscegenation" in 1971) and art. 3, sec. 33 (repealed 1999), in *Constitution of the State of South Carolina, Ratified in Con-vention, December 4, 1895* (Abbeville, S.C.: Hugh Wilson, 1900), 11, 18; Ala. Const., art. 4, sec. 102 (repealed 2000). Most of these clauses prohibited marriages between "whites" and "negroes," but South Carolina's constitution also included a clause deny-ing persons convicted of a long list of crimes, including "miscegenation," the right to vote. On the history of this clause, see James Lowell Underwood, *The Constitution of South Carolina* (Columbia: University of South Carolina Press, 1994), 4:109–19.

43. *In re Hobbs*, 12 F. Cas. 262, 262 (C.C.N.D. Ga. 1871) (No. 6550).

44. *Ex parte Lou Brown* (C.C.W.D. Tex. 1877), 5 *Central Law Journal* 149; *Ex parte Francois*, 9 F. Cas. 699, 700 (C.C.W.D. Tex. 1879) (No. 5047).

45. *Ex parte Kinney*, 14 F. Cas. 602, 603 (C.C.E.D. Va. 1879) (No. 7825).

46. *Pace v. Alabama*, 106 U.S. 583 (1882).

47. *Pace*, 106 U.S. at 584; *Pace v. State*, 29 Ala. 231 (1881). For interpretations, see Novkov, *Racial Union*, 58–65; Wallenstein, *Tell the Court*, 110–14, 120–21; and Rachel F. Moran, *Interracial Intimacy: The Regulation of Race and Romance* (Chicago: University of Chicago Press, 2001), 79–81.

48. John R. Tompkins to Jos. Kinney, February 13, August [no day date], and January 5, 1883, PCF.

49. *Pace*, 29 Ala. at 232.

50. John R. Tompkins to Wm. B. Woods, April 5, 1882, PCF. A handwritten copy of the brief is in PCF; a printed copy, entitled "Brief of Jno. R. Tompkins, for Plaintiff in Error," is in File Copies of Briefs, 1882, vol. 12, October Term 1882, pp. 806–949, at the U.S. Supreme Court Library in Washington, D.C. References below are to the printed copy.

51. Brief for Plaintiff in Error, 4–5.

52. Brief for Plaintiff in Error, 1, 6–7.

53. *In re Ah Fong*, 1 F. Cas. 213, 214, 218 (C.C.D.Cal 1874) (No. 102); *Ho Ah Kow v. Nunan*, 12 F. Cas. 252, 255 (C.C.D.Cal. 1879) (No. 6546); Brief for Plaintiff in Error, 6.

54. *Pace v. Alabama*, 106 U.S. 583, 584–85 (1882); Tompkins to McKinney, Febru-ary 13, 1883, PCF.

55. As Maureen McNeil notes, the idea of nature "haunts and animates the contem-porary Western world in countless ways": for an introduction, see her discussion in *New Keywords: A Revised Vocabulary of Culture and Society*, ed. Tony Bennett, Lawrence Gross-berg, and Meaghan Morris (New York: Blackwell Publishing, 2005), 235–39.

56. *West Chester and Philadelphia Railroad Co. v. Miles*, 55 Pa. 209, 213 (1867). For an analysis of this case, see Barbara Young Welke, *Recasting American Liberty: Gender, Race, Law, and the Railroad Revolution, 1865–1920* (Cambridge: Cambridge University Press, 2001), 328–34.

57. The *West Chester* passage was cited, for example, in both *State v. Gibson*, 36 Ind. 389, 404–5 (1871) and *Green v. State*, 58 Ala. 190, 194 (1877).

58. *Scott v. State*, 39 Ga. 321, 323 (1869); *Ex parte Francois*, 9 F. Cas. 699, 701 (C.C.W.D. Tex. 1879) (No. 5047). *State v. Bell*, 66 Tenn. 9, 11 (1872); *Kinney v. Commonwealth*, 71 Va. 858, 869 (1878).

59. Ernst Freund, *The Police Power: Public Policy and Constitutional Rights* (1904; New York: Arno Press, 1976), 717.

60. *Bell*, 66 Tenn. at 11.

61. *State v. Hairston*, 63 N.C. 451, 452 (1869); *Frasher*, 3 Tex. Ct. App. at 263, 278.

62. *Lonas v. State*, 50 Tenn. 287, 310–13 (1871).

63. *State v. Gibson*, 36 Ind. 389, 404 (1871); *Green v. State*, 58 Ala. 190, 194 (1871).

64. *Green*, 58 Ala. at 195.

65. See, for example, *West Chester*, 55 Pa. at 213 (1867); *Cory v. Carter*, 48 Ind. 327, 353–54 (1874); *Plessy v. Ferguson*, 163 U.S. 537, 545 (1896); *Flood v. News and Courier Co.*, 71 S.C. 112, 118 (1905); *Wolfe v. Georgia Railway & Electric Company*, 2 Ga. App. 499, 507–9 (Ct. App. Ga. 1907); *Tucker v. Blease*, 97 S.C. 303, 325–26 (1914); *Tyler v. Harmon*, 158 La. 439, 449–50 (1925).

66. *Plessy v. Ferguson*, 163 U.S. 537, 545 (1896).

Chapter 3

1. An Act to Regulate Marriages, sec. 3, 1862 Or. Gen. Laws 85; H.B. no. 1, "House Bills no. 1–111," Box 13, 1866 Legislature, 4th Session, Record Group 61–117, Secretary of State, Oregon State Archives, Salem.

2. Oregon Donation Land Act, ch. 76, sec. 4–5, 9 Stat. 496, 497 (1850); James Gingles obituary, *Corvallis Gazette,* October 24, 1889, 2; David D. Fagan, *History of Benton County, Oregon* (Portland: A. G. Walling, 1885), 513.

3. David Alan Johnson, *Founding the Far West: California, Oregon, and Nevada, 1840–1890* (Berkeley: University of California Press, 1992), 42–44, 179–81; Gray H. Whaley, "Oregon, *Illahee,* and the Empire Republic: A Case Study of American Colonialism, 1843–1858," *Western Historical Quarterly* 36 (Summer 2005): 157–78; William G. Robbins, "Extinguishing Indian Land Title in Western Oregon," *Indian Historian* 7 (Spring 1974): 10–14; Fagan, *History of Benton County,* 379–80, 393; Janice K. Duncan, *Minority Without a Champion: Kanakas on the Pacific Coast, 1788–1850* (Portland: Oregon Historical Society, 1972), 17–18; An Act to Tax and Protect Chinamen Mining in Oregon, 1856–57 Or. Terr. Laws 13; Or. Const., art. 2, sec. 6 (repealed 1927) and art. 15, sec. 8 (repealed 1946); Of Poll-Tax on Negroes, Chinamen, Kanakas and Mulattoes, ch. 35 (1862), in *The Organic and Other General Laws of Oregon, 1845–1864,* ed. M. P. Deady (Portland: Henry L. Pittock, State Printer, 1866), 815.

4. *Journal of the Proceedings of the House of the Legislative Assembly of Oregon 1864* (Portland: Henry L. Pittock, State Printer, 1864), 57–58.

5. *Journal of the House During the Special Session 1865* (Salem: Henry L. Pittock, State Printer, 1866), 38, 56; Matthew Aeldun Charles Smith, "Wedding Bands and Marriage Bans: A History of Oregon's Racial Intermarriage Statutes and the Impact on Indian Interracial Nuptials" (M.A. thesis, Portland State University, 1997), 52.

6. "Oregon Legislature," *Daily Oregonian,* October 6, 1866; *Journal of the Proceedings of the House of the Legislative Assembly of Oregon* (Salem: W. A. McPherson, State Printer, 1866), 162, 286; *Journal of the Senate Proceedings of the Legislative Assembly of Oregon* (Salem: W. A. McPherson, State Printer, 1866), 236; An Act to Prohibit Amalgamation and the Intermarriage of Races, 1866 Or. Gen. Laws 10.

7. An Act to Prohibit Marriages and Cohabitation of Whites with Indians, Chinese, Mulattoes and Negroes, ch. 32, 1861 Nev. Terr. Stat. 93; An Act to Prohibit Marriages and Cohabitation of Whites with Indians, Chinese and Persons of African Descent, 1864 Idaho Terr. Laws 604; An Act Amendatory of Chapter Thirty, Thirty-one, and Thirty-two, Howell Code, ch. 30, 1865 Ariz. Terr. Sess. Laws 58; An Act to Prevent Intermarriage Between White Persons and Those of Negro, or Mongolian Blood, ch. 83, 1869 Wyo. Terr. Laws 706. During the period covered in this chapter, several western territories had not yet become full-fledged states. Territorial and state legislatures used much the same processes to pass miscegenation laws, and did so for much the same reasons, so I have decided not to emphasize the distinction between the two. For the record, though, Missouri became a state in 1821, California in 1850, Oregon in 1859, Nevada in 1864, Nebraska in 1867, and Colorado in 1876. North and South Dakota, Montana, and Washington all became states in 1889, Idaho and Wyoming in 1899, and Utah in 1896. Oklahoma (1907), New Mexico (1912), and Arizona (1912) did not become states until the twentieth century.

8. Studies of the racialization of Chinese and Japanese Americans in miscegenation law and interracial marriage include Susan Koshy, *Sexual Naturalization: Asian Americans and Miscegenation* (Stanford: Stanford University Press, 2004); Rachel F. Moran, *Interracial Intimacy: The Regulation of Race and Romance* (Chicago: University of Chicago Press, 2001), 28–36; Megumi Dick Osumi, "Asians and California's Anti-Miscegenation Laws," in *Asian and Pacific American Experiences: Women's Perspectives,* ed. Nobuya Tsuchida (Minneapolis: Asian/Pacific Learning Resource Center, 1982), 1–37; Hrishi Karthikeyan and Gabriel J. Chin, "Preserving Racial Identity: Population Patterns and the Application of Anti-Miscegenation Statutes to Asian Americans, 1910–1950," *Asian Law Journal* 9, no. 1 (2002):1–40; and Paul R. Spickard, *Mixed Blood: Intermarriage and Ethnic Identity in Twentieth-Century America* (Madison: University of Wisconsin Press, 1989), 23–158.

9. Randall E. Rohe, "After the Gold Rush: Chinese Mining in the Far West, 1850–1890," *Montana: The Magazine of Western History* 32 (Autumn 1982): 2–19; George Lipsitz, *The Possessive Investment in Whiteness: How White People Profit from Identity Politics* (Philadelphia: Temple University Press, 1998); James M. Schrugham, ed., *Nevada: A Narrative of the Conquest of a Frontier Land* (Chicago: American Historical Society, 1935), 1:137; Verne Blue, "Mining Laws of Jackson Country, 1860–1876," *Oregon Historical Quarterly* 23, no. 2 (1922): 143, 160.

10. An Act to Prohibit Marriages and Cohabitation of Whites with Indians, Chinese, Mulattoes and Negroes, ch. 32, 1861 Nev. Terr. Stat. 93; Anton P. Sohn, *The Healers of 19th-Century Nevada: A Compendium of Medical Practitioners* (Reno: Greasewood Press, 1997), 136; Andrew J Marsh, *Letters from Nevada Territory, 1861–62* (Carson City: Legislative Counsel Bureau, 1972), 449, 499; *Journal of the Proceedings of the House of the Legislative Assembly of Oregon 1864* (Portland: Henry L. Pittock, State Printer, 1864), 29, 38, 57–58.

11. Roger D. Hardaway, "Prohibiting Interracial Marriage: Miscegenation Laws in Wyoming," *Annals of Wyoming* 52 (Spring 1980): 55–56.

12. Julie Novkov, *Racial Union: Law, Intimacy, and the White State in Alabama, 1865–1954* (Ann Arbor: University of Michigan Press, 2008), 5; Eva Saks, "Representing Miscegenation Law," *Raritan* 8 (Fall 1988): 64; Robert G. Lee, *Orientals: Asian Americans in Popular Culture* (Philadelphia: Temple University Press, 1999), 7–8, 85; Karen J. Leong, "'A Distinct and Antagonistic Race': Constructions of Chinese Manhood in the Exclusionist Debates, 1869–1878," in *Across the Great Divide: Cultures of Manhood in the American West,* ed. Matthew Basso, Laura McCall, and Dee Garceau (New York: Routledge, 2001), 131–35.

13. *Debates and Proceedings of the Constitutional Convention of the State of California* (Sacramento: State Office, 1880), 1:633, 639, 647, 2:676, 682; Lee, *Orientals,* 83–84.

14. Jennifer Ting, "Bachelor Society: Deviant Heterosexuality and Asian American Historiography," in *Privileging Positions: The Sites of Asian American Studies,* ed. Marilyn Alquizola, Dorothy Fujita Rony, K. Scott Wong, and Gary Y. Okihiro (Pullman: Washington State University Press, 1995), 271–79; Moran, *Interracial Intimacy,* 30–31. Ting sets her sights well beyond popular imagery, using the concept of "deviant heterosexuality" to offer a wide-ranging critique of Asian American studies scholarship. On popular images of sexual deviance and contagion, see Lee, *Orientals,* 83–105; Nayan Shah, *Contagious Divides: Epidemics and Race in San Francisco's Chinatown* (Berkeley: University of California Press, 2001), 77–105.

15. *Debates and Proceedings* 1:225; Moran, *Interracial Intimacy,* 31; An Act to Amend Sections Sixty-Nine..., ch. 41, 1880 Cal. Code Amend. 3. "The said Clerk," the amendment to ch. 69, sec. 4 read, "shall not issue a license authorizing the marriage of a white person with a negro, mulatto, or Mongolian."

16. It should be noted, however, that Wyoming had also used the term "Mongolian" in its territorial law, which had been passed in 1869 and would be repealed in 1882. See Hardaway, "Prohibiting Interracial Marriage," 57.

17. *Debates and Proceedings* 2:717.

18. An Act Regulating Marriage, ch. 5, sec. 2584, 5–6, 1888 Utah Comp. Laws 92; Miss. Code Ann. 2859 (1892); An Act to Amend section 2853 of Hill's Annotated Laws of Oregon, Relating to Marriages, 1893 Or. Gen. Laws 41; An Act to Prohibit Amalgamation and the Intermarriage of Races, 1866 Or. Gen. Laws 10.

19. See, for example, Jacquelyn Dowd Hall, "'The Mind That Burns in Each Body': Women, Rape, and Racial Violence," in *Powers of Desire: The Politics of Sexuality,* ed. Ann Snitow, Christine Stansell, and Sharon Thompson (New York: Monthly Review Press, 1983), 334–37; Mara L. Keire, "The Vice Trust: A Reinterpretation of the White Slavery Scare in the United States, 1907–1917," *Journal of Social History* 35 (Fall 2001): 6–7.

20. Moran, *Interracial Intimacy,* 35–36.

21. "Aoki Engaged to Daughter of Prelate," *San Francisco Chronicle,* March 3, 1909, 1; "Archdeacon Does Not Approve Alliance," *San Francisco Chronicle,* March 11, 1909, 9.

22. "Brother of Aoki Frowns on the Match," *San Francisco Chronicle,* March 12, 1909, 1; "Don't Want Aoki in Their Town," *San Francisco Chronicle,* March 15, 1909, 16; "Kissing Is Barred," *Morning Oregonian,* March 15, 1909, 2; "Both Families Are

Divided," *Oregonian*, March 25, 1909, 4; "Law Will Block Mesalliance Here," *Oregonian*, March 26, 1909, 3.

23. "Law Will Block Mesalliance," 1, 3; "A Disgusting Spectacle," *Oregonian*, March 26, 1909, 10.

24. An Act to Amend an Act, Entitled "An Act to Regulate Marriage," 1854–55 Wash. Terr. Laws 33; An Act to Amend an Act Entitled an Act to Regulate Marriages, January 23, 1868, in *Laws of Washington: A Publication of the Session Laws of Washington Territory* (Seattle: Tribune Printing, 1896), 2:431.

25. "Stapleton Would Object," *Oregonian*, March 26, 1909, 3; "Tacoma Will Not Say Nay," *Oregonian*, March 26, 1909, 3; "Aoki and Bride to Live on Farm," *Oregonian*, March 28, 1909, 8; "Japanese Succeeds in Winning White Bride," *San Francisco Chronicle*, March 28, 1909, 23.

26. "Becomes Bride of a Japanese," *San Francisco Chronicle*, April 1, 1909, 3; "To Wed Japanese Pastor of Los Angeles," *San Francisco Chronicle*, April 13, 1909, 1; "Deserted by Her Brown Husband," *San Francisco Chronicle*, April 22, 1909, 2.

27. The Nevada law had remained unchanged since its passage in 1861; An Act to Prohibit Marriages and Cohabitation of Whites with Indians, Chinese, Mulattoes and Negroes, ch. 32, 1861 Nev. Terr. Stat. 93.

28. Phillip I. Earl, "Nevada's Miscegenation Laws and the Marriage of Mr. and Mrs. Harry Bridges," *Nevada Historical Society Quarterly* 37 (Spring 1994): 4–6.

29. "Friend of Emery Family Seeks Medical Advice as to Whether Hypnotism Can Explain Girl's Wild Infatuation for Japanese," *San Francisco Chronicle*, March 12, 1909, 1; "Aoki Greets Girl Only for Moment," *Oregonian*, March 27, 1909, 10; "A Disgusting Spectacle," 10; "Wants Freedom From Japanese: Romance of a Seattle Girl Is Quickly Shattered After Wedding," *San Francisco Chronicle*, April 15, 1909, 12; Earl, "Nevada's Miscegenation Laws," 6.

30. An Act to Amend Section 4312 of Chapter 50 of the Revised Statutes of Missouri, 1909 Mo. Laws 662; An Act Prohibiting Inter-Marriage of Persons Belonging to the White Race with Persons Belonging to Certain Colored Races, ch. 266, 1913 S.D. Laws 405; An Act to Prohibit the Marriage of White Persons with Negroes, Mulattoes, Mongolians or Malays, ch. 57, 1913 Wyo. Sess. Laws; An Act Amending Section 4596 of Article I, Chapter 182 of the Compiled Statutes of Idaho, Relating to Marriages of Caucasians with Negroes, Mulattoes or Mongolians, ch. 115, 1921 Idaho Sess. Laws 291.

31. An Act Prohibiting Marriage Between White Persons and Negroes, Persons of Negro Blood, and Between White Persons, Chinese and Japanese, ch. 49, 1909 Mont. Laws 57; An Act to Amend Section 5302 of Cobbey's Annotated Statutes for 1911, Relating to Void Marriages, to Further Regulate the Marriage of White Persons with Those of Alien Blood, ch. 72, 1913 Neb. Laws 216.

32. Earl, "Nevada's Miscegenation Laws," 6–7.

33. *NA*, 288–92; An Act Prohibiting Inter-Marriage of Persons Belonging to the White Race with Persons Belonging to Certain Colored Races, ch. 266, 1913 S.D. Laws 405; An Act to Prohibit the Marriage of White Persons with Negroes, Mulattoes, Mongolians or Malays, ch. 57, 1913 Wyo. Sess. Laws.

34. Howard A. DeWitt, *Anti-Filipino Movements in California: A History, Bibliography, and Study Guide* (San Francisco: R and E Research Associates, 1976), 34, 40, 92;

An Act to Amend Sec. 2166, Rev. Code, 1928, Relating to Prohibited and Void Marriages, ch. 17, 1931 Ariz. Sess. Laws 27; An Act to Amend Sec. 60 of the Civil Code, Relating to Illegal and Void Marriages, ch. 104, and An Act to Amend Sec. 69 of the Civil Code, Relating to Marriage Licenses, ch. 105, 1933 Cal. Stat. 561; An Act Amending Sec. 40-1-2, Rev. Stat. of Utah, 1933, Relating to Prohibited and Void Marriages, ch. 50, sec. 6, 1939 Utah Laws 66.

35. Studies of the racialization of Indians in miscegenation law include Moran, *Interracial Intimacy*, 48–50; Karen M. Woods, "A 'Wicked and Mischievous Connection': The Origins and Development of Indian-White Miscegenation Law," *Legal Studies Forum* 23, nos. 1–2 (1999): 37–70; David D. Smits, "'We Are Not to Grow Wild': Seventeenth-Century New England's Repudiation of Anglo-Indian Intermarriage," *American Indian Culture and Research Journal* 11, no. 4 (1987): 1–32; David D. Smits, "'Abominable Mixture': Toward the Repudiation of Anglo-Indian Intermarriage in Seventeenth-Century Virginia," *Virginia Magazine of History and Biography* 95 (April 1987): 157–92.

36. *NA,* 31.

37. An Act for Suppressing Outlying Slaves, no. 16, April 1691, in *Statutes at Large, Being a Collection of all the Laws of Virginia,* ed. William Walter Hening (Philadelphia: Thomas Desilver, 1823), 3:86; An Act Concerning Servants and Slaves, sec. 16 (enacted 1715), *The State Records of North Carolina,* ed. Walter Clark (Goldsboro, N.C.: Nash Brothers, 1904), 23:65. The Virginia law was short-lived, but versions of North Carolina's prohibition on marriages between Whites and Indians remained on the books into the 1830s. See, for example, An Act Concerning Marriage, ch. 71, sec. 5–6, in *The Revised Statutes of the State of North Carolina, 1836–7,* ed. James Iredell and William H. Battle (Raleigh: Turner and Hughes, 1837), 1:385–87.

38. Peter Wallenstein, *Tell the Court I Love My Wife: Race, Marriage, and Law—An American History* (New York: Palgrave Macmillan, 2002), 13; Woods, "Wicked and Mischievous," 50–52; Smits, "Grow Wild," 3; Ann Plane, *Colonial Intimacies: Indian Marriage in Early New England* (Ithaca: Cornell University Press, 2000), 146–47; Smits, "Abominable Mixture," 157–58.

39. On these relationships, see Sylvia Van Kirk, *Many Tender Ties: Women in Fur-Trade Society* (Norman: University of Oklahoma Press, 1980); Michael Lansing, "Plains Indian Women and Interracial Marriage in the Upper Missouri Trade," *Western Historical Quarterly* 31 (Winter 2000): 413–33; Jennifer S. H. Brown, *Strangers in Blood: Fur Trade Company Families in Indian Country* (Vancouver: University of British Columbia Press, 1980); John Mack Faragher, "The Custom of the Country: Cross-Cultural Marriage in the Far Western Fur Trade," with commentaries by Deena J. González and Sylvia van Kirk, in *Western Women: Their Land, Their Lives,* ed. Lillian Schlissel, Vicki L. Ruiz, and Janice Monk (Albuquerque: University of New Mexico Press, 1988), 199–225; and Tanis C. Thorne, *The Many Hands of My Relations: French and Indians on the Lower Missouri* (Columbia: University of Missouri Press, 1996), 134–76.

40. Woods, "Indian-White Miscegenation Law," 54–58; Moran, *Interracial Intimacy,* 49.

41. An Act for the Orderly Solemnization of Marriages, ch. 3, 1786 Mass. Acts 439; Addition to "An Act to Prevent Clandestine Marriages," sec. 5, 1798 R.I. Pub. Laws 483; An Act for Regulating Marriage, ch. 70, sec. 2, in *Laws of the State*

of Maine, ed. Francis O. J. Smith (Portland: Thomas Todd and Colman, Holden, 1834), 1:419–20.

42. Amy Dru Stanley, *From Bondage to Contract: Wage Labor, Marriage, and the Market in the Age of Slave Emancipation* (Cambridge: Cambridge University Press, 1998), 10–11.

43. Parts of Tennessee had originally been claimed by North Carolina, and the new state relied heavily on North Carolina law. According to Tennessee judge Edward Scott, North Carolina's miscegenation law of 1741, which banned "white men and women intermarrying with Indians, negroes, and mustees, or mulattoes," was in effect in Tennessee until 1821. In 1822, however, Tennessee passed a miscegenation law of its own, which prohibited "any white men or women" from marrying "a negro, mustee, or mulatto" but dropped the word "Indian." An Act Concerning Marriages (1741), ch. 1, sec. 13–14, in Edward Scott, ed., *Laws of the State of Tennessee, Including Those of North Carolina Now in Force in This State* (Knoxville: Heiskell & Brown, 1821), 1:47; An Act to Amend the Law Concerning Marriage, ch. 19, 1822 Tenn. Acts 22.

44. For a fascinating account of the development of the legal concept of "Indian custom" marriage, see Ann Marie Plane, "Legitimacies, Indian Identities, and the Law: The Politics of Sex and the Creation of History in Colonial New England," *Law and Social Inquiry* 23 (Winter 1998): 55–77.

45. Oregon Donation Land Act, ch. 76, 9 Stat. 496 (1850); Robbins, "Extinguishing," 11–13; Whaley, "Oregon," 164–76.

46. Oregon Donation Land Act, sec. 4.

47. Richard H. Chused, "The Oregon Donation Act of 1850 and Nineteenth Century Federal Married Women's Property Law," *Law and History Review* 2, no. 1 (1984): 44–78; James M. Berquist, "The Oregon Donation Act and the National Land Policy," *Oregon Historical Quarterly* 58 (1957): 29–30.

48. *Vandolf v. Otis,* 1 Or. 153 (1854).

49. *Vandolf,* 1 Or. at 155–57.

50. *Morgan v. McGhee,* 24 Tenn. 13, 14 (1844); *Johnson v. Johnson's Administrator,* 30 Mo. 72, 88 (1860).

51. *Meister v. Moore,* 96 U.S. 76, 78, 81, 81, 78 (1878).

52. On the dynamics of White/Indian marriage in the Pacific Northwest, see Whaley, "Oregon," 160–63; Smith, "Wedding Bands and Marriage Bans," 5–31; David Peterson del Mar, "Intermarriage and Agency: A Chinookan Case Study," *Ethnohistory* 42 (Winter 1995): 1–30; and Jean Barman and Bruce M. Watson, "Fort Colvile's Fur Trade Families and the Dynamics of Race in the Pacific Northwest," *Pacific Northwest Quarterly* 90 (Summer 1999): 140–53.

53. "Judge Williams' Opinion," *Oregon Statesman,* December 5, 1854, 2; see also Smith, "Wedding Bands and Marriage Bans," 31–35.

54. An Act to Amend an Act, Entitled "An Act to Regulate Marriage," 1854–55 Wash. Terr. Laws 33. Later that same year, Washington land titles were confirmed when the federal government secured the first formal treaties ceding Pacific Northwest Indian land. See Brad Asher, *Beyond the Reservation: Indians, Settlers, and the Law in Washington Territory, 1853–1889* (Norman: University of Oklahoma Press, 1999), 63–64.

55. See note 7 above.

56. Nevada legislators, for example, engaged in heated discussion about how to treat Indians in the broad-based miscegenation bill they enacted in 1861. One representative objected to naming "Indians" at all, while others railed against "white men living with squaws" who were raising "disgraceful half-breeds"; still others hoped that the passage of a miscegenation law might reduce tensions with local Indians by ending some of the sexual abuse Indian women encountered from White men. Marsh, *Letters from Nevada Territory,* 247.

57. "A Bill to Prohibit Amalgamation and the Intermarriage of Races," H.B. no. 1, "House Bills no. 1–111," Box 13, 1866 Legislature, 4th Session, Record Group 61–117, Secretary of State, Oregon State Archives, Salem.

58. An Act to Prohibit Amalgamation and the Intermarriage of Races, sec. 1, 1866 Or. Gen. Laws 10; "Oregon Legislature," *Oregonian,* October 5, 1866, 2. Washington's 1854 Color Act also set a "one-half" standard for Indians but a "one-fourth" standard for "negroes."

59. "Oregon Legislature," *Oregonian,* October 6, 1866, 2.

60. An Act to Amend an Act, Entitled "An Act to Regulate Marriage," 1854–55 Wash. Terr. Laws 33; Asher, *Beyond the Reservation,* 63–64, 67–68, 71; An Act to Regulate Marriages, January 20, 1866, in *Laws of Washington: A Publication of the Session Laws of Washington Territory* (Seattle: Tribune Printing, 1896), 2:354; An Act to Amend an Act Entitled an Act to Regulate Marriages, January 23, 1868, in *Laws of Washington* 2:431.

61. Asher, *Beyond the Reservation,* 66–67, 71–73. For additional detail on these cases, see Peyton Kane, "The Whatcom County Nine: Legal and Political Ramifications of Metis Family Life in Washington Territory," *Columbia: The Magazine of Northwest History* 14 (Summer 2000), 39–44. The prosecutions had, however, made their point. According to Kane, seven of the nine men who had been indicted married their Indian partners between the indictment and the trial (40, 43).

62. Smith, "Wedding Bands and Marriage Bans," 66–73.

63. *In re Estate of Megginson,* 21 Or. 387, 392 (1891). The quote continues "and bastardized the children."

64. *In re Walker's Estate,* 5 Ariz. 70, 74 (1896).

65. *Banks v. Galbraith,* 149 Mo. 529, 531–32, 533 (1899).

66. "A Real Romance," *Skagit* [Washington] *News,* March 27, 1893, 1. Three years later McBride's ruling would be upheld by the Washington Supreme Court in *Follansbee v. Wilbur,* 14 Wash. 242 (1896).

67. John D'Emilio and Estelle B. Freedman, *Intimate Matters: A History of Sexuality in America* (New York: Harper & Row, 1988), 149–56, 171–73, 208–15.

68. *Walker,* 5 Ariz. at 75. On the Walker case, see Roger D. Hardaway, "Unlawful Love: A History of Miscegenation Law," *Journal of Arizona History* 27, no. 4 (1986) 378–79.

69. *Banks,* 149 Mo. at 537.

70. *Kelley v. Kitsap,* 5 Wash. 521, 524 (1893).

71. Initial estimates of the value of the estate were much higher, ranging from $4,500 to $12,500. I have relied on the figure of $2,528.50 provided by court-appointed assessors. Inventory and Appraisement, June 15, 1920, PaPF; Respondent's Brief, 2–5, November 1, 1920, PaCF; Appellants Abstract of Record, 10–16, September 3, 1920, PaCF.

72. Appellants Abstract of Record, 1–3, 3–7, PaCF; Judge A. M. Hare, Findings of Facts and Conclusions of Law, February 3, 1920, PaPF.

73. *In re Paquet's Estate,* 200 P. 911, 914 (1921).

74. I am grateful to Nancy Cott for pointing this out to me.

75. Respondent's Brief, 7, PaCF. Using typical imagery, they added that the Paquet relationship was "a case where a white man and a full blooded Indian woman have chosen to cohabit together illictly [*sic*], to agree to a relation of concubinage, which is not only a violation of the law of Oregon, but a transgression against the law of morality and the law of nature" (16).

76. Appellant's First Brief, 2, PaCF.

77. *In re Paquet's Estate,* 200 P. at 914.

78. Eva Saks, "Representing Miscegenation Law," *Raritan* 8 (Fall 1988): 39–69; Derrick Bell, "Remembrances of Racism Past," in *Race in America: The Struggle for Equality,* ed. Herbert Hill and James E. Jones Jr., (Madison: University of Wisconsin Press, 1992), 73–82; Cheryl I. Harris, "Whiteness as Property," *Harvard Law Review* 106 (June 1993): 1707–91; George Lipsitz, "The Possessive Investment in Whiteness: Racialized Social Democracy and the 'White Problem' in American Studies," *American Quarterly* 47 (September 1995): 369–87; Patricia J. Williams, "Fetal Fictions: An Exploration of Property Archetypes in Racial and Gendered Contexts," in *Race in America,* 425–37.

79. Respondent's Brief, 6, March 14, 1920; Index to Transcript, 2–3, August 25, 1920, both in *Henkle v. Paquet,* Oregon Supreme Court Case no. 10313, File no. 4267, Oregon State Archives, Salem. R. N. Henkle, a creditor of the estate, had sued to remove John Paquet from his role as administrator of the estate.

80. Decree, June 2, 1924; Bill of Complaint in Equity, 4, 6–7; Stipulation, June 2, 1924; Decree; all in *U.S. v. Paquet,* Judgment roll 11409, Register no. 8-8665, NARA, Pacific Alaska Region, Seattle, Washington. As late as 1928, John Paquet's major creditor complained to a judge that Paquet had repeatedly turned down acceptable offers to sell the land; perhaps he had chosen to live on it himself. Petition of J. S. Cole, June 7, 1928, PaPF.

81. *In re Paquet's Estate,* 200 P. at 913.

Chapter 4

1. Ariz. Rev. Stat. Ann. sec. 3837 (1913); "Appellant's Abstract of Record," August 8, 1921, 1–2, KCF.

2. "Appellant's Abstract of Record," 12–15.

3. "Appellant's Abstract of Record," 16–18.

4. "Appellant's Abstract of Record," 19.

5. Evelyn Brooks Higginbotham, "African-American Women's History and the Metalanguage of Race," *Signs* 17 (Winter 1992): 253.

6. Ariela J. Gross, "Litigating Whiteness: Trials of Racial Determination in the Nineteenth-Century South," *Yale Law Journal* 108 (October 1998): 111–88.

7. Earl Lewis and Heidi Ardizzone, *Love on Trial: An American Scandal in Black and White* (New York: W. W. Norton, 2001), 156–74; Reporter's Transcript, 5:1511–12, MCF.

8. *Wilson v. State*, 20 Ala. App. at 138–39 (Ala. Ct. App., 1924).

9. *Wilson v. State; Jones v. Commonwealth*, 80 Va. at 542 (1885); *Succession of Gilmore*, 5 Pelt. 17 (La. Ct. App., 1921); *Hopkins v. Bowers*, 111 N.C. at 178 (1892).

10. *Hopkins*, 111 N.C. at 178.

11. *Wilson*, 20 Ala. App. at 140.

12. *Linton v. State*, 88 Ala. at 218 (1889); *Bell v. State*, 33 Tex. Crim. at 164 (Tex. Crim. App., 1894); *Hopkins*, 111 N.C. at 178.

13. *Reed v. State*, 18 Ala. App. at 354 (Ala. Ct. App., 1922); *Bartelle v. U.S.*, 2 Okla. Crim. at 85 (Okla. Crim. App., 1908).

14. Ala. Code sec. 5001 (1923); Ind. Code Ann. sec. 2641 (1914); Ore. Rev. Stat. sec. 2163 (1920).

15. George W. Stocking Jr., *Race, Culture, and Evolution: Essays in the History of Anthropology* (1968; University of Chicago Press, 1982), 244–53.

16. U.S. Immigration Commission, *Dictionary of Races or Peoples* (Washington: GPO, 1911), 2; T. H. Huxley, "On the Geographical Distribution of the Chief Modifications of Mankind," *Journal of the Ethnological Society of London*, 2, no. 4 (1870): 406–7.

17. An Act Prohibiting Marriage Between White Persons and Negroes, Persons of Negro Blood, and Between White Persons, Chinese and Japanese, and Making Such Marriage Void, ch. 49, 1909 Mont. Laws 57; An Act to Amend Sec. 5302 of Cobbey's Ann. Stat. for 1911, Relating to Void Marriages, to Further Regulate the Marriage of White Persons with Those of Alien Blood, ch. 72, 1913 Neb. Laws 216.

18. An Act to Amend Sec. 4312 of Ch. 50 of the Revised Stat. of Missouri for 1899, Relating to Marriages and Marriage Contracts, 1909 Mo. Laws 662; An Act Amending Sec. 4596 of Art. 1, ch. 182 of the Compiled Stat. of Idaho, Relating to Marriages of Caucasians with Negroes, Mulattoes or Mongolians, ch. 115, 1921 Ida. Sess. Laws 291; Nev. Rev. Stat. sec 6514 (1912); An Act to Prohibit the Marriage of White Persons with Negroes, Mulattoes, Mongolians or Malays, ch. 57, 1913 Wyo. Sess. Laws 48; An Act to Amend Sec. 60 of the Civil Code, Relating to Illegal and Void Marriages, ch. 104, and An Act to Amend Sec. 69 of the Civil Code, Relating to Marriage Licenses, ch. 105, 1933 Cal. Stat. 561; An Act to Repeal and Re-enact with Amendment Sec. 365 of Art. 27 of the Code of Pub. Gen. Laws of Md. (1924 ed.), title "Crimes and Punishments," subtitle "Marrying Unlawfully," Prohibiting Marriages Between White Persons and Members of the Malay Race and Between Negroes and Members of the Malay Race, ch. 60, 1935 Md. Laws 101.

19. An Act Prohibiting the Inter-marriage and Illicit Cohabitation of Persons Belonging to the Caucasian Race, with Persons Belonging to the African, Corean, Malayan, or Mongolian Race, ch. 266, 1913 S.D. Laws 405; An Act to Amend Sec. 2166, Rev. Code, 1928, Relating to Prohibited and Void Marriages, ch. 17, 1931 Ariz. Sess. Laws 27.

20. An Act to Define Who Are Persons of Color and Who Are White Persons, to Prohibit and Prevent the Intermarriage of Such Persons, and to Provide a System of Registration and Marriage Licensing as a Means for Accomplishing the Principal Purpose, no. 317, sec. 14, 1927 Ga. Laws 272; An Act to Amend Sec. 2166, Rev. Code, 1928, Relating to Prohibited and Void Marriages, ch. 17, 1931 Ariz. Sess. Laws 27; An Act Amending Sec. 40-1-2, Rev. Stat. of Utah, 1933, Relating to Prohibited and Void Marriages, ch. 50, sec. 6, 1939 Utah Laws 66.

21. An Act Providing for Uniformity of Marriage, ch. 55, 1907–8 Okla. Sess. Laws 553; An Act to Prohibit the Amalgamation of the Caucasian Race and Persons of the Negro Race by Concubinage Between a Person of the Caucasian Race and a Person of the Negro Race, Making the Same a Felony, no. 320, 1911 Ark. Acts 295; *A Compilation of the Tennessee Statutes*, ed. Robert T. Shannon, vol. 4 (Nashville: Tennessee Law Book Publishing, 1917), sec. 4178a1 (reinstating a law originally passed in 1866 but omitted from the state's 1884 and 1896 codes); An Act to Preserve Racial Integrity, 1924 Va. Acts ch. 371; An Act to Amend Sec. 5001 of the Code of 1923, no. 214, 1927 Ala. Gen Laws 219; An Act to Define Who Are Persons of Color and Who Are White Persons, to Prohibit and Prevent the Intermarriage of Such Persons, and to Provide a System of Registration and Marriage Licensing as a Means for Accomplishing the Principal Purpose, no. 317, 1927 Ga. Laws 272. In Arkansas, Virginia, Alabama, and Georgia, the one-drop provisions were lodged directly in miscegenation laws, but Oklahoma's miscegenation law of 1907 relied on a race definition embedded in the state's constitution, and Tennessee's one-drop law, which appeared in a section of the state code entitled "Descent and Distribution Among Persons of Color," contradicted the state's miscegenation law, which appeared in the section on "Marriage" and was keyed to the phrase "negroes, mulattoes, or persons of mixed blood descended from a negro, to the third generation inclusive." See *Compilation of the Tennessee Statutes*, sec. 4186.

22. Opinion by Judge Thomas C. Gould of the California Superior Court, in *Murillo v. Murillo*, Los Angeles Superior Court no. D 97714, reprinted in "American Jurists and Lawyers Agree That Filipinos Are Not Mongolians," *Three Stars,* December 1931; Daniel Kwang Lee, "Why Washington State Did Not Have an Anti-Miscegenation Law" (M.A. thesis, Washington State University, 1998), 27.

23. An Act to Amend Sec. 1810 of the Code, ch. 254, 1887 N.C. Sess. Laws 499; An Act to Change the Name of the Indians in Robeson County, ch. 215, 1911 N.C. Sess. Laws 354; An Act to Restore to the Indians Residing in Robeson and Adjoining Counties Their Rightful and Ancient Name, ch. 123, 1913 N. C. Laws 215.

24. An Act Prohibiting Marriage Between Persons of the Indian Race and Persons of the Colored or Black Race, no. 220, 1920 La. Acts 366. A companion law made "concubinage between a person of the aboriginal Indian race of America, known as the red race, and a person of the colored or black race" a felony (No. 230, 1920 La. Acts 381).

25. An Act to Repeal and Re-enact with Amendment Sec. 365 of Art. 27 of the Code of Pub. Gen. Laws of Md. (1924 ed.), title "Crimes and Punishments," subtitle "Marrying Unlawfully," Prohibiting Marriages Between White Persons and Members of the Malay Race and Between Negroes and Members of the Malay Race, ch. 60, sec. 1, 1935 Md. Laws 101.

26. Okla. Const. art. 23, sec. 11 (repealed 1978).

27. Sarah Deutsch, "Being American in Boley, Oklahoma," in *Beyond Black and White: Race, Ethnicity, and Gender in the U.S. South and Southwest,* ed. Stephanie Cole and Alison M. Parker (College Station: Texas A&M University Press, 2004), 105; An Act Providing for Uniformity of Marriage, ch. 55, sec. 12, 1907–8 Okla. Laws at 556.

28. See, for example, *Blake v. Sessions,* 94 Okla. 59 (1923), *Long v. Brown,* 186 Okla. 407 (1939). For a detailed examination of miscegenation law in Oklahoma, see Peter Wallenstein, "Native Americans Are White, African Americans Are Not: Racial

Identity, Marriage, Inheritance and the Law in Oklahoma, 1907–1967," *Journal of the West* 39, no. 1 (2000): 55–63.

29. Scholars have only recently begun to explore this complex history. See Rachel F. Moran, *Interracial Intimacy: The Regulation of Race and Romance* (Chicago: University of Chicago Press, 2001), 50–53, 56–59; Dara Orenstein, "Void for Vagueness: Mexicans and the Collapse of Miscegenation Law in California," *Pacific Historical Review* 74 (August 2005): 367–407; and Martha Menchaca, "The Anti-Miscegenation History of the American Southwest, 1837–1970: Transforming Racial Ideology into Law," unpublished paper presented to the Transnational Exchanges in the Texas-Mexico Borderlands Conference, April 7–8, 2005, University of Texas, Austin, http://www.utexas.edu/cola/depts/history/news/spring_2005/tx_mexico_conf/noformat/news/spring_2005/tex_mexico_conf/ponencia_menchaca.pdf (accessed September 2, 2006).

30. The qualification "explicitly" is important here. As Leti Volpp has pointed out, this generalization only holds true if Filipinos are categorized as Asian Americans rather than Latinos. And Martha Menchaca argues that the determination to bring Mexican Americans under miscegenation law was the motivation for an amendment to Arizona's miscegenation law in 1913. See Leti Volpp, "American Mestizo: Filipinos and Antimiscegenation Laws in California," *UC Davis Law Review* 33 (1999–2000): 833; Menchaca, "Anti-Miscegenation History."

31. Orenstein, "Void for Vagueness," 376–86; Neil Foley, "Partly Colored or Other White: Mexican Americans and Their Problem with the Color Line," in *Beyond Black and White,* 126–30.

32. W. A. Plecker, "Virginia's Attempt to Adjust the Color Problem," *American Journal of Public Health* 15 (February 1925): 113; Brian William Thomson, "Racism and Racial Classification: A Case Study of the Virginia Racial Integrity Legislation" (Ph.D. dissertation, University of California, Riverside, 1978), 288.

33. Karen Isaakson Leonard, *Making Ethnic Choices: California's Punjabi Mexican Americans* (Philadelphia: Temple University Press, 1992), 10, 63, 68–69; Moran, *Interracial Intimacies,* 57–59.

34. On this point, see esp. Foley, "Partly Colored," 123–41, and Ian F. Haney López, *White by Law: The Legal Construction of Race* (New York: NYU Press, 1996), 61–62.

35. Appellant's Abstract of Record, 19, KCF.

36. Appellee's Brief, October 3, 1921, 6, KCF.

37. Appellant's Brief, September 8, 1921, KCF; *Kirby v. Kirby,* 206 P. 405 (1922) at 406. For another account of the Kirby case, see Roger D. Hardaway, "Unlawful Love: A History of Arizona's Miscegenation Law," *Journal of Arizona History* 27 (Winter 1986): 377–90.

38. Franz Boas, "Race," in *Encyclopaedia of the Social Sciences,* ed. Edwin R. A. Seligman (New York: Macmillan, 1930–35), 13:27; Julian S. Huxley and A. C. Haddon, *We Europeans: A Survey of "Racial" Problems* (London: Jonathan Cape, 1935), 107. Emphasis in original.

39. Boas, "Race," 34.

40. Ruth Benedict, *Race: Science and Politics,* new ed. with *The Races of Mankind,* by Ruth Benedict and Gene Weltfish (New York: Viking Press, 1945), 9, 171–72, 98.

41. The background of the case is discussed in the appellate court decision, *Estate of Monks,* 48 Cal. App. 3d 603 (Cal. Dist. Ct. App., 1941) and in extensive local newspaper

coverage, including "Monks-Giraudo Marriage Void, Claim in Gunn's Suit on Notes," *San Diego Union,* August 22, 1939, 1A, and "Trial Concluded in Monks Will Case," *San Diego Union,* October 14, 1939, 1B.

42. Reporter's Transcript, 2:660–67, 3:965–98, MCF; "Mrs. Monks Part Negro, Ex-Nurse Testifies in Estate Controversy," *San Diego Union,* September 14, 1939, 10B.

43. Reporter's Transcript, 5:1511–12, 1525, 6:1900; "Mrs. Monks Backed by Anthropologist," *San Diego Union,* September 29, 1939, 10A; "Mrs. Monks White, Asserts Professor," *San Diego Union,* October 5, 1939, 8A.

44. Reporter's Transcript, 7:2543, 2548.

45. Findings of Fact and Conclusions of Law, in Clerk's Transcript, 81, December 2, 1940, *Gunn v. Giraudo,* 4 Civ. 2832, California District Court of Appeal Records, California State Archives, Sacramento; "Mrs. Lee Wins Monks Estate," *San Diego Union,* January 6, 1940, 1A. Both the California Supreme Court and the U.S. Supreme Court refused to hear appeals of the decision (*Estate of Monks,* 48 Cal App. 2d at 612; *Monks v. Lee,* 317 U.S. 590; *Monks v. Lee,* 317 U.S. 711). In 1945, Monks tried again, this time in a probate court in Massachusetts, where she lost her case in a decision (*Lee v. Monks,* 318 Mass. 513) that downplayed the issue of race; the U.S. Supreme Court refused to grant certiorari in this case, too (326 U.S. 696).

46. As Julie Novkov explains in her study of miscegenation law in Alabama, even when judges ruled in favor of defendants, their actions "reflected assumptions about the legitimacy of the regime of white supremacy and enabled legal state actors to sanitize and rationalize it. These cases, in which the occasional defendant escaped a lengthy prison term because of technical problems in the trial, highlight the contradiction of a commitment to procedural fairness in the midst of a broadly unjust system, evoking Hannah Arendt's analysis of the banality of evil." See Julie Novkov, *Racial Union: Racial Union Law, Intimacy, and the White State in Alabama, 1865–1954* (Ann Arbor: University of Michigan Press, 2008), 24.

47. W. A. Plecker, "Shall America Remain White?" typescript, 8, Box 56, Folder 7, JPP.

48. *Wilson v. State,* 20 Ala. App. at 138–39, 140 (Ala. Ct. App., 1924).

49. I have seen only two miscegenation cases in which the sex of the partners was at issue. In the first, *Williams v. State,* 23 Ala. App. 365 (Ala. Ct. App., 1930), lawyers for Jesse D. Williams, a "negro, or a descendant of a negro" who had married a "white" woman, argued that his conviction should be overturned for several reasons, one of which was that the indictment had failed to specify the sex of each partner to the crime. The appellate court summarily rejected this claim, although it overturned the conviction for other reasons. In the 1951 case of *Griffith v. State,* 35 Ala. App. 582 (Ala. Ct. App., 1951), lawyers for Nathan Bell, another "Negro" man married to a "white" woman, used the same argument, to no better effect.

Chapter 5

1. Southern California Historical Records Survey Project, *Inventory of the County Archives of California, No. 20: Los Angeles County Clerk's Office* (Los Angeles: Southern California Historical Records Survey Project, 1943), 85.

2. Studies of Filipinos and miscegenation law, Filipino intermarriage, and the taxi-dance halls where Filipino men met White women include Rachel F. Moran, *Interracial Intimacy: The Regulation of Race and Romance* (Chicago: University of Chicago Press, 2001), 37–41; Leti Volpp, "American Mestizo: Filipinos and Antimiscegenation Laws in California," *UC Davis Law Review* 33 (1999–2000): 795–835; "Anti-Miscegenation Laws and the Pilipino," in *Letters in Exile: An Introductory Reader on the History of Pilipinos in America* (Los Angeles: UCLA Asian American Studies Center, 1976), 63–67; Nellie Foster, "Legal Status of Filipino Intermarriages in California," *Sociology and Social Research* 16 (1931–32): 447–48; Megumi Dick Osumi, "Asians and California's Anti-Miscegenation Laws," in *Asian and Pacific American Experiences: Women's Perspectives,* ed. Nobuya Tsuchida (Minneapolis: Asian/Pacific Learning Resource Center, 1982), 1–37; Arleen de Vera, "The Tapia-Saiki Incident: Interethnic Conflict and Filipino Responses to the Anti-Filipino Exclusion Movement," in *Over the Edge: Remapping the American West,* ed. Valerie J. Matsumoto and Blake Allmendinger (Berkeley: University of California Press, 1999), 201–14; Barbara M. Posadas, "Crossed Boundaries in Interracial Chicago: Pilipino American Families Since 1925," *Amerasia Journal* 8, no. 2 (1981) 31–52; Linda España-Maram, *Creating Masculinity in Los Angeles's Little Manila: Working-Class Filipinos and Popular Culture, 1920–1950s* (New York: Columbia University Press, 2006), 105–33; Rhacel Salazar Parreñas, "'White Trash' Meets the 'Little Brown Monkeys': The Taxi Dance Hall as a Site of Interracial and Gender Alliances Between White Working Class Women and Filipino Immigrant Men in the 1920s and 30s," *Amerasia Journal* 24 (Summer 1998): 115–34; and Kevin J. Mumford, *Interzones: Black-White Sex Districts in Chicago and New York in the Early Twentieth Century* (New York: Columbia University Press, 1997), 53–71.

3. Foster, "Legal Status," 447–48; Op. Att'y Gen, no. 1-5641, June 8, 1926, Bound Volume 18, Accession no. 95-08-19, California State Archives, Sacramento.

4. Foster, "Legal Status," 444–46, 448; "Anti-Miscegenation Laws and the Pilipino," 66–67; "Life Sentence to Be Imposed on Yatko Today," *Los Angeles Times,* May 11, 1924, 2:17; "Filipinos Can't Marry Whites," *Los Angeles Examiner,* February 26, 1930, 2:1; "Filipino-White Unions Barred," *Los Angeles Times,* February 26, 1930, 2:1.

5. Foster, "Legal Status, 450–52; "Filipino Racial Status in Doubt," *Los Angeles Examiner,* September 6, 1931, 4:12; "Racial Divorce Plea Rejected," *Los Angeles Times,* October 11, 1931, 2:5.

6. Foster, "Legal Status," 449–50; "Filipino and Mexican May Wed, Says Court," *Los Angeles Times,* June 4, 1931, 2:8; "Filipinos Are Not Mongolians Says Los Angeles Jurist," *Three Stars,* July 4, 1931, 5, 33. For a deeper analysis of these cases, see Volpp, "American Mestizo," 813–21.

7. According to the U.S. Census, in 1930 there were 45,208 Filipinos in the United States, 30,470 of whom were in California. U.S. Department of Commerce, Bureau of the Census, *Abstract of the Fifteenth Census of the United States* (Washington: GPO, 1933), 84. According to Linda España-Maram, by 1933, there were 12,000 Filipinos in Los Angeles County alone. España-Maram, *Creating Masculinity,* 20.

8. Aaron M. Sargent, "Survey of Filipino Immigration—Report of Immigration Section," *Transactions of the Commonwealth Club of California* 24, no. 7 (November 5, 1929): 320.

9. Foster, "Legal Status," 443; "Filipinos Can't Marry Whites," *Los Angeles Examiner,* February 26, 1930, 2:1; Constantine Panunzio, "Intermarriage in Los Angeles, 1924–1933," *American Journal of Sociology* 47 (March 1942): 695–97.

10. "Filipinos Can't Marry Whites," 1; "Filipino-White Unions Barred," 1; Foster, "Legal Status," 448–50; "Atty. Gen. Webb Holds Filipinos Mongolian; Manlapit Fights Legal Recognition," *Three Stars,* November 1931, 4; S.V.O. Prichard to Pablo Manlapit, October 29, 1931, reprinted in *Three Stars,* November 1931, 5, 15.

11. James C. Scott, *Seeing Like a State: How Certain Schemes to Improve the Human Condition Have Failed* (New Haven: Yale University Press, 1998), passim.

12. An Act to Legalise Certain Marriages, June 5, 1837, 1837–45 Repub. Tex. Laws 233; Ariz. Terr. Rev. Stat. Sec. 2091 (1887); An Act to Amend and Re-enact Article 94 of the Revised Civil Code of Lousiana, of 1870, 1894 La. Acts 63; *State v. Treadaway,* 126 La. at 305 (1910); An Act Providing for Uniformity of Marriage, ch. 55, sec. 12, 1907–08 Okla. Sess. Laws 553; An Act Prohibiting Marriage Between White Persons and Negroes, Persons of Negro Blood, and Between White Persons, Chinese and Japanese, and Making Such Marriage Void, ch. 49, 1909 Mont. Laws 57.

13. Colo. Comp. Laws sec. 5549 (1921); Md. Code Ann. sec. 365 (1924); Ala. Code sec. 5001 (1923).

14. In Alabama, the standard penalty for a first conviction for "living in adultery or fornication" was a fine of $100 and a sentence of six months in the county jail or at hard labor, but the penalty for living in adultery and fornication "between white persons and negroes" was two to seven years in the penitentiary.

15. Julie Novkov, "Racial Constructions: The Legal Regulation of Miscegenation in Alabama, 1890–1934," *Law and History Review* 20, no. 2 (2002): 227, ftn. 6.

16. Between 1922 and 1928, North Carolina's attorney general reported annual totals of prosecutions of fornication and adultery cases for each fiscal year, running from July 1 to June 30, as follows: 219 (Fiscal year ending June 30, 1923), 220 (1924), 231 (1925), 247 (1926), 201 (1927), 196 (1928). North Carolina Attorney General's Office, *Attorney General Reports and Opinions,* microfilm, Library of Congress, Washington, D.C.

17. *In re Takahashi's Estate,* 113 Mont. at 500 (1942).

18. By my rough count, there were at least sixty-five cases that reached state appellate courts, and these cases are, by definition, just the tip of the iceberg. In the absence of careful state and local studies, no one knows how many cases might have been filed in lower courts. On Louisiana, see Diana Irene Williams, "'They Call It Marriage': The Interracial Louisiana Family and the Making of American Legitimacy" (Ph.D. dissertation, Harvard University, 2007); Michelle Brattain, "Miscegenation and Competing Definitions of Race in Twentieth-Century Louisiana," *Journal of Southern History* 71 (August 2005): 621–58; and Peter Wallenstein, "Native Americans Are White, African Americans Are Not: Racial Identity, Marriage, Inheritance, and the Law in Oklahoma, 1907–1967," *Journal of the West* 39, no. 1 (2000): 55–63.

19. Earl Lewis and Heidi Ardizzone, *Love on Trial: An American Scandal in Black and White* (New York: W. W. Norton, 2001), 50. Leonard Rhinelander lost his case in December 1925.

20. *Inland Steel Company v. Barcena,* 110 Ind. App. 551 (Ind. Ct. App., 1942).

21. *State v. Pass,* 59 Ariz. 16 (1942). As Martha Menchaca notes, one of the most interesting things about the *Pass* case is that despite the court labels, both Frank Pass

and his wife, Ruby Contreras Pass, were, as the court put it, part "Mexican." As the court saw it, however, Ruby's lack of any "Indian" blood allowed her Mexicanness to be read as "Spanish," while Frank, whose father was Mexican, but whose mother was part "English" and part "Indian," was considered "Indian" under Arizona law. See Martha Menchaca, "The Anti-Miscegenation History of the American Southwest, 1837–1970: Transforming Racial Ideology into Law," unpublished paper presented to the Transnational Exchanges in the Texas-Mexico Borderlands Conference, April 7–8, 2005, University of Texas, Austin, http://www.utexas.edu/cola/depts/history/news/spring_2005/tx_mexico_conf/noformat/news/spring_2005/tex_mexico_conf/ponencia_menchaca.pdf (accessed September 2, 2006).

22. Michael Grossberg, *Governing the Hearth: Law and the Family in Nineteenth-Century America* (Chapel Hill: University of North Carolina Press, 1985), 77–78, 93; Chester G. Vernier, *American Family Laws: A Comparative Study of the Family Law of the Forty-eight American States, Alaska, the District of Columbia, and Hawaii (To Jan. 1, 1931)* (Stanford: Stanford University Press, 1931), 1:59.

23. *Eugenics Record Office Bulletin no. 9* (Cold Spring Harbor, N.Y., 1913); Michael Grossberg, "Guarding the Altar: Physiological Restrictions and the Rise of State Intervention in Matrimony," *American Journal of Legal History* 26 (July 1982): 221–24.

24. The proposed law required licensing officials to record, among other things, "the names, relationship, if any, age, nationality, *color,* residence, and occupation of the parties" (my emphasis). Charles Thaddeus Terry, *Uniform State Laws in the United States* (New York: Baker, Voorhis for the National Conference of Commissioners of Uniform State Laws, 1920), 390.

25. Vernier, *American Family Laws* 1:130–39. As Natalia Molina and Nayan Shah have shown, race was a pervasive aspect of the image and administration of public health in this period. Natalia Molina, *Fit to Be Citizens? Public Health and Race in Los Angeles, 1879–1939* (Berkeley: University of California Press, 2006); Nayan Shah, *Contagious Divides: Epidemics and Race in San Francisco's Chinatown* (Berkeley: University of California Press, 2001).

26. Mary E. Richmond and Fred S. Hall, *Marriage and the State, Based upon Field Studies of the Present Day Administration of Marriage Laws in the United States* (New York: Russell Sage Foundation, 1929), 81, 9.

27. Studies of the Racial Integrity Act, all of which touch on Plecker's involvement to one degree or another, include Pippa Holloway, *Sexuality, Politics, and Social Control in Virginia, 1920–1945* (Chapel Hill: University of North Carolina Press, 2006), 32–51, 59–67; J. Douglas Smith, *Managing White Supremacy: Race, Politics, and Citizenship in Jim Crow Virginia* (Chapel Hill: University of North Carolina Press, 2002), 76–106; Lisa Lindquist Dorr, "Arm in Arm: Gender, Eugenics and Virginia's Racial Integrity Acts of the 1920s," *Journal of Women's History* 11 (Spring 1999): 143–66; Barbara Bair, "Remapping the Black/White Body: Sexuality, Nationalism and Biracial Antimiscegenation Activism in 1920s Virginia," in *Sex, Love, Race: Crossing Boundaries in North American History*, ed. Martha Hodes (New York: NYU Press, 1999), 399–419; J. David Smith, *The Eugenic Assault on America: Scenes in Red, Black, and White* (Fairfax: George Mason University, 1993), 13–22, 50–58; Paul A. Lombardo, "Miscegenation, Eugenics, and Racism: Historical Footnotes to *Loving v. Virginia,*" *UC Davis Law Review* 21 (1988): 421–52; Richard B. Sherman, "'The Last Stand': The Fight for Racial Integrity

in Virginia in the 1920s," *Journal of Southern History* 54 (February 1988): 69–92; Gregory Michael Dorr, "Segregation's Science: The American Eugenics Movement and Virginia, 1900–1980" (Ph.D. dissertation, University of Virginia, 2000), 449–554; and Brian William Thomson, "Racism and Racial Classification: A Case Study of the Virginia Racial Integrity Legislation" (Ph.D. dissertation, University of California, Riverside, 1978).

28. Sherman, "Last Stand," 71; W. A. Plecker, "Racial Integrity Act of 1924," in *Annual Report of the State Department of Health and the State Health Commissioner to the Governor of Virginia for the Year Ending June 30, 1927* (Richmond: Department of Health, 1928), 156–57.

29. Va. Code Ann. sec. 4546 (1918); "Bureau of Vital Statistics Finds Solution [to] Puzzle," *Richmond News Leader,* August 4, 1923, 22; Va. Code Ann. sec. 67 (1918); W. A. Plecker, "Racial Integrity Law," Appendix X, *Report of the State Board of Health and the State Health Commissioner to the Governor of Virginia for the Biennium Ending June 30, 1925* (Richmond: Supt. Public Printing, 1925), 377; "Report of the Bureau of Vital Statistics for the Year Ending December 31, 1929," *Virginia Health Bulletin* 23 (February 1931), 119.

30. For more about the influence of eugenics in Virginia and elsewhere, see Dorr, "Segregation's Science," and Alexandra Minna Stern, *Eugenic Nation: Faults and Frontiers of Better Breeding in Modern America* (Berkeley: University of California Press, 2005).

31. Walter Ashby Plecker, *Eugenics in Relation to the New Family and the Law on Racial Integrity Including a Paper Read Before the American Public Health Association* (Richmond: Supt. Public Printing, 1924), 6; Plecker, "Virginia's Attempt to Adjust the Color Problem," *American Journal of Public Health* 15 (February 1925): 111; Plecker, "Racial Integrity Law," 377; "Bureau of Vital Statistics Favors Race Integrity Bill," *Richmond Times Dispatch,* February 17, 1924, 6; Plecker, "Shall America Remain White?" typescript, 6, Box 56, Folder 7, JPP.

32. Plecker, *Eugenics in Relation,* 4–5; [Plecker] to Editor, *Survey Graphic,* March 13, 1925, Box 56, Folder 2, JPP.

33. Thomson, "Racism and Racial Classification," 207–8, 251–52; "Major Activities of the Virginia State Department of Health," *Virginia Health Bulletin* 25 (September 1933), 5.

34. During the years between 1896 and the formation of Plecker's Bureau of Vital Statistics in 1912, for example, no state agency had been charged with tracking births or deaths in Virginia. See Thomson, "Racism and Racial Classification," 207.

35. Plecker, "Adjust the Color Problem," 114.

36. Sherman, "Last Stand," 77; "Major Activities," 5.

37. Sherman, "Last Stand," 77–78; Lombardo, "Miscegenation, Eugenics, and Racism," 434; W. A. Plecker to Hon. Harry E. Davis, Cleveland, Ohio, October 4, 1924, Box 56, Folder 1, JPP.

38. "Racial Passports," *Virginian Pilot and Norfolk Landmark,* February 19, 1924, 4.

39. W. A. Plecker to C. W. Garrison, State Health Officer, Little Rock, Arkansas, January 5, 1925, Box 56, Folder 2; W. A. Plecker to Hon. Harry E. Davis, Cleveland, Ohio, October 4, 1924, Box 56, Folder 1, both in JPP; Lombardo, "Miscegenation, Eugenics, and Racism," 434–35.

40. W. A. Plecker to Dr. F. M. Register, State Registrar, Bureau of Vital Statistics, Raleigh, N.C., August 9, 1924, Box 56, Folder 1, JPP.

41. Lombardo, "Miscegenation, Racism, and Eugenics," 435 and ftn. 74; Thomson, "Race and Race Classification," 152–61; Smith, *Managing White Supremacy*, 89–90.

42. An Act to Amend Sec. 5001 of the Code of 1923, no. 214, 1927 Ala. Gen. Laws 219; An Act to Define Who Are Persons of Color and Who Are White Persons, to Prohibit and Prevent the Intermarriage of Such Persons, and to Provide a System of Registration and Marriage Licensing as a Means for Accomplishing the Principal Purpose, no. 317, 1927 Geo. Laws 272.

43. An Act to Define Who Are Persons of Color, sec. 14, 1927 Geo. Laws 272. In the end, though, the state legislature declined to pass any appropriation to support the racial registration system, and it was never put into effect. Thomson, "Racism and Racial Classification," 160–61.

44. Lombardo, "Miscegenation, Eugenics, and Racism," 447–49; Smith, *Managing White Supremacy*, 89–92; Dorr, "Segregation's Science," 488–94; Smith, *Eugenic Assault*, 62–70; Holloway, *Sexuality, Politics, and Social Control*, 63–65.

45. Plecker to Davis, October 24, 1924.

46. An Act to Preserve Racial Integrity, ch. 371, sec 4, 1927 Va. Acts 534.

47. W. A. Plecker to W. B. Hesseltine, August 21, 1924, Box 56, Folder 1, JPP.

48. Plecker, "Racial Integrity Law," 376; handwritten note on W. A. Plecker to the Clerks of Rockbridge, Amherst, and Augusta Counties, April 29, 1924, Box 56, Folder 1, JPP.

49. W. A. Plecker to Mrs. Robert H. Cheatham, April 30, 1924; W. A. Plecker to Mrs. Mary Gildon, April 30, 1924; both in Box 56, Folder 1, JPP.

50. Plecker to Garrison; "Dr. Plecker Writes of Irish in History of Irish Creek Indians," *Rockbridge County News*, September 25, 1924, 1; Plecker, "Report of the Bureau of Vital Statistics... 1928," 10; W. A. Plecker to W. H. Clark, Irish Creek, Virginia, July 29, 1924; Plecker to the Clerks of Rockbridge, Amherst, and Augusta Counties, April 29, 1924; all in Box 56, Folder 1, JPP.

51. "Report of the Bureau of Vital Statistics for the Year Ended December 31, 1928," *Virginia Health Bulletin* 22 (January 1930): 11 (emphasis mine). For accounts of these cases, see Sherman, "Last Stand," 80–82; Lombardo, "Miscegenation, Eugenics, and Racism," 440–42; Smith, *Managing White Supremacy*, 92–94; and Smith, *Eugenic Assault*, 71–76.

52. "Woman, Listed Negroid, Wins Right to be Called 'White,'" *Richmond News Leader*, November 18, 1924, 1, 4; "Woman, Listed Negroid, Wins Right to be Called 'White' in Integrity Case," *Richmond Planet*, November 29, 1924, 5. For a fascinating account of how Alabama judges struggled with similar difficulties created by the rise of eugenics-based hereditary definitions of race, see Novkov, *Racial Union*, 116–47.

53. Sherman, "Last Stand," 80–81; "Woman, Listed Negroid," *Richmond News Leader*, 4; Asst. Atty. Gen. Leon M. Bazile to John Powell, November 26, 1924, Box 56, Folder 1, JPP.

54. For an astute analysis of the power and the problems of the OMB classifications, see Michael Omi, "Our Private Obsession, Our Public Sin: Racial Identity and the State: The Dilemmas of Classification," *Law and Inequality* 15 (Winter 1997): 7–23. On race in the administrative state, see Barbara Young Welke, *Recasting American*

Liberty: Gender, Race, Law, and the Railroad Revolution, 1865–1920 (Cambridge: Cambridge University Press, 2001); Lucy E. Salyer, *Laws Harsh as Tigers: Chinese Immigrants and the Shaping of Modern Immigration Law* (Chapel Hill: University of North Carolina Press, 1995); Erika Lee, *At America's Gates: Chinese Immigration During the Exclusion Era, 1882–1945* (Chapel Hill: University of North Carolina Press, 2003); Mae M. Ngai, *Impossible Subjects: Illegal Aliens and the Making of Modern America* (Princeton: Princeton University Press, 2004); Martha Mabie Gardner, *The Qualities of a Citizen: Women, Immigration, and Citizenship, 1870–1965* (Princeton: Princeton University Press, 2005); Molina, *Fit to Be Citizens?*; and Novkov, *Racial Union.*

55. "Report of the Bureau of Vital Statistics for the Year Ended December 31, 1929," *Virginia Health Bulletin* 23 (February 1931): 119; "Woman, Listed Negroid," *Richmond News Leader*, 4; Russell E. Booker Jr., director of vital statistics, quoted in Smith, *Eugenic Assault*, 90. On the Monacans, see Samuel R. Cook, *Monacans and Miners: Native American and Coal Mining Communities in Appalachia* (Lincoln: University of Nebraska Press, 2000), esp. 84–134.

56. Virginia R. Domínguez, *White by Definition: Social Classification in Creole Louisiana* (New Brunswick: Rutgers University Press, 1986), 36–45; Michelle Brattain, "Miscegenation and Competing Definitions of Race in Twentieth-Century Louisiana," *Journal of Southern History* 71 (August 2005): 642, 656–57.

57. "Report of the Bureau of Vital Statistics for the Year Ended December 31, 1929," *Virginia Health Bulletin* 23 (February 1931): 119. Like most other states, California had a law prohibiting "cohabitation and adultery" that might have served as the vehicle for the criminal prosecution of interracial couples in much the same way that illicit sex laws did in southern states such as North Carolina (see note 16 above), but this law seems to have been enforced very rarely. The California state attorney general's report for 1928–28, for example, lists every criminal case that reached the state's district court of appeal between July 1, 1926, and June 30, 1928, including, according to my count, 79 convictions for robbery, 53 for murder, 30 for embezzlement, 23 for rape, 7 for incest, and 6 for sodomy. During this same period, there were only 2 appeals of convictions for adultery. State of California, Office of the Attorney General, *Biennial Report of the Attorney General of the State of California, 1926–28* (Sacramento: Supt. State Print., 1928), 86–99.

58. Cal. Civ. Code sec. 60 (1923).

59. An Act Providing for the Registration of Marriages, Births, Divorces, and Deaths, ch. 356, sec. 1, 1858 Cal. Stat. 342; An Act to Amend Sec. 69 of the Civil Code of California, Relating to Marriage Licenses, ch. 241, 1907 Cal. Stat. 305.

60. Panunzio, "Intermarriage in Los Angeles," 690–701. In all his statistics, Panunzio differentiated native-born whites from foreign-born whites, but I have combined the two groups to get the totals given here.

61. Panunzio, "Intermarriage in Los Angeles," 692–93, 698. These are my calculations, using the totals provided by Panunzio. Miscegenation law was not, of course, the only factor that determined these marriage rates. Sex ratios, patterns of residential segregation, cultural preferences for in-group marriage, and a variety of other considerations played a part.

62. At least one source suggests that Filipino men who wanted to marry White women had to file affidavits first, presumably attesting to the fact that they were

not "Mongolians." See "Filipino Marriage Balked," *Los Angeles Times,* February 11, 1930, 2:5.

63. At about the same time, the U.S. naturalization bureau decided that White women who married Filipinos would lose their U.S. citizenship. See "Marry Filipino, Lose Citizenship," *Los Angeles Examiner,* August 12, 1930, 1:4; "Anti-Miscegenation Laws and the Pilipino," 70.

64. Bill of Exceptions, 14–15, April 30, 1932, in Transcript on Appeal, RCF.

65. "Rajah's Son Can't Wed: Scion of Noble House in India Twice Disappointed by Refusal to Grant Santa Ana Marriage License," *Los Angeles Times,* February 10, 1930, 14; "Negro and White Fiancée Denied License to Wed," *Los Angeles Times,* February 11, 1930, 2.

66. "Negro and White Fiancée," 2.

67. See, for example, "Are Filipinos Mongolians? Los Angeles Judge to Decide Little Brown Brother Color," *Three Stars,* May 1931, 1, 5; "Filipinos Are Not Mongolians Says Los Angeles Jurist," *Three Stars,* July 4, 1931, 5, 33.

68. "Girl Fights for Right to Wed Filipino," *Los Angeles Examiner,* October 12, 1931, 2:1; "Couple's Marriage Plans Meet New Legal Barriers," *Pasadena Post,* April 12, 1932, 2:1; "Filipino, Malay, or Mongolian? Wedding Waits," *Los Angeles Examiner,* April 12, 1932, 2:1; "Marriage License Denied Pasadena Girl and Filipino," *Los Angeles Examiner,* April 20, 1932, 1:5; Primo E. Quevedo, "Atty. Gladys T. Root, & George B. Bush Defend Filipino Race in High American Court," *Three Stars,* June–July 1932, 21. The *Roldan* case has attracted surprisingly little historical attention, but brief accounts are available in Osumi, "Asians and California's Anti-Miscegenation Laws," 19–20; "Anti-Miscegenation Laws and the Pilipino," 68–69; and Volpp, "American Mestizo," 795–96, 821.

69. Root's opening brief was reprinted in full in "American Jurists and Lawyers Agree That Filipinos Are Not Mongolians," *Three Stars,* December 1931, 37 (my emphasis).

70. "American Jurists," 37.

71. Appellants' Opening Brief, 5–6, June 17, 1932, RCF; U.S. Webb, June 8, 1926, in Attorney General Opinions, 1906–55, 483, Accession no. 95-03-19, Department of Justice, Administrative Services Division, Legal Support Unit, California State Archives, Sacramento.

72. Petition for Hearing by Supreme Court, 22, March 11, 1933, RCF.

73. Findings of Fact and Conclusions of Law, 6–9, April 8, 1932, Transcript on Appeal, May 20, 1932, RCF; *Roldan v. Los Angeles County,* 129 Cal. App. 267, 268, 270 (Cal. Dist. Ct. App., 1933).

74. Quevedo, "Atty. Gladys T. Root," 21; "The Mongolian Case," *Three Stars,* June–July 1932, 5; de Vera, "The Tapia-Sakai Incident," 208.

75. Certificate of Registry of Marriage, April 12, 1933, County of Los Angeles, Registrar-Recorder/County Clerk's Office, Norwalk, California; "Filipino and White Girl Finally Wed," *Los Angeles Examiner,* April 11, 1933, 1: 10; Roldan obituary, *Pasadena Star-News,* August 21, 1975, D6; Deborah Buckelew, "'Lady in Purple' Still Downtown," *Civic Center News,* May 24–June 13, 1977, 13, clipping in Gladys Root, California Biography File, History and Genealogy Department, Los Angeles Public Library; Cy Rice, *Defender of the Damned: Gladys Towles Root* (New York: Citadel Press, 1964), 63–64.

76. "Anti-Miscegenation Laws and the Pilipino," 69; Osumi, "Asians and California's Anti-Miscegenation Laws," 20–21.

77. William H. Jordan, "State Measure Bans Filipino, White Unions," *Los Angeles Examiner*, January 19, 1933, 1:3.

78. The justices split 4–3, deciding by a one-vote margin not to hear the appeal on March 27, 1933, *Roldan v. Los Angeles County* at 273; "Filipino, White Marriage Upheld," *Sacramento Bee*, March 30, 1933, 12.

79. "Marriage Ban Bills Passed," *Los Angeles Times*, April 6, 1933, 1:2; "Rolph Signs Ban on Mixed Marriage," *Los Angeles Examiner*, April 21, 1933, 1:3.

80. An Act to Amend Sec. 60 of the Civil Code, Relating to Illegal and Void Marriages, ch. 104, 1933 Cal. Stat. 561; Volpp, "American Mestizo," 822–23.

81. An Act to Amend Sec. 69 of the Civil Code, Relating to Marriage Licenses, ch. 105, 1933 Cal. Stat. 561.

Chapter 6

1. An Act Prohibiting Marriage Between White Persons and Negroes, Persons of Negro Blood, and Between White Persons, Chinese and Japanese, and Making Such Marriage Void, ch. 49, 1909 Mont. Laws 57; An Act to Prevent Miscegenation, ch. 164, 1909 N.D. Laws 202; An Act Prohibiting the Intermarriage and Illicit Cohabitation of Persons Belonging to the Caucasian Race with Persons Belonging to the African Race, ch. 196, 1909 S.D. Laws 297; An Act to Amend Sec. 4312 of Ch. 50 of the Revised Stat. of Missouri for 1899, Relating to Marriages and Marriage Contracts, 1909 Mo. Laws 662; Nev. Rev. Stat. sec. 6514–17 (1912); Phillip I. Earl, "Nevada's Miscegenation Laws and the Marriage of Mr. and Mrs. Harry Bridges," *Nevada Historical Society Quarterly* 37 (Spring 1994), 7.

2. *NA*, 297–98, 302–4.

3. *NA*, 299.

4. On Jack Johnson, see Al-Tony Gilmore, "Jack Johnson and White Women: the National Impact," *Journal of Negro History* 58 (January 1973): 18–38; Gilmore, *Bad Nigger! The National Impact of Jack Johnson* (Port Washington, N.Y.: Kennikat Press, 1975); Thomas R. Hietala, *The Fight of the Century: Jack Johnson, Joe Louis, and the Struggle for Racial Equality* (Armonk, N.Y.: M. E. Sharpe, 2002); Randy Roberts, *Papa Jack: Jack Johnson and the Era of White Hopes* (New York: Free Press, 1983); Geoffrey C. Ward, *Unforgivable Blackness: The Rise and Fall of Jack Johnson* (New York: Alfred A. Knopf, 2005); David J. Langum, *Crossing Over the Line: Legislating Morality and the Mann Act* (Chicago: University of Chicago Press, 1994), 179–86; Kevin J. Mumford, *Interzones: Black/White Sex Districts in Chicago and New York in the Early Twentieth Century* (New York: Columbia University Press, 1996), 3–18; Gail Bederman, *Manliness and Civilization: A Cultural History of Gender and Race in the United States, 1880–1917* (Chicago: University of Chicago Press, 1995), 1–20; and Randall Kennedy, *Interracial Intimacies: Sex, Marriage, Identity, and Adoption* (New York: Pantheon Books, 2003), 79–85.

5. "Mrs. Johnson Tries Suicide; Pugilist's Wife, Tired of Being Social Outcast, Shoots Herself," *New York Times*, September 12, 1912, 6.

6. "Reflections on a Suicide," *New York Times*, September 14, 1912, 12.

7. "Mrs. Johnson Tries Suicide," 6; Hietala, *Fight of the Century,* 55–56, 59–60; Ward, *Unforgivable Blackness,* 249–57, 289–95.

8. Hietala, *Fight of the Century,* 61.

9. "Jack Johnson," *Crisis,* December 1912, 72. On Black public opinion about Johnson, see Gilmore, "Jack Johnson and White Women," 22–29.

10. Hietala, *Fight of the Century,* 61.

11. "Will Marry Miss Cameron; Jack Johnson Declares Wedding Will Take Place Before End of Week," *New York Times,* December 3, 1912, 1; Langum, *Crossing Over the Line,* 181–86; Hietala, *Fight of the Century,* 61–62, 65–69.

12. Ward, *Unforgivable Blackness,* 319–22; "Johnson Weds White Girl," *New York Times,* December 4, 1912, 2.

13. Langum, *Crossing Over the Line,* 185.

14. *Proceedings of the Fifth Meeting of the Governors of the States of the Union Held at Richmond, Virginia, December 3–7, 1912* (Madison, Wisc.: Cantwell Printing Company, 1912), 200.

15. "Jack Johnson Again," *New York Age,* December 12, 1912; Gilmore, "Jack Johnson and White Women," 30–32.

16. "Messrs. Blease and Johnson," *Crisis,* January 1913, 124, reprinting an article from the *New York World.*

17. *Congressional Record,* 62nd Cong., 3rd Sess., December 11, 1912, 502; "Attacks Johnson Marriage; Georgian Asks Congress to Forbid All Such Unions," *New York Times,* December 12, 1912, 24.

18. *Congressional Record,* 62nd Cong., 3rd Sess., December 11, 1912, 502; Gilmore, "Jack Johnson and White Women," 32; Hietala, *Fight of the Century,* 71–72.

19. William Monroe Trotter to Oswald Garrison Villard, February 12, 1913, fr. 930, Part 11, Series B, Reel 2, NAACP-MF.

20. "Intermarriage," *Crisis,* April 1912, 296–97; *NA,* 299–311; Gilmore, "Jack Johnson and White Women," 33.

21. At the end of 1912, when the Jack Johnson scandal broke, the NAACP had 3 branches and 329 members; at the end of 1913, it had 10 branches and 1,100 members; by 1919, it would have 310 branches and 91,203 members. Manfred Berg, *The Ticket to Freedom: The NAACP and the Struggle for Black Political Integration* (Gainesville: University Press of Florida, 2005), 23.

22. David Levering Lewis, *W.E.B. Du Bois: Biography of a Race, 1868-1919* (New York: Holt, 1993), 425; House Committee on the District of Columbia, *Intermarriage of Whites and Negroes in the District of Columbia and Separate Accommodations in Street Cars for Whites and Negroes in the District of Columbia,* 64th Cong., 1st sess., 1916, 23. Michele Mitchell aptly described this dynamic as the politics of racial destiny in *Righteous Propagation: African Americans and the Politics of Racial Destiny after Reconstruction* (Chapel Hill: University of North Carolina Press, 2004), 8–13. For more on Black opinions on interracial marriage and miscegenation law, see Charles F. Robinson II, *Dangerous Liaisons: Sex and Love in the Segregated South* (Fayetteville: University of Arkansas Press, 2003), 114–28, and Renee C. Romano, *Race Mixing: Black-White Marriage in Postwar America* (Cambridge: Harvard University Press, 2003): 82–108.

23. W.E.B. Du Bois, "Extract from 'Marrying of Black Folk,'" clipping, fr. 918, 916, Part 11, Series B, Reel 2, NAACP-MF; Mark Robert Schneider,"*We Return Fighting*":

The Civil Rights Movement in the Jazz Age (Boston: Northeastern University Press, 2002), 36–41; Charles Flint Kellogg, *NAACP: A History of the National Association for the Advancement of Colored People*, vol. 1, *1909–1920* (Baltimore: Johns Hopkins University Press, 1967), 14–19, 67–88; Berg, *Ticket to Freedom*, 13–17.

24. Lewis, *Biography of a Race*, 477–78; Berg, *Ticket to Freedom*, 18. Two especially insightful analyses of the discourse of respectability among African Americans are Kevin K. Gaines, *Uplifting the Race: Black Leadership, Politics, and Culture in the Twentieth Century* (Chapel Hill: University of North Carolina Press, 1996) and Mitchell, *Righteous Propagation*, 9–11, 80–85.

25. Berg, *Ticket to Freedom*, 40–43; Kellogg, *NAACP*, 45.

26. *NA*, 222, 247–65.

27. Ill. Rev. Stat. ch. 89 (1874); An Act to Amend Sec. 6 of ch. 169, of the Compiled Laws of 1871, no. 23, and An Act to Amend Sec. 1 and to repeal Sec. 31 of ch. 170, of the Compiled Laws of 1871, no. 24, 1883 Mich. Pub. Acts 16.

28. *NA*, 255–64; An Act to Repeal Secs. 4008, 6987, and 6988 of the Rev. Stat. of Ohio, 1887 Ohio Laws 34.

29. *NA*, 248–51, 287–88; Emma Lou Thornbrough, *The Negro in Indiana Before 1900: A Study of a Minority* (1957; Bloomington: Indiana University Press, 1993), 268–69.

30. W.E.B. Du Bois, "Intermarriage," *Crisis*, February 1913, 181.

31. Nathaniel Sawyer to May Childs Nerney, December 29, 1913, fr. 485–86, Part 12, Series D, Reel 6, NAACP-MF.

32. William Monroe Trotter to Oswald Garrison Villard, March 16, 1913, fr. 959; NAACP to Charles T. Hallinan, April 11, 1913, fr. 964; both in Part 11, Series B, Reel 2, NAACP-MF; *NA*, 303–4.

33. New York Senate Bill no. 158, January 15, 1913, ms. copy in NAACP Intermarriage File, fr. 923–25, Part 11, Series B, Reel 2, NAACP-MF.

34. Cosmopolitan Society of America, "To the New York State Legislature Senate Committee on Resolutions," January 1913, fr. 1017; Franklin D. Roosevelt to Oswald Garrison Villard, January 30, 1913, fr. 928; both in Part 11, Series B, Reel 2, NAACP-MF.

35. Ohio House Bill 27, January 1913, typed copy, fr. 970; Harry E. Davis to May Childs Nerney, March 8, 1913, fr. 953; both in Part 11, Series B, Reel 2, NAACP-MF.

36. Davis to Nerney, March 8, 1913; Douglass Men's Club, resolutions against the intermarriage bill, copy, n.d., fr. 931; Cleveland Association of Colored Men to Ohio legislators, March 8, 1913, fr. 954; M.C.B. Mason to Oswald Garrison Villard, March 11, 1913, fr. 957; Charles W. Chesnutt to W.E.B. Du Bois, April 28, 1913, fr. 968; all in Part 11, Series B, Reel 1, NAACP-MF.

37. NAACP to Chairman of California Senate Committee on Education, March 3, 1913, fr. 935; May Childs Nerney to Charles T. Hallinan, April 11, 1913, fr. 964; NAACP national office to Senator Harry Rosenhaupt, June 2, 1913, fr. 972; all in Part 11, Series B, Reel 2, NAACP-MF.

38. Joel E. Springarn, file note on conversation with Franklin Delano Roosevelt, January 27, 1913, fr. 16; May Childs Nerney to James C. Waters, April 15, 1914, fr. 6; both in Part 11, Series B, Reel 3, NAACP-MF (emphasis mine); Kennedy, *Interracial Intimacies*, 257–58.

39. Kellogg, *NAACP*, 103, 175–76, 180–81; House Committee on D.C., *Intermarriage*; Dickson D. Bruce Jr., *Archibald Grimké: Portrait of a Black Independent* (Baton Rouge: Louisiana State University Press, 1993), 211–12. Rosetta E. Lawson, who also testified at the hearing, limited her comments to the issue of streetcar segregation.

40. Du Bois, "Intermarriage," 180; Mia Bay, *The White Image in the Black Mind: African-American Ideas About White People, 1830–1925* (New York: Oxford University Press, 2000), 196–98; Franz Boas, "The Real Race Problem," *Crisis*, December 1910, 23; W.E.B. Du Bois, "Races," *Crisis*, August 1911, 157.

41. "Along the Color Line," *Crisis*, April 1912, 231; "Along the Color Line," *Crisis*, August 1911, 144; "The Horizon: Ghetto," *Crisis*, September 1917, 264; Bay, *White Image*, 198.

42. Harry E. Davis to James Weldon Johnson, March 6, 1925, fr. 203; Melville Jacobs to NAACP, February 12, 1939, fr. 561; both in Part 11, Series B, Reel 3, NAACP-MF.

43. Gilbert Jonas, *Freedom's Sword: The NAACP and the Struggle Against Racism in America, 1909–1969* (New York: Routledge, 2005), 12.

44. For example, between 1900 and 1950, the Boston marriage license registry reported 138 marriages between Black men and White women, but only 13 marriages between White men and Black women. Ray Stannard Baker, *Following the Color Line* (New York: Doubleday, 1908), 172; Paul R. Spickard, *Mixed Blood: Intermarriage and Ethnic Identity in Twentieth-Century America* (Madison: University of Wisconsin Press, 1989), 272–74.

45. "Champion Jack Johnson Denies Charges Against Him in the Daily Newspaper," *Chicago Defender*, October 26, 1913, 1.

46. The NAACP files include a typescript of the entire text of William Lloyd Garrison's argument for repealing the Massachusetts miscegenation law, originally published in the *Liberator*, on February 24, 1843; fr. 11, Part 11, Series B, Reel 3, NAACP-MF.

47. NAACP to California Senate, March 3, 1913, fr. 937; NAACP to Wisconsin Senate Committee on Judiciary, January 25, 1917, fr. 22; both in Part 11, Series B, Reel 3, NAACP-MF.

48. On Black opposition to interracial marriage, see Mitchell, *Righteous Propagation*, 197–217, and Gaines, *Uplifting the Race*, 125–27.

49. Du Bois, "Intermarriage," 180.

50. W.E.B. Du Bois, "Sex Equality," *Crisis*, January 1920, 106; NAACP to California Senate, March 3, 1913; Committee on D.C., *Intermarriage*, 22.

51. Committee on D.C., *Intermarriage*, 17; Du Bois, "Extract from 'Marrying,'" fr. 918; NAACP to California Senate, March 3, 1913.

52. Wendell P. Dabney, testimony before Ohio House Judiciary Committee, March 3, 1925, fr. 228, Part 11, Series B, Reel 3, NAACP-MF.

53. Langum, *Crossing Over the Line*, 179; Mumford, *Interzones*, 10–13, 169–71.

54. "Negroes Charge Klan Conspiracy in Anti-Intermarriage Bills," NAACP press release, February 24, 1927, fr. 349, Part 11, Series B, Reel 3, NAACP-MF.

55. The defense of marriage grew especially strong roots in African American political discourse in these years. Gaines, *Uplifting the Race*, 78–80, 122–25; Mitchell, *Righteous Propagation*, 202–3.

56. Committee on D.C., *Intermarriage,* 12–14. Grimké could ground his argument in personal experience as well as political conviction: the son of a White South Carolina planter and his mixed-race slave, Grimké had also been married, briefly, to a White woman. See Bruce, *Archibald Grimké,* 1–4, 37–42.

57. Du Bois, "Intermarriage," 180.

58. Committee on D.C., *Intermarriage,* 19; "Prominent Iowa Leaders of N.A.A.C.P. Fighting Inter-Marriage Bill," clipping from *Pacific Defender,* April 2, 1925, fr. 238; "Tells Why Colored People Oppose Anti-Intermarriage Laws," NAACP press release, June 5, 1925, fr. 234; both in Part 11, Series B, Reel 3, NAACP-MF. Interestingly, many Black *opponents* of interracial marriage also relied on arguments about the need to protect black womanhood. Mitchell, *Righteous Propagation,* 208–9.

59. On the racial structure of the discourse of "white slavery," see Mumford, *Inter-zones,* 14–18.

60. Instructions to Michigan Branches, April 12, 1921, fr. 86, Part 11, Series B, Reel 3, NAACP-MF; *Sixteenth Annual Report of the National Association for the Advance-ment of Colored People for the Year 1925* (New York: NAACP, 1926), 23.

61. Laurence J. Moore, *Citizen Klansmen: The Ku Klux Klan in Indiana, 1921–1928* (Chapel Hill: University of North Carolina Press, 1991), 1–3; Nancy MacLean, *Behind the Mask of Chivalry: The Making of the Second Ku Klux Klan* (New York: Oxford University Press, 1994), xi–xvii; Shawn Lay, ed., *The Invisible Empire in the West: Toward a New Historical Appraisal of the Ku Klux Klan of the 1920s* (Urbana: University of Illinois Press, 1992), 1–9. On the NAACP's campaign against the Klan during the 1920s, see Schneider, *"We Return Fighting,"* 231–48.

62. "Prominent Iowa Leaders," April 2, 1925; Davis to Johnson, March 6, 1925; "Mich. Legislature Kills Anti-Intermarriage Bill," clipping from *Pittsburgh Courier,* May 16, 1925, fr. 273, Part 11, Series B, Reel 3, NAACP-MF. The Ohio bill would have criminalized both marriage and "carnal knowledge" between "any person of pure white blood" and "a person of another race or a person having a distinct and visible admixture of the blood of another race," with "race" defined to include "the Mongolian or yellow, the Ethiopian or black, the American or red, and the Malay or brown." Ohio House Bill 218, 1925, fr. 268–69, Part 11, Series B, Reel 3, NAACP-MF.

63. "New Bills Reported To N.A.A.C.P. From New Jersey, Pennsylvania & Maine," Press Release, February 25, 1927, fr. 350; Walter White to George W. Crawford, January 20, 1927, fr. 305; James Weldon Johnson to George S. Brookes, February 15, 1928, fr. 431; "Michigan Anti-Intermarriage Bill 'Quietly Expired,' NAACP Told," NAACP press release, fr. 402; typescript of Michigan Senate Bill no. 61, February 8, 1927, fr. 320; all in Part 11, Series B, Reel 3, NAACP-MF.

64. William P. H. Freeman to James Weldon Johnson, February 4, 1927, fr. 316; "Senate Rejects 'Klan' Measures," clipping from *Providence Journal,* February 3, 1927, fr. 317; both in Part 11, Series B, Reel 3, NAACP-MF. In Ohio, NAACP organizers had discovered that the Catholic Church was one of their best allies even before the resurgence of the Klan. See M.C.B. Mason to Oswald Garrison Villard, March 11, 1913, fr. 957, Part 11, Series B, Reel 2, NAACP-MF.

65. Both Barbara Bair and J. Douglas Smith have emphasized the extent to which the Anglo-Saxon Clubs of America, the sponsor of Virginia's Racial Integrity Act, tried to distance itself from Klan politics even as it drew on the Klan roots of its major

supporters. See Barbara Bair, "Remapping the Black/White Body: Sexuality, National-ism, and Biracial Antimiscegenation Activism in 1920s Virginia," in *Sex, Love, Race: Crossing Boundaries in North American History*, ed. Martha Hodes (New York: NYU Press, 1999), 400–404; J. Douglas Smith, *Managing White Supremacy: Race, Politics, and Citizen-ship in Jim Crow Virginia* (Chapel Hill: University of North Carolina, 2002), 78–80. Julie Novkov explains that in Alabama a similar process took place, as "populists who sought to seize the mantle of reform through the gaudy and flamboyant use of rhetorical and real racial violence" lost out to "conservative Democratic elites," who offered a more "sani-tized" and "rationalized" version of the white supremacist state. Novkov, *Racial Union,* 8.

66. "Charges U.S. Postal Frank Used to Disseminate Anti-Negro Propaganda," NAACP press release, March 25, 1925, fr. 624; James Weldon Johnson to Florence Kelley, Apr. 18, 1925, fr. 656; James J. Davis to James Weldon Johnson, March 28, 1925, fr. 643; Arthur E. Cook to James Weldon Johnson, April 3, 1925, fr. 647; all in Part 11, Series B, Reel 3, NAACP-MF.

67. Proposed Senate Bill no. 9394, fr. 112; Transcript of telephone conversation with Capper, fr. 135; both in Part 11, Series B, Reel 3, NAACP-MF; Glenda Eliza-beth Gilmore, *Gender and Jim Crow: Women and the Politics of White Supremacy in North Carolina, 1896–1920* (Chapel Hill: University of North Carolina Press, 1996), 71.

68. On the UNIA, see Tony Martin, *Race First: The Ideological and Organizational Struggles of Marcus Garvey and the Universal Negro Improvement Association* (Westport, Conn.: Greenwood Press, 1976); Judith Stein, *The World of Marcus Garvey: Race and Class in Modern Society* (Baton Rouge: Louisiana State University Press, 1986); Bay, *White Image,* 202–15; Bair, "Remapping the Black/White Body," 399–419; and Schneider, *"We Return Fighting,"* 125–44.

69. W. A. Plecker to J. Griswold Webb, March 3, 1926, Box 56, Folder 3, JPP; Amy Jacques Garvey, *The Philosophy and Opinions of Marcus Garvey, or Africa for the Afri-cans* (1923–25; Dover, Mass.: Majority Press, 1986), 240.

70. Martin, *Race First,* 314–33; Schneider, *"We Return Fighting,"* 136–37; Edward A. Williams, "Racial Purity in Black and White: The Case of Marcus Garvey and Earnest Cox," *Journal of Ethnic Studies* 15 (Spring 1987): 121–22.

71. See also Marcus Garvey, "Essays on Race Purity by Marcus Garvey," in *The Marcus Garvey and Universal Negro Improvement Association Papers,* ed. Robert Hill (Berkeley: University of California Press, 1989), 4:217–20.

72. Marcus Garvey to Earnest S. Cox, June 24, 1925, in Hill, *Garvey Papers,* 201; "Negroes Indorse State Racial Integrity Law," clipping from *Richmond Times-Dispatch,* August 15, 1925, Box 56, Folder 8, JPP; Williams, "Racial Purity in Black and White"; Bair, "Remapping the Black/White Body," 406–7.

73. Bair, "Remapping the Black/White Body," 405, 409–10, 414; Martin, *Race First,* 274–80; Schneider, *"We Return Fighting,"* 136–37, 142; Gaines, *Uplifting the Race,* 120; Williams, "Racial Purity in Black and White," 121–25.

74. W.E.B. Du Bois, "Opinion," *Crisis,* May 1924, 8; Garvey, "Essays on Racial Purity," 220; Marcus Garvey, "W. E. Burghardt Du Bois as a Hater of Dark People," in A. Garvey, *Philosophy and Opinions,* 310–11; Martin, *Race First,* 307.

75. Du Bois, "Sex Equality," 106; "Negroes Want Racial Integrity, Too," *Richmond Planet,* February 11, 1928, 4; Martin, *Race First,* 15; Mitchell, *Righteous Propagation,* 190–92, 219–39.

76. NAACP to California Senate, March 3, 1913.

77. Estelle B. Freedman and John D'Emilio, *Intimate Matters: A History of Sexuality in America* (New York: Harper and Row, 1988), 172–73, 222–23, 233–35.

78. Freedman and D'Emilio, *Intimate Matters*, 265–73; Christine Stansell, *American Moderns: Bohemian New York and the Creation of a New Century* (New York: Metropolitan Books, 2000), 225–72.

79. Gaines, *Uplifting the Race*, 166–69; Lewis, *Biography of a Race*, 435, 451.

80. Josephine Schuyler, "An Interracial Marriage," *American Mercury*, March 1946, 274. For the public presentation of the marriage, see "An Interracial Marriage" and George Schuyler, *Black and Conservative: The Autobiography of George S. Schuyler* (New Rochelle, N.Y.: Arlington House, 1966), 163–64; for interpretations of the growing misery that lay beneath the public image, see Kathryn Talalay, *Composition in Black and White: The Life of Philippa Schuyler* (New York: Oxford University Press, 1995), and Kennedy, *Interracial Intimacies*, 339–66.

81. George S. Schuyler, *Racial Intermarriage in the United States* (Girard, Kans.: Haldeman-Julius Publications, 1929), 12; G. Schuyler, *Black and Conservative*, 169.

82. G. Schuyler, *Racial Intermarriage*, 5, 30, 6–12, 8; Kennedy, *Interracial Intimacies*, 354.

83. G. Schuyler, *Racial Intermarriage*, 28.

84. George S. Schuyler, *Black No More: Being an Account of the Strange and Wonderful Workings of Science in the Land of the Free, A.D. 1933–1940* (New York: Macaulay, 1931); Kennedy, *Interracial Intimacies*, 344–53; Schuyler, "A Negro Looks Ahead," *American Mercury*, February 1930, 218, 220; Schuyler, "The Caucasian Problem," in *What the Negro Wants*, ed. Rayford W. Logan (1944; Notre Dame: Notre Dame University Press, 2001), 290, 297–98.

85. J. A. Rogers, *As Nature Leads: An Informal Discussion of the Reason Why Negro and Caucasian Are Mixing in Spite of Opposition* (Chicago: M. A. Donahue, 1919); Rogers, *Sex And Race: Negro-Caucasian Mixing in All Ages and All Lands*, 3 vols. (New York City: J. A. Rogers Publications, 1940–44); Rogers, *Nature Knows No Color-Line: Research into the Negro Ancestry in the White Race* (New York: Helga M. Rogers, 1952). Quotes are from Rogers, *Sex and Race* (St. Petersburg, Fla.: Helga M. Rogers, 1967–72), 1:2, 19.

86. Rogers, *Sex and Race* 2:295.

87. Rogers, *Sex and Race* 3:99; 2:295; 3:158.

88. Rogers, *Sex and Race* 3:84, 82, 102, 227, 142.

89. Bruce, *Archibald Grimké*, 113–17; Archibald H. Grimké, "The Heart of the Race Problem," *Arena*, January 1906, 29–33; W.E.B. Du Bois, "Black France," *Crisis*, March 1922, 199.

90. Rogers, *Sex and Race*, 3:18, 3:20.

91. American Civil Liberties Union, *The Story of Civil Liberty—1929–30* (New York: ACLU, 1930), 34; American Civil Liberties Union, *Black Justice* (New York: ACLU, 1931), 19.

92. Gunnar Myrdal, *An American Dilemma: The Negro Problem and Modern Democracy* (New York: Harper and Brothers, 1944), 60, 587.

93. Samuel Walker, *In Defense of American Liberties: A History of the ACLU*, 2nd ed. (Carbondale: Southern Illinois University Press, 1999), 60.

94. *People v. Wilkerson,* 99 Cal. App. at 124 (Cal. Ct. App., 1929); "State Marriage Laws Force Couple to Travel 2800 Miles," *Pacific Citizen,* October 8, 1949, 1.

95. *Whittington v. McCaskill,* 65 Fla. 162 (1913); *In re Takahashi's Estate,* 113 Mont. 490 (1942); *People v. Godines,* 17 Cal. App. 2d 721 (Cal. Dis. Ct. App, 1936).

96. *Kinney v. Commonwealth,* 71 Va. at 866 (1878).

97. See, for example, Of Offences Against Morality and Decency, ch. 7, sec. 3, 1877–78 Va. Acts 301; An Act in Relation to Marriage and Divorce, Miss. Rev. Code, ch. 42, sec. 1147 (1880); An Act Prohibiting Marriage Between White Persons and Negroes, Persons of Negro Blood, and Between White Persons, Chinese and Japanese, and Making Such Marriage Void, ch. 49, sec. 5, 1909 Mont. Laws 58.

98. An Act to Prevent the Evasion of Laws Prohibiting Marriage, no. 110, Vt. Acts & Resolves 148; An Act to Make Uniform the Law Relating to Marriages in Another State or Country in Evasion or Violation of the Laws of the State of Domicile, ch. 360, Mass. Acts 302. Both laws used language offered by the Conference of Commissioners on Uniform State Laws, which had, in August 1912, proposed a model act "On the Subject of Marriages in Another State or Country in Evasion or Violation of the Laws of the State of Domicile." The model act was proposed a few months before the Jack Johnson episode, so it is important to note that the commissioners were well aware that their model law would, among other things, "give full effect" to the miscegenation laws of many states "by making void all marriages contracted in violation of such prohibitions." *Proceedings of the Annual Conference of Commissioners on Uniform State Laws* 22 (1912): 127–30.

99. *In re Takahashi's Estate,* 113 Mont. at 495 (1942).

100. *Ex Parte Kinney,* 14 F. Cas. at 607 (C.C.E.D. Va. 1879) (No. 7825); *State v. Tutty,* 41 Fed. Cas. at 760 (C.C.S.D. Ga. E.D., 1890); *Estate of Wilbur,* 8 Wash. at 37 (1894); *Succession of Gabisso,* 119 La. at 713 (1907); *Eggers v. Olson,* 104 Okla. at 301 (1924).

101. *State v. Tutty; Succession of Gabisso; In re Takahashi's Estate; Kinney v. Commonwealth,* 71 Va. at 865–66 (1878); *Jackson v. Jackson,* 82 Md. at 30 (1895); *Goldman v. Dithrich,* 131 Fla. at 416 (1938).

102. *State v. Tutty.*

103. *State v. Kennedy,* 76 N.C. at 252 (1877); *Greenhow v. James' Executor,* 80 Va. at 640–41 (1885); *Eggers v. Olson,* 104 Okla. at 299–301 (1924).

104. *State v. Hand,* 87 Neb. 189 (1910); *Estate of MacKay,* 3 Coff. Prob. at 321 (Cal. Sup. Ct., 1894); *People v. Wilkerson,* 99 Cal. App. at 125 (Cal. Ct. App., 1929).

105. "Anti-Miscegenation Laws and the Pilipino," in *Letters in Exile: An Introductory Reader on the History of Pilipinos in America,* ed. Jesse Quinsaat (Los Angeles: UCLA Asian American Studies Center, 1976), 69; Megumi Dick Osumi, "Asians and California's Anti-Miscegenation Laws," in *Asian and Pacific American Experiences: Women's Perspectives,* ed. Nobuya Tsuchida (Minneapolis: Asian/Pacific Learning Resource Center, 1982), 22; An Act Amending Section 40-1-2, Revised Statutes of Utah, 1933, Relating to Prohibited and Void Marriages, ch. 50, 1939 Utah Laws 66. Rachel Moran notes that this incident did not end here; another California legislator subsequently, but unsuccessfully, tried to pass a bill that would have declared interracial marriages made in other states void if they would have been void if made in California. See Rachel F. Moran, *Interracial Intimacy: The Regulation of Race and Romance* (Chicago: University of Chicago Press, 2001), 39.

106. On the significance of the military as an arena for interracial marriage, see Romano, *Race-Mixing*, 12–27, and Alex Lubin, *Romance and Rights: The Politics of Interracial Intimacy, 1945–1954* (Jackson: University Press of Mississippi, 2005), 96–122.

107. The Buakens' story can be followed in Iris Brown Buaken, "My Brave New World," *Asia and the Americas*, May 1943, 268–70; Iris B. Buaken, "You Can't Marry a Filipino; Not if You Live in California," *Commonweal*, March 16, 1945, 534–37; and Manuel Buaken, *I Have Lived with the American People* (Caldwell, Id.: Caxton Printers, 1948).

108. Buaken, "Can't Marry a Filipino," 534.

109. For more on the contradictions that faced Filipinos who served in the U.S. armed forces during World War II, see Linda España-Maram, *Masculinity in Los Angeles's Little Manila: Working-Class Filipinos and Popular Culture, 1920–1950s* (New York: Columbia University Press, 2006), 152–63.

110. Buaken, "Can't Marry a Filipino," 535.

111. Buaken, "Can't Marry a Filipino," 536.

112. Walter White to Secretary of the Navy James Forrestal, December 20, 1945, fr. 13; Secretary of War Robert P. Patterson to Walter White, March 5, 1946, fr. 56; James D. Givens's comments on Request for Permission to Marry, January 9, 1945, fr. 51; all in Part 9, Series B, Reel 15, NAACP-MF; Brenda Gayle Plummer, "Brown Babies: Race, Gender, and Policy After World War II," in *Window on Freedom: Race, Civil Rights and Foreign Affairs* (Chapel Hill: University of North Carolina Press, 2003), 67, 75–78.

113. Robert Bradford to NAACP Headquarters, October 28, 1946, fr. 77; Marie Druax to NAACP Headquarters, October 14, 1946, fr. 80; Julia E. Baxter to Marie Druax, November 14, 1946, fr. 79; all in Part 9, Series B, Reel 15, NAACP-MF.

114. Franklin H. Williams to John W. Morris, March 23, 1948, fr. 117, Part 9, Series B, Reel 15, NAACP-MF.

115. "Estimate 550 Japanese Girls Wed to GIs Before Deadline: Majority of Marriages Between Nisei Personnel, Japanese Nationals," *Pacific Citizen*, August 23, 1947, 2; "Masaoka Says GI Brides Law Discriminatory," *Pacific Citizen*, May 17, 1946, 1; "Soldier Brides Act of 1947," *Pacific Citizen*, December 17, 1954, C7.

116. "Report 1300 Nisei Soldiers Married Japanese Brides During Occupation Period," *Pacific Citizen*, September 27, 1952, 2; Elfrieda Berthiaume Shukert and Barbara Smith Scibetta, *War Brides of World War II* (New York: Penguin Books, 1989), 217; "GIs Query Washington JACL Office on Soldier Bride Act," *Pacific Citizen*, September 30, 1950, 7; "National Legislative Progress Report #4," JACL, Anti-Discrimination Committee, Washington Office, March 2, 1949, Box 132, Folder 11, FCP.

117. J. Robert Smith, "Nazi Virginians Separate Man and Ofay Wife," *Afro-American and Richmond Planet*, June 18, 1938, 1–2; Buaken, "Can't Marry a Filipino," 535, 534; Buaken, "My Brave New World," 268.

118. Irving G. Tragen, "Statutory Prohibitions Against Interracial Marriage," *California Law Review* 32 (1944): 276, 279; Eugene Marias, "A Brief Survey of Some Problems in Miscegenation," *Southern California Law Review* 20 (1946): 222; Harry L. Gershon, "Restrictive Covenants and Equal Protection—The New Rule in Shelley's Case," *Southern California Law Review* 21 (1947–48): 368.

119. *Smith v. Allwright*, 32 U.S. 649 (1944); *Shelley v. Kraemer*, 334 U.S. 1 (1948); *Sweatt v. Painter*, 339 U.S. 629 (1950); *McLaurin v. Oklahoma State Regents*, 339 U.S. 637 (1950); *Brown v. Board of Education*, 347 U.S. 483 (1954); Berg, *Ticket to Freedom*, 109–11; Mark V. Tushnet, *The NAACP's Legal Strategy Against Segregated Education, 1925–1950* (Chapel Hill: University of North Carolina Press, 2004), 100–101, 135–37.

120. Greenberg, *Crusaders in the Courts*, 81; Tushnet, *NAACP's Legal Strategy*, 102, 145. Indeed, as Risa Goluboff has recently argued, during World War II, the NAACP had also made labor rights cases a significant part of its civil rights caseload. See Risa L. Goluboff, *The Lost Promise of Civil Rights* (Cambridge: Harvard University Press, 2007), 198–216.

121. Cassandra E. Maxwell to W.A.C. Hughes Jr., October 21, 1939, fr. 609, Part 11, Series B, Reel 3, NAACP-MF.

122. Thurgood Marshall to A. L. Emery, January 20, 1944, fr. 670; Emery to Marshall, January 5, 1944, fr. 671; both in Part 18, Series A, Reel 3, NAACP-MF; Findings of Fact and Conclusions of Law, December 13, 1943, Transcript of Record, 31, Stevens v. U.S., no. 2941, Record Group 276, Records of the U.S. Courts of Appeals, NARA—Rocky Mountain Region, Denver. Although the court referred to the couple by the racial designations quoted in the text, Emery told Marshall, with emphasis, that *"both are and were mixed bloods."*

123. Milton R. Konvitz to A. L. Emery, April 12, 1944, fr. 702; William H. Hastie telegram to Milton R. Konvitz, April 7, 1944, fr. 704; both in Part 18, Series A, Reel 3, NAACP-MF. Emery proceeded with the case anyway, and did indeed lose in federal district court. See the accounts of the case in Peter Wallenstein, *Tell the Court I Love My Wife: Race, Marriage, and Law—An American History* (New York: Palgrave Macmillan, 2002), 174–79, and Phyl Newbeck, *Virginia Hasn't Always Been for Lovers: Interracial Marriage Bans and the Case of Richard and Mildred Loving* (Carbondale: Southern Illinois University Press, 2004), 90–92.

124. Robert L. Carter to Lewis B. Stewart, June 3, 1946, Part 2, Box B 82, Folder: Legal File: Intermarriage General, 1946–49, NAACP-LC.

125. Greenberg, *Crusaders in the Courts*, 71–72.

Chapter 7

1. The most detailed accounts of the *Perez* case are Dara Orenstein, "Void for Vagueness: Mexicans and the Collapse of Miscegenation Law in California," *Pacific Historical Review* 74 (August 2005): 367–407; Mark Brilliant, *Color Lines: Civil Rights Struggles on America's "Racial Frontier," 1945–1975* (New York: Oxford University Press, forthcoming); Fay Botham, "'Almighty God Created the Races': Theologies of Marriage and Race in Anti-Miscegenation Cases, 1865–1967" (Ph.D. dissertation, Claremont Graduate University, 2005), 19–78; and Ben Field, *Activism in Pursuit of the Public Interest: The Jurisprudence of Chief Justice Roger J. Traynor* (Berkeley: Berkeley Public Policy Press, 2003), 19–44.

2. As Dara Orenstein notes, Sylvester Davis's own uncle had been married in Mexico for this reason. Orenstein, "Void for Vagueness," 386.

3. Orenstein, "Void for Vagueness," 372–73, 386–88; Allison Varzally, "Romantic Crossings: Making Love, Family, and Non-Whiteness in California, 1925–1950," *Journal of American Ethnic History* 23 (Fall 2003): 10.

4. George H. Gallup, *The Gallup Poll: Public Opinion, 1935–1971* (New York: Random House, 1972), 2:1572.

5. Orenstein, "Void for Vagueness," 367–68, 371–74.

6. Cal. Stat., Civil Code sec. 60 (1937); Jean Simon, "Marriage Recorder Uses 'Sixth Sense' to Determine Race," *Los Angeles Sentinel,* December 23, 1948, 2 (emphasis added); Orenstein, "Void for Vagueness," 368, 377–87; Mark Brilliant, "Color Lines: Civil Rights Struggles on America's 'Racial Frontier,' 1945–1975" (Ph.D. dissertation, Stanford University, 2002), 128; Kevin R. Johnson and Kristina L. Burrows, "Struck by Lightning? Interracial Intimacy and Racial Justice," *Human Rights Quarterly* 25 (2003): 533–36. Orenstein aptly describes the racial classification of Mexicans as "white by default," noting that it was highly unstable.

7. Orenstein, "Void for Vagueness," 394.

8. Orenstein, "Void for Vagueness," 374–75.

9. One study of Los Angeles marriage licenses found, for example, that for the period between 1924 and 1933, of the 11,016 marriages involving at least one "Mexican" partner, only 1 was to a "Negro." Data for the early 1940s do not seem to be available, but during the period between 1948 and 1951, the first three years in which interracial marriage was legal, another study found 32 marriages between "Mexicans" and "Negroes." Constantine Panunzio, "Intermarriage in Los Angeles, 1924–33," *American Journal of Sociology* 47 (March 1942): 692; John H. Burma, "Research Note on the Measurement of Interracial Marriage," *American Journal of Sociology* 57 (May 1952): 587, 589.

10. See *Lopez v. Seccombe,* 71 F. Supp. 769 (1944); *Westminster v. Mendez,* 161 F. 2d 774 (1947); and Vicki L. Ruiz, "South by Southwest: Mexican Americans and Segregated Schooling, 1900–1950," *OAH Magazine of History* 15 (Winter 2001): 23–27.

11. Dara Orenstein, "Between the Lines: Mexicans, Miscegenation and *Perez v. Sharp,*" December 2002, unpublished paper in the possession of the author, 10.

12. "Catholics Start Attack on Statute," *Los Angeles Tribune,* August 23, 1947, 12; Orenstein, "Void for Vagueness," 388.

13. Theodore LeBerthon to Matthew Ahmann, August 10, 1959, 2, Catholic Human Relations Council Correspondence, 1959–63, in Series 10, Box 2, National Catholic Conference for Interracial Justice Records, Marquette University Department of Special Collections and Archives, Milwaukeee, Wisconsin; Ted LeBerthon, "Council of All Races," *Interracial Review* 18 (October 1945): 150–52. See also "Declaration of Principles of the Catholic Interracial Council of Los Angeles," LACIC papers in the possession of Michael Engh, Department of History, Loyola Marymount University.

14. Shana Beth Bernstein, "Building Bridges at Home in a Time of Global Conflict: Interracial Cooperation and the Fight for Civil Rights in Los Angeles, 1933–1954" (Ph.D. dissertation, Stanford University, 2003), 98–163. For a full account of the battles over race in this period of Los Angeles history, see Kevin Allen Leonard, *The Battle for Los Angeles: Racial Ideology and World War II* (Albuquerque: University of New Mexico Press, 2006).

15. "Los Angeles Council Urges Permanent FEPC," *Interracial Review* 17 (October 1944): 159; LeBerthon, "Council of All Races," 150–51; LeBerthon to Ahmann, August 10, 1959, 2–4.

16. LeBerthon to Ahmann, August 10, 1959, 4–6; A. V. Krebs Jr., "A Church of Silence," *Commonweal* 16 (July 1964): 474; George H. Dunne, *King's Pawn* (Chicago:

Loyola University, 1990), 4, 211; Frances J. Weber, *His Eminence of Los Angeles: James Francis Cardinal McIntyre* (Mission Hills, Calif.: Saint Francis Historical Society, 1997), 474–75.

17. "Interracial Marriage Ban to Be Attacked," LACIC press release, April 4, 1947, LACIC papers in the possession of Michael Engh, Department of History, Loyola Marymount University; LeBerthon to Ahmann, August 10, 1959, 3; Petition for Writ of Mandamus, Memorandum of Points and Authorities and Proof of Service, August 8, 1947, PeCF.

18. This, for example, is the phrasing in Marshall's Petition for Writ of Mandamus, 2.

19. Petition for Writ of Mandamus, 4. For an argument that religion was central to the *Perez* case from its inception to its outcome, see Botham, "Almighty God," 23–76.

20. Compare John LaFarge, *Interracial Justice* (1937; New York: Arno Press, 1978), 143–48, and *The Race Question and the Negro: A Study of the Catholic Doctrine on Interracial Justice* (New York: Longmans, Green, 1943), 192–98, to Marshall's Petition for Writ of Mandamus, 3. For more on LaFarge, see David W. Southern, *John LaFarge and the Limits of Catholic Interracialism, 1911–1963* (Baton Rouge: Louisiana State University Press, 1996), esp. 113 and 227, and Dunne, *King's Pawn*, 98–99.

21. George H. Dunne, "The Sin of Segregation," *Commonweal*, September 21, 1945, 542.

22. Quoted in Southern, *John LaFarge*, 274, 112–13.

23. *People v. Oyama*, 29 Cal. 2d 164, 177 (1946). The vote was 5–0, though two justices had not participated in the case, and Roger J. Traynor's terse concurrence seemed to signal considerable discomfort with the court's reasoning. See Mark Brilliant, "Color Lines," 96–127.

24. Petition for Writ of Mandamus, 5b; Memorandum of Points and Authorities, 4, 6, PeCF.

25. LaFarge, *Race Question and the Negro*, 77–81, 102; Joseph F. Doherty, *Moral Problems of Interracial Marriage* (Washington: Catholic University Press of America, 1949), 35–38, 115; and "Interracial Marriage," *America*, October 16, 1948, 36.

26. *Black's Law Dictionary*, 4th ed. (St. Paul, Minn.: West Publishing, 1951), 1177; and *Webster's New International Dictionary*, 2nd ed., (C. G. Merriam, 1946), 1631.

27. *Norman v. Norman*, 121 Cal. 620 (1898); *Meyer v. Nebraska*, 262 U.S. 390, 399 (1923).

28. The failure of civil rights organizations to come to Marshall's aid has been noticed by nearly every scholar who writes about the case. Fred Fertig of the JACL did, however, loan Dan Marshall his personal collection of materials on interracial marriage for use in his brief. The national office of the ACLU, unable to find a lawyer who could write a brief in time, left the task to its Southern California office, which never filed the brief it evidently planned to write. Fred Fertig to Roger Baldwin, September 17, 1947, ACLU; Ernest Besig to Frances Levenson, August 29, 1947; Levenson to Besig, September 11, 1947; Levenson to Besig, September 23, 1947, all in Series 1, Box 558, Folder 21, ACLU. Later, both the JACL and the ACLU claimed more credit than they actually deserved for their participation in the case. See ACLU *Annual Report, 1948–49* (New York: ACLU, 1949), 29; "Interracial Marriage Issue on Block," *Pacific Citizen*, August 26, 1955, 5.

29. "The Shape of Things," *Nation,* October 16, 1948, 415. It should be noted that there is, as yet, no clear evidence that Marshall asked anyone but the LACIC for anything more than informal support. Marshall's personal papers have been destroyed, and in their absence we are left with little more than speculation. Perhaps Marshall desperately wanted—but could not secure—help from the civil rights organizations of his day (Though I could find no evidence of an approach from him in the papers of the NAACP or the ACLU); perhaps he made a strategic decision that the freedom of religion argument should be kept separate from civil rights claims in this case; perhaps he wanted a victory that the LACIC could call its own.

30. Joseph T. McGucken to Daniel G. Marshall, April 26, 1947, Box 17, Folder 29, John LaFarge Papers, Georgetown University Special Collections, Washington, D.C.

31. Return by Way of Demurrer, October 6, 1947, 6–7, PeCF.

32. Respondent's Brief in Opposition to Writ of Mandate, October 6, 1947, 61–97, PeCF.

33. Respondent's Brief, 97–116; quotes on 98, 116, 102.

34. Oral Argument in Support of Petition, October 6, 1947, 3, PeCF.

35. Oral Argument in Support, 4, 5, 7.

36. Oral Argument on Behalf of Respondent, October 6, 1947, 3–4, PcCF.

37. J. Edward Johnson, *History of the Supreme Court Justices of California* (San Francisco: Bender-Moss, 1963–66), 2:191–92; Roger J. Traynor, "The Mind Counts," *Catholic University Law Review* 20 (Winter 1970): 259–69; Traynor, "Badlands in an Appellate Judge's Realm of Reason," *Utah Law Review* 7, no. 2 (1960): 164; Traynor, "*La Rude Vita, La Dolce Giustizia;* Or Hard Cases Can Make Good Law," *University of Chicago Law Review* 29 (Winter 1962): 231; Field, *Activism,* 30–34, 38–40, 121–25.

38. Oral Argument on Behalf of Respondent, 6.

39. "State Court Hears Attack on California Intermarriage Ban: Dan Marshall Leads Assault on Nazi-Like Law," *California Eagle,* October 9, 1947, 1, 8; Grace E. Simons, "County Insults Race at Court Hearing in Intermarriage Suit," *Los Angeles Sentinel,* October 9, 1947, 1; "No Place for Racism," *Los Angeles Sentinel,* October 16, 1947, 7; "Supervisors Duck the Issue," *Los Angeles Sentinel,* December 11, 1947, 7.

40. Petitioners' Reply Brief, November 3, 1947, 4, 44, 24, 40, PeCF.

41. *Perez v. Sharp,* 32 Cal. 2d 711. "Sharp" is William G. Sharp, the county clerk of Los Angeles when the California Supreme Court took its final action in the case. Sharp's name is given in the *California Reporter,* and I have used it here, but the suit had originally been filed against Sharp's predecessors, John F. Moroney and Earl O. Lippold, so it is also cited in various documents and news reports as *Perez v. Moroney* and *Perez v. Lippold.* Andrea Pérez spelled her name with an accent mark. Unfortunately, none of the legal documents, even the published report of her case, included the accent; since cases take their names from the published record, the case is always referred to as "Perez"; I have reluctantly continued that tradition here.

42. *Perez,* 32 Cal. 2d at 714, 716, 717, 725.

43. *Perez,* 32 Cal. 2d at 721, 729, 731.

44. *Perez,* 32 Cal. 2d at 736–37 (my emphasis). According to Ben Field, Roger Traynor's law clerk, Don Barrett, had unsuccessfully urged Roger Traynor to take a position similar to Carter's. See Field, *Activism,* 37.

45. *Perez,* 32 Cal. 2d at 742, 745, 751, 759, 762, 759, 752, 742. For fascinating details on the dissenting justices, see Orenstein, "Void for Vagueness," 379–86, 399–401.

46. *Perez,* 32 Cal. 2d at 740, 744. Ben Field has suggested that Dan Marshall's religious liberty argument may have been designed especially to appeal to Justice Edmonds, who was both an ideologically unpredictable member of the California Supreme Court and a Christian Scientist who was known to have strong feelings about religious liberty. See Field, *Activism,* 36–37.

47. See, for example, "National Affairs: Races: The Person of One's Choice," *Time,* October 11, 1948, 27; "The Shape of Things," *Nation,* October 16, 1948, 415; "Mixed Marriages Upheld by Court," *New York Times,* October 2, 1948, 13; "Inter-racial Marriage Ban in State Voided," *San Francisco Examiner,* October 2, 1948, 4.

48. Robert F. Drinan, "Triumph over Racism," *America,* January 22, 1949, 430.

49. Grace E. Simons, "Calif. Kills Ban on Intermarriage: California Sanctions Mixed Marriages," *Los Angeles Sentinel,* October 7, 1948, 1.

50. "Another Hurdle in Racial Ban," *Korean Independence,* October 6, 1948, 1.

51. "The Shape of Things," 415.

52. Marjorie McKenzie, "Pursuit of Democracy," *Pittsburgh Courier,* December 16, 1948, 15–16. McKenzie, who lamented that the NAACP "has not bothered about the illegality of laws against intermarriage, despite all its expertise on the Fourteenth Amendment," nonetheless believed the NAACP spokesmen who told her, inaccurately, "that no defendant with a valid case has sought aid."

53. "Affirmation in the Courts," *Pacific Citizen,* October 2, 1948, 4; John R. Williams, "Mixed Marriage Ban Outlawed in California," *Pittsburgh Courier,* October 9, 1948, 5; Lawrence E. Davies, "Mixed Marriages Upheld by Court," *New York Times,* October 2, 1948, 13.

54. "Race Law Decision Awaited," *Los Angeles Examiner,* October 2, 1948; "Intermarriage Ban Continues Clerk Reports," *California Eagle,* October 7, 1948, 1; Marriage License Bureau Clerk Says Ruling Against Ban Not Law Yet," *Los Angeles Tribune,* October 9, 1948, 1.

55. "County Re-Opening Intermarriage Case," *Los Angeles Sentinel,* October 21, 1948, 9; *Perez,* 32 Cal. 2d at 763; "California High Court Reaffirms Its Decision on Intermarriage," *Los Angeles Sentinel,* November 4, 1948, 1; "County Attorney Wipes Out Ban on Racial Marriages," *California Eagle,* November 4, 1948, 5.

56. "No Run on License Bureau by the Interracial Lovelorn," *Los Angeles Tribune,* November 6, 1948, 3; "Marriage Recorder Uses 'Sixth Sense' to Determine Race," *Los Angeles Sentinel,* December 23, 1948, 2; "You're Just a Clerk, Miss Rice," *Los Angeles Sentinel,* December 23, 1948, 25.

57. "County Appeals Intermarriage Case to U.S. Supreme Court," *Los Angeles Sentinel,* November 25, 1948, 1; "Plan to Appeal Marriage Ruling," *Pittsburgh Courier,* November 27, 1948, 1; "Law on Intermarriage," *Pacific Citizen,* December 11, 1948, 7.

58. "Couple to Wed; Battle for Intermarriage," *Los Angeles Sentinel,* December 16, 1948, 9; Al Wirin to Clifford Forster, November 30, 1948; Forster to Wirin, December 6, 1948; both in Series 1, Box 564, Folder 32, ACLU.

59. "Pair Who Upset Marriage Curb Given License," *Los Angeles Times,* December 14, 1948, 2:31; Orenstein, "Void for Vagueness," 404–7. Dan Marshall went on to other legal triumphs, including winning a temporary stay of execution for accused atomic

spies Julius and Ethel Rosenberg in 1952. But his willingness to defend interracial couples in the 1940s and accused Communists in the 1950s eventually cost him the support of both his law school and his law partners; he spent the rest of his life struggling to make a living in an increasingly isolated private practice. See Botham, "Almighty God," 38–41, and Orenstein, "Void for Vagueness," 404, ftn. 82.

60. "Statutory Prohibitions Against Interracial Marriage," *Wyoming Law Journal* 3 (Spring 1949): 162.

61. *Shelley v. Kraemer*, 334 U.S. 1.

62. "Wed to White Girl, Gets 5-Year Term," *New York Times,* December 19, 1948, 36; "Facing Prison for Marrying White Girl; Says He's Indian," *Pittsburgh Courier,* December 25, 1948, 5; "The Children's Children," *Time,* December 27, 1948, 18. Detailed accounts of the case include F. A. Behymer, "Mississippi Blood Test," *Negro Digest,* June 1949, 15–20; and Victoria E. Bynum, "'White Negroes' in Segregated Mississippi: Miscegenation, Racial Identity, and the Law," *Journal of Southern History* 64 (May 1998): 247–76; see also Phyl Newbeck, *Virginia Hasn't Always Been for Lovers: Interracial Marriage Bans and the Case of Richard and Mildred Loving* (Carbondale: Southern Illinois University Press, 2004), 92–94.

63. *Knight v. State,* 207 Miss. at 568–69 (1949); Bynum, "'White Negroes,'" 276.

64. "The California Marriage Decision," *Interracial Review* 22 (January 1949): 3–4; "Minutes of the Meeting of the Committee on Race Relations," March 1, 1949, Series 1, Box 77, Folder 21, ACLU, quoted in Bynum, "'White Negroes,'" 249, ftn. 6. Although the NAACP Legal Defense Fund tracked the *Knight* case, it does not seem to have been among the groups eager to take part. As the LDF's Constance Motley explained to an NAACP member who had asked her to do something about "this outrage," the LDF took the position that "there is nothing that we can do specifically for Mr. Knight unless our aid is sought directly by him or someone on his behalf." See Blanch Bloch to NAACP, circa December 31, 1948, and Constance Baker Motley to Mrs. Robert Briggs, January 6, 1949, both in Part 2, Series B, Box 82, Folder: Legal File: Intermarriage General, 1946–49, NAACP-LC.

65. PE, 70; *Jackson v. State,* 37 Ala. App. at 521 (1954); *Jackson v. State,* 260 Ala. 698 (1954).

66. *Brown v. Board of Education,* 347 U.S. 483 (1954); Risa L. Goluboff, *The Lost Promise of Civil Rights* (Cambridge: Harvard University Press, 2007), 240–41; quoted in Waldo E. Martin Jr., *Brown v. Board of Education: A Brief History with Documents* (Boston: Bedford/St. Martin's, 1998), 204. See also Randall Kennedy, *Interracial Intimacies: Sex, Marriage, Identity, and Adoption* (New York: Pantheon Books, 2003), 24–25.

67. E[arl E.] P[ollock], Conference Memo, November 1954, Box 162, Folder: Supreme Court, Conference Memos, O.T. 1954, Misc. no. 118, EWP; H[arvey] M. Grossman, Conference Memo, November 3, 1954, Box 1157, Folder: O.T. 1954, Office Memos, no. 118 Misc., WODP; *Jackson v. Alabama,* 348 U.S. 888 (1954). The three justices who voted to hear the case were Hugo Black, William O. Douglas, and Earl Warren. Several justices recorded the vote in their docket sheets; Docket, Box C 71, Folder 4, OT 1954, Misc. 118, TCCP; and Docket, Box 1157, Folder: O.T. 1954, Office Memos, no. 118 Misc., WODP. For more on the Jackson case, see Novkov, *Racial Union,* 256 60.

68. The most detailed accounts of the *Naim* case are Gregory Michael Dorr, "Principled Expediency: Eugenics, *Naim v. Naim,* and the Supreme Court," *American Journal*

of Legal History 42 (1998): 119–59; PE, 73–94; Dennis J. Hutchinson, "Unanimity and Desegregation: Decisionmaking in the Supreme Court, 1948–1958," *Georgetown Law Journal* 68 (1979–80): 61–68; and Philip Elman, "The Solicitor General's Office, Justice Frankfurter, and Civil Rights Legislation, 1946–1960: An Oral History," by Norman Silber, *Harvard Law Review* 100 (1986–87): 845; but see also Newbeck, *Virginia,* 103–16.

69. The court granted Ruby Naim an annulment, but not the divorce she would have preferred. Dorr, "Principled Expediency," 130–35.

70. Samuel Walker, *In Defense of American Liberties: A History of the ACLU*, 2nd ed. (Carbondale: Southern Illinois University Press, 1999), 217; PE, 77–78; David Carliner, "Memorandum re: Ruby Naim v. Ham Say Naim," n.d.; David Carliner to Edward J. Ennis, March 9, 1954; both in Series 3, Box 1106, Folder 22, ACLU.

71. Dorr, "Principled Expediency," 135; David Carliner to Herbert Levy, September 3, 1954, Series 3, Box 1106, Folder 22, ACLU.

72. Levy to Carliner, November 30, 1954; Carliner to Levy, November 24, 1954; Carliner to Levy, February 16, 1955; all in Series 3, Box 1106, Folder 22, ACLU.

73. Carliner to Levy, November 24, 1954; Carliner to Levy, August 18, 1955; both in Series 3, Box 1106, Folder 22, ACLU; "Solicitor General's Office," 845; PE, 84–87; Hutchinson, "Unanimity and Desegregation," 61–62. Phyl Newbeck offers an especially cogent explanation of these procedures in *Virginia,* 110–11.

74. Carliner to Levy, June 24, 1955; Levy to Carliner, June 29, 1955; Carliner to Levy, July 20, 1955; Levy to Carliner, August 2, 1955; Will Maslow to Carliner, July 12, 1955; Carliner to Levy, July 12, 1955; Levy to Roger Baldwin, August 2, 1955; Carliner to Levy, August 18, 1955; all in Series 3, Box 1106, Folder 22, ACLU; Statement as to Jurisdiction, August 31, 1955, Record Group 267, Box 1306, Folder 366, NARA, Washington, D.C.

75. Carliner to Levy, August 18, 1955, Series 3, Box 1106, Folder 22, ACLU. The absence of these groups from the briefs is all the more puzzling because the JACL, which provided the necessary addresses, predicted enthusiastic acceptance of the ACLU's invitation to join in the brief. See Tats Kishida to Mike Masaoka, July 27, 1955, Box 545, Folder 4, FCP. When I spoke with David Carliner in September 2004, he could no longer remember whether he had received any responses from his overtures to these groups.

76. "They're Bound to Win," *Baltimore Afro-American,* June 25, 1955, 4.

77. Herbert Levy to Thurgood Marshall, April 12, 1954, Series 3, Box 1106, Folder 22, ACLU.

78. Mike Masaoka to George Inagaki, July 25, 1925, Box 545, Folder 4, FCP. Masaoka went on to add, inaccurately, that "the NAACP unofficially has already joined in legal and strategy discussions on the case."

79. Roy Wilkins, "Statement on Interracial Marriage for the Magazine *Behind the Scene,*" September 6, 1955, Part 2, Box A 496, Folder: General Office File, Publicity, General, 1955, July–Sept., NAACP-LC; PE, 84, 133–34, 147; Kennedy, *Interracial Intimacies,* 270; Newbeck, *Virginia,* 109; Peter Wallenstein, *Tell the Court I Love My Wife: Race, Marriage, and Law—An American History* (New York: Palgrave Macmillan, 2002), 184–85.

80. Carliner to Levy, July 20, 1955; Levy to Carliner, August 19, 1955; Sol Rabkin to Alan Reitman, August 25, 1955, all in Series 3, Box 1106, Folder 22, ACLU; Elman, "Solicitor General's Office," 846.

81. Carliner to Levy, July 20, 1955, Levy to Carliner, November 22, 1955; both in Series 3, Box 1106, Folder 22, ACLU.

82. S[amuel] A. S[tern], Conference Memo, October 1955, Box 167, O.T. 1955, Appellate no. 366, EWP; A[lan] J. M[oscov], Conference Memo, October 23, 1955, Box 268, Folder 11, O.T. 1955, no. 366, HHBP; Hutchinson, "Unanimity and Desegregation," 62–64; Dorr, "Principled Expediency," 122, 145–46, 148–58.

83. Frankfurter Memo, Friday, November 4, 1955, File 4040, Reel 139, fr. 150–51, FFP; Hutchinson, "Unanimity and Desegregation," 64–65; Dorr, "Principled Expediency," 119, 150–53. Frankfurter had been alerted that the case might be arriving at the Court by his ex-clerk, Philip Elman. Elman, "Solicitor General's Office," 846; Dorr, "Principled Expediency," 148.

84. Conference List, O.T. 1955, no. 366, Box 143; Docket Sheet, O.T. 1955, no. 366, Box 369, both in EWP.

85. Frankfurter Memo, Friday, November 4, 1955, File 4040, Reel 139, fr. 150–51, FFP. These drafts are collected in Box 147, O.T. 1955, Folder 3, no. 366, TCCP.

86. Docket Sheet, O.T. 1955, no. 366, Box 369, EWP.

87. *Rescue Army v. Los Angeles,* 331 U.S. at 584 (1947).

88. *Naim v. Naim,* 350 U.S. 891 (1955).

89. Elman, "Solicitor General's Office," 847.

90. Carliner to Levy, November 14, 1955; Levy to Carliner, November 21, 1955; Carliner to Levy, January 25, 1956; Levy to Carliner, February 6, 1956; all in Series 3, Box 1106, Folder 22, ACLU; PE, 91–93.

91. *Naim v. Naim,* 197 Va. at 735 (1956): Arnold Snow, "State's High Court Spurns U.S. Order," *Richmond Times-Dispatch,* January 19, 1956, 6; "Virginia's Top Tribunal Rejects Order of U.S. Supreme Court," *Richmond Times-Dispatch,* January 19, 1956, 12; Dorr, "Principled Expediency," 156–57; Newbeck, *Virginia,* 115.

92. See, for example, Docket Sheet, March 2–9, 1956, Box 1163, Folder O.T. 1955, no. 366, WODP; Docket Sheet, March 2, 1956, Box 264, Folder 13, O.T. 1955, Appellate no. 366, HHBP; Docket Sheet, March 2–9, 1956, Box 369, Folder O.T. 1955, Appellate no. 366, EWP.

93. According to Gerald Gunther, a relieved Frankfurter later reflected on the Supreme Court's refusal to hear either *Jackson* or *Naim.* "We twice shunted it away," Frankfurter told federal judge Learned Hand, "and I pray we may be able to do it again, without being too brazenly evasive." Gerald Gunther, *Learned Hand: The Man and the Judge* (New York: Alfred A. Knopf, 1994), 667.

94. *Naim v. Naim,* 350 U.S. 985 (1956). On this seeming unanimity—and the sharp conflict that lay beneath it—see Dorr, "Principled Expediency," 158.

95. Draft Dissent, 5, Box 167, Folder O.T. 1955, Appellate no. 366, EWP; Bernard Schwartz, *Super Chief: Earl Warren and His Supreme Court—A Judicial Biography* (New York: NYU Press, 1983), 161.

96. Carliner to Rowland Watts, March 13, 1956, Series 3, Box 1106, Folder 22, ACLU.

97. Masao Satow to Min Yasui, December 21, 1964, Box 545, Folder 4, FCP.

98. Sol Rabkin to Alan Reitman, August 25, 1955, Series 3, Box 1106, Folder 22, ACLU.

99. These criteria, which had originated with Sanford Kadish, a professor of law at the University of Utah, are listed in PE, 132; see also Newbeck, *Virginia,* 95–96.

100. Memo on Miscegenation Laws, October 2, 1963, Box 545, Folder 4, FCP.

101. "Most of Summer Marriages Between GIs, Japan Girls Not Faring Well, Says Writer," *Pacific Citizen,* November 1, 1947, 2; Elfrieda Berthiaume Shukert and Barbara Smith Scibetta, *War Brides of World War II* (New York: Penguin Books, 1989), 203–8; Paul R. Spickard, *Mixed Blood: Intermarriage and Ethnic Identity in Twentieth-Century America* (Madison: University of Wisconsin Press, 1989), 132–35.

102. "Senate Passes Amendment to Soldier Brides Act," *Pacific Citizen,* July 19, 1947, 1; "Soldier Brides Act of 1947," *Pacific Citizen,* December 17, 1954, C7; "President Signs New Bill for Nippon Brides," *Pacific Citizen,* August 26, 1950, 8; "Army in Japan Drops Ban on GI Marriages," *Pacific Citizen,* September 30, 1950, 4; "800 War Brides Pass Through Seattle in One Year as Non-Quota Immigrants," *Pacific Citizen,* February 12, 1954, 2; Tamotsu Murayama, "20,000 War Brides in America," *Pacific Citizen,* June 3, 1955, 2; Shukert, *War Brides,* 209–16; Spickard, *Mixed Blood,* 133.

103. "Report 1300 Nisei Soldiers Married Japanese Brides During Occupation Period," *Pacific Citizen,* September 27, 1952, 2; Shukert, *War Brides,* 217.

104. Susan Koshy, *Sexual Naturalization: Asian Americans and Miscegenation* (Palo Alto: Stanford University Press, 2004), 11–12, 16, 22; Caroline Chung Simpson, *An Absent Presence: Japanese Americans in Postwar American Culture, 1945–1960* (Durham: Duke University Press, 2001), 151, 165–85; Robert G. Lee, *Orientals: Asian Americans in Popular Culture* (Philadelphia: Temple University Press, 1999), 161–72.

105. Tamotsu Murayama, "20,000 War Brides in America," *Pacific Citizen,* June 3, 1955, 2; Larry Nakatsuka, "Slur Against Interracial Marriages," *Pacific Citizen,* August 19, 1955, 1, 3.

106. William Marutani to Patrick Okura, January 3, 1964, Box 545, Folder 4, FCP.

107. Kumeo Yoshinari to Min Yasui, December 19, 1964; Min Yasui to Frank Chuman, January 19, 1965; Masao Satow to Min Yasui, December 21, 1964; William Marutani to Masao Satow, December 29, 1964; all in Box 545, Folder 4, FCP.

108. Pat Coontz to Leanne Golden, circa January 24, 1961; Richard Daly to Melvin Wulf, January 28, 1961; both in Series 3, Box 1114, Folder 17, ACLU.

109. The most detailed accounts of the *Bridges* case are Phillip I. Earl, "Nevada's Miscegenation Laws and the Marriage of Mr. and Mrs. Harry Bridges," *Nevada Historical Society Quarterly* 37 (Spring 1994): 1–17, and Newbeck, *Virginia,* 84–88.

110. Frank Johnson, "Law on Miscegenation Picketed by Organizer," *Nevada State Journal,* December 12, 1958, 20; "No License, Clerk Tells Labor Chief," *Nevada State Journal,* 1, 7; "Nevada Won't Allow Bridges to Wed Nisei," *New York Times,* December 10, 1958, 1, 28; Earl, "Nevada's Miscegenation Laws," 8–9. The wording of Givens's questions echoed that of the Nevada miscegenation law, which had been amended in 1911 to read "It shall be unlawful for any person of the Caucasian or white race to intermarry with any person of the Ethiopian or black race, Malay or brown race, Mongolian or yellow race, or the American Indian or red race, within the State of Nevada." Nevada Rev. Stat. sec. 249 (1912).

111. Quoted in Earl, "Nevada's Miscegenation Laws," 9. The newspapers that covered the incident give several slightly different accounts of who said what during this interaction; I have relied on Earl's interpretation here.

112. "Law Overturned; Bridges Weds," *Nevada State Journal*, December 11, 1958, 1, 7; "Bridges Gets License," *New York Times*, December 11, 1958, 30; "The Death of a Bad Law," *Pittsburgh Courier*, December 20, 1958, 12; Earl, "Nevada's Miscegenation Laws," 9–10; Newbeck, *Virginia*, 85.

113. "Statute on Miscegenation Gets Some Rude Treatment," *Nevada State Journal*, December 14, 1958, 14; "No License," 7; Johnson, "Law on Miscegenation," 20; "Mixed Marriages—And an Exception," *Newsweek*, December 22, 1958, 20; "Nevada Marriage Law Upset," *Pacific Citizen*, December 12, 1958, 1; "Death of a Bad Law," *Pittsburgh Courier*, December 12, 1948, 12; "Bridges Case Given Study By Clerks," December 13, 1958, 1; "Reno Still Saying 'No' to Interracial Marriage," *Las Vegas Sun*, December 13, 1958, 3; Ed Olson, "All Ends Well as Bridges Weds in Reno," *Las Vegas Sun*, December 11, 1958, 2.

114. Cornelius Steelink to Leanne Golden, December [10], 1959, Series 3, Box 1111, Folder 28, ACLU; Exhibits B and C, in Abstract of Record on Appeal, OCF; George Wilson, "Miscegenation Law Challenged," *Arizona Daily Star*, November 18, 1959, B1. The most detailed accounts of the *Oyama* case are Newbeck, *Virginia*, 79–84, and Roger D. Hardaway, "Unlawful Love: A History of Arizona's Miscegenation Law," *Journal of Arizona History* 27, no. 4 (1986): 377–90.

115. Steelink to Golden, December [10], 1959; "High Court Won't Hear Marriage Ban Protest," *Arizona Daily Star*, November 26, 1959, B1.

116. Complaint, 1, in Abstract of Record on Appeal, OCF; "Suit Wants Marriage Ban Lifted," *Arizona Daily Star*, December 12, 1959, B1.

117. Declaratory Judgment and Decree for Permanent Injunction, December 23, 1959, 2–3, Abstract of Record on Appeal, OCF; "Miscegenation Ban Held Unconstitutional," *Arizona Daily Star*, December 24, 1959, A4.

118. Dick Alexander, "After Winning Court Fight, Oyama, Mary Jordan Wed," *Arizona Daily Star*, December 29, 1959, A8.

119. Steelink to Golden, December [10], 1959; Rowland Watts to Frank J. Barry, January 12, 1960, Series 3, Box 1111, Folder 28, ACLU.

120. Notice of Appeal, January 27, 1960, OCF. Phyl Newbeck explains that although Watts didn't know this, Pima County officials themselves believed the law unconstitutional, and regarded the entire proceeding as "friendly litigation." Newbeck, *Virginia*, 81–82.

121. Appellant's Opening Brief on Appeal, June 8, 1960, 15, 34–38, OCF.

122. Appellees' Answering Brief, September 19, 1960, 31, OCF.

123. An Act to Repeal Secs. 4008, 6987, and 6988 of the Rev. Stat. of Ohio, 1887 Ohio Laws 34.

124. "Senate OKs Inter-Racial Marriages," *Klamath Falls Herald and News*, March 21, 1951, 2; "Lifting Marriage Bar," *Oregonian*, March 28, 1951, 18; Matthew Aeldun Charles Smith, "Wedding Bands and Marriage Bans: A History of Oregon's Racial Intermarriage Statutes and the Impact on Indian Interracial Nuptials" (M.A. thesis, Portland State University, 1977), 150–57.

125. "Mixed-Marriage Proposal Beaten," *Oregonian*, February 1, 1951, 1; "Senate Okehs Removal of Miscegenation Ban," *Oregonian*, March 25, 1951, 1; "Senate Votes to Permit Inter-Race Marriages," *Salem Statesman Journal*, March 21, 1951, 5.

126. "Senate Votes," 5; "Marriage Law Clears Hurdle," *Oregonian*, March 13, 1951, 8; "Senate OKs," 2; "Senate Okehs," 1; An Act Relating to Marriages, ch. 455,

1951 Or. Laws 792; "Ban on Mixed Racial Marriages Removed by Bill," *Oregon Voter,* March 31, 1951, 255; Smith, "Wedding Bands," 158–65.

127. Frank Chuman to Mike Masaoka, April 28, 1955, Box 545, Folder 4, FCP; ACLU, *42nd Annual Report* (1961–62), 50–51; Hardaway, "Unlawful Love," 386–88; Newbeck, Virginia, 87–88, 100.

128. Richard Daly to Melvin Wulf, January 28, 1961, Series 3, Box 1114, Folder 17, ACLU; Masao Satow to Min Yasui, December 21, 1964, Box 545, Folder 4, FCP; Alice Kasai, "Repeal of Utah Mixed Marriage Ban Held Likely," *Pacific Citizen,* February 1, 1963, 1; "Utah Repeals Anti-Miscegenation Law for Only Civil Rights Action This Session," *Pacific Citizen,* April 19, 1963, 1; "All Mixed Marriage Bans Lifted," *Pacific Citizen,* June 16, 1967, 1, 6; An Act Amending Sec. 30-1-2, Utah Code Ann. 1953, Relating to Prohibited Marriages; Providing for the Removal of Certain Racial Restrictions from Marriages, ch. 43, 1963 Utah Laws 163.

129. Min Yasui to Frank Chuman, January 19, 1965, Box 545, Folder 4, FCP.

130. Megumi Dick Osumi, "Asians and California's Anti-Miscegenation Laws," in *Asian and Pacific American Experiences: Women's Perspectives,* ed. Nobuya Tsuchida (Minneapolis: Asian/Pacific American Learning Resource Center, 1982), 25.

131. *Freedom's Frontier,* pamphlet, 1954, Carton 25, NAACP-WC; "NAACP Calls for Sweeping Legislative Program in California," November 23, 1958, fr. 565, Part 25, Series C, Reel 9, NAACP-MF.

132. Terea H. Pittman, "Of Pressure and Progress: An Annual Summary," 1959, Carton 25; Edward P. Elliott to Everett P. Brandon, December 17, 1958, Carton 42, Folder 1, both in NAACP-WC; "Miscegenation Repealer Successfully Passes Assembly," *NAACP News* {West Coast Regional Branch}, February 18, 1959, fr. 600, Part 25, Series C, Reel 9, NAACP-MF; An Act to Repeal Sec. 60, and to Amend Sec. 69, of the Civil Code, Relating to Miscegenation, ch. 146, 1959 Cal. Stat. 2043.

133. Earl, "Nevada's Miscegenation Laws," 15; Newbeck, *Virginia,* 84, 88; "Nevada Passes Moderate FEPC Act, Repeals Miscegenation Act," *NAACP News,* March 20, 1959, fr. 607, Part 25, Series C, Reel 9, NAACP-MF; "Japanese-Americans Hit Miscegenation Law," *Idaho Daily Statesman,* February 10, 1959, 2; Masao Satow to George Sugai, February 24, 1959, Box 545, Folder 4, FCP; "Idaho Repeals Miscegenation Act," *NAACP News,* March 20, 1959, fr. 608, Part 25, Series C, Reel 9, NAACP-MF.

134. An Act Relating to Marriages, ch. 455, 1951 Or. Laws 792; An Act Amending Sec. 32-206, Ida. Code, An Act Relating to Miscegenation and Marriages Between First Cousins, by Deleting and Eliminating Therefrom the Provision Making Marriages Contracted of White Persons with Mongolians, Negroes or Mulattoes Illegal and Void, ch. 44, 1959 Idaho Sess. Laws 89; An Act to Repeal Sec. 60, and to Amend Sec. 69, of the Civil Code, Relating to Miscegenation, ch. 146, 1959 Cal. Stat. 2043; An Act Amending Sec. 30-1-2, Utah Code Ann. 1953, Relating to Prohibited Marriages; Providing for the Removal of Certain Racial Restrictions from Marriages, ch. 43, 1963 Utah Laws 163; An Act to Repeal Secs. 48-106, 48-107, 48-108, 48-109 and 48-110 of the Rev. Code of Montana, 1947, Relating to Miscegenous Marriages Within the State of Montana, ch. 4, 1953 Mont. Laws 4; An Act Relating to Marriage, Prescribing Certain Marriages as Being Void and Prohibited, and Amending Sec. 25-101, Ariz. Rev. Stat., ch. 14, 1962 Ariz. Sess. Laws 21; An Act to Repeal NRS Secs. 122.180 and 122.190 Relating to Unlawful Miscegenetic Marriages, ch. 193, 1959 Nev. Stat. 216; An Act

Concerning Marriages, and to Amend the Law Relating Thereto, ch. 124, Colo. Sess. Laws 334; Repeal of Mixed Race Marriage Restrictions, ch. 243, 1963 Neb. Laws 736; An Act to Repeal Secs. 14-0304, 14-0305, 14-0326 and 14-0327 of the N.D. Rev. Code of 1943 Relating to Miscegenation, ch. 126, 1955 N.D. Laws 157; An Act to Repeal Subsection (4) of Sec. 14.0106, and Sec. 14.9901, of the S.D. Code of 1939, Relating to Mixed Race Marriages, ch. 38, S.D. Laws 71.

135. Miscegenation Law Repealed, ch. 4, 1965 Wyo. Sess. Laws 3; An Act to Amend An Act Entitled "An Act Regulating the Granting of Divorces, Nullification of Marriages, and Decrees and Orders of Courts Incident Thereto," ch. 15, Ind. Acts 24.

136. "Lifting Marriage Bar," *Oregonian,* March 28, 1951, 18.

137. My calculations here depend on U.S. Census data for 1960. University of Virginia Library, Geospatial & Statistical Data Center, Historical Census Browser, http://fisher.lib.virginia.edu/collections/stats/histcensus/php/state.php (accessed July 10, 2006).

138. Mike Masaoka to George Hasegawa, May 11, 1959, George Hasegawa to Mike Masaoka, April 4, 1962; Mike Masaoka to Hasegawa, April 11, 1962; all in Box 545, Folder 4, FCP.

139. Petition for Writ of Mandamus, 4, August 8, 1947, PeCF.

Chapter 8

1. Transcript of Record, 55, 23, 26, McLCF.

2. Transcript of Record, 30, 23, 31.

3 Transcript of Record, 40–45, 50–52, 54, 36–40.

4. Transcript of Record, 55; Fla. Stat. sec. 798.05 (1959).

5. Fla. Stat., ch. 741, sec. 741.11–741.16 (marriage) and ch. 798, sec 798.04 (living in adultery) (1959).

6. Transcript of Record, 26, 33, 83, 85.

7. PE, 95–96; Phyl Newbeck, *Virginia Hasn't Always Been for Lovers: Interracial Marriage Bans and the Case of Richard and Mildred Loving* (Carbondale: Southern Illinois University Press, 2004), 118.

8. *McLaughlin v. Florida,* 379 U.S. 184 (1964); *Loving v. Virginia,* 388 U.S. 1, 12 (1967).

9. Newbeck, *Virginia,* 89.

10. *Pace v. Alabama,* 106 U.S. 583 (1882).

11. *In re Paquet's Estate,* 200 P. 911, 913 (1921); *Jackson v. Denver,* 190 Colo. 196, 199 (1942).

12. *Stevens v. U.S.,* 147 F. 2d 120, 123 (10th Cir.) (1944); *Naim v. Naim,* 87 S.E. 2d 749, 754 (1955).

13. Respondent's Brief in Opposition to Writ of Mandate, 54, 59, October 6, 1947, PeCF; Petitioners' Reply Brief, 26, November 3, 1947, PeCF; *Perez v. Sharp,* 32 Cal. 2d 711, 726 (1948).

14. When David Carliner filed his jurisdictional statement on behalf of both these organizations with the U.S. Supreme Court in *Naim,* he made the bold statement that "the issue posed by this appeal—whether a state may restrict the right to marry upon the basis of race—has never been passed upon by this Court." Statement as to Jurisdiction, 7, August 31, 1955, Naim v. Naim, Box 1306, Folder 366

O.T. 1955, Record Group 267, U.S. Supreme Court Appellate Case Files, NARA, Washington, D.C.

15. Robert L. Carter to Lewis B. Stewart, June 3, 1946, Part 2, Box B 82, Folder: Legal File: Intermarriage General, 1946–49, NAACP-LC.

16. Jack Greenberg, *Crusaders in the Courts: How a Dedicated Band of Lawyers Fought for the Civil Rights Revolution* (New York: Basic Books, 1994), 102.

17. Robert W. Saunders Sr., *Bridging the Gap: Continuing the Florida NAACP Legacy of Harry T. Moore, 1952–1966* (Tampa: University of Tampa Press, 2000), 83; Greenberg, *Crusaders,* 270–81, 285–90.

18. Stewart E. Tolnay and E. M. Beck, *A Festival of Violence: An Analysis of Southern Lynchings, 1882–1930* (Urbana: University of Illinois Press, 1995), 38; Paul Ortiz, *Emancipation Betrayed: The Hidden History of Black Organizing and White Violence in Florida from Reconstruction to the Bloody Election of 1920* (Berkeley: University of California Press, 2005), xiv, 61; Ben Green, *Before His Time: The Untold Story of Harry T. Moore, America's First Civil Rights Martyr* (New York: Free Press, 1999), 1–10, 48–51, 54–58, 68–71.

19. Greenberg, *Crusaders,* 93–99, 133–35, 140–42.

20. David R. Colburn, "Florida Politics in the Twentieth Century," in *The New History of Florida,* ed. Michael Gannon (Gainesville: University Press of Florida, 1996), 358–64; Saunders, *Bridging the Gap,* 65–89; Marvin Dunn, *Black Miami in the Twentieth Century* (Gainesville: University Press of Florida, 1997), 171–223; Clarence Taylor, *Black Religious Intellectuals: The Fight for Equality from Jim Crow to the Twenty-First Century* (New York: Routledge, 2002), 94–106.

21. Fla. Stat. sec. 798.01, 798.02, 798.03 (1959).

22. Judge Morris Ploscowe, who published an extensive study of sex laws in 1951, concluded that there were only five U.S. states that did not criminalize adultery, but "at least ten" that did not criminalize fornication. Morris Ploscowe, *Sex and the Law* (New York: Prentice-Hall, 1951), 145.

23. Fla. Stat. sec. 798.04, 798.05 (1959).

24. Jack Greenberg, *Race Relations and American Law* (New York: Columbia University Press, 1959), appendix A26, 396.

25. Ploscowe, *Sex and the Law,* 281.

26. *McLaughlin v. State,* 153 So. 2d 1, 2.

27. American Law Institute, *Model Penal Code and Commentaries (Official Draft and Revised Comments),* Part 2 (Philadelphia: American Law Institute, 1980), 434–46.

28. Andrew D. Weinberger, "A Reappraisal of the Constitutionality of Miscegenation Statutes," *Cornell Law Quarterly* 42 (1956–57): 221, 224; Greenberg, *Race Relations,* 345–46; Gerhard O. W. Mueller, *Legal Regulation of Sexual Conduct* (New York: Oceana Publications, 1961), 12.

29. "Intermarriage and the Race Problem—As Leading Authorities See It," *U.S. News and World Report,* November 18, 1963, 84–93.

30. Gunnar Myrdal, *An American Dilemma: The Negro Problem and Modern Democracy* (New York: Harper & Brothers, 1944), 61–62; "How the NAACP Stands on Intermarriage," *U.S. News and World Report,* September 2, 1963, 9.

31. Saunders, *Bridging the Gap,* 76–77, 85, 169, 171; "A Great Loss," *Miami Times,* January 16, 1992, 4A; "NAACP Wants Law Center Named for G.E. Graves," *Miami Times,* January 30, 1992, 6B; J. Clay Smith, *Emancipation: The Making of the Black*

Lawyer, 1844–1944 (Philadelphia: University of Pennsylvania Press, 1993), 51; "Drive for Integrated Facilities in Miami," *New Pittsburgh Courier,* November 21, 1959, 11; "Fla. Masons Aid Arrested A & M Students," *New Pittsburgh Courier,* May 6, 1960, 4; "Some Integrate Without Incident, Others Fight It: Segregation Paradoxical," *New Pittsburgh Courier,* August 27, 1960, 8; *Rice v. Arnold,* 45 So. 2d 195 (Florida 1950); *Rice v. Arnold,* 54 So. 2d 114 (Florida 1951); *Gibson v. Florida Legislative Investigation Committee,* 108 So. 2d 729 (Florida 1959); *Gibson v. Florida Legislative Investigation Committee,* 126 So. 2d 129 (Florida 1961); *Gibson v. Florida Legislative Investigation Committee,* 372 U.S. 539 (1963); *Gibson v. Florida Legislative Investigation Committee,* 153 So. 2d 301 (Florida 1963).

32. Although, as Peter Wallenstein explained, the *McLaughlin* case was "crucial" to the collapse of miscegenation law, it has attracted surprisingly little attention from historians, much less, for example, than *Perez, Naim,* or *Loving.* Wallenstein, *Tell the Court,* 211. The most detailed accounts to date are Newbeck, *Virginia,* 117–31; PE, 94–107; and Moran, *Interracial Intimacy,* 92–95. For those who want to pursue the subject, the best starting places are the case file, which is housed in the U.S. Supreme Court Library, and contemporary coverage in the *Miami Times,* the *Miami Herald,* and the *New York Times.*

33. Motion to Quash Information, April 11, 1962, and Minute Entry, April 12, 1962, Transcript of Record, 5–6, McLCF; Fla. Stat. sec. 798.05 (1959).

34. Fla. Stat. sec. 1.01 (6) (1959); *Perez v. Sharp,* 32 Cal. 2d 711, 731.

35. Transcript of Record, 17, 34, McLCF.

36. Transcript of Record, 34, 60–63.

37. Transcript of Record, 68–70, 84.

38. Transcript of Record, 22–23.

39. Transcript of Record, 82–85, 74.

40. Transcript of Record, 93–94; PE, 99–100.

41. Transcript of Record, 93, 97–98.

42. Brief of Defendants-Appellants, 16–17, McLCF. A copy of this brief was included as Appendix A to the Florida state Brief of Appellee submitted when the case reached the U.S. Supreme Court.

43. Brief of Defendants-Appellants, 9–11. The phrase "constitutionally an irrelevance" comes from *Edwards v. California,* 314 U.S. 160, 185 (1941), in which the U.S. Supreme Court had used the authority of the commerce clause to strike down a California law designed to stop indigents from coming into California. In a concurring opinion, Justice Robert H. Jackson had written that "being without funds is a neutral fact—constitutionally an irrelevance, like race, creed, or color."

44. Brief of Appellee, 4, McLaughlin v. Florida, Florida Supreme Court Case File 31.906, Series 49, Carton 2824, File Folder 31906, Florida State Archives, Tallahassee.

45. Brief of Appellee, 5.

46. In the 1940s, the Florida NAACP had led the fight to deny Caldwell a coveted federal appointment. See Saunders, *Bridging the Gap,* 23; Colburn, "Florida Politics," 357–59; Anna Rothe, ed, *Current Biography: Who's News and Why 1948* (New York: H. W. Wilson, 1948), 84–86; Eleanora W. Schoenebaum, ed., *Political Profiles: The Truman Years* (New York: Facts on File, 1978), 79–80.

47. *McLaughlin v. State,* 153 So. 2d 1, 2, 3 (1963).

48. PE, 97–98; Newbeck, *Virginia,* 121; Greenberg, *Crusaders,* 160–61. According to Phyl Newbeck, it was Coleman who persuaded Pollak to enter the case.

49. William Marutani confidential letter to Patrick Okura, January 3, 1964, Box 545, Folder 4, FCP.

50. Brief for Appellants, 14, August 24, 1964, McLCF. It is worth noting, however, that in the 1917 case, NAACP lawyers had sharply differentiated housing rights from interracial marriage. "The cases upholding statutes against miscegenation are . . . irrelevant," they had argued, "since marriage is a matter of status in which the interests of the State are vitally concerned." Citing *Pace* as their source, they repeated the then-authoritative conclusion that these "statutes are equal in their operation since they impose no penalty upon the members of one race for doing that which is lawful for members of the other race." *Buchanan v. Warley,* 245 U.S. 60, 64 (1917).

51. Brief for Appellants, 16–17, 25, 19.

52. Brief for Appellants, 27–30.

53. Brief for Appellants, 20.

54. Brief for Appellants, 20, 13. On the phrase "constitutionally an irrelevance," see ftn. 43 above.

55. Anthony Lewis, "Court Considers Race Marriages," *New York Times,* October 14, 1964, 34; "Arguments Before the Court: Miscegenation," *United States Law Week,* October 20, 1964, sec. 3, 3137–38.

56. Compare Fla. Stat. sec. 741.12 to 798.05 (1959); Newbeck, *Virginia,* 128–29; PE, 100–102.

57. Jerry Blitzin, "Supreme Court Is Hearing 1962 Miami Beach Case," *Miami Herald,* October 14, 1964, 2A; Response of Appellee to Jurisdictional Statement, 7, September 30, 1964, McLCF. Mahorner had handled the case at the Florida Supreme Court level, too.

58. Response of Appellee, 15, 5.

59. Response of Appellee, 13, 3, 4.

60. "Arguments Before the Court: Miscegenation," 3138; Brief of Appellee, 55.

61. Brief of Appellee, 38.

62. Ed Cray, *Chief Justice: A Biography of Earl Warren* (New York: Simon & Schuster, 1997), 451; Handwritten Notes, October 16, 1964, Box 1880, Folder: O.T. 1964, Argued Cases, no. 11, WODP.

63. Handwritten Notes; C[harles] R. N[esson], "Memo to the Files: Re McLaughlin v. Florida," Box 218, Notebook on O.T. Term 1964, Case no. 11, John Marshall Harlan Papers, MC 071, Department of Rare Books and Special Collections, Princeton University, Princeton, New Jersey; Del Dickson, ed., *The Supreme Court in Conference (1940–1985)* (New York: Oxford University Press, 2001), 694, and ftn. 144. The justices also considered basing their decision on an earlier Supreme Court decision that had affirmed a lower-court injunction that prevented Louisiana from enforcing a state law prohibiting interracial boxing matches; *State Athletic Commission v. Dorsey,* 359 U.S. 533 (1959).

64. *McLaughlin v. Florida,* 379 U.S. 184, 188, 191–93 (1964).

65. *McLaughlin,* 379 U.S. at 187.

66. *Naim v. Naim,* 87 S.E. 2d 749, 754 (1955); *State v. Brown,* 108 So. 2d 233, 234 (1959); *McLaughlin v. State,* 153 So. 2d 1, 2 (1963).

67. *McLaughlin,* 379 U.S. at 187, ftn. 6., and at 196, 198.

68. Alabama, Arkansas, Delaware, Florida, Georgia, Indiana, Kentucky, Louisiana, Maryland, Mississippi, Missouri, North Carolina, Oklahoma, South Carolina, Tennessee, Texas, Virginia, West Virginia, Wyoming.

69. *Jones v. Lorenzen,* 441 P. 2d 990 (Okla., 1965); *Hibbert v. Mudd,* 187 So. 2d 503 (La. Ct. App., 3rd C., 1966).

70. *Naim v. Naim,* 197 Va. 80, 90 (1955). The hostility of the Virginia Supreme Court of Appeals made a deep impression on David Carliner. As he told Gregory Dorr in an interview conducted in the 1990s, "I was never treated with such hostility anywhere as I was by that Court. The fact this was a Chinese-white marriage didn't make any difference; they saw black all over the place. And they treated me as if I were a piece of shit." Gregory Michael Dorr, "Principled Expediency: Eugenics, *Naim v. Naim,* and the Supreme Court," *American Journal of Legal History* 42 (1998): 142.

71. Simeon Booker, "The Couple That Rocked Courts," *Ebony,* September 1967, 78. The story of *Loving v. Virginia* has been told and retold in a wide variety of formats. Recent examples include Newbeck, *Virginia*; Peter Wallenstein, *Tell the Court I Love My Wife: Race, Marriage, and Law—An American History* (New York: Palgrave Macmillan, 2002) and Wallenstein, "Interracial Marriage on Trial: *Loving v. Virginia,*" in *Race on Trial: Law and Justice in American History,* ed. Annette Gordon-Reed (New York: Oxford University Press, 2002), 177–96; Robert A. Pratt, "Crossing the Color Line: A Historical Assessment and Personal Narrative of *Loving v. Virginia,*" *Howard Law Journal* 41 (1998): 229–44; as well as the TV movie *Mr. and Mrs. Loving,* starring Timothy Hutton and Lela Rochon, which first ran on the Showtime Network in 1996 and has since been reissued in both video and DVD format, and even a book for juveniles, Karen Alonso, *Loving v. Virginia: Interracial Marriage* (Berkeley Heights, N.J.: Enslow Publishers, 2000). In legal scholarship, see the essays collected in the *Howard Law Journal* 51 (Fall 2007) and the *Wisconsin Law Review* 2007, no. 2; Walter Wadlington, "The *Loving* Case: Virginia's Anti-Miscegenation Statute in Historical Perspective," *Virginia Law Review* 52 (1966): 1189–223; and PE, 107–20.

72. Booker, "Couple," 78–80; Pratt, "Crossing the Color Line," 234–35, 244; "The Crime of Being Married," *Life,* March 18, 1966, 85–91. The phrase "part negro and part Indian" comes from Mildred Loving's first letter to the ACLU asking for help (see Newbeck, *Virginia,* 136, for the text). Mildred Loving's multiracial background was widely reported at the time, and almost as widely ignored; the state of Virginia considered her "colored," a label it linked to its one-drop standard of blackness so as to emphasize blackness and erase Indianness. The Lovings' lawyers did little to challenge this presumption, and neither have most of those who have written about the case. It is only very recently that scholars have begun to investigate the significance of the "Indian" aspects of Mildred Loving's identity. For an especially striking discussion, see Arica L. Coleman, "Notes on the State of Virginia: Africans, Indians and the Paradox of Racial Integrity" (Ph.D. dissertation, Union Institute and University, 2005), 226–49.

73. Newbeck, *Virginia,* 11–12; Transcript of Record, 2–5, LCF; David Margolick, "A Mixed Marriage's 25th Anniversary of Legality," *New York Times,* June 12, 1992, Law, B7; Wallenstein, "Marriage on Trial," 177–78, 183.

74. Leon M. Bazile to John Powell, November 26, 1924, Box 56, Folder 1, JPP; W. Hamilton Bryson, ed., *Legal Education in Virginia, 1779–1979* (Charlottesville:

University Press of Virginia, 1982), 83–86; Richard Lee Morton, ed., *Virginia Lives: The Old Dominion Who's Who* (Hopkinsville, Ky.: Historical Record Association, 1964), 60; Newbeck, *Virginia*, 14–15, 138.

75. Transcript of Record, 6, LCF; Newbeck, *Virginia*, 14; Va. Code Ann. (Michie 1950), sec. 20-58, 20-57, and 20-59.

76. Transcript of Record, 6.

77. In 1964, a leading Black newspaper explained that "scary states use all kinds of subterfuges to prevent mixed marriage cases from being appealed to higher courts on their merits. For example, the charge would be changed to disorderly conduct and a small fine imposed." "Intermarriage, Ho Hum," *Baltimore Afro-American*, December 5, 1964, 5. Jack Greenberg gives additional examples in *Race Relations*, 347–48.

78. Pratt, "Crossing the Color Line," 237. On one of these visits, in March 1959, they were arrested yet again. See Newbeck, *Virginia*, 15.

79. Margolick, "25th Anniversary," B7; Newbeck, *Virginia*, 135–42; Wallenstein, "Marriage on Trial," 184–85; Walleinstein, *Tell the Court*, 218; Motion to Vacate Judgment and Set Aside Sentence, November 6, 1963, Transcript of Record, 7–8, LCF; "Pair Files Suit to End State Ban," *Richmond News Leader*, October 28, 1964, 23; PE, 109–11.

80. Transcript of Record, 16.

81. *Loving v. Commonwealth*, 206 Va. 924, 929–30.

82. "Virginia Case May Be Key to Upsetting Miscegenation Laws," *Civil Liberties*, September 1966, 5; PE, 113–14; Newbeck, *Virginia*, 147–60.

83. Public commentary on the case emphasized the plight of Richard Loving (and so did the Lovings' lawyers in the Supreme Court), but in private, the lawyers remembered that Richard was extraordinarily, even painfully, shy; it was Mildred who did most of the talking. Newbeck, *Virginia*, 17–18.

84. Brief for Appellants, 11, 8, 9, 15; February 17, 1967, in *LB*, 741–88.

85. Brief for Appellants, 40, 15, 17, 20, 22–23.

86. Brief for Appellants, 24–27.

87. Brief for Appellants, 32–34.

88. Brief for Appellants, 34; Newbeck, *Virginia*, 150–54, 161–68.

89. Newbeck, *Virginia*, 155–56.

90. Brief of Amicus Curiae, Urging Reversal, February 16, 1967, in *LB*, 925–45.

91. Brief of Amici Curiae Japanese American Citizens League, 3, February 17, 1967; Brief of the National Association for the Advancement of Colored People as Amicus Curiae, 5, February 28, 1967, Brief of N.A.A.C.P. Legal Defense and Educational Fund, Inc. as Amicus Curiae, 2, 6, all in *LB*, 847–924.

92. Brief on Behalf of Appellee, 9, March 20, 1967, in *LB*, 789–845.

93. Brief on Behalf of Appellee, 32, 38, 50.

94. Brief on Behalf of Appellee, 38, 40, 46–50.

95. Brief of the State of North Carolina as Amicus Curiae, 6, 4, January 24, 1967, in *LB*, 951–58.

96. Oral Argument, 2, 3, 8 in *LB*, 959–1007; Newbeck, *Virginia*, 140–41, 154–59.

97. Oral Argument, 8, 9, 12.

98. *Loving v. Virginia*, 388 U.S. 1, 1 (1967); *Loving v. Virginia*, 386 U.S. 952 (1967); "U.S. Supreme Court Calls Nisei to Argue Loving Case," *Pacific Citizen*, March 31, 1967, 1; Oral Argument, 14–16.

99. See *Griffin v. County School Board of Prince Edward County,* 377 U.S. 218 (1964); Newbeck, *Virginia,* 171.

100. Oral Argument, 20.

101. McIlwaine admitted that, when it came to some of the other provisions of Virginia's miscegenation law, especially 20-54, the section that defined "white" persons and limited the marriage of Whites to other Whites, "I myself could find a number of constitutional objections." Oral Argument, 18.

102. Oral Argument, 22–23, 38–39, 41, 33, 18, 34–36.

103. Handwritten Notes, Loving v. Virginia, April 14, 1967, Box 1379, Folder: O.T. 1964, Argued Cases, no. 395, WODP; Interview with Benno Schmidt, 1975, Columbia University Oral History Collection on Microfiche (New York: Columbia University Oral History Research Office, 1984), 142, 306, 173–74, 197–99, 308; *Loving v. Virginia,* 388 U.S. 1, 13 (1967). The justices' reactions and Warren's responses can be followed in considerable detail in Box 620, no. 395, Loving v. Virginia, EWP.

104. *Loving,* 388 U.S. at 8.

105. *Loving,* 388 U.S. at 6, 7, 12.

106. *Loving,* 388 U.S. at 12. The phrase "basic civil rights of man" comes from *Skinner v. Oklahoma,* 316 U.S. 535, 541 (1942), a case involving an involuntary sterilization law in which the U.S. Supreme Court had described marriage and procreation as "basic civil rights of man." "Marriage and procreation," the Court had explained, "are fundamental to the very existence and survival of the race."

Chapter 9

1. Interview with Benno Schmidt, 1975, Columbia University Oral History Collection on Microfiche (New York: Columbia University Oral History Research Office, 1984), 245–46, 308–9; Warren's penciled edits to Schmidt's June 5, 1967, draft of the *Loving* opinion, Box 620, no. 395, Loving v. Virginia, EWP. One of the very few scholars to have noticed, and emphasized, Warren's reluctance in this regard is Andrew Kull in *The Color-Blind Constitution* (Cambridge: Harvard University Press, 1992), 170–71.

2. Harlan's famous comment was made in the 1896 case of *Plessy v. Ferguson,* in which the U.S. Supreme Court upheld a Louisiana law that required racial segregation in railroads by a vote of 7 to 1. Justice Harlan, the lone dissenter, told the court that "the white race deems itself to be the dominant race in this country. And so it is, in prestige, in achievements, in education, in wealth and in power. So, I doubt not, it will continue to be for all time, if it remains true to its great heritage and holds fast to the principles of constitutional liberty. But in view of the Constitution, in the eye of the law, there is in this country no superior, dominant, ruling class of citizens. There is no caste here. Our Constitution is color-blind, and neither knows nor tolerates classes among citizens." *Plessy v. Ferguson,* 163 U.S. 537, 559.

3. Simeon Booker, "The Couple That Rocked Courts," *Ebony,* September 1967, 80; Brief for Appellants, 13, 20, August 24, 1964, McLCF; Brief of N.A.A.C.P. Legal Defense and Educational Fund, Inc. as Amicus Curiae, 6, in *LB,* 905–24; "The Right to Marry," *New York Times,* June 20, 1967, 38.

4. *McLaughlin v. State,* 172 So. 2d 460, 461 (1965).

5. Petition for Alternative Writ of Mandamus, 1, October 26, 1967; Respondent's Brief, November 24, 1967; Brief in Support of Petition for Alternative Writ of Mandamus, October 27, 1967, all in Van Hook v. Blanton, Florida Supreme Court Case no. 36, 790, Series 49, Carton 3069, Florida State Archives, Tallahassee. "Florida's Attorney General Doesn't Want Mixed Marriages," *Miami Times*, December 1, 1967, 13; *Van Hook v. Blanton*, 206 So. 2d 210 (1968).

6. *Davis v. Gately*, 269 F. Supp. 996 (D. Del.) (June 26, 1967); *Zippert v. Sylvester* (W. D. La.) (August 9, 1967), 12 Race Rel. Law Reporter 1445; "Judge in Arkansas Rules Against Miscegenation Law," *New York Times*, September 26, 1968, 31.

7. "Mississippi Allows a Mixed Marriage," *New York Times*, August 3, 1970, 1; Peter Wallenstein, *Tell the Court I Love My Wife: Race, Marriage, and Law—An American History* (New York: Palgrave Macmillan, 2002), 235–36; Phyl Newbeck, *Virginia Hasn't Always Been for Lovers: Interracial Marriage Bans and the Case of Richard and Mildred Loving* (Carbondale: Southern Illinois University Press, 2004), 198–99.

8. *U.S. v. Brittain*, 319 F. Supp. 1058 (N.D. Ala, E. Div.) (1970); "Alabama Marriage Law Contested," *Richmond Times-Dispatch*, December 4, 1970, A13; "U.S. Challenges Law Against Miscegenation," *New York Times*, May 21, 1971, 79; Julie Novkov, *Racial Union: Law, Intimacy, and the White State in Alabama, 1865–1954* (Ann Arbor: University of Michigan Press, 2008), 272–74; Newbeck, *Virginia*, 206–10.

9. *Brittain*, 319 F. Supp. at 1061.

10. "First in S.C," *Richmond Afro-American and Richmond Planet*, June 24, 1967, 2; Chester Higgins, "Mixed Marriage Ruling Brings Mixed Reaction in Dixieland," *Jet*, June 29, 1967, 23–24; PE, 119–20; Wallenstein, *Tell the Court*, 226–27.

11. "Tennessee Issues License for Interracial Marriage," *New York Times*, January 12, 1968, 32; "Mississippi Allows," 1.

12. "Maryland Repeals Law Banning Mixed Marriage," *Jet*, March 23, 1967, 3; An Act to Repeal Sections 393 and 398 of Article 17 of the Annotated Code of Maryland (1957 Edition), title "Crimes and Punishments," subtitle "Crimes and Punishments," subheading "Marrying Unlawfully," ch. 6, 1967 Md. Laws 15.

13. An Act Relating to Statutes Which Apply Discriminately on the Basis of Race, Color, Creed, or National Origin, 1969 Fla. Laws ch. 69-195; An Act to Repeal Section 563.240, RSMo 1959, Relating to Intermarriage Between White and Negro Persons, H.B. 569, 1969 Mo. Laws 579; An Act Relating to Marriage, ch. 45, 1969 Okla. Laws 46; An Act Adopting Title 1 of the Family Code, ch. 888, sec. 6, 1969 Tex. Laws 2733 and ch. 889, sec. 2, 1969 Tex. Laws 3024–25.

14. An Act Deleting Provisions Which Are Racially Discriminatory, ch. 49, sec. 5, 1974 Ky. Acts 50; An Act to Amend and Reenact Article 94 of the Civil Code of Louisiana, Relative to the Prohibition of Marriage Between Persons Related to Each Other and the Marriage of Persons of the White Race with Persons of Color, Providing That There Is No Longer a Prohibition of Marriage Between Members of the White Race and Persons of Color, no. 256, 1972 La. Acts 679–80; An Act to Amend G.S. 51-3 to Remove References to Race and to Clarify Its Provisions, ch. 107, 1977 N.C. Sess. Laws 111; An Act to Repeal Section 20-7 of the Code of Laws of South Carolina, 1962, Relating to Miscegenation and Exceptions, no. 1198, and An Act to Repeal Section 20-8 of the Code of Laws of South Carolina, 1962, Relating to the Performing of Marriage Ceremonies Involving Miscegenation, no. 1199, 1972 S.C. Laws 2378, 2379;

An Act to Amend Section 9…and to Repeal Certain Laws, to Delete References to the Black, Colored, or Negro Race and Mulattoes, act 253, sec. 5, 1973 Ark. Acts 842, 845; An Act to Repeal Code Section 53-106, Relating to the Registration of Individuals as to Race, no. 543, 1979 Geo. Acts 948; An Act to Repeal Tennessee Code Annotated, Sections 36-402 and 36-403, Relative to Abolishing Anti-Miscegenation Laws, ch. 79, 1979 Tenn. Pub. Acts 126; An Act to Amend Chapter 1, Title 13, Delaware Code, Relating to Marriage, ch. 472, 1986 Del. Laws 895. In Mississippi and Alabama, miscegenation laws were dropped during regular recodifications, so that neither the Mississippi Ann. Code of 1972 nor the Alabama Code of 1975 contained miscegenation laws.

15. *McLaughlin v. State,* 172 So. 2d 460, 461 (1965); An Act Relating to Statutes Which Apply Discriminately on the Basis of Race, Color, Creed, or National Origin, ch. 69-195, 1969 Fla. Laws 770-71.

16. Talbot D'Alemberte, *The Florida State Constitution: A Reference Guide* (New York: Greenwood Press, 1991), 12; Lewis L. Laska, *The Tennessee State Constitution: A Reference Guide* (New York: Greenwood Press, 1990), 155; John W. Winkle III, *The Mississippi State Constitution: A Reference Guide* (Westport, Conn.: Greenwood Press, 1993), 142. The North Carolina provision was dropped when a new state constitution was proposed in 1970.

17. Benedict Anderson, *Imagined Communities: Reflections on the Origin and Spread of Nationalism,* rev. ed. (London: Verso, 1991), 204.

18. Carol A. Horton, *Race and the Making of American Liberalism* (New York: Oxford University Press, 2005), 192–93, 199–204; Paul Finkelman, "Review of *The Color-Blind Constitution,*" *Northwestern University Law Review* 87, no. 3 (1992–93): 945.

19. Hazel Erskine, "The Polls: Interracial Socializing," *Public Opinion Quarterly* 37 (Summer 1973): 292.

20. Jack Ludwig, "Acceptance of Interracial Marriage at Record High," in Alec M. Gallup and Frank Newport, *The Gallup Poll: Public Opinion 2004* (Lanham, Md.: Rowman & Littlefield, 2006), 223.

21. Jerold D. Cummins and John L. Kane Jr., "Miscegenation, the Constitution, and Science," *Dicta* 38 (January–February 1961): 51; Alexander M. Bickel, "Integrated Cohabitation," *New Republic,* May 20, 1964, 4 (my emphasis).

22. See, for example, the LDF Brief for Appellants in *McLaughlin,* August 24, 1964, 8, 25, McLCF, and the ACLU Brief for Appellants in *Loving,* February 17, 1967, 1, in *LB,* 741–88.

23. Brief of the National Association for the Advancement of Colored People as Amicus Curiae, 5, February 28, 1967, *LB,* 887–904; Brief for Appellants, *Loving,* 1; Brief of N.A.A.C.P. Legal Defense and Educational Fund, Inc. as Amicus Curiae, 14, February 20, 1967, *LB,* 905–24; "Justices Upset All Bans on Interracial Marriage," *New York Times,* June 13, 1967, 1, 28; Anthony Lewis, "Decision on Race," *New York Times,* December 13, 1964, 4:6.

24. Quoted in Wallenstein, *Tell the Court,* 228.

25. *Perez v. Sharp,* 32 Cal. 2d 711, 717.

26. *Loving v. Virginia,* 388 U.S. 1, 11 (1967), and citing *Hirabayashi v. U.S.,* 320 U.S. 81, 100 (1943).

27. Erskine, "Polls," 292; Ludwig, "Acceptance of Interracial Marriage," 223.

28. Robert A. Pratt, "Crossing the Color Line: A Historical Assessment and Personal Narrative of *Loving v. Virginia*," *Howard Law Journal* 41 (1998), 240; Newbeck, *Virginia,* 173, 188; Booker, "Couple," 80.

29. David Margolick, "A Mixed Marriage's 25th Anniversary of Legality," *New York Times,* Law, June 12, 1992, B7.

30. These numbers come from a table I constructed on February 5, 2007, at SDA: Survey Documentation and Analysis, http://sda.berkeley.edu, using GSS data from the 1990s and the variables "race issues" and "favor law against racial intermarriage."

31. Margolick, "Mixed Marriage's 25th Anniversary"; Newbeck, *Virginia,* 219.

32. Sharon M. Lee and Barry Edmonston, "New Marriages, New Families: U.S. Racial and Hispanic Intermarriage," *Population Bulletin* 60 (June 2005): Figure 1, p. 11, 24. (Neither of the overall figures includes "Hispanic intermarriage.")

33. Table 1, Race of Wife by Race of Husband: 1960, 1970, 1980, 1991 and 1992, July 5, 1994, U.S. Bureau of the Census, http://www.census.gov/population/socdemo/race/interractab1.txt (accessed Feb. 14, 2007); Table 52, Married Couples by Race and Hispanic Origin of Spouses: 1980 to 2003, in Statistical Abstract of the U.S., 2004–5, http://www.lexisnexis.com; Lee and Edmonston, "New Marriages," 15.

34. Erksine, "Polls," 289. Among Blacks, opinion was much more sharply divided. While 24 percent of southern Blacks and 17 percent of northern Blacks agreed that intermarriage would "hurt," 28 percent of southern Blacks and 43 percent of northern Blacks believed intermarriage would "help."

35. Poll by Princeton Survey Research Associates, April–May 1999, in People and the Press 1999 Millenium Survey, http://www.lexisnexis.com.

36. Nancy G. Brown and Ramona E. Douglass, "Evolution of Multiracial Organizations: Where We Have Been and Where We Are Going," in *New Faces in a Changing America: Multiracial Identity in the 21st Century,* ed. Loretta I. Winters and Herman L. De Bose (Thousand Oaks, Calif.: Sage Publications, 2003), 111–24; Francis Wardle, "History of Contemporary Multiracial Movement, Part 1," *Interracial Voice,* n.d., http://www.webcom.com/~intvoice (accessed January 31, 2007).

37. Ramona Douglass, "Loving Conference Highlights," 1997, Association of Multi-Ethnic Americans, http://www.ameasite.org/lovconf.asp (accessed January 31, 2007); Brown and Douglass, "Evolution," 114.

38. Ken Tanabe, "Love's Forgotten Laws: A Project to Raise Awareness of Racial Sex and Marriage Restrictions in American History" (Thesis, Parsons School of Design, Spring 2004), 4; Loving Day, http://www.lovingday.org (accessed January 31, 2007).

39. Carlos A. Fernández, "Government Classification of Multiracial/Multiethnic People," in *The Multiracial Experience: Racial Borders as the New Frontier,* ed. Maria P. P. Root (Thousand Oaks, Calif.: Sage Publications, 1996), 24–34; Rainier Spencer, "Census 2000: Assessments in Significance," in Winters and De Bose, *New Faces,* 99–100.

40. *Zablocki v. Redhail,* 484 U.S. 374, 383 (1978); *Turner v. Safley,* 482 U.S. 374 (1987); *Moore v. East Cleveland,* 431 U.S. 494 (1977); *M.L.B. v. S.L.J.,* 419 U.S. 102 (1996); *Boddie v. Connecticut,* 401 U.S. 371 (1971).

41. For more on the same-sex marriage cases of the 1970s, see Peggy Pascoe, "Sex, Gender, and Same-Sex Marriage," in *Is Academic Feminism Dead? Theory in Practice,* ed. Social Justice Group at the Center for Advanced Feminist Studies, University of

Minnesota (New York: NYU Press, 2000), 86–129, and George Chauncey, *Why Marriage? The History Shaping Today's Debate over Gay Equality* (New York: Basic Books, 2004), 89–92.

42. *Baker v. Nelson,* 291 Minn. 310, 315 (1971); *Singer v. Hara,* 11 Wash. App. 247, 252, 259 (Wash. Ct. App., Div. 1) (1974).

43. Chauncey, *Why Marriage?* 93–94, 119.

44. *Baehr v. Lewin,* 74 Haw. 530, 563, 570, 581, 570 (1993).

45. *Goodridge v. Dept. of Public Health,* 440 Mass. 309, 327–28 (2003).

46. Finkelman, "Review," 943–45; Steven F. Lawson, *Civil Rights Crossroads: Nation, Community, and the Black Freedom Struggle* (Lexington: University Press of Kentucky, 2003), 144.

47. Jeffrey O. G. Ogbar, *Black Power: Radical Politics and African American Identity* (Baltimore: Johns Hopkins University Press, 2004), 64–67, 123–25, 143–44, 150–53, 156–58; Lawson, *Civil Rights Crossroads,* 144–52.

48. Randall Kennedy, *Interracial Intimacies: Sex, Marriage, Identity, and Adoption* (New York: Pantheon Books, 2003), 108–23; Malcolm X, *By Any Means Necessary* (New York: Pathfinder, 1992), 9; Renee C. Romano, *Race Mixing: Black-White Marriage in Postwar America* (Cambridge: Harvard University Press, 2003), 216–47.

49. Jonathan Feldman, "Review Essay: Race-Consciousness versus Colorblindness in the Selection of Civil Rights Leaders: Reflections upon Jack Greenberg's *Crusaders in the Courts,*" *California Law Review* 84 (1996): 153–55, 160–62; Neil Gotanda, "A Critique of 'Our Constitution is Color-Blind,'" *Stanford Law Review* 44 (November 1991): 1–68.

50. See Terry H. Anderson, *The Pursuit of Fairness: A History of Affirmative Action* (New York: Oxford University Press, 2004), and pages for "Transracial Adoptions" (http://www.uoregon.edu/ adoption/topics/transracialadoption.htm) and "The Indian Child Welfare Act (ICWA)" (http://www.uoregon.edu/~adoption/topics/ICWA.html), both in Ellen Herman, Adoption History Project, http://www.uoregon.edu/~adoption/index.html (accessed February 12, 2007).

51. Angela D. Dillard, *Guess Who's Coming to Dinner Now? Multicultural Conservatism in America* (New York: NYU Press, 2001), 48–98; Horton, *Race,* 191–94, 199–202, 221–22, 227–29; Anderson, *Pursuit of Fairness,* 189.

52. Ward Connerly, *Creating Equal: My Fight Against Race Preferences* (San Francisco: Encounter Books, 2000), 206.

53. Connerly, *Creating Equal,* 23, 76–77; Connerly, "*Loving* America," *Interracial Voice,* September–October 2000, http://www.webcom.com/~intvoice (accessed January 31, 2007); Connerly, "Don't Box Me In: An End to Racial Checkoffs," April 16, 2001, American Civil Rights Coalition, http://www.org/dont.htm (accessed January 31, 2007).

54. Using Lexis/Nexis's page for Federal Case Law, I searched for "Loving v. Virginia" under "Supreme Court Cases" from 1967–2005 and received 78 hits. Using the same page, I searched for "Loving v. Virginia" under "District Courts" from 1967–2005 and received 362 hits (both searches conducted on January 12, 2007). On the significance of *Loving* as legal precedent, see, in addition to the essays cited in chapter 8, Randall Kennedy, "How Are We Doing with *Loving?* Race, Law and Intermarriage," *Boston University Law Review* 77 (October 1997): 815–22; Allison Moore,

"*Loving's* Legacy: The Other Antidiscrimination Principles," *Harvard Civil Law–Civil Liberties Review* 32 (1999): 163–200; and the essays in "Symposium: Law and the Politics of Marriage: *Loving v. Virginia* After Thirty Years," *Howard Law Journal* 41 (1997–98): 215–347.

55. *In re Adoption of Gomez*, 424 S.W. 2d 656 (Tex. Civ. App. 8th D.) (1967); *Compos v. McKeithen*, 341 F. Supp. 264 (E.D. La.) (1972); *Palmore v. Sidoti*, 466 U.S. 429, 431, 433–44 (1984); and *Bob Jones University v. U.S.*, 461 U.S. 574, 605 (1983); Kennedy, *Interracial Intimacies*, 372–89; Renee Romano, "Immoral Conduct: White Women, Racial Transgressions and Child Custody Disputes, 1945–1985," in *"Bad" Mothers: The Politics of Blame in 20th-Century America*, ed. Molly Ladd-Taylor and Lauri Umansky (New York: NYU Press, 1998), 230–51.

56. See note 40 above.

57. *Roe v. Wade*, 410 U.S. 113, 153 (1973); *Bowers v. Hardwick*, 478 U.S. 186 (1986).

58. *Regents of the University of California v. Bakke*, 438 U.S. 265, 356 (1978). Brennan, who was writing in dissent from a decision that upheld a White student's challenge to a California university's affirmative action program, was joined by Justices Byron White, Thurgood Marshall, and Harry Blackmun.

59. *Wygant v. Jackson Board of Education*, 476 U.S. 267, 314 (1986). Stevens was dissenting from a decision in which the Court struck down an affirmative action policy in a case involving teacher layoffs.

60. *Adarand v. Pena*, 515 U.S. 200, 272 (1995). Ginsburg was dissenting from a decision that struck down an affirmative action plan in federal contracting; she was joined by Justice Stephen Breyer. Interestingly, in this decision, both groups of justices, the conservative majority and the liberal minority, claimed to approve, in theory if not in practice, of governmental action to remedy "lingering effects of racial discrimination."

61. *Regents of the University of California v. Bakke*, 438 U.S. 265, 307 (1978); Powell was writing for the Court.

62. *Fullilove v. Klutznick*, 488 U.S. 448, 524, 525 (1980). Both justices were dissenting from an opinion upholding a set-aside program for minority businesses.

63. See, for example, *Miller v. Johnson*, 515 U.S. 900, 904 (1995), a voting rights case.

Conclusion

1. Jay Taylor, "Bedroom Doors, Battle Lines: Interracial-Marriage Vote Masks Deep S.C. Divisions," A1, 10; S.C. Const, art. 3, sec. 33 (repealed 1999), in *Constitution of the State of South Carolina, Ratified in Convention, December 4, 1895* (Abbeville, S.C.: Hugh Wilson, 1900), 18; Sid Gaulden, "Marriage Bill's Obsolete Language Struck," *Post and Courier* [Charleston, S.C.], February 4, 1999, and "House Votes Out Ban on Interracial Nuptials," *Post and Courier*, February 6, 1998, both at http://www.lexisnexis.com.

2. Julie Novkov, *Racial Union: Law, Intimacy, and the White State in Alabama, 1865–1954* (Ann Arbor: University of Michigan Press, 2008), 275–78; Robin DeMonia, "Alvin Holmes' Grand Stand for Fairness," *Birmingham News*, August 30, 2006, http://www.al.com/opinion/birminghamnews/rdemonia.ssf?/base/opinion/1156929476222610.xml&coll=2 (accessed February 2, 2007); "N.A.A.C.P. to Appeal Interracial Marriage Ban," *New York Times*, November 8, 1998; "AEA Poll Finds Support for Erasing Interracial Marriage Ban," AP State and Local Wire, December 1, 1998, http://www.

lexisnexis.com; "NAACP Seeking to Overturn Ban on Mixed-Race Marriage in Alabama," *San Francisco Chronicle,* November 7, 1998, A11; Ala. Const., art. 4, sec. 102 (repealed 2000).

3. "AEA Poll"; "Alabama Considers Lifting Interracial Marriage Ban," March 12, 1999, CNN, http://www.cnn.com/US/9903/12/interracial.marriage (accessed February 2, 2007).

4. Andrew J. Skerritt, "Couples Find Interracial Marriage Draws Mixed Acceptance Locally," *Herald* [Rock Hill, S.C.], March 8, 1998; "Groups Are Against Interracial Marriage Amendment," *Birmingham News,* August 27, 2000, both at http://www.lexisnexis.com.

5. Gaulden, "House Votes"; Multiracial Activist, Legislative Hit List, circa 1999, http://multiracial.com/site/content/category/6/18/29 (accessed February 1, 2007).

6. Taylor, "Bedroom Doors." A10.

7. Taylor, "Bedroom Doors," A10; Mark Pratt, "S.C. Interracial Couples Say Discrimination Prevalent," AP State and Local Wire, September 25, 1998, http://www.lexisnexis.com.

8. "Ban Is an Embarrassment," *Herald,* February 12, 1998; "Interracial Marriage Court Should Throw Out Suit Challenging Amendment," *Birmingham News,* October 9, 2000, both at http://www.lexisnexis.com.

9. Gene Owens, "Alabama Voters to Decide Fate of Miscegenation Ban," October 23, 2000, Stateline, http://www.stateline.org/live/ViewPage.action?siteNodeId=136&languageId=1&contentId=14152 (accessed Feb. 2, 2007); Bob Johnson, "Alabama to Decide Whether to Repeal Last Ban on Interracial Marriage," AP State and Local Wire, October 5, 2000; Phillip Rawls, "Siegelman Urges Passage of Amendment Two," AP State and Local Wire, October 31, 2000, both at http://www.lexisnexis.com.

10. Sybil Fix, "Victims Rights Stay Put; Constitutional Issue: South Carolina Voters Defeated the Amendment Tuesday by a Margin of About 18,000 Votes," *Post and Courier,* November 5, 1998; "Jay Reeves, "Voters Send Mixed Signals with Votes on Interracial Marriage Ban, Courts," AP State and Local Wire, November 9, 2000; "Rejecting Racism Voters Bury Interracial Marriage Ban," *Birmingham News,* November 10, 2000, all at http://www.lexisnexis.com.

11. "Holmes Files Bill to Remove Ban on Interracial Marriages and Provide Equal Protection," AP State and Local Wire, January 28, 1999, http://www.lexisnexis.com; C. Barillas, "Alabama Finally Moves to Revoke Miscegenation Law," March 12, 1999, Data Lounge, http://archive.datalounge.com/datalounge/news/record.html?record=4026 (accessed December 1, 2004).

12. Robin De Monia, "First Step Taken to Repeal Interracial Marriage Ban," *Birmingham News,* March 11, 1999, B1.

Index

Note: Page numbers in italics indicate illustrations

CPSIA information can be obtained
at www.ICGtesting.com
Printed in the USA
BVOW03s1556281217
503797BV00002B/3/P